PELICAN BOOKS

THE WORKER AND THE LAW

Professor K. W. Wedderburn was born in 1927 in Deptford. He was educated at Askes Hatcham Grammar School, Whitgift School, and Queens' College, Cambridge. After reading Classics, he took a double-starred first in Law, and was called to the Bar in 1953. For twelve years until 1964 he was a university lecturer in Law and a fellow of Clare College, Cambridge. He was then appointed the Cassel Professor of Commercial Law in London University, a chair which he holds at the London School of Economics. In 1967 he was one of an international team working on comparative labour law at the University of California, Los Angeles. In 1969–70 he was Visiting Professor at Harvard Law School.

Professor Wedderburn has written textbooks and many articles on legal topics, and takes an interest in the social sciences generally. He is a staff panel member of the Civil Service Arbitration Tribunal, and Deputy Independent Chairman of the London, and the Provincial, Theatre Councils. He has written on problems of disarmament, and also on higher education generally. He was recently appointed Editor of the *Modern Law Review* from July 1971.

He is married, and has three children by a previous marriage.

K. W. WEDDERBURN

THE WORKER AND THE LAW

SECOND EDITION

PENGUIN BOOKS

Penguin Books Ltd, Harmondsworth, Middlesex, England
Penguin Books Inc., 7110 Ambassador Road, Baltimore, Maryland 21207, U.S.A.
Penguin Books Australia Ltd, Ringwood, Victoria, Australia

—

First published 1965
Reprinted 1968
Second edition 1971

—

Copyright © K. W. Wedderburn, 1965, 1971

—

Made and printed in Great Britain
by Hazell Watson & Viney Ltd,
Aylesbury, Bucks
Set in Linotype Times

CONTENTS

PREFACE TO THE SECOND EDITION

THIS book aims to set out a simple account of the relationship between British workers and the law. It sketches the development and current state of our 'Labour Law'. Until ten years ago little was heard of this topic as such in Britain; but today it is of special interest, not merely by reason of its obvious importance in many problems of industrial relations, but also because of the lessons which it has to teach about the place of law in all our lives and about the interplay between law and the social forces which go into its making.

Moreover, the developments which have occurred since the first edition in 1965 have put some of the main issues of Labour Law on everyone's lips. Was the Donovan Report right to reject compulsory legal enforcement of collective agreements? Should the law 'do something' about unofficial strikes? What should a man's rights be when a merger makes him redundant? It is not possible to understand the content – and often the very language – of trade disputes and other employment problems without some understanding of the law that influences both strategy and attitudes. There has, therefore, been created in this decade a new recognition of the coherence of Labour Law as a subject of study. An introductory book such as this aims to sketch the territory falling within the boundaries of the subject and to provide some perspective for discussions about its reform.

The book is written both for the general reader and for the student of our social and legal system. The former will, it is hoped, find in it a general guide to the impact of law on the field of employment. The latter will find an introductory account of the whole subject into which the works cited in the notes and bibliography will take him further.

The text of this edition is completely revised. It has had to take account of the yearly, indeed monthly, changes in Labour Law over the last five years. New statutes, such as the

Redundancy Payments Act, 1965, have added to the *floor of rights* for workers. Urgent problems of technological change have prompted such measures as the Industrial Training Act, 1964. Since 1966 we have had the Prices and Incomes Acts saga. But recently, of course, attention has mainly been focused upon the Report in 1968 of the Royal Commission on Trade Unions and Employers' Associations under Lord Donovan, and, no less, on the Evidence to it and the Research Papers prepared for it and the legislation which was to follow. The preparation of this edition was undertaken as the proposed reforms were awaited; but it was not until May Day 1970 that there was made available the Industrial Relations Bill, 1970 (in the pages that follow called the '1970 Bill'). During the same period the Courts, the new Industrial Tribunals, the National Insurance Commissioners, the Industrial Court and various other bodies have been making new decisions about workers' rights and duties. The picture is not what it was in 1965. Nor have all the different parts changed in a harmonious and consistent way. Indeed, one member of the Commission, Mr Wigham, wrote at the time the Report was published:

A thing that worried me all through the deliberations ... was this: supposing we made all the right recommendations and supposing the Government gave effect to them all in legislation, how long would it be before the judges turned everything upside down? ... The ingenuity of lawyers is endless.

That ingenuity seemed likely to be further tested by plans of the new Conservative Government elected in June 1970 to introduce sweeping legislation in this area. What follows aims to elucidate the bases from which the law sets out into the seventies.

Law is not a mystery; it only uses long words. But an understanding of the technical structure of the law is necessary for an understanding of its development. When an account is given, therefore, of important developments (as in the chapters concerned with industrial conflict and strikes) the reader will find an elementary exposition of the law as lawyers argue it and as judges interpret it. Technical detail is avoided; but we can understand the social significance of the doctrines expounded by judges only by resolutely entering the muddy waters of the law itself and emerging on the other side, not by skirting round them. But technical law by itself is useless, at best an arid game played by keen minds in court rooms and academic ivory towers. To understand its significance we must look at its historical and social setting, we must question what are the value and policy judgments enshrined within the propositions of law, and we must ask what is done in other countries about the problems revealed. As far as is possible in an introductory work, that has been the aim in what follows. The law is stated as in July 1970, except for such few later references as are indicated.

My thanks are owed to very many people – lawyers, trade unionists, students, managers, and others. I should like to mention my special gratitude to the following: Professor O. Kahn-Freund, to whom I, like every student of our Labour Law, owe a great debt; Professors Benjamin Aaron, Xavier Blanc-Jouvan, Gino Guigni, Thilo Ramm and Folke Schmidt, Dr P. O'Higgins, Brian Thomson, David Lea, Peter Pain, Albert Blyghton, and Paul Davies (whose help has been invaluable); my publishers Penguin Books for help, guidance and forbearance; Mrs J. Bruce, Joyce Bannister and Mrs D. Deamer for their help in typing; the Librarian of the Middle Temple; Marie Catterson, Ken Schwartz, Harvey Shulman and Gary Gerlach for timely assistance; and most of all my wife Frances, who alone knows the problems which attended the writing of this edition and without whose patient help and support it could never have been attempted. For the imperfections that remain I am, of course, responsible.

K. W. WEDDERBURN

London
August 1970

GLOSSARY OF ABBREVIATIONS

A.E.U.	Amalgamated Engineering Union
All E.R.	All England Law Reports
A.S.S.E.T.	Association of Supervisory Staff Executives and Technicians
A.S.T.M.S.	Association of Supervisory Technical and Managerial Staff (1967 amalgamation of A.S.S.E.T. and Association of Scientific Workers)
A.U.E.F.W.	Amalgamated Union of Engineering and Foundry Workers (A.E.U and foundry workers, 1968)
A.U.E.W.	Amalgamated Union of Engineering Workers (1970; A.U.E.F.W. plus D.A.T.A. and C.E.U.)
C.A.	Court of Appeal (England and Wales)
C.B.I.	Confederation of British Industries
C.E.U.	Constructional Engineering Union
Ch.	Chancery Division (High Court)
C.I.M.	Commission for Industry and Manpower (1970)
C.I.R.	Commission on Industrial Relations (1969)
D.A.T.A.	Draughtsmen's and Allied Technicians' Union
D.E.P.	Department of Employment and Productivity (before 1968, Ministry of Labour)
E.E.F	Engineering Employers' Federation
E.E.T.U.–P.T.U. (or E.P.T.U.)	Electrical Electronic Telecommunication Union and Plumbing Trades Union
E.T.U.	Electrical Trades Union (after 1968 E.E.T.U.–P.T.U.)
G.M.W.	See N.U.G.M.W.
H.L.	House of Lords (Law Lords; final appeal court for England, Wales, Scotland and Northern Ireland)
I.L.O.	International Labour Organization
I.P.C.S.	Institute of Professional Civil Servants
I.S.T.C.	Iron and Steel Trades Confederation
I.T.R.	Industrial Tribunal Reports
J.I.C.	Joint Industrial Council
K.I.R.	Knight's Industrial Reports
N.A.L.G.O.	National Association of Local Government Officers

N.B.P.I.	National Board for Prices and Incomes (1965)
N.J.A.C.	National Joint Advisory Council
N.U.B.E.	National Union of Bank Employees
N.U.F.L.A.T.	National Union of Footwear, Leather and Allied Trades
N.U.G.M.W.	National Union of General and Municipal Workers
N.U.P.E.	National Union of Public Employees
N.U.R.	National Union of Railwaymen
N.U.T.	National Union of Teachers
N.U.V.B.	National Union of Vehicle Builders
P.C.	Privy Council, Judicial Committee (appeals from some Commonwealth courts)
P.O.E.U.	Post Office Engineering Union
Q.B.	Queen's Bench (Division of High Court)
S.O.G.A.T.	Society of Graphical and Allied Trades
T.G.W.U.	Transport and General Workers' Union
T.S.S.A.	Transport Salaried Staffs Association
T.U.C.	Trades Union Congress
U.I.S.	Union of Insurance Staffs
U.P.W.	Union of Post Office Workers
W.L.R.	Weekly Law Reports

CHAPTER 1

THE FOUNDATIONS OF LABOUR LAW

MOST workers want nothing more of the law than that it should leave them alone. In this they can be said to display an instinct that is fundamental to British industrial relations. So marked is the characteristic that on some occasions the foreign observer looks in vain for what he would recognize as 'Labour Law' in Britain (and though what follows is based largely on English law, most of it applies equally to the separate Scottish legal system).

There are indeed many matters on which less firm 'law' in either decided cases or legislation is to be found in Britain than elsewhere. There are, of course, statutes on particular matters – the Factories Act, 1961, on safety in factories; the Trade Union Acts, 1871 to 1913, on trade unions. But we have no complete labour law code; and one expert has written:

When British industrial relations are compared with those of the other democracies they stand out because they are so little regulated by law.[1]

In 1965 there was appointed a Royal Commission under Lord Donovan to inquire into these problems, the fifth such Commission in a century but the first since 1906. Its terms of reference were wide (including consideration of all 'relations between managements and employees', as well as the place of trade unions and employers' associations 'with particular reference to the Law'). After an extensive research programme, it reported in June 1968.[2] During and since that period the air has been thick with projects for the reform of Labour Law; for this is a time when we have:

reached a point at which these old traditions have to some extent been abandoned in the face of new developments and the policy of what has been called abstention or non-intervention has, as a result, become controversial.[3]

13

The controversy is largely between those who wish to tear up the old system and turn to the tidy answers of legal regulation and those who, whatever their ultimate preferences, feel that the best course now in Britain is to modify and reform the existing voluntary institutions of collective bargaining. That was the fundamental choice to be made by – as we shall call it – the 'Donovan Report' of 1968.

But, it must be appreciated, the law has for many years had, and still has, things to say about relations and conditions at the place of work, and neither worker nor employer expects it to be silent. If wages are not paid, can the employer be forced to pay? If so, how much? Can the employee be compelled to work or punished for not working? Has the worker a legal claim to his job, or for compensation for loss of his job; and what are his legal rights when he is unemployed? Can the employer be forced to negotiate with a union? Can he sue a trade union if its members strike contrary to an agreed procedure? Is it lawful for the union to organize a '100 per cent' membership at a place of work? Can an employer be punished for running an unsafe factory? Can the worker get compensation for injury suffered at work? Can a factory inspector compel the employer to allow him into the factory? Can a worker ever compel a trade union to accept him into membership? Can he sue the union if he is expelled? These are the questions which concern the relationships between employer, employee and trade union.

The social meaning of the answers given to these questions can, of course, be affected strongly by the different legal sanctions attached. For example, there is a radical difference between prosecuting men who go on strike for a criminal offence and their employer suing them for breach of contract. In the first case, the wrongdoing (if they have committed a crime) is so dubbed because the acts done are regarded as wrongs against society generally, and the sanction is punishment by way of fine or imprisonment. In the second, there is failure to keep a bargain with another person, usually remedied today by payment of damages to him. There is another type of civil wrongdoing which, in a way, falls between the two: i.e. if a person commits a 'tort'. Such wrongdoing may be thought of as a civil wrong other than a breach of contract, from slander and negligent injury of another person to violent assault and fraudulent deceit practised on another. One act may fall into all three categories – e.g. if an employer fails to provide a safe machine for an employee, a lapse from which the worker suffers injury, this may be a breach of contract on the part of the employer, *and* a tort against the worker (for which he can also get damages – possibly higher damages), *and* a crime if the lapse is prohibited by the Factories Act. It is never enough to call an act 'unlawful'. We must know what kind of illegality is in issue.

The courts have never developed a special separate code of law to deal with contracts of employment. The legal relationship between worker and employer is governed by the ordinary law of contract, based on principles propounded by the judges, to govern various types of transaction, from hire-purchase to sea voyages. Because there is a contract of employment recognized by the common law, the worker can take the employer to court if he fails to pay the wages, and the employer can sue the worker if he breaks his obligations under the contract. Such labour law as there is in this country rests heavily upon that legal phenomenon, the individual contract of employment, in which the two sides (the employer and individual employee) are looked at by the law as equals to a legally enforceable agreement. Even recent legislation like the Contracts of Employment Act, 1963, uses the same language. The English lawyer does not look first at the relations between 'the workers' and their employers. His primary concern is this individual contract between the employer and each employee. The rules of law dealing with it are largely judge-made, though Parliament has begun now to take a greater interest. We must, therefore, analyse it closely in Chapters 2 and 3. But in all social relationships people more often than not avoid standing on their legal rights, and certainly avoid enforcing them in the courts (if only because it is still expensive to do so). Most employers would be appalled at the idea of issuing writs against their workers; and most workers refused their wage would go first not to a solici-

tor but to their shop-steward. Similarly, the principles governing the law between the member and his union (dealt with in
Chapters 9 and 10) are based on the same common law doctrines of contract, together with certain Acts passed to
supplement them. But trade union affairs are not conducted
primarily with reference to legal principles. The law tends to
make its appearance only when things go radically wrong.

There are, as has been said, some situations into which the
law obtrudes much more obviously, directly, and regularly –
certain areas, for example, in which Acts lay down rules about
conditions of employment. Women's hours of work, or deductions from the wages of manual workers, for instance, receive
special statutory protection; and the safety, health, and welfare
of employees have, since early in the nineteenth century, been
the object of such Parliamentary intervention. Recent Acts
such as the Factories Act, 1961, Offices, Shops and Railway
Premises Act, 1963, and Employers' Liability (Defective Equipment) Act, 1969, carry on that tradition. Factory accidents are
a cause, also, of much litigation in the courts. Every year
thousands of employees injured at work, often advised and
backed by their trade unions, bring successful legal actions
against employers who have failed to observe the safety level
demanded by the Acts or by the common law. There are also
the Acts that establish the modern system of insurance that
aims to provide social security for those who suffer industrial
injury. This topic of safety at work is examined in Chapters
5 and 6. Statute also intervened in 1965 to provide 'redundancy
payments'; and the Industrial Relations Bill, 1970 (the '1970
Bill') proposed to protect 'unjust dismissal' of employees
(Chapter 3). The Race Relations Act, 1968, extended the policy
of racial equality to employment (Chapter 2), while the Equal
Pay Act, 1970, foreshadowed the end of discrimination at work
against women (Chapter 5). Statutory interventions of this kind
have gradually built a *floor of rights* into the employment relationship of each worker, whether he is a union member or not.
Such Acts are quite different from laws which try to regulate
the structure, methods or outcome of collective bargaining
between employers and trade unions, from which Labour Law

in Britain has been in modern peacetime remarkably free, at least until the Prices and Incomes Act, 1966 (Chapter 4).

It may be useful at this stage, therefore, to indicate the areas which properly fall within the province of labour law and which will be dealt with in this book. They are:

(a) The employment relationship between worker and employer. We shall describe the individual contract of employment on which that rests, and the problems of job-security connected with its termination.

(b) The area of collective bargaining between trade unions and employers and the legal effect, if any, of the collective agreement.

(c) The statutory control of certain conditions of employment by Parliament. In respect of safety, in particular, statutes make a complex pattern with the judges' rules of law.

(d) The law concerning strikes, lockouts, and industrial conflict generally. Here judges' law and statute law have played a role in establishing the modern position.

(e) The law about the status and membership of trade unions, which is intertwined with the law about industrial conflict.

We shall discuss the topics in that order.

NON-INTERVENTION BY THE LAW

But, it may be asked, if there is all this law governing the contract of employment (however little it is used in practice), and all these Acts and judge-made legal rules about safety at work or redundancy, what is meant by those who have talked of the 'non-intervention' or, as the leading authority, Professor Kahn-Freund, put it, the 'abstention' of the law from our industrial relations? The answer lies in the development of collective bargaining in Britain during this century. Today collective negotiation between trade unions and employers is the most important factor in determining the wages and terms of employment of a majority of workers. Collective bargaining is remarkably widespread in Britain today, directly affecting some

75 per cent of the workforce compared with a mere 35 per cent at most in the U.S.A. Yet here it owes very little to the law. Even those who are not integrated into the bargaining process are plainly affected by its backwash upon the general level of wages; and most observers accept that collective bargaining has come to stay. It is true that the Webbs in 1902 predicted that the trade unions' 'method of Collective Bargaining' might in time encounter increasingly such serious difficulties as to 'lead to its suppression by some form of compulsory arbitration; that is to say, by Legal Enactment'.[4] But the opposite has happened so far in Britain. Legal enactment has *not* been the modern method. Voluntary collective bargaining has developed in a system which depends very little on the law, which is covered by very few decisions of the judges, and which is controlled by statute very little, if at all. Events in 1969, as we shall see, confirmed this tradition. In other countries with comparable economic systems (such as the United States, Australia, Sweden, West Germany) the 'collective agreement' and the process which produces it are more regulated by legal sanction. Sometimes this is done by special agencies, Labour Courts or administrative Boards, to control the parties and the outcome of the bargaining.

In Britain, as we shall see in Chapter 4, the collective agreement is not normally enforceable by legal sanction. The agreements made and the resolutions passed at the various levels (Joint Industrial Councils, district committees, shop-floor conferences, or other joint bodies) do not follow lawyers' lines or distinctions. Many of them are informal trade practices or local bargains struck by shop stewards; and there is little recognition in Britain of the distinction which lawyers apply (and which labour law systems in other countries apply where lawyers have been more prominent in industrial affairs) between the negotiation of new agreements and the interpretation of existing agreements, between 'conflicts of interest' and 'conflicts of rights'. Often an 'agreement' here is not so much a final settlement as a stage in a continuing negotiation. If this is offensive to legal minds, nevertheless the flexibility of the system has great merits. The Donovan Report proposed not its replacement but its reform; and the Report amply supports the comment of two leading authorities: 'It is a well established fact that collective bargaining does not thrive on a diet of principles'.[5]

There is, of course, a case for making some of the British agreements more detailed and more precise; and the Donovan Report stressed the need to extend, reform and rationalize the institutions of British bargaining. In particular, it recommended management to initiate the development of agreements at factory or company level. For it is at this level, and often at shop-floor level, rather than on the national plane, that many critical bargains are struck in Britain today. The new-style productivity agreement at factory level should, the Report said, include written and precise clauses, wherever possible, dealing with pay; linking improvements in conditions with improvements in methods of operation; providing for speedy and fair 'procedures' for settlement of grievances, including matters of discipline and dismissal; and for regular 'joint discussion' about safety at work. Such agreements should be registered with the Department of Employment and Productivity. (In 1968, the 'D.E.P.' with a 'Secretary of State' took over the old Ministry of Labour, and in what follows the terms are, it is hoped, used with chronological accuracy, except that sometimes reference is made simply to 'the Minister'.) Not that new advances cannot be made also at national level. The Report commended the chemical industry national agreement of 1967 which sets out national guidelines within which plant bargaining operates and which, interestingly, distinguishes the procedures to be used in disputes about interpreting the agreement from those to be used in new negotiations.[6] To assist the new developments the Report proposed the setting up of a new body which was established as the Commission on Industrial Relations ('C.I.R.') in 1969. Such a body, the Report envisaged, would not be concerned with 'short-run improvement of the country's economic position' and 'incomes' policy . . . revised at fairly frequent intervals' which came within the province of the National Board for Prices and Incomes (the 'N.B.P.I.') after 1965. The C.I.R. would be concerned with the 'reconstruction of industrial relations'. Nor did the Report (with the exception of the dissent of Mr Shonfield) believe that the C.I.R. should operate by use of legal sanction. Lord Tangley thought it should have certain powers; and Lord Robens, Sir George Pollock (an ex-president of the Employers' Federation) and Mr Thompson (a banker) thought power to de-register unions should be within its province. But the majority, Lord Donovan (a judge), Professors Clegg and Kahn-Freund (two academics), Mr Woodcock and Lord Collison (two trade unionists), Miss Green (a schoolmistress) and Mr Wigham (Labour Correspondent of *The Times*) firmly opposed legal 'teeth' for the C.I.R. The composition of the Commission is not without interest when we come to see the unanimous views which it expressed (with only marginal dissents from Mr Shonfield) about the proposals to make collective agreements 'binding in law' (Chapter 4).

It would clearly be extremely difficult to reduce the patchwork quilt of British industrial negotiation to clear lines of academic or legal principle. Like the trade union movement which is woven into it, it cannot be understood apart from its history. The crazy-paving pattern of workers' trade unions has recently received much publicity and we return to the problem in Chapter 10. But at the outset we may note that there were still 534 trade unions by 1969 with a total of over ten million members; yet 42 per cent of them had fewer than 500 members each. At the 1970 Congress 150 unions were affiliated to the T.U.C. comprising 9,402,170 members; but seven of these had over half the total membership – the top three (T.G.W.U., A.U.E.F.W., and N.U.G.M.W.) three and a half million members. The number of affiliated unions had fallen by five since 1969 through mergers and the dissolution of small unions (the 12 members of the London Jewish Bakers wound up their organization); but the membership rose with the accession of more white collar bodies, notably the N.U.T. with 318,000. The first Whitley Committee, which was set up in 1916 to consider 'relations between employers and employed', recommended the establishment in each industry of organizations representative of workers and employers. Since the First World War industry has been covered by a network of such bodies, at least as far as manual workers are concerned; and the Ministry of Labour told the Donovan Commission of about 500 industry-wide negotiating arrangements for manual workers, to which must be added thousands of local arrangements. Yet they have been set up, and this complexity of unions has been accommodated into them, without peacetime legal compulsion of any kind. Such a development is little less than a triumph of empiricism.

This system, of course, can only function without undue friction when parties representing workers and employers are acceptably identified, and agree to come together. The strains of the system are, therefore, especially illustrated in those areas where union membership is still not easily accepted by employers. An authoritative survey in 1967 for the Royal Commission by Professor Bain revealed that, whereas five out of ten manual workers belong to a trade union, only three out of ten white-collar workers do so (most of these being in public employment).[7] The rapid increase of the white-collar proportion in the workforce – soon more than half the workers will be in that category – makes this low proportion of union members disturbing for those who, like the Commission, wish to strengthen and reform collective bargaining.

But what happens if employers refuse to negotiate, either locally or at national level? In the United States it has since 1935 been possible for representative unions to *compel* an employer to negotiate (though there has been a heavy price for that power by way of legal strings on the unions themselves and on their bargaining strength). But there is no such legal remedy in Britain. Nationalized corporations are under a legal duty to negotiate with such unions as each thinks appropriate. But in practice even that exceptional duty is scarcely enforceable in court. In 1970 a member of the Guild of Telephonists, from which the Post Office withdrew recognition after forty years when its members refused to approve a merger with the Union of Post Office Workers, failed in his attempt to compel the Post Office to go on negotiating with a union which it no longer deemed appropriate. Indeed, unions have even sought a foreign tribunal. The United Kingdom has ratified the I.L.O.

conventions of 1948 and 1949 on 'Freedom of Association' and the 'Right to Organize and Collective Bargaining'. But such conventions do not become law in Britain merely because the Government 'ratifies' them. An Act would be needed for that; and none has been passed. The conventions state that workers shall have the right to 'join organizations of their own choosing' and enjoy 'adequate protection against acts of anti-union discrimination'. Complaints can be made to the Committee on Freedom of Association of the I.L.O. In one complaint made in 1954, the Committee said, 'as the Government makes clear, in the United Kingdom the question of actual union recognition by the employers for the purpose of collective bargaining is left to be settled freely by the parties concerned.' In 1962 the National Union of Bank Employees, refused recognition by nearly all the big banks, complained of this refusal, and, in particular, of 'staff associations' which, the N.U.B.E. claimed, infringed the ban put by the 1949 Convention on employers promoting associations of employees dominated by the employers, tame 'company unions'. The British Government, at the request of the I.L.O., set up an inquiry under Lord Cameron. But his unsatisfactory conclusions did not settle the matter. (They were not, of course, legally binding.) The N.U.B.E. had to struggle on and win recognition for itself. In 1967 N.U.B.E. members took selective strike action to compel recognition by the many banks that still refused it. The idea that white-collar workers were not 'militant' was dead. After further strike threats, the Committee of London Clearing Banks agreed in 1968 to the setting up of national negotiating machinery, comprising employers, the N.U.B.E. and the staff associations.

Many employers have objected to recognition of white-collar trade unions, especially on such grounds as that 'supervisors are part of management' or that there is a 'special relationship' between these workers and employers. The Donovan Report dubbed this attitude 'increasingly unrealistic and out of date'. In private manufacturing industry, only 12 per cent of such workers were organized in 1968. This is not unrelated to the resistance of employers. There are still employers who say of recognition what the chairman of the Society of Independent

Manufacturers said of his own firm to the Donovan Commission: 'We manage without it'.[8] At the 1970 N.U.B.E. conference the president still complained bitterly of the 'outdated, feudalistic methods' by which some leading banks still refused full recognition to the union. The struggle between the banks and insurance companies and the unions, as a *Financial Times* article put it, 'over the years has been neither honourable nor clean'.[9] We return to the difficult problem of union recognition in Chapter 4. In its first reports published in December 1969, the C.I.R. took a firm stand on the issue. An insurance company was urged to accord limited recognition to U.I.S. which organized 16 per cent of its employees. In another case, rejecting the refusal of a firm to recognize a union for its foremen, the C.I.R. said:

We do not agree that there is a special relationship between employer and staff workers which is incompatible with their representation by a trade union.[10]

But when firms rejected C.I.R. recommendations, as these did, what was to be done? Both political parties inclined favourably to the idea that a legal duty to recognize should be enacted. This attractive solution was treated with caution by the Donovan Report and by observers who feared the importation of regulation by the back door and the mass of legalistic hair-splitting which surrounds the 'duty to bargain in good faith' in the U.S.A.[11] Nevertheless the Industrial Relations Bill introduced by the Labour Government in 1970 (to which for brevity we shall refer as 'the 1970 Bill') proposed such a duty. Whether a new law on recognition would reinforce or obstruct the working of the British system of industrial relations is an open question, likely to depend, as we shall see (p. 165), on the precise formulation and range of the statute. At present, the voluntary nature of the system is still its dominant characteristic.

THE REASONS FOR NON-INTERVENTION

Why has the British system developed in this way? A comprehensive answer to that question would need to review the entire social history of Britain in the nineteenth century; but one potent factor is undoubtedly the fact that judicial legal *intervention* in that century was inimical to the trade unions. As we shall see in Chapters 7 and 8, it was the judges who repeatedly declared trade unions and their activities criminal during the first half of that century. When statutes of 1859, 1871, and 1875 were fought for and enacted to relieve the growing unions from the worst consequences of criminal liability, the judges turned to the development of civil liability. For example, the liability for criminal 'conspiracy' was excluded from trade disputes in 1875; but the courts replied by creating and extending civil liability for the *tort* of 'conspiracy' to do damage to another. In 1901 they imposed the new civil liabilities in an extended form on union funds. In 1906 the unions extracted the protections of the Trade Disputes Act from a Liberal government; but the judges reacted by invalidating political activity by unions, a ruling for which yet another protecting statute had to be passed in 1913. Until the First World War, the judges (with few notable exceptions) proved, as Professor Kahn-Freund puts it, that 'the attitude of the courts reflected that of the middle class'.[12] 'You cannot,' said Lord Justice Lindley in 1896, 'make a strike effective without doing more than is lawful.'

The labour movement had acquired considerable industrial strength as the nineteenth century drew to its close. Skilled and semi-skilled workers were organized in 'New Model' unions; and, later, the general unions organized the unskilled. The new union strength came to be allied to the weapons of political democracy as the vote was extended to various groups of workers in 1867 and 1884, and the Labour Party grew from its strange amalgam of trade union members and Fabians after 1900. But these new avenues of political strength were scarcely ever used for any purpose in industrial conflict other than the protection of the industrial movement against the interventions of the judges. Indeed, industrial strength had secured protection before political democracy brought forth a Party based upon an appeal to working men. By 1969, that Party's Government, in its desire to initiate new legal intervention, ran into the full scale opposition of the industrial movement.

The Acts of 1871, 1875, and 1906 all aimed largely to *remove* liabilities which judgments had imposed upon the unions; and that is, as we shall see, the reason for their being expressed in a language that establishes formally 'privileges' or 'immunities' in a trade dispute. Whereas the factory reformers and trade unions had united during the nineteenth century to obtain positive legislation upon factory conditions at work – on safety, health, or the protection of child and women workers – the statutes on industrial conflict took this negative, or in appearance 'abstentionist', character. That is why the problems of safety and the like are today regarded as more appropriate for legislation than collective bargaining, but the reverse is true of wages, hours, and so on, where autonomous collective bargaining between unions and employers is the objective and the rule. Already there have been some changes in the 'mix', and in Chapter 5 we shall ask whether this line will continue to be drawn at the place history has laid it down. It is, of course, often difficult to know whether new problems should be tackled by one method or the other (e.g. should the problems of redundancy, low-paid workers, equal pay, or unjust dismissal be solved by voluntary collective bargaining, or by compulsory statute law? Or, if by both, what should be the relationship between the two methods?). At any rate, the Acts of 1871 to 1906 pushed back from trade disputes the illegalities which hamstrung the unions. There was not so much an 'abstention' on the judges' part as an exclusion of them. Trade unions and their supporters used political power to exclude them by legislation which enacted non-intervention.

What is remarkable here, however, is the phenomenon that after the First World War many judges themselves seem to have reconsidered their position and their policy. Employers in the post-war period, and particularly after the defeat of the unions in the General Strike of 1926, became rather less eager to solve labour problems in the courts; they wanted work not writs. And judges began to ask where interventionist policies had led them. After all, a court that intervenes in an industrial conflict cannot be 'neutral'; it will take one side or the other. Intervention in economic conflict must be for one side, against the other. In 1920 Lord Justice Scrutton, a great judge and no radical in social attitudes, expressed the new thoughtful concerns when he said:

The habits you are trained in, the people with whom you mix, lead to your having a certain class of ideas of such a nature that, when you have to deal with other ideas, you do not give as sound and accurate judgments as you would wish. This is one of the great difficulties at present with Labour. Labour says 'Where are your impartial Judges? They all move in the same circle as the employers, and they are all educated and nursed in the same ideas as the employers. How can a labour man or a trade unionist get impartial justice?' It is very difficult sometimes to be sure that you have put yourself into a thoroughly impartial position between two disputants, one of your own class and one not of your class.[13]

His Lordship was, of course, making no accusation or admission of 'bias', a word which implies something like conscious fraud. Rather, he was beginning to see, as he put it in 1933, that these 'elaborate new systems' of collective bargaining 'bewilder people like myself who have not known of them'. He was recognizing that judges are men, and like other men their decisions are influenced by the social background they have known and the unconscious premises they acquire. Self-awareness of this kind was rare among judges before 1920. Even today it is not always apparent. Judges who reviewed with such refreshing frankness the unhappy story of the battles between the courts and the unions were likely to abstain from interventions of quite the kind in which their brethren had indulged in the earlier period.

THE CHANGE IN JUDGES' POLICIES

But, it will be asked, how can judges 'abstain' or 'intervene'? Are they not there to apply the law? No doubt – but the application of the principles of the common law gives the judges frequent opportunities to *develop* them in different directions. Let us take, as an example from Labour Law, conspiracy.

A combination to do an unlawful act (e.g. to commit assault) has long been held by judges to be, in itself, a punishable criminal conspiracy, even before the act is done. But they also held combinations to 'molest' others to be criminal even if the acts to be done were not in themselves unlawful. In 1872, gas workers organizing a strike were convicted of criminal conspiracy under that heading. Three years later an Act abolished criminal conspiracy charges in trade disputes, except where the act to be done would itself be criminal. But the judges decided that there was a *civil* liability for conspiracy, to pay damages to the person maliciously injured or molested, and the Act had not abolished that! So they allowed actions against trade unionists which imposed on them in civil law the conspiracy liability which the Act had abolished in criminal law. In 1895 unionists who posted a 'black list' of blackleg workers were made liable for a 'conspiracy to injure'; in 1892 and 1902 the circulation of lists of strikers and trouble-makers by employers' associations was held not unlawful because the employers were defending legitimate self-interest. In 1892, traders who undercut competitors were held not liable for conspiracy because they were pursuing legitimate objects of their own. At the turn of the century the judges were, in fact, willing to choose some lawful economic or social ends as less 'legitimate' than others.

The story begins with *Quinn* v. *Leathem*, 1901, where union officials had objected to Leathem's employment of non-union workers in his fleshing business. A lengthy dispute ended in the officials demanding the men's dismissal; nothing else would suffice. When Leathem refused, the union approached a butcher who was one of Leathem's customers and, under threats of a withdrawal of labour from his shop, got him to stop dealing with Leathem. The latter sued for conspiracy, alleging a 'combination to injure'. No unlawful act had been done. The defendant unionists argued that they were pursuing their legitimate interests, like trade competitors. Moreover, they argued, in the remarkable case of *Allen* v. *Flood*,[14] four years earlier the majority of the Law Lords had decided that a union official calling a strike to injure his employers was not civilly liable, even if he was malicious, as he had done no act unlawful in itself. Nevertheless, the Lords found for Leathem. This was a combination, they considered, not an individual act; and its objects were not the furtherance of legitimate objects; it was a combination to injure.[15] The reasoning in the judgments was vague, and from 1901 all strike activity ran the risk of encountering this liability for the tort of conspiracy from which plaintiffs could obtain damages and injunctions. In 1901, the *Taff Vale* decision allowed such damages to be enforced against the funds of the unions.[16] From the ensuing uproar emerged the Act of 1906, replete (so it was thought) with defences against these new liabilities, as we see in Chapters 7 and 8.

But after the war a new wave of judgments began. After a period of uncertainty from 1918 to 1920, cases were decided that applied the liabilities restrictively. In 1921, showing a very different spirit from that of 1901, the Court of Appeal accepted the objective of comprehensive union membership at a place of work as legitimate, Lord Justice Younger warning that the court must be 'vigilant' not to be misled by 'prepossessions' about the issues. In *Reynolds* v. *Shipping Federation*, 1924, an agreement between the seamen's union and employers' federation blacking men in a breakaway union was held to be legitimate, as showing 'a desire to advance the business interests of employers and employed alike by securing or maintaining those advantages of collective bargaining and control'. Any remaining doubts were settled in the great *Crofter* case of 1942.[17] In the Outer Hebrides island of Lewis, local weavers of tweed cloth made their product from yarn imported through the docks from the mainland. But in larger mills on the island cloth was woven from more expensive yarn supplied by local crofters. Most mill workers were in the Transport and General Workers union, as were the dock workers. The union wanted to secure 100 per cent membership and also a wage increase. The mill owners refused, pointing to the difficulties of local competition. Eventually, the defendants, who were officials of the T.G.W.U., arranged for the dockers to put an embargo (without any breach of their employment contracts) on the yarn going to the local weavers. The weavers alleged that the whole arrangement was a conspiracy to injure; but the House of

Lords said that it was not. All the parties were pursuing their legitimate interests, the mill owners to increase their control of the market and their profits, the union to improve wages and extend membership – all, said Viscount Simon, 'to create a better basis for collective bargaining. ... A combination with such an object is not unlawful, because the object is the legitimate promotion of the interests of the combiners.' The union could use the dockers to help the mill workers; and any combination between employers and union could not be invalid merely because each has, in Viscount Maugham's phrase, 'his own axe to grind'.

Mr Justice Evatt had pointed out in Australia ten years before that it is logically possible to see union action to secure 100 per cent membership in two different ways – 'first as a combination for the purpose of damaging or injuring the non-unionists, secondly as a combination to protect or advance the interests of the union'. In 1901 it was natural for judges to take the first view. By 1942, *Quinn* v. *Leathem* had to be regarded as a case where the court took that view of the particular facts. Courts felt themselves free to say that (whatever was said in 1901) if the predominant motive disclosed were of the second type (as it could usually be said to be once trade union objectives were accepted) there could be no liability for conspiracy to injure. Thus even a decision of the House of Lords (the final court of appeal) can be vastly reinterpreted forty years later, and the law can subtly shift its meaning. Lord Wright remarked in the *Crofter* case that the law

has for better or worse adopted the test of self-interest or selfishness as being capable of justifying the deliberate doing of lawful acts which inflict harm, so long as the means employed are not wrongful ... we live in a competitive or acquisitive society, and the English common law may have felt that it was beyond its power to fix by any but the crudest distinctions the metes and bounds which divide the rightful from the wrongful use of the actor's own freedom.

Judges now placed workers' collective interests on a level as valid as those of employers; they themselves abstained from the battle, so long as each side pursued self-interest by acts lawful in themselves. Lord Wright even added: 'The right of workmen to strike is an essential element in the principle of collective bargaining.'

It is not without interest to note that the development towards a more liberal view of 'legitimate objects' took place in decisions of 1924 and 1942 where the big battalions of labour and capital stood together against, respectively, the small union or small producer. No doubt this made it easier for the courts than if the facts had disclosed a straight conflict between workers and employers. Still, the development took place and the legal principle grew into something new.

In Chapter 8 we shall investigate more closely the modern developments of judge-made law, and look again at the principles of conspiracy and other torts. In fact the era in which statutory, enforced non-intervention was matched by judicial 'abstention', to underpin the voluntary system of industrial relations, appeared to come to an end with the House of Lords' decision in *Rookes* v. *Barnard*, 1964.[18] New liabilities there outflanked the 1906 Act to such an extent that a new Act protecting trade unionists was fought for and enacted in 1965. But the novelties of judge-made law were not at an end, most of them (though not all) extending new risks to workers' industrial action. By 1970, as Chapter 10 reveals, some judges were making startling innovations in trade union law; and new judicial attitudes to strikes, as Chapter 8 shows, meant that even as the print dried, whole passages in the Donovan Report itself were obsolescent in the face of them.

MODERN LABOUR RELATIONS AND THE LAW

It has been in an atmosphere of legal non-intervention that modern collective bargaining has grown. But in the last decade the pressures to change that context into one of legal regulation have increased – and met with increasingly fierce resistance. Such a phenomenon cannot be divorced from the tensions and conflicts of interest that still lie beneath the surface of a more affluent society. The contest has, indeed, been played out at so many levels of society that the brief description possible here must necessarily be selective. The conflict has begun to pervade modern British society.

First, there developed the problems of 'planning'. For many years until 1965, Government interventions on collective bargaining took forms compatible with a voluntary system, from fiscal measures to restraints on wages in the public sector (as in the *Dudfield* case, p. 190) or 'background' information sent to voluntary arbitrators who were (and are) still independent in their decisions. Except in wartime arbitration was not compulsory. But pressure grew for the 'planning of wages', to match the planning of capital resources in the 'public interest'. Eventually (after a joint T.U.C.–C.B.I.–Government 'Declaration of Intent', well meaning, but variously interpreted), the N.B.P.I. was established as an advisory body. But the policy took legislative form in the Prices and Incomes Acts 1966 to 1968, which gave powers to Government to stop or to delay pay increases. But, as we see in Chapter 4, the next period from 1970 may well be one of smaller governmental power, especially after the advent of a Conservative Government in 1970 pledged to abolish what is left of the prices and incomes legislation. The policy of State control of wages is not only difficult to reconcile with a voluntary system of industrial relations. It may also forget that in a capitalist economy no easy equivalence can be made between planning the commodity of capital resources and their price and planning the 'commodity' of human labour; for, as Marx put it, 'whereas labour power is a commodity only in the hands of its seller, the wage-labourer, it becomes capital only in the hands of its buyer'. And, of course, as the reports of the N.B.P.I. have shown, the 'public interest' is a difficult concept, on which even 'reasonable' men can disagree in any concrete situation.

Secondly, the tensions expressed themselves in the development of bargaining institutions. The Donovan Report, in a unanimous analysis, laid bare the strain which exists between the 'formal' pattern of national agreements and 'informal' plant bargaining. In the latter, shop stewards elected directly

by and responsible to (often propelled by) the workers themselves, have extracted from management better employment
conditions than the national minima, especially in areas and
times of full employment:

The formal and informal systems are in conflict. The informal
system undermines the regulative effect of industry-wide agreements ... Factory bargaining remains informal and fragmented,
with many issues left to custom and practice ... Any suggestion
that conflict between the two systems can be resolved by forcing
the informal system to comply with the assumptions of the formal
system should be set aside. Reality cannot be forced to comply
with pretences.

Hence, the Report's central thesis emerged that collective
bargaining must be extended and reformed at *factory* level. To
some this was a disappointment. It was already clear that no
such reform could be achieved by a short swipe of the legal
axe; but they had equated in their minds the notions of 'more
law to control unions' and 'reform of industrial relations'. The
power of this widely-promulgated fallacy is nowhere seen
more clearly than in the proposals that collective bargains,
freely entered into, must be made compulsorily 'binding' in
law (which the Report rejects). This remedy confuses the symptoms with the malady. If (which is not universally accepted)
there is a special British problem of short unofficial strikes,[19]
it springs from defects in the institutions which do not allow
for adequate expression of workers' influence in quick and early
negotiation of problems. The negotiation of 'productivity'
bargains with more rational grievance procedures is urgent.
But tough bargaining also brings new problems. For example,
workers are widely challenging the right of management to act
(e.g. by changing methods of work) before negotiation when
they, the workers, are told to 'exhaust the procedure' before
they act (e.g. strike). This argument about managerial rights to
change the *status quo* will assume the centre of the bargaining
stage in the seventies. But this is only a new facet of the
customary struggle to gain a sharing of power at the workplace. As Professor Allan Flanders puts it:

The trade unions in exercising their own functions necessarily limit the managerial rights of the employers. ... How far in practice they attempt to extend their 'frontier of control' depends partly on their power and partly on whether they consider it expedient to acquire the responsibilities involved.[20]

What, thirdly, were the pressures from the political parties, the C.B.I. and T.U.C.? Before the Donovan Report appeared, the Conservatives published *Fair Deal at Work* as the 'basis' of their policy. This made some proposals which were in accord with Donovan and the Labour Government's still-born '1970 Bill' (though with significant differences of detail), such as extending the *floor of rights* to include a right for workers to challenge unjust dismissals before statutory tribunals (Chapter 3). For the rest, it aims at changes promoted and underpinned by new legal regulation across the board of labour relations – the Registrar to control rules of trade unions compulsorily registered and incorporated; 'Industrial Courts' to enforce agreements; a duty to recognize trade unions; severe liabilities for many types of strike (all 'sympathetic' strikes for example); a power for the Minister to obtain injunctions against strikes, and so on. As Mr Robert Carr put it, there was 'a fundamental difference' between the Report and this approach to 'comprehensive legislation as an instrument of modernization', though the main object was to 'deter' rather than to 'punish'.[21] The Labour Government waited until after the Report and then published a White Paper, *In Place of Strife*. This adopted most Donovan recommendations – to establish the C.I.R.; to demand registration of company agreements; to legislate on unjust sackings; to establish new powers for the Registrar and a new Review Tribunal on trade union rules; and so on. (It is parenthetically interesting to note that the Labour Government White Paper appeared to think that some legislation of the past, such as the Redundancy Payments Act, 1965, evinced an 'alternative view' to the doctrine of non-intervention so that there were 'two conflicting philosophies'. This is not the case. A statutory *floor of rights* and legislation supplementary to industrial relations on such matters as safety or training do not 'conflict' with state non-intervention in collective bargaining, as we shall see in Chapter 5. They supplement and support the voluntary system.)

But in three respects the Labour Government went further. It proposed to enable the Secretary of State after consulting the C.I.R. (a) to order an employer to recognize a union, and (after consulting the T.U.C.) to order a *union* to be excluded from negotiation in an inter-union dispute; (b) to order strikers to return to work for 28 days if there had been a 'breach of procedure' or 'inadequate discussion' and to impose conditions, including the *status quo*, on management; and (c) to order a 'secret ballot' of members before an official strike. The orders would be enforced by financial penalties. Employers reacted with mixed feelings; many of them disliked compulsory strike-ballots which, with reason, they saw as likely to increase, embitter and prolong strikes. The trade unions vigorously opposed the new legal powers against unions and workers. The T.U.C. had already launched a 'major initiative', as the *Financial Times* described it, to reform union structure, called conferences of unions in six industrial sectors, and published *Action on Donovan*. The C.B.I. had begun its own deliberations; and the T.U.C. and C.B.I. had jointly agreed to promote certain central Donovan recommendations.

Suddenly, in what the T.U.C. called an 'overnight' decision, the Government announced in – of all things – the Budget Speech, April 1969, that it intended to pass an 'interim' Bill including, mainly, two of the novel sanctions (or 'penal clauses' as they came to be called), (a) and (b) above.[22] The Prime Minister spoke of 'industrial anarchy' and of the need to have 'legislation on the Statute Book by the Summer recess' of Parliament. But the trade union movement had exploded in united opposition to the Bill and its 'penal clauses'. It was never very clear how these were supposed to work; for so ill-prepared were the proposals that within a few days Mrs Castle, the D.E.P. Secretary of State, had said that imprisonment would not be used as a sanction, only 'attachment of earnings'. But, realizing that this touched the most tender nerves (the traditional fear of working men that industrial discipline would be enforced by impounding future wages) she said in Parliament:

I am ready to discuss alternatives with the T.U.C. ... The way ... might be to see that any payments levied on strikers did not go to the state but to a fund to serve some purpose beneficial to workers as a whole – [laughter] ...[23]

The T.U.C. General Council or its sub-committee met again and again with the Prime Minister and his advisers for over two months. In early June, a special conference of unions was called, a step unprecedented in the post-war era. That conference approved the T.U.C. *Programme for Action* whereby further powers were to be given to the Council enabling it to move in to settle unofficial stoppages of inter-union disputes. Sanctions here are, as we shall see (Chapter 10), wholly voluntary. (Later, these powers were ratified by changing the T.U.C. rules at the 1969 Congress.) But the Prime Minister said there was a 'missing link' in such proposals. There was no 'automatic application' of T.U.C. rules against 'recalcitrants'. The T.U.C. Council all firmly insisted that 'the major fallacy' in Government thinking was 'the belief that the imposition of automatic sanctions would solve disputes'. The Government was not alone. But, after a fierce debate, by 18 June the Government was 'prepared to recognize they had learned a lot'. The T.U.C. agreed to add a 'binding undertaking' to the new programme, pledging that unions should be obliged to secure a return to work wherever the T.U.C. did not consider that 'unreasonable'. Agreement was reached on that and the Government agreed to drop its legislation on 'penal clauses' during that Parliament. Both sides hailed the concordat as a 'victory for good industrial relations'. As the Summer recess closed quietly around Whitehall, one wondered what the battle had been about after all. Yet, after it, nothing could ever be quite the same.

In the year which followed, while politicians talked of legal interventions (for, as one Donovan Commissioner has written, 'whenever they see anything going wrong, their first instinct is to pass a law to stop it')[24] other developments occurred which will have a lasting effect. First, the national bodies pushed ahead. The joint discussions of the T.U.C. and C.B.I. reached what *The Times* called 'a high level of agreement' by the spring of 1970 on such issues as reform of disputes procedures, new local arbitration techniques, and the like. The C.B.I. moved slowly; but by the same date it had produced a significant report on disputes procedures and set up working parties to re-examine other aspects of the Donovan proposals. It showed many signs of increased influence among its 104 affiliated bodies. Other sectional employers' bodies ranged from shrill calls for statutory intervention to the thoughtful report by Mr Lowry for the Engineering Employers' Federation, *Greener Grass?*, which warned against amateurish borrowing of American legal regulation.[25]

But the spotlight was on the T.U.C. After their first success in a demarcation dispute at Willenhall Motor Ltd in September 1969, Mr Victor Feather (T.U.C. Secretary) and his slender staff attempted almost impossible feats of conciliation and mediation. An analysis of newspaper reports alone for the last quarter of 1969 reveals at least twelve important stoppages in which T.U.C. intervention was decisive in either ending or severely curtailing the dispute,[26] ranging from 300 clerks at a brake factory involved in inter-union wrangles, to 3,000 broadcasting staff, 125,000 miners and 120 tobacco workers engaged in other intractable strikes. Although the number of working days involved in strikes increased sharply in the first half of 1970, the T.U.C. continued to register successes; and in May, shortly after T.U.C. intervention had dramatically headed off a national newspaper stoppage, the Prime Minister himself said there was 'some support' for the estimate that T.U.C. activity had saved 'two million man-days', silencing Conservative Opposition laughter with the remark: 'the newspapers which support them are not laughing today'. These interventions sometimes succeeded alongside and in step with efforts by D.E.P. conciliation officers, sometimes a Court of Inquiry (p. 396), and usually the particular union concerned.

But the T.U.C. had its failures. In several unofficial strikes, for example in the motor car industry, it tried unsuccessfully to secure a return to work. Moreover, an official dispute between S.O.G.A.T. and the newspaper proprietors closed down national newspapers just eight days before the June 1970 General Election – though T.U.C. intervention secured a settlement where none seemed possible. There were those who said the T.U.C. could not deal with disputes between two of the giant unions (though machinery for this had existed long before 1969: p. 469). Also, where a union had lost the loyalty and support of a group of workers, the T.U.C. naturally had a harder task. It failed, for instance, to secure a speedy return to work by blast-furnacemen at Port Talbot in 1969. The state of mind of those workers was well summarized by one who said (pausing to apologize for the blasphemy): 'If Jesus Christ ... asked us to go back we wouldn't go.' *The Times* said the strike was 'the result of incompetent labour relations over a long period',[27] a verdict to which a Court of Inquiry only added indictments of management, union and workers alike. But in May 1970, Mr Feather succeeded in acquiring the confidence of unofficial strikers at Pilkingtons after a savage dispute in which thousands of workers had renounced their own union, the G.M.W. (p. 463). He was prepared to go straight to the men involved. It is difficult to believe that in that situation, as the D.E.P. Court of Inquiry mumbled through its formal ritual of investigation, intervention by any other body could possibly have secured a return to work. As we shall see, p. 464, that did not solve all the problems; But then, a return to work is not, contrary to conventional wisdom, always the highest virtue. Many stoppages can be avoided; but sometimes a stoppage leads the parties to face the real problems as nothing else could.

So the T.U.C. increased its role in the system for ironing out disputes. At the same time it engaged upon a critical review of its own structures (setting up a new Collective Bargaining Committee) and of the rules of its affiliated unions. To that we return in Chapter 10. In the very same period, after September 1969, the C.I.R., whose work had been hindered by the struggle between the Government and the T.U.C., began on cases referred to it by the D.E.P. Nine months later, twenty-five such references had been made. Recognition problems were the sole or partial content of nine; eleven others related to a particular firm's difficulties in industrial relations; and five, of great moment, related to general questions – about the hotel and catering industry (where bad conditions and inadequate collective bargaining lay behind recent litigation: p. 334); the shipbuilding industry; the general position of and facilities for shop stewards; the provision of training in industrial relations; and the formulation of a code of practice to guide (or, as the 1970 Bill proposed, to govern: p. 169) the disclosure of information by employers to their employees and unions. The C.I.R. made a promising start quickly on the particular problems; and its reports were awaited with interest on those five sensitive general issues.

With Mr Woodcock (ex-General Secretary, T.U.C.) as Chairman, the Commission comprised an ex-Secretary of the mineworkers' union, an ex-personnel director of Fords, and a Professor of Industrial Relations. They set out to use informal and relaxed methods. An extreme example occurred in the thirteen-week-old strike for union recognition against the tough management of an East Kilbride factory, where the Commissioner in charge of the inquiry arranged for management and union officials to meet for the first time ever – *in Paris*! Negotiations began; a full recognition and bargaining agreement was made; and (after a ten-day dispute about its application) four months after their first meeting the two sides held a celebration dinner (this time in Scotland). The Report showed that in earlier days management had 'had to concentrate, to the virtual exclusion of all else, on increasing output'. Before the dispute, workers' problems 'had been largely shelved under the pressure of the more immediate need to meet production targets'.[28]

The C.I.R., like the T.U.C., has not always been successful. Some employers, urged to recognize unions, have resolutely refused (as in the case of the insurance company, p. 23). Faced with such a result, the C.I.R. has had power only to persuade them (in one case successfully, after a ballot of the employees). We have already seen that the 1970 Bill proposed to give the C.I.R. power to recommend to the D.E.P. Secretary of State legal enforcement of recognition (p. 34; and p. 165 below). But the status of the Commission, as a body which is established by law but which does not aim to use legal 'teeth' or sanctions, may be judged from the fact that both unions and employers began to seek its assistance. The first request to the D.E.P. for reference of its problems (including unions and 'staff association' recognition) to the C.I.R. actually came from an *insurance* firm, Commercial Union, in April 1970. Part of the reputation of the C.I.R. was undoubtedly acquired in the prolonged strike at the Birmingham Qualcast works in 1970, a dispute involving 25 Indian workers allegedly 'poached' by one union from another, with unsustained allegations by the workers of racial discrimination, overlapping union structures, and lack of proper disputes procedures. The C.I.R. played a major role in easing the intense human and industrial problems created by these factors. Any proposal to put such questions into a system of courts with lawyers has, in the British context, a crude look when placed beside the patient inquiries of such a sophisticated body as the C.I.R.

Meanwhile, however, the Labour Government had been promoting legislation. The *floor of rights* was to be increased by legislation on equal pay for women (p. 234), new medical services and safety committees at work (p. 254), and regulation of 'labour-only' practices in the construction industry (p. 64). The N.B.P.I. was to be merged into a new Commission for Industry and Manpower (p. 216). Workers' representation on employing boards was to be part of the scheme for nationalization of the ports (p. 45). Wages were to be open to attachment for debt (p. 224). Merchant seamen were to have less archaic laws controlling their rights (p. 389). None of these Bills, it will be noted, set out to regulate the structure of collective bargaining. All except the first and the last two lapsed when a General Election was held in June.

But on May Day, 1970, the Government at last produced its Industrial Relations Bill (the '1970 Bill'), which also lapsed in the same way. It contained none of the 'penal clauses' of April 1969; nor did it propose to enact the proposals for compulsory registration of unions, or control of union rules by the Registrar or a Review Board (p. 430). Instead, it concentrated upon proposals for definitions (e.g. of 'trade union' p. 411); a legal duty to recognize where the C.I.R. so recommended (p. 165); disclosure of information by employers, and registration of agreements (p. 169); amendments of trade dispute law (p. 384); a new *floor of rights* for workers unjustly dismissed (p. 142); the right of workers to join independent trade unions (p. 79); trade union accounts (p. 419); and the jurisdiction of industrial tribunals (p. 149). Around such proposals – and around the matters omitted from the 1970 Bill – will the debate about labour law revolve in the seventies. That debate has to take account of new aspirations among workpeople. As Mrs Castle told the Institute of Directors, power in the unions has

returned to the grass roots whence it came. We have got to accept ... that workpeople have a veto which they are increasingly prepared to exercise; in other words that management these days can no longer function by the arbitrary exercise of traditional prerogative but only by winning the consent of its workpeople.[29]

No law can guarantee that consent.

The strange year which preceded the 1970 General Election saw the thwarting of an attempt to introduce hasty labour legislation. Because of that, the roles of the T.U.C. and the C.I.R., and even of the C.B.I., were able to expand without cracking the system. But the task of reforming and expanding collective bargaining, to which the Donovan Report called its audience, still remains. The Conservative Government was elected in June 1970 on a programme for extensive legislation for controlling trade unions and regulating industrial relations. In the face of the Dock Strike in July, however, the new Secretary of State, Mr Carr, adopted traditional methods of conciliation which helped to promote a negotiated settlement. He appeared to be certainly no more 'interventionist' than his Labour predecessor; and it is for speculation whether he really wished to have at hand new powers to seek court injunctions against the trade union in the 'national interest'. Yet *Fair Deal At Work* envisaged that and many other similar new laws which would touch the whole structure of collective industrial relations. Such laws could impede the reform of collective bargaining which some of their authors hope to achieve; for British trade unions are likely to oppose on into the 1970s Bills which seem to them more inimical than the ill-fated measure of 1970. Moreover, the very attempt to promote legal sanctions into a primary role in the British system of industrial relations is unlikely to be either wise or effective. For, as two authorities put it in 1969:

These short cuts are in fact blind alleys. The law has a part to play, but it cannot enforce a regulative order where none exists.[30]

THE WORKER AND THE COMPANY

The worker is recognized by the rules of law that deal with his employment and his trade union. He was until 1967 (with two trivial exceptions) not known at all to company law. Even in 1967 the Companies Act demanded merely annual disclosure of overall pay-roll figures and the number of 'employees' earning more than £10,000 a year. But there are aspects of company law which it is fitting to mention briefly in a book concerning labour law.

First, an employer will usually be a registered company or some other corporation. The 'employer' and the worker, on the so-called 'individual' level, are already disparate in that the former is a fiction endowed with personality by the law. The company is in law a *separate* person from its shareholders or directors. In 1961, for example, a Mr Lee had been killed piloting a plane owned by his New Zealand company in which he owned 2,999 shares and his solicitor one. He was a director, and was also employed by the company as chief pilot. The Privy Council found that he was an employee of the company; for the company was a separate legal person and employed him, even though he (as director for the company) negotiated the terms with himself (as employee).[31] The company is, then, a personified aggregation of capital. The worker is a human person. But each is one person in law. So the 'employer' is already an association to which the law gives a legal personality. The workers' *trade union* is the equivalent of the company in social fact: whether it has a similar legal 'personality' has been a matter of doubt, as we see in Chapters 7 and 10.

Behind the legal person, 'the company', stand its shareholders, who own shares in it; its creditors who lend to it; and its directors, who manage it and owe their duties to it. The directors owe 'fiduciary' duties to their company which, unless expressly modified by agreement, are very strict – e.g. not to make secret profits from their position – and of which many directors are wholly ignorant. This, in itself, can create a problem for industrial relations with 'top people' in white collars. If a trade union finds directors doing work which makes them eligible for membership, can it try (by lawful means) to force them to join up? Or will the court stop the union from making the directors become trade unionists and, as it were, sit on both sides of the collective bargaining table at the same time? In a 1963 case the majority of the Court of Appeal thought the directors could make no objection; no breach of fiduciary duty *necessarily* arose from joining the union; and anyway, a company can, and often does, *waive* the directors' fiduciary duties. On the other side, there is no objection to a union's buying shares and attending the shareholders' meeting to question directors of a company with which it has a dispute.

These, then, are the characters who alone appear in the drama of company law. The employee is nowhere in the programme. His omission is not logically necessary. In West Germany, for example, workers' interests are recognized as among the objects which management may pursue. The extent to which English company law excludes the employee, however, may be judged by the case of *Parke* v. *Daily News*, 1962.[32] There, the directors of the company which owned the *News Chronicle* had negotiated the sale of the paper's goodwill to close it down. Their company owned the newspaper as its major asset, for which some £2 million was paid by the purchasers. The directors determined to pay the bulk of this money as a gift to the employees who had to be made redundant (the Act of 1965 was not yet passed) by way of compensation. A shareholder challenged their decision in court and succeeded in obtaining an injunction to stop the payments to the employees.

The shareholder's complaint was based on two rules of law. First, a registered company, except when authorized by its constitution, can make gifts of corporate property only if they are made in good faith, reasonably for the benefit and prosperity of the company, and incidental to its business. As a judge said in 1883: 'There are to be no cakes and ale except such as are required for the benefit of the company ... charity has no business to sit at boards of directors *qua* charity.' Invalid gifts are *ultra vires* acts, and cannot be adopted even by the shareholders' meeting. Secondly, the duty of directors is to consult the best interests of the company, and that, in English law, means the interests of the *shareholders*, on a long-term view. They may take account of the interests of employees not directly, but only indirectly as they reflect upon the interests of their shareholders.

All these principles, claimed the plaintiff in the *News Chronicle* case, had been broken by gifts to the ex-employees. Mr Justice Plowman agreed with him. The directors had acted honestly; but were motivated by a predominant desire

to treat the employees generously, beyond all entitlement . . . The view that directors, in having regard to the question what is in the best interests of their company, are entitled to take into account the interests of the employees, irrespective of any consequential benefit to the company, is one which may be widely held ... But ... in my judgment such is not the law ... the defendants were prompted by motives which, however laudable, and however enlightened from the point of view of industrial relations, were such as the law does not recognize as a sufficient justification.

But do not company directors commonly speak, as did Mr Harold Wincott, Editor of the *Investor's Chronicle*, in 1960 to the Jenkins Committee on company law, of having 'three co-equal interests to serve – those of the shareholders, the employees and the customers' and of the *partnership* between management, investors and workers? In the face of such assertions, workers may well feel resentment when the court has to apply rules of company law, as in the *Parke* case, which show that they have no legal rights in the enterprise. There has, therefore, sprung up over the last five years a lively debate about the reform of company law and even its very 'philosophy'.[33] But the Jenkins Committee of 1962 thought it was outside the scope of a body reviewing company law; and the matter is considered by the Donovan Report as a question of 'workers' participation *in management*'. But the problem is wider than that.

In fact, 1970 saw general agreement that, in Professor Walker's words: 'We are on the brink of a new phase in our thinking about industrial democracy'.[34] There was less agreement about what 'industrial democracy' means. To some it meant effective consultation; for others it could not exist in any form 'except in a context of full employment' in society.[35] Then there is the school which links 'partnership' to profit-sharing, and sometimes to workers' shares (which workers show a tendency to sell as soon as they can). The Liberal Party, like the Gaullist programme in France, points along this road to an eventual sharing of industrial power. Next come the advocates of 'workers' directors'. Twenty years of such experiments in Germany on 'supervisory boards' (not the equivalent of an executive board of directors) – one-third of the board except in steel and coal where worker and union representatives constitute one half – suggest that workers' participation in management

still has a rather limited scope within the Federal Republic of Germany ... such co-determination by employees' representatives as exists has been achieved only at the price of fostering oligarchic tendencies.[36]

A great majority of the Donovan Commission recommended that workers' directors should not be a compulsory feature of British company law, rightly in the view of the present writer. Many issues of company law would be raised which will no doubt feature in the next review of that area of law which the Conservative Government intends to institute. Would such directors have a 'dual' loyalty? Or more divided loyalties than some company directors enjoy now (e.g. the director nominated by a large shareholder or creditor)? Can such a scheme work without a 'two-tier' system of company boards (like the German)? Who would appoint them, for how long and in what numbers? What would their precise functions be, and who could ensure that they would be invited to informal meetings where decisions were *really* taken? The Donovan Report thought that new law of this kind might 'direct attention from the urgent task' of reconstructing collective bargaining, though some Commissioners wished to facilitate voluntary experiments. If German experience is relevant, it may have more to offer in the office of 'Labour Director' on the coal and steel management boards.

It may be easier to experiment along 'worker-director' lines in public corporations, where shareholders have been eliminated. Thus, the British Steel Corporation has increased to sixteen the workers appointed to the various boards controlling the industry and has produced an experimental 'job specification' for their work. The trade unions fought successfully for clauses in the Ports Bill, 1970, whereby their members would have been represented on the port boards, both national and local. It is true that unions have to be careful in such experiments, because 'participation may lead workers to become alienated from their union as well as from management'.[37] But the public sector seems to offer more opportunities for sharing power at all levels, shop-floor as well as board-room, as in the case of the T.G.W.U. shop stewards representing London Transport (now G.L.C.) busmen who from 1970 have negotiating rights over a wide area of managerial decisions.

Such shop-floor arrangements will, perhaps, be more characteristic of the British way to 'industrial democracy', namely the way of extended collective bargaining. The 'Task Force' under Dean Woods reported to the Canadian Government in 1968:

The basic contribution of industrial democracy has been to reduce the disparity between the rights of the individual as a worker and his rights as a citizen. The curbing or elimination of arbitrary authority in the hands of management has been one of the greatest contributions of unions and collective bargaining.

But the Transatlantic concept of 'industrial democracy', although it includes bargaining over more topics than has until recently been the case in Britain (after all, as there was no free National Health Service, it is hardly surprising that unions demanded medical insurance in the U.S.A.), nevertheless still rests upon the basic notion that management should retain extensive rights to act first even if the union may 'grieve' later. In Britain managerial prerogative to act is under more severe question in the seventies. Power over the *status quo* at work is being sought by workers today. The view is current that collective bargaining can build 'industrial democracy', not from the board-room down but from the shop-floor up.[38] In this process, the law might have a distinctive part to play, either by reform of 'company' law[39] or more generally. It could provide that employers should recognize their workers' trade unions and disclose to them information sufficient to make bargaining meaningful. Such disclosure can sometimes be won by agreement, as in the case of a Norfolk road haulage firm which in 1969 agreed to open its books to the union regularly. But the 1970 Bill proposed to enact a code of law on both matters (p. 165) to provide, as it were, a floor of practice for employers who would otherwise impede collective bargaining. The opportunity to pioneer such laws in the Companies Acts was lost in the sixties. Now in the seventies, legal obligations about disclosure of information will bridge the old categories of labour, company, or even monopoly law.

Disclosure is also the first of the obvious items on the agenda concerning the institution which will dominate the remaining decades of the century, something which (as Mr Wedgwood Benn put it in 1968) will reduce national governments 'to the status of a parish council' – the international, multi-national or 'global' corporation. Already about a quarter of Britain's exports are 'internal' transactions of international corporations; one in ten of Scotland's workers is employed by an American firm; foreign firms in Britain more frequently refuse to bargain (p. 166); and there are more companies than nations in the world with incomes higher than the gross national product of Ireland. No international mechanism for control of such enterprises is on the horizon (least of all in such groupings as the European Community where such control is discouraged by the Rome Treaty). When 400 draughtsmen at Fords, Dagenham, insisted in 1969 on a management pledge that transfers of work to Fords, Germany, would not cause them redundancies, they were illustrating the primary need for compulsory disclosure of plans by international enterprises. Moreover, there is urgent need to discover where and how international management makes decisions. to whom it owes its loyalties; and how to control its activities. Such laws are urgent at a national level, and the Bill on the Commission for Industry and Manpower, 1970, would, had it been enacted, have enforced certain disclosures by companies with more than £10 million in assets.

Despite joint action across frontiers, 'the scope for international trade union action is necessarily limited' (*T.U.C. Economic Review* 1970). Unions in both the motor-car and chemical industries have recently discussed collaboration and joint action. In 1968, workers at St Gobain subsidiaries in Italy and the U.S.A. launched simultaneous successful strikes. European unions increasingly refuse to countenance overseas subcontracting of work. Engineering workers' leaders in Britain and Germany have met (the German leader remarking: 'We cannot strike in sympathy with our British colleagues because our laws prevent that' – a fact illustrated once more in the British dock strike of 1970 when only German and Spanish port workers handled diverted cargoes). Workers at Heathrow blacked an American airline, and the A.E.U.F.W. decided to boycott General Electric goods to support striking American workers. But the muscle behind these moves is, so far, minute in the face of the power of giant global enterprises. Mr Paynter, a member of the C.I.R., has said that this 'movement of economic power' will make the proposals made in Britain for legislation on collective agreements

even more irrelevant – if that is possible – than they are now ... the law would be more appropriately employed in trying to establish some form of democratic control over the action of the large international enterprises. Their arbitrary decisions are likely to become the main source of disputes in industry.[39]

The international enterprise now adds a new dimension to the relationship between the worker and the company and a new challenge to both collective bargaining and labour law.

Notes to Chapter 1

1. Phelps Brown, *The Growth of British Industrial Relations* (1959), p. 355. The best textbook is now H. A. Clegg's *The System of Industrial Relations in Great Britain* (1970).
2. *Report of Royal Commission on Trade Unions and Employers' Associations*, 1965–8, Chairman: Rt Hon. Lord Donovan, 1968, Cmnd 3623. For the Research Papers (Numbers 1 to 11) see *Report* Appendix 4. The *Evidence* was published by H.M.S.O., 1965 to 1967. For brief accounts of the findings see: Folke Schmidt (1969) 32 *Modern Law Review* 65; and on various aspects (1968) VI *Brit. J. Industrial Relations* 275–359. See too O. H. Parsons, *The Donovan Report* (1968).
3. O. Kahn-Freund, *Labour Law: Old Traditions and New Developments* (1968), p. 9.
4. S. and B. Webb, *Industrial Democracy* (1914 edn), p. 814.
5. Ross and Hartman, *Changing Patterns of Industrial Conflict* (1960), p. 174.
6. On earlier chemical procedures, and on other industries, see K. W. Wedderburn and P. L. Davies, *Employment Grievances and Disputes Procedures in Britain* (1969, U.C.L.A.), Chapters 4–7.
7. G. S. Bain, 'Trade Union Growth and Recognition', *R. C. Research Paper No. 6* (1967). See too on bank workers, O. Robinson (1969) VII *Brit. J. Industrial Relations* 19.
8. *Evidence to Royal Commission*, Day 32, p. 1375.
9. J. Elliott, *Financial Times*, 18.5.70.
10. C.I.R. Report 1, *Associated Octel Ltd*, Cmnd 4246, p. 3.
11. See H. H. Wellington, *Labor and the Legal Process* (1968), Chapters 1–3; K. W. Wedderburn, 'British Unions Beware', *New Society*, 4 December 1969.
12. O. Kahn-Freund, 'Labour Law' in *Law and Opinion in England in the 20th Century*, ed. Ginsberg, p. 241. See for the cases, K. W. Wedderburn, *Cases and Materials on Labour Law* (1967), Chapter 4.
13. (1923) *Cambridge Law Journal*, p. 8.
14. [1898] A.C. 1.
15. [1901] A.C. 495.
16. [1901] A.C. 426.
17. *Reynolds* v. *Shipping Federation* [1924] 1 Ch. 28; and *Crofter Hand Woven Harris Tweed* v. *Veitch* [1942] A.C. 435.

18. [1964] A.C. 1129 (H.L.); see Chapter 8. Also *Torquay Hotel Co.* v. *Cousins* [1969] 2 Ch. 106 (C.A.).

19. See H. A. Turner, *Is Britain Really Strike Prone?* (1969), discussed in Chapter 8. For a critical analysis of Turner, see W. E. J. McCarthy (1970) VIII *Brit. J. Industrial Relations* 224.

20. A. Flanders, *Trade Unions* (1968), pp. 79–80.

21. *The Times*, 31.7.68. See also p. 180 [and now Appendix, p. 485].

22. For what follows see *The Times* 9 April to 19 June 1969; and the T.U.C. *Report*, 1969, pp. 202–225, from which quotations are taken unless otherwise specified.

23. *The Times*, 17.4.69. On the ambiguities in *In Place of Strife* see R. C. Simpson (1969) 29 *Modern Law Review* 420.

24. E. Wigham, *The Times*, 1.5.70.

25. J. P. Lowry, *Greener Grass?* (1970, E.E.F.).

26. See *The Times* and *Financial Times* for 18, 20, 30 Sept., 23, 24, 25, 28, 31 Oct., 5, 13, 14, 15, 27 Nov., and 12, 14, 18 Dec. 1969.

27. *Sunday Times*, 27.7.69; *The Times* 5.8.69.

28. C.I.R. Report 5, *B.S.R. Ltd*, Cmnd 4274 (1970).

29. *Financial Times*, 7.11.69.

30. Alan Fox and Allan Flanders (1969) VII *Brit. J. Industrial Relations* 180.

31. *Lee* v. *Lee's Air Farming Ltd* [1961] A.C. 12 (P.C.).

32. [1962] Ch. 927. (By a voluntary arrangement later made with many shareholders the directors managed to make some £900,000 available for the ex-employees.)

33. For the literature see: L. C. B. Gower, 'The Future of Company Law in a Mixed Economy', *Modern Company Law* (1969, 3rd edn. Gower, Park, Weaver and Wedderburn), p. 60.

34. *Industrial Democracy, Fantasy, Fiction or Fact?*, K. F. Walker, (Times Management Lecture 1970), p. 36.

35. E. Fletcher, discussing Prof. Walker's lecture, *The Times*, 4.3.70; and L. Cannon, *ibid*: 'I choose a word between consultation and participation, the word *involvement*'.

36. F. Furstenberg, 'Report on Workers' Participation in Management in Germany' (1969) 6 *International Instit. for Labour Studies* 94, 147.

37. G. Strauss and E. Rosenstein, 'Symposium on Workers' Participation' (1970) 9 *Industrial Relations* 117, 214; see *ibid.*, J. Schregle 117–22 on different meanings of 'participation'. See too F. Emery and E. Thorsrud *The Form and Concept of Industrial Democracy*, Tavistock Institute (1970).

38. See *Industrial Democracy* (Labour Party Working Party Report, 1967); *Institute for Workers' Control*, 'The Way Forward for Workers' Control', H. Scanlon (1968); and *Trade Union Register 1970* (ed. Coates, K., Topham, T., and Barratt Brown, M.), Part II.

39. K. W. Wedderburn, 'Company Law Reform' (Fabian Society, 1965, Tract 363).

40. *Industrial Law Soc. Bulletin* (1969), Supplement to No. 5, p. 32.

CHAPTER 2

THE CONTRACT OF EMPLOYMENT

FOR the English lawyer the fundamental institution to which he is forced to return again and again is the individual contract of employment. This makes inevitable a certain unreality; for the common law sets up a model of an individual contract which is a 'voluntary relationship into which the parties may enter on terms laid down by themselves within limitations imposed only by the general law of contract'.[1] The agreement is thought of as one attained after a bargain. Few contracts of employment are arrived at in that manner. They are not made after a protracted haggle between employer and employee at the factory gates. The accepted rights of the parties are often found in the result of collective negotiations between employers and trade unions rather than in any individual bargain; and on rare occasions are even imposed by Parliament in statutes; to those two matters we turn in succeeding chapters. But the legal starting-point is always the individual worker's contract of employment – which he invariably has with his employer, though he is often unaware that it exists. Even without collective or statutory intervention, the lawyer's model of this freely bargained agreement is misleading; for many terms of agreement are imposed by the more powerful individual of the two, the employer. Indeed, in practice, the worker's social 'rights' – as he would think of them – often depend more upon practice and power at the workplace than upon law, as in the case of a worker dismissed for throwing a sponge at the foreman (though he missed) whose reinstatement was secured by the shop steward largely on the argument – not wholly unfamiliar to the lawyer – that the punishment was out of step with a case three years before in which a man was only suspended for throwing a sponge at the foreman (which hit him).[2] But the employment contract knows little or nothing of such matters. The language of 'agreement' used in the court-room is bound to have a hollow ring to a servant sued for the enforcement of what he felt to be an imposed obligation; and we shall see that the courts' interpretation of the 'agreement' and 'intention' has frequently resulted in a legal consolidation of the superior disciplinary and other powers of the employer.

Furthermore, the general law of contract concerning employment still rests largely on judicial decisions of the eighteenth and nineteenth centuries. But direct litigation has been relatively infrequent between employer and employee in the last fifty years. In consequence, the legal authority on many incidents in the employment relationship is contained in cases decided more than a century ago. As we shall see, the courts, though bound by the principles expressed in the older cases, may attempt to apply them in new ways more consistent with current social conditions; but it is not always easy to predict just how far, or in what ways, the judges will modernize their application; and on some matters the precedents can be simply irrelevant. Similarly, the same principles have caused problems in many of the cases before Industrial Tribunals on redundancy payments. A society in which the agricultural labourer and domestic servant predominated was wont to produce litigation concerned with them. In one modern textbook, therefore, the student who today asks after the legal rights of an employee dismissed for immorality, incompetence, or neglect is referred to eleven judgments, four before 1779, four before 1862. The legal rights of the industrial worker still have to be based to a great degree upon reinterpretation of those cases. The collective procedures arranged between management and union, the local, area, divisional, or national committees, and (perhaps above all today) the 200,000 local shop stewards elected by the workers themselves, to whom complaints about a grievance or dismissal might be taken, have little part initially in the legal discussion.

WHO IS A 'SERVANT'?

The common lawyer has for centuries referred to the parties as 'master' and 'servant'; and although modern usage has gradually replaced those terms with the more egalitarian 'em-

ployer' and 'employee', the latter's contract is still usually referred to as a contract of 'service'. As such, it is distinguished
from other contracts, such as one of partnership, or one in
which an employer has work done by a self-employed 'independent contractor'. The difference between the contract of
service and 'contract for services' has taxed the ingenuity of
judges. 'It is often easy to recognize a contract of service when
you see it,' said one, 'but difficult to say wherein the difference
lies.' Sad to say, by 1970 even recognition has become harder.
Yet the concept of 'servant' is critical in many areas of law.
A master, for example, is 'vicariously' liable for the tort of a
wrongdoing servant, in addition to any liability of the servant
himself, if the servant acted in the course of the employment,
e.g. a delivery man who carelessly knocks you down driving
his van on the delivery round. He also owes *to* his servants a special duty to provide a reasonably safe system of
working.

The development of the law was here again greatly influenced by propositions established in cases dealing with agricultural or manual labourers and domestic servants; and perhaps for that reason more than any other, the residual test
which the courts employed was the right to control the *manner*
of executing the work, the right to say both what shall be done
and how it shall be done. The courts also take account of other
factors such as the power of dismissal; the right of selection (for
example, of a driver for a hired vehicle); the character of the
task; the method of payment and the right to withhold it – all
are relevant to the decision of fact whether the contract is one
of 'service' or not. In 1924 one judge said that 'the final test, if
there be a final test, and certainly the test to be generally
applied lies in the nature and degree of detailed control over
the person alleged to be a servant'.[3]

But today the other factors are often critical. One commentator has said the control test, although it may sometimes be a
determining factor, 'can no longer be treated as the decisive
test in all circumstances'.[4] In 1966 a judge, agreeing that the
test is 'not as determinative as used to be thought', added that
of course 'the greater the degree of control exercisable by the

employer the more likely it is that the contract is one of service'. The Lord Chief Justice said in 1965 that the control test was clearly *not* 'the determining test' in a case where an engineer employed by a local council had his manner of work controlled by a consultant from outside the council's staff. Since the council retained complete power over his appointment (though not his selection), his dismissal, his salary and other payments, he was, the Court of Appeal found, still the council's 'servant'.[5]

When judges have to decide which of two persons is the 'master' in law, where one has lent a servant to the other, they have said that unless the general employer proves that the right to control the manner of the work in fact passed to the borrower he remains the 'master' in law. In one case, in 1947, for example, the Mersey Docks and Harbour Board hired out a mobile crane to a company, and sent one of their skilled men to work it, providing in the contract of hire that he was to be the company's servant on the job. He was indeed told by the company what to pick up with the crane; but when he injured a third party by driving it into him, the House of Lords decided that the Board remained vicariously liable as his employer. It retained the right to control the manner of his work.[6] What is at stake in these cases is often of course a battle between insurance companies, for when one says a company 'is liable' one usually means that its insurance company must pay up; but the courts take no account of this. Where a servant goes to work for a short time 'on loan' to another firm and is paid by them, with his national insurance cards transferred to them, he nevertheless remains the servant of the original employer, unless he has agreed to a transfer.[7] Moreover, the 'master' today is frequently a corporation – a limited company or a public corporation – a separate person in law. In such a case, as in any big organization, the servant may be bound to obey the commands of a superior servant – a foreman or manager. But the superior servant will not himself become in law the master of the servants beneath him in the hierarchy; he gives the orders on behalf of the master. Both are servants of the corporation.

The 'control test' may have been easy to use when the work done was manual or simple; but it becomes rather unreal when the work is highly complex, especially if the worker knows more about it than anyone else and might give, as it has been said, a 'sturdy answer' to anyone who told him *how* to do it. The problems grew in cases concerning alleged vicarious liability of hospitals for their staff. Whereas earlier cases had suggested that no such liability could arise, by 1942 the Court of Appeal was ready to treat nurses, radiographers and house doctors as occupying the position of 'servants' of the hospital. In later cases, encouraged no doubt by the structure of the National Health Service, the court has extended this principle to surgeons, at least as long as they are on the staff and not specially engaged by the patient. 'It is,' said Lord Justice Somervell in 1951, 'also important to remember ... that the principle *respondeat superior* (i.e. the master's vicarious responsibility) is not ousted by the fact that a "servant" has to do work of a skilful or technical character for which the servant has special qualifications.'[8] No doubt; but the servant's 'duty to obey commands' in regard to the *manner* of his work can surely mean little in such a context. No surgeon could be so instructed by the Chairman of the Hospital Board! The result is no doubt just, since the patient can sue the hospital; but the 'control test' fits awkwardly into the argument.

Some judges have therefore turned to a different test. Lord Justice Denning contrasted in 1952 the ship's master, chauffeur, and reporter on the staff (all servants) with the ship's pilot, taximan, and newspaper contributor (all independent contractors), saying: 'One feature which seems to run through the instances is that, under a contract of service, a man is employed as part of the business, and his work is done as an integral part of the business; whereas, under a contract for services, his work, although done for the business, is not integrated into it but is only accessory to it.'[9] This so-called 'organization' test can be valuable. It approximates to the economist's distinction between the contractor who operates as an independent enterprise, and the man who sells his labour as service to the enterprise of another. But it cannot be used in all cases. There may be no 'organization' or 'business', and yet a man may be employed as a servant.

Moreover, the need to reassess the common law concept of 'servant' is emphasized by the fact that the judges have been so influenced by it that they tend to make use of it in areas where it is doubtfully appropriate. When statute talks merely of 'clerks or servants', it may cause little surprise if judges give to the words the common law meaning. Thus, under the Companies Acts, the preferential claim for wages (up to £200) allowed to servants on a winding-up was denied in 1965 to a gang of workers supplied to the company under a 'labour-only' contract. The same test has been carried over, with more questionable advantage, into the interpretation of modern social security law and of other statutes.

Since the National Insurance Act, 1946, and now under the Act of 1965, every citizen is either non-employed, self-employed, or 'employed' – i.e. 'gainfully occupied in employment in Great Britain being employment under a contract of *service*'. An employed person pays the lower contribution and can claim unemployment benefit, if qualified, when unemployed, or industrial injury benefit if injured in his work. Did a music-hall artiste, part of a 'comedy duo', fall into this third category when engaged under a weekly contract by which he could be transferred to another theatre? He was prohibited from appearing elsewhere, undertook to cause no danger to persons in the theatre, to pay penalties if he failed to appear, and was required to obey the regulations of the management. He gave the management control over anything to which they objected in the act, and the right to demand different songs, or a reasonable response to encores. The Court agreed with the Minister of Pensions (who has had primary jurisdiction over this question under the Acts) that this was not a contract of service because, in the last resort, the artiste retained control over the manner in which he performed his act. A different result was reached in 1966 in the case of a trapeze artiste who provided her own apparatus and act but was also obliged to help move the circus tents and to act as an usherette. The judge held that she was a 'servant' largely because she carried out her duties overall 'as an integral part of the business of the company'.[10] In 1963 a transport worker was injured when pursuing, on his motor-cycle, his spare-time occupation as trade union 'sick-steward'. Was he injured in the course of employment under a contract of service? He was held to be a servant of the *union* at the time of injury. The judge commented: 'the nature of the control which is required in order to bring the employment within the scope of the contract of service varies almost infinitely with the general nature of the duties involved.'[11] At this point the 'control test' has become nearly fictional. Indeed in many of the social security decisions both of the courts and of the Minister, one suspects that the decisions pay much more attention to social policy (and rightly so) than to the outdated formulae of the old common law.

The modern decisions, however, show an ever-increasing confusion over this fundamental concept of our labour law. Three cases in 1968 showed the difficulty of predicting who is and who is not a servant. An actor who taught at a school of drama on a part-time basis and to his own syllabus was held by the Minister to be a self-employed person. He appealed to the High Court where the judge, referring to all the possible tests (including 'what in modern parlance is called economic reality'), held that the Minister was right, clinching his argument with the comment that otherwise a barrister teaching part-time at a university, in the evenings or over weekends, would become an employee of the university 'when in truth his own profession as a barrister made manifest that he was a self-employed person as every practising barrister necessarily is'.[12] On the other hand, a woman interviewer who was from time to time engaged to interview persons according to a pattern set by a market research company but who could work as and when she chose, her contract containing no provisions about time off, sick-pay, holidays, dismissal, and no prohibition against working for others, was held to be employed under a series of contracts of service and therefore in 'insurable employment'.[13] Although she had a 'limited discretion' in the work, she was not, the judge thought, 'in business on her own account' nor did she 'provide her own tools or risk her own capital'.

This last factor was important in the third curious but important judgment, *Ready Mixed Concrete Ltd* v. *Minister of Pensions*.[14] An 'owner-driver', L., was engaged to drive a lorry with a rotating drum for delivering concrete to the company's customers. A complicated contract declared him to be an 'independent contractor'; but, as the judge said, this could not be final (especially for insurance purposes) since if 'the relation is that of master and servant, it is irrelevant that the parties have declared it to be something else'. The system of 'owner-drivers' had been initiated by the concrete company. L. contracted with the company for the carriage of the concrete; entered into a hire-purchase contract (with an associated company) for the lorry, which was painted in the company's colours; agreed to wear a uniform, to drive up to certain maximum hours, and to carry out orders 'as if' he were an employee. He was to maintain the lorry, and was paid on a mileage basis. The judge appeared to use neither the 'organization', nor the old form of the 'control' test. Instead, he held that even if there be control, that is not *sufficient* to create a contract of service unless the *other* provisions of the contract are consistent with that result. He thought that L. was not an employee but a 'small businessman', especially since he 'owned the instrumentalities' (as the American law has it) of the operation. In truth, he was the owner in name only; for the hire-purchase had five years to run and the company had an option to take the lorry at market price after that. It is easy to agree with the comment that in this judgment 'the form in which the arrangement was cast has been allowed to prevail over the substance', and that it affects in a 'radically new way' a problem fundamental to labour law.[15] The *Ready Mixed Concrete* judgment has been influential in later cases, an influence unlikely to be beneficial. For this unhappy decision can only help to spread the dangerous practice of 'self-employment' on which comment is made below (p. 61).

It might be preferable if the courts, instead of applying the old distinction between servant and independent contractor to modern welfare laws, developed in each area a concept of 'employee' appropriate to its needs. Such a development has occurred abroad, for example in Sweden where social security law uses rather different notions from those used in the Labour Courts. Already in 1950 a judge remarked that a person 'employed' for national insurance purposes need not fall into that category for the purpose of income tax. An investigation of British labour law statutes prompts the same conclusion, that new concepts are needed.

Various statutes have laid down their own meaning of 'employee' within their scope; and whereas the courts appear to have been constricted by the one meaning of servant, statute law presents a patchwork of various definitions – some very wide. The Industrial Courts Act, 1919, under which much voluntary arbitration takes place, applies to any person under a contract with an employer 'whether it be a contract of service or of apprenticeship or a contract personally to execute any work or labour'. Thus it appears to include 'independent contractors' who are 'self-employed'; and the Wages Councils Act, 1959, is in similar terms. Others are narrower – for example the definition in the Employers and Workmen Act, 1875, which applies only to a 'workman', i.e. a person who is 'a labourer, servant in husbandry, journeyman, artificer, handicraftsman, miner, or otherwise engaged in *manual* labour' (except a domestic or menial servant), whether it be under a contract of service or one 'personally to execute any work or labour' (i.e. an independent contractor within the prescribed range). This definition is, as we shall see in Chapter 5, critical in the statutory regulation of payment of wages. The Trade Disputes Act, 1906, the vital statute in industrial conflict, applies to 'workmen', defined as 'persons employed in trade or industry'. The usual modern definition of 'employee' is used in the Contracts of Employment Act, 1963, and the Prices and Incomes Act, 1966, namely, any person 'who has entered into or works under a contract with an employer, whether the contract be for manual labour, clerical work or otherwise, be expressed or implied, oral or in writing, and whether it be a contract of service or of apprenticeship'. The Redundancy Payments Act,

1965, uses the same definition with the addition of words apt to include dismissed employees ('or worked under') for whose benefit the Act was passed. It is hardly surprising in view of this variation that Acts which, like the Shop Clubs Act, 1902, regulate the conditions of employment of 'workmen' or which, like the Industrial Training Act, 1964, provide for boards for training 'persons employed or intending to be employed' in different industries *without* defining the critical words, leave considerable uncertainty. It is to be hoped that Parliament will continue to elaborate a series of definitions suited to the needs of the various areas of labour law. The 1970 Bill proposed to make a start by creating a new category of 'worker' of which it would have made use in amending the definitions of trade union (p. 410) and trade dispute (p. 327), and which it would have inserted into the Industrial Courts Act, 1919. Such a 'worker' would be a person who works or seeks to work either (a) under a contract of employment (as defined in the Redundancy Payments Act, 1965); or (b) under any other contract personally to do work (manual, clerical or otherwise); or (c) in employment under a Minister of the Crown or government department (other than the armed services). This category of 'worker' would be very useful. But in the 1970 Bill itself, most of the provisions still applied only to 'employees' or servants in the strict sense. We are likely to struggle for a long time yet with the common-law concept.

There are certain groups of persons who at first sight seem to be 'servants' but who for various reasons of policy are excluded from the category. For instance, a police constable is not a servant when engaged in the performance of his duties and is not, therefore, the employee of his local watch committee. The committee is not, therefore, legally liable for his torts (e.g. wrongful arrest) – though the Police Act, 1964, has introduced a special new liability for policemen's acts on the part of chief constables whereby the citizen can now get damages out of police funds. But most workers – from factory operatives to nurses, from dustmen and typists to chauffeurs and house surgeons, white-collar or blue, black-coated or shirt-sleeved – can still be brought under the old common-law meaning of 'servants'. Unless there is a different meaning because of an Act or some other special rule, it is to that legal concept that our discussion of the worker, or employee, is assumed to relate in what follows.

SELF-EMPLOYED WORKERS AND LABOUR-ONLY CONTRACTS[16]

But we must interject at once that this assumption is bigger than many people realize. In truth, a spectre is haunting labour law, the spectre of 'self-employment'. The growth of this practice is not unrelated to the new confusion about the definition of 'employee' or 'servant' in the courts. The problem stems from the fact that more and more workers who *look* like employees are adopting, or being given, the position of 'self-employed' persons. For many years this problem has plagued some sectors of industry, notably the building industry and engineering firms which employ 'contract draughtsmen'. The latter have been vigorously opposed by the trade union (D.A.T.A.) and two fierce strikes in 1966 forced English Electric in effect to eliminate 'self-employment' among their draughtsmen. A similar attempt by a builders' union to challenge what can be a form of 'self-employment' (workers supplied under 'labour only' sub-contracts) failed, as we shall see (p. 350), when the sub-contractors obtained an injunction to stop the strike. Had the workers been 'employees' proper, the Trade Disputes Act, 1906, might have prevented such legal action (see Chapter 8).

Apart, therefore, from the impact of such arrangements upon good industrial relations, there are various legal consequences which flow from an industrial worker becoming 'self-employed', words normally associated with the white-collar consultant or the one-man business. The worker becomes, for example, entitled to pay income tax not under P.A.Y.E. but in arrears under 'Schedule D', with better opportunities for claiming expenses. One builder, Mr Jessop, who gave his workers the choice of being self-employed or being paid union rates (below their normal earnings) said in 1966:

'They are better off self-employed. I have given them the
services of my accountant and ... they are saving £3 a week
tax.' Reports have appeared of workers made bankrupt through
failure to put aside sums towards Schedule D tax. The worker
has to pay the higher self-employed State insurance contribution; but he often forgets that he loses his claim to many
benefits (e.g. unemployment and industrial injury benefit: see
pp. 122 and 287). Evasion of insurance and tax payments has
been alleged to be widespread among self-employed workers,
especially the so-called 'Bedouin' workers who travel from site
to site in the building industry.

The 'employer' makes certain savings, for example in his
administrative work. The stability of his labour force may
decrease; but his workers, if their 'self-employed' status is
upheld, fall outside a vast range of modern labour law legislation. Such statutes, stricken with an apparent myopia, continue to concentrate upon the 'employee' proper. Thus the
'employer' of self-employed workers is relieved of his obligations under the Contracts of Employment Act, 1963 (p. 117)
and the Redundancy Payments Act, 1965 (p. 125). In order to
make the Industrial Training Act, 1964, bite, special Orders
have had to be made. An amending Bill was proposed in 1970
to extend the 1964 Act to the 'self-employed'. Moreover, it
seems to be almost a matter of chance whether or not a worker,
either 'self-employed' or one whose labour is supplied by
another, falls within the protection of health, welfare and safety
legislation or Orders made under it (see Chapter 6). In 1967, a
worker who had fallen from a roof was held by the Court of
Appeal to be able to claim damages from his employing sub-
contractors (who were insolvent) but not from the main contractors; but the House of Lords by careful re-interpretation of
the Building Regulations allowed his action against the latter.[17] Regulations passed to protect 'workmen employed' by a
company do not, it was held in 1959, protect the self-employed.
At common law, the employer owes a lower duty to the self-
employed independent contractor. Thus, a judge held in 1967
that a timberman paid on a daily basis who agreed to remain
self-employed in a small timber business was not owed the duty

in respect of a 'safe system of work', to which an employee is entitled (see p. 265) and therefore, when injured by a tree felled by an unsupervised method, failed in an action against his 'employer'.[18]

The figures for self-employment in Britain overall in the early sixties were uncertain; but with the Selective Employment Payments Act, 1966, a new wave began. The new tax, S.E.T., was levied on the number of *employees*! A director of 'Labour Force' (an agency supplying self-employed building workers) said soon afterwards: 'Since S.E.T. we have been at our wits' end to know how to deal with demand.' By July 1969 the President of the Building Employers' Federation said self-employment had grown at an 'alarming rate' and the industry was 'literally breaking into pieces – little one-man pieces'. A committee, under Professor Phelps-Brown, sat from 1967 to June 1968 to consider the building industry's problems. It made various recommendations, including a statutory register of those 'genuinely in business on their own account'; new legal provision that anyone who paid for construction work by an unregistered person should be deemed to be his employer for all purposes; and extensions of liability in respect of accidents.[19] The committee found that of the 1,850,000 workers in construction in 1966 some 147,000 were self-employed workers, an increase of 60 per cent over 1961. Up to 200,000 operatives worked under 'labour-only' sub-contracts. The problems are complicated in that some of these are employees of the 'labour-only' contractor. Others (about 100,000 the committee estimated) are self-employed workers merely supplied by the contractor acting as an agency. This is especially the case where the workers do specific jobs as a 'gang', the gang leader sometimes being given a lump sum for distribution as 'wages'. By 1969, the estimate of construction workers supplied under various types of 'labour-only' contracts rose to 250,000; and the Inland Revenue estimated that up to £3 million had been lost in taxes for 1967 because of the failure by contractors to complete returns on sums paid to such workers. The spokesman of the Inland Revenue Staff Association spoke in 1969 of '300,000-plus of these self-employed people who are involved in what I call financial fiddling'. The Finance Act, 1970, would, but for the General Election, have required builders using labour-only workers from an unregistered source to pay over normal income tax to the Revenue at the standard rate on sums paid out. *Registered* contractors would be treated as the employers of the workers concerned. The register was to be set up under the Construction Industry Contracts Bill. That Bill (with certain exceptions) would have exacted a levy on subcontractors, 'labour-only' suppliers, and agents of self-employed gangs who were not registered but who carried on defined operations in the construction industry. The levy was meant to make up for lost statutory contributions (from national insurance and redundancy contributions to S.E.T.).

But this method of registration-plus-penalties would not cure all the problems. Even though conditions as to insurance cover were imposed upon admission to the register, it would be difficult to enforce the continuous maintenance of proper policies by a registered sub-contractor. The Bill would not have applied to firms whose *business* did not include the erection of buildings. Lastly, the Bill did nothing to alter the status of the self-employed building worker and, therefore, nothing to improve the position in respect of safety, which the Phelps-Brown Report had made a high priority. These proposals for legislation lapsed in 1970. There is, therefore, a chance to do better. But voluntary action was taken by the Joint Industry Board in electrical contracting which gave a lead by adopting new Working Rules in 1970 prohibiting anyone within its scheme (which means, effectively, the industry) from working for 'labour-only' firms or free-charging agencies, or as a self-employed worker.

But the practice of self-employment is not confined to the building industry. At various T.U.C. conferences, speakers have mentioned agriculture, shipbuilding and other industries. In 1969 the Inland Revenue Staff representatives spoke of self-employed barbers who 'rented' chairs; waiters who 'rented' tables; and commercial travellers who are self-employed.[20] That gangs of 'highly-skilled labour' are customarily supplied to big firms in the electronics industry was confirmed by an unsuccessful appeal against training levy before an Industrial Tribunal in 1967 by On-Line Electronics Ltd, whose sole business was the supply of such labour. As is usual, an Order had been made for the relevant industry dealing with 'employees', and within its terms the gangs were held to be the employees of the company (though a further group of 'freelance', presumably self-employed, workers were not brought within the scheme). Solicitors have made clerks into self-employed contractors. The writer met an industrialist in engineering who remarked in 1968: 'Of course all my fitters are self-employed men. We have no union trouble.'

There should also be remembered the related problem of private fee-charging agencies which supply workers, often part-time. Great legal difficulty can arise in assessing whether such a worker is self-employed or, if not, who is the employer. In Europe considerable concern has been shown about '*le travail interimaire*' (though European agencies seem often to charge the worker, which is not British practice). An O.E.C.D. Report on 'Part-Time Employment' in 1968 made proposals for new laws about part-time workers; and the I.L.O., in Convention 96, called for legal regulation of the agencies. Although minor changes have been made (for example by national insurance regulations deeming certain clerical staff to be the 'employees' of firms to whom they were supplied by some types of agencies), the Labour Government did not introduce legislation. In 1969, the Government told the T.U.C. that, though legislation was still a 'live' issue, it had to await (*inter alia*) the report of the Royal Commission on Local Government to decide the appropriate mechanism for control! Yet in 1968 the N.B.P.I. had put the case for a 'fully developed State employment service' in its Report on Office Staff Employment Agencies (No. 89). The labour force should not be 'fragmented' between private agencies and the state employment offices. In 1970 a new drive to improve and publicize the services of the state employment offices was begun by the D.E.P. A statute regulating the fee-charging agencies would be a welcome complement in the drive against 'self-employment' and its associated problems.

Staggeringly, the Donovan Report contains no detailed discussion whatever of any of these problems. Nor have Ministers or the courts consistently leaned against the rising tide. The decisions on National Insurance classification and loans of servants include statements by judges that the question 'contract-of-service-or-not?' must be tested as a matter of law, not merely by reference to the descriptions used by the parties. But increasingly the legal test has become obscure; and in borderline cases, as in the *Ready Mixed Concrete* case, judges sometimes are much too willing to categorize a worker as an independent contractor. In July 1970, three High Court judges ruled in an appeal from an industrial tribunal decision that workmen paid a flat rate by Labour Force Ltd and sent to work for contractors who paid a higher sum to the company, the workmen paying their own income tax and insurance contributions, were not the 'employees' of Labour Force Ltd. That company was not, therefore, liable to pay some £120,000 industrial training levy payable on 'employees'.[20a] Such decisions subvert the 1964 statute which might otherwise help the building industry to acquire the trained workers which it needs. Mr Justice Cooke stressed that the parties did not intend to make any contracts of service, while Mr Justice Fisher even laid stress on the fact that if the men were 'employees' the tax and insurance arrangements would be illegal – so they could not be 'employees'.

Furthermore, in 1965, the Minister of Pensions decided to classify as self-employed a slater and tiler who was told by the employer (Marley Tile Ltd) that he would be treated as a 'sub-contractor' (he used his own tools and paid his own tax and insurance contributions) for purposes of industrial injuries benefit (see p. 287). But in 1966, the Industrial Court, faced with workers similarly designated by building employers (W. Creighton Ltd), found that 'the relationship between the Company and the workers ... is by way of contract of service ... that the expression "self-employed" is a misdescription of the true position of the said workers'. Their trade union could, therefore, make use of a procedure available to representative organizations of workers under contracts of employment in section 8, Terms and Conditions of Employment Act, 1959 (see p. 200).[21] Perhaps it is no accident that the Industrial

Court, normally a voluntary arbitration tribunal, which sits with a legal president and lay 'wing-men' representing employers and employees, appreciated the true problem and broke through to reality while the ordinary courts hang back. On the other hand, the legal position of every worker cannot be left to the outcome of litigation, however sensible the tribunal. Nor can 'genuine' self-employment be made illegal. The little man who paints the fence cannot be made into a criminal because he prefers not to work for another. Mr R. Carr, M.P., the Conservative Party spokesman, who became D.E.P. Secretary of State in 1970, declared in March 1967 that, 'providing the rules defining self-employment are properly drawn, every man and women has a right to be self-employed, if they want to be'. But what are 'the rules' to be? There are few more baffling or important questions in labour law than how to allow the genuine practice of self-employment and even 'labour-only' contracting (which in some cases the Phelps-Brown Committee even commended) without permitting it to be a legal device for evading laws passed to protect workers, for avoiding taxes, for destroying industrial relations, and for encouraging management to attack trade union organization to gain an advantage over more conscientious competitors. As a first step, the legislature could at least see to it that *each* statute expressly brings within its scope those groups of 'self-employed' workers (and their employers) whom it does not wish to see escape on a mere technicality.

THE FORMATION OF THE CONTRACT OF SERVICE

The layman tends to think of a contract as a formal document but the contract of employment may be made by word of mouth, or partly in writing or partly oral, or even by implication. Where there is a clear agreement on certain terms which the parties intend to be legally binding, there the law finds a bargain enforceable as a contract. Furthermore, the parties may spell out only some of the terms and leave the rest to silence; but the court will, whenever it can, supply the missing terms, relying sometimes on customs or practices to which the parties must have referred – as the leading judgment has it, where, if some 'officious bystander' had suggested this is what they meant, 'they would testily suppress him with a common "Oh of course!" '. This willingness of the courts to uphold agreements by filling out gaps left by the parties is understandable; but it is a method, as we shall see, whereby the courts can mould the obligations of the parties. The terms of the employment should be set out clearly, and legislation has made a meagre attempt to promote that aim in the Contracts of Employment Act, 1963. Although the courts will occasionally fill out gaps, the agreement must not be so uncertain that the court is unable to give it a clear meaning. If the parties contract for services to be rendered at a 'West End salary to be mutually arranged between us', as in a case of 1902, there is no enforceable contract. But recently the courts have leant towards upholding contracts of employment wherever, by reasonable common sense, they could give a meaning to apparently vague terms. In 1958, coal mining deputies bound to work 'such days or part days in each week as may reasonably be required by the management' were, in *N.C.B.* v. *Galley*, sued for breach of contract when they refused to work certain Saturday shifts. The Court of Appeal decided that their obligation was one to work a reasonable number of days, and on the evidence the court was prepared to say that their refusal was unreasonable.[22] Certainty of terms by itself is not enough. Unless the agreement is made in a sealed deed, there must, in order for it to be enforceable, be 'consideration' advanced by each party; that is to say, each party must contribute his part to the bargain as the price of the other's promises. In the usual case, for example, the employee's promise to do the work matches the employer's promise to pay the wages. The exact moment of formation of the contract can at times be important. Thus, a dock worker presented himself to dock employers as allocated by the Board under the Dock Workers Order, 1967 (p. 82), who gave him documents welcoming him as their employee. Later the same day, it was discovered that the worker's union membership had lapsed and the employers 'returned' the worker to the Board. But in doing so, they broke the contract already made by the agreement earlier in the day.[23]

Certain parties have at common law, however, only a limited capacity to contract. Of these, two require brief mention here – infants and the Crown. The Courts upheld contracts of service as binding on the infant if they were on balance beneficial to him, even if particular terms operated to his disadvantage. The same principle applied to contracts of apprenticeship (under which in return for the services of the apprentice the master agrees to instruct and teach him in his trade), and to analogous contracts. These common-law rules came to be supplemented by a series of statutory restrictions over the employment of young persons and children (touched on in Chapter 5), such as the Children and Young Persons Act, 1963, one effect of which is to restrict within extremely narrow limits the legality of employing at all any person under the compulsory school leaving age, currently fifteen years.

In an age when the teenager enjoys greater affluence and emancipation, the age of majority (for centuries twenty-one years) had to be lowered. In 1970, therefore, it became eighteen years by statute and full contractual capacity is now acquired at that age. Below eighteen years the old common law still applies. Thus, in 1965, a 'Bohemian' young man living on social security benefit, a son of Charlie Chaplin, was held by two judges in the Court of Appeal to a contract whereby the defendants were to publish a book, *I Couldn't Smoke the Grass on My Father's Lawn*, which would be ghost-written for him. The text put the son in a very bad light and might expose him to libel actions; but these judges held that the contract 'enabled him to make a start as an author' – 'The mud may cling but the profits will be secured' – and was a benefit even though the text had neither 'taste nor decency'. Yet the son was trying to repudiate the tasteless contract into which he had been led by what Lord Denning, M.R., who dissented, called 'financial inducements on all hands'. Quite how such a muddy start could be beneficial to his career as author was unexplained. But after 1970, a young man of eighteen would have no similar chance to disclaim a contract on grounds of lack of benefit.

The position of the Crown – that is of all Ministries and

Government Departments – is still a matter of some dispute. In 1947, the Crown Proceedings Act made clear that the citizen can sue the Crown for breach of contract. But has the civil servant any contract of service on which he can sue? Two answers receive support in the judges' decisions. First, where nothing is said concerning security of tenure, the Crown can undoubtedly dismiss at pleasure. Some cases go so far as to hold that this prerogative to dismiss at will overrides even express terms of a contract of service, and cannot be restricted except by a statute, so that the Crown is able to ignore the terms of the agreement at its pleasure.[24] The legal actions for wages in the 'pay pause' of 1961 brought by two industrial civil servants against their Government employers, discussed in Chapter 4, p. 190, might have decided whether a civil servant had a contract; but, as we shall explain, their actions failed for other reasons. Recently the Privy Council supported the Crown's right to dismiss at pleasure. But the same court (in which the Law Lords sit) suggested in 1970 that, while employed, the Crown employee had a contractual right to his salary just like any other employee.[25] It is to be hoped that the House of Lords will establish at least that minimal right. The 1970 Bill proposed to include Crown employees (other than the armed services) within its new employment rights (e.g. protection against unjust dismissal). A general statute defining the special privileges (if any) of the Crown as employer would be timely. After all, there is little reason why a worker employed on two weeks' notice by the Crown should suffer the legal disability of not being able to sue for his wages or of being open to instant dismissal without redress. Of course, in practice he will be protected by his trade union and the consultative and other procedures established by the Whitley Councils and institutions of collective bargaining that honeycomb the civil service. But, as we shall see, these exist largely outside the law and can rarely improve his legal rights in any way. Lord Goddard remarked in 1957 that, though in law insecure, the established civil servant is after probation in fact 'secure in his employment till he reaches retiring age, apart, of course, from misconduct or complete inefficiency'.

(His Lordship should perhaps have added, also, an exception to accommodate the decisions of those who investigate 'security', whose procedures have owed more to the Star Chamber than to any due process of law. Unhappily the 1970 Bill would have refused any protection to a worker unjustly dismissed if a Minister merely 'certified' that his dismissal was 'for the purpose of safeguarding national security' – a power of extraordinarily wide scope which the Bill would not even have confined to Crown employment!)

The cloak of the Crown covers government departments and other bodies which act for the Crown. But there is no such protection for the commercial public corporations – the National Coal Board, Gas and Electricity Councils, and the like. Even if controlled by government departments, they are in law separate entities, which, subject to any provisions in each controlling statute, employ their employees on the same conditions as any other corporation, as far as the law is concerned.

PUTTING THE EMPLOYMENT TERMS ON PAPER

By 1955, the occasions on which the law demanded any written document in employment were very few – for example, by statute in the cases of seamen on merchant ships, and drivers of hackney carriages; and apprenticeship contracts, which before 1814 had to be made by deed, are still required by the courts to be in writing. But the ordinary worker's contract of employment could be made without any written document. Today the worker in the factory frequently receives a booklet containing the firm's Regulations or the 'Works Rules', often unaware that in law he is thereby given sufficient notice to make the contents binding on him, whether he has read them or not. Some companies go further and ask employees to sign something referring to the Works Rules book. In the absence of misrepresentation a man is normally bound by a contract he signs. Cases before the Industrial Tribunals have revealed the remarkable ambit of such conditions. For example, in 1968 an I.C.I. Works Rule was found to give management the right to transfer workers 'to another job with a higher or lower rate of pay, whether day work, night work or shift work', and employees of British Railways were required to 'reside at whatever places may be appointed'.[26] In such cases these written terms of the contract were clearly binding. Even words in a notice at the place of work, displayed in such a way that they give reasonable notice to the employees of terms of employment, may be sufficient – 'cogent evidence of a contract based upon those rules,' said Mr Justice Blackburn in 1875, 'and it is not to be assumed even if the servant could not read that such rules would not be binding upon him'. Higher up the hierarchy, of course, white- or even blue-collar workers often have a more formal letter or written form of contract today.

The Contracts of Employment Act, 1963 does not make new demands on the form of the contract itself; that is, a good contract can still be *made* by word of mouth. But in section 4, the Act does require every employer to give each employee 'written particulars' of certain terms of his employment. This document must be presented not later than thirteen weeks after the commencement of the employment. The 'particulars' must specify the detailed terms on a number of matters: date of commencement; terms of remuneration; hours, holiday, incapacity in case of sickness and injury and pay during such periods; pensions and pension schemes; and periods of notice – a list to which the Minister can add other items. The 1970 Bill proposed to add minor additions to this list. (But it would not have demanded, as it might have done, a written description of the worker's job. Lack of such a statement often creates difficulty. Where, for example, an employer wanted to move a salesman who was in charge of the office which was being closed down, the court in 1969 accepted that he was not being moved to appropriate duties in another office but dismissed by reason of redundancy (p. 125) because he was more than a 'salesman'; he had 'managerial' duties at the office, and the need for such managers had declined.)[27]

Where there is no agreed term in respect of any of the matters listed, the Act requires that fact to be stated; the attention of the employees will thereby be drawn to it. The employer is under an obligation, too, to notify the employee within *one month* of changes in the terms. Many 'particulars' issued to workers do not seem to comply with these demands. And the expectation that the Act might lead to tough union bargaining, in particular at plant level, on some of the fringe benefits specified, to ensure that nothing gained in past practices is lost in the written documents, does not seem to have been realized; for workers and shop stewards do not seem to take special interest in the written particulars.

These provisions of the Act are excluded if the employee is employed under a written contract, of which he has a copy, or has reasonable access to a copy, and which contains all the particulars required by the Act. This is more likely to be the case with 'staff' or white collar workers. But, where the contract itself is not in writing, the 'written particulars' are not the contract. They are evidence, but 'not even conclusive evidence of the terms', as Lord Chief Justice Parker said in 1967. Six months before that, an Industrial Tribunal was convinced by Mr Charnley, a metal worker, that his 'normal' working hours included 10 hours obligatory overtime even though his particulars said they were 40 hours as specified in the Works Rules. As we shall see (p. 128) the point affects calculations on redundancy payment; and in most cases the worker is unable to convince the tribunal that his contractual terms are different from those stated. The Act envisages, it will be recalled, that the employee is just handed the particulars; it makes no provision for consultation or bargaining. In almost feudal language, it tells the employer to 'give to the employee' his written particulars of employment.

At first sight section 4 appeared likely to let loose a flood of paper in every factory in England, Wales and Scotland. But three factors weighed against this. First, a number of employees are specifically excluded from its scope. These include dockworkers and seamen, and, on this matter of written particulars, employees who are close relatives (spouse, parent, son, or daughter) of an employer. The Minister has power to extend or vary the list of exceptions. Furthermore, though the statute itself is silent on the point, it does not seem to bind the Crown.

Secondly, since the Act allows the employer to delay for thirteen weeks after the commencement of the employment, some workers may never receive particulars, such as workers employed for short periods in the building industry. Pleas to the Donovan Commission to reduce the period fell on deaf ears. Thirdly, the statute enacts that the written statement given to the employee satisfies the Act, either for all or any of the particulars required in it, if it refers the employee 'to some document which the employee has reasonable opportunities of reading in the course of his employment or which is made reasonably accessible to him in some other way'. This section is an extreme example of the language of 'individual contract'. The other 'document' will, of course, very often be a collective agreement. Indeed, the section goes on to provide that if the employer, in referring the employee to it, 'indicates' that future changes will be recorded in that document, or 'recorded by some other means', he is relieved of any further obligation to notify changes. The written document will, therefore, in many cases amount to no more than a statement referring the worker to a copy of the (changing) terms agreed with the trade union, made 'reasonably accessible' perhaps in the foreman's office. Such a device can, of course, also be employed where the other document is not a collective agreement at all. The worker may be surprised by what he finds, as were two Scottish estimators who claimed that they were 'dismissed' for redundancy purposes by being told to transfer to work of a much lower grade. The Court of Session rejected their claim since their written particulars incorporated the management's 'Rules Governing Employment' among which one rule stated: 'A worker may be transferred from one occupation to another carrying a lower or higher rate of pay without notice and at the discretion of the management'.[28]

The Act originally imposed certain criminal sanctions upon employers who failed to give proper written particulars. But in the absence of an effective Ministry inspectorate, this was a useless remedy, for who was going to prosecute on such a matter? The Redundancy Payments Act, 1965, was, therefore,

THE NATURE OF THE CONTRACT

used to amend the 1963 Act by excluding the criminal provisions. Instead, jurisdiction is given to Industrial Tribunals to which an employee may complain about failure to issue, or either side may complain about the accuracy of, the written particulars. The tribunal has power to issue, amend or substitute particulars in the appropriate cases. A doubt remains as to whether the procedure is available to an *ex*-employee even though he is not specifically included in the definition of employee under the 1963 Act (see p. 59). Scottish tribunals have been willing to recognize him; and the 1970 Bill proposed to remove this ambiguity. On principle a failure to issue particulars cannot now affect the enforceability of the contract; and a County Court decision in 1968 to the contrary appears to overlook the disappearance of the criminal sanction. The number of such cases is small (only 53 of 7,689 cases heard by tribunals in 1968 came under this heading), and very few succeed. But, as we shall see, the written particulars can be of vital importance evidentially to the dismissed employee, especially in claiming a redundancy payment. More attention to their terms before dismissal, therefore, by workers and their union representatives might strengthen their hands at a later date.

THE NATURE OF THE CONTRACT

The modern law regards a contract as a set of voluntary but enforceable promises under the protection primarily of the civil law. Few breaches are today criminal. Yet it is not often realized how modern this image is as far as employment is concerned. From the Statute of Labourers, 1351, onwards various enactments subjected workmen who failed to fulfil their duties to the master employing them to criminal penalties, including imprisonment. Similar penalties did not attach to employers who broke their contracts and, as the Webbs remarked, 'it is difficult in these days, when equality of treatment before the law has become an axiom, to understand how the flagrant injustice of the old Master and Servant Acts seemed justifiable even to a middle-class Parliament'.[29] Some statutes related to particular groups of workers; others to workmen generally. In the nineteenth century, consolidating and amending statutes continued this policy. It is only just over one hundred years ago that a chainmaker, engaged to work at fixed rates for an indefinite period on fourteen days' notice, was convicted and sentenced to two weeks' hard labour for absenting himself. He had left after giving fourteen days' notice demanding an 'advance of wages'. Benches of justices scarcely favoured the worker; and in 1854 over 3,000 workers were imprisoned for leaving or neglecting their work. In 1867 the Master and Servant Act revised the law and made it somewhat less harsh but retained the sanction of imprisonment for 'aggravated misconduct'. Prosecutions under the 1867 Act were used to the full against the increasingly militant trade union movement; in 1872 the figures reached 17,100 prosecutions and 10,400 convictions.[30]

In 1875 all these laws were swept away under the mounting pressure of an organized labour movement. Since then criminal liability for breach of contract of service as such has been rare, confined in effect to the two cases of danger and of public utility workers, which are discussed in relation to strikes in Chapter 8.

During this period also another obsolete concept affected the law: '... ideas which had come down from the days of serfdom and villeinage lingered on, so that a master was regarded as having a proprietary right in his servant'.[31] Therefore, if a stranger wrongfully injures the servant, in addition to his liability to the servant, he can be liable also to the master because he has damaged the latter's 'property'. Seeking to curtail such feudal concepts, the judges have recently stated that the second action is available only in the case of 'menial' or domestic servants. Both the Law Reform Committee and the Law Commission have recommended that this obsolete action be abolished. But any amending legislation would have to deal with the awkward problem: What should be the rights of an employer (if any) in respect of sums paid (as wages or voluntarily) to an employee while the latter is off work because of injury by another person?

In place of those outmoded conceptions of villein status and criminal sanctions, the modern law of employment emphasizes the personal and voluntary exchange of freely-bargained promises between two parties equally protected by the civil law alone. That model is, of course, suffused with an individualism which necessarily ignores the economic reality behind the bargain. The parties are not equal, even in their ability to go to law. But the emphasis upon this theoretical basis of the modern law can be found both in statutes and in the decisions of the judges, sometimes in an extreme form. A contract of service is personal and cannot, for example, be transferred from one employer to another without the consent of the employee. As we have seen, one employer may have the right to 'lend' a servant for a period to another; but the servant does not then for all purposes become the servant of the borrower as far as his rights are concerned, unless he consents, for he is not a chattel. And in 1940 the House of Lords refused to sanction the transfer of employees' contracts from one company to another under powers in the Companies Act which allowed for transfers of all rights and liabilities on an amalgamation, for 'the right to choose for himself whom he would serve', said Lord Atkin (in language that it is not unconnected with the other events of 1940), '... constituted the main difference between a servant and a serf'. Yet the same servant would not have possessed any legal right to prevent precisely those same changes in economic terms in the employing company, so long as the means used (change of name, or a share 'take-over') avoided this particular type of amalgamation which required a formal transfer of service contracts from one company to another.

Similarly, the death of a party to the contract will in the ordinary case be an event which automatically terminates the contract, as will illness, incarceration, or similar hazards which are of a probable duration sufficient to destroy the substance of the contract; for personal service by the employee is, in the absence of agreement to the contrary, its essence. Where, as in the case of a drummer in a pop group who was schizophrenic, the worker becomes unfit and there is 'no reasonable likelihood' that he will be able to resume work within the near future or substantially to perform his contract, the contract terminates by reason of 'frustration'.[32] So, Mr Jones, a steel wagon burner, had to stop work for six months in 1966 through hypertension, and a month later had to leave work because his condition became chronic. While he was away in 1967 the works closed down; but the High Court agreed with a tribunal decision that he could have no redundancy payment because his contract had terminated long before the closure which would otherwise have operated as his dismissal in a redundancy. Illness is not usually a *breach* of the employment contract, unless, of course, the worker *guarantees* to do something without fail, e.g. appear on a particular day. Although the contract can be affected by a statute, it cannot be terminated or stopped merely at the whim of the Government. A County Court judge in 1966 rightly rejected the view that a Government policy statement on incomes policy (before the statute of 1966, see p. 211) could 'frustrate' a contract for wages above the level desired by the Government.

The same approach emerges in respect of remedies. Today the primary remedy for breach of a contract of service is damages. The courts refuse to order 'specific performance' of such a personal contract. For example, they will not order the *reinstatement* of a wrongly dismissed employee. So strongly have the judges held to this view that they applied it even under the wartime Order (1305) which forbade strikes and lockouts and ordered compulsory arbitration of disputes. They refused to construe the Order as giving even the National Arbitration Tribunal, as it then was, the power to grant what Lord Chief Justice Goddard called

a remedy which no court of law or equity has ever considered it had power to grant. ... A court of equity has never granted an injunction compelling an employer to continue a workman in his employment or to oblige a workman to work for an employer.[33]

Modern conditions require drastic reconsideration of this refusal, as we shall see in the discussion of 'unjust dismissals' (p. 137).

The judges have also refused in modern times to use the

remedy of 'injunction' (an order prohibiting the defendant from doing certain acts) as a roundabout way of granting specific performance. An injunction can be obtained only if the judge exercises his discretion in favour of its award; only if damages are not an adequate remedy; and only if there is a 'negative stipulation' to which it can attach – e.g. 'I agree to work for Jones for two years and not for anyone else'. Even then, there can be no injunction if its effect would be to enforce the contract of service as such rather than encourage the defendant towards its performance. This was the issue in 1937 between Bette Davis and a film company for whom she had agreed to act exclusively for a certain period, with a negative stipulation attached. The judge granted an injunction in narrow terms, stopping her acting for other companies. As he put it, the defendant would be able to 'employ herself both usefully and remuneratively in other spheres of activity, though not as remuneratively as in her special line. She will not be driven, although she may be tempted, to perform the contract.' But in 1967 a judge refused an injunction against four musicians ('The Troggs') to stop them breaking a contract whereby they promised to employ no person except the plaintiff as their manager. The group – 'simple persons of no business experience' – had to have a manager, so that an injunction would amount to an order to have the plaintiff. When we come to Chapters 7 and 8 we shall find a quite different use of the injunction – to stop strikes which are held to involve a tort or some other wrong beyond mere breach of the employment contract. This use of 'labour injunctions' has increased in a disturbing manner since 1960.

Finally, it must be noted that, for all its archaic qualities, the individual contract of personal employment remains a useful and flexible legal device. Systems of law, such as the American, which have more or less lost it in the quest for collective reality, lack a legal tool of great utility. Thus, many incidents of a *floor of rights* can be given legal expression through the individual contract even if they concern collective questions. The 1970 Bill proposed to outlaw the 'yellow dog' contract banning union membership and give a right to belong to an 'independent' trade union to all employees with a few exceptions (which, oddly, included domestic servants, close relatives, and those working for less than 21 hours a week). That right was to be a compulsory term in every contract of employment (and stated in the written particulars). Neither the employer nor his agents were to prevent or deter the employee joining such a union, to penalize him for doing so, or compel him to join a union that was not 'independent' (though he could require the employee to join a particular *independent* union, i.e. make a 'closed shop' arrangement a term of the employment: p. 460). If the employee proved to an industrial tribunal (p. 149) that action to his detriment had been taken, it would be for the employer to show that he had not been penalized because of his union membership. If he had been, the employee would recover compensation.

These sensible proposals were marred by two faults which could be put right in any similar sections in another Government's legislation. First, the drafting was defective. Action by third parties other than the employer's agents (e.g. persons with whom he was associated in an employers' association) was not covered. The definition of 'independent' (*not under the domination or control of an employer*) was weak when compared with the I.L.O. Convention 98, which forbids employers 'to support workers' organizations by financial or other means *with the object of* placing ... [them] under the control of employers'. Secondly, the Bill fell into the trap awaiting those who use the personal employment contract as a legal vehicle. Traditionally only the parties to a contract can sue for its breach. Thus, although the employee could sue, the Bill would give no right of action to the trade union as such. But why should this not be allowed in this case? When statute uses this vehicle for social reform, it need not be bounded by the old common law frontiers.

This should be remembered when discussion begins (as it no doubt soon will) concerning new rights of civil liberty for workers. The individual contract will be a useful weapon for reform. For example, a compulsory term might protect the worker, as the Italian Labour Law statute of 1970 provides, from certain types of surveillance by audio-visual and electronic devices. Already at the 1970 conference of the Institute of Professional Civil Servants extreme concern has been voiced by those in a position to know about the compilation of information about individual workers on computers and the use of 'bugging' devices; and cases have been alleged in which lists of 'subversive' workers kept by police have been consulted by employers. There is room, in civil liberties and many other matters, for statutory expansion of the individual employment contract. But the old attitudes, such as that which refused reinstatement as a remedy, will need to be reviewed.

CONTRACT AND STATUS

Those attitudes have so dominated the courts that judges have been reluctant even to grant the remedy of a 'declaration' in cases of personal contracts. Such a remedy merely declares the rights of the parties without any order of the court for their fulfilment. Now, if one side refuses to perform a contract, it usually gives to the injured party the option to regard it as at an end, if he wishes. If he insists on pursuing and affirming the contract despite the breach, the contract remains alive and the repudiation is what one judge called 'a thing writ in water'. If he accepts the repudiation, the contract ends, and his remedy is to sue for damages. But the employee, for his part, appears usually to be compelled to accept the dismissal and sue for damages, an old principle confirmed by a case in 1968 involving 'The Kinks' (pop groups having made a major contribution to recent employment litigation).[34] In no case is a declaration appropriate. 'Normally', as Lord Keith put it in *Vine* v. *National Dock Labour Board*,[35] 'and apart from the intervention of statute, there would never be a nullity in terminating an ordinary contract of master and servant. Dismissal might be in breach of contract and so unlawful, but could only sound in damages'. There would be no scope for a declaration. Where the plaintiff acts in a dual contractual capacity, one of which allows for a declaration (e.g. as a member of and as an employed official of a union), the court has been careful to confine declaratory remedies so as not to extend them to the employment contract.[36]

But in *Vine*'s case statute *did* intervene. The plaintiff was a registered dockworker under the scheme established by an Act of 1946 and Order of 1947. Under the scheme a registered dockworker was relieved of the worst effects of casual labour by being paid by the Dock Labour Board if there was no work; but if there was work he was allocated to a registered employer. A registered dockworker's relationship with his local Board was regulated closely by the order; if he failed to fulfil his obligation he might be suspended, or in some cases dismissed. (The 1967 Order, as we see later, p. 138, has given new safeguards in this respect.) Vine had refused an order to report for work and he was given seven days' notice. He sued the N.D.L.B. for damages and a declaration, alleging that the dismissal was wrongful because the Order gave no power to delegate functions to a committee, as the local Board had done in his case. The House of Lords accepted this allegation and awarded both the damages *and* the declaration, even though the latter went some way towards forcing his employment on the Board. Viscount Kilmuir, Lord Chancellor, said:

This is an entirely different situation from the ordinary master and servant case. ... Here, the removal of the plaintiff's name from the register being, in law, a nullity, he continued to have the right to be treated as a registered dockworker with all the benefits which by statute that status conferred on him.

Similarly in 1969 a dockworker obtained a declaration that he was employed (p. 68). Under the 1967 Order he could not be given notice without the consent of the local Board. The dockworkers' scheme shows that a worker with a statutory status is in a rather different position from the worker under a mere contract.

Cases which suggested that the judges might be willing to break with the past and embark on the course of granting declarations more widely appear to be explicable only as special contracts where the employment was in effect permanent and terminable only for misconduct and a few other stated reasons.[37]

But as demands for 'job-security' increase, the common law is likely to be overtaken by statutes which introduce a general form of 'reinstatement' as a remedy. Other countries, from Germany to the U.S.S.R., have adopted it as a remedy in employment; but in many of these, including Germany, it does not operate in practice without the agreement of employers. Polish law adopted the remedy in 1956 because money could not always compensate a worker who had lost not just wages, but perhaps pension rights, housing assistance, seniority rights, and so on. Yugoslav courts have power to reinstate a worker to a post of 'the same level of appropriate professional skill' if his job has been abolished. Clearly, to administer such a jurisdiction, one needs tribunals of practical wisdom and understanding.

But until 1970 no pressures prevailed upon the British Parliament to introduce general statutory schemes in which employment was forced on either employee or employer. The theme underlay even the Reinstatement in Civil Employment Acts, passed between 1944 and 1950, which imposed certain duties on former employers of men returning from the wartime armed forces and later from conscription to reinstate them. The ultimate remedy under the Acts was a fine on the ex-employer and compensation to the ex-employee, not reinstatement. Similarly, under complex conditions enacted by the Disabled Persons (Employment) Act, 1944, an employer of more than twenty workers may be compelled to employ a quota of disabled persons, and an obligation not to discontinue the employment of such a person so as to fall below the quota is imposed. Disabled workers on the register number some 650,000, and in February 1970, 62,082 of these were unemployed although 'suitable for ordinary employment'. Once again, however, the ultimate legal sanction is *not* enforced employment or any reinstatement of the disabled worker, but a fine on the employer. In a similar manner, the pressures put upon any unemployed worker in social security statutes to take a particular job have never gone to the length of permitting anyone to order him into a particular employment. They do, however, as we shall see, include withdrawal of benefit where he refuses 'suitable' employment.

Even under the Race Relations Act, 1968, enacted after the Street and P.E.P. Reports had disclosed extensive racial discrimination in employment, a similar policy appears.[38] The Act prohibits discrimination by less favourable treatment or segregation on grounds of race, colour, ethnic or national origin in respect of (among other matters) refusal or omission to employ, provision of different conditions of employment or work, and dismissal. Both an employer and any other person 'concerned' with employment (e.g. an agency) are affected; but for the first four years certain small businesses are excluded. Similarly an employer is exculpated if in good faith he refuses employment or selects someone for work for the purpose of securing 'a reasonable balance of persons of different racial groups'. This unhappy section is perhaps made tolerable only by the fact that all persons 'wholly or mainly educated' in Britain are treated as in the *same* 'racial group', so that it will hardly ever apply to the 35 per cent of the one million immigrant family population who are under 16 (about one-half of whom were born in Britain) and will gradually cease to have any application. Shipowners, however, are given special permission still to discriminate in respect of sleeping or mess rooms and sanitary accommodation. Complaints on employment are referred by the Secretary of State for Employment either to special industrial committees, or (where no such suitable body exists) to the normal statutory conciliation committees, or the Race Relations Board. Only if a complicated procedure of conciliation fails can the Board finally bring a civil action in the County Court for damages on behalf of the grievant. An injunction may be granted (including, it seems, even a mandatory injunction ordering the employer to stop discrimination in hiring) but only where the defendant has engaged in the past in the 'same kind' of discriminatory conduct and is likely to engage in it in future. In the face of the difficulties of proof and the complexities of procedure involved, judicial intervention by way of injunction is likely to be negligible. The Act emphasizes conciliation rather than legal sanction, and much may depend on the specially-constituted industrial committees. Some unions have been active in rooting out discrimination. In the first year of the Act, 819 employment complaints were referred to the D.E.P., of which 186 could be passed on to suitable industrial machinery. Discrimination was found in 5 per cent of these cases (none in the 14 claims against trade unions); and although a third of the complainants appealed from industrial committees to the Board, no case ended up in court.

The effect of the Race Relations Act, 1968, in setting a floor for racial equality at work is likely to be far wider than these figures indicate. And it is notable that the ultimate availability to the Board of an injunction against a racially biased employer is a step adopted even on this specially dangerous social evil with carefully constructed safeguards.

One oddity remains to be mentioned here. The Employers and Workmen Act, 1875, on abolishing the criminal remedies, gave a special jurisdiction to magistrates in cases involving less than £10 in disputes between employers and manual workers (a jurisdiction aimed at inexpensive resolution of such legal actions which has decreased in importance as the value of money has fallen and legal aid for actions in other courts has been introduced). County courts too were given a wide jurisdiction, including the power to order performance in the form of a pledge to pay a penalty on breach. It is true that such an order depends on the consent of the defendant; but it is interesting that such a remedy was thought possible in 1875, and, though not much used in practice, remains extant today.

RESTRAINT OF TRADE

One other legal principle serves to illustrate the manner in which the roots of the common law governing the contract of service lie deep in the individualist concepts of *laisser faire*, the principle of 'restraint of trade'. Although the parties are in theory normally free to decide on what obligations they will, the judges have always refused to enforce certain agreements on grounds of 'public policy'. For example, the courts have refused to enforce a contract which in substance is one of slavery. An agreement, therefore, to work for an employer until a money-lender agrees you can stop and to assign all your property and future salary to him in return for the loan is not enforceable as having servile incidents. No one seems ever to have raised this point in connection with some of the severe Works Rules mentioned earlier. The matter is one of degree, however; and the principle would not extend to the employment of a driver at whose inquest in April 1970 it was discovered that he had worked an average of 92 hours a week in the fortnight before he died, the coroner remarking, 'I thought slavery in this country had been abolished'. Contracts with severe terms may be upheld, such as the contract by a son promising to transfer his property to his father, give up his swindling friends, never become bankrupt, borrow or drink to excess, or live or go within eighty miles of Piccadilly Circus, in return for a settlement of his debts, which was upheld in 1919, the judge saying 'eighty miles was not too wide having regard to the nature and extent of the mischief to be avoided'.

Similarly the judges have always refused to enforce a covenant which unduly restrained trade. The principles on which they have acted have varied in response to the changes in the social pattern that governed their thinking. In the time of Elizabeth I they held void all such restraints. By the eighteenth century they allowed 'partial restraints'. In the nineteenth century, they regularly treated trade unions as bodies based on 'illegal' agreements because they acted in restraint of trade. Were they to uphold such agreements, said Lord Chief Justice Campbell in 1855, they

would establish a principle upon which the fantastic and mischievous notion of a 'Labour Parliament' might be realized for regulating the wages and the hours of labour in every branch of trade all over the empire. The most disastrous consequences would follow to masters and to men, and to the whole community.[39]

In 1894, however, the courts turned to the modern doctrine that an agreement in restraint of trade is unenforceable when it is 'unreasonable' in the sense of unreasonably protecting one party or putting unreasonable burdens on the other, or unreasonably infringing any interests of the public. By 1900, an illegal restraint was not in any way a crime; it carried merely the civil consequences that the agreement could not be enforced by a court, unless, at least, the judge was prepared to 'sever' the illegal part. This flexible weapon of 'severance' allows the judge to excise the illegal portion of a clause if it is separate and of 'trivial importance, or merely technical, and not a part of the main purport and substance' of the agreement.[40]

Under the modern doctrine, the employer can impose conditions on the employee's future work or competition only where they are a reasonable defence of proprietary interests of his own, in particular trade secrets or business connections. Mere knowledge by the servant of special methods of organization is not enough, and his knowledge of business connections (e.g. customers) must be such that he could make use of it later. Take a promise not to enter the trade within so many miles and for a certain period. The more skilled the servant, the higher up the hierarchy of a firm he is, the more confidential the knowledge he possesses, the more likely is the restraint to be valid. But as the time of the restraint lengthens or the spatial area grows, the weight of the onus on the employer to justify it as 'reasonable' grows too. Thus, in 1964 the Court of Appeal upheld a clause restraining for two years a salesman from canvassing anyone who was a customer of the employer in any area, but disallowed a clause restraining a traveller from dealing with persons in the districts which he visited (whether customers of the employer or not) for three years. The latter went further than a reasonable protection. So, in 1965, clauses which aimed to stop the manager of a credit betting-shop from working in any other such business within twelve miles for three years were held unreasonable; for he rendered no 'personal service' to customers which impinged on the goodwill of the firm. But in a decision of 1970, the Court of Appeal found reasonable and enforceable against a mere milk roundsman a clause banning him for one year not only from canvassing, but also from selling 'milk or dairy' products to any customer whom he happened to serve in his last six months as rounds-man for the dairy.[41] To hold the latter reasonable might be thought to forget what Lord Justice Denning said in 1956:

During the last forty years the courts have shown a reluctance to enforce covenants of this sort. They realize that a servant has often very little choice in the matter. If he wants to get or to keep his employment, he has to sign the document which the employer puts before him; and he may do so without fully appreciating what it may involve. Moreover, if these covenants were given full force, they would tend to reduce his freedom to seek better conditions, even by asking for a rise in wages; because if he is not allowed to get work elsewhere, he is very much at the mercy of his employer.[42]

Rarely, the courts ignore the employment aspect and apply the less strict test appropriate to a vendor of a business, as when the Court of Appeal enforced in 1969 severe restraints on competition against an employee who was a 'genius' as a designer of ladies' garments but who had also contracted to sell a major shareholding which he owned in the business. The judges looked to the substance and applied 'vendor and purchaser standards' (though one also took note that the employee was 'not a good time-keeper and was inclined to be gay in his personal life', ultimately getting the sack after being convicted of possessing cannabis.) But the more rigorous approach has been maintained in most recent decisions. In *Kores Manufacturing Ltd* v. *Kolok Manufacturing Ltd*, 1958,[43] two neighbouring manufacturers in the same line of business had agreed that neither would employ a servant employed by the other within the preceding five years. The Court of Appeal refused to regard the agreement as reasonable. It did not distinguish between skilled and unskilled workers; no time limit was imposed for the contract; each of the employers could not have made an agreement with his employees binding them not to work for the other, since no trade secrets had to be protected. What they could not legally do directly with the employees they could not legally do indirectly between themselves, merely in order to create a constant supply of labour. Moreover, in the *Kores* case, the court showed interest in the separate test of 'reasonableness in the public interest'. In all but one case this century the courts have tended to hold that what was reasonable as between the parties was not unreasonable merely because some interest of 'the public' was damaged. But in *Bull* v. *Pitney-Bowes*, 1966,[44] an employee had been required to enter the firm's pension scheme, one rule of which provided that all rights to a pension would be cancelled if the committee decided that a retired worker was engaging in any activity 'in competition with or detrimental to the interests of' the employer. The plaintiff retired after twenty-five years with the firm; but his pension was cancelled under the rule. The judge held that the rule was invalid as an unreasonable incident of the employment relationship; and (most important) the decision was based primarily upon 'a principle of public policy and I emphasize', he said, 'the word "public"'.

In 1963 the 'retain and transfer' rules of the Football Association, in accordance with which the Association, League, and clubs controlled the employment of players, were challenged in *Eastham* v. *Newcastle Utd F.C.*[45] Eastham had become a professional player at the age of nineteen and his first League Club was Newcastle United. His action was brought during a period of conflict between the players and their union and the League, the Football Association, and many of the clubs, over pay and over the 'retain and transfer' system, later changed as a result of this case. Under the scheme as it then stood the 'retain and transfer' scheme meant that a player in Eastham's position was effectively prevented by his club from playing for almost any other club throughout the world. If he refused to re-sign for the club retaining him he need not be paid even his wages. Control of the transfer rested in the club and the League. 'The transfer system', said the judge, 'has been stigmatized by the plaintiff's counsel as a relic from the Middle Ages, involving the buying and selling of human beings as chattels; and, indeed, to anyone not hardened to acceptance of the practice it would seem inhuman and incongruous to the spirit of a national sport.' The judge concluded that even taking account of the special needs of the game, the scheme operated to an unjustifiable degree in restraint of trade. Eastham therefore became entitled to a remedy against his club to declare the restrictions void. But he also asked for a declaration against the League and the Association. With those two bodies, however, he had no contract of employment. What right did he have to challenge *their* arrangements? In a novel extension of the remedy, the judge went on to declare that Eastham must be given a declaration against them too. The court could grant a declaration 'not only against the employer who is in contractual relationship with the employee but also against the association of employers whose rules or regulations place an unjustifiable restraint on his liberty of employment'.

If this approach is maintained in later cases, it could, by leaving behind the old focus of the contract of employment, place in the hands of the employees entirely new weapons with which to challenge employers' agreements in restraint of trade. It cannot, of course, extend the area of what is meant by 'restraint of trade' today. For instance, many of the agreements declared void by the new Restrictive Practices Court, under the Act of 1956, would not necessarily be unlawful at common law – that is why the Act was passed. And the 1956 Act expressly excludes restrictions which relate to employment from the restrictions which the Act puts within the purview of that Court. In a suitable case, however, where the old common-law doctrine of restraint of trade has something on which to bite, the *Eastham* case gives the employee the right to take the initiative. Paradoxically, however, the same case re-emphasized another principle established in 1920, namely that no action in tort lies for a conspiracy to use 'unlawful means' (discussed later at p. 376) merely because defendants have made use of a scheme in restraint of trade to the damage of the plaintiff. Yet a person deliberately injured by the operation of a scheme which is prima facie void by reason of the 1956 Act can sue in tort for damages or even an injunction. That was one of the grounds of the Court of Appeal's decision in *Daily Mirror Newspapers Ltd* v. *Gardner*, 1968,[46] where the *Daily Mirror* obtained an injunction against a Federation which, in a dispute about profit margins, decided that its members (retail newsagents) should boycott the paper for a week and sent out 'stop notices' for them to forward to the wholesalers. The injunction lay against this tortious use of 'unlawful means', i.e. a plan which appeared to infringe the 1956 Act (though the Restrictive Practices Court had not considered the matter). No doubt an employee deliberately injured might seek a similar remedy.

Notes to Chapter 2

1. Mansfield Cooper and Wood, *Outlines of Industrial Law*, 1966, p. 2.
2. W. E. J. McCarthy, 'The Role of Shop Stewards', *Royal Commission Research Papers, No. 1* (1966), p. 18.
3. McCardie J. in *Performing Right Soc. Ltd* v. *Mitchell* [1924] 1 K.B. 762 at p. 767.
4. P. Atiyah, *Vicarious Liability in the Law of Torts* (1967), p. 48.
5. *Morren* v. *Swinton and Pendlebury B. C.* [1965] 1 W.L.R. 576.
6. *Mersey Docks and Harbour Board* v. *Coggins & Griffith Ltd* [1947] A.C. 1; see too the same result on 'continuity' of employment: *Alexander* v. *McMillan* (1969) 4 I.T.R. 171.
7. *Duckworth* v. *Farnish Ltd* (1970) 5 I.T.R. 17 (C.A.); and *Smith* v. *Blandford Gee* [1970] 3 All E.R. 154: apparent master stopped from denying his status as employer.
8. In *Cassidy* v. *Min. of Health* [1951] 2 K.B. 343 at p. 351.
9. *Stevenson Jordan & Harrison Ltd* v. *Macdonald & Evans* [1952] 1 T.L.R. 101, at p. 111.
10. *Whittaker* v. *Minister of Pensions* [1967] 1 Q.B. 156. See for other Ministers' Decisions under the National Insurance Acts, Wedderburn, *Cases and Materials on Labour Law*, pp. 10, 26.
11. *A.E.U.* v. *Min. of Pensions* [1963] 1 All E.R. 864, Megaw J.
12. *Argent* v. *Minister of Social Security* [1968] 3 All E.R. 208.
13. *Market Investigations Ltd* v. *Minister of Social Security* [1968] 3 All E.R. 732.
14. [1968] 2 Q.B. 497. See generally C. Drake (1968) 31 *Modern Law Review* 408.
15. G. de N. Clark (1968) 31 *Modern Law Review* 450 at p. 453.
16. See: G. de N. Clark, 'Industrial Law and the Labour Only Sub-Contract' (1967) 30 *Modern Law Review* 6; and P. Samuel and R. Lewis, 'Building's Bedouin Arabs', *Personnel*, April 1968.
17. *Donaghey* v. *Boulton & Paul* [1968] A.C. 1.
18. *Inglefield* v. *Macey* (1967) 2 K.I.R. 146; C.L.Y. 2726. See too *Quinn* v. *Burch Bros.* [1966] 2 Q.B. 370 (C.A.).
19. *Report of Committee of Inquiry under Professor Phelps Brown*, Cmnd 3714 (1968, H.M.S.O.), see Appendix III, R. Rideout; and R. Lewis (1969) 32 *Modern Law Review* 75.
20. T.U.C. *Report*, 1969, pp. 519–20, C. T. H. Plant.

20a. *Construction Industry Training Board* v. *Labour Force Ltd* [1970] 3 All E.R. 220.

21. See Wedderburn, *Cases and Materials on Labour Law*, p. 10. See too P. O'Higgins (1967) *Cambridge Law Journal* 27.

22. [1958] 1 All E.R. 91.

23. *Taylor* v. *Furness Withy Ltd* (1969) 6 K.I.R. 488.

24. See *Riordan* v. *War Office* [1959] 3 All E.R. 552; [1960] 3 All E.R. 774. But see Logan (1945) 61 *Law Quarterly Review* 240, 'A Civil Servant and his Pay'.

25. *Att.-G. for Guyana* v. *Nobrega* [1969] 3 All E.R. 1604 (P.C.); *Kodeeswaran* v. *Att.-G. of Ceylon* [1970] 2 W.L.R. 456 (P.C.).

26. *Briggs* v. *I.C.I.* (1968) 3 I.T.R. 276; *Miller* v. *British Railways Workshops* (1968) 3 I.T.R. 89; *Murray* v. *Robert Rome* (1969) 4 I.T.R. 20 (by N.J.C. Rules plumber had to work wherever sent); Wedderburn and Davies, *Employment Grievances and Disputes Procedures in Britain*, Ch. 2.

27. *Hall* v. *Farrington Data Processing Ltd* (1969) 4 I.T.R. 230.

28. *I.C.I.* v. *McCallum* (1969) 4 I.T.R. 24.

29. S. and B. Webb, *History of Trade Unionism* (1920), p. 249.

30. See D. Simon in *Democracy and the Labour Movement*, ed. J. Saville, Chapter 6, 'Master and Servant'.

31. Lord Goddard C.J. in *Jones Bros. (Hunstanton)* v. *Stevens* [1955] 1 Q.B. 275 at p. 282.

32. *Condor* v. *The Barron Knights* [1966] 1 W.L.R. 87.

33. *R.* v. *N.A.T. ex parte Horatio Crowther Ltd* [1948] 1 K.B. 424 at p. 431. But see G. de N. Clark (1969) 32 *Modern Law Review* 532.

34. *Denmark Productions Ltd* v. *Boscobel Productions Ltd* [1968] 3 All E.R. 513, explained by M. Freedland (1969) 32 *Modern Law Review* 314. But compare, *Marriott* v. *Oxford and District Co-op Soc.* [1969] 3 All E.R. 1126 (C.A.), and *Saunders* v. *Paladin Coachworks* (1968) 3 I.T.R. 51, which suggest the courts are not strictly applying this old rule in redundancy cases.

35. [1957] A.C. 488 at p. 507; p. 500. See too the rights of a teacher to have a local authority's decisions taken in accordance with the procedures of natural justice, even though he has no contract with the authority, the rights resting upon the statutory position of the council: *Hannam* v. *Bradford City Council* [1970] 2 All E.R. 690 (C.A.).

36. *Taylor* v. *N.U. Seamen* [1967] 1 All E.R. 767.

37. *McClelland* v. *N. Ireland General Health Services Board* [1957] 2 All E.R. 129 (H.L.). See now *Vidyodaya University of Ceylon* v. *Silva* [1964] 3 All E.R. 865 (P.C.).
38. See B. Hepple, *Race, Jobs and the Law in Britain* (2nd ed. 1970; especially Chapters 2, 5 and 6); and his critique of the 1968 Act, (1969) 32 *Modern Law Review* 181.
39. *Hilton* v. *Eckersley* (1855) 6 E. and B. 47 at p. 66.
40. Lord Moulton in *Mason* v. *Provident Clothing Co.* [1913] A.C. 724 at p. 745.
41. *Strange* v. *Mann* [1965] 1 All E.R. 1069; *Home Counties Dairies Ltd* v. *Skilton* [1970] 1 All E.R. 1227 (C.A.).
42. *M. & S. Drapers* v. *Reynolds* [1956] 3 All E.R. 814 at p. 820.
43. [1959] Ch. 108.
44. [1966] 3 All E.R. 384.
45. [1964] Ch. 413.
46. [1968] 2 Q.B. 768; see (1968) 31 *Modern Law Review* 440 (Wedderburn); (1968) *J. Bus. Law* 345 (Korah); and *infra* p. 359.

CHAPTER 3

JOB-SECURITY AND UNEMPLOYMENT

WE must investigate the obligations of employer and employee under the contract of employment in order to understand the ways in which the contract can come to an end and the consequences of its termination. The obligations under this contract, as in any other, may be either expressly stated or implied by the law. Any breach of contractual obligations gives the injured party a claim for damages as compensation for his loss. If it is a very serious breach he may also have the right to end the contract, e.g. by summary dismissal. Apart from summary termination, a contract of employment can usually be terminated by notice given by one party to the other. Termination of the employment leads us to discuss modern statutes on unemployment and 'job-security'.

IMPLIED OBLIGATIONS IN THE CONTRACT

The demand for written particulars in the Contracts of Employment Act, 1963, should help to define with greater clarity the obligations of employer and employee. As we have seen, the written particulars are, however, not conclusive. And the problems of real life are always sufficiently unpredictable to bring to light gaps in the express terms of any contract. In such a case the courts can imply a term; for

it is well recognized that there may be cases where obviously some term must be implied if the intention of the parties is not to be defeated, some term of which it can be predicated that 'it goes without saying'; some term not expressed but necessary to give to the transaction such business efficacy as the parties must have intended.[1]

But, of course, the parties have usually not considered the matter at all. That is why there is a gap in the terms expressly agreed. In deciding what the 'intention of the parties' must have been, the courts can, in practice if not in theory, exercise considerable control over their rights, perhaps to the surprise of one or other of them. For instance in a case of 1926, a mine had become so dangerous that the owners (who were not at fault) decided, after complaints by the men, to close it for repairs. Could the men claim their wages when they were ready to work? The contract said nothing about such a situation. The Court of Appeal felt that it must have been the 'intention' of both parties that the owners should not bear all the loss due to the operation of natural forces but that it should be divided between the parties. Previous cases where the employer had for business reasons *chosen* to close down were different, said the judges; here, no wages were payable. The judges' 'business efficacy' test to imply what 'goes without saying' and thereby to discover the parties' common intention no doubt left the miners with many hard things to say. For if 'natural forces' had surprisingly produced a profitable crop of diamonds it is clear that the judges would not have held that miners should share the fortuitous riches. It is to be noted, as the Court of Appeal re-emphasized in 1968 when rejecting in a redundancy case an alleged implied right of employers to send Liverpool workers in their fire alarm factory to work in Barrow, that the implication of a contractual term is a 'question of law'.

Similarly, what happens if the worker is temporarily off sick and nothing has been expressly agreed? How many of the 948,000 employees who on 1 June 1968 drew sickness benefit could demand their wages or even part of their wages? In the past it has been a vexed problem. In 1960 the High Court upheld the claim of a manager employed under a written contract on a salary and production bonus, who had been too ill to work for two months. His contract stated that he should be paid these sums while an employee, and the judge refused to imply any further term whereby payment should be suspended during the period of illness.[2] But in other cases the opposite conclusion has been reached and, although there is no doubt now a stronger presumption that pay continues than once was the case, the matter is always to be determined by the construction of the particular contract of service. The matter should,

we saw, be mentioned in the 'written particulars'. Practice undoubtedly varies, as do the expressly agreed terms of employment; and the Ministry of Pensions and Ministry of Labour
surveys in 1964 disclosed that in 1961 only about a fifth of the
male workers incapacitated by sickness actually received
employer's sick pay and that only just over fifty per cent of
employees were covered by provision for any payments when
they were sick. The reports showed that of the men, only 29
per cent could receive payments beyond 13 weeks; for 24 per
cent the period was 'discretionary'. Workers sick for long
periods were often struck off the employer's books; and we
have already noticed that a prolonged illness which looks like
being a very serious interruption of the worker's capacity automatically terminates the employment contract. Sick-pay
schemes have increased in number but so have sick workers. A
report in June 1968 showed that 311 million working days were
lost in 1966 from sickness. Epidemics can be disastrous; an in-
fluenza outbreak in 1962 caused a loss of 4 million working
days in one month. As Professor Turner has said: 'An effective
anti-influenza serum would probably be of more measurable
benefit to the economy than an effective anti-strike law'.[3] Some
collective bargains do now govern the problem of sickness and
their provisions allow for flexibility. Thus, one 1970 case revealed that a worker of 64 was paid for five months but was
then, while still sick, transferred under an agreement with his
union to a 'holding' department, which meant his contract was
suspended without pay but not terminated.[4] The employer's
refusal to take him back for work in July was, therefore,
wrongful. Despite such arrangements, there is perhaps a case
for a statutory minimum period for the right to wages in sickness. Recently complaints have been heard that some workers
have made use of social security benefit for feigned 'sickness'
as part of strike activity. Whether this is a serious problem is
not clear. But were Britain to experience stoppages in the
ostensible form of a mass 'sick-out' (as the U.S.A. did in 1970)
no doubt both matters might receive legislative attention.

Sometimes the court accepts as proved a custom, it may be
of the trade or the locality, which answers a question on which

the contract is silent. Where the parties can be taken to have contracted on the basis of the custom (and where nothing in the express contract contradicts it), and the custom is 'reasonable, certain and notorious', the court will enforce it. Local custom is now less important than it once was. But customs can be decisive even for industrial workers. In *Sagar* v. *Ridehalgh*, 1931, the Court of Appeal allowed customary deductions for bad workmanship from a weaver's wages, Lord Justice Lawrence saying: 'A Lancashire weaver knows, and has for many years past known, precisely what his position was as regards deductions for bad work on accepting employment in a Lancashire mill.'[5] So in *Bective Electrical Ltd* v. *Warren*, 1968,[6] an electrician who objected for 'domestic and travelling' reasons to being moved to another place of work found that the court decided 'it was well known and accepted and was the custom that somebody shop recruited' (as he was) 'would be bound within reason to go where he was sent'. But, after an extensive review of the judicial decisions, a tribunal in 1969 refused to accept as an implied term a customary right for bookmakers to 'lay off' a manager in a week when there was no racing, and added that the right to lay-off, an 'obscure' subject, could not be implied into 'a contract of employment at fixed or guaranteed periodic wages'.[7]

Where the practice is not so general as a local or trade custom, however, it is not clear how far the courts demand proof that the worker knew of a practice of the place of work before he is bound by it. In 1918, for example, one judge refused to imply terms into contracts of employment saying: 'None of the plaintiffs when they entered the employment ... had ever heard of that practice ...'. On the other hand, in *Sagar* v. *Ridehalgh* Lord Justice Lawrence also said that, even apart from the custom, it was immaterial whether the worker knew about the practice of deductions, because 'he accepted his employment on the same terms as to deductions for bad work as the other weavers at the mill'. The second approach will probably be adopted by the court wherever a worker joins an enterprise already operating and where, he must know, practices exist concerning certain matters on which nothing has been said. In

1966, an Industrial Tribunal found that an electrician at Dungeness Power Station on accepting a new higher rate of pay applicable to a 'travelling' man under the National Working Rules (whom the employer was therefore entitled to send to any site in the country), even if he was unaware of the new obligation, 'had taken advantage of the better terms ... for nearly five years and must be taken to have agreed to them'. But another tribunal rejected an alleged custom of the dredging industry that workers were 'interchangeable' in duties as not binding upon a lorry driver who had been assigned to pipelaying, in the absence of evidence that he had accepted that arrangement. This difficult question arises again when we analyse the collective bargain.

In addition to the test of 'business efficacy' and the incorporation of custom, the courts will sometimes decide on the implication of a term according to their view of needs of the type of contract before them. The House of Lords in *Lister* v. *Romford Ice and Cold Storage Co. Ltd*, 1957, had to construe the duties of a lorry driver and his employer.[8] Although a minority was prepared to develop implied terms by reference to 'drivers of motor vehicles and their employers generally', the majority of the Law Lords required 'very compelling evidence' to imply 'some quite novel term' into the relationship, outside the duties which had already been recognized in earlier cases.

This chapter can do no more than summarize the most important incidents so far recognized by the courts. In each example the principles set out state, as it were, the incidents which the common law expects to find in a contract of employment. They are open to alteration by the express agreement of the parties (subject to the rules of illegality and public policy). In many cases they form the legal basis of the employer's disciplinary powers over the employee. Statute limits those powers on occasion and trade unions or shop stewards limit their exercise in fact, but the law begins with the contractual duties that follow.

THE EMPLOYER'S OBLIGATIONS

The employer's primary obligation is to pay the wages, salary, or other payments agreed upon in the contract. Today the wages are often compounded of a national rate (collectively agreed) plus local bonuses. The Donovan Report gave as a typical example the total pay, £31, of a fitter, made up of £11 under national time rate, over £8 under national overtime and night rates, and nearly £12 bonus under local factory agreements. Other, rather feudal, additions to this obligation, such as the duty to provide medicines, were said by judges of the early nineteenth century to be obsolete, and the duty to pay wages is now the employer's main duty. It appears that the master must reimburse the servant against loss or expenses incurred in properly performing the employment, even if the servant innocently does unlawful acts authorized by the employer. The employer is under a general duty not to require his servant to do any act which is unlawful. But his duty is limited to reasonable care in respect of the servant's *safety*. Thus, when in 1965 a director of a Brighton 'Wimpy Bar' called on the plaintiff, an assistant manager, to come and 'back up' the manager who was being threatened by three youths 'larking about', the latter could not, in the absence of proof of negligence, claim 'reimbursement' as an indemnity for the broken leg which the youths caused him. But that case went to the very verge of another principle which forbids the employer to give orders which import grave danger to the servant's person or health. Thus, in 1970 Wing-Commander Donovan recovered damages against his employers, Invicta Airways, after walking out in the face of orders which the trial judge thought lawful, but which the Court of Appeal held demanded 'wholly unwarrantable risks' in flying, for the sake of speed and economy, and were therefore improper. A curious refinement on the obligation not to order the servant to take unlawful action was made in 1970 in *Buckoke* v. *G.L.C.*[9] The defendants had made regulations for their firemen expressly leaving it to their discretion whether to drive across a red traffic light, even though such an act is clearly a crime as much for drivers of fire engines in emergencies as it is for anyone else. The firemen objected to being put in this ambiguous position. But Mr Justice Plowman refused to regard the regulations as unlawful. They were 'not a command to break the law but a command to take care' if, in the discretion placed upon them, the firemen decided to break it. Quite what his Lordship would have made of an employer's instruction to employees to 'take care' if they decided to steal customer's goods in an emergency is not wholly clear.

The employer is, however, not normally obliged to provide work. So long as he pays the agreed wage he can, if he wishes, keep the servant idle. But the law departs from this rule in cases where the very nature of the contract means that the employee is deprived of the chance to earn anything on his side if there is no work: where, for example, a servant agrees to render services at piece-rates, or exclusive services on commission. Frequently such problems are solved by 'guaranteed week' payments bargained with unions; but otherwise, in such cases, failure to provide work can be a breach of contract by the master. These cases may be seen as illustrations of the more general principle obliging each party not to impede the performance of the contract. The law does not, however, put on the employer any duty to assist the worker after performing the job, e.g. by providing a testimonial. The most important remaining duty of the employer today developed by the judges is the duty to provide reasonably safe working conditions for the employee. This matter is considered later, however, in Chapter 6, in conjunction with the statutory rules on safety.

THE EMPLOYEE'S OBLIGATIONS

The employee's main duties may be classified under the headings (i) to give 'faithful and honest service', (ii) to use reasonable skill and care in the work, and (iii) to obey reasonable lawful orders and not commit misconduct.

Under the first heading the servant must not make use of any information or material confidential to the employer, such as using trade secrets or canvassing clients for a business he aims to set up at a later date. An assistant solicitor who, while still employed, made an arrangement with the firm's biggest client to do his work after leaving the firm and then left, taking the firm's secretary, was held in 1967 to be liable in damages of £500 to his employer.[10] Nor do the requirements of collective bargaining provide any defence, as employees discovered in 1945 when they disclosed information about the business to trade union officials which the officials needed to prepare for bargaining. The line over which the employee must not step can be, in this area of law, very difficult to draw. But if the servant uses the employment improperly for his own purposes and makes a secret profit, the sum can be claimed by the master, a principle applied in 1951 to the analogous case of an army sergeant who used his uniform to make £20,000 by the sale of illicit spirits in Egypt.[11] The courts, although very reluctant to restrict a worker's spare-time activity, once even extended the duty of good faith that far to restrain skilled workers whose spare-time work on valves for deaf-aids for another manufacturer in direct competition could have seriously damaged their employer's business, even though they disclosed to the competitor nothing confidential.[12] The legal result is the same where workers' spare-time jobs incapacitate them in their work.

The duty does not prevent an employee using information which is essentially his own skilled knowledge. And in 1967 the Court of Appeal decided that the employee could disclose even confidential information when an over-riding 'public interest' demanded it (e.g. in cases of the employer's fraud, crime, or, probably, arrangements restricting trade subject to statutory regulation).[13] But, oddly, the courts refuse to allow as a defence, if confidential information has been improperly revealed, the fact that the information has already been made public by a third party. Indeed, the courts have over recent decades expanded the remedies for preventing employees and others (including third parties) from breaking any kind of 'confidence' received from the plaintiff.[14] This approach has materially restricted the employee's rights in his invention. Today, where the invention relates to his employment duties in any way those rights belong to the employer. Thus, in 1956 a technician employed to advise on 'all technical matters' by a firm making, among other things, soda syphons was compelled by the court to assign the patent in his new method of dispensing soda water to the employer.[15] In white-collar employment express terms in the worker's contract sometimes increase his rights. But the courts have restricted such clauses to their narrowest ambit in order to protect the employer's right ('inherent in the nature of the contract' of employment) to own the inventions, even where patents were registered in the joint names of both parties.

The problem of the employee's invention is bound to be a vexed one in any industrial society, whether capitalist or socialist. But in other countries, from Sweden, Germany and Holland to Poland and other socialist countries, employees have rights to compensation or payment for their inventions which the employer cannot exclude. The Secretary of the Institute of Patentees called for reform of the law in 1965, writing 'the Common Law ... is weighted against the employee inventor'. A Private Member's Bill of that year failed to reach the statute book. By 1969, a 'Committee on Patents' was sitting and assured the T.U.C. it would give 'full and sympathetic consideration to the place of the employee-inventor in the general context' of its review. It is time sympathy gave way to new laws. The Donovan Report said nothing about this question, which is surely germane to the encouragement of innovation and efficiency.

Despite extensions of the duty of faithful service the courts have in another respect narrowed its range. There seems to be no implied duty on the employee to disclose any misconduct of his *own* to his employer (e.g. his past breach of faithful service if they are negotiating new terms).

The duty under the second heading requires the servant to exercise reasonable care and skill in performing his work. In *Lister* v. *Romford Ice and Cold Storage Co. Ltd*, 1957,[8] Lister was the company's lorry driver. One day in the slaughter-house yard he backed the lorry carelessly into another employee (who happened to be his father). The latter successfully sued the company for damages; it was 'vicariously' liable for its driver's carelessness. Before 1948 he might well have failed, because

103

the courts, in decisions dating from 1837, had decided that a servant could never recover damages against the master for the carelessness of fellow-servants in 'common employment' with him – on the ground that each servant 'impliedly agreed' to take the risks of the other's negligence! The doctrine was first modified and finally, in 1948, abolished by statute. But in *Lister's* case, the employer's insurance company, which met the damages, used its right to have an action brought in the employer's name (a normal clause in such policies) against the driver. He, they alleged, had broken his duty to use care in his work; and for that breach he must pay his employer the sum paid out in damages to his father – in effect an indemnity for the damages. By three to two, the Law Lords rejected the argument that an 'implied term' should allow the driver to have the benefit of the employer's insurance policy. This would be a 'novel' term of employment contracts. Therefore, the driver must reimburse the 'employer' (in truth, the insurers). Viscount Simonds perhaps overstated the psychological effect of their Lordships' legal decisions on workers in real life when he argued:

... now to grant the servant immunity from such an action would tend to create a feeling of irresponsibility in a class of persons from whom, perhaps more than any other, constant vigilance is owed to the community.

The master (or his insurers) probably cannot get a full indemnity if his fault contributed to the accident. But the only reason why no outcry followed the *Lister* case was a gentlemen's agreement among the insurance companies not to bring such actions for indemnity. But this is a slender protection for the employee.[16] Statutory protection is needed, at least to limit the amount of damages recoverable against the employee or, better, to give him the benefit of any insurance. The employer, after all, can always dismiss him; that is the real sanction against carelessness.

The contractual duty of care is owed only in relation to the work which the employee is engaged to do, not to other jobs which he may do as a favour for the employer. Further, no

general duty requires him gratuitously to disclose defe
might make him lose the job (as in the case of a go............ ...
1872 who said nothing about being a divorcee); but his failure
to do so may mean that he is careless of his own safety
(as in the case of a building worker who failed to disclose he
was an epileptic), a point to which we return in Chapter 6.

SUMMARY DISMISSAL OF EMPLOYEES

Together with the remedy of damages, the employer sometimes
has available the additional remedy of summary termination
of the contract, i.e. without any notice. In theory, either party
may, if he so elects, treat the contract as at an end whenever
the other commits a breach going 'to its root' (though as we
saw, p. 81, the employee may have no choice). Where, for
example, the negligence constitutes a very serious breach
matched not against the consequences that in fact occur (for
these may be unforeseeable, as if the servant drops a parcel
that explodes) but against the nature of the contract and the
probable consequences (as if a signalman fails to work a
signal), the master may dismiss summarily. Repeated carelessness is more likely to allow for summary dismissal.

The same question of degree is raised in connection with the
third category of an employee's duties, those of obedience and
good conduct. He is obliged to be present at the place of work;
and, as Mr Justice Blackburn said in 1873, 'it is for the workman to explain why he was absent'. A strike is, therefore, a
breach by those participating unless some excuse can be found,
whether it be an unlimited strike or, as with Coventry car
workers in 1967, 'guerilla strikes' for fifteen minutes each hour.
He is also, as we said on p. 100, obliged to obey all lawful and
reasonable orders of the master. Miners who in 1894 refused to
descend in a cage with non-union men were held liable in
damages; and the courts refuse to accept union solidarity as
any answer to a breach of contract. It is to be noted here that a
renunciation by a party in advance of duties which will arise
at a future date operates as what the law calls 'anticipatory
breach' there and then; the other party need not wait to see if

he changes his mind but can proceed to his remedies (e.g. summary dismissal) at once.

Whether any act of misconduct is serious enough to give the employer the right to dismiss on the spot is a question to which the answers of the judges have reflected changing social conditions. An element of lack of fidelity still leads to a strict view. So, in 1966, a bookmakers' manager was held to have been lawfully dismissed summarily after borrowing £15 from the money in his charge, knowing that the employer would disapprove of the practice of inserting an I.O.U. and replacing the money later. And an engraver who did work during his employment hours for rival firms was guilty of similarly serious misconduct in the eyes of a tribunal in 1967. In many older cases wilful neglect, immorality or inebriation (especially on the part of domestic servants), was regarded as justifying summary dismissal. In *Turner* v. *Mason*, 1845, a maid who wanted to go and see her dying mother left the house against her employer's orders. The court upheld the summary dismissal in judgments full of the unattractively robust common lawyer's thinking of the day. The defence, said Baron Alderson, 'does not show that the mother was likely to die that night'. And even if it had done so, this was a 'mere moral duty'; the master still had the right always to dismiss the servant for any wilful disobedience.[17] The Court of Appeal was faced with the same principle, but modernized its application, in *Laws* v. *London Chronicle Ltd*, 1959,[18] when an employee of a newspaper disobeyed the order of the managing director to stay where she was and followed her immediate superior, the advertising manager, out of the room after a scene between the two men. While accepting the principle in *Turner* v. *Mason*, the court felt that its application required attention to modern social conditions. Disobedience was a breach of contract, but today 'one act of disobedience or misconduct can justify dismissal only if it is of a nature which goes to show (in effect) that the servant is repudiating the contract, or one of its essential conditions'. Gross insubordination is likely more easily to render even one act a repudiation. Thus, in *Pepper* v. *Webb*, 1969,[19] a gardener, who had got used to working on his own while his employer, a Major Webb, and his wife (respectively described as 'a perfectionist' and 'exacting') were in the West Indies, three months after their return refused to put in some plants before leaving work on a Saturday. In reply to the Major's remonstrations, he cried: 'I couldn't care less about your bloody greenhouse and your sodding garden', and strode off. The Court of Appeal held that the Major acted lawfully in instantly dismissing him for the wilful disobedience. It must, however, be noted that the gardener had been acting in 'unsatisfactory' ways during the three months before this explosive incident. But for that, the decision might be thought rather old-fashioned. A few swear words would not have altered the decision in the *Laws* case.[20]

Where the employee is properly dismissed for misconduct his wages may even be forfeited. If the contract expressly states that this shall be so, it is enforceable unless possibly the sum involved is an unconscionable penalty on him. Where there is no express clause, he can claim the wages that have accrued due to him; but if the service was to last for a definite period (e.g. one month) that is unexpired, and the wage is to be paid for the whole work or whole period the law may still be that he is entitled to nothing at all for work done. Moreover, the worker may even have to pay damages to the employer, as in *Pepper* v. *Webb* where the gardener had to pay £49 for losses on his tied cottage (such as a new key).

In apprenticeship contracts the rule has for centuries been modified so that the master cannot normally dismiss even for misconduct which 'goes to the root' of the contract, the master being left to his remedy of damages – or under the old law 'moderate chastisement'! The old law on infant apprentices was that the master (because of his 'quasi-parental' position) could not even sue for damages; but modern writers suggest that this remedy may be available although, if the apprentice is under eighteen, only if the contract is for his benefit. A jurisdiction of magistrates to order an apprentice to perform his contract and imprison him in default was abolished by the 1969 statute which provided for the lowering of the age of majority to eighteen years. But if an apprentice makes it impossible for the master to teach, the latter has a good cause for not performing the contract, as when an apprentice to a pawnbroker became a habitual thief. In most modern apprenticeship contracts, the master is given an additional express right to dismiss for misconduct. Some employers put obstacles in the way of union organization of apprentices; this makes all the more odd the Act of 1965 which permits a written contract made after the Act to waive apprentices' rights to redundancy payments. But much of the law is now as outmoded as the system of apprenticeships itself. Some estimates put Britain's needs as the training (and retraining) of over one million workers in the next decade. Government Training Centres have doubled in number since 1964, and are planned to expand from 45 (with 16,000 trainees a year) in 1969 to 54 (20,000) in 1971. Under the Act of 1964, Training Boards had by 1970 been set up for 28 industries covering over 15 million workers. The numbers being trained or retrained have been estimated at 1·5 million – of whom about half a million are apprentices – but that includes a very wide range of people. The Donovan Report doubted whether the 'urgency and scale of the problem' had yet been grasped. A report on the advisory Central Training Council proposed that it be given greater influence and powers, including the supervision of 'the adequacy of the educational content' of training courses; for while Governments boast of the increase in numbers, less is heard about quality. Acts like that of 1964, at least, are of greater importance than the old apprenticeship laws.

In all types of employment contract, express clauses frequently increase the area of the master's right to dismiss. B.O.A.C., for example, under one agreement in 1949 acquired the right summarily to dismiss an employee for drinking intoxicating liquor or taking drugs to excess, and for any conduct 'likely to be prejudicial to the interests of the Employers'. We have already met express clauses which give the employer the right to move a worker many miles (p. 72); but in their absence, the courts will restrict any *implied* term on such a matter to a narrow compass, e.g. restricting a building contractor's right to demand that his plumber move to another site 'to other sites within what one might call commuting distance'.[21] So, too, a contract sometimes contains an express clause providing for its suspension (as in the case of the sick-pay scheme, p. 97). But without an express clause or a clear custom giving the right to suspend, one party cannot suspend the employment against the other's wishes. An employer who 'suspends' his servant without an express right to do so must pay the wages due; and the law has, on the other side, not given to workers the right unilaterally to suspend the contract by collectively withholding their labour. But the relationship of the employment contract and the strike remains rather uncertain, even in 1970.

The view that a trade dispute itself leads to 'suspension' of contracts of employment has been put to the House of Lords, where it was not accepted, and was equally rejected by the Scottish Court of Session in litigation about a lockout.[22] The traditional view has been, as we saw, that a strike is usually a breach of contract. A 'go-slow' usually is a breach (since the work is slower than it should be), but a 'work-to-rule' (which is an unusually meticulous observance of the work-rules) is not. An 'overtime ban' is a breach only if the contract makes overtime obligatory. Other industrial actions are harder to fit into legal categories (such as the 'administrative restrictions' adopted by Pearl Insurance agents in 1966, or Pressed Steel draughtsmen's decision in 1967, after exhausting negotiating procedure, to 'work without enthusiasm').

But does a strike notice (equivalent in length to that needed to end the contract: p. 116) cure the breach? The usual view is that it does not necessarily do so. Sometimes the notice really *is* a notice to terminate the contracts of employment and some unions have given notice of official strikes in this form (e.g. the miners and cine-technicians). Then there is no breach because the contracts terminate with the strike. The Merchant Shipping Act, 1970, gives seamen a statutory right to strike on giving 48 hours' notice, after mooring, to 'terminate' their contracts. But most unions and strikers do not regard a strike notice as equivalent to asking for the workers' cards. It is just a notice announcing a withdrawal of labour. Such a notice is in legal terms usually notice of *breach*, though (as with other breaches) the employer can waive the breach. Thus, in *Rookes* v. *Barnard*, 1964, Lord Devlin said the object of the threat to strike was 'to break the contract by withholding labour but keeping the contract alive for as long as the employers would tolerate the breach'. And Lord Justice Donovan (as he then was) had said in the Court of Appeal that the employer usually waives a breach because he 'does not want to lose his labour force; he simply wants to resist the claim'. Lord Denning has also agreed that the normal strike notice was a notice of breach.[23]

In *Morgan* v. *Fry*,[24] lockmen in the T.G.W.U. employed by the Port of London Authority decided to take action against a small breakaway group. Fry (a T.G.W.U. official) sent a notice to the P.L.A. stating that, as from a date two weeks ahead, his members would be 'instructed not to work with ... non-trade unionists' but would otherwise carry out duties 'as far as possible'. The lockmen were obliged to give only one week's notice to terminate contracts; but clearly that was not a notice of termination. Unhappily, the three judges of the Court of Appeal, though all agreeing that Fry had done no wrong, analysed the notice in different ways. Lord Justice Russell gave it the usual status of a notice of impending breach. But Lord Denning held that a 'lesser notice' than notice to terminate but of equivalent length is, by implication, enough to *suspend* the contract 'during the strike', and it 'revives again when the strike is over'. This remarkable novelty in the law of implied terms sounds attractive. But the Donovan Report carefully considered and rejected the very proposal that it should be introduced into the law by statute (para. 943). Its argument is convincing. Does the doctrine apply to all strikes – even those in breach of agreed 'procedures'? Does it apply to other action, e.g. go-slow? Can an employer dismiss an employee for misconduct during the 'suspension'? Can strikers 'moonlight' (take other jobs) while on strike? What happens if the strike is never settled? Lord Denning's judicial innovation answers none of these problems. His well-intentioned attempt to find a legal basis for the 'right to strike' creates more difficulties than it solves.

Lord Justice Davies made use of a similar but different method of finding that there was no breach, which is of general interest. It is not always easy to know what constitutes an act of 'disobedience' in a real situation of industrial conflict. For example, take the employer who says: 'Move that bale', and the worker who replies: 'Sorry, can't touch that; the union says those bales are black'. If the employer insists, the worker will be in breach for, we have seen, union orders are as such no defence (though nothing in our law prevents a modern judge from taking account of union orders known to the employer in deciding whether his disobeyed instruction was both lawful and *reasonable*). But suppose the employer says: 'Oh all right, we'll have to see about it later; get on with the rest of the work'. There are two possible legal analyses. First, this may be a breach which the employer has waived. Or secondly, it may be that the parties have 'negotiated' varied or new employment terms. It is always open to parties to vary by agreement the terms of their contract. In *Stratford Ltd* v. *Lindley*, 1964,[25] a similar argument was raised by lightermen who had instructions from their union not to handle certain barges. Their employment was by *daily* contract. It was argued that the employers, since they knew of the embargo before they took the men on each day, must have agreed to new daily terms of employment which excluded work on these barges. The House of Lords rejected the idea and refused to treat them as accepting a 'conditional offer' to work on new terms Despite the embargo, the employer 'expected his normal reasonable orders to be obeyed', said Lord Donovan. But in *Morgan* v. *Fry*, Lord Justice Davies suggested that the notice given was in a sense 'a termination of the existing contract and an offer to continue on different terms. In the present case this was accepted by the [employers]'. This valuable legal device may be of great importance since it may permit interpretation of many a strike notice so as to escape from the category of 'notice of breach' into the lawful territory of 'an offer to work on new terms'. We shall see, when we discuss Industrial Conflict in Chapters 7 and 8, that the existence of a breach may today turn out to be more important than any waiver of it.

Lastly, even where the breach is serious, the common law does not demand that the employer inform the servant of the reason for his dismissal. Even if the employer does not at the time know of any misconduct, the dismissal is justified if it turns out later that there are in fact good grounds for dismissal. In some other relations, a person may be required by law to observe the rules of 'natural justice' before terminating a relationship (e.g. the watch committee which exercises its statutory power to dismiss a chief constable), but, as Lord Reid has said, 'the question in a pure case of master and servant does not at all depend on whether the master has heard the servant in his own defence: it depends on whether the facts emerging at the trial prove breach of contract'. So in 1967, the British Museum trustees were upheld in the dismissal of a principal scientific officer of the National History Museum without holding any sort of inquiry. Thus it will be seen that using the language of an agreement between equals the law protects in great measure the employer's power over the worker. In practice, although the employer sometimes finds he has to give reasons to the local employment exchange, trade union pressure has been the avenue for the ordinary worker to know of such reasons. But now, as we shall see, statute is gradually supplementing that with a new *floor of rights* for the worker in regard to job-security.

DAMAGES FOR BREACH OF THE CONTRACT

How much is recoverable for breach of the contract? The ordinary rule is that the compensation meets the loss arising naturally in the ordinary course of things, or any special loss in the contemplation of the parties as the result of breach. Thus, under the second principle, an actor can recover damages for his loss of opportunity to put his name in lights; under the first, the wrongly dismissed employee always claims wages to which he would be entitled and any other similar actual loss. Since, as we shall see, the worker may be entitled to only short notice to terminate his employment, the wages recoverable will relate only to that period. Moreover, in *Lavarack* v. *Woods*,

1967,[26] a majority of the Court of Appeal, in a harsh interpretation of the principles, held that damages cannot take account of discretionary bonuses which the worker would almost certainly have received, since, as Lord Justice Diplock put it: 'The law is concerned with legal obligations only ... not with the expectations, however reasonable ... that the [employer] will do something that he has assumed no legal obligation to do.' A more liberal attitude was displayed by the court in *Dunk* v. *Waller and Son Ltd*, 1970,[27] where defendant employers had terminated a four-year apprenticeship contract under which a 'reasonable and obliging lad' attended part-time courses which he appeared likely to fail, whereas the apprenticeship was terminable only for misconduct. While the trial judge would grant only nominal damages, the Court of Appeal took account of the 'special character' of apprenticeship 'entirely different' from ordinary employment: of the loss of earnings undergone during the four years; the instruction and training of which the dismissal deprived him; and the loss of *future prospects* for obtaining a better job afterwards, as Lord Justice Widgery said: loss of 'a status in the labour market'. They therefore awarded him £500. Some of the reasoning in the *Dunk* judgment might well lead to a different result in cases such as *Lavarack*, even though there an ordinary employee was involved.

The amount of compensation an employee can obtain may be further reduced by two other considerations. First, he is under a duty 'reasonably to mitigate his loss'. If after dismissal, therefore, he refuses to take another suitable job, he will be penalized to the extent of the wage he did earn or could have earned by taking such a job – though it will not normally be reasonable to expect him to take work at a much lower wage nor, the courts have now added, with any 'important reduction in status'. Where there is a labour shortage, the employer need have little fear of this remedy, therefore; and as the T.U.C. Report, 1963, said: 'the opportunity to obtain damages would be illusory in areas of high employment'.

Secondly, the damages are meant to compensate the worker for his exact loss, and not to punish the master. On this ground, the courts have held since 1955 that where the sum lost through dismissal (e.g. wages) would have been taxed, but the damages receivable by the dismissed worker would not be taxed, the employer need pay as compensation only that sum *less* the amount the worker would have paid as tax on his wages. This, said the courts, must be done to stop the worker making a profit out of the action, for any damages he recovers will remain in his hands free of tax. This means, however, that the employer need pay the employee less than would have been payable had the employment continued; and the 'slice' which before would have gone as tax to the revenue he now keeps. Then, in 1960, Parliament decided that all sums paid on removal from employment (often the form legally taken by 'golden handshakes' paid, for example, to redundant directors) must be taxed in the hands of the recipient *except* for the first £5,000. In *Parsons v. B.N.M. Laboratories*, 1963,[28] The Court of Appeal held (logically perhaps) that if the damages were under £5,000, then the wrong-doer employer still paid damages *net* of the tax; but the basis of computation must change for any 'slice' over £5,000. The damages that represented an excess over £5,000 had to be paid gross, without deduction for tax, because this sum was taxable in the hands of the plaintiff! This bizarre result can give pleasure only to an accountant.

The court went on to an equally strange, but much less defensible, decision. In the same case, the plaintiff had drawn £59 unemployment benefit after his dismissal. The court argued that this too must be deducted from the damages. But in the State insurance scheme, the employer's contributions do not, as the judges said, return to the unemployed worker as a form of 'wages'. The scheme shows no indication that (as Lord Justice Sellers asserted) 'he should get the benefit of it if he finds it necessary to put one of his employees into unemployment' by wrongful dismissal. Anyway, both the employee and the State have contributed too. Moreover, the court distinguished the State scheme from an ordinary insurance policy, payment under which would not be deductible from damages since they would derive from the worker's own 'thrift'. Such judicial thinking can only be termed a Samuel Smiles view of State unemployment insurance. Later cases have held that discretionary State benefits (National Assistance as it was) are not to be deducted. It is difficult to see why any social insurance benefits should be deducted from the compensation payable by a man who has, in breach of his legal duty, 'found it necessary' to dismiss a worker into unemployment. Indeed the logic of a House of Lords decision in 1969 on related matters happily makes the whole of the *Parsons* decision doubtful.[29] In 1969 an English judge refused to deduct retirement pension benefits. The law in Scotland and Northern Ireland does not seem to follow the pattern of *Parsons*.[30] But in the *Dunk* case, the Court of Appeal made the customary English deduction from damages for unemployment benefit received by the apprentice. Statute should intervene to impose a different solution (as in the case of industrial injury benefit: p. 284).

Where it is the worker who breaks the contract, the employer can recover the loss naturally arising from the breach. In *N.C.B.* v. *Galley*,[31] the Coal Board claimed against deputies who refused to work Saturday shifts damages for the entire loss of production caused. That sum might have been recoverable against each worker had the strike been a tortious conspiracy, as we shall see in Chapter 8; but the Court of Appeal decided that here the measure of damage against each man was, for breach of contract, no more than the net loss suffered through losing *his* output, or (where, as here, the worker was not directly related to production) the cost of replacing him with another deputy on the day in question. This small sum (here £3 18s. 2d.) would be awarded in respect of the repeated breaches on Saturdays up to the date of the writ, but not later. The practice of suing strikers for damages, rare in most industries, had always been more common among coal-owners and this survived nationalization. In the early sixties, however, policy changed, and the N.C.B. representative before Donovan was ironically among the witnesses who most strenuously insisted upon the harm done to good industrial relations by such legal actions brought by employers. Some foreign legal systems in which actions for damages against employees have been more common than in Britain have even found it necessary specially to limit the damages recoverable; for example, in Sweden the maximum was fixed in 1928 as two hundred crowns (now about £15). Because of their special position a limit of this kind is enacted in the 1970 Act for merchant seamen (p. 389). Without the policy apparent in the *Galley* decision, Britain would no doubt need such a law for all workers.

NOTICE

The period of employment is usually not a fixed time and each party can normally end the contract where no ground exists for summary dismissal only by giving notice to terminate it. The length of notice will be that expressly set out; or if none is expressly agreed, that implied by any custom; or, otherwise, the reasonable period for ending the particular job. As we have seen, the master can, in practice, also end it on the spot by paying the wages in lieu of proper notice, since the sum lost over the period of notice which should have been given will normally be the full extent of the loss suffered by a worker wrongly sacked. The contract may, of course, provide different periods of notice for employee and employer. Or it may exceptionally exclude the right of one, or both, to give notice at all, as in the case of a clerk employed by the Northern Ireland Health Service Board in 1957. The House of Lords held that, though the clerk could resign on one month's notice, the employing Board's power to sack her was restricted to grounds set out (e.g. inefficiency) and it could not give her notice whenever it wished.[32]

Customs still receive judicial attention, as in the County Court decision, 1959, that club band musicians are entitled to two weeks' notice. Where there are neither customs nor express terms, the court has had to decide in each case what is 'reasonable' notice. This is often hard to assess; but one can say that the higher the status of the worker the longer is the notice a judge is likely to find 'reasonable'. So cases have decided that a weekly-paid foreman and a hairdresser's assistant were entitled to receive one week; a shop manager one month; a travelling salesman of high-class ladies' foundation garments three months; a cinema controller six months; and a steamer's chief officer one year. Two newspaper editors were in 1916 and 1908 held entitled respectively to twelve and three months.

Notice to terminate is a formal legal act. When given, it should always be in unambiguous terms, to make clear for example that it is a notice to quit. It is a 'unilateral act', as Mr Justice Diplock called it in 1959: '... like a notice to quit a tenancy, once given it cannot in my view be withdrawn save by mutual consent'. Thus, when Bailey Ltd tried in 1969 to rely upon a notice given by their employers' association to the trade union ending an old agreement on working conditions as a notice to terminate the individual contract of Mr Morris, one of their boilermakers, the Court of Appeal rejected their contention because Morris had never been given any formal notice. Lord Justice Winn who had noted that the union Rule Book said 'working men have been ground down and held down by laws made and administered by ... The Ruling Class', tartly remarked that 'this man ... will no longer have occasion to feel' that in this case.[33] (Of greater legal interest, the court left open the question whether and when a union can be the agent to receive dismissal notices applicable to its members.) A distinction is drawn in practice in modern redundancies between agreed periods of formal notice (when wages in lieu of the period can be paid if the employer chooses) and more informal periods of 'warning' of impending dismissal (during which time off to seek other work is sometimes allowed). The decisions on redundancy (p. 129) have upheld this distinction between the two in law.

After the Contracts of Employment Act, 1963, the period of notice will usually be expressly stated in the written particulars. But the Act also extended new protection to employees by laying down minimum periods of notice.

The compulsory statutory *minima*, where notice can be given to terminate the contract, are now as follows:

(i) The employer must give at least one week's notice to an employee after his continuous employment for 26 weeks: two weeks' after two years; four weeks' after five years. (The 1970

Bill proposed to amend 26 to 13 weeks, and to add periods of six weeks after ten years and eight weeks after fifteen years.)

(ii) The employee must give at least one week's notice after 26 weeks' continuous employment.

Of course, these minima will be displaced if a particular contract imposes a longer period; and in many written particulars the period of notice required of certain workers has been contractually made equivalent to those periods imposed on the employers by the statute. Thus in *Pepper* v. *Webb*, 1969, the gardener was entitled to receive but also bound to give three months' notice.

The employment *contract* cannot exclude the minimum notice provisions; but a puzzling phrase in the Act states nevertheless that either party may waive his right to notice 'on any occasion' – an undesirable loophole which allows for pressure on the non-union worker. The Act applies only where some notice is required; but after 26 weeks' continuous employment the employer is prohibited from evading the Act by employing the worker on a short contract that ends without notice. But employees engaged on contracts of a fixed duration of 5 weeks or above (i.e. the contract ends after 5 weeks without notice) fall outside the Act, since in every 5-week contract they have more 'security' of employment than the Act could provide (though, if needed, continuous 5-week contracts can be used to compute 'continuity'). 'Continuity of employment' is rather a legal puzzle under the statute. It is continuity of *employment*, not necessarily of contract. So, a break from Friday evening to Monday morning should be ignored. The concept has been used also to test rights to redundancy payments; most of the tribunal decisions fall under that rubric but apply to the 1963 Act equally. The worker can count any week in which he is either employed under a contract involving at least 21 hours' normal work or actually employed for 21 hours; and weeks when he has no contract but in which he is absent through sickness or injury (up to 26 weeks); or on account of a temporary cessation of work (other than strikes); or where a special 'custom or arrangement' provides that he is still employed, also count towards continuity. Tribunal decisions upon these complicated provisions are numerous and not always consistent. Two 1967 decisions show that the 26-week limit on sickness does not apply if the employee's *contract* continues despite his illness; and that a 'temporary cessation' of work can include workers made unemployed by strikes in which they took no part. The High Court decided in 1968, where a riveter had been employed for forty years by the same ship-repairers but had regularly been 'laid off' for periods of seven to forty days, that his service was continuous.[34] Cessation meant cessation of the job, not of the business; and 'temporary' had to be judged not by whether the parties thought the relationship was ending at the time, but with 'hindsight' as to whether the interruption appeared temporary on *re-engagement* of the worker. The House of Lords vigorously upheld this approach (as against the opposite view which Scottish courts had taken) in *Fitzgerald* v. *Hall Russell Ltd*,[35] where a welder was employed from 1958 to November 1962; re-employed in January 1963; and dismissed in 1967. The welder was held to have nine years' continuity, the eight-week break caused by shortage of work at the respondents' shipbuilding yard being seen as a temporary cessation of *his* work looking back at the dismissal and re-employment. But if, on looking back, it appears that the *employee* intended to make a permanent break with the employer, but is re-employed some weeks later, the court may still hold that, although there was a temporary cessation of work, the worker was not absent from work *on account of* that cessation, as in Mrs Newsham's case, 1969.[36] An even larger number of decisions have concerned those parts of the Act which aim to preserve 'continuity' of service when ownership of a business changes. Here again the concepts are basically the same in the Redundancy Payments Act, 1965. The main question is whether there has been merely a transfer of assets (when the statutes do not preserve continuity) or transfer of 'a business' (when they do), which 'must be a question of fact and degree in every case'.[37]

The problem of 'continuity' is particularly awkward where a worker works for more than one company in a group of companies. To him it often looks like one 'employer'; and so, in common sense, it is. But of course each company is a separate legal entity or 'person' and therefore a separate employer. In 1965, amendments were made which, it was hoped, would plug loopholes in the 1963 scheme and by which it was laid down that service with 'associated' companies was to be regarded as service with one employer for continuity purposes. The trouble is, however, that this is much too narrow. 'Associated' companies are defined to mean only 'subsidiary' and 'holding' companies within the Companies Acts, and (although that definition includes any 'body corporate', i.e. public corporations as well as private sector companies) it applies only where one company holds half the equity shares of another or controls the composition of its board of directors. In 1969, in a case about redundancy payments (see p. 125), Mr Collins was employed from 1951 to 1965 by the Southern Electricity Board. A collective agreement with the unions provided that workers could be transferred to other Boards but were not to lose any rights, such as holiday or pension rights, by such transfer. In 1965 he was transferred to the Central Board; but after six months he was transferred back to the Southern Board. The High Court held that the transfer had broken his continuity; so in 1965 he went back to square one! Lord Chief Justice Parker said that, although 'all my sympathy is for' Mr Collins, these were not 'associated' companies. What is more, the collective agreement did not save him, because it preserved accrued rights to benefits but not continuity under the *statutes*. He was not 'absent' on account of any temporary cessation of work. Nor would the court see this as an 'arrangement or custom' whereby he was regarded as 'continuing in the employment of his employer'. When he left Southern, he might never have come back; and when he went to Central, the agreement did not provide that he should be regarded as still employed by Southern. Such are the hazards of the method of statutory control over employment when it ousts collective agreements. The decision indeed struck such a serious blow at the industry's arrangements that the Minister in March 1970 made an Order (as he has power to do, p. 134) removing this category of employee from the redundancy statute altogether in favour of a scheme agreed between the employers and the union.

Weeks spent on strike or locked-out do not count towards continuity; but neither do they break continuity. The 1963 Act attempted to make strikes in breach of employment contracts break continuity; but, as we have seen, this included most strikes where the worker did not give notice to terminate. And if he did terminate, he broke continuity anyway. So in 1965 an amendment repealed this futile attempt in the 1963 Act to penalize strikes and restored the policy of statutory 'neutrality' towards them, so that now they count neither for nor against continuity. The Donovan Commission was pressed by certain witnesses to reintroduce automatic rupture of continuity or some similar sanction by deprivation of benefits for strikes and other industrial action in breach of agreed procedures. But the Report rejected the idea. The deterrent effect could not work twice; once a worker lost his 'seniority' he would 'cease to be interested in the threatened penalty' on the next occasion. The cooperation of employers would be needed but they would have every incentive to 'condone' the impropriety of the strike when it was being settled. Further, the risks to older workers would be 'intolerable' when the 'fruits of a life-time's work' could be lost 'through participation in an action which may be over in an hour. The history of our law ... shows that where the penalty is too harsh it will not be imposed.'

When the statutory rights to notice arise, the 1963 Act lays down minimum sums which must be paid during the relevant period. In effect, these provisions mean that the worker will get his normal remuneration (even during periods when there is no work for him to do or when he is sick or on holiday during the period); where pay varies with work done, the employer pays the average of the previous four weeks; and where there are no normal working hours but the worker is ready and willing to do reasonable work, the average of the previous twelve weeks is paid. Where a factory has been slowly in decline, the averages may, therefore, be rather depressed. The Act thus departs very little from the normal legal rule that the worker is entitled to something like his wage during

121

the time of notice. 'Remuneration' has, however, a wider meaning than payment for work done. In 1969 the High Court decided that it included sums paid to the employee to keep up his car which he was required to use in his work (see p. 229).

The statutory compensation cannot be used to overlap with damages recovered at common law for wrongful dismissal, but there may be cases where extra damages can be recovered under one or other heading (as where the worker has a right only to reduced sick pay under his contract but claims under the Act). All such claims are made still in the ordinary courts (not, as is often thought, the Industrial Tribunals to which the 1970 Bill proposed to give concurrent jurisdiction, p. 149). Finally, the Act reserves the common law rights of the parties to terminate without notice, for example summary dismissal in a proper case.

UNEMPLOYMENT BENEFIT

An employee under 65 (60 for women) who has the necessary contributions (at least 26 contributions paid and 50 paid or credited in the preceding year) has, since the National Insurance Act, 1946, been able to claim unemployment benefit for days on which he is unemployed. The same is true under the 1965 Act (to which Acts of 1966 to 1969 have added). He is not, however, normally able to claim for the first three days, nor able to draw benefit for longer than 312 days, after which he must requalify with 13 more contributions. In June 1969 the Government announced increases which would make the benefits £5 for single men, and £8 2s. 0d. for a married couple, per week (with additional dependants' allowances). But this flat-rate has since 1966 had added to it a graduated 'earnings-related' benefit. This benefit is one-third of normal weekly earnings between £9 and £30. But the maximum *total* benefit must not exceed 85 per cent of average weekly earnings. Furthermore, the graduated benefit is not paid until the thirteenth day of unemployment and stops after 156 days. This now-fashionable notion of 'earnings-related' benefits (which also applies to sickness benefit) has carried over the inequalities of the labour market into social security. The worker who benefits least from it is the low-paid worker. And for the really long-term unemployed man, it offers an unkind cut-back to flat-rate benefits after six months' lack of work.[38] The National Insurance Act, 1966, also introduced a change in regard to workers 'suspended' by their employers without pay. It provided that, for earnings-related benefit, no day is 'treated' as a day of unemployment for such a person unless it is the seventh day or later of the suspension. After protests, the Government decided in 1968 not to extend this rule to the flat-rate 'for the time being'.

As under all State insurance schemes since 1924, the employee can suffer disqualification for various reasons under the 1965 scheme. Disputes on such questions under the Act go from local officers to local tribunals, and then to National Insurance Commissioners (who must be barristers of at least ten years' standing). Those arising from strikes we deal with in Chapter 8. The worker can lose his benefit for a period in the discretion of the tribunal of up to six weeks, if he refuses approved training or has failed without good reason to carry out reasonable recommendations of the employment exchange which were aimed at helping him find 'suitable employment'; or without good cause has refused the exchange's recommendation of 'suitable employment'.

The Act is careful to state that a job is deemed not to be 'suitable' if it is a vacancy consequent upon a trade dispute; or if it is in the worker's usual occupation at worse wages or conditions than he might expect to earn in his district; or in another district in his usual occupation at a lower rate than is generally observed by 'good employers' or in collective agreements with unions. (After a reasonable time, however, employment at such generally observed rates is not deemed 'unsuitable' merely because it is in some occupation other than his usual one.) Despite these protections, the qualifications put the unemployed worker under considerable pressures. Take Decision R (U) 15/62: a builder's labourer with cardiac debility and registered as a 'light labourer', after five years mainly without work, was offered a job as a trainee operator at a low rate. He said he could not manage on the wage, and wrote: 'give me a job where I can live and not starve and I will do it.' But the Commissioner accepted the principle as settled that the 'question whether a claimant would have been worse off financially by accepting a situation is not in itself relevant to the question whether he is disqualified'. He no longer had a 'usual' occupation, and was disqualified. Union policy was no defence to a joiner who refused a 'suitable' job which provided for no free tea breaks (R(U) 9/64). But where none of the statutory provisions on 'deeming' apply, the Commissioners can consider all the circumstances in deciding on suitability (such as an employer offering pay well below rates agreed with a union: R(U) 5/68).

The unemployed worker can also be disqualified for up to six weeks if he voluntarily left his job without 'just cause' or lost it 'through his misconduct'. The Commissioners have held that it is 'just cause' to leave voluntarily in order not to have to join a trade union.[39] Though it obviously overlaps with breach of the employment contract, 'industrial misconduct' has its own meaning and must be interpreted by the statutory tribunals, not by reference to the judges' principles. A Commissioner said: 'It is the duty of the statutory authorities to make up their own minds on what constitutes misconduct, in an industrial sense ... irrespective of the conclusions which may have been reached by the employers or by a court of law.' Misconduct outside work – though not before the job began – may be relevant; and hearsay evidence can be admitted when it would be excluded in the courts.[40] So, the judges' principles govern breach of contract and dismissal; the Commissioners decide 'misconduct' if social security rights are in issue.

In some respects the Commissioners' decisions are more harsh than the judges' decisions; and they are certainly as legalistic. Further, there is a discretion allowed to the tribunal. For example, in 1959 a group of workers stopped work after alleging that the foreman was retaining a cash rebate on their P.AY.E., found the work-site closed the next morning, and received their cards and wages: the argument was only settled a month later. The claimant, the shop steward, was disqualified from benefit for 'misconduct' (for the matter should have been taken up via the union, not a stoppage, said the Commissioner), but only for three days as the men had been 'grievously provoked'. And the Commissioners (from whom there is no appeal to ordinary courts even on points of law) have the advantage of not being strictly bound by their own decisions, and sometimes cut adrift from principles which have become an encumbrance. Thus, recently they have destroyed a long-standing artificial interpretation of 'suspension' (R(U) 7/68), and reversed decisions on trainees in receipt only of expenses so as to categorize them as 'qualifying for', and not in, employment (R(U) 3/67). There are judges who will envy this power to innovate so easily.

A disqualified unemployed worker may still be able to obtain discretionary 'supplementary' benefit for himself and his family. The National Superannuation Bill, 1970, proposed, over strong trade union objections, to reduce the rate of such benefit for the disqualified worker to two thirds the normal rate. Such a reduction could adversely affect a worker trying to make up his mind whether alternative employment is satisfactory when the insurance officer has already decided that it is 'suitable' and should have been accepted. Any such punitive provisions certainly invite a reconsideration of the grounds for disqualification.

REDUNDANCY PAYMENTS

Since December 1965, a new tribunal has had jurisdiction to decide rights which may involve problems of 'misconduct' and the like. The Industrial Tribunals have jurisdiction under a number of modern statutes (from disputes about training levies, for which they were set up, to disputes on what is 'dock work' or selective employment tax). Their most important jurisdiction, however, is over disputes under the Redundancy Payments Act, 1965, decisions being enforceable through the County Courts and open to appeal on points of 'law' only – not of 'fact' – to the High Court.

The rationale of the curious Act of 1965 is still shrouded in mystery. Undoubtedly it arose from the fact that collective bargaining had not developed rapidly enough to deal with the problems of unemployment caused by technological change. But it has been variously explained as intended to promote 'labour-mobility' (in the Donovan Report); as relieving 'hardship'; and as protecting a worker's 'property in his job'. Some features of the Act could be said to promote, but others to obstruct, each one of these objectives. Indeed, in January 1965, when both trade unions and employers were luke-warm about it, the *Financial Times* thought 'the Government has given priority to the wrong measure'; it should have given priority to better social security schemes to encourage labour mobility. That case is still arguable today. Even the word 'redundancy' is peculiarly English. It is untranslatable exactly into French or German and it is not the same as the American 'mass lay-off'. It reflects a management idea, of course – redundancy implies 'superfluity', but of workers not of directors.

The basic feature of the Act is an obligation on any employer to make an employee a redundancy payment if after two years' continuous service the employee is *dismissed by reason of redundancy* as defined by the Act[41] (excluding certain groups such as spouses; domestic servants who are close relatives; employees on fixed contracts of two years or more who waived their rights; and National Health Service, Crown and registered dock employees – all of whom now, however, have equivalent schemes in operation). So long as he notifies the office of the Department of Employment as Regulations require, the employer recovers a rebate, now reduced by the amending Act of 1969 to one half of each payment. Rebates come from the national fund financed by levies on all employers. (If the employer is insolvent, redundant workers have rights to claim from the Minister.) The fund has continuously gone 'into the red' and the figures show why. At first, Government estimates that the fund would need to provide £15 million and employers £10 million in 1966 were nearly correct. But as unemployment rose £50 million was paid in 1967 (£38 million rebated from the fund) to 240,000 redundant workers. In 1969, 250,764 payments swallowed up nearly £62 million (£38·5 million rebated). From 1966 to August 1970 nearly £250 million had been paid to just over one million workers.

The technicalities of the statute are such that from the outset the tribunals were swamped. In 1967 they heard 10,818 cases, and 9,759 in 1969. Each tribunal has a lawyer as chairman (appointed by the Lord Chancellor) and two 'wingmen' (one each from panels of employers and employees appointed by the D.E.P. Secretary of State after consultation with T.U.C. and C.B.I.). The backlog of cases in England and Wales and in Scotland was reduced from 3,006 at the end of 1967 to 2,391 in March 1970. The energetic President of the English tribunals reorganized their structure, setting up regional centres, with some thirty panels and, by 1970, nine permanent chairmen; removing some of the part-time chairmen who obstructed the drive towards informality, as one did, by insisting on asking a dismissed woman who had made a technical error in naming her employer: 'Madam, do you want to amend your pleadings?' – when all she could say was: 'I want my money'. In 1965 the Minister of Labour had promised that the tribunals would be 'easy of access ... speedy ... with less formality and expense' than the courts. But in 1966 the time from first complaint to a decision was on average 10 weeks;[42] and this appeared, if anything, to have increased by 1969. Cases appealed to the High Court – which since 1965 have run at a regular average of about one per cent of tribunal cases – seem to involve about ten to twelve months from complaint to decision; longer still, of course, if appeals go on to the Court of Appeal, or to the House of Lords. One case, for example, about 'continuity' and 'temporary cessation' of work, involved a dismissal in March 1967, followed by decisions by a tribunal in July 1968; the High Court, April 1969; and the Court of Appeal, January 1970. Our survey of about 1,000 cases in 1966 showed that three questions accounted for 75 per cent of the issues argued, namely (i) 'dismissal'; (ii) 'redundancy' and (iii) offers of 'alternative engagement'. The evidence suggests that this picture has changed very little. We concentrate here, therefore, on those issues, with brief comment on other aspects of the Act.

First, however, how is the payment computed if it is due? With maxima of twenty years and £40 a week, there is paid: − for each year of service between 41 and 65 years one and a half weeks' pay; for each between 21 and 40, one week's pay; for each between 18 and 20, half a week's pay. (A worker made redundant after 64 (59 for women), however, gradually has these rights reduced to zero at pensionable age − a harsh tapering-off resented by older workers who see others with less seniority receiving larger payments). A week's pay is computed by reference to the same criteria as the rules for compensation in the 1963 Act (p. 121) in the last weeks before redundancy. Once a payment is made, continuity is broken. The main problem relates to pay for 'normal working hours'. Overtime pay falls within this formula usually only when the overtime is obligatory. The tribunals and courts have leaned heavily in favour of saying that local overtime arrangements go to 'co-operation not contract', because men are not normally bound to work the overtime.[43] As we shall see, in one case the local agreement was said to be a 'gentlemen's agreement' (p. 192). These payments must be given (with a written statement) whether or not the worker gets another job at once elsewhere. For the purpose of the Act is:

to compensate for loss of security and to encourage workers to accept redundancy ... compensation for loss of a right which a long term employee has ... a right analogous to a right of property in his job. (The Tribunals' President, 1968)

As Lord Denning pointed out in 1969 this 'is not unemployment benefit ... It is compensation to the employee for loss of his job'. And the Solicitor General, in speaking on the Bill, said its 'whole philosophy' was that a job was a 'valuable thing' for which a man should receive compensation if it was ended 'by reason of redundancy'.

We now turn to the main problems.

(i) There must be a *dismissal* proved by the employee. The Act extends the meaning of 'dismissal' to include any act by or 'event affecting' the employer which operates to terminate the contract (except for death about which special provision is

128

made, and change of ownership when continuity of service can be preserved) or any breach by the employer (except lock-outs) which allows the worker to leave without notice. Otherwise dismissal is interpreted in the usual way, and the employee must prove it strictly. If, as in *Morton Sundour Fabrics* v. *Shaw*, 1967,[44] employers warn an employee in the velvet department that they will soon close it down and he later gives notice, having found another job, he is not 'dismissed'; but his less enterprising brethren who wait to be dismissed will receive payments even if they then find other jobs at once. The D.E.P. National Joint Advisory Council booklet on redundancies in 1969 asks employers to give 'as long advance warning as possible' of redundancy. Such communications may put the long-service worker in an awkward dilemma. Similarly, in the cases discussed on p. 108 about moving workers to other sites, the order to move is a dismissal if the employer has no right to give it under the contract of employment, but not otherwise (as in the 1967 decision on a 'travelling' construction worker liable to work wherever required 'anywhere in the United Kingdom'). A dismissal was upheld in 1969 even though a farmworker had persuaded the employer to dismiss him. But in 1967 a worker away sick had his job completely changed (a serious breach by the employer), returned to work and gave in his notice in protest: result – no 'dismissal'. The Court of Appeal applied a more realistic test in 1970 when, faced with an employee loaned in a slack time 'for a few days' to another firm who found no work or pay available for him on returning to his employers, it decided that he was faced with a repudiation by the employers. Thus, when he sent a letter giving 'notice', he counted as 'dismissed' because the Act includes a case where the employee terminates the contract, being entitled to do so because of the employer's repudiation (though, strictly, the Act speaks of him terminating *without* notice').[45] Dismissal is a 'unilateral' act, distinguished from changing or leaving your job by 'mutual agreement' (Tribunal 1967). In *Marriott* v. *Oxford & District Co-op. Soc.*, 1969,[46] the Court of Appeal refused to accept as a mutually agreed 'variation' of employment terms a foreman's continuing to work for a few weeks under protest, until he found another job, after receiving a letter informing him of a reduction in grade and wages the following week. The decisions in the lower Courts had classified this as a 'consensual varia-tion' of the terms. But Lord Denning led the judgment of the Court of Appeal back to real life by deciding that this was 'termination' by the employer; the foreman had never 'agreed' to terms 'dictated' to him by the employer.

(ii) The Act states that dismissal is by reason of *redundancy* if it is 'attributable wholly or mainly' to the fact either (a) that the employer ceases temporarily or permanently to carry on the business altogether or in the 'place' of the employee's employment, or intends so to cease; or (b) that the require-ments of the business for employees to carry out 'work of a particular kind' have ceased or diminished (generally or in that 'place') or are expected to do so. In 1966 the writer predicted this definition would 'provide a lawyers' field-day'. It has. Unless the contrary is proved, the Act presumes against the employer both that employment has been continuous *and* that the dismissal was by reason of redundancy. But despite the latter presumption, courts have significantly reduced the burden on an employer. In *North Riding Garages* v. *Butter-wick*, 1967,[47] a manager who had worked at a garage for thirty years was dismissed by the new bosses after a take-over. They introduced quite new methods of work. He claimed that needs for his 'particular kind' of managing had diminished. But the High Court disagreed. One must look, said Mr Justice Widgery, 'at the overall requirements of the business' for work of any kind (here workshop-managing); and an employee 'is expected to adapt himself to new methods and techniques'. This narrow reasoning has dominated later cases. For example, the owners of the 'Star and Garter' at Blyth converted it into 'The Steamboat Inn' and installed a discotheque. They also wished to instal 'young blondes' as 'Bunny girls'; and they dismissed Mrs Ward, a barmaid. The tribunal awarded a pay-ment. The case came to the High Court twice, in 1968 and 1970; and each time the judges said the tribunal's approach of contrasting 'a barmaid of a very quiet bar' with attendants of 'more glamour and younger, who might attract the young, or old perhaps, to the premises', was the wrong approach: 'it is not a question of whether the requirements for a barmaid of her type had declined but whether the particular kind of work' ceased or diminished. The reason for the dismissal was essentially to 'get younger and more attractive staff', a reason 'quite inconsistent' with a diminution in the requirements for work of that *nature*. That was not 'redundancy'.[48] So if relief of 'hardship' be an object of the Act, this case shows it has not attained its goal. But if it can be shown that existing terms of employment would cause the need for workers to diminish, a dismissal effected to try to enforce management's offer of new terms is attributable to redundancy.[49] The court will not allow 'minute details of distinction', as was said where a one-eyed carpenter and joiner was refused a payment after being moved to a building site where he could no longer avoid the dangers to his eye which habitual indoor sites had put at a minimum. The tribunal awarded a payment; but an appeal succeeded in 1968 because the *overall* need for carpenters on all the sites had not diminished. 'Redundancy', then, is an even more technical and narrow concept than appears at first sight from the Act.

The Act also provides that no employee is entitled to payment if dismissed in circumstances which allow for his summary dismissal, i.e. 'misconduct' by way of breach (with the exception that this does not apply to strikes *after* the employer has given notice). In such cases the Act says he must be given written reasons for the dismissal if the employer still gives him normal notice – but, oddly enough, he need not be given reasons if the employer gives shorter or no notice! An employer seeking to rely on misconduct must, the judges have said, prove the contractual terms strictly. But why should the Act deal expressly with 'misconduct'? If that is the reason for the dismissal, surely it is not one 'by reason of redundancy'. The reason seems to be, as a tribunal held in 1969, that even if the dismissal is *mainly* attributable to redundancy, no payment need be made if the employee is open to summary dismissal. Here the misconduct must be proved by the employer on the evidence.

But worse is to follow. What does 'attributable' to redundancy mean? If there is some patent reason for the dismissal then the Act does not apply even if the business is being closed down. Thus an early tribunal decision accepted that a lady's dismissal was prompted by other motives ('she knew too much' about certain matters and there were 'personal reasons flowing from the familiar terms on which she and [a Director] had at one time worked'). But must such other motives be substantiated as facts, or will the employer's genuine belief suffice? If the latter, the employer can easily leap over the hurdle of the statutory presumption. The former seems the better view, as it did to Lord Denning. But he was outvoted by two Court of Appeal judges in *Hindle* v. *Percival Boats*, 1969,[50] in which a skilled woodworker employed for twenty years on boat-building suffered the same fate as the garage manager after a take-over and a shift to boat-repairing occurred in the firm. At this time the introduction of fibreglass boats had led to a decline in woodwork on boats. There was less need for his 'kind of work'; neither he nor any other of the seven woodworkers were replaced after their dismissal. The management dismissed him, however, on the ground that he was a thorough but a 'slow' and 'unprofitable' worker. The majority judges held that all the employer need do is convince the tribunal (as here) that the *main* ground on which he dismissed was 'genuine'. It mattered not that he was mistaken in fact. The Act does not deal with cases, said Lord Justice Sachs, of 'ill health or a deterioration in the employer's views of the capabilities of the employee'. Nor does it apply if the employer wants 'to see if someone else can do the job better; it could indeed be industrially unfortunate if it puts a brake on employers seeking to get the best man for any given job.' Lord Justice Widgery added that the employer's evidence as to his belief would often, though not always, be important: he might think the employee 'a bad influence', or 'suspect him of pilfering' or want to 'replace him by a younger employee', in which case he 'does not assume the obligation of proving that his suspicions were well founded' or his actions reasonable. Even in a redundancy situation, then, all the employer needs to prove is a genuine belief that the worker is ill, too old, unprofitable or suspect. Judicial adoption of managerial prerogatives has made nonsense of the Act's protection of the worker's 'right analogous to a right of property in his job'. As the Act says nothing about the principles or policies for *selecting* the workers to be dismissed in a redundancy (e.g. it does not insist on 'last in: first out') it is always open to management to select workers who might be brought under the retrograde *Hindle* principles.

(iii) Thirdly, the employer is afforded a defence, even in a redundancy dismissal, if he (or when 'he' is a company, his holding or subsidiary 'associated' company) has, before termination, either *offered re-engagement* on the same terms, or offered *in writing* (oral offers will not do) to re-engage the worker on terms which, though differing from the previous employment, will take effect within four weeks and will constitute 'suitable employment in relation to the employee'. If the worker accepts he is taken never to have been dismissed, but if he 'unreasonably refuses' such an offer, he is disqualified. The interpretation of 'suitable' and 'unreasonable' was left to the tribunals, except that where a change of ownership has occurred – when as we saw, p. 119, continuity is normally preserved – the worker cannot make that the ground of a 'reasonable' refusal (an important limitation in a take-over or merger).

Judges have held that the 'offer' need not set out all the employment terms. It need only contain 'adequate material' to enable the worker to decide, and 'sufficient detail to show differences between the proposed contract and the old one'.[51] But in 1970 a tribunal thought the offer must be available for the worker with an opportunity to make his decision at the time of, or after, his notice of dismissal. Many tribunal decisions have considered suitability and reasonableness together, for example, justifying refusals of a job involving longer travel for older women workers; work involving 'loss of position' or status; work far away which might cause the worker's wife to break up his marriage; work involving a move at the time of a child's 'eleven-plus' examination; night-shift work when his wife was in poor health; work at worse wages and conditions. Yet a list of opposite results can be given in cases which differ little: refusals unjustified where the new job meant a wife could not continue to go home to cook lunch for her husband on a diet; where the new wages would be materially lower than the old rates; where extra travelling time of two hours and costs of ten shillings would be involved; and so on. All relevant factors are to be considered, including family commitments and, it seems, social 'status'. Thus, the High Court, 1969, decided that an offer of a position in a mobile pool of teachers was not 'suitable' to a man who had been headmaster of a boys' school for ten years, even if his old pay were guaranteed, Lord Chief Justice Parker saying:

a director under a service agreement ... is offered on dismissal a job as a navvy, and it is said: but we will guarántee you the same salary ... I should have thought such an offer was plainly unsuitable.

Yet where a chargehand (supervisory) shipwright was, on the closing down of a dockyard, offered work as a shipwright in another yard, the decision was different, even though extra time and expense in travelling were involved and the work would not include duties as a chargehand, by reason of which he would lose his chargehand allowance (which he had normally received, though it was not guaranteed, in the old job). The tribunal held that the offer was *suitable* to him, even though it meant reverting to use of his tools from being in charge of sixteen other men. The High Court upheld the decision, Mr Justice Bridge saying this was not a case where, as in the headmaster's case, the offer was 'manifestly unsuitable'.[52]

Finally, alternative offers must be made by the employer himself or an 'associated company', not by a stranger. Thus, television employees dismissed by commercial companies in 1967 and 1968, who took jobs in the same studios under new companies the very next day, were paid large redundancy payments – 'obviously absurd ... lump sums,' said *The Times*, 'for losing jobs which they have not lost'. As for voluntary agreements, there is a procedure whereby the Secretary of State can remove workers from the scope of the Act altogether, i.e. by Order if all the parties to a collective agreement request him to make it and if disputes remain referable to the Industrial

Tribunals. The workers are left to their 'rights' under the agreement. This offer to give a primary role to voluntary agreements if the parties in industry so wish has not been taken up. Apart from the case of the electricity workers (p. 120) the only use of this procedure has been an Order to secure continuity for, and bring within collective agreements, employees in companies connected with Centrax Ltd in 1969 which were not technically 'associated'. At the time it was reported that the D.E.P. was asking that collective agreements should be binding contracts before an Order would be made; but that requirement is not present in the Act.

In 1963 a survey disclosed that, whereas the majority of employees in the public sector was covered, out of 20 million employees in private industry only 1·75 million enjoyed any redundancy schemes or similar policies. But such schemes have multiplied and the number of collective agreements has increased. A British Institute of Management survey in 1969 found that many companies today at least had 'policies' (usually 'last in – first out'). About one half had schemes or agreements whereby payments exceeded the amounts payable under the Act (though the same number paid nothing to workers who left after 'warning' and before formal notice – a remarkably high figure). It is interesting that a tribunal had to remind parties to a collective agreement in 1967 which purported to alter the rules about re-engagements that this could not alter the workers' legal rights unless an Order had been made about the agreement. Similarly, voluntarily-agreed payments must presumably be accompanied by the necessary written calculation if the money paid is to be in satisfaction of the statutory rights as well.

Two possible loopholes are plugged by extraordinarily complicated provisions in the Act. First, where *after* being given notice of dismissal workers go on strike, an employer can serve a 'notice of extension' which, if all the complex time limits are observed, can have the effect of obliging the workers to come and work out their unworked notice *after* the strike is over! By this time industrial relations will be so strained that the section is unlikely ever to be used. Secondly, the whole Act could be evaded if an employer could substitute for 'dismissal' weekly 'lay-offs' or 'short-time' (defined respectively as entailing no remuneration or less than half the worker's normal pay). Periods of 'lay-off' or 'short-time' (or 'LOST' periods) may be combined; and if they run for four consecutive weeks or six broken weeks in 13, the worker can claim redundancy payment (provided he navigates the maze of procedures which include giving in 'notice of claim' within four weeks of the LOST periods, and such notice to quit as his contract requires). Other rules prevent certain LOST periods being used, however, including periods 'attributable' to strikes in any trade or industry, *whether in Great Britain or elsewhere* (apparently from Tokyo to Timbuktoo – a provision implying an unusual legislative insistence upon the international solidarity of workers' interests). Even after he goes through all these hoops, a worker may fail if the employer serves a counter-notice that work is to be expected again within the month. The failure of the Act to compensate workers prejudiced in earnings by LOST periods (sometimes to a greater degree than colleagues entitled to redundancy payments who could get new jobs) has been one reason for demands from unions, notably the T.G.W.U. and A.U.E.W. in 1970, for new schemes of 'lay-off' pay from certain employers. This will, no doubt, be one of the questions, together with the basic definitions, such as 'redundancy' itself, and matters such as the current six-month time limit on claims, which will be considered for reform in an amending Bill about which the Labour Government had already had consultations in 1969.

It is small wonder that this complicated statute, hurriedly enacted, has given rise to so many cases in the tribunals. More surprising is the fact that only a minority bring in the lawyers (in 1966, lawyers appeared in 14 per cent of employees' cases and 26 per cent of employers'; in 1968, 21 and 29 per cent respectively) – though the number may now be on the increase. Most claims are conducted by applicants in person; and an important regulation allows for the payment of expenses to such applicants (including loss of earnings) and the expenses of their witnesses. Even in the decisions *reported* in 1967 (those selected for the Reports are likely to be legally more complex), 30 per cent were presented in person. Trade union officials argued 26 per cent of all cases in 1966, and 20 per cent of *reported* tribunal decisions in 1968; and many of those will, of course, have been 'test' actions.[53]

As for the rationale of the Act, it does not always promote mobility of labour (indeed workers may want to hang on until formal notice, and long-service workers will not want to lose their rights by rupturing continuity by moving). It does not always relieve 'hardship' (especially when offers of alternative employment are found 'suitable' in odd circumstances). The consequences in this area are so uncertain that the Labour Government had commissioned a special study of them. (Significantly, regulations made under a special statute have established a scheme of additional *weekly* payments to supplement the incomes of mineworkers made redundant between July 1967 and March 1971 in the declining coal industry.) And in the light of such decisions of the appellate courts as the *Hindle* case, it certainly does not protect a 'property' in the job. The Act is, in fact, a curious legal raft of intricate construction on to which some rather arbitrarily selected workers can clamber from the waves of unemployment. What more then does the law say about 'job-security'?

UNFAIR DISMISSAL AND JOB-SECURITY

Generally the law does little more to secure 'job-property' in Britain. In particular, there is no general legal protection against 'arbitrary' or 'unjust' dismissal from work. As we have seen, the ordinary worker is not even entitled to a reason (except in rare cases, such as when given proper notice on a dismissal for misconduct that disqualifies him from redundancy payment – though the employer *always* has to tell the D.E.P. in advance of his reason for dismissals if he wants to recover his rebates). The power of the employer to dismiss is limited by liability for wrongful dismissal in damages of no large amount, as we saw, which cannot include any sum for the worker's injured feelings or any specially outrageous circumstances. The power to *select* for dismissals is in law his alone. Good grounds to justify summary dismissals can be discovered by him after the event. No declaration (let alone reinstatement) is usually available to an employee; nor is he entitled to a hearing about the cause for his dismissal, unless he is within a narrow range of 'office' holders with statutory rights (such as a chief constable: p. 112): or a checkweigher in coal mining: p. 231).

One exceptional statutory scheme is of special importance. The Docks scheme (now the 1967 Order) as we saw in *Vine's* case (p. 82), gives registered dockworkers a special status. The regulations provide that a permanent dockworker may be dismissed by his employer either on notice, but only with the consent of the local Board, or summarily, in which case, on appeal, the Board has power, after a hearing, to uphold the dismissal, dismiss him with due notice, suspend him for five days, or *'reinstate him* with his former employer' with a retroactive right to wages. An employer may also suspend him for alleged 'misconduct' for five days; but he can again appeal to the Board and the suspension 'has no effect pending' its determination. A 'temporarily unattached' dockworker employed by the National Board (which can in extreme cases remove a name from the registers) enjoys different and less stringent protection. Appeals lie from all Boards to an appeal tribunal. Various permanent dockworkers who led unofficial strikes have successfully appealed against individual suspensions; but, in February 1969, London dock employers took mass disciplinary action against 3,074 workers. The chairman of the local Board said: 'If we dealt with each appeal it could take six or seven years'; but he felt it would be unfair to hear only a few. By March, mass discipline seemed to be ineffective. The union (T.G.W.U.) protested that the scheme had never envisaged mass dismissals; the employers wanted the law amended to give them the right of three days' suspension without appeal. By the summer of 1969 another 1,000 men were threatening to strike, with union support, because the employers refused to keep 60 men in employment while their dismissal was discussed, and threats of disciplinary action were again heard which sounded as unreal as those of February. In March 1970, employers were held by the Hull Board to have acted outside their rights under the Order in purporting to dismiss, as a disciplinary penalty, 2,000 of their dockworker employees for taking part in two unofficial one-day strikes, and to 'return' them to the Board's pool of un-allocated workers. The Docks Order thus provides considerable job-security for those who enjoy the status of registered dock-worker. But it is the product of the struggle to end casual labour in the docks; and its precise mechanism could not be easily transferred to other industries.

Meanwhile other workers have no such rights. Even elected shop stewards have none. Yet they are essential to modern negotiations – as the Donovan Report put it, with the support of its research surveys, 'an accepted, reasonable and even moderating influence; more of a lubricant than an irritant' – and in most European systems their counterparts receive special protection from dismissal (as in Germany or in France, where since 1959 protection extends for six months to *ex*-representatives of workers and to candidates for the office). Sackings or suspensions of British shop stewards are a regular phenomenon. Sometimes they follow fierce strikes, as when 27 of the 29 stewards were dismissed after a four-week strike, making 83 strikes in the year among 1,250 workers in a factory where they had become an 'endemic feature of factory life accepted by *both* sides as ... largely inevitable'.[54] More often they cause more strikes. The biggest employers in a Dorset village dismissed 46 workers for taking part in an official strike in 1965, and the union's officer claimed these included key union figures in the works, saying: 'This is Tolpuddle all over again' (the village a few miles – and 135 years – away: p. 308).[55] An appendix to the T.G.W.U. evidence to the Donovan Commission told the story of a firm which in 1965 allegedly broke a national agreement by introducing new piece-work rates without warning, 'then locked-out for five weeks workers who objected ... and finally singled out a union official [chief shop steward] for dismissal.' Nor are white-collar staff exempt. The cases of nursing staff who had been dismissed for reveal-ing dreadful conditions in a Cardiff hospital, and of art teachers who were dismissed (or some not re-employed) in

Guildford and Hornsey colleges after supporting or sympathizing with students, are but recent illustrations.[56] Of course: 'In practice many employees enjoy much greater security against dismissal than is implied in the law' (Donovan Report). If they did not, the system would have broken down because, a N.J.A.C. Report of 1967 estimated, out of three million dismissals every year, something up to 500,000 are for 'misconduct' and about 9 per cent of strikes seem to be associated with such dismissals.[57]

Other countries have long made use of laws to extend a worker's floor of rights to include protection from unjust dismissal. In France, apart from protection of workers' representatives, the employer can in some cases be liable in damages for an improper 'abuse' of his right to dismiss. Dismissals which contravene trade union rights or in short illness or pregnancy are invalid. Further, the *conseils de prud'hommes* (equal numbers of employers and workers with – to unbelieving Anglo-Saxon eyes – *no legal chairman*!) provide cheap, local tribunals in most areas for disputes on *individual* employment matters. Since 1951, German law has forbidden the dismissal of a worker after six months' employment if it is 'socially unjustified'. The law says reinstatement is a remedy; but courts usually give damages. The employer must show *in fact* that the reason for dismissal relates to personal conduct of the employee (which can, however, include 'trouble-making') or to pressing needs of the enterprise. Also, he must consult the Works Council on dismissals and, in addition, the local government office in cases of mass dismissal. The 1965 French decision in which a secretary's dismissal was really caused by the wife's '*jalousie ombrageuse*' (jealousy that made her prone to take umbrage) and that of 1960 in which an employee was dismissed by reason of his divorce from the niece of the company chairman, in both of which the dismissals were declared improper and damages had to be paid,[58] contrast starkly with the British lady who in 1966 did not even get her redundancy payment: p. 132. In the U.S.A. squads of private 'grievance arbitrators', often professors, decide complaints about unjust dismissals brought under collective agreements to which, since

1947, statute has attached contract status (though this does not help the low-paid millions outside the bargaining system). The usual American view (not today unchallenged) of disputes arising out of such agreements is that 'a good arbitrator is probably better able to cope wisely with this sort of agreement than is a good judge'.[59] Reinstatement is regularly ordered. In Italy principles that grew out of the better collective agreements were enacted in a statute of 1966. Certain reasons (as in all such systems) are declared invalid; and otherwise a dismissal must have a 'just cause'. In Sweden the system of bargaining, centralized in a small country, limits the employer's power to dismiss by agreed principles for selections in redundancies; and a variety of other matters is supervised by the Labour Market Board which organizes retraining, rehousing, removal allowances and the like.

Many European laws resemble the principles of I.L.O. Recommendation 119, accepted by the British Government in 1964 with reservations, including the need to keep the 'ultimate right of the Crown to dismiss at pleasure' – an odd desire when some of the dismissal procedures in British Government Departments are excellent illustrations of the 'salutary effects of formal procedures in preventing arbitrary dismissal' (1967 N.J.A.C. Report). The I.L.O. recommends that dismissal should be limited to 'valid' reasons related to the conduct or capacity of the worker or the firm's needs. Certain reasons should be invalid, such as trade union membership, workers' representation, race, colour, and so on. Selection in redundancies should be conditioned by criteria precisely stated in advance and might include efficiency, seniority and family considerations. The 1967 Report thought that efforts should probably be made in Britain to reach such goals by voluntary action, with legislation only if they failed. The Donovan Report (with two dissentients) thought the balance of the argument went the other way and recommended new laws. The Conservative *Fair Deal at Work* had already proposed – albeit sketchily – legislation. The Labour Government's *In Place of Strife* took the Donovan view; and the 1970 Bill proposed legislation.

Before passing to that, it must be observed that many dismissals *are* tested already in procedures either 'internal' to a company or as part of collective agreements in an industry or district.[60] But these are inadequate in scope and – conversely to the old common law – while easily providing reinstatement rarely provide compensation for the unjustly dismissed. Industry-wide procedures often deal with dismissal badly and slowly; they operate best when specially constructed for the purpose. But most of such procedures are not available to non-unionists. In only a very few instances is the dismissal suspended while the case is heard. 'Internal procedures' appeared to exist in only about one fifth of British firms in the late sixties. Many are rather primitive ('the managing director's door is always open'). There are just a few examples of what Dr Plumridge has called 'participative structures', including one firm where disciplinary questions are largely decided by a group of five of whom three are shop-stewards. It is in this respect that the whole 'public sector' (comprising both Government and nationalized enterprise), contrasts so markedly, with its special procedures incorporating

(a) ... written notice of disciplinary action; (b) the right of appeal at successive levels; (c) the opportunity of a ... hearing and ... a trade union representative ... (d) final decisions by an executive (or appeals) authority.[61]

The Donovan Report was convinced of the need for legislative intervention because of the inadequacy of procedures; the crisis which dismissal brings to a worker (his life 'is no less at stake if he is being dismissed for alleged ... misconduct than if ... dismissed for redundancy'); the problem of the non-unionized workforce; and the possibility of reducing strikes associated with dismissals. The 1970 Bill proposed to establish a right to appeal against unfair dismissal to an industrial tribunal. Some current estimates put the possible yearly hearings as high as 150,000; and even if this is too high, the tribunals will clearly have to be expanded once again. The problems of finding suitable chairmen and wingmen will redouble.

More important, any new law will run into a well-known list

of problems. The main features of the Labour Government's 1970 Bill are worth discussing, therefore, partly because they illustrate the new issues which the law on job-security is likely soon to encounter in Britain.

(i) *'Employees'* covered by the Bill would have had the same definition as in the redundancy statute of 1965 (p. 60), with certain excluded categories such as dockworkers. Some of the categories are hard to understand, e.g. close relatives; domestic servants; those ordinarily working outside Great Britain except on ships; and an employee with less than two years continuous service (continuity having the usual meaning: p. 118). That the employer should be allowed to dismiss the worker employed for only eighteen months on grounds that would be unlawful six months later seems absurd. The Donovan Report saw 'no justification' for this limitation. The Secretary of State would have power to limit or reduce the period. But it should not be enacted at all. Moreover, much litigation could be avoided by extending the protection from the outset to the 'self-employed' worker.

(ii) *'Dismissal'* – which is for the employee to prove – would arise if the contract (a) is 'terminated by the employer'; or (b), being for a fixed term, expires (unless in a fixed term of two years or more the worker 'agreed in writing' to exclude his rights, a strange invitation to pressure by employers which even includes apprenticeships); or (c) is terminated by the employee where the employment could not be expected to continue with reasonable goodwill because of employer's 'conduct' of which the reason was a *disqualified* ground (below (iii)). This is both wider and narrower than the 1965 Act. It gives, in the spirit of the I.L.O. Recommendation 130 on Grievance Procedure Standards, protection against disqualified unfair discrimination at work. But it might not cover every case of the employee giving in notice in the face of other breaches by the employer amounting to 'repudiation' of the contract. We have already seen that 'national security' dismissals are excluded (p. 71). In an attempt to exclude problems of collective industrial conflict, as is the tradition in such floor of rights statutes (p. 121) the Bill would exclude all dismissals in the form of a 'lock-out'. (It

143

need not have gone so far. What if an employer locks out a group of militant Irish workers saying 'I will have no more Irish workers here'? Had the dismissals not been a 'lock-out', within a complicated definition in the 1963 Act, they would have been invalid (see (iii)). So too, a dismissal during a strike does not count unless the worker proves that one or more of his fellow strikers were not dismissed and the reason is a *disqualified ground*. A special problem can arise if there is a 'closed shop' or if workers refuse to work with another man on grounds that fall within the *disqualified* list, so that the employer dismisses him. The Donovan Report and *In Place of Strife* both took the view that, since the ultimate decision was the employer's for the advantage of his business, he should remain liable for any unfair dismissal in such cases. The C.B.I. strongly opposed this; and *Fair Deal at Work* pledged the Conservative Party to rights of action against union or workers for 'coercion'. The 1970 Bill followed the Donovan view. But it did not include provisions, as that Report proposed, to integrate the new law on dismissals with cases of expulsion from a union. Whatever form it takes, a new statute is bound to encounter problems. What if a disgruntled group threaten, as in the Pilkington strike 1970 (p. 463), to resign from their union and form a 'splinter' organization, but are then dismissed, or made redundant, or 'laid off' for a long period?

Lastly, the 1970 Bill made no provision about lay-off or short-time. These (together with disciplinary 'suspensions' allowed by clauses in the contract which did not become dismissals within the provision about 'goodwill') could allow extensive power to employers to penalize workers unfairly without technically 'dismissing' them within the Act.

(iii) '*Unfair*' dismissals were defined in three ways. First, if the principal reasons are proved by the *employer* to relate to the employee's capability to do his work; or to his conduct (other than a *disqualified ground*); or only to his redundancy (that is, where selection for the redundancy dismissals was applied equally and not applied in a discriminatory way against him on *disqualified grounds*),[62] then the dismissal is not unfair. Secondly, however, the Bill would designate as unfair dismissals shown to be made on the following *disqualified grounds*: (a) Membership of or activity for an 'independent' trade union (p. 80), refusal to join a non-independent union, or acting or seeking election as a workers' representative, unless the worker took time off for the activities as a representative or for the union work without his employer's consent; (b) making a bona fide complaint against an employer; (c) professing or practising a religion, or supporting a political party or doctrine (or not doing either of these), unless it had been agreed in writing that the employee should profess the religious or political doctrine; (d) being of a particular colour, race, ethnic or national origin; a man or woman; or of a particular marital status (unless a particular status has been agreed in writing as a requirement of the employment). It is, of course, already unlawful to discriminate on grounds of colour, race and ethnic or national origins in dismissing an employee, under the Race Relations Act, 1968 (p. 84).

But a curious exception would limit the disqualified grounds merely to (a) for workers whose employer has less than four employees and for employees who reach 65 years (60 for women) or other normal retiring age in their undertaking. (How can it profit the statute to allow a sixty-five year old Jew to be discharged solely on ethnic grounds?) Claims that overlap the Race Relations Act 1968 would go to the tribunal first. There is, however, a good case for requiring further notification to the Race Relations Board of any complaint involving racial discrimination so as to further the work of the Board.[63]

Thirdly, where the reason for dismissal is not a *disqualified ground* but relates to the employee's capability or conduct, he can still succeed in proving unfairness if he proves the employer acted '*unreasonably*' in dismissing him. What that means is entirely in the lap of the tribunals. Presumably this would allow the tribunal to take its own view of the reasonableness of the employer's Works Rules. Such, at least, ought to be the law.

The Bill spoke throughout these provisions of the 'reason' or 'principal reason' for the dismissal. The better reading of its provisions indicates that they do not incorporate the thinking of the *Hindle* case (p. 132) and that the employers' subjective beliefs, e.g. as to the worker's capability to do his work, would not be as overriding as that case suggested in redundancy claims. Nevertheless, this might, no doubt, be one of the many points of law appealed to the High Court under such a statute. One defect in the Bill, however, which would severely impede the chance of a worker proving that an employer had acted 'unreasonably' (whether subjective or objective tests are employed) is the absence of an obligation on the employer to provide a written statement of reasons for dismissal. Even if the employee requested such a document, he would still have no legal right to it, though no doubt a refusal to commit reasons to paper at the time might reduce the credibility of an employer's evidence at the hearing.

(iv) *Remedies* for unfair dismissal would include both reinstatement and compensation. The claim, however, must be made within fifteen days – a very short period – or six months in exceptional cases. A claim settled by re-engagement within six months means that the interim period counts again towards continuity so long as no redundancy payment was made. In a successful claim, the tribunal could have ordered reinstatement, either with the employer or with 'an associated employer', and, so long as the employee agreed to reinstatement, either to his job or another job which the tribunal regarded as 'reasonably *suitable* to him'. Thus, for the first time in Britain, a tribunal would have obtained jurisdiction to order reinstatement against the wishes of the employer, though his views must be heard before pronouncing such a verdict. But if the employer failed to comply with a reinstatement order 'wilfully and without reasonable excuse', the tribunal would award extra compensation to the worker if that were appropriate. So even here the last word would be with the old tradition, compensation not forced employment.

On reinstating, the tribunal could award a sum representing lost 'remuneration' reduced by the amount received as unemployment benefit or supplementary benefit, though the Bill was silent as to reductions in respect of tax (a thoroughly unsatisfactory clause which would have made the position described on p. 114 even worse, as the right to claim damages in breach of contract was expressly saved by the Bill). If the worker were not reinstated he was to get compensation – two thirds of the total of eight weeks pay plus two weeks pay for every year of continuous employment after the first up to twenty. The computation otherwise followed the lines of redundancy payments, with a proposed maximum of £1,280. The sum might be reduced by reason of the employee's conduct or increased (to a maximum supplementary £640) because the dismissal was so 'flagrantly unjust' or 'injurious to the employee' that the normal compensation would be inadequate. The extra compensation awardable in the face of a wilful refusal to obey an order to reinstate could be up to £2,640; but that figure seems a low price for an employer who (by hypothesis) arbitrarily ejects a worker from his livelihood and flouts a legal order to restore him. In a Bill which failed to propose proper limits to the new flood of 'labour injunctions' against trade union officials (see p. 374) it seems odd that such acts by an employer should not be counted a serious contempt of court.

Lastly, the Bill did not deal at all with insolvent employers. The 1965 statute gives workers a residual right to recover from the D.E.P. redundancy payments due from insolvent employers, against whom the D.E.P. can then claim. But no other payments are so secured (except the small sums in company liquidations: p. 56). Thus, when financial difficulties overcame Handley Page in 1970, workers' claims of up to £2 million were said to be outstanding, only a small part of which were redundancy claims. Compensation for unfair dismissal should, at least, be a debt that receives preference.

(v) *Voluntary procedures* would not, however, have been entirely replaced by the 1970 Bill's proposals. As the Donovan Report had suggested, the new law would yield to voluntary agreements between employers and trade unions so long as they met certain standards. The Secretary of State could designate such an agreement by Order so long as it was 'on the whole as beneficial' to employees as the new law about unfair dismissals (including compensation arrangements); provided for 'arbitration' by an independent person 'in appropriate cases'; and made its procedures available to *every* employee covered by it (a condition plainly intended to allow non-unionists to use such procedure unless the agreement expressly excluded them).[64] If either employers or unions wished to revert to the law, the Minister would decertify the agreement by Order. Such provisions would match the little-used sections of the Redundancy Payments Act, 1965 (p. 134). The mechanism would have preserved, as is desirable, the primacy of voluntary procedures; but it could give rise to industrial problems. A worker in an 'exempted' factory has to use his domestic voluntary procedure. His colleague at a neighbouring works, with no designated machinery can, if his shop steward can get no redress for him, go to the statutory tribunals. If the latter succeeds but the former fails in his claim, the former is likely to grumble that he was not allowed to put his case to the statutory tribunal, especially if he is a non-unionist who objects to the way the union runs the designated domestic procedure.

(vi) *Appeals* from the Industrial Tribunals would, as usual, lie on points of law to the High Court. But here a critical omission in the 1970 Bill becomes important. Experience in Britain in redundancy cases accords with that in other countries (e.g. in Germany) in suggesting that ordinary courts almost of necessity make a legal maze out of such labour legislation. (If one feature of the law of the U.S.A. is to be adopted, it will hopefully be the wise decision of its superior courts to refuse to be entangled in reviewing the decisions of local arbitrators.) Private arbitrators in Britain have provided a contrast. They are already used on occasion in voluntary procedures. (The D.E.P. has a list from which they can be provided, though quite how this is drawn up might merit investigation.) In our 1966 survey it was found that private arbitrators (usually not lawyers in Britain up to now) reported quickly (on average 21 days from appointment) and could judge 'fairness' in an informal way against local background. To infuse a similar atmosphere, the Donovan Report proposed to introduce a *conciliation* stage into the industrial tribunals' procedure after the fashion of the French labour courts. Although the

Government accepted this idea, with modifications, it nowhere appeared in the Bill. It is true that regulations might modify the tribunals' procedure so as to move in this direction. But that would be an unsatisfactory way to introduce something which is much more than a minor procedural change. Without a *conciliation* stage as mandatory in unfair dismissal cases, we can expect the legal arguments to become more complex and the appeals to the High Court to multiply. A new law on unjust dismissal should introduce a compulsory *conciliation* procedure, thereby moving the focus of the tribunals' work in this area away from adjudication, which would be reserved for the difficult cases where no agreed compromise could be reached.

Jurisdiction of Industrial Tribunals: In its evidence to the Donovan Commission in 1965, the Ministry of Labour said:

The nucleus of a system of labour courts exists potentially in these tribunals.

Since then the Tribunals have not merely been expanded in number and streamlined in structure, as we have seen, in order to deal with claims about industrial training levies, written particulars (p. 75) and redundancy payments (p. 127). There has also been a continuous policy of adding to their jurisdiction in almost any statute dealing with industrial matters. Thus, the tribunals deal with certain disputes about Selective Employment Tax, and with the definition of 'dockwork' under the Docks and Harbours Act, 1966; and they will deal with disputes arising under the 1970 Equal Pay legislation (p. 234). The Donovan Report proposed to expand their jurisdiction so as to take all *individual* cases stemming from employment contracts (such as actions for wrongful dismissal now heard in ordinary courts). The 1970 Bill proposed to permit regulations extending the jurisdiction to all such actions for damages (other than damages for injury from accident), with appropriate provision to deal with the concurrent jurisdiction of County Courts and High Court. The tribunals would thereby have a scope rather similar to the French *conseils de prud'hommes*.

We have already noted that the tribunals try to be speedy and informal. (They do not apply ordinary rules about evidence or costs; indeed, expenses are paid to witnesses.) But insufficient research has yet been done on the relative merits in both respects of the tribunals and of an improved system of County Courts, on the one hand, and an extended system of voluntary arbitration on the other. Little concrete discussion of such problems, for instance, seems to have preceded the allocation of equal pay disputes to the tribunals (p. 235). It is perhaps too easily assumed that the presence of the two 'wingmen' necessarily makes the tribunals more 'down to earth' bodies than ordinary courts. But, perhaps, because of the difficulty of recruiting active wingmen to serve with continuity the evidence suggests that the influence of legal chairmen is often dominant. Even when, as on occasion happens, the laymen outvote the chairman, they risk expressing their conclusions in words which allow for an appeal on a point of law to the High Court (precisely what happened in the case of Mrs Ward: p. 130).[65] Laymen often do not understand that a point of 'law' includes any point of interpretation of a statute or contract. Indeed, some questions now put to the tribunals seem to invite such an appeal. Why, for example, is a tribunal better equipped than the County Court to decide (as in 1969 one was asked to do) whether, for training levy purposes, the Plas Machynlleth Fox Destruction Society, having only one employee, is engaged in an activity 'by way of business'? Was it perhaps inevitable that in 1969 and 1970 appeals were taken to the High Court from a tribunal decision about the Industrial Training Order for hotels on the meaning of 'immediate consumption', and to the House of Lords on the meaning of 'industry or commerce'? [65a] Sometimes a tribunal is just not referred to binding High Court decisions so its decision has to be appealed, and sent back for a second hearing.[66]

The T.U.C. opposed the extension of tribunal jurisdiction because it saw this as the thin end of the wedge which would 'involve interpretation of collective agreements', and suggested that far from becoming 'Labour Courts' they should be renamed Employment Tribunals and kept away from collective industrial relations. There is indeed good ground for thinking that the tribunals work less well as they move away from strictly individual employment problems. They were, for example, between 1968 and 1970 presented with difficult cases on the meaning of 'dock work'. As was to be expected, one leading case ended in the Court of Appeal on whether work on timber near docks was work on 'cargo ... in the vicinity of' docks.[67] But while that case was grinding its way through the appellate courts, an industrial battle was fought about what was 'dock work'; the Bristow Committee considered the whole question; after its report the Secretary of State announced that she would reconsider the statutory definition, while the committee went on to consider the role of the tribunals in interpreting it. The real problem concerning the relative work-boundaries for dock, road haulage and other workers is one appropriate for negotiation and, perhaps, arbitration, not adjudication; and it is perhaps a pity that the policy of trying to turn the tribunals into Labour Courts ever brought them into the matter at all.

The industrial tribunals have proved to be a useful device for dealing with certain problems affecting individual employees quickly and informally. Their President has strenuously tried to adapt them to that role. They would perform better if there were more chairmen (who should not always be lawyers), more continuity in the wingmen, and far *less* scope for appeals to the ordinary Courts. After all, no appeal lies on points of 'law' from National Insurance Commissioners (p. 123). They may just be able to cope with burdens of a general law about unfair dismissal and possibly, in 1975, about equal pay. But an extended jurisdiction with much more work and many more issues of legal complication may break their backs.

Job-Security and Job-Control: A statute in the seventies on unfair dismissals will clearly revolutionize the standards of 'job-property' in Britain and cause the sixties, when a headline could still read 'Worker dismissed for wearing beard', to seem like the era of industrial feudalism. The idea of property-rights in employment has made considerable strides. One pioneer study on 'ownership of jobs' stated in 1964:

Workers do in fact tend to regard themselves as having some kind of right of possession in a job and to devise institutions which wrest control over incumbency from the hands of the employer and which express objectively a vesting of property-like rights in the worker.[68]

Such ideas are encouraged by guarantees of employment such as the Derbyshire firm which, secure in its long-term contract to supply iron tunnels for the London Victoria underground line, agreed with its foundry workers to guarantee wages and employment for three years from 1963. But these offers are always conditional upon a no-strike guarantee in return, and workers who think they are safe against redundancy may easily lose the guaranteed jobs, as in the case of Clydeside workers whose employers withdrew a two-year employment guarantee because they went on strike for one day in 1969 against the Government proposals made in *In Place of Strife*.

It is, of course, true as *The Times* Labour Correspondent, Mr Wigham, wrote in July 1966 that 'if the worker owns his job, or has rights in it analogous to property rights, then he owns something which is as important a part of an undertaking as the things the shareholder owns'. Clearly that is so; but that part is presumably what conventional wisdom refers to when it speaks of the 'partnership' in industry. If, moreover, this concept is taken seriously, the 'right to work' (a phrase often used by lawyers to mean merely the right *not* to be a member of a trade union in a 'closed shop' factory) must, when cleansed of mystification, acquire a different meaning – namely the right to have appropriate work available. Before 'rights analogous to property' in jobs can be meaningful, full employment must be secure. Not everyone, of course, sees the matter this way. Sir George Pollock, then Director of the British Employers' Confederation, remarked in 1964:

I do not consider myself that a man has a vested interest in a particular job but I think he has a stake in a company or an industry to which he has devoted years of his working life.

Like Mr Wigham he was a member of the Donovan Commission, but unlike him he dissented from the proposal to establish at this juncture statutory tribunals to deal with unjust dismissals; to do so 'might damage relationships between employer and employee where there is a comparatively small labour force', he thought. (Yet the evidence suggests that it is the small employer who resists trade unionism and who acts arbitrarily against 'troublemaking' workers.[69])

The goal of 'job-security', therefore, leads to a consideration of other, sometimes conflicting, goals. As we have seen, policies of efficiency and managerial rights have often dominated in the courts (though less in the tribunals) in decisions about redundancy. Mobility of labour, to which the 1965 Act may not have contributed in great measure, is another professed social objective; yet, in the face of the real problems of changing jobs disclosed by the Social Survey Report of 1966 (45 per cent of workers would rather take a less 'suitable' job in their own area than face the prospect of moving), the legislative support for that goal is minimal as far as the workers are concerned, tiny allowances for removal and grants for training. The evidence suggests that the effects of unemployment are less harsh than in the past. But few workers would find acceptable the headline 'Why Unemployment Doesn't Matter Any More' (*Sunday Times*). In February 1966, 328,000 wholly unemployed faced 373,000 vacancies for jobs. In February 1970, 606,000 unemployed faced 250,000 vacancies; and by April the *Financial Times* commented that 'the public is now apparently complacent about rates of unemployment which a generation ago might have produced riots.' An announcement by G.E.C.–E.E. in 1969 that employment in its plants on Merseyside, where general unemployment stood at 3·8 per cent, would be cut by 5,500 jobs produced militant plans to take over the factories, though these were later voted down at mass meetings of workers. In 1970, the closing of a large factory in Bakewell, Derbyshire, was fought tooth and nail by workers who came from a quarter of the town's families, one man of 59 saying:

Who will give work to a man of 60? Besides there's nothing else round here ... When you are with a firm so long and suddenly told you are no longer needed it is like a death in the family.[70]

It is not surprising that demands have recently been made for a general and more liberal system of 'severance' payments, especially by A.S.T.M.S. At the 1968 T.U.C. conference the resolution was passed which called on the Industrial Reorganization Corporation to consider job-security of workers when reviewing the case for a merger. (The redundancies at Woolwich after the G.E.C.–A.E.I. merger were fresh in delegates' minds.) The proposed Bill to set up the Commission on Industry and Manpower (C.I.M.) would have facilitated such policies. The T.U.C. *Economic Review*, 1970, calls for collective agreements which provide severance, resettlement and travelling allowances for workers dispossessed of employment through such reorganization, and for the Government to secure from companies assisted by public funds a 'binding undertaking' (the phrase was no doubt carefully chosen: p. 35) to make such agreements.

In the seventies, faced with control of jobs, workers may decide that they should have a voice in the matter. What if labourers prefer to share their 'property' among the existing workforce, perhaps without overtime? In June 1964 a shop stewards' committee representing 1,250 motor car workers decided to impose a limit on piece-workers' earnings and thereby avoid redundancy and excessive short-time workings. Behind the determined unofficial strike of 1,300 blast-furnacemen at Port Talbot in July 1969 stood not just a demand for an increase of £1 a week, but the employers' 'green book' proposals to increase productivity but reduce the 16,000 workforce by 5,000 between 1969 and 1971. These workers wanted a say in the amount of job-property and its distribution. Some writers see these developments as 'forcing the issue of workers' control into the daylight' and find in the management reaction to them the workers' 'support upon which shop stewards have been able to build their partial controls in day-to-day activities'.[71]

In other words, new thinking on our laws about dismissal cannot avoid the most fundamental issues concerning industry, management and the worker. We have to decide to what extent the existence of a job, in which the worker is to have this 'property', is limited by management considerations such as cost. We have to decide to whom, in a modern society, jobs really 'belong'. Questions of 'industrial democracy', already touched upon (p. 44) tend here to break down the boundaries of labour law and company law. Moreover, it is by no means clear how the competing claims of job-security, efficiency, re-training, mobility and productivity will affect the 'mix' of the methods of collective bargaining and legislation within British labour law in the future. The Donovan Commission recommended, in effect, that the emphasis should be laid upon the reform and extension of collective bargaining, though legislation will clearly have new roles as well. We therefore turn in the next two chapters to the present role that these two methods play in the regulation of the worker's employment.

1. Lord Wright in *Luxor Ltd* v. *Cooper* [1941] A.C. 108 at p. 137.
2. *Orman* v. *Saville Sportswear Ltd* [1960] 1 W.L.R. 1055.
3. *Is Britain Really Strike Prone?* (1969), p. 35.
4. *O'Reilly* v. *Hotpoint Ltd* (1970) 5 I.T.R. 68.
5. [1931] 1 Ch. 310; see Wedderburn, *Cases and Materials on Labour Law*, p. 290, note.
6. (1968) 3 I.T.R. 119 (D.C.); and see *Parry* v. *Holst Ltd* (1968) 3 I.T.R. 317 (D.C.).
7. *Jones* v. *H. Sherman Ltd* (1969) 4 I.T.R. 63.
8. [1957] A.C. 555.
9. [1970] 2 All E.R. 193.
10. *Sanders* v. *Parry* [1967] 2 All E.R. 803.
11. *Reading* v. *A.G.* [1951] A.C. 507.
12. *Hivac Ltd* v. *Park Royal Scientific Instruments Ltd* [1946] Ch. 169.
13. *Initial Services Ltd* v. *Putterill* [1967] 3 All E.R. 145 (C.A.).
14. *Cranleigh Precision Engineering Ltd* v. *Bryant* [1964] 3 All E.R. 289; and see *Printers and Finishers Ltd* v. *Holloway* [1965] R.P.C. 239; *Seager* v. *Copydex* (No. 2) [1969] 2 All E.R. 718 (C.A.).
15. *British Syphon Co. Ltd* v. *Homewood* [1956] 2 All E.R. 897.
16. See Lord Gardiner (1959) 22 *Modern Law Review* 652 at p. 654.
17. (1845) 14 M. and W. 112, at p. 115, p. 117. Note: the maid would have 'just cause' today for leaving work for social security purposes: R(U) 32/59.
18. [1959] 1 W.L.R. 698.
19. [1969] 2 All E.R. 216 (C.A.).
20. See *Hewitt Ltd* v. *Russell* (1969) 4 I.T.R. 260 (woman who lost temper and 'had words' with manager, and left 20 minutes early: *held* not to have renounced contract).
21. Parker L.C.J., *Ingham* v. *Bristol Piping Co.* (1970) 5 I.T.R. 218, 221; *Charles* v. *Spiralynx Ltd* (1970) 5 I.T.R. 82 (C.A.: no implied right to move workers to factory five miles away); but see *Murray* v. *Robert Rome* (1969) 4 I.T.R. 20.
22. In *Stratford* v. *Lindley* [1965] A.C. 269, 315 (and see the pleadings: (1965) 28 *Modern Law Review* 206; *Evidence to Royal Commission*, Day 31, 1966, para. 56): *Jas. Cummings* v. *C. Connell & Co. Ltd*, 1969, S.L.T. 25 (employer's notice of 'suspension' of employment in lock-out held to be a breach; the

employment was guaranteed for 18 months, but that does not seem critical in all of the Court of Session's reasoning).

23. See *Rookes* v. *Barnard* [1964] A.C. 1129, 1204 (H.L.); [1963] 1 Q.B. 623, 682 (C.A.); *Stratford Ltd* v. *Lindley* [1965] A.C. 269, 285 (C.A. and H.L.). See Wedderburn, *Cases and Materials on Labour Law*, p. 525; Grunfeld, *Modern Trade Union Law*, p. 330.

24. [1968] 2 Q.B. 710 (C.A.); see P. O'Higgins [1968] *Cambridge Law J.* 223.

25. [1965] A.C. 269 (H.L.). Cp. *Saxton* v. *N.C.B.* (1970) 5 I.T.R. 196.

26. [1967] 1 Q.B. 278; But see, too, *White* v. *Bloomfield*, 1966, *Guardian*, 8 December (Wedderburn, *Cases and Materials on Labour Law*, p. 179).

27. [1970] 2 All E.R. 630 (C.A.). Contrast the willingness to add money for future damage more liberally in cases of breach of contract by expulsion from a trade union; *Edwards* v. *S.O.G.A.T.* [1970] 3 W.L.R. 713; *post p. 448*.

28. [1963] 2 All E.R. 658; [1964] 1 Q.B. 95.

29. *Parry* v. *Cleaver* [1969] 1 All E.R. 555 (H.L.).

30. See *Hewson* v. *Downs* [1970] I.Q.B. 73; J. P. Casey (1969) *Juridical Review* 206 (Scot.); *Fitzpatrick* v. *Moore* [1962] N.I. 152.

31. [1958] 1 W.L.R. 16.

32. *McClelland* v. *N.I. General Health Services Board* [1957] 2 All E.R. 129.

33. *Morris* v. *Bailey Ltd* [1969] 2 Lloyd's Rep. 215 (C.A.).

34. *Hunter* v. *Smith's Dock Ltd* [1968] 2 All E.R. 81; and *Thompson* v. *Bristol Channel Ship Repairers Ltd* (1970) 5 I.T.R. 85 (C.A.).

35. [1969] 3 All E.R. 1140 (H.L.).

36. *Newsham* v. *Dunlop Textiles Ltd* (1969) 4 I.T.R. 268.

37. *Lloyd* v. *Brassey* [1969] 1 All E.R. 382 (C.A.); *Kenmir Ltd* v. *Frizzell* [1968] 1 All E.R. 414.

38. On the Act of 1966 see J. Reid (1966) 29 *Modern Law Review* 537.

39. R(U) 38/53.

40. R(U) 10/54 quoted; 8/57; 2/60; 7/57; 20/59; 17/64.

41. See Wedderburn (1966) 29 *Modern Law Review* 55. On mobility of labour and the Act of 1965, see C. Drake and M. Freedland in No. 5 *Bulletin of Industrial Law Society* 2, 23.

42. For a survey of a sample of the tribunals' decisions up to January 1967 and some later statistics, see Wedderburn and

Davies, *Employment Grievances and Dispute Procedures in Britain* (1969).

43. *Turriff Ltd* v. *Bryant* (1967) 2 I.T.R. 292; contrast *Merseyside Transport* v. *Kelly* (1968) 3 I.T.R. 112. A way out of this problem, by restricting the meaning of 'normal hours' to hours normally worked, was rejected in *Lynch* v. *Dartmouth Auto Castings* (1969) 4 I.T.R. 273.

44. (1967) 2 I.T.R. 84. As to problems as the date of termination, see R. Rideout, 'The Industrial Tribunals' (1968) 21 *Current Legal Problems* 178, 185.

45. *Duckworth* v. *Farnish Ltd* (1970) 5 I.T.R. 17 (C.A.).

46. [1969] 3 All E.R. 1126 (C.A.). See too, *Lowe* v. *East Lancs. Paper Mill Ltd* (1970) 5 I.T.R. 132.

47. [1967] 2 Q.B. 56.

48. *Vaux* v. *Ward* (1868) 3 I.T.R. 385; (1970) 5 I.T.R. 62. See too, *Jones* v. *Star Associated Ltd* (1970) 5 I.T.R. 178 (manager of bingo casino and film theatre diverted to managing only the theatre; no redundancy despite reduction in earnings; the 'overall requirements' of the business for this kind of work had not diminished; 'they have increased', *per* Lord Parker, C.J.).

49. *Dutton* v. *C. H. Bailey* [1968] 2 Lloyd's Rep. 122 (boiler-makers).

50. [1969] 1 All E.R. 836; 4 I.T.R. 86 (C.A.); *Kirkby* v. *Fred Peck* (1970) 5 I.T.R. 229. But employer's mistake of law has no such effect: *Mumford* v. *Boulton Paul* (1970) 5 I.T.R. 222.

51. *Johnston* v. *St Cuthbert's Co-op Assoc.* (1969) 4 I.T.R. 137 (Ct. Session); *Havenhand* v. *Thos. Black* [1968] 1 W.L.R. 1241.

52. *Collier* v. *Smith's Dock Ltd* (1969) 4 I.T.R. 338; *Taylor* v. *Kent C.C.* [1969] 2 All E.R. 1080. See too *N.C.B.* v. *Williams* (1970) 5 I.T.R. 71; and on different approaches to 'suitable' employment in Scotland, *Carron* v. *Robertson* (1967) 2 I.T.R. 484; and *Williamson* v. *N.C.B.* (1970) 5 I.T.R. 43.

53. Compare European labour courts and tribunals: Blanc Jouvan, X., et al., *Labour Courts and Grievance Settlement in Four Western European Countries* (forthcoming ed. Aaron); McPherson and Meyers, *The French Labour Courts* (1966).

54. W. E. J. McCarthy, *The Role of Shop Stewards* (1966), p. 23.

55. *Guardian*, 17.9.65.

56. *The Times*, 10 to 25.6.68; 16 to 19.12.68; 28.3.69; and *The Hornsey Affair*, Students and Staff of Hornsey College (1969).

57. 'Dismissals Procedures', Committee of the National Joint Ad-

visory Council (N.J.A.C.) of Ministry of Labour (1967), p. 1 and Appendix 1; and see Part II on other countries.

58. M. Panayotopoulos, *Le Controle Judiciaire du Licenciement dans le Droit des Pays Membres de la C.E.E. et de la Grèce* (1969), p. 193.

59. H. H. Wellington, *Labor and the Legal Process* (1968), p. 105.

60. Much of what follows is based upon Wedderburn and Davies op. cit., chapter 7.

61. T.U.C. Evidence to Royal Commission, para. 337.

62. For difficulties that could arise, see *McKillen* v. *Turner (Metals) Ltd* (1966) 1 I.T.R. 303.

63. See B. Hepple, *Race, Jobs and the Law* (1970), p. 241.

64. This compulsion on a union to service non-members might cause problems: G. de N. Clark, *Remedies for Unjust Dismissal* (P.E.P. 1970), pp. 62–64.

65. Later evidence tends to confirm Wedderburn and Davies, op. cit., pp. 248–51; 261–3.

65a. *Hotel and Catering Industry Training Board* v. *Automobile Proprietary Ltd* [1969] 2 All E.R. 582 (H.L.), a decision that members' clubs could not be engaged in 'industry or commerce'. This so undermined the statute that an amending Bill was hastily prepared; but it lapsed with the 1970 General Election.

66. *Seymour* v. *Barber and Heron Ltd* (1970) 5 I.T.R. 65.

67. *N.D.L.B.* v. *Bland Ltd* [1970] 2 All E.R. 577 (C.A.; tribunal upheld, Lord Denning M.R. dissenting).

68. F. Meyers, *Ownership of Jobs* (U.C.L.A. 1964), p. 112.

69. *Donovan Report*, paras. 214–24; *T.U.C. Report*, 1967, para. 33, pp. 130–32. For a stimulating off-beat discussion of 'Ownership of Work' by a psychologist, see R. Holmes (1967) V *Brit. J. Industrial Relations* 19.

70. *Sunday Times*, 15.2.70.

71. K. Coates and A. Topham, *Industrial Democracy in Great Britain* (1968), p. 210 (new ed., 1970: *Workers' Control*).

CHAPTER 4

COLLECTIVE BARGAINING AND THE LAW

THE ordinary worker scarcely recognizes his individual contract of employment, which is so vital to the lawyer whom he or his employer consults in time of trouble. But he will frequently be sharply aware of an agreement between his union and the employer, or a group of unions and employers' associations. By combination the workers attempt to restore to themselves some equality of bargaining power. Yet the position of such 'collective agreements' is not certain in English law. Two different questions arise: (i) Is such an agreement legally a contract, enforceable between the 'collective parties' (between unions and employers or associations of employers)? (ii) How far does the collective agreement control in law the terms of the individual contract of employment? But before answers can be attempted to these questions it is necessary to describe the general relationship of our law to the machinery of collective bargaining.

THE CONTEXT

' "Collective bargain" is a term coined by Beatrice Webb,' said the Donovan Report, 'to describe an agreement concerning pay and conditions of work settled between trade unions on the one hand and an employer or association of employers on the other. Thus it covers any negotiations in which employees do not negotiate individually, and on their own behalf, but do so collectively through representatives.' Agreements reached after such bargaining directly affect the terms of employment of well over two thirds of our working population. In no other country is there such a varied and intricate web of bargaining machinery. It emerged from 150 years of development. Even before 1824, when the first dent was made in the illegality of trade unions, groups of workers (printers, brush-makers, and cabinet makers, for example) were negotiating 'lists of prices' with employers; and with the growth of unions in the nineteenth century, first skilled craft workers and later the unskilled groups forged from a sharp class conflict at first tacit, later explicit, recognition, and then the chance to negotiate on hours and wages. Whereas the Royal Commission in 1869 spoke of 'codes of working rules', by 1894 a Commission was discussing 'collective bargaining'. The original Whitley Committee of 1916 inaugurated a new era of voluntary joint negotiation, in both the Civil Service and industry. Seventy-three Joint Industrial Councils were set up between 1918 and 1921. Today there are over 200. And there are about 500 separate industry-wide negotiating arrangements for manual workers alone.

This transition to collective bargaining occurred in a period of the sharpest industrial warfare in which, as we shall see, the law was deeply involved. It was, undoubtedly, partly as a reaction against that legal warfare and the legal attacks in nineteenth-century courts on the unions that the modern structure of collective negotiation was built on the autonomous actions of the parties rather than on legal devices. In 1911, a year of savage conflict and just after severe judicial interventions, Winston Churchill said: 'It is not good for trade unions that they should be brought in contact with the courts, and it is not good for the courts'. In the First World War membership of workers' unions doubled; and the practice of bargaining flowered until, as Professor Phelps Brown puts it, 'it came about that the typical British bargaining unit, which in 1914 was still made up of certain occupations in one district of one industry, had become by the end of the war the whole of the wage-earners in the whole of an industry'.[1]

Yet the system did not, as in smaller countries with later industrialization such as Sweden, become completely centralized. The T.U.C., founded in 1868, had, and has, even after its changes of Rules in 1969, largely coordinating functions.

The first national employers' federation was formed in 1919 (this became in 1965 the C.B.I.); but by then a network of committees, conferences, Joint Industrial Councils (J.I.C.) and the like were springing up, some industry-wide, some company-

or even plant-based. Industry-wide agreements on both substantive (wages, bonus, etc.) and procedural (redress of grievances) issues have, especially in the period after the Second World War, come to be supplemented by a system of 'informal' negotiations at plant level, usually with shop stewards. We have already noticed the modern importance of bonuses negotiated by shop stewards (p. 100); and the Donovan Report suggested that

the practices of the formal system have become increasingly empty while the practices of the informal system have come to exert an even greater influence on the conduct of industrial relations throughout the country.

This is clearly true of some industries, especially where shortage of labour has led to local 'bidding-up', and where formally agreed procedures are outmoded and cumbersome (e.g. engineering); but in others the doctrine needs application with caution, and national negotiations or procedures are more dominant (e.g. local government, or chemicals other than I.C.I.). The Donovan Report stated that the first priority is:

a change in the nature of British collective bargaining, and a more orderly method for workers and their representatives to exercise their influence in the factory ... if possible, without destroying the British tradition of keeping industrial relations out of the courts.

It was to press forward with this job that C.I.R. was set up. Along with its work of inquiry, and the roles of the other voluntary bodies already described (p. 30) have gone significant developments in trade union bargaining practice. In many unions the old gaps which often appeared between the officials who negotiated and the workers who waited outside the bargaining room with their elected shop stewards have been closed by incorporating stewards in bargaining teams and repeated consultation with members on the terms of proposed agreements. The A.U.E.F.W. and T.G.W.U. have been in the forefront of this plan. A ballot of London dockers in 1970 led first to a rejection but later to an acceptance of employers' offers. A bargain struck in this way will, it is hoped, stick better for the ballot. Workers at Fords voted to prefer a management offer to their stewards' claim, and the unions supported their choice. The reform of procedures has been more difficult. The 1970 Bill proposed to introduce compulsory registration of procedure agreements with the D.E.P. A voluntary beginning had been made in 1969 when the Department secured registration of agreements covering over a third of the workforce. But, although such registration can remind management of its responsibility to initiate clear comprehensive 'factory agreements', too much emphasis on written agreements can ignore the unwritten basis of 'custom and practice' on which it often suits *both* sides to proceed in industrial arrangements. Many useful deals are made 'on the nod' which might be more difficult to concede on paper. But grievance procedures need to be clear, and the C.B.I. 1970 report on *Grievance Procedures* concluded

their existence and method of operation must be clearly understood by all concerned and this is best achieved by reducing procedures to writing.

It is, thus, hard to generalize about British collective agreements, which words can refer to anything from a resolution of a J.I.C. down through district or company agreements to 'practices' arranged on the shop floor. As far as grievance procedures go, systems vary from joint committees at one end to what are still, in theory, hearings conducted by employers (engineering) at the other. But in practice, vast numbers of disputes are hammered out in these procedures. However, delays can be considerable, especially under the old 'York Agreement' of 1922 in engineering, Works Conferences sometimes taking four weeks, and the later steps to Central Conference anything from 10 to 23 weeks. Delays in the two building industry procedures in 1961–66 were smaller, cases reaching even the National Joint Council on average within a month. Yet that industry suffered from serious outbreaks of strikes over grievances; many grievances fell outside the procedures; and the main causes of strikes probably lay in those grievances, in the wage-structure and poor organization overall of management and workforce. Despite the procedures a short stoppage became a recognized way of settling a grievance – one reason why the Donovan Report put such emphasis on urgent reform of some procedures. But in all industries 'procedure' is crucial. In coal mining, 10,000 disputes were settled at pit meetings in 1964; only 73 by 'umpires' on final appeal.[2]

The remarkable development of flexible patterns of collective machinery in Britain happened largely without the aid of the law, or even the lawyer's distinction between 'disputes of interest' and 'disputes of right'. The T.U.C.'s *Action on Donovan* in 1968 said it might be possible to distinguish between them 'theoretically, but they cannot be readily distinguished in practice'. Professor Flanders says:

Most important, perhaps, is our lack of concern for the distinction between conflicts of interests and conflicts of right, which is fundamental in European labour law; or between negotiation and grievance procedure, as in the United States. So long as the agreed disputes procedure is followed through the various stages, we are not particularly interested in whether new substantive rules are being made or old ones applied: the main thing is to find an acceptable, and if possible a durable, compromise by means of direct negotiation between representatives of the two sides.[3]

'The tendency', one authoritative research paper reported to the Royal Commission, 'is to regard procedures as all-purpose arrangements to be used flexibly as particular situations arise and as commonsense seems to dictate'.[4] There is, in fact, much to be said for the view that – even in systems where the distinction is dominant – 'legal' proceedings properly adapted to employment disputes (with conciliation built in) would not be essentially different from many industrial negotiations 'in procedure'[5] – although the distinction has now received official blessing from the I.L.O. but at a level of no great intellectual sophistication.[6] If there is a profound distinction (as most lawyers think) between the two types of dispute, it is unlikely to be introduced as a fundamental feature of even reformed British procedures. On the other hand, we have seen that some issues require specially devised procedures, e.g. dismissal (p.

142). Similarly, the parties in deciding cases in voluntary industrial procedures sometimes go to great lengths to avoid the
creation of strictly binding 'precedents' so as always to retain
the ability to treat each case on its merits,[7] though we saw
that departure from 'precedent' can sometimes be as much an
argument in the factory as everywhere else (p. 51).

Legal Duties to Recognize and Bargain: As we have seen,
there has been no legal right in Britain for the worker even to
join a trade union, let alone have it recognized by the employer.
The 1970 Bill proposed to introduce a right for the employee to
join an independent union (p. 80), a right which would be of
value to that minority of workers who, the Donovan Report
confirmed, still work for employers who forbid or discourage
union membership. Only the nationalized corporations have
been placed under a legal duty to consult or bargain; and even
then the various statutory duties direct boards to seek consultation, or to negotiate with unions which appear to them to
be appropriate or representative. These duties could scarcely
ever be enforced by action in the courts and depend on the
Board's choice of union. Where the N.C.B. will negotiate with
only the N.U.M. and not with another union, as in 1963, or
where three white-collar unions, as in 1969, compete fiercely
for recognition by the British Steel Corporation, a strike may
result or be threatened. The Minister might make a direction
in an extreme case; or even, as we saw in Chapter 1, a complaint be made to the I.L.O.; no one would expect a writ.
Similarly there is no legal right for workers to bargain. Trade
unions have to win recognition; and many members still feel
that what has been won by strength is more safely held than
recognition which the law imposes and which the law might
take away. Even under the 'Fair Wages' condition imposed on
employers who take on government contracts ('The contractor
shall recognize the freedom of his workpeople to be members
of trade unions') the Industrial Court decided in 1964 that
employers were justified in refusing to negotiate with a small
union which was not accepted by the A.E.U. and the National
Confederation in the industry (p. 204).

Some employers in recent years have maintained refusals to recognize and bargain with unions. The T.U.C. Report 1967 revealed that the areas in which trade union organization is noticeably difficult are those involving small firms; women workers; firms with high labour turnover; firms in foreign ownership or control (a resolution in 1968 called for a special law about these); and white-collar workers (for many years banks and insurance companies for example had refused to recognize). To this list later studies have added others, such as the distributive trades, catering and hotels, agriculture, laundries, hairdressing and construction (industries with over six million employees) in which to the inherent difficulties of organization have also often been added the hostility of employers. Foreign firms create special problems. One American-owned factory in Stockport was the subject of a week of protest strikes by workers throughout the town (a rare event in Britain) by August 1967; ten months before 145 men had been dismissed after a dispute about non-recognition and non-union labour. *The Times* called it 'one of the most bitter industrial clashes of recent years'; there were violent demonstrations; and the company twice claimed damages successfully against the police under the Riot Damages Act, 1886, (which led to demands from the local authority for reform of the Act). By December the company's American President announced that the firm would close down. Foreign firms always have the ultimate sanction of taking their capital elsewhere.

We have already seen that the C.I.R. has attempted to persuade firms which refuse to recognize and treat with trade unions (p. 38). But so far it has often been rebuffed. Demands that there should be a *legal* duty to bargain, even in the attenuated form of a condition on limited liability registration for companies, were rejected by the Donovan Commission, which preferred the way of persuasion through the C.I.R. The Commission, however, did think that, if an employer refused recognition or evaded 'effective bargaining', the union should have the right to have compulsory arbitration on its claims (for higher wages and so on). The Commission overlooked that even this reform would require a legal definition of the duty to bargain 'effectively'. It is partly the jungle of law about the 'duty to bargain in good faith' which has brought lawyers into the very bargaining room in the U.S.A.

The 1970 Bill proposed a further step towards the legal duty. In the event of non-recognition, the Secretary of State would confer with the T.U.C. and the C.B.I. and have a discretion then to refer the union request for recognition to the C.I.R. The intention here appears to be to exclude difficult cases of inter-union rivalry which should be settled by the T.U.C., for the Bill said nothing about situations where two unions claim the right to be recognized – except for a vague right of the C.I.R. to impose 'conditions'. Some commentators wish to import the American 'exclusive bargaining agent' system where workers elect a union by majority. But the Donovan Report showed that binding majority votes would be inimical to industrial relations in such situations. The American system was introduced, in 1935, to deal with mass, not minority, non-recognition by introducing *election* units. In many industries, the election units do not now correspond to either the bargaining or the contract units. 'Coalition' and 'co-ordinated' bargaining among unions and 'multi-employer' bargaining means that practice is very different from the paper scheme. In any case, in Britain, even to try and draw 'unit' boundaries would be a legal nightmare. (See p. 466; and now p. 517.)

The 1970 Bill proposed the following scheme: If, after a reference, the C.I.R. indicated that the employer ought to recognize the union which made the request, the Secretary of State could (but need not) make an Order compelling the employer to recognize. The C.I.R. might, if it wished, take ballots among the employees to help it reach a decision about advising the Minister. If the employer did not comply, the union could make a complaint to be heard by a Complaints Tribunal of the C.I.R., consisting of members of the Commission itself and assessors specially appointed after consultation with the T.U.C. and C.B.I. If the Complaints Tribunal found the case proven, it would make a 'declaration'; and at that point the union could present a claim to the Industrial Court for arbitration on the claims which it wished to make on the employer (whether they related to wages, hours, or even procedural matters such as new grievance machinery). If the Industrial Court thought the claim should be met, it would make an 'award' which in this case (exceptionally, see p. 200) would make the terms claimed into terms and conditions of employment in the individual employment contracts of the employees involved.

This involved procedure unhappily contains problems. We mention only three. First, the compulsory terms at the end of the day could be superseded by an agreement between the employer and an *individual* employee. It would be rather absurd to impose the terms collectively only to allow an employer to lean on each worker enough to obtain his agreement to displace them. Secondly, the declaration of the C.I.R. Complaints Tribunal was not to be challenged in the ordinary courts – except that within six weeks an appeal could be made to the High Court on a *point of law*. This defect is highlighted by the third and critical problem. The definition of *recognition* of a union, to which the employer's duty relates, included

the taking by the employer of all such action by way of or with a view to the carrying on of *relevant negotiations* with the trade union as might reasonably be expected to be taken by an employer ready and willing to carry on such negotiations.

Relevant negotiations were defined as relating to terms and conditions of employment; to making procedure agreements; or to any *matters* to which procedure agreements can relate. Procedure agreements were defined as relating to these *matters*: machinery for consultation or arbitration about terms and conditions; facilities for union officers or workers' representatives; procedures concerning dismissal, discipline or grievances; or – *'recognition of trade unions'*. The definition was, thus, not only circular; it would also provide food on which appeals to the High Court could feed for many years.

In fact, it is questionable whether these long sections of the Bill would have been worthwhile, unless at least the decision of the C.I.R. were to be made as unassailable as that of a National Insurance Commissioner (p. 288). Recruitment to a union often follows recognition, it is true; but enforced recognition might sometimes prop up a flabby union structure. If a legal duty is required, it must concentrate upon supporting trade unionism in the area of white-collar workers – and there, unfortunate as it may be, there is currently a tough competition for members among many different unions.

White-collar workers will become the majority of the workforce before 1990. Their unionization has often been opposed by big employers and even associations, such as the Engineering Employers' Federation. Only 30 per cent of them (against 51 per cent of manual workers in 1968) were unionized and many of these were in the 'public sector': only 12 per cent in manufacturing. What was thought to be a boom in white-collar unionism since 1948 turns out to be an increase in the workforce to nearly nine millions, but the unions did 'little more than keep abreast of the increasing white-collar labour force and the density of white-collar unionism has not increased significantly since the post war period'.[8] Even though the growth of white-collar unionism exceeded that of manual unions by thirty times between 1948 and 1964 this was not enough to stop the overall 'density' of unionization in Britain falling from 45.1 to 42.6 per cent in the same period.

The 1970 Bill proposed two other new legal pressures to promote collective bargaining – first, as we have seen, to allow for compulsory registration of procedure agreements with the D.E.P.; secondly, to enforce *disclosures of information* by employers. This, as we saw in Chapter 1, is an important matter in relation both to 'industrial democracy' and to international companies. The Bill would have had the C.I.R. publish a 'code of practice' indicating what type of information ought to be disclosed to trade union representatives. Once Parliament had approved such a code, an employer in bargaining would be under a duty to disclose information within the principles of the code without which the union would be 'to a material extent impeded' in negotiating. Exceptions eat into the value of this duty, excluding disclosures against the interests of national security; of information communicated to the employer 'in confidence' (a wide range); or of information disclosure of which would seriously prejudice his business. The Secretary of State could make regulations requiring similar disclosure to employees and trade unions by all or by designated groups of employers. A union in dispute with an employer could complain of his failure to disclose information to the Industrial Court. The first remedy would be a declaration. Then, if the employer still did not disclose, the Court might on a second complaint make an award imposing compulsory terms in the individual employment contracts of employees concerned; but this would only be done where the negotiations about those terms would have been assisted by disclosure of the information. There are, once again, defects in this cumbersome procedure; but in this case at least an appeal to the ordinary courts was not apparently envisaged.

Such laws would be quite novel. Their danger is that they may release unforeseen pressures for further legal regulation of collective labour relations. In the past, not only has there been no such regulation, but after 1924 the ordinary courts displayed for forty years a certain desire not to obstruct the voluntary developments. Since in that year a judge made it clear that such combinations were not unlawful as a 'conspiracy', the unions have met fewer legal obstacles in the path of organizing '100 per cent union membership' at a place of work (at least until some judgments in the 1960s to be described in Chapter 8). Contrary to their previous attitudes to industrial conflicts, many judges from 1920 onwards developed the law's doctrines in such a way as to interfere little during the next three decades with the autonomous interplay, or if need be the conflict, of the industrial parties, an 'abstentionist' flavour which matched the newly emergent pattern of national collective bargaining. In fact, the legislation of 1906 which was the resulting balance of a sharp class conflict in which 'the law' was used against the unions was later rationalized into the more metaphysical doctrine of the 'abstention of the law' as we have seen. Curiously enough, the extra-legal structure of voluntary negotiation, and later of joint consultation, grew to have a rather 'official' look. This could mislead even the lawyers. In 1953, for instance, the Divisional Court faced a case in which the judge had granted leave for a remedy appropriate only to statutory and similar bodies against the National Joint Council for Dental Technicians. The judges said:

> I think that, possibly, the court when giving leave thought that the National Joint Council by reason of its name was a statutory body [and] they are in no sense a public body ... People are not compelled to abide by their decision. This is a private tribunal set up as arbitrators by agreement between the parties.[9]

Interestingly enough the ordinary remedies seem to be available under the Arbitration Act, 1950, in respect of such decisions. The High Court will, however, set aside an arbitrator's award only in rare cases, such as a clear error of law or fact in the award. But if the arbitrator had been appointed by the Secretary of State, even at the request of the parties, by virtue of his powers under the Acts of 1896 or 1919 (see p. 396) then the Arbitration Acts have always been excluded and access to the ordinary courts rendered virtually impossible.

ARE COLLECTIVE AGREEMENTS CONTRACTS?

Remembering the great variety in types of collective agreements, we turn now to our question: are they enforceable as legal contracts? Until 1969 it had never been decided whether an employer who, say, employs a greater percentage of women in the plant than that agreed with the union, could be sued by the union; nor (and this is the practical question) whether a union which has agreed not to take strike action – either at all, or before an agreed procedure is exhausted – can, if it does so, be sued by the employer for breach of contract (for damages or an injunction or both). The answer depended on two things; first, the general, judge-made law of contract; second, section 4(4) of the Trade Union Act, 1871. The matter is an explosive question of current politics. The view of the trade union world in Britain is, without doubt, that collective agreements are not legal contracts in this country and that no legal action can therefore be brought if a union fails to observe agreed procedure. But in recent years lawyers have begun to ask: 'Why not? There is the document, signed and agreed. Is it not, prima facie, a contract?'

The English law of contract says that a bargain is a contract provided that there is apparent in the agreement an 'intention to be legally bound'. Is such an intention to be found in collective agreements? It is true, as Mr Justice Megaw insisted in *Edwards* v. *Skyways Ltd*, 1964,[10] that whereas domestic or social agreements are presumed not to be so intended, serious business agreements are in general presumed to give rise to legal obligations. He, therefore, upheld a negotiated promise by an employer to make payments to redundant employees as enforceable by the employees, even though the employer always described the payments as 'ex gratia'. That was a contract with each employee who accepted. What then of collective agreements?

Putting aside the relatively unimportant s.4(4) of the 1871 Act, the Donovan Report summed up the opinion which most commentators held by saying:

In this country collective agreements are not legally binding contracts. This is not because the law says that they are not contracts or that the parties to them may not give them the force of contracts ... It is due to the intention of the parties themselves. They do not intend to make a legally binding contract and without both parties intending to be legally bound there can be no contract in the legal sense. ... This ... intention and policy that collective bargaining and collective agreements should remain outside the law is one of the characteristic features of our system of industrial relations ... It is deeply rooted in its structure.

Professor Kahn-Freund had advanced this opinion in 1954, changing his previous view to the contrary, and in 1968 summed up the point by saying: 'That intention (to create legal relations) just does not exist although there is nothing to prevent the parties from making their agreement into a legal contract ...'[11] On 27 February 1969, as the writer was hurrying to hear a lecture on this theme by the same authority, he read with astonishment in an evening newspaper 'Fords sue two giant unions – for breach of agreement. Injunction granted!' In *Ford Motor Co. Ltd* v. *Amalgamated Union of Engineering and Foundry Workers and Transport and General Workers' Union*,[12] 1969, the point was put to the test.

The injunction had been *granted* under a special procedure, namely the 'interlocutory' jurisdiction of judges to give such a remedy for a few days without even hearing the defendants – *ex parte*. Not until the Monday did the hearing begin with the defendant unions present, and for four days argument continued as to whether this interlocutory injunction ordering the unions not to do certain acts (including supporting strike action by their Ford members) should be extended until the 'trial' of the action. Interlocutory proceedings are theoretically meant to hold the balance of the *status quo* until trial, and the proceedings are normally on written affidavit, without witnesses in person (and without cross-examination). Thus, the judge can form only an 'interim' view of the facts. But in labour matters, it is often the injunction which the employer wants far more than damages at any subsequent trial, as we shall see in Chapter 8. At any rate, a mandatory injunction was granted by the court for a week until Mr Justice Geoffrey Lane decided on 6 March that no good grounds for it existed in law. In so deciding the High Court confirmed that collective agreements were presumptively not contracts.

The *Ford* case was an odd one in which to test the point. Agreement had been reached in 1955 whereby a joint negotiating committee (N.J.N.C.) was set up at Fords, the trade union side consisting of one representative of each of the many unions (15 in 1969) whatever its membership among the workforce. It was signed by Ford managers, by accredited officers of each individual union, and the chairman and secretary of the union side of the N.J.N.C. In 1967, an agreement similarly signed was made concerning new conditions of employment and providing that variations of the agreements should be negotiated 'through the medium of the N.J.N.C.'. Early in 1969, Fords proposed variations and the union side of the N.J.N.C. after long discussions ultimately voted by a narrow majority in favour of accepting the proposals; but the delegates of the defendant unions (who represented some two thirds of Ford workers) opposed or abstained from votes of acceptance. But Fords put up a Notice on 12 February signed by Fords management spokesman and the officials of the

N.J.N.C. announcing new terms as agreed. The new terms involved fundamental changes in employment terms, including an obligation to give 21 days' notice of strikes (though this was not in the Notice) and the so-called 'penal clauses' whereby workers taking action in breach of the grievance procedure agreed in the 1955 and 1967 agreements (where it was also agreed there should be no strikes before procedure was exhausted) would lose holiday bonuses and entitlement to 'lay-off' pay. To the latter, many workers objected violently. At lay-delegate meetings and through shop stewards this opposition boiled up, and by 21 February strikes had begun. Five days later the two defendant unions made it official for their members. The result was 'a massive stoppage of work at the majority of the Ford plants'. Six days later Fords issued their writ and obtained an *ex parte* interlocutory injunction. It is noteworthy that they did not sue the workers involved for breach of employment contracts, perhaps for obvious reasons as there were some 35,000 workers involved. Nor did they sue the officials who organized the strike (see Chapter 8). Fords sued the unions as such for breach of contract, an action never before heard with full argument in an English court.

The judge faced three main problems. The unions denied ever having broken any of their agreements with Fords. On this point, he reached no conclusion; and it remains a matter for argument, the unions maintaining that they did nothing wrong, the management (and the Press) tending to assume they were in breach of some obligation or other in the agreements. Secondly, the judge agreed that no agreement of the N.J.N.C., whether by majority or unanimous, could bind the unions automatically. Indeed, the 1955 and 1967 agreements had been sent round for individual signatures by the various unions. Therefore there was no 1969 agreement, since no such signatures had been obtained. But, thirdly, what of the 1955 and 1967 agreements which Fords alleged the unions had broken? Were they contracts? The judge mentioned such slender indications as there were in previous case law.[13] In 1904 a local agreement between a baker and the East London Bakers Union was perhaps treated as an enforceable contract by the Court of

Appeal. (There was no final decision, and the case involved proprietary interests in trade labels). In other cases, 'justification' for procuring breach of a contract (see p. 349) was found by judges in a pre-existing collective agreement (but the doctrine of 'justification' is certainly not limited to enforceable contracts). In a case in July 1926 a case for breach was settled on terms which seemed to show that the court as well as the trade union which made the agreement thought it was 'binding' (but these words were only a settlement as agreed by those parties; and the union was floundering in the wake of the General Strike). On the other side, however, the cases to be cited were equally inconclusive. In 1931 a Law Lord had said collective agreements could not be enforced by legal action by a union but by calling a strike; and in 1956, Mr Justice Pearson had treated an agreement *settling* a strike as 'a gentleman's agreement' not intended to be legally enforced.

The judge (noting that the parties had said nothing about their intentions expressly) took note, as is usual, of 'all the surrounding circumstances' to ascertain the common intention. For where no express words appear, it is the objective manifestation – what the reasonable man would think the parties meant, knowing what they knew – to which an English court looks. (This is a rather different question from one put by a commentator who criticizes the decision: i.e. 'What were the intentions *at that time* [1955] *of these parties*?' – a difference which may vitiate most of the criticisms.)[14] The judge then read passages of the Donovan Report such as that quoted above. He also quoted the Evidence of the C.B.I. which was based (as was that of every employers' association) on the assumption that, if collective agreements were to be generally enforceable at law, a 'radical' change in the law would be needed. (The 1894 Royal Commission had said much the same in a different context.) The T.U.C. Evidence was to the same effect, as was the Ministry of Labour's Evidence to the Commission, the Ministry's Industrial Handbook of 1961, the passage written by Professor Kahn-Freund in 1954, and a statement by Lord Justice Pearson presiding over the Inquiry into the Electricity Supply Industry in 1964:

... the three-year (collective) agreement was not intended to be legally binding but the parties, by entering into it, assumed a moral obligation as is usual in industrial relations.

From this it was clear that the climate of opinion was almost unanimous to the effect that no contractual force was normally intended. So, a reasonable man would not think these parties meant to make a legally binding contract. Exceptionally, such an intention is apparent, as in the Boot and Shoe Industry agreements of 1898 and 1910 when a trust deed under seal was executed, which the judge agreed was a binding document. (Some collective agreements are stamped; but whether that imports a similar appearance of intention to be legally bound remains for argument.) It is said, too, that unions have made agreements recently which both sides know are intended to be legally binding, such as that made between Henry Wiggin and three unions in 1967, though this rests, it seems, partly on an opinion given to the company after the agreement that it 'is enforceable in the British courts'.[15] This 'climate of opinion' on both sides of industry in 1955 and 1967 was known to the Ford and union negotiators; they 'must have been aware of current attitudes and developments ... that is their job ... we are dealing on either side in this case with people who are in the top rank ... of their jobs'. No one from Fords had sworn to a positive intention to create legal obligations. Criticisms have been made of this part of the judgment where the judge looked for any indications of the *actual* states of mind of the bargainers. But such criticism may treat as the core what was only a necessary penumbra of the judge's reasoning. Having found that, from an objective assessment, no reasonable man would conclude that an agreement of this kind made in this social climate was to be enforceable in the courts, naturally he turned in fairness to see whether the actual parties had said or done anything which would rebut that conclusion. Finding, on the contrary, that they had done nothing of the sort, he was fortified in his interpretation.

Moreover, although clauses about wages and so on were specific, many others were 'aspirational clauses drawn in vague terms' (the parties agreed 'to achieve efficient production by all reasonable means') which the parties cannot really have expected to enforce in a court. He therefore concluded:

> The fact that the agreements prima facie deal with commercial relationships is outweighed by the other considerations, by the wording of the agreements, by the nature of the agreements, and by the climate of opinion voiced and evidenced by the extra-judicial authorities. Agreements such as these, composed largely of optimistic aspirations, presenting grave practical problems of enforcement and reached against a background of opinion adverse to enforceability, are ... not contracts in the legal sense and are not enforceable at law. Without clear and express provisions making them amenable to legal action, they remain in the realm of undertakings binding in honour.

Those who think the *Ford* judgment has created 'privilege' for collective agreements should remember that it is open to such parties to agree on enforceability if they wish. And it is arguable that the 'climate of opinion', so clearly illustrated by the judges, goes back much further than the post-war period; for in the ten years to 1935 seven Bills were introduced in Parliament to *change* the law so as to make some collective agreements enforceable; and, while it is true the debates do not always distinguish our problem from other related problems, it is not difficult to find an air of the same 'climate' in the speeches. Furthermore, there are a number of other 'commercial agreements' which the courts have leaned against putting into the category of contracts – arrangements for government subsidies; agreements with statutory suppliers of water or electricity; agreements with the Post Office. The fact is that the collective agreement is not a commercial contract; Isadore Katz called it 'at once a business compact, a code of relations, and a treaty of peace', and in Britain it is frequently part of constant and dynamic negotiation. Even the arbitrators called in to decide disputes shy away from legalism; or as Mr Jack Scamp said in arbitrating a disputed interpretation of agreements between British Railways and the unions:

> I have not attempted to make a legal interpretation of the agreement. It was not conceived, drafted or to be implemented by law-

yers. It attempted to record the understanding of each of the parties as to what was contemplated. I have therefore directed my attention to what I conceive to be the spirit and intention of the agreement.

A host of legal problems would arise if collective agreements were enforceable as contracts, or in respect of a particular agreement expressly made enforceable. A new necessity would arise to distinguish 'consultative' from other bodies with power to bind the parties. Then, who are the 'parties'? A party to a legal contract must be a human person or legal 'person' (e.g. a company). A registered union may have status, though this is doubtful (p. 445); an unregistered union at the moment does not have it. An unincorporated association making a 'contract' can cause the gravest procedural difficulties. The legal problems become almost insoluble in an agreement (to take an example from an arbitration before the Industrial Court) between 'the Workpeople's side and the Employer's side of the National Joint Council for the Inland Waterways Industry'. How far, next, would courts go in trying to enforce vague phrases encouraging 'efficient production' or 'emphasizing the value of consultation' (Engineering agreements); and if they tried to enforce them would not their industrial value be lost?

Nor is it true, as is commonly believed, that unions would necessarily be liable for unofficial actions or, even, all the actions of shop stewards. If unions guarantee that no breach will occur, then of course they are liable if there is one; so too, if (as in a film industry agreement) they agree that the employers' obligations are contingent on the union members complying with the agreement. Occasionally clauses go even further, as in the Boot and Shoe agreement: 'Both parties undertake to use such means as are at their disposal to ensure its due observance by all employees whether members of their respective organizations or not'! But where (as in food manufacturing) the union agrees not to *instruct* members to strike or (as in cable-making) to 'exert every effort to ensure that no stoppage of work or any unauthorized action shall take place', the matter is different. Only if someone acting within the authority which he had as an agent of the union acted contrary to those clauses would the union be liable. It was established as early as 1906 that branch officials do not bind the union in every action they choose to take; and that the union is only liable by virtue of 'ratification' if subsequently it adopts the act done without authority with full knowledge of the facts. Merely to pay strike-pay to men who have already terminated their employment contracts is not enough to establish that liability. Then, there is the difficulty of knowing just when parties can withdraw from any particular agreement (e.g. can they get out by resigning from the employers' or union federations that made it?). As for remedies, damages (of vast proportions against unions) might be recoverable; but sums fixed in advance as payable on breach, as in the Boot and Shoe agreements, are not recoverable if they are 'penal'. An injunction might lie, especially in interlocutory cases; and although this remedy lies always in the court's discretion, one certain consequence of making collective agreements into contracts would be an even more vigorous reappearance of the 'labour injunction' in Britain.

Lastly, there is one curious but relevant statute. The well-known rule enacted in 1906, that trade unions cannot be sued for torts, does not apply; for what we are discussing is not tortious civil wrongdoing but breach of a contract. But the Trade Union Act, 1871, Section 4, provided: 'Nothing in this Act shall enable any court to entertain any legal proceedings instituted with the object of directly enforcing or recovering damages for the breach of ... (4) Any agreement made between one trade union and another.' Because of the archaic definition of 'trade union' (see p. 410), many employers' trade associations have been 'trade unions' in law. An agreement between workers' unions and a trade association may fall, therefore, within Section 4 of the 1871 Act. If collective bargains were ever held to be contracts by the judges, the Act of 1871 would prevent *direct* enforcement of such agreements. Agreements between a union and one employer, or a group of employers not a 'trade union', would not be affected; and since company and factory agreements are now critical, the section is less important today than ever. But where it applies any legal proceedings for *direct* enforcement would encounter difficulties. It would be a very strange situation. As we shall see in Chapter 9, the Courts have often allowed the remedies of declaration or injunction as 'indirect' enforcement not forbidden by other paragraphs of the section. But the Court of Appeal in 1922 considered that neither remedy could be allowed under paragraph (4), since, as Lord Sterndale, Master of the Rolls, put it: 'I cannot see a much more direct way of enforcing an agreement than by an injunction to prevent a person from breaking it.' The Donovan Report, with three dissentients, recommended the repeal of section 4 altogether. The 1970 Bill proposed to amend the definition of trade union so as to exclude employers' associations (p. 411) and to stop Section 4(4) applying to agreements between those associations and unions.

Quite apart, however, from the 1871 Act, we conclude that very few collective agreements are enforceable as legal contracts. Certainly current British industrial practice is based upon that view; and any appellate judgment which struck at the *Ford* decision would, as the Donovan Report hinted, strike at deep roots, and sensitive nerves, of the very structure of our industrial relations. Statutory intervention might cause a breakdown.

Should Collective Agreements be enforceable? The Donovan Report rejected all the proposals for methods of enforcing collective agreements now – with the exception of two dissentients on unofficial strikers losing seniority rights, and of Mr Shonfield. The latter went so far as to conclude that if only agreements were contracts, judges would, by interpreting phrases like 'the union will use its best endeavours', build up 'a body of useful case law'. The lawyer's vision of the maze of decisions likely to eventuate becomes a nightmare when Mr Shonfield's proposals go on to demand that unions must demonstrate that they had 'not connived' at the 'use of its authority' by officials or shop stewards to 'defeat the purposes' of the agreement. The consequence of such a law in the unofficial strike of Swedish miners, which dragged through the dark December of 1969, was that the local union official, having to use his best endeavours, was the only man at work! His ability to help settle the strike was not thereby increased. Lord Donovan's own short personal Appendix shows how he was gradually convinced that no sensible way could be found to enforce agreements in law. As the Report says, to make existing agreements into contracts would need a statute 'attaching the force of law to the terms of a bargain contrary to the wishes of the parties ... a new departure in the law of contract ... a breach with a long tradition of our industrial relations'. Further, at present, enforcing bad procedures would clearly inhibit their reform; and 'no proposal' for sanctions 'is practicable if it assumes that the employer takes an active part' in enforcement (for employers, on the whole, do not want to sue). A sanction against a trade union where members have acted unofficially could only operate by making unions act against such members – what Lord Devlin once called making them industry's policemen. But there was no evidence that this would help with unofficial strikes. Direct fines or penalties against workers are rejected, a conclusion much affected by the failure of such methods in wartime, such as the famous prosecution of Kent miners in 1942 which resulted in the Minister having to settle the strike by negotiating inside a Kent gaol (Report, Appendix 6). (As we see later, though, (p. 385) seven Commissioners proposed a less direct sanction and four of these thought the C.I.R. should have power even to *deregister* a union which persistently broke agreements.) Automatic sanctions by loss of social security or seniority rights were also rejected (p. 121). Thus, although the Report wished to reduce unofficial strikes and was not 'in principle' opposed to legal sanctions, it found no such means of any utility. As for compulsory strike-ballots and 'cooling-off' periods, the Report swept both aside with brief pertinent argument. In his authoritative modern textbook, Professor Clegg remarks that:

It is foolish to suppose that a statute giving binding force to procedure agreements could accomplish a reduction in the number of unconstitutional strikes so long as the system of collective bargaining itself is promoting an increase. That is so evident that the volume of support for the proposal is puzzling.[15a]

Unhappily, before 1968 the Conservative Party in *Fair Deal at Work* had committed itself to putting 'collective agreements on a par with any other type of contract – no more and no less', which was said (incorrectly) to mean that legal enforceability would be the rule rather than the exception. (The A.E.U. in supplementary evidence to the Royal Commission explained that it would withdraw from certain agreements if they were made legally enforceable.) Both individuals or unions and employers' associations could be liable, the latter if they had not done *all in their power to prevent a breach* (which presumably means expelling any member who threatens a breach). The union could then sue the members. The chief plaintiff was to be the employer. New Industrial Courts, local and national, would have power to grant injunctions, including cases where the Minister applied for one to stop a strike or lock-out likely to endanger the national interest, in which case he could order a secret ballot of workers as to whether an employer's 'last offer' should be accepted. (The 'last offer' procedure is borrowed from part of the Taft-Hartley law in the U.S.A. where, oddly, in the same period there was considerable questioning of its suitability. Clearly, the methods of bargaining used by an employer can be materially affected if he believes such a law will be used.) Mr Robert Carr, it is true, has said that he sees the main purpose *not* to 'punish breaches' but to act as 'preventive medicine'. Workers' opposition is so strong that the result would very likely be just the opposite. The Minister could get an injunction under the *Fair Deal* proposals in certain other cases; e.g. if parties refused to accept certain arbitration awards, and in 'national emergencies'. Later, a system of legally regulated bargaining 'units' was suggested. The proposals of the C.B.I. have been rather different. They at first concentrated upon the need to select industries. The Government should take power to impose procedures and enforce them in selected areas where strikes are specially damaging; but it is not clear what sanction is envisaged. By 1970, the C.B.I. was reconsidering the question and set up a new working party. An influential report on procedures was produced by a committee steered by

Mr Lowry, who had recently reported cautiously on any attempt to transplant American law into the body of British industry (p. 36). Unfortunately, other peripatetic advisers, mainly lawyers, repeatedly dashed back home with snippets of the U.S. laws, ready to paste them on to the British statute book. But some industrialists had, by the summer of 1970, become more wary. It was a time when the negotiations to reform the 1922 engineering procedures had become deadlocked, and the unions had begun to threaten to give notice to terminate those agreements which covered two million workers. No law could force them to make a new agreement; and leaders of two large unions said they would not enter into legally binding agreements. By July 1970, a new C.B.I. working party was reported to be urging that the impending new laws should have a 'catalytic rather than a compulsive effect'. Instead, therefore, of compulsory binding collective agreements, they were apparently more interested in compelling unions to register and in giving the Registrar power to control union rules and to penalize unions in certain situations so as to weaken the opportunities for strike action. The C.B.I. also pressed on the new Conservative Government the desirability of introducing any such rigorous laws step by step so that the effect of one measure could be assessed before others were implemented. It was, no doubt, unfortunate that the new Government had entered office with the scrawny albatross of *Fair Deal at Work* tied up in one package of proposals, ready without adequate research) for immediate legislation.

Curiously, the Labour Government's *In Place of Strife* was also more interventionist than the carefully argued Donovan Report. Although it proposed to retain the *non*-contractual character of the collective agreement (unless the parties agreed otherwise in writing) it proposed three powers of intervention for the Secretary of State, as we saw: p. 34. Sanctions were to be enforced through an 'Industrial Board', and made practicable against individuals by way of 'attachment of earnings' in the County Courts. It was this proposal, perhaps, more than any other which served to provide the T.U.C. with a unified movement on which to base its opposition that ultimately, as we saw in Chapter 1, caused their withdrawal. Oddly enough, it was only a few weeks after the publication of *In Place of Strife* that the Report of a Committee on Enforcement of Judgment Debts was able to state that the previous 'apprehension' of the T.U.C. about attachment of earnings (expressed to the previous committee of 1934) had been relaxed to the point where the T.U.C. was able to accept 'attachment of earnings' on certain conditions, namely a 'reasonable limit' on the earnings available, and attachment to apply to all forms of income.[16] The legislation to allow such deductions was passed in 1970 (Chapter 5). Also, the 1970 Bill had proposed a sensible confirmation of the law, namely that a collective agreement should be presumed *conclusively* not to be intended to be a legally enforceable contract unless (a) it is in writing; and (b) it contains a provision 'which (however expressed) states that it is the intention of the parties' that it should be an enforceable contract in whole or in part. (Unhappily, this admirable formula could be wrecked by the two words 'however expressed', for lawyers would still be able to argue that the agreement *as a whole* 'expressed' such an intention! Why should not the parties be compelled to put the simple formula: 'This is a Legally Binding Contract' at the head of the agreement, if that is their intention?)

It is, of course, true that Britain stands almost alone in presuming that collective agreements are not contracts. But a closer inspection of other European systems reveals that, whereas in some the contractual status of agreements does have a real practical importance (e.g. in Sweden and Germany), in others it is in practice of no great moment (e.g. in Italy and France).[17] In so far as the collective contract is the basis of the 'peace' obligation, its function is clearly to reduce the power of the trade unions. The German courts have added a tort liability in strikes; and there the metal workers were made liable in 1958 for breaking their peace obligations by taking a strike ballot and in 1964 (at the instance of Fords) for making strike preparations. Whether the Taft Hartley Act, 1947, benefited or harmed the system in the U.S.A. by grafting contractual status firmly on to collective agreements is hotly debated by

American commentators. Professor Harry Wellington said to the Donovan Commission:

... what is accomplished by making the collective agreement an enforceable contract? ... The answer, it seems to me, is that little, if anything, positive comes out of this, while a great deal detrimental to the system of private ordering results. Accordingly, on balance, I would favour not making the agreement enforceable ... When we bring the law to bear there is pressure towards uniformity and it tends to undermine the benefits that come from diversity.[18]

Since diversity and flexibility are the virtues most envied in the British system by some whose laws try to systematize industrial life into neat legal packages, it is to be hoped that future governments will pay heed both to the Donovan Report and to the expert evidence given to it by such foreign observers. On one thing, however, we can be sure: the debate about the legal status which collective agreements *ought* to have is not yet over. Indeed, it has become a curious national obsession.

IS THE UNION AN AGENT?

It has been suggested that, although the collective agreement may not be a contract between the 'collective parties', it is intended to be itself an enforceable contract between the employers and the union members represented by the bargaining officials. The member could not normally enforce a contract made between two other persons, for English law does not allow a third party to derive rights or duties from a contract. But the third party can sue as principal if one of the contracting parties was contracting as his agent. The union, they say, is the agent of its members. This would produce the startling result that the worker could sue for the agreed wage, as a principal and a party to the collective agreement itself. That is quite contrary to the usual understanding, and to one legal decision. In 1924, the Court of Appeal decided that an agreement between a provincial trade union and a London trade union agreeing to reciprocal rights of membership could not be enforced by a provincial member when he moved to London. Not only was this agreement 'between one trade union and another' within the 1871 Act; it was also an agreement to which the provincial member was a third party, since unions did not normally make such agreements as agents for their members.[19]

That case is not, of course, concerned with an ordinary collective agreement. Further, some judges have spoken of union representatives on bargaining bodies as agents authorized 'to bind the trade union as a whole and the members individually'.[20] Employers' associations are often accepted as acting as agents for the member companies. Also, some collective agreements even state that they are between the association representing *its* members and the trade union 'representing the members thereof' and the undertakings are made by 'the union and its members' (film agreement of 1958).

But the opposite view still holds the field. Other judicial discussion, the Donovan Report, and all our statutory machinery, seem to treat the union as a principal, not an agent. If it were an agent, a hundred legal puzzles would emerge. For example, we would ask: What is the position of non-unionists in the trade? Usually a union does not bargain for its members alone (though one Civil Service union began to do so in 1963). It seeks to affect conditions throughout the industry. But surely it is not the 'agent' for those who chose not to join. What of those, moreover, who join the company, or the union, later? They might 'ratify' the agreement; but if they were not born or were otherwise unable to contract when the agreement was made, the law concerning 'ratification' prevents their so doing. What of infant workers? They are bound by the agreement only if it is on balance beneficial. Just what is the extent of the officials' authority as 'agents' of members? Can the union member withdraw the authority of the 'agents'? Presumably, in order to do so he must resign from the union. If so, how can a non-unionist be a party to the contract? These, and other legal conundra, make the 'agency' solution inelegant, uncertain, and, in industrial terms, unreal.

Some cases which look like 'agency' cases turn out not to be. In *Edwards* v. *Skyways Ltd*, 1964, some have seen an example of the agency approach. The Air Line Pilots Association officials had bargained new terms by which pilots who agreed to give up certain pension rights were entitled to receive certain payments from the employer. A pilot won his action to recover his payment. But he had to *elect* to take these payments; and the judge saw the negotiated terms as a standing offer put out by the company, which the ex-pilot then accepted. This interpretation does also mean that the company could have lawfully revoked the 'offer' so long as it had acted before the ex-pilot's election. The case is not, as it stands, authority for an 'agency' approach. As we saw in *Morgan* v. *Fry* (p. 110) some judges are making use of this elementary legal concept of a 'standing offer' to analyse difficult industrial situations. An Industrial Tribunal in *Joel* v. *Cammell Laird*, 1969,[21] was prepared if necessary to use the same concept to bind two workers to a collectively negotiated 'Package Deal', the terms of which they knew and accepted by working on them for over two years. But there were better grounds for the decision: see p. 188. However, no rule of law *prohibits* an agency here. In 1962 officials of A.C.T.A.T. were treated by a court as the agents of three named members on whose behalf they tried to negotiate with an employer the settlement of a debt in a dispute that led to the 'blacking' of the employer. The distinguishing mark of such cases is that the officials are negotiating with employers on behalf of a few particular members. They do not involve collective agreements of which the object is to establish a pattern for the industry, district, or factory. Perhaps then even a local plant agreement, for example, for overtime or wage rates, could be seen in this light. But this would mean that members were, as principals, party to shop agreements and able to sue on them as such. It is not thought likely that a court would often take that view. Many legal problems which we are about to mention could not have arisen if the officials at national bargaining level were always agents. The employee is not normally treated by the courts as a principal who can immediately sue for the new wage agreed between his unions and the employers.

COLLECTIVE AGREEMENTS AND THE CONTRACT OF EMPLOYMENT

How then does the collective agreement affect the worker's legal terms of employment? For it is meant to do so – on hours, wages, holidays, sick pay, and now productivity, pensions and redundancy. The national or district agreement is meant to have, as Professor Kahn-Freund says, a 'normative effect', to provide a code for the industry. Yet the contract of employment is not compulsorily subject to collective terms. British collective agreements do *not* have an *automatic* effect upon employment contracts. But the best way to ensure that they do have an effect is to see that the contract of employment incorporates the collective terms *expressly*. So in *N.C.B.* v. *Galley* in 1958, the mining deputies' contracts stated that their wages were regulated by the 'national agreement for the time being in force', and that the other terms of their contracts were subject to the terms of the current ancillary collective agreements.[22] An express reference to the collective agreement must be clear. Employment at the 'going rate', for example, has been held not to be enough. But there is no objection to the terms of employment changing automatically with changes in the collective agreement. Such arrangements are facilitated by the permission to refer to 'another document' in Section 4 of the Contracts of Employment Act, 1963, and to indicate in advance that its terms will change. The main ground of decision in *Joel* v. *Cammell Laird*, 1969, (p. 187) was that written 'memoranda' given under Section 4 to the workers bound them to the 'Package Deal' (which entitled employers to move them from repair work to shipbuilding) by reason of a clause that said that all documents relating to the 'basis of payment' under employment contracts were available at the Time Office. The Package Deal was such a document and was therefore incorporated into the employment terms from the time it came into force in 1965.

We have had occasion to note some of the redundancy cases in which the courts have held that contracts of employment incorporated from collective agreements rights for the employer to move the worker to another site or to regrade him to another job.[23] But suppose the worker's contract says nothing about collective agreements. Can the latter operate so as to bring an *implied term* into his contract – something that 'goes without saying', as Lord Wright put it in the case quoted on p. 95? It cannot be implied in order to affect any term to which he has expressly agreed. Thus, in 1945 a mason alleged that he was being paid at a rate less than that agreed by the district's Joint Council; but his action for breach of contract was bound to fail because he had contractually agreed to take a lower rate. Wherever there is the slightest conflict, therefore, English law still says that the individual contract of employment prevails over the collective agreement. But if the express terms do not cover the point, the court may take the view that the employer and employee must have adopted this collective term as governing their relations, as they did in a case as early as 1858 about rates of pay. In 1933 a mate's written contract with his shipping company had added to it by the court certain rights to shore leave set out in the National Maritime Board's Year Book; 'he assumed ... he was being engaged ... upon the terms and conditions of [the Year Book] ... a perfectly familiar form of engagement which had been applied to him on many occasions before.' Moreover, as we saw (p. 117) once the terms of a collective agreement have been incorporated into a worker's contract, the termination of the collective agreement does not necessarily terminate or change his individual contract. Such a result would have to be provided for in the terms; and even then difficult questions could arise, such as the extent to which the union could act as his agent to receive notice of dismissal.

It is not clear, as we have seen (p. 98), how far the knowledge of the worker will regulate the implication of terms into his contract. But it is plain that after terms of a collective agreement have been acted on by an employer for a period, it is much easier to imply them, by practice or even 'custom', into the worker's contract – or, as we have seen, the court may now treat the worker as 'accepting' a standing offer of which he must know. Where that is so, the inclination of the English lawyer is normally to imply the term into the contracts of *all* workers – union members and non-unionists alike. In 1937, a county court judge refused to discriminate between the two in respect of customary bonus payments and added that he would have refused to imply another alleged custom that only union men should receive extra, since that would be 'unreasonable'! The unionists' reply no doubt would have been that it was more unreasonable for non-members to share the benefits when they did not share the burden of contributions to union funds.

But not every usage or customary practice of long standing will become a contractual term. It must be 'intended' to become one. For example, in 1963 Charles Grieve sued his employers, Imperial Tobacco Company, for a bonus which had been withheld from him because he had taken part in a strike. The company had paid an annual bonus for fifty years and the workers had come to expect it. But there had been no negotiations with the union about it; and on eleven occasions the directors had withheld the bonus from striking employees. The county court judge decided that there was no implied term in Grieve's contract which entitled him to the bonus. The company had never intended the payments to be more than gifts; and 'mere repetition of gratuitous payments cannot convert that which is gratuitous into a contractual obligation'. The result is to be contrasted with that reached in *Edwards* v. *Skyways*, 1964, (p. 172), where the promises of payments to be made to certain redundant pilots were held to be sufficiently serious in intention to be contractual offers even though the payments were always called 'ex gratia' by the company. The fact of negotiation with union representatives was clearly an element of importance there.

What happens, however, where a new agreement, or new arbitration award, is made at collective level? If the worker is clearly employed on whatever are the collective terms 'in force from time to time', the new terms are automatically transmitted from collective down to individual level. But when that is not so, can the new terms be incorporated into his contract of employment? In *Dudfield* v. *Ministry of Works*,

1964, a lift-attendant member of the T.G.W.U. was employed by the Ministry as an established chargehand. He received a copy of rules applicable to him which referred to the wages to be paid as those agreed by the Miscellaneous Trades Joint Council for Government Industrial Employees. In 1952, the Council ratified a new agreement establishing a new wage rate until April 1960 and six-monthly reviews thereafter. In October 1961 an increase of two shillings a week was agreed. But two months previously the Treasury had informed the unions and the Council that there could be no further wage increases in the industrial civil service during the 'pay pause'. Dudfield now sued for the increase which the Ministry said it could not pay. The High Court judge held that the functions of the Joint Council were not executory but 'purely consultative'. Its decision could not create legally enforceable rights as such. There was a long-standing practice whereby the employer and workers had recognized the rates agreed by the Council for many years; but there was no implied obligation that the employer must observe a new agreement. Furthermore, the Ministry could not pay any wages except such as the Treasury authorized. In a case heard at the same time, an Admiralty employee sued on similar facts except that the new rate had been awarded in a voluntary arbitration by the Industrial Court after disagreement. The judge refused to imply a term that the rate to be paid was such as might be agreed or awarded on arbitration: '... he was entitled only to such sums as were directed to be paid in Admiralty Fleet Orders.'[24] But in each case one must look closely at the collective bargaining machinery. In *Brand* v. *L.C.C.*, 1967, for example, the L.C.C. and its staff associations had agreed that the decisions of a National Joint Council should determine workers' pay rates, subject to a 'rounding-off' adjustment. Increases were regularly approved in a resolution passed later by an L.C.C. committee. In July 1966 the Council agreed an increase of approximately seven per cent. The L.C.C. resolution was not passed until October, by which time it was caught by a provision of the Prices and Income Act, 1967, permitting the employer not to pay. But the County Court judge held that, despite the need for the subsequent 'rounding-off' and resolution, the L.C.C. was bound contractually to the *worker* 'as soon as the award of the N.J.C. was made' in July.[25]

Even bigger difficulties can arise where, as is not uncommon, local agreements have been made which are not the same as the national agreement. In 1964, Reginald Clift, an ambulance driver, sued his employers, West Riding County Council, for an alleged underpayment according to the 'scheduled rates' for stand-by duties. The defendants proved that they had in 1955 negotiated a local agreement with the union to which Clift belonged, under which the rates for stand-by duties were modified. The court decided that the rates of pay to which he and other drivers in a similar position were entitled were those fixed by the local agreement.

But in calculating 'normal' working hours for the calculation of redundancy payments the courts have adopted rather a different posture. It is no doubt understandable that, when faced with the ordinary situation of a nationally agreed guaranteed week (say, 40 hours) and locally arranged overtime with a ceiling (up to, say, 51 or, in one case, 84 hours in all), judges should insist that the 'normal' week is still the lower figure because the overtime is not obligatory.[26] Indeed, in some of these cases the local agreement just could not be made contractual because the written particulars unambiguously incorporated the 40-hour national working week as 'normal hours'. But that did not seem to be the case in *Loman and Henderson* v. *Merseyside Transport Services*, 1968,[27] where union officials of road haulage workers, whose national agreement guaranteed a 41-hour week, had made a local agreement in 1963 whereby their payment was to be 'on the basis of a 68-hour guaranteed week'. The employers' argument that this agreement was 'in the nature of a gentleman's agreement for ironing out local difficulties' was accepted, Lord Chief Justice Parker being able to 'see at once why a local agreement of this sort is not made contractually binding but is adopted as a gentleman's agreement. If local legally binding agreements were made departing from the National Agreement, it would undoubtedly create demands for a complete overhaul of the National Agreement ... these local arrangements are useful to iron out local labour difficulties . . . employers, as it were, assume ex gratia an obligation to pay . . . on the basis of a 68-hour week, whilst . . . there is no obligation on any workman to work the 68-hour week.' But British industry is riddled with local agreements which 'depart from' national agreements. It will be interesting to see whether the judges maintain this attitude if presented with another Mr Clift, who stands to gain, not lose, by the incorporation of the local agreement into his contract.

Two other problems add to the area of uncertainty. First, not every collective term is appropriate for incorporation into the individual contract of employment. Some of them will be only a code agreed between the collective parties. For example, it is not easy to incorporate into any individual worker's contract the clauses: 'Each Trade Union party to this agreement may have Shop Stewards' (Vehicle Building 1961) or 'the proportion borne by the aggregate number of boys to the aggregate number of men [in certain departments] shall not exceed one boy to every four (or fractional part of four) men' (Boot and Shoe 1962). These are matters between the unions and the employers. Other clauses could be incorporated only with some semantic juggling: e.g. 'No female shall be allowed to use nails longer than $1\frac{1}{4}$ inches' (Packing-case Agreement, 1942). Many other clauses (quite apart from wages, hours, and the like) are capable of being incorporated, e.g. 'Secretaries of Line Committees shall be allowed free rail travel on the Region concerned when engaged in the execution of their secretarial duties' (Railways 1960). With minimum ingenuity this could be expressed as an implied term of the individual contract of employment of each Secretary if the lawyers so desired. Presumably, too, a '100 per cent membership' agreement can become an individual obligation to join a union if incorporated into the employment contract.

The judges have on occasion suggested that they will not extend the area over which terms are deemed appropriate for incorporation into the individual employment contract so as to affect the rights and duties of the employee. In 1966 the Court of Appeal refused to bind a teacher by an arbitration

193

clause in the statutorily regulated 'Burnham' agreements so as to disallow his right to sue for salary in the courts. The arbitration clause was 'designed to prevent disputes arising between teachers' associations and local authorities', i.e. at collective level.

This question is likely to become more rather than less important. Take *Camden Exhibition and Display Ltd.* v. *Lynott*, 1966.[28] The defendants were shop stewards, employees of the plaintiffs, whose written particulars stated that rate of wages, hours, and holiday pay, were 'in accordance with the ... working rule agreement' of the N.J.C. Rule 6(a) stated:

Overtime required to ensure the due and proper performance of contracts shall not be subject to restriction, but may be worked by mutual agreement and direct arrangement between the employer and the operatives concerned.

As part of a dispute about wage increases the defendants had helped to organize an overtime ban. Had they induced the employees to break their contracts? Lord Denning, Master of the Rolls thought they had. Whereas in 'an ordinary contract of employment' a man is not bound to do overtime, here they were bound by the incorporation of this clause. But Lord Justice Russell thought that Rule 6(a) was not appropriate for incorporation. It was an agreement between the members of the N.J.C. who agreed to impose no ceiling on overtime hours and leave them for each man to agree individually. But Lord Denning saw the Rule differently. The first half meant not only that the unions would impose no restriction on overtime but also that the workers would not 'officially or unofficially impose a collective embargo' on overtime when required. In other words, he made the Rule appropriate for incorporation by distinguishing sharply between *collective* and *individual* action by workers.

This point is very relevant to the problem of the collective clause prohibiting strikes, either altogether or before the exhaustion of a grievance procedure. Professor Kahn-Freund has expressed the view that it 'must be quite exceptional' for such a clause to be incorporated into individual employment con-

tracts; but this opinion may well have been overtaken by
events. In the leading case of *Rookes* v. *Barnard* in 1964,
defendant's counsel *conceded* that the draughtsmen employed
by B.O.A.C. were individually bound by the terms of a 'no-
strike' clause in the collective agreement. In future cases, defendants will therefore not be bound by anything decided in the
Rookes case. It is noteworthy, too, that the collective agreement in *Rookes* v. *Barnard* stated: '*The employers* . . . and the
employees . . . undertake that no lock-out or strike shall take
place.' Such a wording is much more appropriate for incorporation than, say: 'The Trade Union agrees that no strike
shall be called.' On these words the obligations may be said to
be reserved to the collective parties who must do their best to
have the members follow their lead. Some commentators, however, argue that, whatever the wording, the 'no-strike' clause
is appropriate only at the collective level, and should not be
made binding on the individual worker as such. They would
point to the interpretations of certain statutes (p. 203), which
indicate that 'no-strike' or 'procedure' clauses do *not* become
terms of individual employment (though that argument is
weakened by clauses in the 1970 Bill which speak of procedure
clauses as able, to some unspecified extent, to be 'terms and
conditions' of the employment). They would also add that a
strike is essentially a collective act. What is it, indeed, that
the worker is obliged not to do, if the procedure clause is binding on him? Presumably, he can still give notice to quit; and
to go on strike without notice is a breach of contract anyway.
What *could* be added by the incorporation of a 'no-strike' or
'procedure' clause to the content of the worker's obligations?
The only answer to this question seems to be an argument analogous to Lord Denning's in the *Camden* decision – i.e. that
the 'no-strike' clause at individual level imports an obligation
not to combine *collectively* to give notice to quit. This is such
a formidable limitation on a man's liberty of action that one
wonders whether judges would accept it lightly. Of course, if
the suggestion made by Lord Denning in *Morgan* v. *Fry*
(p. 110) is correct – namely that a doctrine of 'suspension' of
employment contracts exists, contrary to the usual view – then

the incorporation of a 'no-strike' clause would appropriately limit the novel worker's right to suspend his employment contract.

In truth, apart from the exact wording of the clause, the question of the incorporation of 'no-strike' clauses becomes the question of policy, whether the worker's liability in damages is to be extended by this method as a way of restricting the legality of strike action. It is rather unlikely that judges would think such incorporation exceptional. They would approach the problem with the view, it is thought, that a 'no-strike' clause is not so different from 'penal clauses' withdrawing benefits (bonuses or holiday pay) in the event of certain strikes or, as in recent agreements negotiated by the electricians' union, providing for agreed 'fines' against strikers – all of which can easily be made appropriate to the individual contract. But would the logical consequence also be drawn? If a 'procedure' clause is implied into a worker's contract, then, if the procedure has been exhausted, presumably he has a contractual *right* to strike. Today when procedures often take months, sometimes years, to exhaust the problem is largely academic; but if grievance procedures were ever reformed, it could become a point of some legal consequence.

The second problem arises if the worker takes employment on terms which conflict either with the collective agreement, or with his contract of union membership (e.g. if he takes a lower wage than that specified in the earlier agreement). The law is uncertain; but it seems improbable that any court would today hold that his contract of employment itself was invalid. On the other hand, there is some support in the cases for the view that the union might be legally justified in persuading the other party with whom it had made the earlier agreement (that is, the employer or the worker, respectively, in our examples) to terminate the subsequent employment which undercut the agreed rates.

The judicial atmosphere concerning implication of the collective terms into the worker's contract of employment undoubtedly undergoes changes. The written particulars under the 1963 Act may not (as they should) solve most of the problems; and the question of what is 'appropriate' is bound to present profound issues of policy.

STATUTORY INTERVENTIONS

As Professor Kahn-Freund has said: 'All statutory methods of fixing wages and other conditions of employment are by the law itself considered as a second best. All British labour legislation is, in a sense, a gloss or a footnote to collective bargaining.'[29] The Donovan Report stated: 'Parliament has long been committed to the view that the best means of settling such questions is voluntary collective bargaining.' There have, therefore, been few attempts to make collective agreements compulsorily binding by statute over any area of employment. An Act of 1934 which made it possible for the Minister to do this in the cotton industry with the agreement of both unions and employers was revoked in 1957; and only a few examples exist today. Under the Dock Workers' Order 1967 the dockers' rates of remuneration and their other conditions of service shall be 'in accordance with the national or local agreements for the time being in force'. Such statutory enforcement of collective bargaining is exceptional though there are, of course, other employees whose conditions of employment are affected by special statutory machinery which incorporates elements of collective bargaining (such as school teachers).

Similar exceptions relate to social security legislation under which it is possible for the Minister, if he thinks it expedient, to make an Order approving and giving legal force to a scheme agreed between employers and unions for supplementary benefits and contributions such as certain agreements between the N.U.M. and the N.C.B.

Such rare exceptions apart, Parliament, until 1966, had, over the past sixty years, in peacetime intervened in the sphere of collective bargaining merely to pass statutes which facilitate or prop up the machinery of autonomous negotiation. Thus the Conciliation Act, 1896, and the Industrial Court Act, 1919, aimed to provide not a code of compulsory arbitration, but means to improve conciliation (bringing the parties together) and the machinery of voluntary arbitration (for deciding between them on the merits). The 1896 Act empowers the Minister to inquire into a dispute in existence or likely to exist between employers and workmen or workmen and workmen, to bring the sides together, or to appoint a conciliator if asked by either side, or an arbitrator if asked by both. The most important legacy of the Act is the nation-wide conciliation service of the D.E.P. whose staff is obliged to be fully informed about industrial relations, has been called in to promote productivity bargaining and incomes policy alongside its old task of helping in the formation and maintenance of voluntary joint procedures throughout industry, and participates directly in the settlement of hundreds of disputes every year. In 1966, 310 of their 447 formal interventions succeeded; but the conciliation service 'oils the wheels of voluntary proceedings far more than the statistics tell'.[30] The Ministry of Labour told the Royal Commission: 'It is well known that [the] facility for informal consultation is readily available and sometimes advice given in this way has a preventive value.' The Donovan Report in a now forgotten passage proposed that the hard-worked Industrial Relations Officers of the Ministry be given new powers to help investigate strike-prone localities or factories. But in 1968 there seemed to be only about 55 such Officers. Plans existed to treble their numbers; but the internal structure of the D.E.P. was reorganized and the Industrial Relations Officers were submerged into other branches. Indeed, by August 1970, the patiently constructed conciliation service was in jeopardy for its very existence.

In 1919 the need for a standing arbitration body was felt and the Industrial Court was set up. It is, in effect, a permanent arbitration body with a full-time president, independent chairmen, and representatives of employers and employees on its panel. It sits in divisions, usually composed of the 'collective bargaining' pattern of one employer, one employee, and an independent chairman. The Minister can refer to the Court any 'trade dispute' reported to him by a party only if both parties consent; and where machinery for arbitration already exists, the Minister cannot refer to the Court unless that

machinery has failed. The supremacy of voluntary arrangements is, therefore, safeguarded under this Act; the only real
exception to that principle created by the statute is the Minister's power to appoint, on his own initiative, a court of inquiry
merely to report on a dispute. The findings of the Industrial
Court, or of arbitrators who can, under the Act, be similarly
appointed only with the parties' consent, are not in any sense
'law'. The Industrial Court is not in a legal sense a 'court' at
all, and its ordinary arbitration decisions, as we saw in *Faithful*
v. *Admiralty*, are not automatically binding on contracts of
employment. The Court decided 857 voluntary arbitrations
between 1946 and 1966; single arbitrators 610. Most of the
former were about disputes over claims (for higher wages,
etc); the latter involved about an equal number of claims and
of grievances over discipline or other employment disputes.
Arbitrators are used locally and their reports are not published. Industrial Court awards are published; but normally
the Court does not give reasons. Professor Folke Schmidt has
described the work of the Court as 'the adjustment of the
relations of the parties with a view to the future' (rather than
a search for legalistic 'rights') – which he sees as 'the great
strength in the English system of arbitration'.[31] Moreover, the
Court – and especially its President – has taken pride in its
independent status as arbitrator between the parties who have
voluntarily come for a decision. The Donovan proposal that
'all arbitrators' be bound by law to consider government
'incomes policy' would drastically change the Industrial Court's
character and, probably, the confidence of parties who go to it.

Under the pressure of war in 1915, and again in 1940, forms
of compulsory arbitration were introduced. Both sides of
industry agreed to Order 1305 in 1940, which set up a National
Arbitration Tribunal. The Order (which was especially unpopular after abortive attempts to prosecute North Thames
gas workers and London and Liverpool leaders of a dock
strike in 1950 and 1951) was revoked in 1951 and replaced by
Order 1376, which retained certain features of compulsory
arbitration, though not the illegality of strikes. Under it, certain
types of 'disputes' or 'issues' could be referred by the Minister

to an Industrial Disputes Tribunal (after first attempting a settlement via voluntary machinery). The awards of the Tribunal became compulsory implied terms of all relevant contracts of employment. Although the Order gave rise to legal problems, such as the definition of an 'issue', its procedures were popular with many trade unions, especially those which felt unable to use the strike weapon, or those to whom recognition was refused by employers and who could often bring such employers before the Tribunal. In 1958, however, the Government, under pressure from employers' organizations, revoked the Order and for some months put nothing in its place. (The proposals in 1970 to use compulsory arbitration as the sanction for non-recognition or non-disclosure (pp. 167 and 170) are in direct descent from Order 1376. As we see next, those proposals also drew on the example of the exceptional jurisdictions of the Industrial Court.)

In 1959, the Terms and Conditions of Employment Act, however, established a method of 'extending' by law voluntary collective agreements. Under it a 'claim' can be reported to the Minister by either a trade union or an employers' association representing a 'substantial proportion' of workers or employers in a trade, industry, or section or district of a trade or industry, that a black-sheep employer is not observing the 'recognized terms or conditions' (that is to say, the terms or conditions collectively bargained between the representative parties). The Minister must (as is usual in our legislation) try to settle the claim by negotiation; but if he fails he must refer it to the Industrial Court. If the Court finds that the black-sheep employer is in fact observing terms and conditions for his workers less favourable than the 'recognized' terms, it will make an award compelling him to observe the better terms in the employment of all his workers of the description covered by the claim (whether union members or not). In this case the Industrial Court makes an exceptional, legally enforceable, award. Its decision under this jurisdiction becomes a compulsory implied term in each worker's contract of employment. Since the worker himself cannot initiate the proceedings – only his union, or an employers' association, can do so – the result is an interesting method of amending the individual contracts via collective machinery. The Act should mean that the award must remain an implied term of employment until overtaken by a new collective agreement or a new award. That is surely its objective. But a county court judge in 1964 accepted the notion that an employer might 'contract out' of an award by a subsequent contract with his workers. That would be a highly unfortunate interpretation in view of the pressure which such an employer could put upon workers to contract out. But the Industrial Court itself sometimes seems to assume that it can order for the future. In 1964, for example, it made an award (3006) in one complaint brought against a small Yorkshire employer, Wain, by the Laminated and Coil Spring Workers Union (down to 226 members in 1970). They complained that he had not recently paid the recognized holiday pay to a spring fitter and a spring viceman who had been employed there for some twenty-five years. Wain had in fact previously observed the recognized terms (negotiated in 1962 and 1963 between the union and the Manufacturers' Association) though he did not normally acknowledge union communications. The Court found the case proved and made a backdated award requiring 'the Employer to observe the recognized terms and conditions of employment (*and any subsequently agreed amendments thereto*) as respects all employees from time to time employed by him'. But in award 3142 of 1967, the Court reminded a union that it cannot backdate the award beyond the date when a complaint was made to the employer.

Between 1959 and January 1968, 151 such cases were heard by the Industrial Court in 75 of which the union was successful. A number of these successes – five of the latest sixteen – involved apprentices or young workers, such as the award against Littlewood's Pools (3135) who were paying less than the recognized rates to some lithographic journeymen and an apprentice. One award of 1967 was almost agreed in advance by the two sides (3137); they went to the Court in order to have its award with which to stand firm against the Government's attempt to stop an increase because of incomes policy! Where employers have won, they have in 25 cases shown that they were not engaged in the 'industry' covered by the agreement. For example, the Building Trade Operatives failed to prove that Lord Newborough was in the 'building industry' so as to enforce national rates in respect of Mr Jones, his maintenance foreman on his estate at Llanwnda (3164). Similarly in award 2994 of 1963, the Variety Artistes Federation failed against the B.B.C., partly because its agreements with the I.T.V. companies were not made with a representative employers' body, but partly also on the B.B.C. argument that there was no 'industry' because it was 'unique'. So far, so good. But a further development of this line of thinking has caused the Court to hold that employees cannot be the subject of a claim even if they are in the industry if they are workers not within the *language* of the original collective agreement. Thus, because the agreements for guaranteed employment stated they applied to 'manual workers of federated firms' the T.G.W.U. lost a case against Brook Motors, a firm not in the employers' federation (3168). But one of the major objectives of the Act was to allow the union to claim against the non-federated, and often non-unionized, firm!

The escape route of observing terms 'not less favourable' than the recognized terms of employment, has been the ground of success by employers in 43 cases in the same period. But 'it is not entirely clear whether the court judges [the] argument ... according to the particular terms in issue or the whole range of employment conditions. In many cases it does the former.'[32] The 1970 Bill proposed that the Court be required to judge on the employment conditions taken as a whole. But where the Court finds against the employer it will not be inhibited from making an award because of some present uncertainty in the recognized terms. Thus in making an award (3056) against a small Urban District Council in 1965 the Court stated that it could not say what the overtime rate of pay should be; under the agreement that must be determined by negotiation or by a 'conciliation committee'. In such a case, the 1959 Act plays a part in forcing negotiations on an employer.

Lastly, what are 'terms and conditions of employment'?

After initial hesitation, the Court decided in 1965 that union claims to have 'Procedure Agreements' enforced must fail. These claims, that Newtown Polishing Ltd (3069) or Fairview Caravans Ltd (3059) were not observing the agreed methods of recognition and negotiation with the union or its shop stewards, were about provisions which were not 'terms or conditions of employment' at all within the Act. The same reasoning was repeated in the Tilestone Tiles Ltd award (3105) in 1966. It had been anticipated by Lord Justice Denning in 1955, deciding a case under Order 1376 in which he said that an agreement for settling disputes 'is not, properly speaking, one of the "terms and conditions of employment" at all. It is only machinery for settling a difference.' These decisions restrict the 1959 Act and the terms which it can compulsorily imply into employment contracts to the substantive parts of collective agreements, as against the procedural parts. We saw (p. 195) that such decisions might be used as analogies in the argument about the propriety of incorporating 'procedure' or 'no-strike' clauses into employment contracts. In this connection, it must be noted that a 1969 award, N.A.L.G.O. and Walsall B.C. (3190), appears to say that the Court included National Joint Council procedures for deciding disputes about allowances as within the scope of 'terms and conditions'. But there the Court, according to its habit, gave no reasons; whereas in the Newtown Polishing case it exceptionally explained its award.

By an express provision of the Redundancy Payments Act, 1965, the jurisdiction of the Industrial Court is preserved in a claim under the 1959 Act even if the claim includes complaints that the employer is not making proper redundancy payments. Perhaps the only disadvantage suffered by the workers is that the Court will probably not give a reasoned award; whereas an Industrial Tribunal must give a reasoned decision. As a matter of fact, there is a good case for saying that the practice of not giving reasons, easily defensible in voluntary arbitrations, ought to be jettisoned by the Court in special jurisdictions leading to legally enforceable awards. The 1959 Act, then, is a buttress to autonomous bargaining. It takes for granted a system of voluntary bargaining by 'representative' parties in the industry, and builds on that. It is the nearest the English law ever comes to the practice, common in Europe, of extending a collective agreement by law to cover a whole industry. No such general extension is possible in Britain; but each lagging employer may be dealt with separately where there are 'recognized' terms and conditions in the industry.

THE ENCOURAGEMENT OF FAIR WAGES

Two other pieces of legal machinery encourage collective bargaining. The first rests upon the 'Fair Wages Resolution' passed by the House of Commons, originally in 1891, and in its present form in 1946. Such a Resolution is by itself not 'law' in the strict sense; it is not an Act, merely a direction to the executive by the House of Commons. The current Resolution sets out the conditions – such as the right of workers to join trade unions, which we have met already, (p. 165) – which must be observed by firms to which public contracts are awarded, and which they must guarantee that sub-contractors will observe. Similar conditions are imposed by local authorities.

One Fair Wage condition obliges the contractor to observe terms and conditions, both in respect of wages and otherwise, not less favourable than those recognized in collective bargaining by representative union and employers' associations in the trade or industry. Once again, collective bargaining is taken for granted and its standards are the norm. This obligation the employer must observe in respect of all his employees at the place of work used to execute the contract; and he must be shown to have complied with it for three months. He must display a notice of the Resolution at every place of work concerned. In the case of any 'question' arising as to whether the Resolution is infringed, the dispute is to be referred by the Minister to an independent tribunal, which in effect means the Industrial Court. In 1964, a white-collar trade union used this procedure to complain against a firm, alleging breach of Fair Wages conditions. (The firm was eventually found by the Industrial Court to have failed to display proper notices, but not to have broken its duty to allow freedom of union organization among workers.) The firm resisted the right of the Industrial Court to hear the case, and the union consequently asked the ordinary court of Queen's Bench to compel the Industrial Court to hear the case. The judges held that the Industrial Court had jurisdiction. It was a term of the contracts between the Ministry of Health and the firm that, if the Minister of Labour decided to do so, he could refer questions under the Fair Wages Resolution to the Industrial Court. But, they went on, the Industrial Court could not be *ordered* to act because in this situation it does not act as a body exercising its statutory powers; it is merely a private tribunal for arbitrating disputes, as it were, doing the Minister a favour. The judges could not compel such a private tribunal to sit.[33] Similar arguments lay behind the failure of the B.B.C. to obtain a declaration in 1966 to stop the television technicians' union proceeding in the Industrial Court. A declaration *is* the proper remedy to stop a private arbitrator exceeding his jurisdiction; but Mr Justice Megaw decided that no point of jurisdiction was raised, only 'questions' of interpretation of the Resolution which the Court could decide for itself. (Under its current charter and licence the B.B.C. has ceased to be bound by the Resolution.)

The tribunal's award is an ordinary arbitration award and does not have any automatic legal effect. The sanction against the employer, in effect, is the ultimate loss of government contracts. Nor does the display of the notice necessarily help the worker. In *Simpson* v. *Kodak*, 1948,[34] a worker employed at some £6 7s. 6d. a week claimed that the proper Fair Wage minimum had for months been £8 18s. 0d., the figure negotiated between his union and an employers' association and accepted by the then National Arbitration Tribunal. The judge refused to imply the higher wage into the worker's contract merely because the employer displayed a Fair Wages notice at work. Indeed, he thought that if the worker could know about such matters via the notice and still accepted wages lower than the recognized rates, this must be 'strong evidence' that he was choosing to accept the wages as a compliance by the employer with Fair Wages standards! Such is the weakness, in the absence of statutory compulsion, of the ordinary 'implied term' when it meets any obstacle in the form of an express term – here the express wage of £6 7s. 6d. Moreover, although in theory the Resolution is a powerful defence for workers employed by contractors with Government, it is noticeable that only 31 cases on it came before the Industrial Court between 1946 and 1967. Whether this is because the Resolution is not enforced or very well enforced is not clear.

But in some cases the Fair Wages clause has been brought more fully into the sphere of law. Certain statutes make compliance with this standard the condition of a licence, subsidy, or similar privilege. For example, it is a condition of obtaining a licence to operate a passenger bus service. Failure to observe the recognized terms allows a trade union to complain to the licensing authority and, eventually, to take the case to the Industrial Court as the T.G.W.U. did successfully in 1968 in the case of Greyhound Luxury Coaches Arbroath (3163). The sanction here is the suspension or revocation of the licence. The worker's protection rests in the hands of his union to set in motion the legal machinery.

Sometimes, however, statutes take a further step. For example, where a company other than a professional carrier employs drivers to drive its own lorries for the transport of goods, observance of fair wages has since 1938 been imposed by statute. Failure to observe 'fair wages' (of which one of a number of tests in this case is the collectively agreed rate) can be a criminal offence; but in this case, either a workers' union or the worker himself can complain to the Minister, who may eventually refer the matter to the Industrial Court for a decision. Twelve of the 19 cases taken to the Court between 1946 and 1966 were begun by individual workers. And here the Court's award is legally enforceable as a compulsory implied term of the worker's contract of employment. Then – and only then – the lorry driver can sue for the fair wage. The Fair Wages clause becomes 'law' in the full sense.

Similar statutes allow certain workers eventually to enforce recognized terms as compulsory implied terms of their employment in the sugar industry, in television, and in the film and cinematograph industry. A different, but analogous, scheme applies to civil aviation. The worker was in the film industry in *Simpson* v. *Kodak*; but no award of the Industrial Court had been obtained, so that the express terms of the employment still held sway and the worker was without remedy in the ordinary courts. Once such an award has been obtained, however, the employer and employee cannot under these statutes vary it by agreement, for they all make it quite clear that the parties (in effect, the employer) cannot evade them by 'agreement'. Thus such workers are clearly in a better position *legally* than the employee who works under an ordinary collective agreement untouched by statute.

Lastly, however, it was suggested to the Royal Commission that the logic connecting these statutes is 'rather slender'. There are many firms in receipt of government subsidies and the like which do not have laid upon them the reciprocal legal duty to observe 'fair wages'. The Commission was asked to recommend that all assistance of this kind should entail a 'fair wages' condition (including a formal, instead of as now informal, condition against racial discrimination), and that the remedies available should be made into a more regular pattern, with the union always having the right to apply for rescission of the subsidy or licence.[35] But unaccountably the Donovan Report made no such proposal.

MINIMUM WAGE LEGISLATION

Britain does not have a legal minimum wage for all workers, as some countries do. This point we consider again in Chapter 5. But since 1909 minimum wage legislation has attempted to protect special groups of workers who are thought to be relatively unable to protect themselves. At first it applied to the 'sweated trades'; today it is supposed to apply where union organization is weaker. Two statutes, the Wages Councils Act, 1959, and the Agricultural Wages Act, 1948 (with the Scottish

Agriculture Act, 1949), govern the current situation. Apart from agriculture, the industries in which Wages Councils fix compulsory minimum wages are specified in Orders made by the Ministry of Labour. Fifty-four Wages Councils covered some three and a half million workers by 1970, of whom about two and a half million were in the catering, distributive, or hairdressing trades, in half a million establishments.

The Minister (now Secretary of State) has to decide whether to establish a Wages Council for an industry; the initiative may come either from him or from a Joint Industrial Council in the industry; and he must be assisted, in most cases, by the report of a commission of inquiry. (The 1970 Bill would have substituted the C.I.R.) The critical questions to be decided are whether adequate bargaining machinery exists, or is likely to cease to exist, or be adequate; and whether a reasonable standard of remuneration exists or is likely to be maintained for the workers concerned. On the first, the relevant considerations include not only the scope of the machinery and the agreements made but also the extent to which there is non-observance in fact of those agreements in the industry. It is only if the Minister is satisfied that no adequate voluntary bargaining exists in the industry that he will establish a Wages Council for it. Even then he must publish his intention to do so, so that objections can be received; and the Order must be laid before Parliament.

The way in which the Wages Council is planned to be a substitute for collective bargaining is apparent once more, however, in the constitution of the Council. It consists of employers' and employees' representatives, chosen after consultation, and independent members, in equal numbers. The voting is effected by 'sides', and the independent side does not vote in practice if the rest of the Council agrees. The Council may submit wage regulation proposals to the Minister for fixing by Order the workers' remuneration generally, or pay for a group of workers; or payments in particular circumstances (e.g. for sickness, injury, or for a guaranteed week); and proposals, also, for fixing holidays and holiday pay in the trade. Although the Council cannot deal with other conditions of work, its flexible control over remuneration (including over-time, piece, and time rates, and other payments) gives it a powerful influence over them and it can initiate an inquiry into conditions generally if it thinks this should be done. The Minister cannot amend the Council's published proposals; he must accept or refer the proposals back to it for reconsideration, and most Wages Councils have a tradition of independence from Government control. This can lead to a series of references to, and stubborn unamended resubmissions by, a Council, as in the case of the Industrial Canteens and Wool Reclamation Councils during the 1961 'pay pause', when the Minister gave way but postponed the date of the Order. Similarly, in 1966 and 1967 the Government felt compelled to ask a number of Wages Councils to refrain from making proposals inconsistent with the 'incomes policy'. But the (now defunct) Prices and Incomes Act, 1968, gave power to impose a legal 'standstill' on Wages Orders (and Agricultural Wages Orders – the Agricultural Wages Board makes its own Orders without reference to the Minister). The N.B.P.I. in Report 27 on the pay of workers in Retail Drapery and similar trades in 1967 made a number of drastic proposals to change the structure and powers of Wages Councils which it appeared to see as enemies of effective national 'incomes policies' because many workers in their industries earned more than the minimum but often received increases as though they did not.

If and when an Order is made by the Minister, or by the Agricultural Wages Board, it has the force of law. Its terms become compulsory terms of the contracts of employment between all employers and workers specified in it, laying down a regulatory code for the entire trade. Employers are so informed; they must display a notice of the new terms and keep records to prove their compliance; and they cannot avoid the compulsory terms by contract with the employees. The worker has the right to sue for breach of contract to recover any under-payment below the statutory rate up to six years back; and he has the right to be awarded up to two years' back pay in less expensive summary proceedings in which the employer is prosecuted for the crime of infringing the Order –

an unusual mixture of criminal punishment and civil compensation in English legal procedure. In addition, the Secretary of State appoints Wages Inspectors under this legislation. The Inspectors have extensive powers to enforce the minimum wage Orders, powers, for example, to enter premises and demand records, and they may both prosecute offending employers and institute actions against them in the name of underpaid workers.

In 1969, some 8,564 complaints were received, the wages of over 271,000 workers examined, and £171,000 arrears paid to 13,000 workers. There were only 146 Inspectors, yet they conducted 50,000 inspections among the half-million workplaces available – about one a day for each Inspector. The importance of the inspectorate lies perhaps in its ability to persuade employers who are often ignorant of the statutory rates to pay them; and legal action is taken only when the offences appear deliberate or repeated. Certainly the figures for litigation make one *hope* that this is so. In 1969 there were no prosecutions (ten in 1964); and civil proceedings against three employers yielded £24 12s. 2d.!

The substitutive character of the legislation is best gauged from the use by the Secretary of State of his power to vary the scope of or to abolish a Wages Council, either on his own initiative or on the recommendation of joint bodies in the industry. The abolition of a Wages Council is a success for autonomous collective bargaining. In one sense, the first objective of any Wages Council should be to commit suicide. Since 1946, fifteen Wages Councils have been abolished in industries ranging from tin box, and fustian cutting, to cutlery, and drift nets mending. The Donovan Report and the 1970 Bill proposed to give power to the Secretary of State to abolish wherever a trade union convinced him that the workpeople no longer needed the council to maintain reasonable wages. The constitution of a Wages Council itself shows that it can be a training ground for bargaining; and as the process of stimulating collective bargaining goes on, industries can reach the stage where in some parts the statutory wage regulation is still critical, while in other sectors autonomous collective negotiation forges ahead. The 1959 legislation made the Wages Councils and the exceptional jurisdiction of the Industrial Court under the Terms and Conditions of Employment Act mutually exclusive. The Report and the Bill also proposed amendments so that, when higher rates have been negotiated voluntarily in a section of a trade, the union could use the extension procedure against a 'lagging' employer before the formal abolition or variation of the Council. But the Donovan Report also supported a complaint by some unions that the Wages Council system could sometimes act not as a stimulant to collective bargaining but as a barrier to union recruitment and voluntary negotiation. But a revised structure for Wages Councils, when it comes, is more likely to be affected by the outcome of current debates about a minimum wage (p. 259) since most of the workers concerned fall into the low-paid category. About 10 per cent of them still in 1969 earned less than £15 a week; and until 1970 the basic agricultural rate for a 43-hour week was still £13 13s. 0d. Small wonder that the N.B.P.I. was asked in March 1970 to study the problems of half a million workers on poverty wages, including some, such as laundry workers, under Wages Councils. Whatever else the latter have done, as the Donovan Report showed, they have not solved the problem of low pay.

PRICES AND INCOMES POLICIES

The year 1966 marks a watershed. In that year a new type of legislation on collective bargaining made its appearance, one whereby the Government attempted to control 'awards and settlements' that are the outcome of collective bargaining. The Government had, of course, for long been in the business of influencing it in a host of ways – fiscal measures; resistance to wage increases where the Government was, or stood behind, the employer; even distribution of statistics to 'inform' arbitrators. But broadly, from the days of the Labour Government's 'wage freeze' in 1948 to the era of the Conservative administration's 'Three Wise Men' and 'National Incomes Commission', the special institutions set up were not accompanied by powers of legal intervention. The method of a special Commission to report and influence 'public opinion' had become normal before the N.B.P.I. was set up in April 1965. In 1964, the Government had said that this machinery would be backed by compulsion only if the 'voluntary method' failed; and in a 'Joint Declaration of Intent', the T.U.C. and employers undertook to cooperate to give 'effective shape' to the machinery to keep increases in incomes and prices in line with efficiency and productivity. The T.U.C. had already established its own scrutiny of wage claims, and, though not accepting the same 'norms' for rises in every case as the Government would like, it tried to obtain by consent a co-ordination and, in places, restraint in wage demands, not wishing (as it said in November 1966) to replace 'one kind of authoritarianism by another'. At the same time the Government began to institute a voluntary system whereby employers notified it of wage and price increases. Thus, throughout the period, voluntary action was encouraged.

But in 1966 the first Prices and Incomes Act was enacted. Its form was changed late in the day in the face of an economic crisis to include Part IV which was operative only for one year. This Part (so obscure in places as to lend credence to the apocryphal story that it had to be drafted over the weekend while the Prime Minister was returning from a visit to Moscow) gave the Minister power to ban wage increases outright. Its defects were such, however, that a number of actions were brought in the courts to enforce contracts for increases which it was meant, but failed, to stop. Apart from that twelve-month legislative maverick, however, the Act did mainly three things which have remained the chief headings of discussion about legislation ever since. Since we have not heard the last of incomes policy, a summary of them is worth-while.

First, Part I established the N.B.P.I. on a statutory basis, allowing the Government to refer any 'question' on incomes, employment terms, or prices to it. The statute gave the N.B.P.I. powers to compel testimony on pain of a fine which, although a big union did once threaten not to appear, have never had to be used. The job of the Board as set out in Part 1 was to examine the 'question' with reference to the current White Paper expressing Government incomes policy.

Secondly, the core of the Act was Part II, to be brought into effect by Order for twelve months (first done in August 1967). Its sections give to the Secretary of State a set of 'weapons' which he can fire off; but, contrary to popular belief, until he pulls the relevant trigger, by Order or directive, no *legal* obligation rests on anyone (either to abstain from, or even to report, wage increases). Thus, he can by Order enforce the reporting of any 'claims' about pay or other conditions of employment. Under Section 14 he can order that future awards and settlements be reported within seven days, in which case they must not be implemented until notified and for a further 'standstill' period of thirty days or longer if referred to the N.B.P.I. In practice, what was used was neither of those sections, but Section 15 under which he can give a 'direction' putting a legal 'standstill' on the implementation of an award or settlement referred to the N.B.P.I. as a 'question' under Part I. This basic structure was parallel to a set of sections on prices and charges.

How long could this 'standstill' last? Under the 1966 Act the maximum period was three months (or four under Section 14, the extra thirty days normally applying to that section). But the 1967 and 1968 Acts, apart from extending control over dividends, also extended the basic standstill period first to six months and then to eleven months from *reference* to the Board where the N.B.P.I. made an 'adverse recommendation' in regard to the increase. But various loopholes had now appeared. For example, if a collective settlement had already been implemented the Secretary of State seemed to have no power to fire his weapons. The 1967 Act therefore forged a new one which he could trigger off to apply Section 15 to a settlement 'by reference to a date not more than three months' before he acted *'as if'* it had not been implemented; and in this case the extended period of standstill began with the date of the *direction* (which could 'come into force' at a date later than either its own publication or the reference to the Board). These retroactive directions were used in a number of cases, such as the municipal busmen's agreement. But the criteria enforced in Government White Papers began to clash with reality to such an extent that in January 1969 the N.B.P.I. Report (101) on agricultural workers accepted that their increase could not satisfy them but asked the Government to make an exception and not use its powers, which it agreed to do.

Thirdly, what was the sanction for breach of a standstill? The civil consequences were for a while obscure: but the 1967 Act made it clear that a contract of employment became invalid only in respect of the amount of the remuneration 'in excess of the restriction', no right to which could exist. Also, it is noticeable that disputes about 'standstill' restrictions or differences of opinion about their effect were always stated to be included within the legal concept of 'trade dispute' (see Chapter 7), and that Section 16 of the 1966 Act was stated not to give rise (except for the liabilities next set out) to 'criminal or tortious liability for conspiracy or any other liability in tort' (a material point on strikes in Chapter 8: p. 385). That Section made it a crime for (a) an employer to implement the wage-increase during a standstill, and (b) any person or trade union to take any action, including strike action, 'with a view to compel induce or influence' an employer so to do. The penalty was a fine of £100 (or for companies £500). Proceedings, however, could not be brought without the consent of the Attorney-General. The offence in (b) is committed only if committed with the stated end 'in view'. Thus when a group of drivers withdrew extra working which they alleged was the price of their frozen productivity increase, they could easily argue that they were not committing any crime. They were just freezing their end of the bargain.

Moreover, pay increases awarded unilaterally by employers do not seem to be pay 'settlements' caught by Section 16. Some employers resorted to non-cash bonuses – 'ranging from holidays in Bermuda to washing machines', the *Financial Times* reported in 1966. Most important, however, the section itself states that it is *not* unlawful, once the standstill period ends, for an employer to pay 'any sum in respect of remuneration for employment at an earlier time', i.e. during the standstill period.

Since that is lawful, it follows that it is no contravention of the section to put pressure (even by striking) on the employer *during* the standstill period with a view to inducing him to promise that, once the period ends, he will *then* pay retrospectively. The ban then becomes not so much of a 'standstill' as a dam of limited duration. This tactic was successfully employed by some unions. For example, municipal bus workers received retrospective payments of money 'frozen'; and in Report 68 the N.B.P.I. to whom pay agreements between certain employers and the draughtsmen's union had been referred on a standstill direction, remarked despairingly that the employers

have indicated their intention of making the payment retrospectively on the expiry of the standstill regardless of what our judgment may be.

Many employers also opposed the Acts. The C.B.I., however, at the same time called for strengthened 'reserve powers' for the Government for the period following devaluation. The terminology of 'reserve powers' has been used on all sides to fit the Acts into the philosophy of a voluntary system. But their effect was, of course, to create a widespread belief that it is illegal to have pay increases or, at least, not to report them whether or not the Minister fired off a Part II weapon (an interesting psychological effect of law on social attitude which those who like the policy tend to commend as the benefit of 'reserve powers' and those who dislike it tend to call a 'confidence trick'). 'Reserve powers' clearly have a direct effect upon the 'voluntary' character of bargaining. The best illustration arose when late in 1968 Mrs Castle, after weeks of negotiation over an agreed rise of 3d. an hour for building workers, produced a compromise whereby the parties agreed to accept a 1d. cut per hour in the settlement, the 'reserve' threat being that if this was unacceptable the whole 3d. would have to be put under standstill. Indeed the semantics of incomes policy came to resemble those of Humpty Dumpty in *Alice*. It therefore comes as a breath of fresh air when someone puts clearly what is involved in the enforcement of incomes policies. Thus, Mr Shonfield has said:

Labour is really being asked to give its consent to a particular type of social order. There is no reason why it should willingly do so – or for that matter why the owners of capital should positively assent to any alternative proposed. They may, of course, be compelled to do so. But what a fully fledged 'incomes policy' really implies is the equivalent of a new Social Contract: it presupposes a society in which the different interest groups have marked out a sufficient area of agreement about the present distribution of wealth to deny themselves the right to try, in the future, to obtain certain advantages at each other's expense ... a practical approach to a more rational wages policy must be deliberately and extensively political. It must stand ready to include in the bargain a wide range of issues concerned with the ordinary man's notions of social justice ... it seems unlikely that people in a democratic society will accept a policy of wage restraint unless the composition of all other domestic incomes which affect costs, however remotely, is brought under close and expert scrutiny.[36]

We have seen that the imposition of incomes policy by law must affect the very institutions of collective bargaining. These damaging effects, together with the doubt whether the policy could be made effective by law, led the Labour Government to announce that it would 'de-escalate' statutory controls after 1969. The Conservative Opposition also opposed the Acts and planned to replace the N.B.P.I. with a Productivity Board (in the context of their more legalistic code for industrial relations). In 1970 the Labour Government published a Bill to merge the N.B.P.I. and the Monopolies Commission into a Commission on Industry and Manpower. The C.I.M. would have considerable power to investigate, control prices charged by, and demand disclosure from large companies; but none of the 'standstill' powers over collective agreements were to remain. The only powers over incomes would be those of obtaining advisory reports and the Minister's power to demand advance notification of 'claims'. At the same time, the voluntary bodies were adapting their policies, the T.U.C. merging its Incomes Policy Committee into the new Collective Bargaining Committee after the 1969 Congress had voted for the repeal of the Prices and Incomes Acts lock, stock and barrel.

But until the C.I.M. Bill became law (it lapsed with the

General Election and the new Conservative administration's plans do not appear to include the establishment of such a powerful body) the Government claimed it must have, as a 'bridging operation', some reserve powers. De-escalation was not, apparently, the same as disarmament. An Order was therefore made just before all the 'standstill' statutes lapsed at the end of 1969, preserving the *original* Part II of the 1966 Act for a further twelve months.[37] Thus, for the period to the end of 1970 the Government retained its power to fire the old weapons for a three, or four, months' standstill; but *without* the power, it seemed, given under the 1967 Act to catch settlements already implemented, and with the same possibilities, as the C.B.I. immediately warned employers, for retrospective settlements after the standstill. Although many wage claims were made and met in the first six months of 1970, the Government did not use its reserve powers. Critics had argued that incomes policy not only had not helped the lower-paid (for whom it was said to be partly devised) but gave rise to inflationary effects and a 'neurotic atmosphere' in relations between Government and trade unions; and by May 1970, the Director-General of the National Economic Development Council ('Neddy') said a legally-backed wage freeze was impractical, poor psychology and bad economics.[38]

In a society which is still as unequal as Britain in its distribution of wealth (perhaps in this context a more important factor than 'incomes') laws which allow a Government to ban or hold up agreed wage increases can hardly be popular. Nor is there yet the consensus on which any 'new Social Contract' can be based. As has been said in the United States:

No stretch of psychological analysis concerning the spur of ambition, the spice of constant emulation, the staleness and flatness of uniformity, can prevail against the universal conviction that the maximum of human happiness is not promoted by great, glaring, permanent inequality.[39]

The attempt to introduce incomes policy 'guidelines' has been more or less given up in the U.S.A. Nevertheless there is concern about the way in which collective bargaining can be accommodated to the community's need to avoid inflation (whether or not 'wage-push' is the primary cause). The interesting proposal has, for example, recently been made that American law, which already enforces bargaining between employers and representative unions 'could compel the parties, as part of the duty to bargain, to discuss in good faith the application to the particular firm of the several flexible guideposts promulgated' by the Government.[40] We are back, therefore, to the reform and modernization of collective bargaining.

The traditional British role for the law, supporting voluntary bargaining by the creation of new institutions, may well have more to offer than blunt legal sanctions wielded by Ministers or judges under Prices and Incomes Acts or through some compulsory contractual status for collective agreements. The lawyer is at his best in collective bargaining when he brings his skills to bear as an auxiliary to help the parties, at his worst when they see him as prosecuting counsel in wig and gown. After the lawyer has forgotten the case or the Minister has forgotten the 'standstill' Order, the parties in industry will still be there in the factory getting on with the negotiations as best they can. As Dean Shulman of Yale Law School said in 1955:

But the courts cannot, by occasional sporadic decision, restore the parties' continuing relationship; and their intervention in such cases may seriously affect the going systems of self-government. When their autonomous system breaks down, might not the parties better be left to the usual methods for adjustment of labor disputes rather than to court actions on the contract or on the arbitration award. I suggest that the law stay out – but, mind you, not the lawyers.[41]

1. Phelps Brown, *The Growth of British Industrial Relations*, p. 362.
2. On procedures and statistics, see Marsh and McCarthy, 'Disputes Procedures in Britain' (1968), *R.C. Research Paper No. 2* (Part 2); and Wedderburn and Davies, op. cit., chapter 5. The *Donovan Report*, Chapters I I to V I I, contains relevant material.
3. Allan Flanders, *Industrial Relations: What is Wrong with the System?* (1965), p. 28.
4. A. I. Marsh, 'Disputes Procedures in British Industry' (1966), *R.C. Research Paper No. 2* (Part 1), p. 18.
5. See Wedderburn, 'Conflicts of Rights and Conflicts of Interests in Labor Disputes' in *Dispute Settlement Procedures in Five Western European Countries* (ed. B. Aaron; 1969), p. 65; and see Sten Edlund, 'Settlement through Negotiation of Disputes', in *Scandinavian Studies in Law*, 1968, p. 11.
6. See the report on Recommendation 130 by J. de Givry, 'Labour Courts' (1968) V I *Brit. J. Industrial Relations*, pp. 364–5.
7. A. I. Marsh, *Industrial Relations in Engineering* (1963), pp. 88–90.
8. G. S. Bain, 'Trade Union Growth and Recognition' (1967), *R.C. Research Paper No. 6*, p. 29.
9. *R. v. N.J.C. for Dental Technicians* [1953] 1 All E.R. 327, 328.
10. [1964] 1 All E.R. 494.
11. *The System of Industrial Relations in Great Britain* (ed. Flanders and Clegg; 1954), pp. 57–8; *Labour Law – Old Traditions and New Developments* (1968), p. 25.
12. [1969] 1 W.L.R. 339; [1969] 2 Q.B. 303.
13. See for most of these Wedderburn, *Cases and Materials on Labour Law*, Chapter 3, Section B, p. 267; cf. the Boot and Shoe Agreement, p. 327.
14. N. Selwyn (1969) 32 *Modern Law Review* 377. See too, B. Hepple, [1970] *Cambridge Law J.* 122.
15. *Sunday Times*, 9 March 1969. See too, Selwyn, op. cit., p. 390.
15a. *The System of Industrial Relations in Great Britain* (1970), p. 469.
16. *Report of the Payne Committee*, Cmnd 3909 (1969) para. 590. Of the twelve members, only two signed the Report without adding notes of reservation or dissent.
17. See *Labour Courts and Grievance Settlement in Four Western*

European Countries (ed. B. Aaron: U.C.L.A.) 1969: lectures by X. Blanc Jouvan, G. Giugni, T. Ramm, Folke Schmidt and K. W. Wedderburn.

18. *Evidence to Royal Commission*, Day 41, p. 1757–8. Compare, too, Allan Flanders' insistence on the need for management to initiate reform, and the marginal relevance of legal sanction, *Collective Bargaining: Prescription for Change* (1968), p. 55 et seq.

19. *Holland* v. *London Society of Compositors* (1924) 40 T.L.R. 440 (C.A.).

20. Sachs J. in *Rookes* v. *Barnard* [1961] 2 All E.R. 825 at p. 827; neither the C.A. nor the H.L. on appeal had to decide this point, but Donovan L. J. clearly had doubts about the agency view: see [1963] 1 Q.B. 623 (C.A.); [1964] 1 A.C. 1129 (H.L.). The matter did not arise for direct decision because counsel *conceded* that a collective clause bound individual workers not to strike; see *post*, p. 361.

21. (1969) 4 I.T.R. 206.

22. *N.C.B.* v. *Galley* [1958] 1 All E.R. 91.

23. See pp 129; and *Parry* v. *Holst* (1968) 3 I.T.R. 317 (moving worker from South Wales to Somerset); *Callison* v. *Ford Motor Co.* (1969) 4 I.T.R. 74 (tribunal: right to regrade).

24. *Dudfield* v. *Ministry of Works*; *Faithful* v. *Admiralty* (1964), *The Times*, January 24.

25. *The Times* (1967), October 28. See too R(U) 11/64 (collectively agreed 'disappointment money'; term to pay it to casual worker 'implied from the course of conduct').

26. See *Pearson* v. *William Jones* [1967] 2 All E.R. 1062; *Darlington Forge Ltd* v. *Sutton* (1968) 3 I.T.R. 196.

27. (1968) 3 I.T.R. 108; see (1969) 32 *Modern Law Review* 99.

28. [1966] 1 Q. B. 555 (C.A.) (the defendants were protected by the Trade Disputes Act, 1906, on any view: see p. 332).

29. *The System of Industrial Relations in Great Britain*, ed. Flanders and Clegg, p. 66.

30. Wedderburn and Davies, op. cit., p. 222–3 (from which many of the other statistics in this part of the chapter are taken).

31. Folke Schmidt, 'Conciliation, Adjudication and Administration: Three Methods of Decision Making', in *Dispute Settlement Procedures in Five Western European Countries* (ed. B. Aaron; 1969), pp. 52–60.

32. Wedderburn and Davies, op. cit., p. 206.

33. *R. v. Industrial Court, ex parte A.S.S.E.T.* [1965] 1 Q.B. 377.
34. [1948] 2 K.B. 184.
35. K. W. Wedderburn, *Evidence*, Day 31, 1966, p. 1281.
36. A. Shonfield, *Modern Capitalism* (1965), pp. 218–19.
37. Prices and Incomes Act, 1966 (Continuation Part II) Order 1969, S.I. 1830; see *Productivity, Prices and Incomes Policy After 1969* (Cmnd 4237).
38. Dr J. Bray, *The Times*, 16.12.69; F. Catherwood, *Financial Times*, 11.5.70. And see R. Lipsey and A. Parkin, 'Incomes Policy: A Reappraisal', (1970) 37 *Economica* 115; N. Bosanquet, *Pay, Prices and Labour in Power* (Young Fabian Pamphlet 20, 1969).
39. F. W. Taussig, *Principles of Economics* (1911; 1936 ed.), p. 207. On inequality in Britain see the summary of recent writing by R. Blackburn in Chapter 1 of *The Incompatibles* (1967; ed. R. Blackburn and A. Cockburn) showing that as far as wealth is concerned, in the words of Professor J. E. Meade, we live, not in a semi-socialist state, but in an anti-socialist state'. See too, *Poverty and the Labour Government* (Child Poverty Action Group Pamphlet 3, 1970).
40. H. H. Wellington, *Labor and the Legal Process* (1968), p. 324.
41. H. Shulman, 'Reason, Contract and Law in Labor Relations' (1955) 68 *Harvard Law Review* 999 at p. 1024.

CHAPTER 5

STATUTORY CONTROL OF EMPLOYMENT

APART from the Acts of Parliament just discussed, the function of which has been largely, as we saw, to underpin collective bargaining, statutory control over employment has fallen for historical reasons into two main categories: (A) regulation of the payment of wages; and (B) control of conditions at work. Of these the second provides us with much the greater volume of legislation, ranging from the welfare and safety of workers to hours of work in certain cases. In the latter area there has been a fluctuating boundary between the methods of legal enactment and autonomous bargaining. There is today a huge amount of statute law about safety and accident prevention at work – a body of law of the highest importance – and some modern examples of its operation in relation to both judge-made law and the judges' interpretation of the Acts appear in the next chapter on 'Compensation for Injury at Work'.

A. Payment of Wages

Truck: From 1464 onwards a continuous succession of statutes tried to stop the abuses which in the nineteenth century were described as the 'Truck' and 'Tommy Shop' systems. 'Truck' describes any system whereby the worker is paid in something other than coin of the realm (e.g in kind); and, in Dr Batt's words: ' "Tommy Shop" was the name given to a shop, generally run by the employer or his relatives, where the vouchers or credits given in lieu of wages could be exchanged for goods, often of inferior quality ... the opportunities for abuse in the hands of unscrupulous employers or their managers make the whole system stink.'[1] Practices of this kind were manifold; and we still have on the statute-book Bradlaugh's self-explanatory Payment of Wages in Public Houses Prohibition Act,

1883. The general abuse of the truck system was struck at by an Act which repealed previous partial measures in 1831. There was rising resentment at the operations of certain 'truck-masters', especially among small employers; and the Act itself was the result of both new trade union pressure, liberated by the first legalization in 1825 of rudimentary union organization, and the dislike of some larger employers, one of whom introduced it into Parliament.[2]

The effect of the Truck Act, 1831, is to enforce payment of wages to workmen in cash and not in kind. The wages of any 'artificer', said the 1831 Act, 'shall be made payable in the current Coin of this Realm only and not otherwise'. Any contract to the contrary is 'illegal, null and void' and the employer commits a crime. The employer must not impose any restrictions as to where or how the wages shall be spent; nor can he recover the price of any goods supplied on credit to the worker, nor even set off sums allegedly owing for goods supplied. The 1831 Act was not very successful in practice. Amending statutes to improve it did not succeed until Bradlaugh got an Act on to the statute book in 1887.

After that date the Truck Acts applied to all 'workmen' as defined in the Employers and Workmen Act, 1875. This definition of 'workmen' comprises, in effect, all *manual workers*', except domestic or menial servants. (But 'servants in husbandry' could still be provided with 'food, drink not being intoxicating, a cottage or other allowance or privileges' as part of the remuneration; today the Agricultural Wages Board has power to define and value such wages in lieu of cash so that they cannot be used to avoid the minimum wage.) The test in regard to 'manual labour' is whether that is the substantial part of the employment or whether it is merely ancillary to the job. So, judges have at various times decided that bus drivers with repairing duties are, but a tram driver and a bus conductor are not, 'manual workers'; a grocer's assistant and a hairdresser were not, but a seamstress was. (The same test is used in defining a 'factory': p. 275). Even 'domestic servant' has caused difficulty. In 1940 a stoker-mechanic who lived in at a hospital, tended the boilers, and assisted the engineers was held to be a 'domestic' servant so as to fall outside the Acts. Lord Justice Du Parcq said this was a domestic establishment no less than a 'boarding school' or a 'residential college in a university'.

Everybody who has been into large country houses knows that many of them built in comparatively recent days relied on coal fires for their heating but now one will find that in many of them central heating has been adopted and where there is central heating there are boilers and boilers need attendants.[3]

The 1875 definition of 'workmen', however, although confined to non-domestic manual workers, extended beyond a 'contract of service'; it expressly included a 'contract to execute any work or labour'. Thus the term 'workman' bears a very peculiar meaning here, one apt to include, for once, the self-employed man. Yet there is no intrinsic reason today for a prohibition that applies only to manual workers and not to white-collar workers. Indeed, the former may well be better defended against abuses by a strong union than the latter. The Act of 1831 allowed the employer to make certain deductions (e.g. for medical attendance; food on the premises if agreed by special contract; rent for a dwelling; provender to beasts); and later statutes have added more, e.g. deductions for income tax; national insurance; deductions under the dockworkers' pension scheme; certain superannuation deductions from wages fixed by a Wages Council; and, after 1958, deductions for maintenance to a wife where the earnings are attached by the courts – the last being an exception to yet another Act of 1870 forbidding attachment of wages. As we saw (p. 184) a movement of opinion allowed Parliament to enact in 1970 a new extension of attachment of wages for the enforcement of civil debts. By an irony of history, the traditional objections of the trade unions were replaced by protests from the Association of British Chambers of Commerce at the prospect of employers becoming debt-collecting agencies with all the trouble that might entail as a worker moved from job to job. Indeed, in so far as the new Act is effective in facilitating enforcement of debts against workers to the last penny, it may blunt one of the major deterrents against the hire-purchase or credit salesman who knows that a family cannot really afford what he induces them to buy. While the Lord Chancellor, Lord Gardiner, enthused over the reform – England is 'almost the only civilized country which has still got imprisonment for debt' – others wondered whether this was another neat legal idea which would promote very different social policies from those intended by its authors. It is to be hoped that it does not assist Britain down the path to the American condition where the person most frequently found among bankrupts (now over 200,000 a year) is an industrial worker in his late thirties, married over twelve years, with four dependants, earning over £40 a week.

Apart from the statutes allowing deductions, however, which include special disciplinary deductions at work legalized in 1896 (see p. 228), the Truck Acts demand that the full wage be paid in coin or notes (not cheques, money orders or the like). An employer was convicted of infringing this rule in a rare prosecution in October 1969. In 1906 the judges held that the employer cannot even deduct sums owing to himself under a judgment against the worker for breach of his contract of employment. In 1936, after a depression in the trade, employees of a cotton company agreed to take shares in the enterprise and pay for them by deductions from wages; the court held that the Acts had been infringed and the workers could in law recover all the amounts deducted. Lord Justice Scott said:

The money must be paid over so completely and finally that it then and there becomes the workman's very own ... subject to no sort or kind of understanding however tacit ...

The contrast between manual and non-manual workers is odd today. For example, you can pay only your white-collar employee partly in luncheon vouchers. But in 1940, when a workman challenged deductions for meals provided by the employer without special contract, he (and thousands like him) suddenly found themselves able to claim large sums from employers. A hasty Act was passed to protect employers from any other similar claims arising before 1940. When in 1963 proposals were made for incentive payments of trading stamps

225

geared to time lost through accident or injury at work, the difficulty of the Truck Acts was promptly raised. This difficulty at first sight inhibits the spread of the 'check-off', the deduction of trade union dues at source by the employer. The Donovan Report, which had a special research study made of this practice, reported that some two million trade unionists worked under a 'check-off' system, the majority in the public sector, but the rest spread among 1,200 firms.[4] The study showed that there had been a rapid growth of the practice in the 1960s. Some unions prefer the regular contact with members which collection of subscription demands of local officials and dislike the amount of information the 'check-off' gives to the employer. But the efficiency and stability of the system, especially in a closed shop, led the Donovan Report to recommend it to employers and unions.

The Truck Acts might be a major obstacle in the way of compulsory deductions for a check-off or for other purposes. But various escape routes from the difficulty can be found. One is provided by the House of Lords decision in *Hewlett* v. *Allen*, 1894,[5] where it was held that a subtraction is not improper if it is no more than a payment of part of the wages to a *third person* with the worker's consent. The worker was in that case actually required to belong to a social and accident club, a subscription being deducted from his wages and paid to the treasurer of the club. Other cases have shown that the mere consent of the workman is not enough to bring a case into this escape route; the payment must be at the workman's request to the third person, for as far as the employer is concerned he then pays the wages in full. The Donovan Report thought it clear that a check-off is lawful where the workers request that part of their wages be paid to the trade union. As a decision in 1966 emphasized, where creditors competed for the assets of a shipowner, unpaid contributions of this kind remain unpaid wages. Other deducted contributions commonly found in industry today – to pension schemes and the like – are often justified under the same principle, since the deductions are usually paid to the trustees of the relevant scheme.

Payment by cheque: The insistence of the Truck Acts that

payment of wages to manual workers be in 'coin of the realm' rules out payment by cheque. As a matter of fact, this was not completely the intention of the 1831 Act, which allowed for payment, if a workman consented, by draft or order on any bank within fifteen miles provided it was itself licensed to issue notes. When, later in the century, the Bank of England became the only bank so licensed in England this part of the Act became redundant. After the Second World War some firms experimented with payment by cheque to workers, and in 1956 Pye Radio apparently paid workmen by cheque for some time, without anyone realizing it was wrong. At last the Government sponsored the measure which became the Payment of Wages Act, 1960. After their discussions with the National Joint Advisory Council, however, the Government decided to deal only with the problem of payment of wages in other than coin and notes, and referred the more general problem to a Departmental Committee. There was some dispute in the House about just who wanted the Bill. Mr Robens for the Opposition declared, 'It is not that the workers have asked for this Bill', only to suffer the interruption: 'It may be their wives!' The worker whose wife does not know what he earns figured constantly in the discussions; but he is, as we shall see, safeguarded.

The Act merely introduced a scheme of exceptions to the employer's obligation to pay in coin or notes. The other methods permitted by it are: payment into a bank account, by postal order or money order or cheque. But in all cases, the workman must first make a written *request* for payment by the new method. No compulsion is allowed. Such a request cannot be a condition of employment; and either the worker or the employer can cancel the request or the agreement with four weeks' notice. The worker must be given a statement when paid by the new method clearly specifying any deductions. The only case where he can be forced to accept either a postal or money order is when he is absent, either on duty or sick, but entitled to wages, *unless* he has given notice that he does not wish to receive his wages in one of the new ways.

There is no doubt that the machinery set up by the statute is

227

cumbersome, and it remains questionable whether many manual workers will take advantage of its provisions to request payment by cheque. Employers can perhaps effect some economies by paying in this way and avoid transporting large sums of cash to pay wages and the private armies of guards that are often used; but it seems unlikely that they will press reluctant workers to take cheques if there is any risk to labour relations. Where is the worker to cash his cheque? The local grocer is sometimes reluctant to do so without a discount. Whereas the debates of 1960 abounded with optimistic ideas of extended hours for bank opening, by 1970 the banks opened for shorter hours which were less convenient for workers. Although, therefore, there is a case in logic for the increased use of money orders and cheques, it cannot be said that their introduction into the field of wage payment has been effected by way of any integrated plan of social change.

Deductions at Work: The employer could under the common law deduct an amount from wages for careless work. After all, he has, as we saw, a right to sue for damages for loss caused by the worker's negligence. The Truck Act, 1896, prohibits deductions from wages for such losses except under certain conditions. The Act deals with 'fines', damaged goods, and sums charged for the use of materials; and the same conditions are imposed for payments by the worker as for deductions by the employer.

No contract shall be made for payment or deduction 'in respect of a fine' unless either it is a written contract signed by the workman or a notice of its terms is constantly displayed where the workman can read and copy it. Furthermore, particulars of the specific offences and the amounts must be given; the fine must be imposed in respect of some offence which will cause loss to the employer or 'interruption or hindrance' to his business; the amount must in each case be 'fair and reasonable'; and written notice of each offence and fine must be given to the workman. This particular protection is extended by the Act to shop assistants as well as manual workers. But the courts have interpreted its terms widely. In 1901 workers were fined under a rule posted in the factory demanding 'good order and decorum'. The judges considered that the employer was entitled to fine them for dancing to music in the work-room during meal hours, since the offence was sufficiently specific and the dancing kicked up a dust likely to damage the machines in the room.[6]

Similar conditions are imposed upon payments or deductions in respect of goods damaged by the worker by bad or negligent work: a written contract or notice; a fair and reasonable amount in each case; written particulars on each occasion; and deductions scheduled which must not exceed the actual or estimated loss for which the worker is responsible. Payments and deductions in respect of materials are controlled in like manner. An employer who contravenes the 1896 Act commits a crime and the employee can recover any sums illegally extracted provided that he sues within six months (a relatively short period). It is interesting that the 1896 controls have never been extended to disciplinary 'fines' for conduct at work outside these three areas.

What are the 'Wages'?: The Truck Acts, then, dealt with many of the problems concerning payment of and deductions from wages. They solved some of the questions troubling the worker in Disraeli's *Sybil* who asks: 'What *is* wages? I say 'tain't sugar, 'tain't tea, 'tain't bacon. I don't think it's candles; but of this I be sure, 'tain't waistcoats.' But what *is* the wage? The answer is, that sum agreed between employer and work-man as payable for the work. (It is to be noted that 'wages' can be a narrower term than 'emoluments', under tax statutes, or even 'remuneration' under the Contracts of Employment Act, 1963.[7]) The agreed sum may be expressly agreed or agreed by reference to another agreement, e.g. a collectively bargained rate. Oddly enough, these propositions open up another avenue of escape from the control of the Truck Acts, as the following cases show. In 1945 British Celanese Ltd employed spinners on terms which included notice of one day to terminate, and a right in the employer to 'suspend' a worker for misconduct or disobedience with a proportionate stoppage of his money. A spinner suspended for two days for refusing to clean a machine now claimed his two days' pay as being an illegal deduction.

The Court of Appeal rejected his claim for the simple reason that the wages were never payable. Computation of the wage must precede any question of deductions. Asking whether this could possibly have got to the stage of deductions, Lord Justice Scott answered: 'Clearly not, because you cannot deduct something from nothing. . . . Under the suspense clause the right to wages ceases and the wages are not earned; no deduction can be made from wages which are not payable.' It did not infringe the 1896 Act which was concerned with deductions 'from wages which have been earned under the contract and for which the employer is under a present duty to make payment'.[8]

Similarly, in *Sagar* v. *Ridehalgh*,[9] a case already discussed, the Lancashire weaver claimed that the employer's deductions for faulty work infringed the Truck Acts (the Act of 1831 this time, not the 1896 Act, because the cotton industry in the North of England was relieved of its operation in 1897). The weaver had, it was held, taken his job on the contractual terms which permitted such deductions. This would not be enough by itself to avoid the Truck Acts; but the Court of Appeal held further that these deductions for bad work were not deductions from wages but only a method of calculating wages. Clearly the borderline between the two will always be hard to draw; and the possibilities of abuse by employers remain extensive. The absence of any outcry about such abuses probably testifies both to the rarity of such exploitation by employers and the increased protection against unfair deductions afforded by trade union organization.

Some statutes have, however, gone further in protecting the wage as such. In 1874, for example, an Act prohibited all contracts for 'frame rents' in hosiery manufacture (whereby workers were charged rent for machinery let out to them). Another protection, which originated in legislation concerned with hosiery, silk-weaving, and textile factories, is the 'particulars clause'. Under Section 135, Factories Act, 1961 (which statute also prohibits deductions generally), every textile factory occupier must give to workers written particulars of wage rates and the work to which the rates apply. The section makes very detailed provision, even to the extent of stating that particulars 'shall not be expressed by means of symbols'. The piece-worker especially is thereby protected against any sharp practice or misunderstanding in the calculation of his wage. In origin the 'particulars clause' was aimed at the exploitation and 'sweating' of such workers. Since 1895 the Minister has been able to extend these requirements by Order to other factories, with any necessary modifications; some twenty such Orders between 1900 and 1929 extended the 'particulars clause' to a variety of industries from bleaching and sweetmeats to lampshades and toy balloons. The absence of any new Orders in the last thirty-five years may once again speak to the improvement in consultation and in union organization.

Extensive statutory provisions protect the calculation of wages of miners paid by the weight of material extracted by them. Since 1887, the weighing of coal or other material near the pit-mouth, and such matters as deductions for alien substances, have been controlled by statutes; and also since that year, such miners have had the legal right to appoint, at their own cost, a 'checkweigher', to be elected by a majority of the workers. The employer may (despite the Truck Acts) deduct the checkweigher's wages proportionately from each miner's pay; and he must afford every facility to the checkweigher for examining and testing weighing machines and tubs, and provide a shelter from the weather with sufficient cubic feet for two persons (a friendly touch). The checkweigher must not 'interfere' with the work of the mine (a word which has been held by the judges to include his acting as a union official leading a lawful stoppage of work); but he may be removed only on complaint to a magistrates' court. The system (extended in 1919 to certain other industries) is one rare example of a workers' representative being given statutory protection by our law. What is more, under the Mines and Quarries Act, 1954, the miners have a legal right to appoint one of their number as one of two persons to inspect the mine and its documents to ensure compliance with *safety* regulations.

The Future of the Truck Acts: Despite inquiries by Committees in 1908 and 1961, the structure of these Acts controlling abuses in calculation and payment of wages and deductions from wages bears little relation to present needs. The Donovan Report paid no attention to the general problem, which is odd when it forms part – true, only a small part – of the overall question of 'wage structure' and 'methods of payment' which, again and again, the Report found to be the critical cause of industrial tension, especially in the car industry. Indeed, some of the statutes are just ignored in practice. The best example is, perhaps, the Shop Clubs Act, 1902. This was passed to stop employers (especially in the docks) forcing their workers to join their own 'shop club or thrift fund'; and it was supported enthusiastically by the insurance firms and friendly societies of the day who wished to stop what one M.P. called 'this un-doubted interference with the liberty of the subject'. The Act demands that before an employer can operate such a fund as a compulsory term of the employment of his workmen he must satisfy stringent conditions. These include certification after proof that the fund has a permanent character and that the employer makes a contribution. Furthermore, the views of the workers must be sought and the approval of 75 per cent of them obtained. And rights received some protection on a change of job. The 1902 Act is, in fact, a remarkably early piece of legis-lative protection on 'fringe benefits', at the point where (by reason of the contributions which the workers would make to such a fund) they touch on truck. Yet the Act has gone almost unnoticed, except for express legal exemptions granted to some schemes so as to relieve them from its provisions (notably in the mines, railways, and – ironically – docks pensions schemes).

The Act is highly obscure about which 'thrift fund or shop club' falls within it; and, worse, 'workman' is not defined at all. In 1961, therefore, the Registrar of Friendly Societies re-ported to the Departmental Committee that membership of certified shop clubs numbered only 24,000, but occupational pension schemes were known to cover about 8,750,000 workers, of whom about one million could be said to fall within the Act. A Government Actuary's Report disclosed that by 1966 the figures had risen to 65,000 schemes covering over 12 million workers – but he did not mention the 1902 Act. The Committee concluded that the Act now has little effect and merely recommended its repeal.[10] Surprisingly, no recommendation was made for new legislation to secure for workers an equivalent protection of fringe benefits in modern conditions.

The Committee's Report was, in fact, unsatisfactory. It contains 'elementary errors' and should be quickly 'unheeded and forgotten'.[11] Its philosophy is 'freedom of contract' in employment. Its recognition of trade union and other collective institutions is minimal. The evidence given had shown that there are modern examples of objectionable truck practices of an old-fashioned kind.

In July 1968, the truck problem was referred to a committee of the N.J.A.C. on the proposal of the C.B.I., together with questions on 'relative advantages of different methods of paying wages'. New legislation should concentrate upon protecting the worker not adequately protected by unions and collective bargaining. The Shop Clubs Act was, of course, ahead of its time in protecting fringe benefits like pension rights on change of job. Indeed, advantages like occupational pension rights may be said to give a new dimension to the 'truck' problem. First, there is their loss on change of employment. In 1968 Sir Brandon Rhys Williams, a Conservative M.P., demanded new laws urgently to replace the 'incomprehensible tangle' of the present, to make pension funds 'the inalienable property of the beneficiaries' with 'full transferability ... the main objective'. This would both protect the rights of individual workers and encourage mobility. The T.U.C. had for years pressed the same case. In 1970, the Labour Government expressed willingness to amend its National Superannuation Bill so as to acquire the power to enforce preservation of an employee's pension rights.

But the problems are not confined to preservation on change of job. What about the trustees of pension funds? Should the employees who contribute to their own 'deferred wages' not have some say in who they are and what they do? An obligation to consult employees was to be inserted into the same Bill but it lapsed. Then there is the problem of industrial conflict. One reason why the courts are slow to see a notice of a strike as the same thing as a notice by the men to terminate their jobs and quit is often the simple fact that the men do not intend to lose their pension rights if they can help it. As Lord Pearce said in *Rookes* v. *Barnard* (the big strike case of 1964, discussed later, p. 361), 'neither side wishes the contracts to be determined and the termination of contracts would give rise to confusion in respect of superannuation schemes and other matters'.

Such schemes can add to the employer's armoury in strike situations. In 1964 draughtsmen at a Barrow shipyard who had gone on strike were told that unless they returned they would be given one month's notice, lose their pension rights and be required to join the pension scheme at scratch if re-engaged. And in 1965 when the seven employees of a Scots newspaper went on official strike for their claim for a transferable pension scheme, the employer said: 'I am going to sell the paper. I am certainly not going to give in to these people on the question of a gift.'[12] When additional protection of pension and fringe benefit rights is introduced, the statute should deal with industrial conflict. As we shall see, it is always said to be one of the avowed aims of the Welfare State to remain 'neutral' in industrial conflict, e.g. by not paying unemployment benefit to strikers (see p. 398). Modern legislation should demand that accrued pension rights should not be open to complete obliteration in an industrial dispute.

Equal Pay: The statutes so far discussed deal mainly with the form of wage payment and deductions from wages. But in recent years demands have been made on various Governments to ratify the I.L.O. Convention of 1951 and guarantee payment to women workers of wages equal to those paid to their male counterparts. Indeed, the claim for equal pay for women was first made by the T.U.C. in 1888; but it was not until the 1960s that the prospect of legislation seemed to be a reality. The Labour Government, after promising in 1968 that it was 'anxious' to legislate when circumstances were 'favourable', introduced a Bill at last in 1970. In 1969, inquiries had shown that in about 60 per cent of cases women's rates of pay were less than three-quarters of a man's rate for the same work – often much less, women overall appearing to work for about 60 per cent of the male rates – and that only one woman in ten received equal pay in Britain. The T.U.C. pressed for legislation but also encouraged affiliated unions to press hard in bargaining. That the latter is necessary is apparent in the European Community where a legal requirement of equality, now more than a decade old, has scarcely altered patterns of inequality which are little better than those in Britain, and in the U.S.A. where two Federal and thirty-six State laws appear not to have prevented unequal pay for women workers. Indeed the British Secretary of State described her 1970 legislation as 'a statutory framework, not spoon-feeding'; and the T.U.C. set up a special advisory service to assist unions to obtain true equality for their women members. The *floor* of legal rights which the new statute establishes will not be effective without vigorous collective bargaining to supplement it.

In fact, the Equal Pay Act, 1970, is a very limited measure (though for once the statute does cover both 'employees' proper and self-employed independent contractors and civilian Crown servants – but with a condition of six months' continuous service before claims can be made). First, the statute is to come into force only on 29 December 1975, unless the Secretary of State brings it wholly or partially into effect on 31 December 1973 – a curiously limited set of options. Secondly, the Act does not establish a right to 'equal pay for work of equal value', as the trade unions had demanded. The statute makes it a compulsory implied term of employment contracts that men and women be given 'equal treatment' in the 'same employment'. But this is translated into equal pay in two situations:

(i) where a work study has rated work as being of equal value; and

(ii) where men and women are employed on 'like work' which is defined as *work of the same or a broadly similar nature* without *differences of practical importance* in relation to their terms and conditions of employment. One can only gulp with apprehension at the work for industrial tribunals (to which employee, employer or – very sensibly – the Secretary of State can refer disputes) and for the High Court on the points of law that could arise from this formula.

Thirdly, however, is the statute about 'equal *pay*' or 'equal *treatment*'? Although in places directed to the problem of the former, and specifically allowing a woman (or man) unlawfully paid unequal pay to claim up to two years' arrears of remuneration before an industrial tribunal, the Act is drafted in wider terms. The compulsory term of employment requires *equal treatment* of women and men in regard to 'terms and conditions of employment' generally; and it is only as a form of shorthand that a later section calls this the 'equal pay clause'. Indeed 'damages' may also be awarded by a tribunal for wrongful discrimination. But then the statute excludes a list of matters from the requirements for equal treatment, namely matters regulated by other laws about women's employment (p. 240); special treatment connected with birth; and employment provisions connected with retirement, marriage or death. Thus the Act does not require equal pension rights, though the Labour Government, before it lost office, accepted that such equality should be compulsory later. But otherwise the statute requires equality in that terms and conditions shall not be *in any respect* less favourable for one sex, and appears to include a wide range of terms outside equal wages: e.g. holiday or sick-pay schemes. That interpretation is confirmed when one section tells the tribunal that, in any dispute, it is for the employer to prove that any 'greater remuneration *or other advantage*' enjoyed by one sex as against the other does not infringe the equal treatment obligation. On the other hand, the Act apparently applies its complicated concept of equality only to the *terms and conditions* of employment. This seems to mean the contractually binding terms and conditions. Suppose, therefore, the employer paid discretionary bonuses (such as those about which Mr Grieve complained: p. 190). It is arguable that he could lawfully evade the statute by paying them only to men, so long as the 'terms and conditions of employment' would not be unequal for men and women in like work.

Lastly, the statutory exclusion of discrimination could not, of course, allow for evasion by way of collective agreement. The Secretary of State is, therefore, allowed to refer to the Industrial Court collective agreements which have provisions applying to men or women only, and the Court can declare what amendments are needed if the agreement has not been re-negotiated. The amendments automatically enter any employment contracts affected. While removing inequalities struck at by the Act, they are to 'level up', not down, the provisions of the agreement. But the Court is not to extend a collectively agreed provision to women (or men) which previously applied only to men (or women) and which 'continues to be required' for the category of women or men specified. It will, therefore, be possible, by agreed job categories, still to reserve certain employments for one sex only. The statute deals to some extent in equal *treatment*; but it does not set out to provide equal *opportunity*. Advocates of women's liberation will no doubt argue that it should have aimed at the latter. Indeed if racial discrimination in hiring is unlawful, and if neither race nor sex is to be a valid ground for dismissal, it is not easy to see why, in general, sex should be a valid ground for refusing to hire.

Various other matters of difficulty will arise under the Equal Pay Act. But they will not, on present plans, arise for some years, and there is still time to clarify what is a quite unnecessarily obscure statute. It raises, as we have seen, wide questions concerning equality at work and the general role of legislation in employment. We turn now to the latter question.

B. Statutory Control of Employment Conditions

The method of legal enactment might have become, as the Webbs expected, the dominating influence of our labour law. Early reformers of the nineteenth century turned naturally to it as their method and the trade union movement was not averse to its use. So, as the franchise was gradually extended, the tide of legislation advanced. The area which is today thought proper for statutory control, however, is largely the area which it had come to occupy before the modern era of collective consultation and bargaining began. The statutes on wages illustrate that, as we have seen. Nor was the tide the simple unimpeded flow of progress that some writers have suggested. It is undoubtedly in one sense true, as Sydney Webb put it, that 'this century of experiment in Factory Legislation affords a typical example of English practical empiricism'[13] and that the statutes, which were often tried out on a small area and later expanded to cover a whole trade or industry, constitute (as Professor Kahn-Freund puts it) a process of 'trial and error'. Nevertheless the tide during those years ebbed and flowed and its movement was not unrelated to the strength at different times of groups who called for or resisted reform. Even today certain groups of workers have not been reached by protective Acts which have applied to their fellows in other work for many decades; and we shall see (p. 300) that even now it does not seem to be the objective of Government to reach them all. Although it is not possible here to describe in detail the development of all our factory legislation, certain features of its history must be noticed. The remaining sections of this chapter aim to provide a mere introduction to the development and scope of modern legislation.

The history of protective legislation for workers of the kind we know today may be said to start at the beginning of the nineteenth century. In 1788 a statute attempted to protect the unfortunate boys who were used as chimney sweeps, forbidding use of boys under eight. The struggles and vicissitudes of reform in these matters can be judged very well by the fact that in the 1870s boys were still dying in chimneys; and Lord Shaftesbury, introducing the 1875 Bill that was finally to crush the practice, spoke of magistrates who refused to convict where a boy of eight or nine had been sent up because there was no strict proof that he was under 21. The path of reform legislation was never a smooth one. Even the statutes were often frustrated then (and now) by magistrates whose sympathy with their objectives was slender.

HOURS OF WORK

The first Act controlling hours and conditions for young workers was that passed 'for the health and morals of apprentices and others' in 1802. This was the beginning, as we now see it, of a long battle over hours of work for children,

young workers, and women, all the unhappiest victims of the
savage exploitation of the industrial revolution. True, the Act
of 1802 'was in reality not a Factory Act properly speaking,
but merely an extension of the Elizabethan Poor Law relating
to parish apprentices',[14] but it did limit apprentices' hours to
twelve per day. The Act, like later statutes, was only partially
enforced. In 1833 an Act pressed on to the statute book by
reformers agitating for the Ten Hour Day not only limited
employment in textile factories of those between 13 and 18
years to ten hours and stopped up some more obvious loopholes
previously used by employers, but also provided for the appointment of four inspectors to enforce the Act's provisions.
Those four inspectors were perhaps the most important innovation in British labour legislation. They were not, in the long
run, dominated by the employers, as had been predicted by
the reformers; and the inspectorate has, as we shall see, become a primary agency of enforcing the modern statutes.

But the next fifty years saw a swaying struggle between reformers, workers' unions and factory inspectors on the one
side, and uncooperative employers, many magistrates, and
pressure groups in Parliament on the other. In the Act of 1844
gains and losses for the reformers may both be found; women
workers were brought within the slender protection of the
statute as well as young persons; hours remained at twelve but
children of 8 years might now be employed; and the powers of
inspectors were altered and in some ways reduced. The hours
of women as well as young persons were restricted by 1848 to
ten hours a day, but employers devised methods of evading the
legislation such as the 'relay system' which magistrates usually
refused to stop, so that 'the Ten Hours Act was completely
nullified and it was impossible for the inspectors to detect overtime employment' and 'factory legislation was in perfect
chaos'.[15]

In an amending Act of 1850 permitted hours were even increased though other amendments cut down the evils of irregu-
lar relays. The realities of the fight for control over the appalling hours worked by women and children may be gauged by
the fact that opponents of the reformer Lord Ashley (later

Lord Shaftesbury) asserted that he wished to protect them in order to restrict the hours of adult men who could not work in the factory without the children's help. Restriction of the latter's hours certainly assisted the former in their struggle against the conditions common to the iron temper of the day. In 1842 female workers and males under ten were banned in the mines: and by 1867 factories and workshops other than textiles were brought under elementary statutory control. Only in 1874, however, did a really secure and enforceable ten-hour day for women and young persons appear on the statute book, together with an enforced minimum age of ten for factory employment. The Act of 1878 consolidated the law and may be accounted the first modern Factories Act – all less than a hundred years ago.

It is not surprising that in the years that have followed Parliament has continued the tradition of protecting women and young workers, sometimes in general, sometimes in specific statutes. The hours and conditions of women employed in any 'factory' are caught by a barrage of sections in (now) the Factories Act, 1961. For example, the total hours worked may not exceed nine in a day or 48 in a week; they must begin at 7.0 a.m. or later and end at 8.0 p.m. or earlier (1.0 p.m. on Saturdays); the spells of continuous work are limited; and so on. Some twenty sections of the Act set out exceptions to the rules, or cases in which the Minister can make exceptions if he so decides, each exception dealing with a particular special case. More important, a general exception permits women's overtime outside the hours fixed, within strict limits imposed by the Act (e.g. up to six hours in a week). The Act also protects certain holidays for women and young workers, e.g. bank holidays and Christmas Day. Two statutes, passed in 1920 and in 1936, give effect in English law to I.L.O. Conventions, and under them the employment at night of women or young workers under eighteen years was banned except in strictly specified circumstances. Further, the Mines and Quarries Act, 1954, controls above-ground hours of women, and, of course, continues that prohibition of women working below ground enacted as a result of the Report in 1842 of which 'the details cannot even now be read without pain and shame'. We take for granted that statutory interference with the right to employ women 'dragging trucks of coal to which they were harnessed by a chain and girdle going on all-fours, in conditions of dirt, heat and indecency which are scarcely printable'; yet 130 years ago it represented to many 'the most high-handed interference with industry enacted by the State'.[16]

As for the young, children below the compulsory school age are naturally excluded from most areas of employment. Apart from specific prohibitions such as those concerned with work underground in mines, in factories and industrial undertakings, they may be employed at all only for very limited hours in the two years before school-leaving age (two hours, e.g. on any school day; not before 6.0 a.m., not after 8.0 p.m.); but, once again, there are a number of exceptional rules applying, e.g. to licensed entertainment or street trading (now both governed by an Act of 1963, which was not made effective until 1969). Under the Education Act, 1944, a local authority has power to prohibit the employment of a child if it prejudices his health or fitness to obtain the full benefit of his education. Young persons under eighteen years of age are also protected by a web of enactments similar to but even more extensive than that protecting women workers. The Shops Act, 1950, provides an elaborate code for shop assistants – the young assistants especially – about meal-times, half-holidays, and hours of work generally which are normally limited to a weekly 48 hours, and closely controlled overtime, over the wide area of jobs caught by the statute, much wider than 'shops' would indicate (with very special exceptions for catering and the sale of aircraft, motor, or cycle accessories!). A similar restriction of hours was applied to employment outside shops, ships, agriculture, and factories by an Act of 1938, extended in 1964 to certain premises licensed to sell liquor. The Factories Act, 1961, moreover, continues the statutory regulations in factories of a kind similar to those for women workers. The permitted hours are narrower for workers under sixteen years, and the overtime arrangements excluded; and the Minister can prohibit or restrict overtime for any young persons by Order. A young person can be employed only if certified fit for the work by an appointed factory doctor.

But the 1961 Act contains a plethora of powers for the Minister to make exceptions. For example, he can exempt young workers from various controls over hours after an application from a J.I.C. or from employers or unions, in each case consulting the other side. This exemption applies where he thinks it desirable for 'the efficiency of industry or transport'; other powers apply in an 'unforeseen emergency'. He can also give special authorization for shift-work over slightly longer hours for women or young persons; but before granting certain applications by the factory owner he must consult the workers in a secret ballot conducted, if necessary, by the local factory inspector (a nice mixture of the 'methods' of statutory enactment, collective negotiation, and executive administration). In July 1970 exemption orders were current allowing various types of extended working hours in respect of applications covering 152,600 women and 15,500 young workers between 16 and 18. A comprehensive statement of the law would have to speak of regulations on particular industries as diverse as metal - rod - manufacturing - with - reverberatory - furnaces - in-continuous-use and wire-galvanizing (other than pickling). In some cases there must be a compulsory examination of the young shift-workers by an appointed factory doctor every six months. Other special provisions deal with a huge variety of cases from employment to carry messages to work essential to the continuance of the work of adult workers (when the young person's work-spells may be increased). In addition, the employer must make very clear the periods for which young workers and women are being employed, in a notice affixed in the factory; and in a register which must be available to the factory inspector or factory doctor he must keep prescribed particulars concerning this protected labour force.

The number of exemptions given to employers for women workers nearly doubled between 1964 and 1970. Yet the Donovan Report castigated the 'failure to train' them for skilled work, a failure not unrelated to 'conservatism and prejudice among men'.[17] Moreover, the D.E.P. Report on a *National*

Minimum Wage (1969) confirmed the view that this is an exploited workforce by showing that women and young workers would benefit most through the introduction of a compulsory minimum. An N.J.A.C. Committee considered the hours of work of such workers in 1968. After its report the D.E.P. circulated a discussion document with 'tentative thinking' about the future, based on the idea that restrictions on the hours of work for women should all be swept aside since it is 'no longer possible to sustain the traditional argument' that they stand in special need. Yet it is common ground that women workers are one main group not yet properly organized in trade unions, for which unions may be partly to blame. But neither failures by unions nor a statute on equal pay could justify precipitate destruction of this age-old protection. Those proposals are, one hopes, a mistaken aberration in an area where special groups are still an easy prey for unscrupulous employers, and where one doubts that the scrupulous would wish to see their competitors relieved of the legal duty to observe a decent floor of rights.

But what of men's hours? It has now become orthodox to think that their hours belong, by the light of nature, to the domain of collective bargaining, and to see legislative control as unusual and exceptional. In 1853 and 1855, J. M. Cobbett tried to move Bills which would restrict the hours of working men. (Having protected the women and children, 'the question is now to be, as to the adult male, whether he shall be worked to death or not? – fifteen hours a day! Sixteen hours a day! ... Talk of freedom! The man in the factory is not free.') But the House of Commons thought this legislation would infringe basic principles. As we have noted, the statutory control of hours of women and children strengthened the hand of the men from the earliest Act onwards. The Webbs made famous the remark of the Oldham Spinners' secretary that the men's industrial battle for shorter hours was 'fought from behind the women's petticoats'.

Yet it is often forgotten how ready, even eager, was the union movement in the later nineteenth century to see legislation used to put into effect its demands for shorter hours even for working men. The Miners' Federation, for example, was happy to press its demands for legislation, and the Acts of 1908 and 1919 enacted a maximum daily stint underground, now continued in the 1954 Act as seven hours. The railwaymen, also, had for many years conducted a campaign against the incredibly long hours demanded by their employers. Said an official to a guard who in 1871 had worked eighteen hours and asked when he might be free, 'You've got twenty-four hours in a day like any other man and they are all ours if we want them'.[18]

After a public outcry, in 1893 the Railway Servants (Hours of Labour) Act was passed which for a time gave the Board of Trade certain powers to demand of railway companies reasonable hours for the men. Historians have stressed that in 1890 the T.U.C. itself proclaimed that 'Parliamentary enactment' was the best method for reducing hours; and by the end of the nineteenth century 'the idea of enactment was accepted as an article of faith, but few trade unions continued to believe that there was any foreseeable prospect of getting it'.[19] A 'legal maximum' 40-hour week and 'legal minimum wage for each industry' are still formal T.U.C. objects. The unions did not in principle renounce the method of legal enactment on men's hours. It was ousted by the tactic of industrial pressure and collective bargaining which became more and more the likely source of immediate gains in the twentieth century.

Exceptional areas in which the hours of employment for all workers including adult men receive statutory control today are, in the main, (except for the Shops Act, 1950, protecting shop assistants) occupations where overwork brings special dangers to the men, the public, or both. The Minister has power to make special regulations under the Factories Act, 1961, for industries where risk of bodily injury arises from the work. Miners' hours below ground are as we saw controlled by Acts going back to 1908 (when, in the words of Dicey in 1914, 'modern collectivism' had upset 'the right of a workman of full age to labour for any number of hours agreed upon between him and his employer'),[20] but the maximum can be set aside in times of national danger or grave economic disturbance. To give effect to an I.L.O. convention an Act of 1936 limits the hours of sheet glass workers on necessarily continuous shift and a 1954 Act controls hours in night bakeries (two more restrictions which the 'tentative' D.E.P. proposals would abolish). The Transport Act, 1968, with a view to 'protecting the public against risks which arise in cases where the drivers of motor vehicles are suffering from fatigue', continues the control of hours of drivers of public service vehicles, heavy and light locomotives, goods vehicles, and, now, large motor vehicles. The Act of 1968 bans work by drivers for more than five and a half hours at a stretch or driving for more than ten hours in a day (a period which is later to be reduced to nine). The working day of no driver is to exceed 11 hours (or in certain cases 14) in any 24; and between two working days a driver shall normally have 11 hours' rest interval. In a working week he must not be on duty more than a total of 60 hours, with one full day off. Evasion of previous statutes (by employers and 'cowboy' drivers) led to the Minister being given power to insist upon the installation of automatic recording equipment in the drivers' cabs, but the new Conservative Minister in 1970 made it clear he wanted no such power. The relationship between statutory regulation and voluntary bargaining was well illustrated when these provisions came into force on 1 March 1970. The Act shortened hours, but it did not guarantee earnings. Tough negotiations and some strikes were sparked off when drivers found they might lose money by the change. Most strikes were settled on terms backdated to 1 March.

WELFARE, HEALTH, AND SAFETY

The attempt to control the worst evils of the hours worked by children and young workers in the early years of the nineteenth century constituted a crude attempt to give some protection to their welfare and health. But as the factory system developed and new machinery emerged in the advancing revolution in industry, new dangers to the person of the worker appeared. The new concern about women's conditions of labour in the early 1840s coincided with inspectors' reports of terrible accidents which regularly killed or maimed many workers, especially the many girls and women whose dress made them particularly vulnerable to the dangers of the new machinery. An Act of 1844 demanded the secure fencing of every fly-wheel connected with power, mill-gearing and other dangerous machinery, and forbade the cleaning of machinery in motion. But once again the tide of progress ebbed and flowed. In 1856 the National Association of Factory Occupiers (which Dickens called the 'Association for the Mangling of Operatives') promoted, and a sympathetic Parliament passed, an amending Act which restricted fencing to machinery or mill-gearing with which women or young workers were likely to come into contact in passing or in their ordinary work; and arbitration was provided for by mill engineers who were unlikely to be impartial and were concerned with the working of the machines, not, as the great Inspector Horner bitterly complained, with the prevention of accidents. In spite of such employers' victories, however, and, as Hutchins and Harrison say, 'in spite of the fact that they repeatedly declared that either the Factory Acts must be modified or the industry of England would seriously decline, the next ten years witnessed the gradual extension of the Factory Acts from textile mills to other trades and industries'.[21] A variety of workshops and enterprises was brought within statutes on sanitation and conditions of work; but it was not until 1878 that anything like a modern legislative control appeared on the statute book, and only in that year was the law about secure fencing of machinery restored and made a strict duty on the employer. In 1901, in place of a retrogressive statute proposed by the Government, a new and improved Act was secured by the pressure of Radicals and trade unions (especially the miners and, above all, the cotton unionists, who had the longest experience in factory legislation).[22] The Act also consolidated what had become a jumble of statutes, and remained, with amendments, the basic code until the Act of 1937. Thus, by the time modern collective bargaining came to occupy the territory of workers' pay and related conditions of employment, statute had assumed a firm control of conditions at work affecting the health and safety of certain groups of workers, and no one wished it otherwise.

By the end of the century the battle for statutory safety requirements had been fought and won in very many areas of employment. But many workers remained unprotected. The battles were often prolonged. That waged by Samuel Plimsoll is among the best known. In 1862 Parliament made it even easier to operate a 'coffin ship', and Plimsoll began his furious thirty-year campaign for reform. Reviled and attacked in Parliament and in the courts, he did 'more than any man in this field to create that sense of urgency without which a reform can never reach the Statute Book. It was not facts alone that were needed, but indignation and anger.' Although he was joined by trade union forces, and became President in 1890 of the new National Seamen's Union, 'he disagreed with industrial pressure of this type, preferring that all progress should come by legislation'.[23] His coolness towards industrially militant organization was characteristic of most of the factory reformers in Parliament. Shaftesbury himself wrote often of the 'agitators'; and the Hammonds say:

... Shaftesbury did not like it that the Dorset labourer (on his own estates) had to live on 10s. a week, but he would have disliked much more to see those wages raised by the only method by which wages had been raised in other occupations.[24]

But they add:

He did more than any single man or any single Government in English History to check the raw power of the new industrial system. For the arbitrary rule of capital has been tempered by two forces: one the growing strength of the trade unions, which he watched with dismay; the other the system of Factory Law, the chief credit for which must be given to his courage, his humanity and his patience.

It is hardly surprising that from such a history of struggle, by the unions outside and the reformers inside Parliament, the pattern of protective legislation at the beginning of the twentieth century was patchy. The Act of 1901 rationalized statutory provisions applying to workshops and factories, but many

places of work fell outside these descriptions. The mines legislation protected miners; and an Act of 1900 gave some protection to railway workers. Seamen had at last won the protection
of a proper loadline and the 1894 Merchant Shipping Act has
been subsequently supplemented by six statutes passed after
international conventions.

But although further extensions of legislative protection have
indeed taken place, no general blanket enactment has ever been
attempted covering all places of work though, as we shall see
(p. 258), a general reform and codification is in preparation.
The most important Acts in force today are the Factories Act
(now the Act of 1961), the Mines and Quarries Act, now that
of 1954, and (especially on hours of work) the Shops Act,
1950. To these must be added the Agriculture Act, 1956, and
the Offices, Shops and Railway Premises Act, 1963 – two
statutes which mark belated extensions of protection to
workers in the places named in respect of health, welfare, and
safety. The story of offices legislation began in 1923 when a
Bill was projected to give office workers statutory protection.
Later many efforts were made to introduce such a measure on
the part of the back-bench M.P.s; but they were always lost or,
more often, 'talked out'. Always the Government of the day
resolutely refused to legislate. After the war, the Government
set up a Committee in 1946, but it did not report until 1949.
This (the Gowers) Report recommended legislation, though
not measures as strong as the T.U.C. demanded. At last an
Opposition back-bencher succeeded in having a Bill passed in
1960. That Act was overtaken by the Government measure of
1963. It cannot be accidental that this extraordinary story came
to its conclusion at a time when the white-collar unions organizing office workers were bursting into new strength. Union
strength and protective legislation went hand in hand. Perhaps
the history of Government opposition, too, has influenced the
attitude of the D.E.P. to the enforcement of the 1963 Act. In
1967 it thought there was no 'widespread evidence of bad conditions' in offices, which the T.U.C. dubs a 'rather optimistic
view' (1969 Report).

As in the case of hours of work, some of the modern protections apply only to particular groups of worker – e.g. the duty to provide seats for female shop assistants or the ban on women or young persons working on lead compounds. But, unlike the legislation on hours, statutory enactments protecting groups such as women and young workers are merely an additional code on top of the many more sections and regulations that apply to *all* workers, at particular places of work, whatever their sex or age. Furthermore, under all the Acts the relevant Minister has power to make Regulations. It is impossible to describe briefly even a sample of the statutory sections; and the scope of the continually expanding Regulations made under the Factories Acts alone may be judged from the fact that they occupy over 600 pages of a leading book, from the Tin Plate Manufacture Welfare Order, 1917, to the Ionising Radiations (Sealed Sources) Regulations, 1969. Such Ministerial Regulations are an effective weapon for adapting to the changing needs of individual industries or processes the duty which Parliament intends to impose.

The scope of the Factories Act may be judged from the following description of the first 120 of its 185 sections:

Part I, Health: 11 sections requiring minimum standards on cleanliness, overcrowding, temperature, ventilation, lighting, sanitation, etc.; Part II, Safety: 45 sections demanding the guarding and fencing of prime movers, transmission, and other dangerous machinery, self-acting machines; the proper maintenance and soundness of hoists, lifts, cranes, chains, and lifting tackle, floors and stairs; a safe means of access and place of work 'so far as reasonably practicable'; and imposing duties in regard to dangerous fumes, steam and compressed air apparatus, gasholders, fire escapes and other duties on fire-safety measures, many of which were introduced in 1959; Part III, Welfare (General): 6 sections on drinking water, seating, first-aid, etc.; Part IV: 17 sections on special matters concerning health, welfare, or safety (including protection of eyes; meals in dangerous trades, humid and underground workplaces; and the critical section 76 empowering the Minister when there is 'risk of bodily injury' to persons *employed* to 'make such special regulations as appear to him to be reasonably practicable and to meet the necessity of the case'); Part V: 6 sections requiring notification of accidents, and industrial diseases; Part VI, Employment of Women and Young Persons: 34 sections controlling the hours and conditions of such workers. The 1963 Act on offices contains 24 sections on 'Health, Safety and Welfare of Employees' (General); and 14 sections on fire precautions. The Mines Act, 1954, contains another code covering such matters as ventilation, dust, sanitation, first-aid, washing, drinking-water, vermin, safety in access to work, in shafts, roads, at the workplace, fire, electrical apparatus, blasting, machinery, hours of work, and so on.

If any parts of such statutes have to be picked out as more important than others, we must undoubtedly choose the sections and regulations dealing with safety at work, and, among them, those words which impose strict duties, such as duties to fence dangerous machinery securely. About the most famous of these safety sections, Mr Justice Stable said in 1949: 'The Factories Act is there not merely to protect the careful, the vigilant, and the conscientious workman, but, human nature being what it is, also the careless, the indolent, the inadvertent, the weary and even perhaps in some cases the disobedient.'

The Acts are there primarily to stop accidents and (perhaps as important today) industrial diseases; and the judges have recognized that aim. In 1952 Lord Denning said the Factories Act 'is intended to prevent accidents to workmen, and I think it should be construed so as to further that end'; and Lord Reid said in 1963 of the Building Regulations: 'their primary purpose is to prevent accidents by prescribing appropriate precautions'. We shall in the next chapter ask how far in recent times the judges have always kept that end in view.

ENFORCING THE STATUTES

What means exist to ensure compliance with the Acts, and what happens if one is broken? The following are the main methods of enforcement:

(i) *Prosecution.* The first method of enforcement is to prosecute and punish the man who fails to observe his duties under the Act and Regulations made under it. Usually this will be the factory 'occupier' (normally the employer); but some duties are laid by the Act and the Regulations upon the worker too (e.g. he must not 'wilfully misuse' a proper safety appliance or 'wilfully and without reasonable cause' endanger himself).[25] The parent of a young person improperly employed can also be fined. In 1969, 2,657 prosecutions were brought by factory inspectors against firms or persons, and 2,482 convictions obtained, 1,705 for breach of safety duties. Although these figures show a 35 per cent increase over 1967, even today prosecutions are, however, only brought in the worst cases (the absolute totals are almost exactly the same as in 1963) and are heard in magistrates' courts. This is somewhat surprising in view of the danger to life involved in many breaches of the statutes; and the low fines imposed prompt the suggestion that indictment and prison sentences might be more appropriate if the criminal law is to be used seriously as a method of accident prevention. An action by seven workers against Central Asbestos Ltd in 1970, in which they were awarded over £86,000 damages after contracting asbestosis, revealed that the company had been convicted of breach of the safety regulations (pleading guilty) in 1964 – eleven years after factory inspectors first 'drew the attention' of the company to excessive asbestos dust at its plant. (Magistrates also have a power to make safety *orders* in respect of premises; but this promising jurisdiction seems to be little used.) In general, the maximum fines which can be imposed for breach of the safety requirements of the Factories Act, 1961, are £300 and (for an employee) £75, wherever a contravention is 'likely to cause the death of or bodily injury to any person'. The average fine for factory offences in 1969 was £34. It may be felt that the price of human life is not held high in these figures.

(ii) *Civil Action.* Where a breach of the statute has caused injury to a worker, he may be able to sue for damages the person responsible for the breach. Under the 1961 Act that is usually the 'occupier' of the factory. We deal with the problems of such actions in the next chapter.

(iii) *Workers' Representatives.* A method of enforcement so

251

far rarely used in Britain is inspection by workers' representatives. We have already noticed the examples of safety inspectors and the checkweighmen whom miners are entitled to appoint (see p. 231). Such representatives can bring day-to-day pressure to bear both on employers *and* on fellow workers. In other countries greater use is made of this institution. In Ireland a law of 1955 establishes workers' safety committees. In Sweden, the Workers' Protection Act, 1949, gives to workers' delegates in all employments statutory powers, protection against victimization, and special access to the Government inspectors. The Act also establishes compulsory joint committees on safety in all larger enterprises. The law is supplemented by collective agreements. British industry has many joint consultative committees concerned with safety; the number of safety committees voluntarily established has been rising, e.g., in factories employing more than 50 workers from 2,220 in 1966 to 5,470 in 1969. A further 4,017 such firms have 'consultative' committees which deal with safety. But the inspectorate's surveys show that more than one half of such firms still lack any joint committee; and not only the small firms come out badly. In factories where over 500 persons work, only one in five have committees. Whatever the reason, voluntary committees have not been effective in Britain to stop an increase in accidents. The survey of industrial accidents by Mr J. L. Williams concludes on this point:

This [the Swedish] agreement was reached *after* the introduction of statutory provisions compelling employers and employees to establish safety organization at the workplace. The British critics of such legislation on the ground that the voluntary spirit would be stifled should take note.[26]

(iv) *Safety Supervisors.* In a few cases English statute law demands that the employer appoint some qualified person to look after safety matters at work. The Coal Mines Act, 1911, initiated such rules in the mines; and Regulations under the Factories Acts made for the pottery industry require the occupier to appoint someone 'to see to the observance of these Regulations throughout the factory' by means of 'systematic inspections'. The Construction Regulations, 1961, provide that an employer of more than twenty workers in building operations or engineering construction must appoint a safety supervisor of suitable experience and qualifications. The main problem in such appointments is the relation of such supervisors with the employer who employs them and who is responsible for the work. As Mr Williams remarks: 'The real weakness is the inability of the regulations to protect the person appointed.'[27]

(v) *Administrative Inspection.* Inspection is a valuable method of enforcement, if only because it is bound to concentrate upon prevention of breaches (and therefore of accidents) rather than on legal action afterwards. Inspectors are appointed under the Factories Act, 1961; Mines and Quarries Act, 1954; Shops Act, 1950; Baking Industry Act, 1954; Railway Act, 1900; Agriculture Act, 1956; and Offices, Shops and Railway Premises Act, 1963. The four factory inspectors of 1833 have grown to a force which early in 1970 numbered 618 (including the new 'specialist' inspectors and 22 extra fire inspectors). This is still below the authorized strength. The Chief Inspector had said in 1968 that he 'expected' an actual strength of 550 by summer 1968; but his Report for that year lamented that recruitment 'barely made good wastage'. By 1969 the Mines Inspectorate numbered 152. In 1964 the Chief Factory Inspector wrote: 'He would be a poor factory inspector who confined his efforts merely to seeing that there was compliance with the law, for the law, after all, lays down only minimum standards ... [he] has both to enforce the law and to act as a consultant and adviser to industry.'[28]

This is, indeed, the understandable philosophy of the inspectorate; and the same Inspector described the job in 1966 as one of 'education, exhortation and enforcement'. But the last often seems to be rather a poor relation. The insistence upon 'education' has led two experienced commentators to ask whether the same philosophy has not been proved to be inadequate in respect of drunken driving by the breathalyser:

... it has plainly produced a dramatic result in the number of road traffic accidents ... because there stands behind the breathalyser a real threat of prosecution and punishment. No such threat stands at present behind the Factories Act.[29]

The legal powers of an inspector are extensive. He may enter, inspect premises and documents, take samples, require information, and prosecute. The chief inspector also generally appoints the factory doctors; they, too, descend from the 1833 Act, with its 'certifying surgeon' for the child workers; but their role has been extended. (In 1970, it was planned to replace them with a full occupational medical service.) Local authorities and fire authorities also have certain inspection functions. Under the Offices, Shops and Railway Premises Act, the factory inspectors enforce the Act over premises occupied by the Crown, local authorities, the Atomic Energy Authority, and most railway premises; while local authorities are responsible for inspecting most other offices and shops. It would have been wiser to allocate all inspection to a unified Factory and Office Inspectorate, especially since the Act gives power to the enforcing authority to exempt individual premises from certain standards of hygiene and sanitation. The 1967 Report said that the Offices Act had 'added greatly to the inspection load' and inspections were possible only once in four years. The answer to that is obviously to double the size of the inspectorate. Indeed, such an increase is urgent, when employees of a prosecuted butcher were said by the bench to have been working in 'an appalling condition of unbelievable squalor'. By 1969, 1,603 local authorities were employing 5,175 inspectors but 'few inspectors are employed full-time on this work'. They had to cope with 750,000 registered premises with some 8 million employees; and claimed to have given a 'general inspection' during 1968 to 258,000 (60,000 by Factory Inspectors) with 660,000 visits in all. The Report complacently observed that 'good progress continued to be made in the enforcement' of the 1963 Act: 'No new problem came to light'. Meanwhile, the annual record of accidents continued at some 19,000 injured (39 fatally), 699 from machinery in motion. Prosecutions rose from 116 in 1965 to 589 (86 per cent successful) in 1968. Administrative inspection remains essential to enforcement of statutory standards. But there should be a unified Inspectorate. It should have more men (and women) to staff it. And it should be better paid.

But the battle to reduce accidents at work is being lost. In 209,000 workplaces covered by the 1961 Act, 'serious' accidents to workers (defined by the arbitrary test of three days' absence) rose in 1968 to the staggering total of 312,430, of which 625 were fatal. In 1969 the figures were 322,390 and 649. In the previous edition of this book, the 1963 figures were given: 204,000 and 610. No doubt, as the Chief Inspector has said, accidents are reported today which 'against an earlier social background would not have resulted in absence or become reportable'. But no such explanation can spirit away an extra 100,000 injured workers per year within six years! Indeed a survey by the Inspectorate mentioned in the 1967 Report revealed that on a sample of construction sites there were, in 1966, 270 reportable accidents, but 2,900 other 'non-reportable' accidents. Mr R. Thompson has said:

The truth of the matter is that many employers not only do not report accidents that occur as the law requires, but they do not even investigate them as a proper accident prevention system requires.[30]

The record of the construction industry (which is within the 1961 Act) is appalling. In 1963 it had some 30,000 accidents, but this rose to 46,500 in 1968 (238 fatal) and 44,570 (265 fatal) in 1969. But this is only one field of casualties. We have already noted the figures for shops and offices. But for 1968 (the latest statistics) we have to add:— Over 140,000 coal miners injured, 851 of them gravely and 115 fatally (the number of serious injuries per thousand miners being much the same as a decade ago); 6,191 railway employees injured, another 659 seriously injured, and 62 killed in accidents; and also, 7,387 agricultural workers injured, 114 fatally. Nor is this the end of the list. Moving a Bill in 1970 to compel trawlers to carry satisfactory safety equipment, the President of the Board of Trade revealed figures which showed that trawlermen are more at risk than the average male worker by a factor of 17 times. That there are many more workers not included in this tally is indicated by the fact that social security benefit for industrial injury at work (p. 287) was drawn by over 937,000 workers in 1968; and in that year some estimates put the real loss of working time through accidents at nearly 22 million days.

There is great concern throughout industry at the dreadful toll which these figures disclose – a human sacrifice to growth, expansion and efficiency – and much voluntary activity is sustained to combat the rising flood of casualties. Both employers and workers who fail to observe safety precautions contribute to it. The Chief Inspector's 1963 Report declared:

... Where safety and health are concerned every man in a factory is both his own and his brother's keeper.

Worst of all is the rise disclosed in the statistics in the rate of accidents among young workers. In 1966 the Chief Inspector said that the rise in young workers' injury rates not only showed 'a wanton disregard of moral responsibility to the young but is also patently bad investment for the future'. A large sector of management was failing in its responsibilities.

Feeling at the T.U.C. conference of 1962 was strong enough to remit to the General Council a resolution calling for new legislation giving to workers' representatives powers of inspection, setting up workers' health and safety committees, and allowing a workers' representative the right to accompany the Factory Inspector. By 1964, the mover had the resolution passed, and in 1966 he commented that in 1927 the Chief Inspector warned employers that, if they did no more to stop the injury rate, compulsory powers would be sought. 'What have we got since that date? Complete and abject failure.' Yet the Minister said almost the same in 1966 in refusing to support a Private Member's Bill. Conference again called for legislation in 1968. But still in 1969 the Government refused to promise a statute.[31] The newspaper headlines rarely speak of these daily injuries. They are recorded in no profit-and-loss accounts, only in the minds of families who grieve for them. Many people in our society shut their eyes to killed and injured workers, as the Victorians shut their eyes to the poor.

On many occasions in recent years, workers have gone on

strike against unsafe conditions, though remarkably sparingly in the light of the accident figures. At times the response of public bodies has seemed negligible. The Donovan Report said nothing. The politicians, on the front benches at least, seemed uninterested. Then, at last, in 1970, the Labour Government published a Health and Safety Bill. This proposed two reforms. First, it would replace 'factory doctors' appointed under the Factories Act with a new employment medical advisory service. With over 30,000 workers a year suffering from various industrial diseases, this would have been a most welcome step which in the long term could have far-reaching effects on health at work. Secondly, the Bill would have allowed the appointment by a trade union 'recognized for the purpose of negotiating terms and conditions of employment' of *safety representatives* at all factories with more than ten workers; and at factories with more than one hundred workers it would compel the formation of joint safety committees. No doubt, as was quickly pointed out, there would be difficulty where no trade union was 'recognized'; or where the recognized union organized only a minority of the workers, or a small craft among them. But the answer seemed simple; the employer could encourage union organization and collective bargaining. The safety representatives would have the right to make inspections every three months, or more frequently in the event of accidents. The representatives had to be persons with five years' employment in industry, over 23 years of age, and, if possible, with two years' employment at the factory concerned. The factory occupier would be guilty of criminal offences if he failed to fulfil his duties under the statute. Unhappily, the Bill did not give to the safety representatives the right to call in the Factory Inspector and (with his consent) have work stopped in the event of serious accidents until an unsafe condition is rectified. But the idea of even having workers' delegates with even the small power of inspection which the Bill proposed struck some people as objectionable. The C.B.I. insisted that voluntary methods were best, recalling that the Minister of Labour in 1966 pledged that the voluntary system would be given a chance to work before compulsion was introduced. The President of the National Federation of Building Trades Employers said the Bill would 'provide increased opportunities for disruptive elements to exploit new areas of industrial life'. The Bill lapsed with the General Election.

Meanwhile, there had been going on since 1967 a review within the D.E.P. to consolidate and extend the various safety statutes. But one consultative document and three years later, the project seemed to have been lost. For in March 1970 the Secretary of State announced that she was setting up a new 'small high-powered body' to investigate the same legislation and to propose new ways of preventing accidents. Mere consolidation of existing legislation was not enough, she said: 'We need to break away from the conventional approach'. But some experienced practitioners took a very different view. One, Mr Woolf, wrote to *The Times*, criticizing the 'pusillanimous' approach of the Inspectorate, the 'pathetic number of prosecutions', and the 'powerless' position proposed for workers' safety delegates, adding:

The Government's indifference to the non-enforcement of the Factories Act is a scandal which is sufficiently exposed by the known facts as to make any further inquiry quite unnecessary.

At the least there seems to be no inconsistency between continued research (even by 'high-powered' bodies) and an increase in the rate of prosecutions to try and enforce the thousands of safety obligations which now go unheeded. Somehow this rising tide of human unhappiness must be stemmed, for in the words of an I.L.O. Report of 1949: 'However one looks at the matter there is no honour or profit in industrial accidents; there is only incredible suffering and loss.'

NEW STATUTORY FRONTIERS?

We may now ask how firmly the boundary of statutory intervention is fixed in our labour law. As we have seen, the areas covered by the tide of statutory reform before the emergence of modern collective bargaining have come to be thought of as appropriate to the method of legal enactment – calculation and payment of wages in Acts from 1831 to 1960; protection of 'sweated' trades in 1909 which becomes the modern Wages Council 'prop' to autonomous bargaining; control of hours and conditions of the weaker groups, young persons and women; and a floor of rights on standards for safety, health and welfare for workers in factories and some other places; plus provision for minimum notice, redundancy payment, rights to appeal from dismissal, and the prevention of racial discrimination at work in the extended floor of rights of the 1960s.

But trade unions, as we saw, did not abandon that method on theoretical grounds; they came to prefer collective bargaining from experience. Even today, however, the roles may be reversed. Thus, on equal pay for women, the trade unions pressed the Government to legislate. Some developments reveal a more sophisticated mixture of the methods of enactment and of union action. In the Health and Safety Bill, 1970, for example, the proposal was to use legislation to compel the establishment of safety machinery; but that machinery would be staffed by appointees of the trade unions recognized for collective bargaining.

There are many other matters which in the seventies will demand careful consideration about the method for reform. If we establish a 40-hour week or a national minimum wage, shall it be done by legislation, or by bargaining, or a mixture? And if the last, what kind of mixture? Trade unions have pressed for a minimum wage statute for many years, arguing as two trade unionists put it in 1968:

Low wages, far from assisting British industry, serve only to accommodate poor management, low efficiency and out-of-date methods.[32]

But few had discussed the relationship of such a statute to collective bargaining. And where is the minimum wage to be fixed? The T.U.C. in 1970 proposed £16.50. The Government and N.B.P.I. proposed £12 in 1967. An interdepartmental Working Party produced a (discussion) 'Green Paper' in 1969, however, questioning the effectiveness of any minimum wage laws in relieving poverty (they have not done so in other countries) and asking whether selective social benefits might not do the job better. Also, the low-paid worker is usually weak and unorganized and needs the help of a third party, e.g. a wages inspector. But when they reviewed the question in 1970, the T.U.C. in their discussion pamphlet *Low Pay,* instead of taking it for granted that a minimum wage should have a statutory basis, probed the alternative of a 'voluntary minimum agreed between the T.U.C. and C.B.I.'. The number of workers affected by a minimum wage would be over 15 million so that the Wages Inspectorate, already under strength, would need augmenting. (Perhaps, they suggested, turning to the answer for which everyone too easily grasps, enforcement could lie with Industrial Tribunals.) In a thoughtful passage, *Low Pay* pauses over the consequences of inviting the State to intervene on a much bigger scale in the wage fixing process; but it is well aware of the 'unsure foundations' of a voluntary system.

The Donovan Report contained disappointingly little analysis of the future relationship of the two methods. One of its research papers, however, proposed that regulation of overtime should be introduced by statutory permits.[33] Once again, the problem of how such legislation would fit into the complex structures of British bargaining was not really solved. Nor are these the only proposals for new legislation which are in the air. Should women be protected further than the four weeks that applies to factory work, in respect of employment after childbirth? After all, an I.L.O. Recommendation stipulates that a woman should be allowed a 'reasonable further period of absence' *beyond* maternity leave if her health or circumstances make it necessary. In Austria, women are entitled to leave of absence of up to one year – and the number of women in the labour force has steadily increased. A much more modest Bill introduced by Lord Balniel in 1962 was voted out by those who said the matter was more appropriate to solution by collective bargaining over a floor of social security rights. Were they correct? As for racial discrimination at work, the 1968 Act, we saw (p. 84), made that illegal; but will that Act be effective? If not, should further action against this curse of modern society be concentrated on statutory or voluntary action?

There is scarcely any legislative intervention in employment conditions that does not affect the bargaining powers of capital and labour. We saw in Chapter 3 that the issues of dismissal and unemployment inevitably led us to the question whether legislation should increasingly intervene. A further parallel with the hire-and-fire problems that emerged in that chapter is presented by the new proposals of legal powers for workers' safety representatives. Once again the questions are raised: what is to be a management function? And how far are workers to share in the control of the process of decision-making, be it accident prevention or dismissals? And as we have seen in Chapter 4 the issues raised by legislative intervention in regard to collective agreements are in the middle of current political debate. Certainly the matters touched on in this chapter suggest that, though statute is plainly a more appropriate method for imposing standards on certain questions (e.g. safety) than on others (e.g. wage rates), the exact boundaries of its intervention are still fluid and open to experiment. Professor Kahn-Freund said of France in 1959 that 'the growth of State-created and State-enforced standards of social policy, including such things as minimum wages, holidays, etc., has led to an impoverishment of collective bargaining'.[34] Since then collective bargaining has developed rapidly in France despite statutory regulation. But it would be well to see that the aims of Donovan are not thwarted by interventions of the State which lead in Britain to an equivalent period of impoverishment in voluntary bargaining.*

* Unhappily the Government seems to intend just such intervention: Appendix, p. 485.

1. Batt, *Master and Servant* (5th ed. 1967), p. 163 n. 2.
2. G. W. Hilton, *The Truck System*, 1960, pp. 101–14.
3. *Cameron* v. *Royal Ophthalmic Hospital* [1940] 4 All E.R. 439, at p. 443.
4. Paras. 718–22; see A. I. Marsh and J. W. Staples in 'Three Studies in Collective Bargaining' (*R.C. Research Paper No. 8*, 1968).
5. [1894] A.C. 383.
6. *Squire* v. *Bayer & Co.* [1901] 2 K.B. 299.
7. *S. & U. Stores* v. *Lee* [1969] 2 All E.R. 417; see *ante* p. 122.
8. *Bird* v. *British Celanese Ltd* [1945] 1 All E.R. 488, at p. 491.
9. [1931] 1 Ch. 310; *ante* Ch. 2, p. 98.
10. *Report of the Committee on the Truck Acts* (1961), para. 62.
11. (1962) 25 *Modern Law Review* at p. 220 (O. Aikin); p. 512 (M. Hickling).
12. *Financial Times*, 17.8.65.
13. S. Webb, Introduction to Hutchins and Harrison, *A History of Factory Legislation*, p. vii (the leading history on the subject).
14. Hutchins and Harrison, op. cit., p. 16.
15. Hutchins and Harrison, op. cit., p. 102; p. 104.
16. Hutchins and Harrison, op. cit., p. 82.
17. See *R.C. Research Paper No. 11*, Nancy Seear, 'The Position of Women in Industry' (1968).
18. *Daily Telegraph*, 19 December 1871, quoted by C. Bassett-Vincent, in *An Authentic History of Railway Trade Unionism*, 1902, p. 38.
19. Clegg, Fox, and Thompson, *A History of British Trade Unions Since 1889* (1964), p. 294.
20. *Law and Public Opinion in England*, p. li.
21. op. cit., p. 119.
22. Clegg, Fox, and Thompson, op. cit. p. 365.
23. E. S. Turner, *Roads to Ruin* (1960), p. 200.
24. J. L. and B. Hammond, *Lord Shaftesbury* (1923), p. 186, p. 153.
25. See on the problems that can arise here *Wright* v. *Ford Motor Co.* [1967] 1 Q.B. 230.
26. J. L. Williams, *Accidents and Ill-health at Work* (1960), p. 432.
27. op. cit. p. 167.
28. R. K. Christy, 'Role of the Inspectorate', *Financial Times* Supplement 15 July 1964. See on 'sociological aspects' of enforcing

the legislation, W. G. Carson (1970) 33 *Modern Law Review* 396.

29. R. and B. Thompson, *Accidents at Work* (3rd ed. 1968), p. 52.
30. *Dissenting Report to the Winn Committee*, Cmnd 3691, p. 170.
31. *T.U.C. Report* (1964), pp. 422–6; *Report* (1966) p. 429; *Report* (1967) p. 608; *Report* (1968), p. 537; *Report* (1969) p. 616.
32. C. Jenkins and J. Mortimer, *The Kind of Laws the Unions ought to Want* (1968), p. 164.
33. E. G. Whybrew, *R.C. Research Paper No. 9*, 'Overtime Working in Britain' (1968).
34. 'Labour Law' in *Law and Opinion in England in the Twentieth Century* (ed. Ginsberg; 1959), p. 252.

CHAPTER 6

COMPENSATION FOR INJURY
AT WORK

THE figures given in the last chapter show how urgent is the need to prevent industrial accidents. But if prevention fails and a worker suffers injury at work, where may he look for compensation? He may receive a temporary payment of his wages (discussed in Chapter 3); but otherwise he has two possible sources of compensation for the loss of his earning power and other injuries: (i) damages in a legal action; and (ii) state insurance benefit. The first category may be divided into actions against those liable to him under the common law; and those liable to him under the protective statutes mentioned in the last chapter.

I. *Legal Action*

(a) *Common Law.* A worker injured on the job by the negligence of another person who owes him a duty to use care can claim damages from that person whoever he is. He may be a fellow-worker, an occupier of premises to which he is sent, the owner's architect, consultant safety specialists brought in by the employer, the owner of machinery, or a manufacturer of appliances which the worker uses; but in the average case he will be the worker's employer. We saw in Chapter 2 how from 1837 onwards the judges decided that a master, although he was 'vicariously' liable to other persons negligently injured by his servant in the course of the employment, was not liable in damages if the person injured was another servant in 'common employment' with the wrongdoer. The servant, said Baron Alderson in 1850, 'contracted on the terms that as between himself and his master he would run this risk'! This judicial reflection of a management ideology remained in our law until finally reversed by statute in 1948. It is today dead and buried, and a worker can sue both the fellow-worker, if he wishes, and the master who is vicariously responsible, claiming compensation for injury caused by the fellow-worker's negligence on the job, so long as the fellow-worker acted within the scope of his employment, a difficult concept which can include cases of breach of an employer's prohibition and, as in 1967, 'exceptional and excessive 'foolhardiness. The employer, of course, is more likely to be insured, as in *Lister* v. *Romford Ice and Cold Storage*: p. 103.

But in the years between 1837 and 1948 the judges began to develop another concept, one fashioned first by the enlightenened Scottish courts. The employer, it was said, owed a *personal* duty to each employee not to expose him to unreasonable risk. In 1880, Parliament permitted the worker to sue an employer in a limited range of accidents despite the common employment doctrine, though it limited damages to three years' wages. The courts developed their own doctrine of the master's personal duty particularly in the 1930s and 1940s when judges, in a liberal period, had grown favourable to claims by injured workers for compensation. This doctrine steered the plaintiff worker around the rocks of common employment because, judges said, he had not impliedly consented to risk the *master's* carelessness.

This employer's duty may be seen either as an implied obligation in the contract of service, or as a duty imposed by law (breach of which is a tort). It continued to develop after 1948 when the employer became vicariously liable for negligent fellow-workers. 'This is fortunate for the injured worker, because it is sometimes easier to show that the employer is guilty of breach of the personal duty than to point to the particular fellow-worker for whose wrongdoing the employer would be vicariously liable, especially if, as Lord Donovan put it in a case in 1969, the facts proved raise against the employer an *inference* 'that the accident must have been due to their default in respect of inspection or maintenance' of apparatus.

What must be shown if the injured plaintiff is to succeed? He must show that he is the defendant's 'servant' – we have already seen that the same duty is not owed to the 'self-employed'; p. 62 – who has been injured by the defendant's breach of the duty. That duty, said Lord Wright in *Wilsons and Clyde Coal Ltd* v. *English*, 1938, is 'to take reasonable care for the safety of his workmen, whether the employer be an individual, a firm, or a company, and whether or not the employer takes any share in the conduct of the operations'.[1] This duty is personal to the master. Therefore he cannot escape merely by entrusting its discharge to independent contractors. He remains liable if the system of working provided for the men is unsafe. The *English* case itself was an excellent illustration, because there the employers were forced by law to delegate management of their mine to a manager; but they were still liable for the unreasonably dangerous state in which he left it and from which the miner, English, suffered his injury.

Lord Wright, in a speech which is regarded as the high point in judicial rejection of the earlier attitudes of *laisser faire*, said the duty covered 'provision of a competent staff of men, adequate material and a proper system and effective supervision'. In 1961 and 1967 judges re-emphasized that an employer must take reasonable care not to expose his employees to 'unnecessary risks, even if it be the risk of injury by criminals' (though in those cases the employers had done all they could). If the master provides incompetent workmates or workmates known to engage in dangerous horseplay, he breaks his personal duty to the other workers; but if he has (or his agents have) no reason to know of their proclivity, he is not personally culpable and is not even vicariously liable if the act is outside the scope of the employment. So, where scrap metal workers jokingly rolled a live shell to and fro and the plaintiff, on being told by another worker: 'Hit it', did so with a sledgehammer, injuring himself in the explosion, he failed in an action against his employers. They knew nothing of the shell or of such jocular habits; and the incitement was an act not within the scope of the employment.

But the duty to provide a safe system of work still rests upon the employer even when men are sent to work outside his works (e.g. on a customer's premises), although what the employer can be expected to know will, of course, be less in such a case than what he must know about his own works. The employer may still be liable (in addition to the occupier if *he* is negligent: p. 264). For example, a window cleaner in 1952 proved that his employers on sending him out to work had failed to lay out a safe system of work and to instruct their workers to use it.[2] The employer must provide not merely proper appliances and the like, but also give adequate instruction to his workers, especially if they are inexperienced. But judges have pointed out that reasonable care is still the test; it is not in itself proof of negligence to show that an employer failed to instruct workers to wear protective clothing. In 1959 Viscount Simonds went so far as to 'deprecate any tendency to treat the relation of employer and skilled workman as equivalent to that of nurse and imbecile child'. If the employer, however, knows of special characteristics possessed by one of his employees, this can step up his duty because the duty is owed to each of them *individually*. Thus, in *Paris* v. *Stepney Borough Council*,[3] the care demanded of the employers for a one-eyed man in the provision of goggles was higher than if they had employed a normal man, for the risk of injury meant more for him, and they knew it. Thus in 1969 an employer was held to be under a higher duty to an apprentice, extending to inquiry as to the young man's experience, (though the result of the case was affected by the latter's misrepresentations on that question); and in 1970 the fact that a worker was unskilled with an imperfect knowledge of English meant that the employers had to increase their efforts to avoid accidents.[4] But the extent to which employers must instruct and enforce instructions is still uncertain. We may contrast the conclusion in *James* v. *Hepworth Grandage*.[5] The worker was burned by molten metal because he was not wearing safety spats. The spats were available and notices advised all workers that they should be worn; but, *unknown* to the employers, who had employed him for four years, this worker was unable to read. The employers were held not liable – a decision which one commentator rightly saw as a reversion 'to the "old" attitudes to safety'.[6] For, as a case of 1969 re-emphasized, where statutory duties have been in issue judges have been more ready to demand a greater degree of instruction and supervision from the employer. In any case, an employer ought to find out when he gives out the written particulars whether he is taking on an illiterate man.

So, the employer's duty is still one to 'take reasonable care for the safety of his workmen', not a *guarantee* of their safety; and it is for the injured worker to prove that the employer failed to take it. This makes the outcome of litigation hard to predict. Negligence is a failure to provide against reasonably foreseeable hazards. But it is a notoriously capricious test, for what one judge thinks foreseeable another may not. Moreover the problem of such cases is so often the problem of *proof*, and the burden is on the worker – as it is on any plaintiff alleging negligence. In a case for breach of statutory duty in 1964, the judge substituted his own inference as to how the injury happened for the worker's own account. Lord Justice Willmer in the Court of Appeal thought this went beyond the limit

beyond which one is not entitled to go in making out a case for an injured workman ... a workman who seeks to recover damages must prove his case. The workman in the present case has not proved how the accident occurred. The Court has had to speculate and this is not sufficient.

In finding evidence to prove his case of negligence the worker has to make bricks out of straw. For example, in another practical joke case, 1969, the worker was seriously burned when X, another workman – 'a "real character" given to playing practical jokes' – kicked a flaming tin at a third man who, in self-protection, kicked it on to the plaintiff. He could prove neither that the employers knew X was a joker nor that X acted within the scope of his employment. But in 1968 a widow of a worker who died of scrotal cancer caused by exposure to oils at work proved the employers were negligent. Their factory doctor had not conducted half-yearly tests, and no warnings of danger were given to workers. Failure to follow the general practice of the trade has long been accounted evidence of negligence (though compliance with it can also leave the master culpable if the court decides that the practice is a negligent one). But in 1960 the House of Lords held that a worker had not proved his case when he showed that his employer did not, as other employers did, provide a barrier cream to guard against dermatitis. The scope of the master's duty has been further restricted by a decision in 1964 that even if some carelessness by the employer is shown, he is liable, not, as had previously been thought, for all 'direct' injuries flowing from that lack of care, but only for damage to the worker of a type which was 'reasonably foreseeable'. But if some type of personal injury is foreseeable a worker who has unknown idiosyncratic peculiarities is able to recover for *all* types of personal injury caused to him by the negligence. Similarly, where a worker eventually suffered cancer as the result of a lip burned by reason of the employer's carelessness; and a worker was injured by frostbite after being sent on a long journey in an unheated van, the employer of each was liable. But if the employer fails to be careful against foreseeable injury, e.g. by splashing with molten liquid, he will not be liable if the worker is hurt by an unforeseeable event, e.g. an explosion caused by the spilt liquid. The new principle has odd results. Employers who were negligent in exposing a worker to the risk of rat-bites were not liable when he contracted a rare disease through coming into contact not with the teeth but with the urine of the rats.[7]

In *Davie* v. *New Merton Board Mills*, 1959,[8] the House of Lords reasserted in a new way the proposition that the master's duty is only one of 'reasonable care'. The worker worked with a drift and hammer and a metal chip flew off the drift into his eye. The employers had bought the drift from suppliers who had bought it from manufacturers; it looked all right but was in fact defective. Now in such a case a worker who can prove negligence against the manufacturers can obtain damages from *them*; but can he also sue his employers? The House of Lords, reversing the trial judge, held that the worker could not sue the employer. The master's duty was not absolute; he could not be liable for the manufacturer's fault. The manufacturer was not his 'delegate' for performing the duty. Of course, if the employer knows of the defect he will be liable; and, where the testing of the tool is then for the employer, the manufacturers may also *escape*, as in a case of 1966. But the employee may not even know who the manufacturer was. The courts saw the unreasonableness of the *Davie* doctrine and held in 1969 that the employer would be liable unless he showed that the fault was the manufacturer's or otherwise proved he was not at fault. The criticism of *Davie* led eventually to the passing of the Employer's Liability (Defective Equipment) Act, which came into force in October 1969. This statute 'deems' that the fault of a third party (identifiable or not) in respect of a defect in equipment which was provided by the employer for the purposes of his business, and injured the employee, is negligence on the part of the employer. No agreement is allowed to exclude this liability; and 'fault' includes breach of both common law and statutory duties. (Unhappily, yet again the statute defines 'employee' to include only those under a 'contract of service or apprenticeship'; the opportunity might have been taken to improve the lot of the self-employed – see p. 265). It is right to reverse *Davie*; for back in 1939 Lord Justice Goddard understood the *English* case to have put on the employer a duty 'to make the place of employment and the plant used as safe as the exercise of reasonable skill and care would permit'. In 1967, the House of Lords had reasserted this rule in regard to the place of work.

Defences: Two defences to liability may affect the worker's legal rights: (i) contributory negligence; and (ii) consent.

(i) Until 1945 a plaintiff who could be shown to have contributed to an accident by his own carelessness was allowed to recover nothing. In consequence the judges in the 1940s often leaned generously backwards to avoid finding carelessness against a worker injured partly by reason of his employer's breach of duty. But in 1945, a law reform Act gave the courts power in such cases of 'contributory negligence' to reduce the damages by the amount they considered just.

(ii) It was, and is, a complete defence to an action for negligence to show that the plaintiff freely encountered and consented to the risk in question. Suppose a worker goes on with his work knowing that the employer has left it dangerous, can this defence of consent be used against him? In *Smith* v. *Baker*, 1891,[9] Lord Bramwell thought it could:

I do so hold, if the servant is foolish enough to agree to it. This sounds very cruel. But do not people go to see dangerous sports?

But the other Law Lords refused to follow this last note of nineteenth-century doctrine. The worker, a navvy, had not 'consented', they said, to stones being slung across his place of work, one of which had hit him. Knowledge does not imply consent to such a superadded risk, especially for a workman who might lose his job if he complains. Most judges could no longer bear the injustice of doctrines of 'consent' in the face of harsh economic reality. Lord Bramwell was, after all, exceptionally steeped in the *laisser faire* ideology of his time and class. (It was he who, faced with a child of four whose fingers had been crushed in 1866 by a dangerous machine left unguarded near the street, said not merely that the child could not sue but that, 'suppose this machine had been of a very delicate construction and had been injured by the child's fingers, would not the child, in spite of his tender years, have been liable to an action as a tortfeasor?' – i.e. for damaging the machine!) Of course, times change and so do judges, though, like the rest of us, they can sometimes lag behind. In the same month that the terrifying figures for factory accidents appeared in 1967, Lord Justice Danckwerts said that in face of his common law and statutory liabilities 'the employer's life is a somewhat hazardous one. Indeed it would be a good deal safer to keep lions or other wild animals in a park than to engage in business involving the employment of labour.' To such conclusions can one be drawn by ignoring the social reality where it is the employer who is (and now must be, p. 295) insured against his liabilities and the worker who is injured.

In the twentieth century 'consent' was thought to be largely dead as a defence in cases involving injured workers. In 1953, a worker was killed in a gypsum mine after he went with his fellows back to work under a 'drummy roof', knowing it to be dangerous, and contrary to the order of the foreman that the roof should be brought down before work proceeded. His widow received damages from the employers, who were vicariously liable for the negligence of the other workers who joined him in the work. Those damages were reduced by 80 per cent on account of his own very serious contributory negligence; but no one raised the issue of 'consent'. More recently court decisions have re-echoed tones of an earlier age. In the case of the man who hammered the live shell the judge thought 'consent' would have been a defence if it had been needed. And an equivalent line of thought appears in cases where 'it is reasonable for the master to leave the servant to choose between running the risk or resigning', as it was put in the judgment against Mrs Vaness in 1965 when she tried to claim that her employers should have protected her against colleagues who so belittled and persecuted her that she came to the verge of a nervous breakdown. Similar tendencies appeared in 1969 cases where it was said not to be negligence for an employer to leave to workers the decision whether to ask for help, or the selection of equipment, about which, in view of the worker's experience, the employers had given no instructions. As we shall see, p. 282, in another field the cases have gone even further.

(b) *Breach of Statutory Duty*. If an employer breaks one of his statutory duties (e.g. to fence a machine) and that breach causes damage to a worker of the kind the statute aimed to prevent, the worker usually has the right to sue the employer for damages. The value of such an action to the worker is that he often does not have to prove negligence as such at all. Many of the duties discussed in the last chapter give rise to such actions, especially those in the Factories Act, 1961, and its Regulations, the Offices, Shops and Railway Premises Act, 1963, and the Mines and Quarries Act, 1954. The standard of such duties varies. Some are strict duties, such as the duty to fence dangerous machinery in the Factories Act, s.14 (which will afford us our main illustration in this section).

As Lord Justice Rigby said in 1898, 'once there has been a failure in the performance of an absolute statutory duty ... there is no need for the plaintiff to allege or prove negligence'. When, therefore, the Factories Act demands that all 'lifting tackle' be of 'adequate strength' (s.26), it cannot be a defence for employers to show that the strength needed for the operation in question was not open to calculation when the worker is injured by failure of the tackle, even though it is also found that the employers were not negligent.[10] Other sections are less strict. For example, s.29 imposes a duty to provide and maintain safe means of access and place of work 'so far as is reasonably practicable'. In a sharply fought case, *Nimmo* v. *Alexander Cowan*, 1967,[11] a bare majority of the Law Lords decided that the burden of proving that it was not reasonably practicable to make the work-place safer is on the 'occupier' of the factory, as are most of the Act's duties, i.e. normally the employer. Lord Upjohn could not 'believe that Parliament intended to impose on the injured workman, or if dead, his widow ... the obligation' of showing how the employer should make the place safer, for 'he is at a great disadvantage compared to the employer'. What is more, in 1969 the House of Lords held further that, under Regulations demanding 'every ladder shall so far as practicable be securely fixed', the employer had the burden of showing that all reasonable steps had been taken to observe this duty – and that might include giving instruction to the workers even if the common law duty would not demand it.[12]

But the Law Lords showed a less liberal spirit in excusing employers who were under a duty to see that the factory floor was 'so far as is reasonably practicable kept free from any obstruction' (s.28). A worker, walking backwards carrying one end of a hot casting in a foundry, fell over scrap metal embedded in sand on the foundry floor. No one suggested the sand could be continuously raked; but the House of Lords did not even think it reasonably practicable to keep such obstructions (if they were such) off the floor during such work.[13] The same section has given rise to problems even in regard to its other, simpler words, such as: 'All floors ... shall be ... properly maintained', that is to say, 'maintained in an efficient state ... and in good repair'. In *Latimer* v. *A.E.C. Ltd*, 1953,[14] storm water flooded a factory floor and, after draining away, left a slippery oily substance over the surface. The employers spread sawdust on the floor but they did not have enough sawdust on the spot to cover the unusually large area affected. A worker slipped on the uncovered part later on that afternoon without carelessness on his own part. He sued for compensation both at common law *and* for breach of the statute. A worker can, as it were, ride both horses at once and needs to get only one past the post to win his damages. But here both fell. The House of Lords held that the Act was not broken. A floor could be 'properly maintained' even though affected by some transient condition. So long as it was of sound construction, it was still in an 'efficient state' even if a temporary danger existed upon it. As for the common law claim the Law Lords thought the employers were not negligent. They were entitled to weigh the seriousness and loss of closing the whole works down and sending the night shift home (which it was claimed they should have done) against the 'inconsiderable' risk of a worker slipping in this way.

The courts have established that an 'obstruction' must be 'something on the floor that has no business to be there' at the time. This restrictive interpretation means that objects properly stored on the floor or otherwise there for normal factory purposes are not 'obstructions'. It was only by a majority of three to two that the Law Lords in 1969 held that the scrap metal was an 'obstruction' on the foundry floor. Under the mines legislation nothing in its 'proper place' can be, the judges have held, an 'obstruction' of the coal mine road. Further, in a factory case of 1968, the Court of Appeal rejected the idea that a cleaner walking to work on the factory roadway was on a 'floor, passage or gangway', the majority saying a 'passage' could not be thirty feet wide. But the cleaner succeeded on the ground that there was a breach of the duty under s.5 to maintain 'sufficient and suitable lighting' in factories where 'persons are working or passing'.

Let us then imagine that a worker has been injured in a factory and follow some illustrations of legal problems likely to arise if he alleges breach of the statute. First, there is the question: does the statute cover that workplace? In 1967, a worker was held not to be working *on* a building within the Regulations when repairing a neon sign *attached* to one. The

Mines Act, 1954, requires every 'surface entrance' to have a barrier to stop persons 'falling down the shaft'; but in 1966 someone who fell down from the cage was held not to come within it since he fell 'from inside the shaft' not from the surface entrance. The Factories Act, 1961, does not apply unless the place is shown to be a 'factory' in law; and the 1963 Act applies only to an office, shop or railway workshop. The definitions are complex, but essentially a factory is a place where, for the purpose of trade or gain, persons are employed in manual labour in the making of an article, altering, repairing, ornamenting, finishing, cleaning, breaking up an article, or adapting it for sale, or for slaughtering cattle. Almost every word in the definition leaves some doubts about its exact meaning. 'Employed' means what it says; so, workers in a prison workshop do not fall within the 1961 Act (even though it binds the Crown). 'Manual labour' was recently reviewed by the Law Lords exhaustively, when they held the words to include repair of television and radio sets since a person is only not within the phrase 'if his occupation is primarily or substantially of a different kind and the manual work that he does is merely ancillary or accessory to that activity'.[15] Particular places are specified in addition as factories (e.g. certain dry docks and laundries); but a place within the precincts of a factory used *solely* for some other purpose is not part of the factory. The decisions make it hard to predict the answers. In 1961 a pump-house which pumped out chlorinated water for distribution to houses was, it was held, not part of a factory; in 1962, a pump-house pumping water *into* a bleaching factory was! In 1966, a separate administration block was held to be part of the factory.

Next, does it matter who the worker is? Suppose he is the visiting window-cleaner or a mechanic come to mend the machine. Some sections and Regulations clearly impose duties in favour of persons 'working', or 'employed' in the factory. Such a term, said the Lord Chancellor, Viscount Kilmuir, in 1962, would cover only those who are working 'for the purposes of the factory', not others; a visiting window-cleaner would be included, but not 'a policeman who enters a factory in pursuit of a felon or a fireman who enters to put out a fire'. In 1967 the House of Lords allowed a worker employed by sub-contractors on, in effect, a 'labour-only' basis to sue under Regulations protecting 'a person employed'; but a Scottish judge in 1969 again refused to allow a visiting fireman to sue as a person working in a factory.[16] Moreover, in the same year Regulations supplementing s.5 of the 1961 Act on lighting for places where 'persons are working or passing' were held not to apply to an ordinary employee who, arriving early at work, tripped as he walked across the dim factory to switch on lights in order to read his paper.

Next, the worker must show that there has been a breach of the relevant section and that this caused damage to him in an accident of the kind which the section aimed to prevent. Let us examine such a claim and the defences to it in relation to the famous 'duty to fence' first introduced in 1844 and, in its strengthened modern form, in 1878. Until the last few years the courts had restricted these vital duties in a strange way. Today there are signs of a change.

The Duty to Fence: Sections 12 and 13 of the Act require all flywheels directly connected with prime movers and all trans-mission machinery to be securely fenced. Then s.14 says:

Every dangerous part of any machinery other than prime movers and transmission machinery shall be securely fenced unless it is in such a position or of such construction as to be as safe to every person employed or working on the premises as it would be if securely fenced.

What is a 'dangerous' part of any 'machinery'? In *Hindle* v. *Birtwistle*, 1897, a flying shuttle flew out of a loom and hit a weaver; it was, said the court, 'dangerous' within a similar section of the 1878 Act 'if in the ordinary course of human affairs danger may be reasonably anticipated from the use of [it] without protection' (keeping in mind the likelihood of carelessness by the worker).[17] From that time on the rather capricious test of 'reasonable foreseeability' of the injury was imported into the section. As for 'machinery', until recently the courts took a narrow view of that word. It does not include machinery being made in the factory nor machinery in the course of installation; but only extends, said two Law Lords in 1964, to 'machinery which has been installed as part of the equipment of the factory' or 'intended to be used in the manufacturing processes'. In the early 1960s judges excluded a cable-way carrying buckets, trucks transporting materials within the factory and a heating fan. But since *British Railways Board* v. *Liptrot*,[18] 1968, most of those decisions are either wrong or suspect. There a mobile crane capable of moving under its own power, which squeezed the plaintiff worker against one of its wheels, was held to be 'machinery' – or at least, that part of it which caused *this* accident was 'machinery'; for, as Lord Pearson said, s.14 is not aimed at protecting 'traffic accidents' (for then the fencing itself might be dangerous to other traffic and need to be fenced, 'and so on ad infinitum'). The fact that the crane could drive outside the factory did not make any difference. The duty to guard 'dangerous' parts of any 'machinery' is absolute; and it is no defence even to show that a secure fence would render the machine useless or, as one case has it, 'a museum piece'.

But the judges raised a new hurdle. The object of the required fence is *'to keep the worker out, not to keep the machine or its products in'*, said Lord Simonds in 1946, in a case where the House of Lords refused damages to a woodworker injured by ejected slivers of wood. The worker had not shown any breach for which damages could be recovered. He had not got into the machine; the machine had thrown out something at him! The courts have made use of this notion to extend the types of occurrence against which the Act, they say, is not intended to guard. In *Close* v. *Steel Company of Wales*, 1962,[19] a bit in an electric drill used by the worker in an instrument workshop shattered and a piece entered his eye. On the facts the courts decided this was not a 'dangerous' part because experience did not suggest that such a forceful fragmentation was likely; that was why goggles were never worn. But a majority of the Law Lords further held that (even if the bit were dangerous) no breach of the duty to fence could have occurred because that duty was aimed exclusively at keeping the worker out, *not* keeping the machine in. In the same year, in *Sparrow* v. *Fairey Aviation*,[20] a worker using a hand scraper had slipped; the tool was thrown against the (dangerous) jaws of the lathe. As a result his hand was thrown on to the face of the chuck (which had not been alleged to be a dangerous part) and was severely lacerated. Again the House of Lords decided that he could not sue. Section 14 imposed no obligation to fence dangerous parts against contact with the tools held by a worker, only against contact with the worker himself! Lord Morris thought that sometimes equipment 'could be so attached to an operator that . . . [it] could rationally be regarded as being a part of him'. In 1964 it had actually been necessary for the Lord Chief Justice, in a case where a worker's hand was nipped between a dangerous machine and material fed into it, to say 'the fact that he wore a glove makes no difference'! The House of Lords agreed with this decision; but questioned whether it would be the same if the material was moving but the machine was stationary, for then 'the "danger" is derived from the moving material rather than from the stationary part of the machine' (Lord Morris)! In 1970, the Court of Appeal managed to save the section from total absurdity by allowing a worker to sue when he was injured in just such a manner, Lord Justice Fenton Atkinson saying, 'it should make no difference in principle whether the bit of the machine is moving and the material is stationary or whether it is the other way about'.[21]

The cases of the early sixties meant, in Mr Howell's words, that 'the protection offered by the fencing provisions of the Factories Act has been pushed back to its narrowest possible limits'.[22] Yet this is a statute of which the admitted and avowed object is accident prevention; and the Government insisted on not varying the words used (and therefore their interpretation) in the fencing section of the 1963 Act. A minority of judges has, it is true, vigorously opposed the development. In the (legislative) House of Lords debate in 1963, Lord Denning said it was a 'disgrace to the law that it should go unremedied'. More recent cases suggest that judges realize they have gone too far. Thus in 1967, a stonemason had his jaw broken when his tie caught in an electric hand tool used to cut granite. He succeeded both at common law and under the statute, the tool being 'machinery', and the judge spent no time dividing the worker from his tie. Moreover in *Millard v. Serck Tubes Ltd*,[23] a man's hand was dragged into a drilling machine in a most unusual fashion. Material called 'swarf' was forced *out* in the course of drilling. His hand got caught in the swarf and was thereby dragged into the machine. He succeeded under s.14. The Court of Appeal, reversing the trial judge, swept aside cases like the *Close* decision. They were pressed in argument with the unusual character of the accident, but this, they said, did not stop it being a 'dangerous' part. Once some kind of damage is foreseeable, there is a duty to fence. If damage occurs through failure to fence, it matters not that the exact type of accident is not readily foreseeable. We may contrast the common law (p. 269).

Fortunately, an attempt by defendants further to limit s.14 has failed. It is not critical that the worker was, at the time of injury, using the machine for unpermitted purposes or was, as in a 1965 case, 'on a frolic of his own'. The decisive decision was *Uddin* v. *Associated Portland Cement Co.*, 1965.[24] A worker in a cement factory climbed on to a platform where he knew he should not go and where a shaft with projecting studs revolved on top of a cabinet. He leaned over the shaft to catch one of the many pigeons which flew about in the roof of the works and which the men fed with corn; and, said Lord Pearce, 'whatever were his designs towards the pigeon which he was stalking they were not actuated by benevolence'. In the result his arm was torn off. Despite this 'action of extreme folly' beyond anyone's anticipation, the plaintiff was held to come within the words 'employed or working on the premises' and was protected even though acting 'entirely for his own ends'. Once a part of machinery was dangerous, the Act protected the 'utterly stupid' as well as the 'slightly stupid' (although, as we shall see, the amount of damages is affected: p. 28). Both the *Millard* and the *Uddin* type of case promote the new policy inherent in Lord Reid's remark in 1967 that the benefit of statutes of this sort intended to protect employees should not be withheld, once it is shown that 'injury was caused by a breach', just because the man 'did not suffer that injury in precisely the way contemplated in the statute'. But it seems a pity that S. 14 itself cannot be urgently amended, without waiting for the new code of safety legislation or an inquiry, to avoid the absurd lines drawn by such decisions as *Sparrow* which deprive injured workers of a remedy.

Section 14 was not the only section to be squeezed. Section 16, for example, demands that all fences be constantly maintained while the dangerous parts are 'in motion or use' (with exceptions for lubrication, adjustment, etc.). Judgments since 1955 have held that a machine rotated on an 'inching button' at five revolutions a minute, and belts pulled round by hand, were *not* 'in motion' within the meaning of the section! In 1964 the Court of Appeal had to accept 'a broad distinction between a thing which is "being moved" slowly and a thing which is "in motion" at a fast pace'. And in 1965 the same court pronounced that one should consider speed, duration, method of starting and *purpose* of using, before deciding whether a machine is 'in motion'. Once again, it is difficult to accept this as the meaning of a safety statute which says merely 'in motion'.

There are fashions and phases in judicial thinking, as in all other things in life. Legal historians may well come to see some of these cases as an unattractive example of legal thinking which, moulded by unspoken premises, becomes almost divorced from the needs of social change. These interpretations of the common law, statutes, and Regulations were for ten years or so increasingly narrow interpretations, as far as the protection of workers is concerned. The feeling seemed to exist that workers' claims for compensation had gone far enough; and scant attention was paid in some decisions to the effect on accident prevention. All is not yet different; but since 1966 some judges have realized how far the process has gone and have tried to save what they can from the wreckage of judicial interpretation of the once 'strict' duty to fence. We cannot tell exactly what are the conscious and unconscious social and psychological pressures which go into such swings of judicial attitude. Perhaps we shall never know until some of the judges (especially appeal judges) encourage closer investigation in the interests of research. Now that it is recognized that policy *does* play a part in judicial decision, it is arguable that machinery should be devised for continuous review of those areas of law in which judges' policies have departed from current social needs. The interpretation of safety statutes has clearly been one such area.

The Careless Worker. The same attitude is apparent in cases where the worker is himself at fault. As we have seen, if the worker does not take due care for his own safety, his damages can since 1945 be reduced for his 'contributory negligence'. In *Uddin*'s case, for example, the plaintiff's damages were reduced by three-quarters. What is carelessness by a worker is often a matter of opinion. But the judges (once again from about 1955) developed two other arguments which can completely destroy the worker's right of action.

First, the worker must, as we have seen, always show that the breach of statutory duty (which we now assume he has proved) *caused* the injury to him. Even if the employer has a statutory duty to see that safety equipment is used, an employee who is also under a statutory duty to use such equipment and fails to do so may well fail to recover any damages at all because the accident is said to have been caused by what was 'all his fault'. If any independent fault causing the accident can be ascribed to the employer, the responsibility will be divided between them. But in *McWilliams* v. *Sir William Arrol Ltd*, 1962, the House of Lords went further.[25] Even if the employer has failed to provide the safety device demanded by the Act, he will escape liability if it can be shown, on a balance of probabilities, that the worker would not have used it, even if it had been provided. There the worker, an experienced steel erector who, not having a safety-belt, fell seventy feet, was dead. Who is to say whether a dead worker would have used a safety belt that was never provided? The House of Lords was prepared to determine 'on the probabilities' this question of hypothetical causation. In the *James* case,[5] the Court of Appeal was prepared to infer in 1967 that the illiterate workman would not have worn safety spats even if he had been told about them expressly because he had failed to inquire about the notices displayed concerning protective clothing! This is a gigantic departure from the old approach, which held, as Lord Justice Hodson put it in 1953, that 'it cannot lie in the mouth of the [wrongdoer in breach of the Act] to say that this was not the cause of the accident on the ground that the probabilities are that the deceased would never have elected to use a belt'. That is exactly what the wrongdoer can now say. The new doctrine of 'hypothetical causation' deprives the habitually careless worker of his right to elect on any occasion to use the safety device. If he is known to be a careless worker who habitually fails to use it, the employer need have rather less fear of a civil action for damages from the worker (or his widow). That is scarcely the way to prevent accidents. Secondly, the Court of Appeal in decisions dating from 1887 held that 'consent' can never be a defence to an action for breach of *statutory* duty. Common employment was still alive; and it was against public policy to allow a worker utterly to 'waive' a statute (though on occasion damages have been cut by 99 or even 100 per cent on account of contributory negligence, so that the result was the same in practice). We have also seen that, after the defeat of Lord Bramwell in 1891, 'consent' had for decades never been used in actions for common law negligence, so it was thought to be a dead or unimportant issue, as such, in all injury cases. It has been resurrected, however, by the House of Lords in 1964, in the rather special case of *I.C.I.* v. *Shatwell*.[26]

Brothers George and James Shatwell, two experienced shot-firers, deliberately engaged in an operation which they knew to be both dangerous and in breach of statutory Regulations. The Regulations put the duty to abstain from it not on the employers, I.C.I., but on them. Both were injured, and George now sued I.C.I. alleging that I.C.I. were 'vicariously' liable for the statutory default of James, their employee acting within the course of his employment. The Law Lords chose to see George as 'consenting' to the risk. His consent was a complete defence as against James, and there was, therefore, no liability for which I.C.I. could be vicariously responsible. This was, it is true, a case of a statutory duty imposed on the *employee*, not

282

the employer; Lord Pearce, for example, insisted that consent could only be

available where the employer was not himself in breach of statutory duty and was not vicariously in breach of any statutory duty ... and where the plaintiff himself assented to and took part in the breaking of the statutory duty in question.

Most Law Lords retained the doctrine that no consent of the worker's could ever excuse the employer for breach of *his* statutory duty. But Lord Reid expressly refused to decide the case where an employer was put into that breach only by the deliberate wrongful act of the worker himself. No doubt the merits of the *Shatwell* case were all against the plaintiff worker. But the Lords, by reviving the old doctrine of consent in even this modified new form, have reopened a door long believed to have been locked. Already, in 1966 two judges have shown a willingness to use the doctrine again even in common law actions. The reasoning of the *Shatwell* case was most dangerous.

Undetected or Fatal Accidents and Amount of Compensation: Next, how much time does the worker have in which to sue? A statute of 1954 reduced the period, for no apparently good reason, from six years to three when the action is one in respect of personal injuries. The time runs from the moment when the damage is first suffered by the worker, not from the time it can be detected. Therefore, if an employer's negligence or statutory default caused a worker to contract a disease, such as pneumoconiosis, which was not detected for (say) five years, it would be too late for the worker to sue. An Act of 1963 aims to set right this anomaly. It provides that the Court may relieve the worker from his disability where 'material facts of a decisive character' were hidden from him during the critical period so long as he has commenced his action within twelve months of discovering them. In 1969 the Court of Appeal liberally decided that this included a case where the worker knew of his injury and that it arose from his work, but could not be expected to know within the three years that it was due to the defendants' negligence and to take the necessary legal advice before he died. In the same year, however, a majority of the same court stopped two widows from adding manufacturers of substances which caused their husbands' cancer as defendants (even though their husbands could have added them) – a much stricter application of the 1963 statute. This problem has been referred to the Law Commission. It should also consider whether, in times when workers discover the effects of industrial accidents or noxious substances eight or (in one case) twenty years later, there is any reason for restricting the time for legal action to *three* years, instead of the *six* which it was before 1954.

An injured worker can claim 'special' and 'general' damages. Special damages include mainly loss of earnings caused by his absence from work. As we have seen in Chapter 2, in discussing damages for wrongful dismissal, damages that represent lost earnings are calculated since 1955 *net* of tax. Since a decision of the House of Lords in 1969, however, the extent of other deductions is uncertain. Money paid to the injured worker by his employer need not be deducted. By virtue of an Act of 1948 fifty per cent of the benefits paid and likely to be paid over five years under the National Insurance Acts (discussed later) is also deductible from the damages. General damages represent an attempt to compensate future losses, disablement, pain and suffering, and so on. The sums awarded by different judges vary very widely. The worker must not exacerbate his losses by staying away from work; in fact, a court may scale his damages down if it finds that he did not mitigate his loss by returning soon enough. If the worker dies, two sorts of action may be brought against a culpable employer. First, since 1934 the worker's own action has survived for the benefit, as it is put, of his 'estate'. Such an action may be thought of as one brought by the worker himself – or, as it were, by his ghost. The estate is entitled to claim for special damages and such items as pain and suffering sustained before the worker's death; and also a sum in respect of his 'loss of expectation of life'. This last sum is invariably a small one, usually no more than £500, and should always be 'moderate'.

The second type of claim that may be brought within three years of the death of an injured worker is one under the Fatal Accidents Acts. Certain relatives (widow, husband, child, parent, grandparent, grandchild, and brother, sister, uncle or aunt and their children) may here claim for the financial loss which they have suffered through his death. The action is in essence one for the loss of a breadwinner who died himself having a right to sue the defendant; and the damages represent the extent of the dependency. Insurance moneys paid to the relatives as a result of death are by statute ignored; but in theory other property inherited from the deceased should be brought into account, though the courts have recently restricted that deduction to any *gain* which thereby occurs and excluded such items as the family home. Otherwise, the damages represent compensation for the loss of 'prospective pecuniary advantage' (but not, except in Scotland, for the emotional or mental distress) suffered by the dependent plaintiff relative. The calculation of this loss of dependency in money terms is often a difficult process, as when the judge has to take account of a young widow's chance of remarriage as a factor reducing damages. In the ordinary case, Lord Justice Wilmer insisted in 1968, 'distasteful though it may be, the task must be faced of assessing that likelihood' of remarriage. In 1970, the Court of Appeal reduced by one sixth the £12,000 damages awarded to a widow of 30 with four children who had testified that she refused to go out with men after her husband's death at work, after she admitted suppressing the fact that she had been sleeping with a man for six months before the legal action, though she had not married him. If the relative benefits from any claim made for the worker's 'estate', this must be taken into account in the claim for loss of dependency to avoid duplication. If the dead man is held to have been contributorily negligent (a question on which, unhappily, his own evidence can no longer be given) all the damages are reduced by the proportion in which he was at fault; and, of course, where he is held to have been solely at fault in causing the accident, nothing is recoverable.

As for the actual sums currently being awarded, the following summaries from *Current Law* give a general idea of the *gross* figures (i.e. apart from cross-allegations of contributory negligence):

June 12, 1969: Former fitter aged 26 earning £15 14s. a week. Left hand crushed; now in fixed claw position. Unmarried; no longer enjoyed going out with girls 'though judge thought he would get over this'. Unemployed and at disadvantage on labour market. Total damages: £3,217.

January 29, 1970: Male steel erector, aged 43 when killed. Claim by widow aged 44, with two dependent children, boys of 13 and 15. Damages to his 'estate': £500. Fatal Accident Acts damages: £15,000.

March 7, 1970. Male foreman, injured at 38, doing important work which he enjoyed. Active man whose recreations included snorkel diving, swimming and dancing. Struck on head by 3-lb. spanner. Severe skull and brain damage, affecting whole nervous and sensory system. Complete loss of taste and smell. Sexually impotent. Impairment of control of right arm and leg. Suffered headaches, depression and loss of concentration. Ten per cent chance of epilepsy. Could swim with difficulty; became very tired. Had lost job with previous employers. Off work nine months; now employed in sitting-down job as component inspector. Continuing loss of earnings £14 a week. Court of Appeal increased judge's award of £9,589 to £15,045.

These are scarcely princely sums. Furthermore, in 1969 the House of Lords, with a determined revival of judicial aloofness, refused to take account of inflation in calculating sums for dependency. Lord Diplock insisted that 'the only practicable course for courts to adopt in assessing damages awarded under the Fatal Accidents Acts is to leave out of account the risk of further inflation'; and 'money should be treated as retaining its value at the date of the judgment'. In criticizing this judgment Professor Alan Day has admitted that to be 'genuinely compensated for loss of prospective earning power' an injured worker 'needs to be given lump sums which at first sight seem enormous'. But courts in other countries give higher damages; and some take proper account of inflation. Although other Law Lords maintained Lord Diplock's view, Lord Reid in 1970 suggested that he took the opposite view. From 1970 it has become compulsory for courts to award interest on the damages awarded, though usually this will apply only to special damages, pain and suffering compensation, and damages under the Fatal Accidents Acts. But should we continue to award damages always as a lump sum? Could they sometimes be regular payments adjusted where subsequently necessary? Such a question is intimately connected with schemes of comprehensive national insurance against injury at work, to which we must now turn.

II. *State Insurance*

National Insurance for Industrial Injuries. Between 1897 and 1945 a series of Workmen's Compensation Acts was passed which put a new principle behind compensation for injured workers. For injury arising out of and in the course of his employment a worker (at first in a limited range but later extending even to lower-paid white-collar work) was to be automatically paid. The need to prove negligence or other default by the employer was removed. By itself this was an important innovation; and the scheme had many merits. For example, many workers received weekly payments as compensation for injury swiftly; and employers were left to make their own arrangements for insurance, which was said to increase their incentive to improve accident prevention, for the insurance companies took a direct interest in how much was being paid to injured workers. But compensation was small, expressed as a fraction of the worker's earnings, normally less than half. If the accident was fatal a lump sum was paid; and a worker could be paid a lump sum in settlement of a disputed claim. Many claims were disputed, and much bitter litigation took place between workers backed by unions and employers supported by insurance companies in cases that frequently went on appeal to the House of Lords. The worker could claim his Compensation Acts benefit only if he elected to waive any claim against the employer for negligence.

Certain industrial diseases were included within the scheme; but it was often alleged that the effect of this was merely to ensure that employers dismissed workers who showed early symptoms of them. Between 1925, when the Acts were consolidated, and 1946, the complaints against the scheme from injured workers and their trade unions grew in volume; and many of the complaints against the conduct of cases and decisions in court undoubtedly contributed to the new social security system being administered by tribunals firmly set apart from the ordinary courts.

In 1942 the *Beveridge Report* recommended that this scheme be replaced by universal insurance against injury at work. The principle of automatic compensation without proof of negligence – which was after all an advanced principle for Parliament to have adopted in 1897 – was of course to remain. But no longer was the scheme to be one of employers' insurance. The State would insure against disability arising from industrial accident or prescribed industrial diseases. This was done in the National Insurance (Industrial Injuries) Act, 1946, which has now been supplanted by the Act of 1965, amended and enlarged in 1966 and 1967. All persons in 'insurable employment' are covered by the Act, and this term includes most workers, the main category being 'persons employed under any contract of service or apprenticeship'. We saw in Chapter 2, p. 52, something of the problems that surround that phrase. A special contribution is payable by employee and employer in respect of industrial injury insurance, the latter deducting the former's sum from wages at source. Apart from certain matters decided by the Minister (such as determination of whether you are an 'employee', on which a right of appeal lies on matters of law to the High Court) disputes are decided under the scheme by tribunals specially set up under the Act. The more important questions, e.g. disputes about eligibility for benefit, are heard by the Commissioners, on appeal from local tribunals. Most important, a Commissioner's decisions are not open to appeal to the ordinary courts, though the latter can review his decision for the purpose of seeing that he has kept within his jurisdiction. An error in the method of computing benefit thus led the Court of Appeal in 1968 to quash a decision of three Commissioners, since they had exceeded their jurisdiction.

Any person insured under the social security schemes is, of course, entitled to claim sickness benefit when unable to work through illness for three days or more; but if he is injured in an accident at work or suffers from a disease prescribed by Regulations, he may be able to claim industrial injury benefit, which is a considerably higher weekly sum. From 1969, the flat-rate benefit is £2 15s. 0d. higher; and special calculations are made in respect of earnings-related benefit so as to maintain the differential. The higher benefit is usually payable for a maximum of 156 days; but if at the end of a period of entitlement to injury benefit (that is, after six months, or on his return to work before that) a worker is fully or partially disabled, he may be able to draw 'disablement benefit'. This is a sum calculated according to his loss of faculty from 100 to 1 per cent (a gruesome table it is: 'Loss of thumb – 30 per cent; guillotine amputation of finger tip without loss of bone – 4 per cent'; and so on). This payment does not depend on loss of earning power. It means, one judge said, 'simply inability to do things'.

But what is the risk against which the national insurance scheme insures a worker? The Act requires that there be either a prescribed disease or a 'personal injury caused by accident arising out of and in the course of the employment'. Each part of this phrase causes difficulty of a kind similar to that caused by phrases in the earlier Acts. An industrial 'accident' or series of accidents must, the Commissioners' Decisions insist, be distinguished carefully from damage caused by a 'process'. An accident is an unexpected 'mishap', an occurrence at a particular time, not a 'process'. But what is an occurrence? Accidents have been held to include the following cases: an ulcer caused by insufficiently large Wellington boots issued for work rubbing an old wound, the penetration of the skin and infection being the occurrence; a psychoneurotic condition and dermatitis caused to a worker by repeated explosive reports from a machine, even though he had (not unreasonably) delayed his claim for two years since he did not realize it was an accident; injury caused to a furniture remover after lifting a wardrobe when he had unknowingly suffered from an insidious heart condition of unknown origin for years past.[27] But the following cases were held to be 'processes' for which injury benefit could not be paid: a foreman incapacitated by a foot condition caused by wearing wet gum boots over a period on the site, the injury being caused by his working conditions; a worker in a chemical factory exposed for eighteen years to substances known to affect the body, who died while off work (as is usual in such cases), the 'indefinite number of so-called accidents' having become a 'process'.[28]

The accident must arise both 'in the course of' and 'out of' the employment. This is the most difficult problem of all. In 1966 the Court of Appeal finally settled the many hearings of the case of Mr Culverwell, a fitter's mate, who was injured while waiting his turn outside a 'smoking booth', five minutes after he should have returned to his work from the tea-break. He was hit by a fork-lift truck. He was denied benefit by the Commissioner because the accident did not arise in the course of his employment; this was no trifling delay; he had interrupted his employment. The Court of Appeal refused to say the Commissioner's decision was so wrong that it must be set aside (unhappily consulting the court decisions from the bad old days before 1946).[29] The decision has a tang of managerial discipline about it. Other decisions apply similar tests with different results, such as the success of an agricultural worker who, while waiting for his tractor to be repaired, went to help unload a vehicle belonging to another farm and had a wheel fall on his leg. The accident was in the course of his employment since he was adopting an attitude of 'mutual helpfulness', whilst there was 'a lull' in his own work, of which his employer would have approved. The line can be fine. Contrast the fireman whose accident fell within the Act, occurring whilst he was playing volley ball in a recreational period (a game he was encouraged but not obliged to play) with the hospital laboratory technician whose accident was held not to arise in the course of his employment. The latter was injured whilst playing football in the lunch hour, a game encouraged by the authorities (especially as he was a member of the hospital team). But whereas the fireman was maintaining his morale and fitness in a period of waiting, the technician was playing for his own purposes during a temporary cessation of his employment.[30]

Misconduct and 'skylarking' at work have caused special problems. An assault on a lighthouse keeper by a colleague who became mentally unbalanced through the work was, but an attack on a foreman by a worker who went mad and then committed suicide was not, in the Commissioners' view, an accident arising out of the employment. The 1965 Act contains a section, first introduced in 1961, which extended the scope of insurance to cover acts of negligence, skylarking and misconduct, and injuries caused by objects, animals, or lightning that were previously excluded. But such an accident must still arise *in the course* of employment and the employee must not contribute to its occurrence by any act outside, or not incidental to, the employment. (This last is a very novel condition, since his contributory negligence as such has not previously affected his benefit rights if he otherwise qualifies.) A decision (3/67) shows how delicate is the test here again. A worker went to have a smoke, with permission, in the corridor where he was hit by a snowball playfully thrown by a young workman. He followed the youth to remonstrate with him but the latter ran into a lavatory, slamming the worker's fingers in the door. He was entitled to benefit. He had not taken himself out of the course of employment as Mr Culverwell had; and following the youth to remonstrate did not contribute to the accident. Although his exact words are not recorded, the Commissioner was convinced he did not chase the youth in order to 'retaliate' (in which case he would have lost his benefit).

The 1965 Act contained certain presumptions which reduce the number of likely disputes. For example, an accident arising in the *course* of an employment is deemed, in the absence of evidence to the contrary, to have arisen *out* of it. If there is such evidence, the claimant is left to prove his case without the assistance of any presumption. An accident is also deemed by the Act to arise out of and in the course of employment even if the employee is contravening statutory or other regulations or his employer's orders, so long as the act is done for the purposes of and in connection with the trade or business and would otherwise be held to arise out of it. But this section is given a narrow meaning. A dock worker in 1966 drove a truck, which he was not authorized to do, and killed himself by driving into the water. The Commissioner said this act was so clearly contrary to the employer's instructions that it fell totally outside the employment; and the High Court refused to quash that decision. The presumption could not help if the act was 'different in kind from what he was employed to do'. (But this is surely a different test from that imposed by the Act.)[31] The Act also provides that an accident counts if the worker is with his employer's permission travelling voluntarily to or from work as a passenger in a vehicle operated by or on behalf of the employer or by arrangement with him, and not in the course of a public transport service, so long as the accident would have arisen out of and in the course of employment if the worker had been obliged to take the ride. Accidents arising out of rescue operations at work are given a similar presumption. But the travelling presumption does not always assist, as in the 1967 case of the home-help injured when she fell in the road while going to the first house at which she was to work that day. Conversely, it is not needed where the travelling is within the scope of the employment anyway, as where a factory worker was cycling to work along the factory road which, though outside the gates, was not a public highway.[32]

The Commissioners have recently shown that they will not be bound by precedents in their decisions which they think should be reconsidered. A more generous attitude, for example, has undoubtedly supervened in regard to acts done for the employee's own purposes. In 1955 a laundry worker injured when going to deposit her personal laundry in a sorting room before clocking-in to work was deprived of benefit; but in 1963 a butcher's assistant hurt while separating chops for his own purchase, a privilege allowed him at wholesale price by the employer, succeeded in his claim.[33] In the important decision R(I)2/63 the Commissioners disapproved the principles enunciated in earlier decisions. The claimant had attempted to relight a cigarette at work when (unknown to him) gas was escaping from an unlit blowpipe, and he was injured by an explosion. It was not enough, said the Commissioner, merely to ask whether the worker did this for his own purposes. The question was: had he done something for his own purposes that went outside the employment risks judged in a broad commonsense way. His act 'converted the danger of an explosion into an actual explosion. It did not make it a different danger or create a fresh one'. Similarly, an approach more liberal than the older cases is apparent in the apprentice's claim (2/68) where he was injured when attending a day-release class at a technical college. His attendance was permitted but not obligatory, and if he chose not to attend he was obliged to go to work. He was entitled to benefit. Many decisions of the Commissioners are characterized by a refusal to lay down 'general tests'; and though this is no doubt prompted by a desire to treat each case on its merits, it makes far more difficult any prediction whether a particular worker will succeed in a claim for benefit or not.

Certain diseases and injuries are prescribed by the Minister in Regulations as within the scope of injury insurance for particular employments although not caused by accidents arising out of and in the course of employment. A number of such Regulations are in force. Pneumoconiosis is prescribed for a range of occupations and byssinosis for some; and special provisions are made for payments of benefits in their case. Forty-four other diseases are prescribed for other occupations, mainly dealing with different forms of poisoning.

From the illustrations already given it is clear that there can be many occasions on which workers suffer an injury or disease at work but fall outside the enhanced industrial benefit. Whether they fall there no doubt sometimes appears arbitrary to the men on the job. As long ago as 1955 a committee proposed that all industrial diseases be included. And many critics argue that the test 'out of *and* in the course of employment' should be replaced by '*or*'. If a man fails to get injury benefit, he draws only the lower sickness benefit. In that case it will be even more important to establish a claim to damages against the employer. Even the higher injury benefit, however, has never, since 1946, risen to so dizzy a height that a worker can ignore his right to compensation from a defaulting employer, especially when only half his State benefit (whichever sort it is) is deducted from the damages.

WHAT NEXT FOR DAMAGES AND INSURANCE?

The legislation of 1946 implemented the suggestion of the *Beveridge Report* that there should be a separate injury insurance covering all workers and paying a higher rate of benefit. The case for a separate industrial benefit rested on three main arguments. (i) Many vital industries were dangerous; special protection was needed if recruiting of labour was to be maintained. (ii) A man injured at work was 'under orders' and deserved special treatment. (iii) An employer ought not to be liable for injuries except where he was at fault in causing them. The third argument gave far too much to those lawyers who often still oppose strict liabilities out of what Mr Munkman called 'the same exaggerated respect for the law of negligence as their predecessors had for the doctrine of "common employment".' Neither of the first two arguments is particularly convincing today. Few men think of the higher insurance benefit when entering on dangerous work. So perhaps there was little to be said in logic even in 1942 for the separate benefit. But the man injured at work is a special phenomenon in our industrial society. We feel – rightly – that we owe him something. The best thing seemed to be to create a State insurance scheme.

Critics have attacked the pattern laid down in 1946. Professor Payne, for example, has suggested that it was a mistake to jettison entirely the old workman's compensation principle of relating compensation to earnings, and placing the cost of compensation on the insured employer.[34] One of the architects of the new wage-related social security benefits, Professor Abel-Smith, has written:

It is impossible with present medical knowledge to make meaningful distinctions between work-generated disability and home-generated disability and the attempt to do so causes thousands of people to have grudges against the whole social security system.[35]

He has argued that compensation 'should not depend upon the wealth or insurance-mindedness of the person responsible for the injury. ... The identification of the negligent should not be used as a means of raising money for disabled people.' In respect of insurance of defendants, it must at once be added that, since he wrote, a welcome statute, the Employers' Liability (Compulsory Insurance) Act, 1969, has made provision whereby every employer carrying on business is to be obliged to take out an 'approved policy' of insurance against liability to his employees for bodily injury or disease arising (unhappy phrase) 'out of and in the course of their employment'. Close relatives are, for no apparent reason, excluded; but otherwise the Act, when effective, should solve the problem of the insolvent or uninsured employer who cannot pay the damages to which his worker is entitled. The Act is likely to be brought into effect by regulations in 1971.

But this will not silence the critics of the action for damages who have in the past few years redoubled their efforts to abolish such actions in favour of a comprehensive insurance system. A moderate adherent of that school, Miss Young, although in favour of proper criminal penalties, has dubbed the civil action

suitable to a horse and cart economy. ... The question of negligence ... should not be tied to financial compensation to the injured or to the initiative of the injured, but should be the responsibility and prerogative of the state itself.[36]

It is often said that such claims for damages, and consequent pressures for employers' safety measures brought to bear by their insurance companies, constitute the 'real incentive for the observance of statutory duties' (Lord Justice Goddard). But a conference of experts held by the Industrial Law Society in 1967 produced the most diverse views about what the practice is. For example, it seems that whether an insurance company varies the premium may depend on whether it has only the safety insurance or has all the different insurance policies, from fire to motor cars, of a company employing workers. It was noteworthy that when the Midland Assurance announced a general increase in rates for employers' liability cover in November 1969, the reasons given related mainly to the rise in damages awarded, the overall increase in accidents and claims, and the addition of interest on damages. The critics, however, have gone much further. They suggest – not without reason – that action in the courts is, in Dr Ison's phrase, a 'forensic lottery'[37] and a prolonged lottery at that. Mr Williams' survey of 1960 suggested that between 10 and 20 per cent of workers injured by accidents claim damages and varying proportions succeed; but he saw many virtues in the civil action, not least its function of preventing similar accidents in future.[38] The critics, however, in contrasting this state of affairs with the social insurance system, sometimes make curious mistakes as when they claim that they wish to abolish the 'adversary system' that goes with the courts. The proceedings before the Commissioners are 'adversary' and some of their decisions also involve anomalies. (Indeed, no social insurance scheme is likely to avoid tribunals to adjudicate disputes.) Going, therefore, beyond this point, and asking with some logic why two men who suffer accidents anywhere, at work or elsewhere, should be treated differently, critics such as Professor Atiyah and Dr Ison have argued that both sets of anomalies should be abolished by replacing both injury benefit and claims for damages by one adequate insurance benefit which applies, under a unified State insurance scheme, to all those who by reason of sickness and incapacity of any kind are deprived of their earning power. With 'more adequate benefits available for all', *The Times* declared in July 1969, 'the action for damages could become redundant'. But any foreseeable State scheme would inevitably be likely to reduce the compensation paid to some injured workers who at present receive industrial benefit from the State and damages (less half the benefit) from the defaulting employer. Many an injured worker would be 'levelled down'.

Professor Atiyah has adopted the view that such a result would in some cases not be unwelcome, for he suggests that there is now a problem of 'over-compensation' for some workers, and says: 'One really shudders to think what a young working class widow ... is going to do with a cheque for

£10,000 under the Fatal Accidents Act.' Moreover, the tort system of liability is 'based on immoral' principles; the liability-insurance system which we now have is 'inefficient and very costly'; the accident insurance system needs to be made 'comprehensive', in particular by deleting distinctions between accident and disease, and improved especially for the man with 'long-term' injuries.[39] But in a conference debating these views Mr Brian Thompson replied that over-compensation was 'neither significant nor typical'; and as for the young widow, 'I shudder if I cannot get her the money'.

If there are a small number of disabled rich men, it may be right to take some of their money and give it to the disabled poor; but why only the disabled rich? What about those who are rich and not disabled? [40]

Claiming many advantages for the civil action he pointed to the many injured workmen whose claims are settled, whereas it is 'very different under the Industrial Injuries Acts ... you cannot negotiate a settlement even on a compromise basis'. Lastly, he was sure that 'sometimes and to some extent' the liability in damages does prevent accidents. It would be quite wrong to abolish it especially when criminal prosecutions were employed only to a 'derisory' extent. The Society of Labour Lawyers has also proposed the use of more serious sanctions against defaulting employers.[41] Their main proposals for reform are, first, the institution of a public insurance authority established on either a national or industry-wide basis. Contributions should be paid by employers and would be increased in the case of a bad accident record. Similarly, an employer with a bad record could be made to pay part of a worker's damages out of the firm's own funds, whether insured or not. Some Canadian experiments suggest that this kind of scheme is workable; and they do not necessarily entail the abolition of the damages action. Secondly, the Labour Lawyers would institute a system of licences to engage in dangerous trades. An employer with a really bad employment record could have his licence withdrawn. Such Draconian measures, however, would not be useful unless his workers could be assured of alternative jobs; it might be better to suspend the licence – but not the workers' wages – while the workers' safety representatives and the Inspector establish the causes of such a bad record.

The feeling that the action for damages involves anomalies has undoubtedly been increased by the curious judicial developments of the 1950s and early 1960s. The worst kind of legalism has pervaded some sections of the safety statutes ('keep the worker out; not the machine in'). The judges in the 1960s seemed to depart from what Lord Wright claimed, in 1951, to be 'a long established tradition of the English common law for the protection of workers'. The change coincided with the growth of a general middle-class feeling that the workers were doing pretty well and perhaps the employer – or his insurers – needed a bit of protection; and secondly, the opportunity for the first time for almost every worker to enforce his rights in a court action, by the addition of a legal aid scheme to the trade union help.

Many observers have long argued that actions for damages *do* help in accident prevention. It may be true that the insured employer is deterred only a little by the prospect of such civil action; but it would be folly to take away even the smallest encouragement towards accident prevention in the present situation. And two experienced observers have said: 'Damages should be increased, especially in more serious cases. ... Punitive damages should be awarded in every case where the employers have been guilty of a grave offence.' [42] They also advocate the restoration of the right to jury-trial. It does seem that damages are low in Britain compared with elsewhere. Commentators in 1967 compared the £13,000 awarded to a 35-year-old widow in Durham with a similar lady's £715,000 for loss of a husband in the U.S.A.; and the £5,000 awarded to a builder for loss of earning ability was compared by an experienced barrister and ex-actuary with practice in other countries, who concluded he would receive about £8,250 in Germany, £10,000 in Switzerland, and about £9,000 in Holland and Norway.[43] The Report of the 'Winn Committee' on Personal Injuries Litigation in 1968[44] (while it felt able to recommend that the prospect of remarriage should no longer be considered for widows' damages) rejected most of the proposals made to it for change, including a proposal for payment of damages in periodical sums (which the Government in fact supported as long ago as 1944), because plaintiffs:

whether or not they are workers or are complaining of an industrial accident would prefer an out-and-out award to periodical variable payments: a lump sum can be used to acquire a business, such as a shop, or to discharge or reduce a mortgage.

The Law Commission is also considering the problem of damages. Furthermore, in 1969, widespread support was forthcoming for the proposal of Professor Atiyah that a comprehensive inquiry is needed by a royal commission (though the writer hastens to add that not all supporters have thereby supported the abolition of damages).

But Professor Atiyah returned to the charge in 1970 with a more general review of the problem. Encouraged by the New Zealand Royal Commission Report of 1967, and that Government's response,[45] favouring an overall State accident insurance system to comprehend road, industrial and other accidents, including criminal injuries, he concludes:

What above all else cries out for reform is the unfairness produced by the lack of integration of the various compensation systems.[46]

In addition to providing further documentation for his earlier views, Atiyah's book enters into the question from which (except for Miss Young) the advocates of exclusive comprehensive social insurance had rather abstained, namely the place of the law and insurance in accident prevention. In this context, the debate has now become sophisticated, ranging far outside the industrial field. Indeed, in the U.S.A. the debate is largely illustrated by motor accident problems. There one of the major developments has been the elaboration of a theory of 'general deterrence' by Professor Calabresi based upon the notion that we should 'let the free market or price system tally the choices'.[47]

General deterrence implies that accident costs would be treated as one of the many costs we face whenever we do anything. General deterrence attempts to force individuals to consider accident costs in choosing among activities.

Elsewhere Calabresi writes that the attack on civil fault liability

leads too often to the simple alternative of social insurance. Such a result would eliminate even the attenuated general deterrence that the fault system accomplishes.[48]

This certainly does not suggest that in the present state of our ignorance we should at once abolish the action for damages for the injured workman; although such an approach probably does give support to certain legal principles criticized above (e.g. the 'hazard' principle, p. 269, which could be said to be necessary for an employer to calculate his 'costs'). But Atiyah is able to respond that in one sense, when financed out of general taxation or on a flat-rate of contribution, all social security 'flies in the face of' the precepts of 'general deterrence' (though he accepts that they may 'creep in again at the back window' via actions for damages and employers' liability insurance).[49] Even those who would not share the assumptions of 'general deterrence', because of their dislike of pricing the cost of workers' accidents on any market principle, cannot overlook the fact that it does not point in the direction of abolishing the civil action.

Rather than abolish the right to damages completely, amending legislation might concentrate upon removing some of the more remarkable anomalies caused by judicial interpretation. In 1964, the Government accepted one Convention and one Recommendation of the I.L.O., with reservations, concerning guarding of machinery in *all* places of work. A new code of safety legislation is, we saw, in preparation. But a senior D.E.P. official in 1968 explained that it could not cover 'everyone working everywhere'; perhaps 'at some stage in the future this may come to pass, but it seems out of the question at the present time'.[50] The draft new code was disappointing; indeed, it did not even restore all the strict duties of the Factories

300

Act or abolish the doctrine of 'hypothetical causation'. And surely the burden of *disproving* negligence could be put upon the employer when the worker is dead or paralysed. Such amendments need not wait upon the new 'inquiry' of 1970, p. 258. At the least, it remains arguable that the time for total abolition of the action for damages will come only when the figure of those maimed and slaughtered at work has been reduced to a much lower level than we tolerate today; when the punishment of those responsible for danger is taken seriously; and when the security afforded to the sick and injured who have through no fault of their own lost the power to earn, compares reasonably with the standard of living enjoyed by a well-paid worker. It is not proven that that time has yet come.

1. [1938] A.C. 57, at p. 84.
2. *General Cleaning Contractors* v. *Christmas* [1953] A.C. 180.
3. [1951] A.C. 367.
4. *Kerry* v. *Carter* [1969] 3 All E.R. 723 (C.A.); *Hawkins* v. *Ian Ross Ltd* [1970] 1 All E.R. 180 (statutory duty).
5. [1968] 1 Q.B. 94.
6. Judith Reid (1967) 30 *Modern Law Review* 455, 461; and see R. W. L. Howells (1970) 33 *Modern Law Review* 89.
7. *Tremain* v. *Pike* [1969] 3 All E.R. 1303.
8. [1959] A.C. 604.
9. [1891] A.C. 325.
10. *Ball* v. *Richard Thomas and Baldwins Ltd* [1968] 1 All E.R. 389.
11. [1968] A.C. 107 (H.L.).
12. *Boyle* v. *Kodak Ltd* [1969] 2 All E.R. 439 (H.L.).
13. *Jenkins* v. *Allied Ironfounders* [1969] 3 All E.R. 1609 (H.L.).
14. [1953] A.C. 643.
15. *Stone Lighting & Radio Ltd* v. *Haygarth* [1968] A.C. 157.
16. *Donaghey* v. *Boulton & Paul Ltd* [1968] A.C. 1 (H.L.); *Flannigan* v. *British Dyewood Ltd*, 1969, S.L.T. 223.
17. [1897] 1 Q.B. 192 at p. 195.
18. [1969] 1 A.C. 136 (H.L.).
19. [1962] A.C. 367.
20. [1964] A.C. 1019.
21. *Johnson* v. *Callow Ltd* [1970] 1 All E.R. 129 (C.A.) [approved, *The Times*, October 23, 1970, H.L.]; but see *Hindle* v. *Porritt Ltd* [1970] 1 All E.R. 1142.
22. 'New Wave of Interpretations of Factories Acts' (1962) 25 *Modern Law Review* 107.
23. [1969] 1 All E.R. 598 (C.A.); see J. Hendy (1969) 32 *Modern Law Review* 438.
24. [1965] 2 Q.B. 582 (C.A.).
25. [1962] 1 All E.R. 623; see Howells (1964) 27 *Modern Law Review* 738.
26. [1965] A.C. 656.
27. R(I) 71/51; 43/55; 12/68 respectively.
28. R(I) 25/52; 7/66.
29. R(I) 4/66; *R.* v. *Industrial Injuries Commissioner, ex parte A.E.U.* [1966] 2 Q.B. 21 (C.A.). For criticism and other cases see Judith Reid (1966) 29 *Modern Law Review* 389.

30. Respectively: R(I) 13/66; 13/68; 2/69.

31. R(I) 1/66; *R.* v. *D'Albuquerque, ex parte Bresnahan* [1966] 1 Lloyd's Rep. 69.

32. R(I) 2/67; 1/68; and see 5/67.

33. R(I) 45/55; 20/63.

34. 'Industrial Injuries' (1957) 10 *Current Legal Problems* 85.

35. *Labour's New Frontiers* (ed. Hall; 1964), p. 126.

36. *Industrial Injuries Insurance* (1964), pp. 172, 173.

37. T. Ison, *The Forensic Lottery* (1967); see too, C. Curson (District Factory Inspector) (1969) 77 *Employment and Productivity Gazette* 624.

38. J. L. Williams, *Accidents and Ill Health at Work* (1960), pp. 270, 281.

39. 'Common Law Damages and Social Security', April 1969, *Law Guardian*, 17, 19–20; *New Law Journal*, 18 September 1969, p. 863; *Industrial Law Society Bulletin No. 6* (1969), p. 10.

40. *Industrial Law Society Bulletin*, ibid., p. 8.

41. Society of Labour Lawyers, *Occupational Accidents and the Law* (Fabian Society Research Pamphlet 280, 1970).

42. R. and B. Thompson, *Accidents at Work* (3rd ed. 1968), p. 61.

43. See *Sunday Times*, 15 and 22.1.67.

44. Cmnd 3691. But see for much less complacent suggestions the dissenting report by R. Thompson at p. 159.

45. See *Personal Injury* (A Government Commentary on the Report of the 'Woodhouse' Royal Commission; Wellington, N.Z., 1969).

46. P. S. Atiyah, *Accidents, Compensation and the Law* (1970), p. 614.

47. G. Calabresi, *The Costs of Accidents* (Yale, 1970), p. 69.

48. 'The Decision for Accidents' (1965) 78 *Harvard Law Review* 713, 744.

49. Atiyah, op. cit., pp. 588–9.

50. No. 2 *Bulletin of Industrial Law Society*, 1968, p. 14, and see discussion pp. 23–5.

CHAPTER 7

INDUSTRIAL CONFLICT AND
THE LAW

IN 1800 trade unions were utterly illegal. The fact remains today a critical feature of their legal situation. The explanation
of this paradox will provide us with the key to the peculiar
structure of our law concerning trade unions and industrial
conflict. The most powerful influence on that law, one that
both underlies the next four chapters and explains much of
what has gone before, has been the union's struggle to emerge
from that illegality.

As we have seen (p. 25), the peculiarity of British law is
not in having the problem. All industrial capitalist countries
have encountered that. The peculiarity was our solution. Unless
that is kept in mind, the character of our law of industrial
conflict will be misunderstood.

The next two chapters, in particular, seek to explain this
critical piece of legal history. For convenience, many of the
matters relevant to the modern right to strike will be discussed
in Chapter 8. But the story in this chapter is an essential preliminary to that discussion. The development of the law will
be presented in the following way:

(i) *The early illegalities:* liabilities of trade unions under
the criminal law, and the problem of an unlawful 'civil status'.
In both cases we shall find that Parliament eventually passed
statutes to provide protection.

(ii) *Taff Vale and the 1906 Act:* the judges reinterpret the
law and the statutes that Parliament has passed. Some of the
interpretations lead to renewed demands for fresh statutory
protection, as in the case of the *Taff Vale* case and the Trade
Disputes Act, 1906.

(iii) *The lawful conduct of strikes:* the law relating to 'peaceful picketing' gives us a particularly good example of the
development of the law and the impact of the 1906 Act, estab-

304

lishing a right for the new industrial labour movement to conduct effective industrial activity.

(iv) *Trade Disputes:* the modern law uses a special concept of 'trade dispute' in establishing that right, the meaning of which is of critical importance today.

Under each of these headings we shall look carefully at the doctrines of law, without undue technicality, but with sufficient attention to the detailed structure of the law to understand its twists and turns.

THE EARLY ILLEGALITIES

In 1800 the Industrial Revolution was in progress; the worker employed by the entrepreneur had begun to replace domestic production. 'There was no proletariat, but the workers in every trade were becoming very much alive to the necessity for defending their standards.'[1] Three things, however, joined to make combinations of workers and anything like strike action totally illegal and criminal – wage-fixing; the judges; and the Combination Acts. First, wages were still in theory to be fixed by State authorities, largely by the magistrates in Quarter Sessions; they were not to be bargained or even left to a 'free market'. Acts of Parliament passed regularly from 1349 onwards had established a system of wage-regulation, and they were not finally abolished until statutes of 1813 and 1824 (although in fact the magistrates had long since ceased to fulfil their wage-fixing functions). New methods of production and the new ideology of 'free competition' which had come with them led directly to the view that these wage-regulating Acts had, as Lord Sidmouth put it, 'pernicious consequences'.

For a time a few groups of workers agitated for the proper operation of the wage-fixing machinery in order to improve, or more often to maintain, their wages; but in the early years of the nineteenth century, as Hedges and Winterbottom say: 'It is not surprising that the working classes sought other means of redress.'[2] That other means was, of course, combination. Between the fourteenth century and 1800, however, statutes had also been regularly passed to make illegal workers' combinations either generally or in various trades ('if workmen do conspire covenant or promise together ... that they shall not make or do their works but at a certain price or rate ... or shall not work but at certain hours and times': 1548). If wages were to be fixed, they must not be collectively bargained!

Secondly, the judges equally saw union organization as a common-law crime, namely that of conspiracy. 'As in the case of journeymen conspiring to raise their wages: each may insist on raising his wages if he can,' said Mr Justice Grose in 1796, 'but if several meet for the same purpose it is illegal and the parties may be indicted for a conspiracy'. The prosecution of the Journeymen Tailors of Cambridge had in 1721 asserted this judge-made liability for conspiracy, one probably independent of the statutes (though that was never entirely clear). The important point about common-law conspiracy independent of any breach of statute where it aims to do no other act unlawful in itself, is, of course, that the illegality rests upon the judge's disapproval of the combination alone.

Thirdly, encouraged by the French Revolution to see all organizations of workers as a potential source of Jacobin revolution, the Government of the day passed the Combination Acts of 1799 and 1800. The 1800 Act rendered criminal all agreements for advancing wages, altering hours, and the like; all attendance at or persuasion to attend meetings for such purposes; and all combinations of this kind. Many prosecutions occurred under these and later statutes. 'The first twenty years of the nineteenth century', wrote the Webbs, 'witnessed a legal persecution of Trade Unionists as rebels and revolutionists.'[3]

Yet various forms of artisans' and workers' clubs, societies, and other organizations persisted and grew, often adopting the form of friendly societies, partly because they really did help their members in old age, sickness, and funeral benefits, partly to avoid the wicked mien of a trade union.

By 1824 reformers imbued with Benthamite philosophy, and led by the Charing Cross master tailor Francis Place, opposed demands for further repression with the argument that all artificial restraints should be lifted. Their argument and tactical skill secured the passage of a Bill repealing the Combination Laws within one week in 1824; but their allies among the working men did not reply by proving true their belief that 'freedom of combination would soon teach the workers its futility for all save quite modest and inoffensive objects'.[4] Quite the opposite; a wave of strikes followed, many of them violent, and a less permissive statute was hastily passed in the following year. That Act of 1825 expressly legalized certain combinations. It dealt with combination by masters and work-men. But equality was merely formal. Although prosecutions against workers were frequent, there is no evidence of such actions against combining employers. The permitted combina-tions for workers were those for the 'sole purpose' of agreeing on *their own* hours and wages, and nothing else. Another section (s.3) of the 1825 Act set out at length a series of vaguely worded criminal offences in respect of pressure brought in industrial conflict by violence, 'threats', 'molestation', 'in-timidation', and 'obstruction'. This Act plus the judges' in-terpretations of the common law remained the basic law until the reforms of 1871–5 which are themselves the basis of the modern law.

In examining the legal history of these fifty years, we are examining a period of remarkable social change and changing fortunes for the emergent trade unions. With the advent of power machinery and the factory system,

Workers forced off the land crowded into towns ... dirty and melancholy assemblages of factories and hovels; the population grew with incredible rapidity; productivity soared; great fortunes were made by some; but the vast majority of the working people became practically slaves of the new machines.[5]

At first, grandiose schemes for huge organizations were attempted. The well-known efforts to set up the 'Philanthropic Hercules' in 1818; the 'Builders' Parliament'; the Owenite 'Grand National Consolidated Trades Union' in 1834 (with Benbow's projected 'Grand National Holiday of the Produc-tive Classes') all crashed in dismal failure. These unions, and their often syndicalist objectives, were met by employers with bitter opposition; and prosecutions helped to deter recruiting. Such prosecutions were not confined to the offences under common law and the 1825 Act. Old Acts that forbade 'unlawful oaths' were unearthed, such as the Act of 1797 (passed after the Nore Mutiny) pressed into service to convict the 'Tolpuddle Martyrs', six unfortunate Dorchester labourers, sentenced in 1834 to seven years' transportation for the mere administration at Tolpuddle of a union oath – in the Webbs' words: 'a scandalous perversion of the law'. In the ten years after the movement towards general unionism broke down, the political programme of the Chartists dominated the working-class scene – a group which fought for Ten Hour and other factory legislation but otherwise played a small role in legal history. The reason for the defeat, it has been said, of this movement of revolt,

in Chartist Britain, as on the revolutionary continent of 1848, was that the poor were hungry, numerous and desperate enough to rise, but lacked the organization and maturity which could have made their rebellion more than a momentary danger to the social order.[6]

British trade unions found both maturity and organization in the New Model unions which arose in the middle of the century. The flavour of revolutionary protest gave way to the tactics of those who felt they were fighting for a stake in society. With the Amalgamated Society of Engineers in the van, tough leaders organized the new craftsmen who were becoming indispensable to an expanding economy. Stable union funds were built up and organization was centralized. The cotton unions, too, emerged from the 1850s in a condition that made it 'clear that the cotton workers had acquired the discipline and training in trade-union principles to enable them to bring consistent and effective pressure upon their employers'.[7] The miners' association even appointed a solicitor in 1844. When the time came there were unions which could effectively resist further extensions of criminal liability, and even, after a national group of leaders emerged, organize evidence to the Royal Commission of 1867 and press for changes in the law. The new societies did not lack militancy in the face of attack by either employers or the courts. The Friendly Societies Act, 1855, appeared to be a haven for them, as far as legal status was concerned, and many registered under it in the hope (forlorn, as we shall see) of acquiring legality.

CRIMINAL LIABILITIES

Apart from the prosecution of trade unionists for oath-taking or conspiracy, most of the legal battles between 1825 and 1859 concerned the interpretation of crimes dubbed 'threats', 'intimidation', 'molestation', and 'obstruction'. A few judges put a narrow meaning on the words, such as Baron Rolfe in 1847 who thought they implied violence or the like. But the vast majority of judges were prepared to convict for any intentional threat or intimidation 'capable of having a deterring effect on the minds of ordinary persons or capable of controlling the free agency of another'.[8]

In 1832 a threat to strike was held to be molestation. In *R. v. Duffield* and *R. v. Rowlands*, 1851,[9] Wolverhampton tinplate workers who were paid less than average rates by a Mr Perry, and obliged to give him six months' notice (compared to his one month's notice to them), were organized in a strike by a London union. Convictions were upheld for conspiracy to molest and obstruct Mr Perry. Mr Justice Erle thought it a molestation and obstruction when 'a manufacturer has got a manufactory and his capital embarked in it ... if persons conspire together to take away all his workmen', and he invited the jury to say this had interfered with Perry's 'lawful freedom of action'. Union officials could not 'molest or intimidate or annoy' the workmen or even induce them not to enter the employer's service. Mr Justice Patteson made it clear there need be no express words of violence or the like before obstruction, intimidation, or molestation were proved. The trade unions were, Mr Citrine observed, 'hamstrung. While a strike to raise wages might be perfectly lawful, it was unlawful to threaten the employer that such a strike would take place, or even peacefully to persuade persons to take part in it.'[10]

In the face of such judgments Parliament, in the Molestation of Workmen Act, 1859, purported to give slight relief, in particular by expressly excluding from criminal liability peaceful persuasion to quit work (so long as it did not induce any breach of contract). But many of the judges' decisions scarcely registered this amendment. In 1868 Vice Chancellor Malins expressed satisfaction that he had jurisdiction to deter by injunction 'misguided and misled workmen from committing these acts of intimidation', i.e. placards 'blacking' an employer who cut wages.

Any picketing was still perilous. Threats to strike for any purpose other than one concerning the workers' own hours or wages were still 'intimidation', as a case in 1867 showed where the strike aimed to force a non-union man to join the union. In the same year, Baron Bramwell (perhaps the authentic voice of *laisser faire*) declared in a prosecution of certain tailors, who had carefully but peacefully picketed masters' shops in London, that such action as theirs was illegal as a conspiracy to 'molest' if it included 'abusive language and gestures', or anything 'calculated to have a deterring effect on the minds of ordinary persons, by exposing them to have their motions watched and to *encounter black looks*'![11] (Proof that history brings some changes was seen in the 1969 march of Welsh strikers who, with no risk of prosecution, sought to deter any potential blacklegs by waving ladies' black tights among their banners.)

Cyril Asquith (later to become an eminent Law Lord) wrote in 1927 of this line of cases: 'It affords an impressive illustration of judicial bias against industrial combination: a bias which has happily ceased to exist decades ago.'[12]

Extensive union agitation secured Reform Acts in 1871 from the large Liberal majority elected on the new urban franchise of three years before. The Acts were based partly on the minority report of a Royal Commission to which the new 'Junta' of union leaders had given evidence. The Trade Union Act, 1871, dealt with civil status; and another Act dealt with criminal law.

The unions, however, did not get all that they wanted in

reform of the *criminal* law. As we shall see, this failure was the price of their apparent victory on civil status. The criminal law statute did repeal the statute of 1825 (and, unfortunately, that of 1859 too); and it confined threats, intimidations, obstruction, and molestation strictly to acts coercing an employer which would allow for a binding over to keep the peace (i.e. *violent* threats and the like) or other specific wrongful acts ('watching and besetting' a man; hiding his tools; and so on). But once again the courts brought down some of the hopes pinned on the statute. The express legalization of picketing by 'peaceful persuasion', gained in 1859, had been lost. Four years later, a court held that if picketing involved a watching which 'occasions a dread of loss', it would still be unlawful. In 1871 itself women were convicted for saying 'Bah' to blacklegs.

But even more important was a prosecution for conspiracy in 1872. Workers in a gasworks supplying 'a great part of what is called the West End of London' had threatened to strike unless a colleague dismissed for union activity was reinstated. They were prosecuted and convicted for common law conspiracy: *R.* v. *Bunn* (1872). There were two strands in the judgment.

One condemned the combination for threatening to call men out in breach of contract – an act which, it will be remembered, was itself still capable of being criminal under the Master and Servant Act and for which, we saw in Chapter 2, p. 76, many prosecutions were brought. But Mr Justice Brett went further with a second argument and spoke of the combination itself as unlawful (even if no act to be done were otherwise unlawful) because it involved a molestation, that is, 'an unjustifiable annoyance and interference with the masters in the conduct of their business ... such annoyance and interference as would be likely to have a deterring effect upon masters of ordinary nerve'.[13] *The Times* of the day commented that the court had 'to maintain the rules of fair fighting, and with whatever reluctance they must be enforced'.[14] The reaction of the trade unions to the revival of conspiracy was one of intense anger, and the London Trades Council held a special meeting to consider their 'critical legal position'.

Almost any action [wrote the Webbs] taken by Trade Unionists to induce a man not to accept employment at a struck shop resulted, under the new Act, in imprisonment with hard labour. The intolerable injustice of this state of things was made more glaring by the freedom allowed to the employers to make all possible use of 'blacklists' and 'character notes'. ... In short boycotting by the employers was freely permitted; boycotting by the men was put down by the police.[15]

The new agitation won, within the surprisingly short time of four years, a new Royal Commission and a new Act. The Unions were delighted with the victory. Working-class power had been used, it was felt, for the first time to extract from the political machinery really successful legal protection for the industrial movement. Selective support had been given to candidates (other than the first few 'Lib-Labs') in the election of 1874, across party lines, according to their answers to certain questions. When the new Conservative government appointed a Commission, the unions were hostile at first. But a year later Disraeli, acutely aware of the strength of the working-class vote, imaginatively offered a Bill which met most of the unions' demands. With a few amendments it passed into law as the foundation of modern labour law. The T.U.C. leaders were ecstatic; a telegram of congratulation was sent to – of all people – a Conservative Minister; an amendment deploring this 'fulsome recognition' of the Government was massively defeated and the retiring secretary George Howell even felt that there was now no further need of the T.U.C. and its Parliamentary Committee. His judgment was erroneous.

The Act – the Conspiracy and Protection of Property Act, 1875 – repealed the Master and Servant Acts; codified yet again the crimes connected with 'intimidation' and picketing; and expressly provided for criminal liability in certain strikes in breach of contract (in public utilities, for example: discussed at p. 388 in Chapter 8). But its most important section invented a golden formula which became the bedrock of British workers' rights to organize and take effective industrial action. Section 3 reversed Bunn's case by providing that in *contem-*

plation or furtherance of a trade dispute no combination to do or procure any act should itself be a criminal conspiracy *unless* the act itself would be punishable as a crime. Common-law 'simple' conspiracy, where the objection was taken to the combination as such, was effectively excluded from trade disputes. Nothing in the section was to affect the law relating to 'riot, unlawful assembly, breach of the peace or sedition, or any offence against the State or the Sovereign'. But simple criminal conspiracy was henceforth banished from *trade disputes*. It was, of course, mainly in trade disputes that the doctrine had been most important. The Act of 1875, with the Trade Union Act, 1871, and the Trade Disputes Acts, 1906 and 1965, are the basic statutes of the modern law. Only after the apparent 'immunity' for conspiracy in 1875 can we begin to speak of a legal 'right' to strike.

THE CIVIL STATUS OF UNIONS

Criminal liabilities were not the only problem for trade unions. In civil law too they had an 'unlawful' status – for example, under the doctrine of 'restraint of trade' (discussed in Chapter 2). Some judges in the nineteenth century even thought that the existence of any association in restraint of trade was criminally 'indictable at common law as tending to impede and interfere with the free course of trade' (Mr Justice Crompton, 1855). By the end of the century this view was rejected. But the same restraint of trade doctrine deprived unions of any lawful *civil* status. For instance, in *Hornby* v. *Close*, 1867, the United Order of Boilermakers, which had registered under the Friendly Societies Acts, wanted the help of the courts to prosecute an official who had embezzled the funds. It was refused. The stage reached in that year by the judges is aptly expressed by Mr Justice Blackburn: 'I do not say that the objects of this society are criminal. I do not say they are not. But I am clearly of opinion that the rules referred to are illegal in the sense that they cannot be enforced.'[16]

Because of the civil status of the association the court could not lend its aid. The unions found themselves without legal protection for money which they had thought safe behind friendly society machinery. After minor statutory amendments about theft and other wrongs, the main reform came in the Trade Union Act of 1871, the year in which the 'Junta' followed the example of certain Trades Councils three years earlier and called together a national Trades Union Congress.

The 1871 Act, still the basic charter of trade union legality, did three things:

(a) First, it relieved the unions from liability for 'restraint of trade'. Their purposes were not to be criminal merely for that reason (it is significant that it was still thought necessary to declare that) nor was 'any agreement or trust' of theirs to be unlawful merely by reason of that doctrine (s.3). We shall see that a century later (p. 459) judges in the Court of Appeal began to put a most odd meaning on this apparently crystal-clear section.

(b) Secondly, as a price for this – but one the unions were very ready to pay – section 4 declared: 'Nothing in this Act shall enable any court to *enforce directly*' certain named internal union agreements (e.g. the member's right to benefit: see Chapter 9), and agreements between one union and another (discussed in Chapter 4). The Act may be said to have instituted the policy of keeping the courts out of union affairs, one plainly dictated by the experience of the fifty years that preceded it. It is the first of the modern Acts that give to the trade unions a legal status in a very peculiar form, namely by way of *'immunity' from judge-made doctrines*. The doctrines themselves (apart from their effect on trade unions) are not affected by the statute; but a special 'immunity' is, in form, provided by the statute as a protection. In substance, behind the form, the statute provides liberties or rights which the common law would deny to unions (in the case of the 1871 Act, the right of lawful civil status). The 'immunity' is mere form.

One of the problems inherent in this way of doing things is that the judges remain in a strategically very powerful position. For if they later decide that the common law doctrine is, after all, rather different from what it is thought to be at the time the statute was passed, then in the light of their subsequent pronouncements as to the 'true' doctrine, the statute itself may come to have a different effect from what it was meant to have – and there may even be need for a new statute.

If we may anticipate a little, it looked at the turn of the century as if this might happen to the 1871 Act in the light of the judges' reappraisal of the 'restraint of trade' doctrine. First, in 1894 (as we saw in Chapter 2, p. 85) the courts finally decided that only 'unreasonable' restraints were void after all. Secondly, some judges suggested that perhaps *not* all trade unions were in unreasonable restraint of trade and therefore unlawful. At least, they suggested that a union might not be unlawful if its committee could not order strikes.

This apparent alleviation by the judges of their illegal status at common law was not, however, welcome to the unions. They had got what they wanted on 'restraint of trade' out of the 1871 Act – namely, an express immunity. Because of s.4, they preferred even to be illegal at common law, and be legalized by that Act, rather than be lawful in the eye of the judges. The first way meant that their contracts within s.4. were not 'directly enforceable' in the courts. Indeed, the change of judicial attitude probably represented 'the judicial tendency to control the internal management of trade union affairs by saving its "legality" at common law.'[17] (Some unions make it clear even today that they *are* in 'restraint of trade', so as to be validated only by s.3 of the 1871 Act. Thereby they have their agreements rendered 'not directly enforceable' under s.4.) The courts have more lately reverted to the earlier attitude; and today most unions, especially if they have rules for calling strikes and disciplining members or if they operate a 'closed shop', are thought to be unlawful at common law by reason of restraint of trade. In that event they are lawful only by reason of the 'immunity' provided by s.3 against restraint of trade. To this we return on p. 456.

(c) The third reform of the 1871 Act, s.6, enabled trade unions, *if they wished*, to register with the Registrar. Certain advantages accrue today from registration, from minor tax benefits and administrative gains to such trivia as a special protection against disorderly conduct in the union's library under a law of 1898. But s.6 said nothing special about the status of a registered union. Registration being voluntary – indeed it is a garb that can be, as Lord MacDermott said in 1956, in the *Bonsor* case (p. 446), donned and doffed at will – it was assumed that the status of a registered union was the same in essence as that of any other unincorporated body, e.g. an unregistered union. Parliament had not in s.6, as it had in the Companies Act nine years before, declared that on registration the association became a separate legal entity or 'person'.

The Royal Commission of 1894, on which Sir Frederick Pollock sat, discussed whether unions *should* be given corporate status on registration, obviously assuming they did not get it under the 1871 Act. (The Donovan Report proposed compulsory registration and incorporation; but the 1970 Bill did not adopt either: (p. 450)). Funds held by an unincorporated group are usually held by its trustees. The 1871 Act demanded trustees to hold the property of a registered union, and even provided that they should be sued in matters concerning its property. But legal action against such funds was – and is – a procedurally difficult matter. To sue all the members is impracticable. Alternatively, a 'representative action' can be brought, *if* the court permits, against some of the members on behalf of the rest if all have the 'same interest in any proceedings'. Such actions can founder easily, if only because it is often easy to show that one member of the class has a *different* 'interest' in the matter. Certainly at the end of the nineteenth century 'the Acts of the 70s were conceived to have made no difference' to union immunity from suit, wrote Lord Asquith; and 'every one must have supposed that actions against unincorporated bodies of large and fluctuating membership, such as Trade Unions, were impracticable'.[18] Indeed, in the bitterly fought case of *Lyons* v. *Wilkins* (1896–9) discussed later, an action against the union itself was begun but dropped for this reason. In 1901 the Law Lords explosively shattered this belief by their judgments in the *Taff Vale* case.

The effect of that judgment, which we next describe, was to lay trade union funds wide open to attack in the courts, as it seemed at the time, almost without limit in situations of severe industrial conflict.

Nothing did more to embitter relations between the courts and the workers than the Law Lords' decision that a registered union could after all be sued. The law had seemed 'so clearly settled to the contrary', wrote Lord Asquith, that 'public opinion was unprepared for any such decision'. Election posters of 1906 depicted a judge handing to an employer a scourge with which to beat workers. The *Taff Vale* case became part of working-class culture, part of the way 'they' treat trade unions if they can. Such feelings have not died. Indeed, as we shall see in the next chapter, the Law Lords in 1964 rendered a judgment which revived once again all the old memories of *Taff Vale*. The legal effect of the *Taff Vale* decision, however, was the passing, in response to persistent trade union demands, of the Trade Disputes Act, 1906. The Act raised strong feelings. Professor Dicey, a leading jurist, castigated it, in tones reminiscent of Baron Bramwell, as 'one of the most outrageous measures ever brought before Parliament'. Speaking to the Women's Liberal Unionist Association on 31 October 1906 in Caxton Hall, he asked his audience, as *The Times* reported, 'to think what it would mean if the terms on which women – domestic servants for instance – laboured were really regulated by the caprice or even the serious doctrine of a trade union'! But the Act was put through by the new Liberal Government, and added a third plank to the Acts of 1871 and 1875 to complete the structure of trade union liberties.

The last ten years of the nineteenth century had seen a sharpening of industrial conflict. The new factor in the situation was the emergence of the New Unions, which organized mainly the unskilled general labourers. 'The labourer', wrote Professor Hobsbawm,

mobile, helpless, shifting from one trade to another, was incapable of using the orthodox tactics of craft unionism. Possessing 'merely the general value of labour' he could not, like the skilled man, buttress a certain scarcity value by various restrictive methods, thus 'keeping up his price'. His only chance therefore was to recruit into one gigantic union all those who could possibly blackleg on him –

in the last analysis every 'unskilled' man, woman or juvenile in the country; and thus to create a vast closed shop.[19]

These unions were constantly embroiled in the legal battles which we must now describe. The period after 1889 – the year of the turbulent dock strike, when, in the biggest fight by an unskilled workers' union so far, the dockers won their 'tanner' (sixpence an hour) – has been called by Mr Saville a period 'of a developing counter-attack by the propertied classes against the industrial organization of the working people'.[20] The law reports provide abundant evidence of that counter-attack. But the most famous battle, when it came, did not involve either one of the New Unions or the old 'aristocracy of labour', the craft workers, but the railwaymen.

In 1900 the Taff Vale Railway had allegedly victimized a signalman, John Ewington, who had led his grade's demands for a wage increase. From this tiny spark a huge conflagration broke out, to which the sour relations between the company and its workers, the prosperity of the company that made it a good target, and the willingness of its manager to import 'free labour' strike breakers and to fan the flames of litigation, all contributed. It was said too by Lord Askwith that the general manager of the railway 'had a passion for litigation'.[21] Mr Justice Farwell held that on various grounds the union officials had been guilty of tortious conduct. The company sought an injunction against the union and its officials.[22] But, it was argued, whatever the liabilities of the officials, the registered union could not be sued as such, for either injunction or damages. It was not a legal entity known to the law. The Court of Appeal unanimously agreed, saying the 1871 Act not only did not infer that the union could be sued, but (if anything) 'the exact contrary'. But the House of Lords restored the trial judge's decision that it could be sued.

Two strands may be found interwoven in the Law Lords' judgments. Some of them (notably Lord Macnaghten and Lord Lindley) thought that the union's registered name could be used in place of 'representative' defendants (though they did not explain how other objections to a 'representative action' might be met). Others (notably Lord Brampton and Lord

Shand) treated the registered union as a 'legal entity' (or 'quasi-corporation') because, they argued, that was the *implied* intention of the 1871 Act. The first view does not make the registered union into a 'corporation' technically, but, whilst leaving it an unincorporated association, achieves the same result in practice. The second view depends on reading into the Act just that corporate status for the registered union which the Act definitely refrained from giving. 'Though not perhaps in the strict sense a corporation', said Lord Brampton, the union was 'nevertheless a newly created corporate body created by statute, distinct from the unincorporated trade union'. As we shall see in Chapter 10, even in 1956 the Law Lords could not agree as to the correct legal analysis of the registered union's exact status; and in 1970 the issue of compulsory registration and incorporation is still with us. But in 1901 all the Law Lords showed a strong determination to reach the conclusion that a registered union could somehow be sued for torts. The decision of the *Taff Vale* case depended on what the Law Lords *read into* the 1871 Act. Lord Chancellor Halsbury, at the risk of assuming his conclusion, expostulated:

If the Legislature has created a thing which can own property, which can employ servants, and which can inflict injury, it must be taken, I think, to have impliedly given the power to make it suable in a Court of Law for injuries purposely done by its authority and procurement.[23]

The unions were not, of course, 'created' by Parliament; the Act had established *trustees* to own property and so on; and the very *question* was whether 'it' existed in law at all! The danger to union funds (including the benefit funds for sickness, old age, etc.) was greatly enhanced by the other developments in the law of conspiracy (already touched on in Chapter 1 and discussed in the next chapter). The A.S.R.S. in fact paid damages to the extent of £23,000 and had to find another £12,000 for costs. An unprecedented protest followed from the labour movement, above all from its rank and file; and after the landslide Liberal victory at the 1906 election, the *Taff Vale* judgment was attacked in the Trade Disputes Act, 1906.

Oddly enough, however – and perhaps unwisely – nothing was done to reverse or even to clarify the judgments concerning the civil status of unions after registration. Instead, such was the shock of *Taff Vale* that the unions and their friends pressed for section 4(1) of the 1906 Act. This proclaims that no action is *ever* to be allowed *against* a trade union and its funds (whether by action against its registered name or by a 'representative action') 'in respect of *any tortious act* alleged to have been committed by or on behalf of the trade union'. This immunity certainly protects trade union funds against actions for damages in tort. And it is complete; it extends outside industrial conflict. Since after 1947 even the Crown can be made liable in tort actions, this immunity can today be criticized as too wide.

Five points should, however, be remembered on this matter: (i) The union is protected by the section, but its officers and members individually are *not*. From 1906 onwards, actions have regularly been brought against union officials; and most unions (and their funds) have not unnaturally backed their men when the latter acted on union business in a conflict. (ii) Nothing in the section prevents actions for breach of *contract* (by an outsider or a member against the union, so long as the 1871 Act does not intervene). (iii) After 1963, some judges began to say that although damages could never be awarded, the words 'alleged to *have been* committed' in the section allowed a plaintiff to obtain an injunction against a union to stop future torts *not yet* committed. Such a result would have been absurd. Not only was s.4 meant to provide, in Professor Kahn-Freund's words, 'the British solution of the problem of the labour injunction'. The courts have discretionary power to award damages in lieu of an injunction, so that the new view would have meant the judges had power to award damages against unions for future but not for past torts! In 1969 the Court of Appeal refused to adopt the new view. The intention of Parliament was clearly that no action of any kind should be maintained for a tort against a trade union defendant.[24] The 1970 Bill proposed to confirm this interpretation – just in case the House of Lords should upset it. (iv) In 1968, however, the

Donovan Report understandably recommended that the protection of s.4(1) be restricted, like the rest of the Trade Disputes Act, 1906, to acts done in contemplation or furtherance of a *trade dispute*. This proposal the Government accepted, adding, of course, that this was acceptable only on condition that 'the definition of a trade dispute is watertight'. As we shall see, p. 327, it may not be the definition so much as the interpretation of it that needs attention. But the 1970 Bill did not include the proposed restriction of s.4(1). (v) Section 4(2) retains the liability even in damages of the union *trustees* (and, thereby, of the funds) in tort actions concerning the union's *property*, except in trade disputes. The law here is in doubt. The usual view is that this liability affects only torts concerned directly with the property (nuisance by disrepair, for example). But a wider construction of the words used, which would increase the vulnerability of union funds, is not impossible. Yet s.4(2) applies only to registered unions; and a wide interpretation of it, the Royal Commission wrote, would produce a 'marked anomaly' between registered and unregistered unions.

In the light of these points, s.4(1) is perhaps less potent a protection than is often thought, and in view of the liabilities of union officers less important in practice than it might be. What matters is the legal liability encountered by union officers and members in the conduct of industrial negotiation and conflict.

CONDUCT OF STRIKES – PEACEFUL PICKETING

Although not used so extensively in modern practice, the right peacefully to picket premises to persuade men not to work, or to urge them not to blackleg and break a strike, is an essential weapon on the workers' side in a trade dispute. The main legal limitation on that right today is section 7 of the Conspiracy and Protection of Property Act, 1875. That section of the 1875 statute codified once again the crimes that had gone under such names as 'threats' or 'intimidation'. It provides that any person commits a crime who (with a view to compelling any other person to do, or abstain from doing, anything lawful) 'wrongfully and without legal authority' does any of five specified things: (i) Uses violence to, or intimidates such other person, his wife, or children, or injures his property; (ii) Persistently follows him; (iii) Hides his tools or other property, or deprives him of them, or hinders their use; (iv) Watches or besets any house or place where he is, or any approach to it; (v) Follows him in the street with two or more others in a disorderly manner. But an express proviso in 1875 permitted 'attending' at or near a place in order merely to obtain or communicate *information*. Attempts were made to go back to the old, wide meaning of 'intimidation'; but in 1891 judges in both England and Scotland held that 'intimidation' must import an act of violence or the like – at least, 'threats which may be supposed to affect a person of common sense and raise a natural alarm of personal violence or of violence to his family'.[25] Although sometimes benches of local magistrates may deviate, this meaning has usually been strictly adhered to, as in the Quarter Sessions case of 1965 where four pickets who, without any threat of violence, had 'frightened' a blackleg into giving his day's wage to the union Benevolent Fund and were acquitted of 'intimidation'. Cases have been very few. (Two pickets at Pilkingtons were convicted under section 7 in 1970 for threats of violence.)

But the liberal interpretations of s.7 were short-lived. In an action heard twice, *Lyons* v. *Wilkins*, the Court of Appeal in 1896 and 1899 rocked the unions back on their heels by declaring peaceful picketing unlawful as a common law 'nuisance' and a statutory 'watching and besetting'.[26] The compulsion need not, the judges said, be aimed at the same person as the one beset (a strange reading of the section). Further, the proviso to s.7 did not contain any exemption for 'peaceful persuasion', as did the old Molestation of Workmen Act, 1859. Persuasion not to work, in which the pickets had here indulged at the works both of Messrs Lyons and of a sub-manufacturer, went beyond merely communicating *information*. Damages and a perpetual injunction were granted. Lord Justice Lindley (by 1899 Master of the Rolls) declared this was an unlawful watching and besetting; for 'such conduct seriously interferes with the ordinary comfort of human existence and ordinary enjoyment of the house beset, and such conduct would support an action ... for a nuisance at common law'. It was in this context that he declared too: 'You cannot make a strike effective without doing more than is lawful.'

In common with the other areas of our law, two developments have since occurred. The courts have taken a fresh look at the problem; and statute has intervened (this time in the Trade Disputes Act, 1906, s.2). But the courts never cleared all the doubts about the common law position, which still governs picketing outside the area of 'trade disputes'. The years 1895 to 1899 saw fierce battles about the employers' importation of 'free labour', workers who ranged from ordinary Irish labourers to thugs like the Deptford 'Eye-Ball Buster Gang'. A crop of decisions in 1899 about picketing of such 'free' labourers re-emphasized the rigid view of *Lyons* v. *Wilkins* that picketing was invariably wrongful as a nuisance and therefore a wrongful 'besetting'. But in 1906, the Court of Appeal in the *Ward Lock* case held that not every peaceful picketing is a nuisance, and (since s.7 did not mean to expand the area of liability for the crimes there described as watching and besetting beyond the area of wrongful *nuisance*) there was not always liability.[27]

It is still not clear how serious an 'interference' picketing may be without falling foul of the judge-made liability for nuisance. Many recent decisions of the Irish courts have reduced rights to picket to derisory proportions; but their logic would not, it is thought, be attractive in England. In 1956, however, the English Court of Appeal, granting a householder an injunction for nuisance against prostitutes who patrolled the street outside his house, treated *Lyons* v. *Wilkins* as an authority without demur, and one judge expressly relied upon it to show that a 'nuisance' could arise even if there were no physical interference with the enjoyment of premises.

But in Britain statute expressly legalized peaceful picketing in 1906. Section 2 was inserted for this purpose into the Act of 1906. 'It shall be lawful', it declares, *'in contemplation or furtherance of a trade dispute'* to attend at or near a house or place 'merely for the purpose of peacefully obtaining or communicating information *or* of peacefully persuading any person to work or abstain from working'. What scope have the courts allowed s.2? Plainly it does not legalize extraneous wrongs, e.g. threats of violence such as were alleged in the fierce building site dispute of 1967, when the workers refused to accept service of writs on the road and men chased them around London to serve them.[28] Nor does it legalize trespass *into* the house or place (e.g. by a 'sit-in' strike). The words are 'at or near', not 'on' or 'in'. But it does allow picketing at a man's home, which four Donovan Commissioners wished to ban. If loitering on the highway is, however, by itself a trespass or 'nuisance' (as it may be) the section must legalize at least that.

But certain forms of 'nuisance' by pickets are not legalized – e.g. 'mass pickets' or obstruction such as that committed by pickets in 1947 who lay down in the road to stop the arrival of lorries at the Savoy Hotel and were prosecuted and convicted. This seems to be because the purpose in such a case is no longer 'merely' one within the permitted range, a restriction the courts have been acute to enforce. Whatever the ulterior motive, the immediate purpose must be no wider than the words quoted. It has recently been suggested that section 2 'would appear to add nothing new to the position at common law' by virtue of the *Ward Lock* case.[29] But recent decisions revive doubts. *Piddington* v. *Bates*, 1960,[30] shows how other legal liabilities can impinge. After employers faced with pickets had rung for the police, a policeman told the pickets that two were enough on the back gate. 'I know my rights,' said a third, and, going to join the other pickets, he 'pushed gently past' the policeman (says the report) 'and was gently arrested'. He was held to have obstructed the constable in the execution of his duty under the Prevention of Crimes Act, because the policeman had acted properly with reasonable grounds for believing there might be a breach of the peace. Section 2 was not argued, but it may be that its words 'It shall be lawful' operate only within the bounds of such instructions from the police.

This conclusion is fortified by *Tynan* v. *Balmer*, 1966,[31] where the defendant led some forty pickets in a continuous circle outside the factory. No serious obstruction of anyone was proved but the Recorder found as a fact that the object of the pickets was to 'seal off the highway' and cause vehicles visiting the factory to stop so as to talk to the drivers. A constable had asked him to move the pickets; he refused; and he was convicted of obstructing the constable in his duty despite section 2. The reason was that the pickets, as Mr Justice Widgery put it, were 'independently of section 2 . . . unlawful and a nuisance'. He affirmed that:

the proper way to approach this question . . . is to ask whether the conduct of the pickets would have been a nuisance at common law as an unreasonable user of the highway. . . . One leaves aside for the moment any facilities enjoyed by those acting in furtherance of a trade dispute, and if one imagines these pickets as carrying banners advertising some patent medicine or advocating some political reform, it seems to me that their conduct in sealing off a part of the highway by this moving circle would have been an unreasonable user of the highway.

In the face of this judgment it is mystifying to understand how the Donovan Report could (apart from the need to legalize picketing of customers) find the law on picketing 'reasonably satisfactory'. Whatever the merits of the facts in *Tynan*, the reasoning of the judgment reduces s.2 to minimal proportions. In convicting for wilful obstruction of free passage on a highway in 1965, Lord Chief Justice Parker stated 'any occupation of part of a road, thus interfering with people having the use of the whole road, is an obstruction'. The test for nuisance on the highway is scarcely less strict, for a 'reasonable' user of the highway does not normally include loitering to advertise medical or political salvation. And a *prospective* nuisance is enough to oust the protection of s.2, since, as *Tynan* shows, the purpose of 'causing a nuisance' is enough to prove that pickets are not acting *merely* for the statutory purposes. The only indisputably lawful pickets after this judgment are those who attend in small numbers near the chosen place and who keep out of everyone's way. Meanwhile, the workers whom they have come to persuade to join them can sweep past in vehicles which the pickets have no right to stop. And yet from 1867 onwards trade unions have tried to obtain the effective right of peaceful and persuasive picketing! The fact is that in practice workmen do picket in rather more effective fashion than the *Tynan* decision allows and sensible experienced police officers often take no action so long as there is no violence or other serious obstruction in fact. The law should surely be amended to make picketing lawful within such limits. Pickets are not selling medicine. They are exercising elementary industrial rights needed to maintain a balance of power in industrial conflict.

SUMMARY

The position bequeathed to us by this curious legal and social history may perhaps be inadequately but usefully summarized as follows:

(a) Criminal liabilities largely ceased to impede trade union activities after the 1875 Act. Crimes like 'intimidation', 'molestation', and 'watching or besetting' were finally pinned down and clarified within narrower limits than ever before. 'Simple' criminal conspiracy was by the same Act excluded from cases where a combination acted in furtherance or contemplation of a *trade dispute*.

(b) The Act of 1871 gave a special immunity to trade unions against the judicial doctrines of 'restraint of trade'. As a price for this certain union contracts were made 'not directly enforceable' by legal action. The same statute allowed for voluntary registration; but the *Taff Vale* case, 1901, gave to a registered union a surprising 'quasi-corporate' status.

(c) The Act of 1906, S.4(1), gave to unions a complete protection against actions based on tort, an immunity which applies whatever the remedy sought. But other actions can be brought, e.g. for breach of contract. Also, an obscure S.4(2) retains liabilities of the trustees except in trade disputes. Moreover union officials and members remain liable to various kinds of civil action: see Chapter 8.

(d) Certain protections were also given by the 1906 Act to individuals when they act in furtherance of *trade disputes*. One such protection appeared to legalize the right of 'peaceful picketing' (s.2). But the ambit of the right to picket is still uncertain because s.2 is ousted if there is an actual or prospective common law 'nuisance'. Other sections protected them from other civil liabilities in trade disputes (discussed in Chapter 8). Without those protections, collective trade union activity would not have been possible without continual risk of illegality. The protections bear the *legal* form of 'privileges' in trade disputes.

TRADE DISPUTES

Both in 1875 and in 1906, then, use was made, in protecting those acting in industrial conflict, of the golden formula: '*in contemplation or furtherance of a trade dispute*'. What does the formula mean? A trade dispute is defined in s.5 of the 1906 Act as being 'any dispute between employers and workmen or between workmen and workmen, which is connected with the employment or non-employment, or the terms of the employment, or with the conditions of labour, of any person'. 'Workmen' here means 'all persons employed in trade or industry whether or not in the employment of the employer with whom a trade dispute arises'. The Prices and Incomes Act, 1966, added (as we saw: p. 214) a dispute connected with that statute.

The whole idea that some disputes are 'trade' or 'industrial' and some 'political' or 'non-industrial' disputes can, of course, be challenged. Many industrial strikes have a high political content; and the definition in the Act has been said to rest on the theory that 'political' and 'economic' disputes are clearly distinguishable, which is today 'plainly untenable'.[32] Yet the distinction is fundamental to our labour law, and despite the conceptual difficulties, it is apparently still accepted by all parties in industry. But the exact interpretation put on it grows daily more important.

On the one hand some strikes are fairly clearly 'political', as when in 1969 workers demonstrated in London against *In Place of Strife* – strikes which, though they were connected with terms of employment, were aimed not at employers or workmen, but at the Government as the other *party*. Similarly the strike of 50 workers in Staffordshire to protest against Mr Enoch Powell's dismissal from the Shadow Cabinet was wholly 'political'. Political and industrial questions, however, have been inextricably mixed up in some of the industrial combat. In 1966, for example, the prolonged strike by merchant seamen was alleged, on its first evening, by the Prime Minister to be 'a strike against the State'; and a few days later he alleged that the union executive was being controlled by a 'tightly knit group of politically motivated men' (an allegation subsequent investigations did little to sustain). There has in fact been a startling recent growth of the false doctrine that strikes 'against the Government' are necessarily outside the area of *trade disputes* (and, indeed, may be illegal combinations: p. 393). That has, on the better view, not been English law. It is the strange doctrine which is at the root of disastrous conflicts which have beset the growth of collective bargaining by public employees in the U.S.A., where Federal or State or, indeed, municipal government servants have no right to strike (though, as the mailmen proved in 1970, they do it). The doctrine, last heard of in the 1926 General Strike (p. 391), flowered in Britain because of a rash of events in 1970 which showed how closely industrial and political problems are intertwined.[33] Mr Clive Jenkins, Secretary of A.S.T.M.S., declared that if a private, rather than a nationalized, concern took over British United Airways (B.U.A.) there might be industrial action by members who worked in the industry. (When criticized for this, he pointed out that managers had been commended who had made it clear they would leave firms on a change of ownership, as in the Rank–De La Rue takeover battle.) Later shop stewards and unions at London Airport declared their opposition to the new Government's plan to hand over air-routes of the nationalized corporations to the 'second force' private airway company. In all major ports dockworkers went on strike demanding full nationalization of all ports, and places for workers on the dock boards, to be accomplished by the Ports Bill which was then before Parliament; and a delegation visited Parliament to lobby. The Secretary of State, Mrs Castle, objected to this 'primitive form of syndicalism'; and the Prime

Minister, Mr Wilson, objected to strikes intended to 'influence legislation'. In another dispute, the London Airport Authority had awarded servicing contracts at London to a foreign firm (G.A.S.). Union members at the airport objected to this and 'blacked' the firm's work. They did not like either the firm or the alleged policy of 'creeping denationalization.' The Authority and the firm eventually obtained an interlocutory injunction (p. 379) against a leading shop steward, counsel alleging that the dispute had nothing to do with the workers' terms and conditions of employment; but the case was never fully argued on both sides. The Press and Ministers were quick to speak of 'abuses' and 'industrial blackmail'; but Mr Watt wrote that all these examples showed that there are purely industrial and purely political decisions; but that

between them lies a large politico-industrial twilight area where it is extraordinarily difficult to see one's way.[34]

If confronted by such problems the judges should illuminate the gloom by the clear light of the statutory definition. Whether Parliament has been influenced or not, that definition lets in disputes *connected with* the matters set out. As we shall see, an additional political element in the dispute (which today is almost inevitable when Parliament so often becomes involved with industrial issues) does *not necessarily* remove the action from the protection of the golden formula into the darkness of common law liabilities. This should be stressed in the forthcoming decade of disputes with international companies, in regard to which the government of the day is bound to have some political policy in operation.

To satisfy the legal definition a dispute must have the right parties, and be 'connected with' the right content. Both of these requirements have caused difficulty. As to parties, there must be a 'workman' on one side at least. Disputes exclusively between employers will not suffice. But the workmen can make their appearance *via* their agents, the trade unions, for it would be 'strangely out of date', as Lord Wright put it in 1942, not to accept a union today as agent of workers it can properly be taken to represent. So, when a union was 'sparring for an opening' in trying to get negotiating rights with an employer, in 1960, there was a trade dispute in existence; and a recognition claim by a union on employers who would not negotiate with unions was in 1968 accepted by a Scottish court as a trade dispute (though as we shall see, to no avail for the defenders: p. 352). But the workman must be employed in 'trade or industry'. Lord Wright thought these words must be understood widely; Lord Goddard was once prepared to include banking within their scope, and Lord Denning to put in 'clerks and shop assistants'. But there are many workers who are probably not protected because they do not work in 'trade or industry' – local government employees or nurses, for example. There does not seem any good reason for their not receiving equal protection with other workers. It has been persuasively argued that 'employed' can even now include a self-employed workman.[35] (The 1970 Bill proposed to enact a Donovan recommendation by replacing the old definition with its new category of 'worker': p. 60). A workman is not put outside the statute merely by being dismissed, even if lawfully dismissed; he can still be the person 'employed' in industry who is party to the dispute.

The dispute must have not merely the right parties, but also the right content. Connection with employment or its terms will obviously include a vast range of industrial questions from pay or safety to the 'closed shop' or recognition of a union. In this way inter-union battles can in law become trade disputes, as in 1921 where disputes between two groups broke out as to which union should recruit at a works. Also, it must be noted that the 'workmen' need not be in the employment of the employer who is a party; and the conditions of labour may be those of any person. Sympathetic strikes are, therefore, clearly included. As is clear from other statutes (p. 136), *any* person need not be construed as meaning only those within the United Kingdom. Whether a court would look abroad is uncertain; but it could be important, e.g. if workers blacked goods from a country discriminating against the employment of coloured workers.

But before 1920 and after 1956 the courts have shown tendencies to restrict the area covered. To some extent, the recent approach of the courts has limited the statutory definition in ways not dissimilar to those envisaged in *Fair Deal at Work* (p. 374). In 1909 in *Conway* v. *Wade* [36] they faced a deceitful threat by a union official to call a strike (which he had no power to call) to put pressure on a worker to rejoin the union and 'punish him' in respect of an eight-year-old fine. The official was outside the Act's protection, said the House of Lords. Neither the intrusion of personal debts nor spite by itself displaces the protections. A trade dispute was declared to exist in 1962 when a union had taken industrial action to force a film producer to pay debts owed to three workers; and again, in 1912, when an official who hated the bandmaster brought out a band on strike for higher wages, for the element of spite had not displaced the trade dispute. What *Conway* v. *Wade* made clear was that the formula cannot extend to a purely personal vendetta. Here we meet the question of 'furtherance or contemplation'. *Conway* v. *Wade* established too that only a dispute already in existence can be 'furthered', and only one imminent or likely can be 'contemplated'. So, where union officials got brewery employees to disclose confidential information to strengthen their hands in preparation for bargaining, the formula did not apply. A trade union official cannot create his own personal dispute and then further it; otherwise, said Lord Atkinson, 'where perfect peace prevailed in any factory ... an intruder, a mere mischief maker, actuated by greed or some feeling of revenge, would be protected'.

In *Huntley* v. *Thornton*, 1957,[37] a worker who refused to respond to the union's call for a one-day strike later became embroiled in a raging dispute with his local branch and its officials. The battle was hard fought, as industrial conflict frequently is. At one point the minutes record him as having waved his arms, thrown down his cards, and stalked out, calling the committee 'a shower' – 'a tolerably accurate account,' the judge felt sure, 'though no doubt much condensed'! In the long and complicated dispute that followed in which neither side pulled punches, recommendations for Huntley's expulsion were made at local and district level, but the Executive Council of the union refused to have him finally expelled. The committee of the local branch purported nevertheless to treat him as no longer a member, and saw to it that wherever he moved in the district the local officials prevented his working, and hounded him out of jobs. Two officials, Mr Justice Harman held, throughout pursued what they thought were proper trade union objectives; but eleven others had gone beyond this, 'thought only of their own ruffled dignity', and pursued 'a grudge'. They were liable in damages of £500 for conspiracy. The judge said there was no trade dispute in existence here; but he was, it is thought, on stronger ground in holding also that this dispute had become the furtherance of a 'personal matter' for these defendants. 'They were', he said, 'not furthering a trade dispute but a grudge and the Act does not protect them.' Contrasting this case with that of the bandmaster, the test emerges whether the *predominant* purpose of the defendants has become one of personal spite or not – not an easy test to apply in real life. But it is clear that once the defendant has proved that the dispute carries all the marks of a trade dispute (a task of which the burden is on him) the plaintiff must prove by clear evidence any allegation of some other predominant motive, as in *Camden Exhibition and Display* v. *Lynott*, where the employers failed to prove an allegation that the overtime ban (p. 194) had been imposed for 'subversive' purposes.

In *Stratford* v. *Lindley*, 1964,[38] the Watermen's Union recruited 3,000 and the T.G.W.U. some 350 of London's lightermen. Bowker and King Ltd – a company run by a Mr Stratford – which employed about 45 T.G.W.U. men, and three Watermen, refused in 1956, 1961, and 1962 to negotiate with the unions; then in 1963 it negotiated an agreement on employment conditions with the T.G.W.U. alone. The Watermen's Union at once put an embargo on the barges hired out and repaired by another of Mr Stratford's companies. This 'froze its business' to put pressure on him and (Viscount Radcliffe said) make an example of him. When its officials were sued for an injunction, the House of Lords found against them on grounds which, as we shall see in the next chapter (p. 349), were not open to any protection under the 1906 Act anyway. But they went on to say that there was, on the evidence presented in these interlocutory proceedings, no 'trade dispute' being furthered by these defendants. In the Court of Appeal, Lord Denning has said that the evidence *prima facie* pointed to a trade dispute. There need be no dispute between any worker and his employer.

Suffice it that the union, on behalf of all its members, desires to be able to negotiate terms of employment and the employer refuses to recognize it. There is thereupon a dispute between employers and workmen which is connected with the terms of employment.

But the Lords took a very different view. This was, they said, mere 'inter-union rivalry', and just a matter of 'prestige' for the Watermen. The agreement with the T.G.W.U., said Lord Reid, settled 'the terms of employment and conditions of labour of all the employees'. On the evidence, none of the three Watermen workers had objected to these terms. The Watermen's Union had made no new approach to Mr Stratford (a point of good manners which plainly weighed heavily with their Lordships). Lord Pearce asserted that the Watermen members employed by Bowker and King 'were, from a practical point of view, adequately protected', and: 'There was here no practical need for any intervention by the defendants'. The Watermen's Union clearly took a different view of the practical needs of their members. It is odd that their Lordships concentrated on the position of the three Watermen employees, for the union, as Lord Denning suggested, could be seen to be acting for its 3,000 members in demanding negotiating rights. 'Workmen', it will be recalled, need not be employed by the employer in question under the definition of s.5. Even more important, the Act says 'connected with' terms and conditions not 'about' them; yet Viscount Radcliffe and Lord Donovan made this unjustifiable translation, turning the Act's 'connected with' into their own 'concerned with' or 'about'. The decision in Stratford is presented by the Donovan Report as though it held merely that the union had not proved 'the existence of any dispute' and might have done so if it had approached Bowker and King yet again. That may have been what the Royal Commission understood the speeches to say; but there is far more in the Law Reports. Indeed the whole tenor of the Law Lords' speeches seemed to put a new restriction on the golden formula. Even if the evidence available did show that this was rivalry between two unions, could it not be analysed as a dispute between 'workmen' (represented by the unions) connected with the employment conditions at Bowker and King Ltd, that is to say, with their negotiation? The Law Lords, to avoid any such content in the dispute, had to say that the evidence available showed a dominant connection with the Watermen's pursuit of 'prestige'! The trade unions received this decision with great anxiety. The rock on which their legal defences had been built suddenly seemed less secure.

In 1969 this anxiety was shown to be justified. In *Torquay Hotel Co.* v. *Cousins*, 1969,[24] the union (T.G.W.U.) was trying to organize hotel workers in Torquay. A local branch began in January 1968. Under a national agreement, another union was assigned the organization of such workers (though a subsequent inquiry revealed that the T.G.W.U. already had 7,000 hotel workers as against the 3,000 of the other union). Together with fellow members of the local Hotels Association, the *Torbay Hotel* had refused recognition to the T.G.W.U. and its local officials, P. and L., called a strike and posted pickets at that hotel. Later C., the General Secretary, heard of the matter from the regional official (N.) and authorized strike pay to the strikers. R., a national official, was also involved. P. told the *Torbay* that it was an 'official dispute'. That weekend newspapers reported statements by X., managing director of the *Imperial Hotel* (the leading hotel in town owned by the plaintiff company) that the Association would 'stamp out' the T.G.W.U. in Torquay and make a stand, though it was never clarified how far these reports were accurate. The *Imperial* employed no T.G.W.U. members. On seeing the reports, some pickets were furious at X.'s intervention, as they saw it, and moved across to picket the *Imperial*. L. claimed that the *Imperial* was now 'in dispute'. P. telephoned a local Esso depot warning them that because of an official dispute with the

Imperial 'supplies of fuel will be stopped being made' there. The Imperial had a contract for the supply of fuel oil, as ordered, with Esso. Esso drivers were members of the T.G.W.U. and it was 'common knowledge' they could not cross the picket line. P. also told the press that X. had intervened, adding 'That means sanctions. ... We can cut off supplies at source and we are going to do that'.

Esso told X. that they could not help him and, in fact, no order for fuel oil was ever placed. X. sought an alternative source and obtained a delivery of oil from Alternative Fuels, a firm in Cheshire with which D. (a local T.G.W.U. official) then had a conversation. The *Imperial* company sued the T.G.W.U., C., R., N., and P. (all full-time officials) and L. (the branch secretary) – see Figure 1. It asked for interlocutory

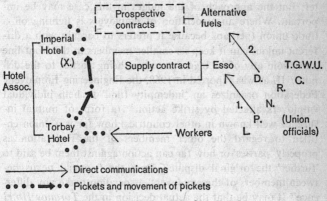

> Direct communications
●●●● ➡ ●● Pickets and movement of pickets

Figure 1. *Torquay Hotel* v. *Cousins*

injunctions to stop the embargo and the picketing that went with it. Incidentally to the other more profound issues in the case (p. 357 and p. 374) the issue arose whether the defendants had acted in furtherance of a trade dispute. Mr Justice Stamp could see no trade dispute, especially because of the inter-union rivalry. But the Court of Appeal said there clearly was a trade dispute in existence at the *Torbay Hotel* about recognition of the union there. That fell squarely within the golden formula.

Nevertheless, 'twixt cup and lip the defendants still failed. There was no dispute, the judges thought, at the *Imperial*. Nor was action taken against the *Imperial* in furtherance of the dispute at the *Torbay*. The action was 'personal', taken to 'punish' X. for his views. The pickets were furthering no trade dispute but 'their own fury'. The court would not accept that, through X., the *Imperial* had taken sides so as to become a party, and did not discuss the problem whether there was a dispute with the Hotels Association, of which the *Imperial* was a most influential member. Two members of the court did, however, note that the *Imperial* had no T.G.W.U. employees.

Of course, once a finding of fact is made that certain persons are only furthering their own 'fury', that is an end to the matter. But the approach of the judges in this case may be important. Where an association of employers is fighting off a trade union (perhaps because it prefers to bargain with a different union) can it keep its smaller members in the front line and avoid any of its bigger members being parties to the dispute? If, as was reported in 1968, the Engineering Employers' Federation organizes an 'indemnity fund' to help individual employers affected by strike action[39] (a form of mutual insurance well known in other countries) how far is a union entitled to regard the other members of the Federation as properly 'parties' or how far can action against them be said to 'further' the original dispute? Does the financial nexus between members of the employers' association make any difference? It may be that the actual decision in the *Torquay Hotel* case depends, like *Huntley*'s, on a finding of fact. But it must be difficult for lawyers in advising pickets to be sure about what will seem mere personal or punitive 'fury' to a judge reading affidavits some weeks or months later.

Even in interpreting the golden formula, then, our labour law has become rather unsettled of late. This review of the basic legal concept of 'trade dispute' reminds us of Professor Kahn-Freund's words: 'It may be possible to carry on with the present law for many years to come but one should at least realize that its foundations are shaky'. But what could we put in place of the golden formula? We might add 'in preparation' to the opening words 'in furtherance or contemplation'; but the definition of the parties and the content did seem, in the 1906 Act, to have outlined an area wide enough for ordinary industrial combat as far as words could do it. The approach of the courts in recent judgments leads to the realization that no formula can be 'watertight' unless it is applied with an understanding that it is not supporting any 'privileges' in trade disputes – or even special 'facilities' as *Tynan*'s case put it. What are at stake are basic liberties of workpeople. Unless the interpreting tribunal adopts that approach, no improvement in the 'definition' of the golden formula will help. For the same formula has been vital to the modern right to strike. To that we turn in the next chapter.

Notes to Chapter 7

1. Milne Bailey, *Trade Union Documents*, p. 4.
2. R. Y. Hedges and A. Winterbottom, *Legal History of Trade Unionism* (1930), p. 8 (the leading account of that history). See too, Wedderburn, *Cases and Materials on Labour Law* (1967), Chapter 4.
3. S. and B. Webb, *History of Trade Unionism* (1920), p. 63.
4. G. D. H. Cole, *Short History of the British Working Class Movement*, p. 62.
5. Allan Flanders, *Trade Unions* (7th ed. 1968), p. 10.
6. E. J. Hobsbawm, *The Age of Revolution* (1962), p. 216.
7. H. Pelling, *A History of British Trade Unionism* (1963), p. 41. See on these unions, H. A. Turner, *Trade Union Growth, Structure and Policy* (1962).
8. Hedges and Winterbottom, op. cit., p. 48.
9. (1851) 5 Cox 404, pp. 432; 436; 463; 466; 493.
10. *Trade Union Law* (3rd ed., M. A. Hickling, 1967), p. 8.
11. *R.* v. *Druitt* (1867) 10 Cox 592, pp. 601–2 (italics supplied).
12. C. Asquith, *Trade Union Law for Laymen* (1927), p. 14.
13. (1872) 12 Cox 316, pp. 348–9.
14. Quoted by Pritt and Freeman, *The Law versus the Trade Unions* (1958), p. 50.
15. S. and B. Webb, op. cit., p. 284.
16. (1867) L.R. 2 Q.B. 153, p. 159.
17. O. Kahn-Freund, 'The Illegality of a Trade Union', (1943) 7 *Modern Law Review* 192 at pp. 201–2.
18. C. Asquith, op. cit., p. 53; p. 56; and see p. 58.
19. E. J. Hobsbawm, *Labouring Men* (1964), p. 181.
20. J. Saville, 'Trade Unions and Free Labour: The Background to the Taff Vale decision', Chapter 9 in *Essays in Labour History* (ed. Briggs and Saville), p. 317.
21. *Industrial Problems and Disputes* (1920), p. 91, an account of the incidents by someone who knew the participants; Lord Askwith was for many years official Conciliator. See too pp. 94–5, where he comments that the cases of this era were decided by 'judges of whom every one had been brought up or practised at the bar at a time when trade unions were unlawful'. This led to a 'mutual shyness', the Trade Unions not trusting 'tribunals' from which they had been excluded'; the judges failing 'to keep in touch ... with events and to overcome prejudices'.

22. See *The Times*, 31 August 1900; and Bealey and Pelling, *Labour and Politics 1900–1906*, Chapter 3.
23. *Taff Vale Railway Co.* v. *Amal. Soc. of Railway Servants* [1901] A.C. 426 at p. 436.
24. *Torquay Hotel Co. Ltd* v. *Cousins* [1969] 2 Ch. 106 (C.A.).
25. *Agnew* v. *Munro* (1891) 2 White 611, p. 615.
26. [1896] 1 Ch. 811; [1899] 1 Ch. 255.
27. *Ward Lock & Co.* v. *O.P.A.S.* (1906) 22 T.L.R. 327 (C.A.); see too *Fowler* v. *Kibble* [1922] 1 Ch. 487 (C.A.); and Wedderburn, *Cases and Materials on Labour Law*, pp. 384, 429.
28. *Bernard Sunley Ltd* v. *Henry*, *The Times*, 8.2.67, and *Financial Times*, 25.1.67.
29. C. Grunfeld, *Modern Trade Union Law* (1966), p. 444.
30. [1960] 3 All E.R. 660.
31. [1967] 1 Q.B. 91 (Div. Ct.).
32. O. Kahn-Freund, *The System of Industrial Relations in Great Britain* (ed. Flanders and Clegg), p. 127.
33. See for what follows, *The Times* and *Financial Times*, 14, 17, 18, 20 and 23 March; 18, 20 and 29 April; 1 and 11 May 1970.
34. *Financial Times*, 20.3.70.
35. See Citrine's *Trade Union Law* (3rd ed., M. A. Hickling, 1967), p. 612.
36. [1909] A.C. 506.
37. [1957] 1 All E.R. 234.
38. [1965] A.C. 269 (H.L.). See Wedderburn (1965) 28 *Modern Law Review* 205.
39. *Financial Times*, 24.4.68.

CHAPTER 8

THE RIGHT TO STRIKE

'WHERE the rights of labour are concerned,' said Lord Wright in the *Crofter* case, 1942, 'the rights of the employer are conditioned by the rights of the men to give or withhold their services. The right of workmen to strike is an essential element in the principle of collective bargaining.'[1] The courts – like collective bargaining – had come a long way since 1900.

To protect such a right is not, of course, to approve (or disapprove) of its exercise in any particular withdrawal of labour. It is to recognize the fact that the limits set to the rights to strike and to lock out are one measure of the strength which each party can in the last resort bring to bear at the bargaining table. Happily, bargaining does not usually come to that last resort. But the strength of the trade union side is bound to be related to the extent to which its members can withdraw or curtail their labour. It is, in this respect, worth noting that although 'strikes' take the limelight there is a gradation of 'workplace sanctions', from the go-slow to 'working without enthusiasm'. The same is true of management; it can, at one end, press down the 'margin of tolerance' about working rules at the workplace[2] (as when the Post Office warned telephonists in 1970 that anyone who struck would not be offered overtime work for six days after returning) and, at the other, lock out workers (a weapon of industrial action not wholly dead as proved in the two-month national lockout of shipbuilding draughtsmen in 1967 when the union paid £250,000 in benefits to members). The employer's power to lock out has been limited only by the need to give appropriate notice for dismissal, or risk an action for breach of contract by each employee. In the last hundred years, the liberty to take strike action has had a more varied fortune.

This is not the place to engage in the complex debate about just how 'bad' or 'good' is Britain's strike record – or, indeed, whether, and when, strikes are 'good' or 'bad'. The orthodox picture of the facts, however, in the words of the Donovan Report is that our

number of working days lost in strikes ... relatively low since 1926 ... in the last decade has been higher than ever before ... the United Kingdom's recent record has been about average compared with other countries. We lost on average (1964–66) 190 working-days for each thousand employees ... over the period in question a comparatively large *number* of strikes for the size of the work force ... the overwhelming majority of stoppages – some 95 per cent – are due to unofficial strikes ... about half of all unofficial strikes ... concern wages (and) 10 per cent ... took place over disciplinary issues.[3]

This analysis of Britain's *special* problem, the large number of short unofficial 'unconstitutional' stoppages (especially in the four strike-prone industries of motors, shipbuilding and repairing, coalmining and the docks) is also the accepted starting point for both *Fair Deal at Work* and *In Place of Strife*. The solution envisaged by the Donovan Report is rapid improvement of collective bargaining especially at factory level. The number of 'official' strikes is relatively stable; but when they are national in extent they naturally change the character of the number of days lost, such as the 4 million days in 1957 and 1·5 million days in 1968, in national engineering stoppages. The annual total for some ten years remained at between 2 and 5 million, but in 1969 it rose to 6·8 and in the first half alone of 1970 the figure was 5 million.

But the orthodox analysis of the *special* British problem has not gone unchallenged. In a fascinating probe into the figures, Professor Turner concluded in 1969 that the evidence for Britain's pattern of conflict being special is 'quite unconvincing'.[4] The assertions about the unusually high record of unofficial and unconstitutional strikes is 'largely unsupported'. (The international statistics are unsatisfactory; and many 'unofficial' strikes were supported later by unions – often 'after they were over'.) The supposedly peculiar costs of British strikes to industry, and even to exports, 'are certainly much exaggerated'. It is clear that:

A strike by a key group in the long chain of production and distribution can put many people out of work in other firms and even other industries. It has a cumulative effect which can lead to disproportionate national cost. (*In Place of Strife.*)

But Turner's analysis rejects the 'marked unanimity of managerial and authoritative muttering on industrial conflict'. The words 'anarchy', 'indiscipline', 'disorder' and 'chaos' are to be found on the lips of all those in authority from the Donovan Report to the Government. These notions, he wrote:

seem to reflect rather a natural distaste on the part of men in authority for the idea that those they administer should sometimes take matters into their own hands than any measured assessment of the actual state of affairs. ... The problem of industrial unrest in Britain may be, not so much that its incidence is high, as that it is *not too well distributed* [italics supplied].

Although in 1969 and the first half of 1970 the number of working days interrupted by strike activity rose to a higher level than during the previous decade, it was still well below the total for some other major industrial countries. The remarkable thing about those who, like Mr Michael Shanks, write about 'the sick man of Europe', and 'the English disease' of which the germ is said to be 'labour unrest', is that they often reveal (as he did) that

with all its inefficiency, our labour does have the advantage that by international standards it is still cheap – at all levels.[5]

It is an 'advantage' which not all workers count as a blessing. Commenting in 1970, Mr Victor Feather pointed out that low basic rates in many industries forced millions of workers to work overtime (the average British worker working 240 days a year compared with 225 in France and Germany) and said that words like 'industrial anarchy' did not reflect the true situation of British industry. The white collar unions have, of course, become more militant; N.A.L.G.O. had its first strike in 1970; and even Civil Service unions began to speak of strike action at their 1970 conferences. Meanwhile, the motor car industry (and especially factories producing components) continued to run a high fever of bad industrial relations.

Both the Donovan Report and Turner,[6] however, join others in rejecting the notion that the whole problem is caused by some conspiracy of 'agitators'. As the Report puts it, 'shop stewards are rarely agitators pushing workers towards unconstitutional action'. Mr Woodcock answered suggestions by the Prime Minister and Minister of Labour in 1967 that a 'red plot' was at work with a blunt: 'Until I see some evidence, I flatly refuse to believe in this nonsense'. The real causes were said by the Donovan Report to lie largely in the failure of our collective bargaining *institutions* to adapt to current needs, and the failure of management to take initiatives on those matters that marked the points of tension (especially structures and methods of wage-payments). High among the priorities for the reformed 'factory agreements', too, is a speedy and effective procedure for settling grievances.

The law, of course, rarely deals with the causes of disputes. Just as a strike 'points to a problem, rather than creates one in the first instance',[7] so the writ and the injunction grapple with the symptoms rather than the causes. But in so far as local, short stoppages are a problem (and there are many such stoppages, it is clear) their prevalence lends a special importance to legal rules limiting strike action at short notice, for they often occur with little formal warning, as indeed do some official strikes called or backed by unions. Moreover, whatever be the true analysis of the detailed figures, about five times the number of working days lost in strikes is lost through injuries, and one hundred times as many perhaps by sickness and injury together. Strikes in fact lose 'something like one hour per head of the working population annually' and the cost of strikes is 'less than one-thousandth of the annual national product' (Turner). Some writers argue that a high strike ratio is a necessary accompaniment of high productivity. We need not venture into choosing between the various analyses. The point is, however, worth putting into perspective. As the T.U.C. put it in 1969:

It is commonly asserted that it is essential to 'do something' urgently about unconstitutional strikes. But there is no case for anyone deciding to do anything without first making a close analysis of the problem and its causes.[8]

This approach contrasts markedly with the common attitude that the 'Law' must root out industrial 'anarchy' after which all would be well in Britain. The facts themselves suggest that no such short-cut can be found to industrial 'peace' (even if that be the overriding objective; for we must remember that in industry, too, we can make a human desert and call it peace). The figures at least make it clear that legal regulation by itself does not necessarily correlate with a low strike record. Some systems with more legal regulation than Britain have far fewer strikes (e.g. Sweden and West Germany); but other countries with closer regulation have a strike record much bigger than ours (e.g. the U.S.A. and Australia where use of legal sanctions in 1969 brought the whole country to the verge of a national stoppage). And some systems of legal regulation forget that a right to strike *is* essential for real collective bargaining. In this chapter we are mainly concerned with that *right* to strike.

'It is our aim', said the American union leader Samuel Gompers in 1908, no revolutionary by any standards, 'to avoid strikes, but I trust that the day will never come when the workers of our country will have so far lost their manhood and independence as to surrender their right to strike'. He was echoed by the English postal workers' leader (by 1969, director of personnel on the British Steel Corporation Board) who declared in 1964 to his members: 'If you give up that right you give up the right to call yourselves free men'.

The emergence of any such 'right' in Britain involved no legal discrimination between 'official' and 'unofficial' strikes, or between 'unconstitutional' strikes (in breach of procedures) and others. Except in so far as the term 'unconstitutional' is used to denote a strike which in some manner constitutes a breach of employment contracts, these are not legal terms. Indeed, as far as 'official' strikes are concerned, it is worth pointing out that the right to strike does not belong to workers organized in an 'official' trade union alone (though, as we shall see, seven Donovan Commissioners wished it to be that way). At present, the protections developed since 1900 apply to any persons acting in furtherance of a trade dispute. We must now investigate their emergence and ask how far they remain effective today. We must first, therefore, look at different types of civil liability: (i) Conspiracy; (ii) Inducing Breach of Contract; (iii) Residual Liability for Economic Interference; and (iv) Intimidation. Around these the modern liberty to take strike action in Britain has revolved. After describing these, therefore, we shall be able to assess the important legal developments that have occurred since the publication of the Donovan Report in 1968.

CIVIL LIABILITIES: (i) CONSPIRACY

A statutory shield against the *crime* of 'simple' conspiracy and a clarification of the crime of 'intimidation' was, as we saw on p. 312, provided in 1875. But liabilities for conspiracy did not disappear as might have been expected. The reaction on the part of the courts was to develop between 1880 and 1906 a new *civil* liability for conspiracy. The intention of Parliament in 1875 was 'entirely to exclude the law of conspiracy from trade disputes, but their intention was defeated by the development of the common law'.[9] The Act was outflanked by judicial development of conspiracy as a *tort*. 'Your Lordships will remember', said Lord Chancellor Loreburn in 1906,

there never had been any attempt to make out any civil liability. ... Then came the new world and the new ideas. ... Decisions were given to the effect that there was a civil liability and therefore the civil responsibility for conspiracy became very serious.[10]

Twenty-six years later, Professor Harold Laski, in a note attached to the Report on Ministers' Powers, pointed out 'that in the history of trade union legislation principles of the Common Law, previously unknown, were invoked to narrow their purposes in a way which defeated the clear intention of those statutes'.

This 'new world' of liability in *tort* struck at any combination to injure, if the judges refused to accept the defendants' objects as 'legitimate'. Anyone who suffered damage could sue

the 'conspirators' for damages. The 1875 Act was of no avail
since it protected only the crime, said the courts. As we have
seen in Chapter 1, p. 24, the courts accepted promotion of
traders' competition (e.g. in price cutting), and employers' other
trade interests (e.g. in cases concerning blacklists of troublesome workers) as legitimate purposes; but from 1890 onwards
equivalent trade union activities all ran into the hazards of the
new liability. They, it seemed, were less legitimate.

We saw in Chapter 1, p. 27, how in *Quinn* v. *Leathem*, 1901,
civil conspiracy was extended by the Law Lords to render unlawful a boycott of Leathem organized by the union when he
would not dismiss non-union men. That was also the year of
Taff Vale. 'The House of Lords', wrote Professor Jenks, 'had
first invented a new civil offence ("civil conspiracy") and had
then created a new kind of defendant against whom it could be
alleged.'[11] Two critical developments, however, in conspiracy
have occurred since 1901, one judicial, and one statutory.

The judicial development was the reflective judicial acceptance, after all, of trade union objects as 'legitimate', in cases
such as *Reynolds* v. *Shipping Federation*, 1924, and the *Crofter*
case, 1942, already described in Chapter 1. By the present day,
judges (some rather reluctantly, others not) are bound to accept
the genuine pursuit of union purposes as proper, including the
'closed shop'. Mr Justice Harman said in 1957: 'It is not for
English lawyers to dislike or distrust the principle of the closed
shop for they are all members of a society which itself lives
and thrives on this principle.'

The modern law was stated by Lord Wright in the *Crofter*
case:

A perfectly lawful strike may aim at dislocating the employer's
business for the moment but its real object is to secure better
wages or conditions for the workers. The true contrast is, I think,
between the case where the object is the legitimate benefit of the
combiners and the case where the object is deliberate damage
without any such just cause ... cases of mixed motives or, as I
should prefer to say, of the presence of more than one object, are
not uncommon. If so, it is for the jury or judge of fact to decide
which is the predominant object.

In *Stratford* v. *Lindley*, 1964, no tort of 'simple' conspiracy by the Watermen's officials was established (even though one Law Lord thought they wished to 'make an example' of the employer) because they acted throughout in pursuance of what they genuinely believed to be their 'fundamental Trade Union principles'.

In 1906, the Trade Disputes Act, section 1, had already anticipated the judges by applying to the novel tort the formula adopted for the crime of conspiracy in 1875. It added to the 1875 statute an amendment to protect the tort of conspiracy. It provided: an act done in pursuance of a combination shall not be actionable (i.e. as a tort) if done in furtherance or contemplation of a trade dispute, *unless the act would be actionable if done without any such combination.*

The 1875 Act had excluded the *crime* of simple conspiracy from trade disputes. The courts replied by introducing, so it seemed, the *tort* of simple conspiracy, in 1901. Parliament responded in s.1 of the 1906 Act by excluding the new tort on the same terms. Then, decades later, the courts took a new look and accepted union objects as legitimate after all. (We see later that the 1970 Bill proposed to replace s.1 with a stronger section to remove doubts raised by cases decided after 1963, especially doubts about the meaning of 'actionable': p. 349.)

This curious interplay of statute and case law, typical of our modern labour law, has produced some odd results. In *Rookes* v. *Barnard*, 1964, the Law Lords were, as we shall see, p. 366, called on to comment on s.1 of the Act. They took the narrowest possible view of the section and insisted that it did no more than protect '*Quinn* v. *Leathem* conspiracies' – i.e. those conspiracies where the defendants are pursuing not legitimate union objects but personal grudges, vindictiveness, or the like, to injure the plaintiff, as their predominant purpose (for that must now be taken to be the 'true' principle behind *Quinn*'s case). Those are the conspiracies, said the Law Lords, which s.1 means to protect, and nothing more. But there is an immediate problem – which their Lordships did not answer. If the defendants are pursuing a grudge or spite, they are not (as we saw in Chapter 7, p. 332) pursuing a trade dispute, if one exists. Now s.1 provides its protection only to those acting in *furtherance* of the trade dispute. In the modern law, therefore, it is scarcely possible for any persons engaged in a '*Quinn* v. *Leathem* conspiracy' to fall within s.1 because they are outside the golden formula. The Law Lords in practice confined the protection of the section to an area where it cannot protect at all! This would not matter if there were no other possible interpretation of it; but, as we shall see when we discuss the *Rookes* case (p. 366), there is another view which would have made all the difference there.

The defendants in *Huntley* v. *Thornton*, 1957, could not receive the Act's protection, and were liable for 'simple' conspiracy because they aimed to injure the plaintiff in furthering their grudge, not union interests (see p. 332). But it may not be easy to define the 'trade union interests' which defendants must show they were genuinely pursuing – though (as in the *Stratford* case) the courts even in the past decade have been quick to accept trade union officials' assertions that they were pursuing union interests as 'genuine'. In 1958 officials of the Musicians' Union were held not liable for combining to organize a boycott of a dance-hall that ran a colour bar among dancers.[12] But the union (which had coloured musician members and argued that musicians could never 'insulate themselves from their audience') was held to have a direct material interest in the boycott, which it was legitimate for them to uphold even though it was not reducible to cash terms. A boycott aimed directly against government policy (e.g. against denationalization) might involve greater difficulty. We have seen that the social climate may be ripe for revival of the idea that a combination 'against the Government' is somehow wrongful (p. 328) and we return to the point later (p. 391). In the *Crofter* case it was said by Lord Maugham that a combination to injure a man *merely* because of his race, religion, or political views would not be justifiable as such within the common law doctrine. But where, as in the ballroom case, the political purpose can be shown to have been genuinely pursued directly to 'advance the welfare of the members' of a union, it is likely now to be justifiable. Such is the limit of civil 'simple' conspiracy today.

The courts have accepted the trade unions as 'legitimate'. Note that the 'conspiracies' we have been discussing were 'simple conspiracies'. No *unlawful* acts or means were involved.

The 1970 Bill proposed to strengthen s.1 by replacing it with a provision which said, in effect, that combinations to act in contemplation or furtherance of a trade dispute would not be actionable as conspiracies (a) if the act would not be a *tort* if done by an individual; or (b) would, if so done, be protected by the 1906 Act, s.3, (p. 350) or the 1965 Act (p. 371). This would be a sensible clarification of 'unlawfulness' for the purpose of conspiracy; but, as we shall see, it may not go far enough (p. 377).

(ii) INDUCING BREACH OF CONTRACT

In *Lumley* v. *Gye*, 1853, the judges reshaped older principles into a modern tort known as causing or 'inducing' breach of contract. It is a tort knowingly and intentionally to induce a third party to break his contract to the damage of the other contracting party without reasonable justification or excuse. Such a general liability was bound to hold profound importance for industrial and commercial law. In two decisions before 1897 the judges showed signs of creating even wider liability for inducing a man not to *make* a contract with another, as well. But the House of Lords rejected that view in 1897. (As we shall see, by 1969 it may have crept in again by a back door.) A contracting party, we may put it, has a right to defend his contract against outside intervention causing breach. But on that basis trade union officials are clearly easy targets for attack. In calling out workers on strike or in procuring them to take other industrial action (e.g. blacking work), they often induce inevitable breaches by the men of their contracts of employment and become liable in damages to the other contracting party – the employers.

The common law offered them no assistance. In 1905 the House of Lords fiercely rejected the argument that defence of trade union principles provided any 'justification' for the tort, in a case where miners had been brought out on strike in the face of very low wage rates. Lord Chancellor Halsbury 'absolutely refused to discuss' any analogy with cases where 'moral or religious grounds' provided justification in law. Only once has the vague defence of 'justification' been allowed in an industrial case – where chorus girls were brought out on strike in breach of their contracts when low wages had forced them into vice to make a living. Sexual corruption 'justifies' inducing breach; but starvation wages alone would not.

By 1906 this tort had become yet another common law liability against which the Trade Disputes Act had to give protection if there was to be any effective right to organize industrial action. Sir Charles Dilke introduced an amendment to section 3 – 'at 5.0 p.m. on a Friday afternoon', Lord Robert Cecil later complained – an amendment which became the first limb of the section and which the Attorney-General accepted as necessary if industrial conflict was to be 'conducted on equal terms'.

The section reads:

An act done by a person, in contemplation or furtherance of a trade dispute, shall not be actionable on the ground only that it induces some other person to break a contract of employment or that it is an interference with the trade, business or employment of some other person or with the right of some other person to dispose of his capital or his labour as he wills.

Thus (within the golden formula of 'trade disputes') the section protects:

Limb 1: Inducing breach of contracts of employment; and
Limb 2: Interference with trade business or employment.

Naturally, Limb 1 does not protect if some other tort is committed as well (e.g. slander or violence); nor if a breach of any contract other than one of employment is induced. So, when in *Emerald Construction Ltd* v. *Lowthian*, 1966,[13] building workers' union officials acted to procure the breach of 'labour-only' contracts, they could not use the section and an injunction was granted to stop them. On the other hand, inducing *any* breach of the employment contract is covered, from a withdrawal of labour to a 'go slow'. The workers themselves

350

can still be liable to the employer in damages for the breach of contract itself (the section does not protect that); but the person who induced the breaches cannot be sued for the higher damages that a tort action might entail, or for any other remedy such as an injunction.

The tort of inducing breach of contracts other than contracts of employment is still, however, a potent and growing weapon in industrial conflict. The wrongdoers are liable only if they intend to induce a breach of a contract of which they 'know'. But the Law Lords have, in *Stratford* v. *Lindley*, 1964, made it clear that they need not know 'all the terms of the contract', but have merely 'sufficient knowledge of the terms to know that they were inducing a breach'. In a now famous passage in the *Emerald* decision Lord Denning took it further:

If the officers of the trade union, knowing of the contract, deliberately sought to procure a breach of it they would do wrong: see *Lumley* v. *Gye*. Even if they did not know of the actual terms of the contract, but had the means of knowledge – which they deliberately disregarded – that would be enough. Like the man who turns a blind eye. So here, if the officers deliberately sought to get this contract terminated, heedless of its terms, regardless whether it was terminated by breach or not, they would do wrong. For it is unlawful for a third person to procure a breach of contract knowingly, or recklessly, indifferent whether it is a breach or not.

And Lord Justice Diplock said:

Ignorance of the precise terms of the contract is not enough ... to show absence of intent to procure its breach. The element of intent needed to constitute the tort of unlawful procurement of a breach of contract is, in my view, sufficiently established if it be proved that the defendants intended the party procured to bring the contract to an end by breach of it if there were no way of bringing it to an end lawfully. A defendant who acts with such intent runs the risk that if the contract is broken as a result of the party acting in the manner in which he is procured to act by the defendant, the defendant will be liable in damages to the other party to the contract.

This was a far cry from the old cases which demanded *real* knowledge and intent. 'Recklessness' had begun to be enough.

As for the need to show an *inducement*, the Donovan Report strove to lead its readers through the narrow passage between that and 'mere advice' which is lawful. For example (it said) if a union official advised a customer about a dispute with the employer and said he should 'consider his business relations with that employer' and called 'attention to the possible dangers for the customer', then, even if the customer broke a contract with the employer in consequence, there would be no tort. Even as the ink was drying on the Donovan pages the courts were showing that this passage could hardly be taken at its face value. In the *Torquay Hotel* case,[14] a much wider notion of 'inducement' was used (as we shall see illustrated by the Alternative Fuels aspect of the case: p. 375). Lord Justice Winn spurned the suggestion that some union officials in that case had done no more than 'warn' or 'advise', saying:

In the ordinary meaning of language it would surely be said that a father who told his daughter that her fiancé had been convicted of indecent exposure had thereby induced her, with or without justification, by truth or by slander, to break her engagement. A man who writes to his mother-in-law telling her that the central heating in his house has broken down may thereby induce her to cancel an intended visit.

Even before the Report, *Square Grip Reinforcement Ltd* v. *MacDonald*, 1968, saw 'the disease of the labour injunction ... spread to Scotland'.[15] Union officials were made liable to an interdict [injunction] because their approach to customers and addresses on sites to men employed by the customers had led those men to support the demands of Square Grip workers for recognition of the union. The men forced the customers to break off deliveries from Square Grip. On the argument that the officials were merely 'informing', Lord Milligan said they knew that the men had already offered to 'black' Square Grip supplies (naturally enough, since they were in the same union); and when even a 'suggestion' was made by someone 'desperately anxious' to produce a result to persons whom he knew were receptive, that was in law an *inducement*. How union officials are ever safely to confine themselves to 'advice' baffles the imagination! They would do well not to rely upon the passage in the Donovan Report, which reflects the older, more liberal attitude of the courts before the 1960s.

We can see the contrast very clearly in two cases – which concern the meaning of 'inducement'; the distinction between *direct* and *indirect* inducement; and the whole nature of this critical tort. First, in *Thomson* v. *Deakin*, 1952,[16] inducing breach of contract was alleged, not by direct persuasion but by *indirect* means. Because D. C. Thomson Ltd ran a non-union shop, the defendant union officials had declared a boycott of them. The officials aimed to force Thomsons out of their anti-union stand by use of the boycott. Bowater Ltd, who had a contract to supply Thomson, learned that their lorry drivers, being union men, would not deliver the supplies, and therefore informed Thomsons that they could not honour the contracts. Thomsons sought an injunction to prevent the officials from continuing this alleged procurement of breaches of the supply contracts. They were not successful. The Court of Appeal decided that the allegation was of indirect inducing. The defendants had not gone to a director of Bowater Ltd and persuaded the company itself voluntarily to stop supplies. They had gone to its servants (their members) instead. To persuade the company's servants was different from persuading the company itself. And an indirect inducement of breach was tortious only if some 'wrongful means' was used in the course of it.

Even so, it was argued, the defendants were liable because their indirect procurement of breach of the commercial supply contracts *was* effected by means wrongful in themselves, namely, the direct procurement of breach of the lorry drivers' contracts of employment (see Figure 2). This might be protected as against Bowater Ltd by s.3, Limb 1, of the 1906 Act. But the men were still breaking their contracts, even if the union officials were protected from action by the employers for inducing breach. The Court of Appeal agreed that had this allegation succeeded, the indirect inducement of breach of supply contracts might have been actionable, provided all the other parts of the tort were proved (such as that the defendants had enough knowledge of the supply contracts, which the Court thought had not been proved). But the Court was not

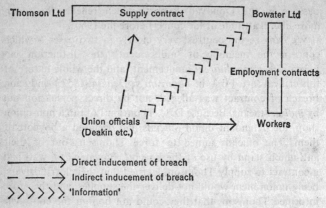

Figure 2. *Thomson* v. *Deakin*

satisfied that the lorry drivers *had* broken their contracts of employment. Bowaters had not ordered the men to load their lorries and, said Sir Raymond Evershed, Master of the Rolls, 'took the line that they would not order any man either to load or to drive paper for the plaintiffs'. Therefore, the indirect procurement of breach of the supply contracts had been accomplished without any 'wrongful means', and was not actionable. It was true, too, that the union officials had informed Bowaters directly of the position and the views of their men; but this was not direct 'persuasion' or inducement, it was mere information (a very different construction from what could be expected in 1970).

The new approach was apparent in the case of *Stratford Ltd* v. *Lindley*, 1964.[17] There, we recall, the Watermen's Union had put an embargo on barges hired out by Stratford Ltd. The Union officials (defendants in the action) had instructed their members employed by the hirers not to handle the barges, in order to put pressure on the Stratford group of companies after the refusal of recognition by another company in it (Bowker and King Ltd). The Union had given notice of this embargo to the Employers' Association, regretting 'any inconvenience' but alleging that it had no alternative action. We saw

in Chapter 7 (p. 333) that the Lords held that this was not a
trade dispute. They also held that an injunction must issue because there had been a wrongful inducement of breaches of the
hiring contracts. They all agreed in rejecting the point which
had convinced a majority of the Court of Appeal, namely that
there was no evidence that the defendants knew enough about
the hiring contracts. They must have had sufficient knowledge,
said the Lords. But then their Lordships separated in their
arguments. A majority held that this was a case of *indirect* inducement. The officials had directly induced their members to
break their contracts of employment with the customers and
there was no trade dispute. This was a wrongful act which led
to the indirect procurement of breach of the hiring contracts
(see Figure 3). In other words, the argument that failed in

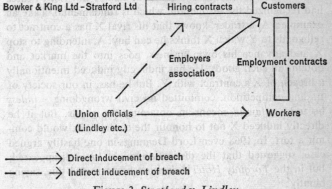

Figure 3. *Stratford* v. *Lindley*

Thomson v. *Deakin*, here succeeded. Lord Pearce, however,
treated this case as one of *direct* inducement of breach of the
hire contracts. He did this because of the notification to the
Employers' Association.

A comparison of the two cases reveals that, of the many
difficult points involved, in 1952 most were decided in favour
of the union defendants, but in 1964 just the opposite occurred.
The notion of 'direct' inducement was extended in 1964 in a
way that became typical of the decisions of the 1960s. 'The

fact that an inducement to break a contract', said Lord Pearce, 'is couched as an irresistible embargo rather than in terms of seduction does not make it any the less an inducement.' (We may contrast the 'information' given Bowaters in 1952.) Lord Justice Jenkins had demanded that the breach be proved to be a 'necessary consequence' of the inducement. In 1964, Lord Pearce thought this might be the law where *indirect* inducement was involved; but for a *direct* inducement it need be shown only that the breach was a 'reasonable consequence'.

Oddly enough (perhaps because of a passage in which Viscount Radcliffe expressed the wish that the law should be less technical), some commentators thought that the *Stratford* decision had in some unidentifiable fashion destroyed the distinction between *direct* and *indirect* inducement, making the latter actionable without proof of unlawful means. But Lord Pearce had recognized the distinction, which is fundamental. Take an example: A, a trader, knows that his rival X has a contract to sell goods to Y which X thinks he can buy. A, intending to stop X and advance his own business, goes into the market and obtains all such goods. He has indirectly induced intentionally a breach of X's contract with Y. But he has, in our society of trading competition, committed no civil wrongdoing – *unless* he used *unlawful* means in obtaining the goods. But if he directly induced X not to honour the contract, he would commit a tort. In 1968 even Lord Denning, in one hastily argued case, suggested that the distinction might have disappeared; but in the *Torquay Hotel*[14] decision he corrected this, saying bluntly:

I went too far when I said ... there was no difference between direct and indirect interference. ... On reading once again *Thomson* v. *Deakin* with more time I find there is a difference ... This distinction must be maintained else we should take away the right to strike altogether. ... A trade union official is only in the wrong when he procures a contracting party *directly* to break his contract, or when he does it indirectly *by unlawful means*.[18]

This, of course, leaves open the difficult problem of what is meant by 'unlawful means' to which we return (p. 376). For the present, it is useful to note one of the three ways in which, despite this reassertion of the traditional law by Lord Denning, the *Torquay* decision increased the legal hazards of union officials. (The other two ways appear on pages 375 and 377.) It will be recalled that some officials had procured Esso to stop supplies (probably directly; or, if not, then indirectly by wrongful means, i.e. inducing the lorry drivers to break their obligations otherwise than in a trade dispute: p. 334). But, it was next argued, no fuel was ever ordered. The court replied that this action was for an injunction to prevent *future* acts which would procure breach of contract *if* fuel were ordered. The question was: had the plaintiffs shown that the officials intended or threatened to do that? But, came the answer, they could not possibly do that. Failure to supply the oil would not be a *breach*. The contract had in it a clause saying that 'neither party shall be liable for any failure to fulfil any term' of the contract if they were prevented by 'any circumstance whatever ... not within their immediate control' (including 'labour disputes' specifically). No previous case had made a defendant liable for this tort unless what he procured was an actionable breach of contract between the parties. But the Court of Appeal refused to let this free the defendants. Lord Denning said they could not rely upon an excuse brought about by their own acts (an argument which may assume the very question whether those acts were wrongful). More important, however, the other Lords Justices held that the tort was still committed even if the 'breach' was not fully actionable, as here, between the contracting parties. The fact that the *Imperial* could not sue Esso for damages because of the clause did not prevent it from suing outsiders who procured such a 'breach', for damages or an injunction. This extension of the judicial doctrine means that the defendant, forbidden in 1966 to turn a 'blind eye' to the contract, by 1969 was told that however hard he looked at it he could not take advantage of a clause which is 'an exception from liability for non-performance'. Lord Justice Russell agreed it would be different for an 'exception from obligation to perform' – i.e. one can still procure a man not to do that which he has no obligation to do. But we shall see (p. 377) that Lord Denning's judgment makes even that doubtful!

357

The judicial extension of this tort of inducing 'breach' of commercial contracts (contracts of supply, hire, repair, sale, etc. regularly made by employers) is a most effective weapon to shrink the legality of union action in trade disputes. Nothing in the Act of 1906 protects that species of tort by name. This is somewhat curious, and it has been argued that the legislature must have intended to protect inducing breach of commercial contracts under the umbrella of s.3, Limb 2 – 'interference with trade, business or employment'. After all, such interference is the main aim of union action. But the House of Lords made it clear in *Rookes* v. *Barnard*, as we see later (p. 368), that Limb 2 does not cover this tort, and the *Stratford* case confirmed that. There arose, therefore, by 1969 an urgent need to reform s.3 if strike action was not to be put at regular risk of illegality. To this reform we return.

(iii) RESIDUAL LIABILITY FOR ECONOMIC INTERFERENCE

Quinn v. *Leathem* (the case of the boycotted meat flesher: *ante* p. 27) had in 1901 revived fears of further liabilities apart from conspiracy. In it Lord Lindley and Lord Brampton thought that 'coercion' could be unlawful in an individual without even any conspiracy or any specifically unlawful act. Sir William Erle as long ago as 1867 had argued that the common law would protect each man's right to the free disposition of his capital and his labour and to 'freedom from interference'. But this seemed to go back to the earlier vague liabilities and the House of Lords' decision in *Allen* v. *Flood*, 1897, was against it.[19] There, new processes had led to disputes between the ironworkers' union and the woodworkers. An official of the former said his men would come out unless the woodworkers were discharged. They were lawfully discharged and sued the official. Workers were, it seems, open to discharge on this work, and able to quit, at the end of the day; so the strike threatened could not have been even a breach of contract. The Law Lords said the official could not be made liable for a tort even if he had acted maliciously and was personally vindictive.

All the acts done and threatened were lawful. Neither malice nor the success of his threat or coercion was enough by itself to create liability.

For a period, however, between 1901 and 1921 it seemed as if English judges were about to ignore this decision in order to intervene in industrial affairs and to dub any economic pressure which they disliked 'unlawful coercion'. In 1919 threats to strike to make a man join the union were so dubbed by Mr Justice Astbury. In 1904 Mr Justice Grantham remarked that the 'House of Lords has been getting round [*Allen* v. *Flood*] so there is little left of that case now'. But in 1921 the tide turned again. A series of decisions by the Court of Appeal confirmed that the English courts were bound by the approach in *Allen* v. *Flood* not to take upon themselves the legislation of rules for economic conflict, either between traders, or between capital and labour. As Lord Justice Atkin said in 1921, to be unlawful in an individual, 'coercion' must be 'intrinsically and irrespectively of its motive a wrongful act'. By 1942 the Law Lords appeared to agree that 'threats' could not be called unlawful merely because a judge disliked them – only if an act itself unlawful were threatened. The opposite view had been denounced by Lord Dunedin in 1925 as 'the leading heresy' and so it remains. Echoes are still heard of the heresy. Lord Devlin said in 1962 that *Allen* v. *Flood* 'dammed a stream of thought that I believe would have had a beneficial effect on the law ... only a tenuous barrier holds back the flow'; and in 1964, that he would leave open the question whether there is a tort of 'malicious interference by a single person with trade, business or employment . . . I mean, putting it shortly, *Quinn* v. *Leathem* without the conspiracy'.[20]

Most modern judges have accepted, however, that the issue is settled for orthodoxy. Interference by itself, without conspiracy, is no tort, malicious or not. It must be repeated, however, that use of *unlawful* means (Lord Dunedin in 1925 said that is a crime or a tort) to damage a man *is* wrongful. Thus, in the *Stratford* case, two Law Lords put their decision on the simple alternative ground that the union officials, unprotected by the 1906 Act, had used tortious means to damage the plaintiff. Similarly, we saw in the *Daily Mirror* case, 1968 (p. 90) a decision where use of arrangements invalid under the Restrictive Practices Act, 1956, was the basis of a tort, a conspiracy to damage the newspaper by *unlawful* interference. But it was not clear in 1906 that this was the limit of liability; and Parliament was understandably in some difficulty to know just what the next judicial development of tort liability might be. After *Quinn* v. *Leathem* anything might happen. That was why Parliament adopted the formula, derived from Sir William Erle's writing, 'interference with trade, business and employment' – and tried to give protection in trade disputes via Limb 2 of section 3 against the prospect of vague liabilities that the judges might impose for any 'coercive' interference. The Prime Minister, Campbell-Bannerman, himself feared that the courts would run a 'coach and six' through the Act unless it were clear.[21] The fears of Keir Hardie led him to reply in *The Times* to a strong letter from Lord Lindley attacking the Bill:

This man and this type of man will have to interpret the act if it becomes law and it is therefore doubly imperative upon us to see that no possible loophole is left whereby they may wriggle out of the plain intention of the Act of Parliament.

But only a few men like Dilke paid the close attention to drafting required if this aim was to be achieved. Yet Parliament tried to achieve it; Limb 2 went further than the proposals of Lord Dunedin's Royal Commission of 1905. Inducing breach of employment contracts (Limb 1) and interference with trade, business or employment (Limb 2) were *both* protected in trade disputes.

For some forty years the law seemed reasonably settled. True, in 1927 after the General Strike a new trade union Act made 'intimidation' a wide offence once again, and included even causing 'reasonable apprehension' of damage to any person's property, including 'his business, occupation, employment, or other source of income'. But this retrogressive statute, redolent of earlier liabilities, was rarely invoked and was repealed totally in 1946. It was universally believed that the law had now laid down (in the 1906 Act and the common law rules) a set of 'Queensberry Rules', within which the autonomous bargaining, and if need be conflict, of the industrial parties should be conducted.

(iv) INTIMIDATION: ROOKES v. BARNARD

In 1964 the Law Lords drove what counsel called a 'coach and four' through the Trade Disputes Act, 1906, in a decision described by Professor Kahn-Freund as a 'frontal attack upon the right to strike'. He added:

One is under the impression that the repressive tendencies of the courts, which in the 19th and early 20th centuries had to be repeatedly counteracted by Parliament, are on the point of being revived.[22]

Rookes was a draughtsman in a London Airport office of B.O.A.C., where the union had an informal (and not wholly clear) '100 per cent membership' agreement. He left the union in 1955 after disagreements with it and local union members took up the issue of his removal from the drawing office. Rookes had been an active member of the union, and there was always some dispute over the circumstances of his resignation. He later accused the union of being too concerned with politics. Union spokesmen said that he insisted on 'direct action' over grievances; and when the union officials and

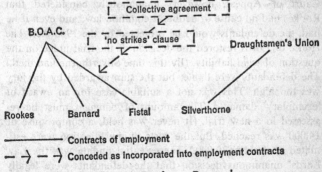

Figure 4. *Rookes* v. *Barnard*

branch members would not agree, he left. No legal point turned on the reason for Rookes' resignation; but feelings among the other union members at B.O.A.C., ran high against him. Barnard and Fistal (two fellow draughtsmen who were local, voluntary union officials) and Silverthorne (a district union official employed by the union, not by B.O.A.C.) organized and conveyed to B.O.A.C. a threat to withdraw labour if Rookes were not removed within three days, as stated in a resolution passed at a members' meeting. Such a strike would have been a breach of contract by each worker – probably for two reasons. There was no proper notice by the draughtsmen to terminate employment; and anyhow 'the object of the notice ... was to break the contract by withholding labour but keeping the contract alive' (Lord Devlin), not to terminate the draughtsmen's employment. But it was also *conceded* by counsel for the defendants that a 'no strikes' clause in another (formal) collective agreement between the unions and B.O.A.C. was incorporated into *each* individual contract of employment (as we saw, p. 195). Rookes was given long notice and lawfully discharged by B.O.A.C. He now sued Barnard, Fistal, and Silverthorne for conspiracy.

Mr Justice Sachs held that he had a good cause of action. After his Lordship's spirited address to them, the jury awarded Rookes £7,500 – a very large sum which went beyond compensation into 'exemplary' damages to punish the defendants. The Court of Appeal, however, unanimously considered that Rookes had no cause of action at common law; and even if he had, the defendants would be protected by the 1906 Act. The House of Lords restored the decision of the trial judge on the question of legal liability. (By this time Silverthorne had died.) The defendants were liable; but the sum awarded by the jury was too high. This was not a suitable case for an award of 'exemplary' damages. The amount of damages must be reassessed in a new trial. (It never was held; a compromise of £4,000 was reached. But the costs of the litigation were estimated at nearly £30,000.) The essential finding was the Law Lords' unanimous decision that the defendants were legally liable, after all.[23] What was the nature of their liability?

'Simple' conspiracy would not do. These defendants were (everyone agreed) pursuing proper trade union objectives. It was not, therefore, the 'closed shop' that vitiated the strike threat in *Rookes* v. *Barnard*. Indeed, in legal terms the case is nothing to do with the closed shop. It is about the right to threaten and organize strikes. And the parties agreed this was a trade dispute. The Act of 1906, s.1, therefore permitted no action for conspiracy unless the act done would be actionable in an individual without any combination. But what liability could be found? Was it really possible that after that Act had stood for fifty years, and twenty years after the *Crofter* case which reaffirmed the modern 'abstentionist' doctrines of conspiracy (see p. 346), a plaintiff could glean from a threat to strike some residual actionable element which no one had ever found before in all the long history of labour litigation? It was indeed possible because for the first time in modern English legal history the judges in the House of Lords were prepared to look at the threat to strike as a threat to do something totally illegal, like violence.

Rookes alleged that he was damaged by civil 'intimidation'. Now the textbooks had relatively little to say about *civil* 'intimidation'. We have already seen (p. 321) that criminal 'intimidation' was tied down to the list set out in the Act of 1875. The rare examples of civil intimidation were cases where A had threatened or used wholly unlawful acts or means. For instance, suppose A threatens to assault B unless B withdraws his regular gifts to C. If C suffers this loss, he can sue A, because A has caused it by threat of violence against B. The latest clear example in the Law Reports was that involving an unduly enthusiastic sea captain who, in 1793, had to pay damages for intimidation to a rival trader. He (A) had fired cannon near to the canoes of customers (B) off the Cameroon coast in order to scare them from trading with his rival (C). Like the other examples in the books, it involved a threat of *violence*. What had that to do with a threat to strike?

Rookes alleged that the threat to strike which had damaged him could be brought under the same principle. He claimed that the trade unionists (A) had threatened to do an 'unlawful' act against B.O.A.C. (B), *viz.* strike in breach of contract, which had damaged him (C). The question therefore arose: is a breach of contract unlawful for this purpose in the same way as violence is unlawful? Threats to do an act which is not in the full sense *unlawful* cannot, the Law Lords agreed, be the tort of intimidation. The step from violence and other illegal acts to breach of contract may not sound a long one. But in law it is. 'In contract,' as one authority has put it, 'no duty common to all is broken, no inherent right invaded: the obligation is self-assumed, the right self-created.'[24] Such rights and duties are usually contrasted with the obligations of the criminal law and of tort law. In English law, no third party to a contract can (as Lord Evershed re-emphasized in the *Rookes* case) sue on that contract. Therefore, the Court of Appeal, which rejected Rookes' argument, insisted that, as between Barnard and B.O.A.C., Rookes (being a third party) could not complain of any breach of the employment contract, still less of a threat to break it. But the House of Lords swept aside this distinction. For the first time they classified breach of contract as similar to violence. (Irish courts had gone that far in 1938 and 1940 in two badly reported cases; but British practice had never been based on those decisions and Irish judgments are, of course, not binding authorities in this country.) The Law Lords said, therefore, that a coercive threat of a breach of contract gave a cause of action just like a coercive threat of violence.

What stands out in the speeches of the Law Lords is their determination to reach this result. 'The injury and suffering caused by strike action', said Lord Hodson, 'is very often wide-spread as well as devastating and a threat to strike would be expected to be certainly no less serious than a threat of violence.' Lord Devlin foresaw that difficulties would be caused by the Lords' decision as far as industrial relations were concerned; but he could not, he thought, therefore 'hobble the common law'. (But he was extending it.) Lord Devlin could find 'nothing to differentiate a threat of a breach of contract from a threat of physical violence', which led Mr George Woodcock to speak with scorn at the T.U.C. of the idea 'that a threat to break an individual contract ... is the equivalent of a threat to bash a man's face to pulp'! The Law Lords even supported their reasoning by drawing an analogy with *Lumley* v. *Gye* in order to defeat the argument that Rookes was a third party to the contract. But that case, as we saw on p. 349, was concerned with the problem whether a third party *defendant* could be liable for interfering with other people's contracts by inducing a breach. Rookes' case was concerned with the question whether a third party *plaintiff* could build a cause of action out of someone's threat to break a contract. The speeches of the Law Lords display the strongest desire to find for the plaintiff. After his retirement in 1964, Lord Devlin said in a broadcast: 'In the common law a question of policy rarely arises'. Whatever the accuracy of this proposition, one such question arose in Rookes' case. It was settled by extending what Lord Justice Pearson had called the 'obscure, unfamiliar and peculiar' tort of civil *intimidation*. The extension depended on the finding that the strike threatened would be in *breach of contract* and that a coercive threat of that kind was a threat of *unlawful* means, just like violence. This common law liability was novel, so much so that Lord Donovan in the Court of Appeal remarked that, if the plaintiff were correct, it was 'astonishing' that no one had discovered the liability before. No one in England had thought of it – ever since 1793.

But plenty of plaintiffs thought of it after the *Rookes* case and issued writs even in the short period before the 1965 Act gave some protection (p. 371). A worker in November 1967 received £1,250 from ten trade union officials in Woolwich power station on facts similar to the *Rookes* case. In August 1966, an *ex parte* injunction ordered officials of three unions to lift a 'blacking' from Olympic Airways planes on a writ alleging 'intimidation, conspiracy and actionable interference' (though after full argument five days later it was lifted). The same 'intimidation' was the tort alleged unsuccessfully in *Morgan* v. *Fry*, 1968,[25] where as we saw (p. 110) two appeal judges held that no breach of contract had been threatened in the union officer's notice of refusal to work with non-unionists from a certain date. The judgment of Lord Denning is notable, too, for the suggestion that even if there had been intimidation there, a defence of 'justification' might have been open to the union official if those organizing the breakaway workers were 'really troublemakers who fomented discord in the docks'. Lord Devlin had mentioned the possibility of a defence of 'justification' but said it did not arise for discussion in *Rookes'* case. Such a doctrine (if it does exist) would give free play to each judge's social policies about 'troublemakers', 'agitators' and even 'anarchists' in industry.

The 1906 Act and Rookes

Why did the 1906 Act not give the trade unionists a defence against Rookes? The Court of Appeal said it did, but the Law Lords thought not. It is, of course, not surprising that the Act does not expressly mention this sort of 'intimidation', since the tort had not been seen in 1906 in this form. The three main arguments were roughly as follows:

(a) Section 1 leaves unprotected an act 'actionable' without combination. But to be 'actionable', an act must cause damage. No damage would have been caused to Rookes by only one draughtsman *without combination* threatening to strike. The Lords disagreed; 'the section requires us', said Lord Reid, not to take 'the precise act complained of', but to think of 'the nearest equivalent act' which could be done by an individual. Other Law Lords thought it was enough that intimidation was 'in its nature' actionable and that s.1 merely protects against '*Quinn* v. *Leathem*' conspiracies, a restriction which reduces the section today almost to nothing, as we saw (p. 348). Both interpretations seem to limit the words of the section, the object of which was to protect strike activity from liability for conspiracy unless *the act* done would be *actionable* in an individual – and 'actionable' must include causing damage.

The second point under the Act was this:

(b) Silverthorne was not a B.O.A.C. employee. So he had no contract of employment to threaten to break. He could not therefore, it was argued, be an 'intimidator', even on the new view of the common law. Perhaps, as a union official he had *induced* breaches of contract by the other employees. But that was what s.3 Limb 1 protected in trade disputes. This argument was, of course, of first-rank importance since it involved a union official doing what officials do every day. The Lords rejected it and found Silverthorne liable with the rest. Only Lord Devlin, however, gave any clear reason for so doing. He said that once the plaintiff had proved 'intimidation' against any defendant, then he could sue 'the doer of the act *and the conspirators, if any, as well*'. That is to say, once one worker threatens to strike, all those 'conspiring' with him are jointly liable too – no matter who they are and whether they are also employees or not.

Both in the *Stratford* case, 1964, and in *Morgan* v. *Fry*, 1968, Lord Denning found it 'difficult to see why Silverthorne was not protected'. The only reason he could find was that Silverthorne was treated as a *conspirator* not an *inducer*. He preferred to treat *Fry* as an *inducer* (and therefore protected) – a good example of the way in which, until the 1965 Act was passed, liability could depend upon the semantic tastes of the judge. This absurd test seemed to encourage an official to be aloof from his members yet militant in leading them, the more easily to be seen as *inducer*, not *combiner*!

But the House of Lords in the *Stratford* case made confusion worse than ever. Lord Pearce there said that if the employer is suing the official who has threatened a strike, no doubt s.3 protects the latter; but that different considerations apply if a *third party* (like Rookes) is suing, for 'the first limb of the section is dealing only with the position between union official or unofficial agitator, and the employer'. In other words, an official is more vulnerable to actions by *third parties* than by the employer! But s.3, Limb 1, says the inducement is not to be 'actionable'. It does not say 'actionable *by the employer*'. Lord Denning in 1968 saw 'no justification for inserting' those words. Although other judges have approved of Lord Pearce's view, it does not seem to reflect the very clear words of the section.

The third point raised in the *Rookes* case on the 1906 Act was this:

THE RIGHT TO STRIKE

(c) Section 3, Limb 2, protects 'interference with trade, business or employment'. That, it was argued, is all that Barnard and the others had done. Not so, replied the Lords. There was 'intimidation' as well; and the word 'only' prevents that tort being covered by *either* Limb 1 *or* Limb 2. But it is then reasonable to ask: If it does not protect an interferer by threats of this kind, what wrongdoing does Limb 2 protect? Their Lordships conclude that the answer today is – *nothing*. Limb 2 was put in as necessary 'if the law should go one way but unnecessary if it went the other way' (Lord Reid). Now that there is no tort of 'malicious interference' with trade (i.e. '*Quinn* v. *Leathem* without the conspiracy' see p. 359) it is 'nugatory' (Lord Evershed) and 'pointless' (Lord Pearce). In that case Lord Donovan had asked pungently in the court below: 'Why bother to enact it?' Is it, he asked, not odd if Parliament has allowed one to 'procure the breach of another's contract with impunity' but 'one cannot even threaten to break one's own'? [26] The result of their Lordships' interpretation was to deprive Limb 2 of any effect at all. 'It may be,' said Lord Devlin, 'that Parliament [in 1906] did not anticipate that a threat of breach of contract would be regarded as an intimidatory weapon.' No one had dreamed it could be so regarded until the present case. No one had ever expected that the judges would equate a threat to walk out on a contract of employment with a threat to punch you on the nose. That is what did the trick.

Uncertainties after Rookes v. Barnard

The astonishment and alarm among trade unionists caused by *Rookes* v. *Barnard* were matched by the many uncertainties that it bequeathed to the law. A 'threat' is, the judges agreed, distinguishable from a 'warning'; but the distinction was – and is – obscure. The plaintiff who can sue for 'intimidation' can be anyone aimed at and injured – customer, worker, employer, etc. – but the range is uncertain. Also, if workers 'strike first and negotiate afterwards', they are not necessarily better off for not threatening first. A court can always (the Lords made clear) treat them as 'impliedly' threatening to continue the strike in breach of contract until their demand is met. 'Implied' threats can have a wide ambit. As we have seen there is apparently available a defence of 'justification', but no one knows how far it will go. Then commentators have doubted whether the new profound illegality of a breach of contract extends to 'two-party' intimidation (where A threatens B to the damage of *B*). The Law Lords' speeches in *Rookes* together with a judgment of Lord Denning's in 1965 make it clear that it does so extend, so that B, threatened by A with a breach of contract, may have actions both for 'anticipatory' breach of contract and for the tort of intimidation. After all, if breach of contract is like violence this would follow. Again the question has been raised: must the person threatened always submit to the threat before there is liability? Most judgments suggest an affirmative answer because in intimidation the damage must be *caused* by the threat. But suppose A threatens B that he will break his existing contract to work for B unless B refrains from offering goods to C. If B submits, C can sue. But if B resists, C will still not get the goods. As we shall see, however, perhaps this must be classed as 'interference by unlawful means' not 'intimidation'. Whatever its name, it may be a tort in both cases, a conclusion which carries grave consequences in labour law.

One other point must be made clear. Certain commentators attempted to say that *Rookes* v. *Barnard* was a very 'special' or unusual case because it involved a breach of an obligation that stemmed from a collective agreement. Indeed Lord Denning tried to confine the decision in that way in 1964 and in 1968. But any such effort to reassess the doctrine of the *Rookes* case runs into two insuperable problems. First, it would not even make much difference if it were correct. What goes for the 'no strikes' clause in the *Rookes* case would go for 'procedure' agreements – always provided that these collective clauses really can be implied into employment contracts (see p. 194). Secondly, and more important, the speeches of the Law Lords do not confine the doctrine of intimidation to threats to break obligations that stem from collective agreements. Indeed, the majority of them insist that they are expounding a doctrine of the common law that applies to all breaches of contract, whether inside or outside trade disputes. A coercive threat to break a contract of employment would plainly, in their view, be capable of being intimidation, whether the breach threatened was to be a strike, a go-slow, or an act of disobedience. The line which they drew was between acts threatened that were lawful and those that were 'unlawful', and they said that any breach of contract fell into the 'unlawful' category. In *Morgan* v. *Fry*, 1968,[25] however, Lord Justice Russell made a fascinating attempt to avoid the unfortunate consequences of these speeches. Contrary to his two brethren, he held that Fry's notice was a threat to induce *breaches* of contract (like the miners of 1894 who refused to go down the cage: p. 105). But he went on to hold that the *Rookes* speeches did not mean that a threat of any and every breach, however trivial, was intimidation. In particular, where, as here, the employers undoubtedly *preferred* the threat of breach to a threat to terminate the employment contracts, he was not prepared to hold that it was intimidation to engage in the first method when the effect of the second (lawful) method would have been exactly the same – i.e. the dismissal of Morgan with notice. The reason behind this seems to be that in intimidation it must be proved that pressure from the threat of unlawful acts *caused* (or *would cause*) the damage. The policy of Lord Justice Russell's judgment is laudable; but it does not seem to be in accord with the *Rookes* speeches. Barnard would, it is suggested, have received short shrift at the Law Lords' hands had he defended himself by saying: 'Oh! but we could have produced just the same effect by threatening to use lawful means'! Their Lordships would probably have remarked pithily that it was a pity for him he had chosen wrongly.

Whatever the uncertainties, a threat to strike in breach of contract could in 1964 be dubbed 'intimidation'. Any other use of such a breach might be seen as unlawful interference with business or unlawful conspiracy. All the new liabilities could be couched in a semantic form which evaded the careful protections of the 1906 Act. By August 1964, *The Times* spoke of 'a real bitterness among many trade union officials who live in anxiety, whether justified or not, lest they be brought before the courts and heavily fined for things they and their predecessors have done with impunity for half a century'. Mr Woodcock, then T.U.C. General Secretary, said to the 1964 conference: 'Really we cannot . . . in this country be responsible to courts, unless those courts are operating the minimum of reasonable sensible laws, related to the circumstances and the functions of trade unions.' In fact, a pendulum that had been still for over fifty years but which in the previous century had swung to and fro between judicial liabilities and statutory protections only to exacerbate industrial relations, had by these ingenious speeches of the Law Lords been set swinging again. And swing it did. For one of the first statutes to be enacted by the new Labour Government was the Trade Disputes Act, 1965.

THE ACT OF 1965[27]

The Act of 1965 set out in one section to provide a traditional type of protection in trade disputes against the new form of liability for intimidation. But, on grounds that were never clear, claimants were allowed six months more in which to issue new writs against persons who had done acts of 'intimidation' before the Act was passed. In those cases the Act was to be no defence. In this six-month period of limbo, in which the ghost of the pristine *Rookes* v. *Barnard* decision had its final fling, many writs were issued or threatened. (*Morgan* v. *Fry*, 1968, was an action begun before the Act was effective.)

The 1965 Act provides in section 1(1):

An act done after the passing of this Act by a person in contemplation or furtherance of a trade dispute (within the meaning of the Trade Disputes Act, 1906) shall not be actionable in tort on the ground only that it consists in his threatening:

(a) that a contract of employment (whether one to which he is a party or not) will be broken, or

(b) that he will induce another to break a contract of employment to which that other is a party.

Some of the wording is not felicitous. For example, it would have been better to make it clear that the statute applies to threats express *and* implied. Again, the limitation imposed in s.1(1)(b) by the words 'to which that other is a party' could be troublesome where an official has applied pressure to one worker which in effect threatens to induce another worker to break his contract in order to damage (say) a customer of the employer. It is not wholly clear that the official is then protected. Nevertheless the object of s.1(1) is clearly to settle the 'Silverthorne problem' once and for all, and give protection to officials in his position – whether in their threats they are regarded as 'conspirators' with the workers, when (a) protects them together with the workers, or as 'inducers' of the workers, in which case (b) protects them. Whichever view of s.3 of the 1906 Act was correct, the 1965 Act seemed to settle that issue at least.

The statute is, however, the very narrowest possible Act which could have been passed to deal with *Rookes* v. *Barnard*. Naturally it applies only within the golden formula of 'trade dispute'. It applies, like the 1906 Act, s.3 Limb 1, only to contracts of *employment*. The defendants in the *Emerald*, *Stratford*, or *Torquay Hotel* cases could get no help from the 1965 Act. It applies, furthermore, only to intimidation as such, by 'threatening'. Therefore, since a breach of contract (of employment or any other kind) remains wholly 'illegal', presumably interference by the use of such a breach, or a combination to promote such breaches, constitute, respectively, interference by, and conspiracy to use, *unlawful means*. We shall see that the expansion of the meaning of this phrase, together with the creation of yet another novel head of judicial liability in tort, is at the heart of many problems of strike law in 1969. The failure of the 1965 Act was its failure to grasp the nettle of the real innovation made in *Rookes* v. *Barnard*, namely the introduction of the total illegality of a breach of a contract in the law of tort. That was the doctrine which needed Parliamentary attention. But, producing their Bill on the same day on which they announced the establishment of the Donovan Royal Commission, the Government could claim that they must not go further than was absolutely necessary to meet the *Rookes* v. *Barnard* decision. Certainly the Act meets that test. Its defects, however, mean that the pendulum stuck half way. Attention shifted in labour law away from the specific tort of 'intimidation' to other related forms of liability. But 'intimidation' was still pleaded in all the major cases after 1965. To these we now turn.

SUMMARY – SO FAR

But first we may summarize the main points already made as follows:

1. *Conspiracy:*
   (a) Civil liability for 'simple' conspiracy, developed by the judges, culminated in *Quinn* v. *Leathem*, 1901; but protection was provided by s.1, 1906 Act in *trade disputes*.
   (b) S.1 was restrictively interpreted (1964); but by now, in cases from 1920 to the *Crofter* case, 1942, judges had accepted union objectives as legitimate for 'simple' conspiracy.
   (c) But none of this affects a conspiracy which aims at or uses *unlawful* means.

2. *Inducing Breach of Contract:*
   (a) Civil liability developed after 1853; but protection is given by s.3, Limb 1, 1906 Act in trade disputes where the contract is one of *employment*. Union officials and others protected; not workers for breach of contract as such.
   (b) Liability remains for inducing breach of 'commercial' contracts, even in trade disputes; this has been widened, – e.g. as regards knowledge, intention, inducement, 'breach', etc.: *Stratford* case, 1964; *Emerald* case, 1966; *Torquay Hotel* case, 1969. But it seems *indirect* inducement is still not a tort unless unlawful means are used.

3. *Residual Liability for Interference:*
   (a) Because of *Allen* v. *Flood,* 1897, and the cases between 1920 and 1942 (*Crofter* case), it became clear that mere 'coercion' by an individual is not a tort. But, again, use

373

    of unlawful means is a tort, and interference by 'unlawful means' was the basis of liability in 1964 and 1968.

  (b) Interpretations of s.3, Limb 2, 1906 Act decided that it protects against *mere* 'interference with trade, business or employment'. Thus, Limb 2 seems to cover only what is already lawful; it does not cover liability in 1(c), nor any other use of *unlawful* means.

4. *Intimidation:*

  (a) On the basis of old cases about threats of violence and the argument in 3(a), *Rookes* v. *Barnard*, 1964, extended civil 'intimidation' to cover threats to strike in breach of contract (a threat to do an 'unlawful' act). The plaintiff can be a third party (worker, supplier, etc.) intentionally injured. But the threat must cause the damage.

  (b) The Act of 1965 protects threats to break, or induce breaches of contracts of *employment* in trade disputes.

CURRENT DEVELOPMENTS OF STRIKE LAW

Strike law, however, has not stopped there, and it is useful now to indicate six areas where the law has developed, or is likely to develop further:

(i) *Golden Formula Again*: Beneath all the problems lies the definition and interpretation of the golden formula of acts done in furtherance or contemplation of a *trade dispute*. We have already noted that the interpretation even more than the definition needs to be made 'watertight' especially if s.4 of the 1906 Act were ever amended (Chapter 7, p. 336). A minority of three Donovan Commissioners thought that demarcation disputes between workmen should not be within the definition; but the majority show that such a proposal is neither necessary nor practicable. *Fair Deal at Work* proposed gigantic restrictions to exclude 'sympathetic' strikes (and lock-outs); 'blacking' goods of customers and suppliers; inter-union disputes; strikes and 'coercive action' to enforce a closed or union shop or 'preventing an employer from employing' types of workers on work they are 'qualified to take'. Under these proposals the golden formula would be turned into an iron chain around the hands of trade union strength at the bargaining table. Of equal importance are the new suggestions that 'political' objectives, or moves directed to influencing the Government, of themselves incapacitate industrial action from falling within the golden formula, even though it is otherwise clearly connected with some person's employment, non-employment or condition of labour (p. 329). The true test is whether the latter *connection* has been *wholly or predominantly* ousted by other objects. If that test were weakened, the golden formula could become valueless in modern society.

(ii) *Inducing Breach of Contracts Not Yet Made:* Whether or not there is a trade dispute, liability for inducing or threatening to induce breach of commercial contracts is now, we have seen, wider than at any time in the past. But one aspect of the *Torquay Hotel* case took liability even further. It will be recalled (p. 334) that a union official, D, had a conversation with Alternative Fuels in Cheshire (the number of their tanker which had got through to the *Imperial Hotel* had been sent through union channels to him), and N. had said 'No further supplies will get through from that area'. Now the *Imperial* never had a contract with Alternative Fuels (and none was needed as Esso supplies recommenced very soon). But the court granted an injunction in respect of supplies from that firm too on this argument: the officials sued had shown an intention to prevent supplies being delivered *if* any such contract were made (especially as 'repercussions' had been spoken of by D. to Alternative Fuels if they made more deliveries). Lord Justice Winn thought it very important that D. had said the Imperial was 'black' without *adding* 'but of course if you have contracted to deliver some more it can't be helped'. D. did not inquire whether there was a contract. On this ground alone an injunction would lie.

But the old law was quite different. In *Thomson* v. *Deakin*, 1952, Lord Justice Jenkins had stressed that general statements such as 'X. is black' were not inducements to unlawful action. And all the books had said that the liability could not arise where no contract existed between the parties. To this the *Torquay Hotel* case adds a critical qualification when the employer is seeking an injunction and alleges that the union officials have shown an intention to procure breach of contracts *if* he makes any. Apparently, in such a case, it will count against the union officials that they do not add, when announcing 'X. is black', some phrase to say: 'But if you have or make commercial contracts with X. we will not make you break them'. This change is crucial, for it could allow injunctions to remove the power behind 'blacking' altogether. It goes far beyond the *Stratford* injunction where the Law Lords granted a remedy against causing breaches of future contracts of the kind *already* existing and broken by reason of the union action. There, breach of an *existing* contract was still the basis of liability. After *Torquay Hotel*, employers who have no existing contracts can, it seems, sue successfully. Once again the Donovan Report was unduly optimistic in stating (without the *Torquay* qualification):

It has, we think, never been illegal ... simply to communicate information to a person in order to persuade him not to enter into or to renew contractual relations with another.[28]

(iii) *Unlawful Means:* Next there is interference or conspiracy to interfere by use of *unlawful* means, illustrated in the *Daily Mirror* case (p. 90).[29] What are unlawful means? A mere restraint of trade arrangement was held in 1920 not to qualify. Nor, it was held in 1959, is the use of perjury to damage a man. But other crimes usually are. Does that include the breach of every statute, however trivial the criminal penalty for breach? The answer is uncertain. In 1955 the Court of Appeal had no difficulty in deciding that crimes by strikers under the Merchant Shipping Act, 1894, (p. 389) were 'unlawful means' for a conspiracy. The increased use of the method of enactment increases the importance of the problem as is shown by experience in such countries as Canada and Australia. Parliament clearly had it in mind in enacting s.16(5) Prices and Incomes Act, 1966, (p. 214) to stop the crime of breaking a 'standstill' order being *unlawful means* in tort cases. Whenever a statute on industrial matters is passed, the question will arise whether a breach of it can be *unlawful means* within the doctrines of the law of tort. The 1970 Bill began to face this problem by proposing to exclude breach of its provisions from that area to prevent new torts being built from it (p. 385).

Even greater difficulty arises in respect to inducing breach of, or breaking, contracts. Suppose a union official induces breach of an employment contract in a trade dispute (or threatens to). He is protected by s.3, Limb 1, 1906 Act (and the 1965 Act) which makes his conduct not 'actionable'. But does it remain an 'unlawful means' for the purposes of other torts (such as indirect inducement of, or interference with, other contracts)? Some judges have said 'yes'. Others have rejected the artificial notion that a man can commit an 'unlawful' act when statute declares it not to be 'actionable'; and that is the better view.[30] But the matter does not end there. Did not *Rookes* v. *Barnard* show that breach of contract was *itself* an unlawful means (apart from the inducement)? If so, use of it must be *use of unlawful means*. Thus a combination to act or make use of any breach of contract, in order to damage X, would be a tort against X to which neither the 1906 nor the 1965 Act provides a defence even in trade disputes. Perhaps because he saw the terrifying results in logic of his decision that breach of contract was equivalent to violence, Lord Devlin in *Rookes* v. *Barnard* expressly said that he was not deciding that point. But he gave no reason. The Donovan Report accepted that the 'possibility' of such liability needs removing by legislation. As we saw (p. 349), the 1970 Bill would remove breach of contract from the area of conspiracies to use unlawful means. Statute needs to go one step further and banish it from the law of tort altogether. Until that is done, any court has ready to hand a weapon to make industrial action illegal, even in a trade dispute.

(iv) *Mere Interference with Contract:* But the biggest innovation is still to come. Despite all his other judgments which have tried to limit the interventionist tendencies in the case law of the 60s, Lord Denning in the *Torquay Hotel* case, 1969, extended liability in a new way. We have seen that mere deliberate interference by lawful means was never a tort; and Lord Donovan repeated this view in the *Stratford* case concerning interference with contract which does not cause any breach. Again stating the law as it was generally accepted to be in 1968, the Donovan Report said: 'Mere interference by itself is not actionable anyhow'.

But in 1969, in the *Torquay Hotel* case, Lord Denning held that it is no longer necessary to prove inducement of breach of contract. 'The time has come', he said, 'when the principle (of inducement) should be further extended to cover deliberate and direct interference with the execution of a contract without that causing any breach'. A person is liable under this new principle so long as he has been guilty of (a) 'interference' (e.g. if he 'prevents' or 'hinders' performance) in the execution of a contract; (b) 'interference' which is 'deliberate' (including turning 'a blind eye'); and (c) 'interference' which is 'direct' interference. This third requirement excludes such cases as the man who indirectly 'corners the market'. And it will exclude union officials where all that they do is inform members, for the interference with commercial contracts will then be indirect. But in real life they are bound to approach other persons 'directly' – employers, customers, suppliers, and so on, persons whom they surely *ought* to inform of impending strike action which clearly has the object of 'hindering' execution of contracts. That is the very object of trade unions' industrial action. They have been doing it for fifty years – and lawfully. They have no other weapon to balance management power. Yet now it is said they can be liable when no *breach* of such contracts has been caused and all their actions have been lawful, if by direct, deliberate acts they 'hinder' performance of any contract. Lord Justice Winn, without finally deciding the whole principle, agreed with Lord Denning that this would be so where a union has caused a customary mode of performing a commercial contract to become unavailable, even if other modes were possible to the parties under the contract.

The dangers of this new doctrine are so great that they cannot yet be gauged. The new doctrine appears to conflict directly with the old principles derived from *Allen* v. *Flood*, 1897. The new doctrine of 'mere interference' is, in truth, a gigantic leap into an unknown future of liability for both commercial and labour law.[31] Paradoxically, it might give a chance to breathe new life into the buried Limb 2 of s.3, 1906 Act (p. 368); though few courts would be likely to consider that a defence if they found that mere interference was really unlawful in itself.

Mere interference, now that it has firm support in the judgments of at least a few judges, is another profound threat to the legality of industrial action. The 1970 Bill failed to propose even the most obvious and moderate reform – protection within trade disputes. Statutory intervention is urgently needed against this wild new swing of the pendulum.

(v) *The Labour Injunction:* Furthermore, there is the problem of the 'labour injunction'. What happens usually is something like this: The employer (or other plaintiff) rushes into court alleging some or (usually) all the torts we have discussed. He is granted an *ex parte* injunction without the defendants being heard (just as in the *Ford* case for 'breach of contract': p. 173). This happened in most of the leading cases. Then a few days later the full argument is heard, the union officials now being represented. Sometimes, as in a case of 1969 against an Oxford district official, if the defendants are quick enough they can get all the merits heard in the one hearing. But some judges (especially in the Chancery Division of the High Court) do not hear the lawyers of the defendants when the employer's *application* is *ex parte*, even if the trade union's lawyers arrive panting at the door of the court. That happened in the *Torquay Hotel* case. After the full argument a few days later, unless the plaintiff has not proved even a case of apparent liability, as in the Olympic Airways case 1966, the court will decide whether to continue an 'interlocutory' injunction 'until trial'. In making such a decision it will only have written affidavits. No witnesses normally appear in person. The judges insist therefore in most of the cases that the 'full facts' will come out at the trial. But in most cases the employer is not interested in the trial for damages: he wants an injunction to *stop* the union's industrial action. So (after two appeals) he retained an injunction in the *Stratford* case in 1964. Then he seems to have done nothing about 'the trial' because in May 1969 the

Watermen's officials applied to have the case dismissed 'for want of prosecution' and the argument about the enormous costs went once more to the Court of Appeal! The 'interlocutory' nature of the injunction 'until trial' is usually mythical. It is usually the major legal weapon of tactical use to the employers (as in the case of a car delivery firm which obtained such an injunction against union officials in 1966 and also issued writs for damages for breach of contracts against its workers, which were promptly withdrawn when the battle was settled by negotiation).

But the courts, by their rules of procedure, have to treat these applications *as if* they were just for temporary injunctions. Therefore, in exercising their discretion whether to grant them they begin with the concept that the '*status quo*' should be preserved (that is, as it was *before* the strike) and that the 'balance of convenience' must be considered. The latter always leads to the conclusion, as in *Emerald*, 1966, that the union's conduct is doing 'grave harm' to the plaintiffs, so that without an injunction they may suffer 'irreparable damage', whereas the union will 'suffer little or no damage' by reason of an injunction. Such a conclusion does not depend, as Lord Donovan suggested to Mr Frank Cousins at one hearing before the Royal Commission, on the judge not being properly 'informed' by the lawyers about union interests. The judges are just not in any position to weigh the intangible but enormous 'damage' which can be done to a union and workers by a court order stopping a strike against the tangible 'damage' to property or contract or profit which the employer or customer claims will be done to him. Because it does not consider the former, the court is almost always bound to conclude that the 'balance' of convenience is in favour of the plaintiff not the union. As was said in the classic American study of the labour injunction:

The injunction cannot preserve the so-called *status quo*. ... The suspension of activities affects only the strikers: the employer resumes his efforts to defeat the strike. ... Moreover, the suspension of strike activities, even temporarily, may defeat the strike for practical purposes and foredoom its resumption, even if the injunction is later lifted.[32]

A similar point has been made by an eminent Canadian Q.C. who added:

The maxim that he who comes to equity must come with clean hands is, to say the least, elastic. ... Is there anything to prevent a judge requiring to know what led to the strike? Strikes are never bolts from the blue.[33]

English judges have not taken that view yet. Nor has much effect been seen in England of the undertaking which a plaintiff must give in order to obtain an interlocutory injunction, namely to pay damages to the defendant for loss caused by any injunction which he should not have had.[34] This may be partly because of the ease with which the plaintiff can now obtain one. For example, early in 1970 Johnson Matthey secured the withdrawal of 'blacking' instructions by union officials when the company pressed for injunctions on grounds of 'conspiracy; nuisance; actionable interference with subsisting trade and/or contractual relations; procurement of breaches of contract; and intimidation'. Their counsel added that unlawful means had been used – 'including threats of violence, blacklisting and industrial action'![35] In April 1970, newspaper distributors obtained injunctions on grounds of 'blacking'. Industrial action and an 'economic blockade' (another favourite phrase in these grape-shot pleadings) became enough almost in themselves to secure an interlocutory injunction from the High Court. In 1969, injunctions were obtained *ex parte* by nine printing and allied companies against trade union officials, who had 'blacked' the handling of work for the companies and appealed to foreign unions for help in the trade dispute, against what the companies' counsel called the 'unlawful blockade of their commercial contracts'.[36]

But even some judges were surprised at the length to which the process was taken in the *Hull Trawler* dispute.[37] In pursuit of a claim for wages and 100 per cent membership, already won in most ports, Hull trawlermen who were members of the T.G.W.U. went on strike. They secured support from other dock workers and loaders (some of them members of two other unions). Three weeks into the strike, on a Monday morning in

March 1970, the trawler owners sought and obtained injunctions *ex parte* against the officials of all three unions. Interference with commercial contracts was one of the many grounds. The owners alleged the matter was urgent since thirty trawlers were about to return with a catch worth £250,000. They had had three weeks to consider legal action; but the judge did not stop to hear the defendants' case, as, in his discretion, he could have insisted on doing.

Moreover, he granted *mandatory* injunctions. A mandatory injunction does not prohibit the defendants from taking actions (as most injunctions do) but orders them to take positive steps. The judge ordered that the officials withdraw various 'instructions, directions or recommendations' concerning the strike. By the Wednesday, the T.G.W.U. applied to the High Court (a different judge because the first was occupied with other cases) for the discharge or variation of the injunctions. The T.G.W.U. officials denied ever giving any 'instructions, directions or recommendations'. But their motion failed on Thursday, except for a minor variation in the orders. The judge pointed out that when orders

took the form of mandatory injunctions forthwith to do certain acts, he did not think the defendants concerned were entitled as of right to come to the same court and invite it to vary or discharge them.

It is true, of course, that a defendant who fails to comply with a mandatory injunction forthwith is normally in contempt of court. Here the owners had obtained mandatory orders against defendants whose case had never been heard, on grounds which they denied; and they now said the officials were in contempt of court for not taking the action ordered. The T.G.W.U. hastened to the Court of Appeal that very afternoon. Lord Justice Sachs thought it 'most unusual to make a mandatory and immediate order on an *ex parte* application ... a very odd procedure'. Lord Justice Russell said it was an 'intolerable situation', and no allegation of contempt of court should be allowed until full argument on both sides. But the Court of Appeal did not discharge the injunctions, saying only that the case should be heard by the original judge on the next day. But he could not hear the case because of 'pressure of business'. It was not heard until the next Wednesday (by which time the officials of the other two unions had given undertakings in order to have the cases against them dropped). After vigorous argument, on the Friday the judge refused to continue the mandatory injunctions any longer – not because they should never have been made (as the T.G.W.U. claimed) but because there had been 'a considerable improvement in the situation especially in the danger to shipping and to life'.

The main improvement had been in the strength of the owners. Able to pay high wages to those who would work, they found some weakening on the part of strikers on £5-a-week strike pay. Press reports spoke of £80-a-week for strike-breakers driven in coach-loads at 50 m.p.h. through the powerless pickets, and of others smuggled ashore in horse boxes. But the owners were dissatisfied and, alleging a 'build up of violence' within a day of the injunctions ending, they obtained leave from the Court of Appeal for a specially expedited appeal against the judge's refusal to continue the mandatory injunctions. Some 700 of the 1,800 trawlermen voted to stay out. But one month after the injunctions were first issued, the owners changed their tack and abandoned their 'expedited' appeal against the judge's refusal to continue the injunctions, counsel saying: 'The strike has been effectively broken'. The defendants denied this; but the injunctions were without doubt one of the factors which weakened the union's position, if only because such orders naturally give to union officials the temporary status of 'wrongdoers'.

These proceedings were, of course, in theory all 'interlocutory'. The owners asserted that they intended to go to trial for 'substantial damages' and permanent injunctions. The Court of Appeal unfortunately made no further comments on the form of procedure, limiting itself to seeking a fair order as to costs. Whether or not this trial ever takes place, it remains the case that British trade union officers who denied the allegations of fact and the arguments of law made against them, were placed for ten days under mandatory orders to do something which, if they were right, could not be done, without ever having been heard on the merits. The procedure alone in the *Hull Trawler* decision did damage to the standing of law in the eyes of many workers. On the substantive law, it is yet another case which shows the scope of liability for interference with commercial contract. In certain respects, therefore, while the politicians argued whether to restrict union rights in the American manner, judge-made common law had already developed restrictions against the legality – or the interim legality, at any rate – of some types of industrial action not dissimilar to the American prohibitions against 'secondary boycotts' and 'hot-cargo' blacking by unions, which were imposed by the Taft–Hartley law of 1947 and tightened still further in 1959. After *Hull Trawler* the common law seemed to offer the judiciary the choice of its own Taft–Hartley English-style.

But in the United States, a Federal statute was passed to stop the labour *injunction* procedure as long ago as 1932. It is time for such a statute in Britain. At the very least no more injunctions should be allowed on an *ex parte* basis in any dispute which appears to be arguably a trade dispute. (If the Court needs guidance on this point, it should have power to consult the C.I.R.) The union should have the merits of actions taken in trade disputes determined at a proper trial. And the interlocutory labour injunction should be abolished.

(vi) *Restoration of the Trade Disputes Acts:* The developments just described show that the pendulum had, by 1970, swung back again towards active intervention by the judiciary under the common law. The three major substantive dangers arose from liability for use of *unlawful* means, apparently including breach of contract; combinations to use such means (tortious conspiracies); and above all, inducing breach of, or interfering with, *commercial* contracts either actual or even prospective. The procedural dangers included the ability of a plaintiff to secure an interlocutory labour injunction, even *ex parte* and in mandatory terms.

Such a summary shows how rapidly the Donovan Report was overtaken by the case law. The Report made two suggestions, neither of them affecting unlawful means as such nor dealing with the procedural problem. First, breach of contract should not constitute unlawful means for conspiracies. This idea was adopted by the Labour Government's 1970 Bill, in respect of trade disputes, in the clause which would replace s.1 of the 1906 Act (p. 385). But the 1970 Bill went further, and, in the manner of s.16(5) Prices and Incomes Act, 1966, proposed that no infringement of the new statute should give rise to criminal or civil liabilities except where the statute *expressly* provides. Thus, an infringement of the statute, even if it amounted to a breach of a term implied into a contract, could not be made *unlawful means* for the purposes of the liabilities just described. This is an important clause, and is a model of the way to avoid an extension by courts of tort liabilities derived from 'unlawful' acts that happen to be breaches of industrial relations statutes.

Secondly, the Donovan Report proposed that the words *of employment* should be dropped from Limb 1 of s.3 of the 1906 Act (and, it followed, from s.1(1) of the 1965 Act). That would mean that in trade disputes inducement of breach of any contract would be protected, and labour injunctions might not be quite so easy to obtain. It is true that a bare majority of seven Commissioners (including Lord Donovan himself) added a rider to this proposal. It should, they thought, apply only to registered unions and employers' associations (they would make registration compulsory) and their officials – or, as Lord Tangley more accurately put it, persons 'acting in an authorized capacity' for such organizations. Such a formula would not only be replete with legal problems (e.g. just who *is* an 'authorized agent' of a union?); it would also change the whole basis of our strike law. Under the Trade Disputes Acts, all persons who act in furtherance or contemplation of a trade dispute have since 1906 been equally treated. The majority seven would in effect restrict legal industrial action to official organizations (registered, they would wish, by State order on State-controlled terms: p. 411). Ordinary workers, unionists and non-unionists, would revert to their status as at 1905.

Oddly enough, the seven Commissioners did not even see their plan 'as a primary means of securing a reduction in ... unofficial strikes'. The minority of five, in one sharp paragraph, proved it to be without 'justification' and 'incompatible' with the Report's proposals for 'reform of the collective bargaining system'. The Labour Government in *In Place of Strife* accepted the logic of the minority and decided that in trade disputes 'inducement of breach of a commercial contract' should be protected by s.3 of the 1906 Act. Of course, even that would have needed the addition of protection against mere 'interference' after the *Torquay Hotel* judgments; but most readers of the White Paper thought that protection was impliedly promised for that.

It was, therefore, little less than astonishing that the same Government's 1970 Bill did not fulfil that promise. It proposed to add to s.3 only a provision to include inducing breach of 'a personal contract for work or services' (as there defined) in addition to employment contracts. The intention of this proposal was said to be the exclusion of liability in such cases as the *Emerald* decision (p. 350) where defendants induced breach of a 'labour-only' contract. (Actually, the proposal would not even do that. A firm supplying a gang of labourers, such as Labour Force Ltd (p. 66), does not, within the definition of the 1970 Bill, 'personally undertake', as an 'individual', to 'perform work or services' in the labour supply contract. The 1970 Bill would protect union officials only if the action were brought *by* a worker taken on as a 'self-employed' worker or as an independent contractor or by his 'employer'. The firm supplying labour is often a party not to any such contract to perform work or services, but only to a contract to supply men who will do so.) The extension of s.3 proposed in this palsied clause of the 1970 Bill was, therefore, minimal and would still leave union officials at the mercy of a labour-only agency which sought an injunction to stop use of industrial action against their operations.

The moral is clear. An amendment to s.3, dropping the words 'of employment' and adding protection for mere 'interference', is the only way in which the pendulum can be brought back into traditional balance. The minority of five Commissioners was right. If any Government seeks precedent, it should remember that the first charter of union rights in 1871 was based more upon minority than majority proposals of the 1867 Royal Commission. Curiously, those who were calling for new legislation against strikes did not seem to notice that the newly extended liabilities of judge-made law had once again, by 1970, threatened the very basis of workers' liberty of industrial action. Without a new statute, the unions and workpeople faced the seventies with risks of illegality redolent of the era from which they thought they had emerged in 1906.

SPECIAL RESTRICTIONS ON STRIKES

Of the many other problems relating to strikes, to most of which the new judgments have some relevance, there are three to which we must briefly make particular reference in this chapter. They are, first, the special legal position of certain groups of workers; second, the problem of a 'General Strike' such as that of 1926, or of a similar stoppage which might disrupt the country or be called 'political'; and third, some topics which illustrate the tradition of Government 'abstention' in regard to strikes and industrial conflict. Under the first heading, we shall without detailed discussion list the main groups, of which the most important are seamen and certain public utility workers. The second problem is perhaps largely of historical importance today. Argument is still heard about whether the General Strike of 1926 was lawful; but unless industrial relations suffer a catastrophic setback, the likelihood of a general strike in modern conditions does not seem great. The third heading expanded considerably with the introduction of the Welfare State. In earlier times the question was simply whether the Government was to intervene directly in industrial conflict. But in modern society the Government must decide how far it can permit measures taken for reasons of social security to affect the relative strength of the parties to industrial bargaining. All three headings will have to be kept in mind in any discussion about reform of the law. Certain groups of workers have long suffered special legal disabilities in regard to bargaining and conflict. We may list them briefly.

(i) *Gas, Water, Electricity.* The Act of 1875 (extended in 1919) makes it a *crime* for any worker employed in these industries wilfully to break his contract of service having reasonable cause to believe that the consequence will be a substantial deprivation of the supply (1875 Act: s.4). The section covers *any* wilful breach, from a strike to a 'go slow'. It causes unions in these industries to give notice of termination of employment contracts before strike action. Recently both gas and electricity workers have been warned that they can be prosecuted if they break the section, the latter by the joint Board on which their union is represented. Some other industries have asked for similar laws. On the same day on which the N.C.B. told the Donovan Commission why it had jettisoned legal suits against strikers, London Transport Board asked for inclusion within a law like s.4, though it could not say whether it would ever prosecute – 'taking proceedings against three or four hundred people may not be valuable'.

(ii) *Strikers Causing Other Danger in Breach of Contract.* Any worker (or indeed, any employer) who breaks a contract of service or hiring with similar cause to believe that he will cause serious bodily injury or serious injury to property commits a crime (1875 Act: s.5); but the Donovan Report confirmed this section has never been used. The Report thought, though, that both s.4 and s.5 had better be 'left undisturbed'. That puts it well.

(iii) *Police.* After the police strike in 1919, statute (now the Police Act, 1964) made criminal actions likely to cause disaffection, breach of discipline, or a withdrawal of services by members of the police force. Police were also forbidden to belong to ordinary trade unions. They are the only employees of civilian status to suffer such severe restrictions. Members of the armed services are in effect deprived of any liberty of strike action because of the relevant statutes, and, although it is not expressly prohibited, they have no right to join a trade union. In other countries policemen and even soldiers can join unions. In 1970, demands for a right to strike were defeated at the Police Federation conference. A union request to organize the armed services (without any right to strike) was rejected; and those Crown servants were, we saw (p. 60), excluded from the proposals in the 1970 Bill.

(iv) *Aliens.* In 1919 also, the Aliens Restriction Act provided that if any alien 'promotes or attempts to promote industrial unrest in any industry in which he has not been *bona fide* engaged for at least two years', he commits a crime punishable by three months' imprisonment. This xenophobic guard against foreign agitators, posted two years after the Russian Revolution, still slumbers on the statute book.

(v) *Seamen.* All seamen were excluded both from the offences created by the 1875 Act, and from its protections, e.g. on criminal conspiracy (and therefore from protection for civil conspiracy added by the 1906 Act, s.1). They were, however, controlled by a severe code of offences in the Merchant Shipping Acts.

Most of the old Acts, especially that of 1894, are, however, to be overtaken by the Merchant Shipping Act, 1970 soon to be brought into effect. There will still be crimes under the new law which inhibit action while at sea, such as concerted disobedience or combinations to impede the progress of a voyage; and recklessly to be absent so as to delay a ship's departure remains a crime for an employed seaman. Furthermore, a ship's master will be able to fine seamen for disciplinary misconduct under regulations made by the Board of Trade, which will also be able to set up ship's committees to exercise disciplinary functions. The Pearson Report, 1967, said successful experiments on a voluntary basis had been made for 'shop stewards' on board ship. But the 1970 Act does not establish any statutory right to workers' representatives on board. It will, however, limit the liability of a seaman for breach of contract by way of absence without leave to damages of £10 (or £100 if special damages are proved); and where he proves the absence was due to accident, mistake or cause beyond his control, the absence 'shall not be treated as a breach' (which implies that it would not be an 'illegal means' for tort purposes). Moreover, the new Act will for the first time apply the Act of 1875 to seamen 'as it applies to other persons' – that is both for and against them. Also, a right to 'terminate his employment' will be given to a merchant seaman which cannot be taken away by his contract, if he leaves the ship when it is in a 'safe berth' in the U.K., and in furtherance or contemplation of a trade dispute provided, *after* mooring, he gives 48 hours' notice before leaving. As we have noted earlier, this is clearly a statutory provision which equates a strike notice and a notice to quit. A seaman, however, always gave notice before striking in order to avoid being an engaged man to whom the crimes of the old laws applied. The real innovation is the legislative protection of the period of 48 hours which his employment contract cannot increase. In the giant seamen's strike of 1966, the men terminated their engagements as their ships docked according to their contracts and refused to sign new contracts. Three thousand at the start became 10,000 within a week, and, after the Pearson Committee of Inquiry had reported, the strike ended in its sixth week with 26,000 seamen on strike from 800 ships.[38] But some of those who did not strike were bound by long-term or 'running' engagements; with the new Act they would have a new right to strike.

(vi) *Civil Servants.* Continental legal systems often put a chasm between ordinary employees and public servants. In English law the main difference relates to the problem whether there is any contract of service for the employee of the Crown (p. 70). It must be remembered that this does not include the nationalized industries, though until 1969 it did include the Post Office. Post Office workers can be liable criminally under an Act of 1953 for endangering or retarding the delivery of the mail even in a trade dispute and the 1969 Act continued those criminal liabilities for such workers on making the Post Office a nationalized commercial corporation. We have seen (p. 60) that the 1970 Bill proposed to include Crown servants in the new category of 'worker' and to insert that word into the definition of 'trade dispute', thereby clarifying the doubt as to whether non-industrial civil servants are 'workmen employed in trade or industry' (p. 330). In the Act of 1927 civil servants were compulsorily segregated into separate trade unions, and all public authorities were forbidden to demand union membership of employees; but that Act was repealed in 1946. A strike among established civil servants would, of course, normally be regarded as a 'disciplinary offence' within the code established under the umbrella of the Whitley Councils; but no special legal problem is involved in that. Although traditionally civil servants have rarely engaged in strike activity (which is to some extent a reflection of the better 'grievance procedures' in the public sector) their militancy is increasing. The early months of 1969 saw the first strike instruction issued by the Institute of Professional Civil Servants and in 1970 both the Society of Civil Servants and the Inland Revenue Staff Federation made arrangements to facilitate strike action.

(vii) *Other Workers*. There are very few other restrictions of importance. Sometimes it is said that 'firemen cannot strike'. But the statutory regulations for the fire services do not in law forbid strikes as such; they only lay down the conditions of the fireman's contract. The only liability likely to arise for firemen would be under (ii) above, if e.g. property were foreseeably put in jeopardy and destroyed after a strike by them in wilful breach of contract. As for other groups, there are a few statutory provisions to be kept in mind for certain workers in industrial conflict. But none involves any major restriction on their liberty to take industrial action.

GENERAL STRIKES, THE STATE AND EMERGENCIES

On 11 May 1926, in the middle of the General Strike, Mr Justice Astbury declared in court:

The so-called general strike called by the Trades Union Congress Council is illegal ... no trade dispute does or can exist between the Trades Union Congress on the one hand and the Government and the nation on the other.[39]

On the same day Sir John (later Viscount) Simon stated:

Once you proclaim a general strike you are starting a movement of ... a wholly unconstitutional and unlawful character.

The T.U.C., which had brought out nearly two million workers in support of the miners in their bitter struggle against wage reductions which the coal owners enforced when a government subsidy was removed, declared:

The General Council does not challenge the constitution. ... The sole aim of the Council is to secure for the miners a decent standard of life. The Council is engaged in an Industrial dispute.[40]

In 1927 Professor Goodhart convincingly argued that this particular dispute and strike remained a 'furtherance of a trade dispute'.[41] The 'political' element had not displaced the industrial content; and the statements of Mr Justice Astbury and Sir John Simon have, as the years passed, acquired increasingly the colour of the context in which they were made. 'What distinguishes a General Strike', wrote Goodhart, 'is that it is more likely to succeed.' The dispute was between coal owners and miners: the Government and the T.U.C. became involved. But just as malice against the bandmaster which was not predominant did not necessarily vitiate the bandsmen's strike in 1912 (see p. 331), so an element of 'political' battle with the Government does not necessarily vitiate the character of a dispute connected with the conditions of labour of miners.

Suppose, however, a non-violent 'general' strike *were* held to be technically not the furtherance of a trade dispute. Would it of necessity then be illegal? Professor Goodhart thought not. It might be 'unquestionably contrary to the spirit of the English constitution but this does not necessarily render it criminal'. Even the 1875 Act, of course, offered no defence against 'offences against the State'; but what offence could it be? Not treason, for this requires a 'levying of war' against the Crown or to intimidate Parliament. Is it sedition? Some of the older definitions might have given colour to that idea. But the modern view is that it requires proof today of some incitement to violence or similar acts done to disturb constituted authority. Short of violence or insurrection, sedition is a charge unlikely to strike home today.

The only crime remaining in the quiver is a general 'common law conspiracy'. It is scarcely believable that the criminal courts would, even in a general strike situation, revert to the gas strike case of 1872 and revive such an offence. We have, however, seen that it is uncertain whether a civil action for tort would be successful if the court decided the unions were pursuing 'political' aims. After *Rookes* v. *Barnard*, 1964, it might be material to consider whether any of the strikers had broken, or threatened to break, their employment *contracts*. And after the *Torquay Hotel* case, 1969, it becomes a possibility that interference with commercial contracts could be relevant. If so, the courts might seize on that element of 'unlawfulness' as tainting the whole combination. What was said by the Attorney-General, Sir Hartley Shawcross, in prosecuting the dock strikers in 1951 gave rise to fears of wide liabilities: '... a strike calculated to cause a breach of contract or ... interfere with or affect the policy of the State ... might constitute a grave criminal offence.' At the time many felt this exaggerated the rigours of the criminal law. When, in the seamen's strike of 1966 (which the union said was for industrial claims for a 40-hour week and better conditions), the Prime Minister declared that this was 'a strike against the State, against the community'; and that a 'tightly knit group of politically motivated men' was 'endangering the security of the industry and the economic welfare of the nation'; and 'what is at issue here is our prices and incomes policy', no one seriously suggested that those organizing the strike could be prosecuted. But we have seen (p. 329) that in 1970 the impropriety of major 'political' strikes was again suggested. Lord Shawcross wrote to *The Times*, in respect of the strikes occurring in the docks and threatened over the B.U.A. takeover, that such purposes were not truly in furtherance of a trade dispute but were 'starkly political'. ('Indeed anarchical.') He stated:

Those trade union officials who incite others to take industrial action for political purposes ... should remember that such action renders officials and unions ... liable to damages ... or penalties (for conspiracy is also a criminal offence) ... it is not only the rule of law but Parliamentary Government itself which is at risk.[42]

Mr Clive Jenkins replied that workers would see this 'pompously rarefied view' as the shaking of a 'meaningless legal tambourine' in our 'integrated pluralistic democracy'. Certainly the law as so stated is both doubtful and disturbing. To dub industrial action taken for political purposes as *per se* criminal conspiracy is a reversion to the 1850s. Yet so ready were some to believe, or establish, this to be the law that, when the Cricket Council announced the cancellation at Government request of the South African tour for 1970, a barrister said he would prosecute the leader of the Stop the Seventy Tour Committee for seditious conspiracy, which he understood to include combinations not only to provoke tumult and disorder but also 'to promote breaches of contract and acts of trespass and to insult or annoy law-abiding people'. Combinations to create violent disorder are, of course, unlawful; and, further-more, after 1964 breach of contract may unhappily add an element of illegality. But otherwise, Professor Goodhart's con-clusion as to the legality of such general or 'political' strikes as that of 1926 seems the preferable view.

Under the Emergency Powers Act, 1920, (amended slightly in 1964), the Government can make a Proclamation and then govern with special powers by Regulation if essential supplies are threatened for the community. The Regulations must be forthwith approved and regularly renewed by Parliament. The powers are extensive, but they expressly stop short of any form of compulsory military service or 'industrial conscription'. This prevents the British Government from using conscription to break strikes. Nor may they make it an offence to 'take part in a strike' or peacefully to persuade any other persons to take part. Since the Act is dealing, by hypothesis, with emergency and general strike situations, it is arguably *implied* that such action is not necessarily always unlawful at common law. Pro-clamations have been issued seven times under the Act and Regulations giving the Government extensive powers, especially allowing them to use troops to run transport or move supplies, on five of those. Since 1945, they were issued in the 1948, 1949 and 1970 dock strikes, the 1955 railway strike and (despite a warning from the union of a general strike if the Royal Navy were used) in the seamen's strike of 1966 when the strike had lasted only eight days. The programme of the new Conservative Government included plans for a new law whereby the

Minister might obtain an injunction against strikes endangering the national interest so as to impose a cooling-off period. There is little, either in the British situation or in the experience with such laws overseas, to suggest that this would further the peaceful settlement of serious industrial disputes. There was, however, a dangerous addition to Government powers tucked away quietly in the Emergency Powers Act, 1964. This made Defence Regulations of 1939 permanent and allowed the armed services to be used without Proclamation or consultation with Parliament on 'urgent work of national importance'. The Government has moved in troops under what must have been these powers to offset the early effects of large strikes. Any extensive use of the powers is bound to result in demands for their repeal. Even in France, where it was once normal, the regular use of troops and conscription to break strikes has been discontinued. It ought not to begin in Britain.

ABSTENTION BY THE GOVERNMENT FROM TRADE DISPUTES

There are two other respects in which the State is often said to express a 'neutrality' in trade disputes.

(a) There has long been provided machinery for conciliation and arbitration. The current Acts, those of 1896 and 1919, have been far more successful in creating useful machinery here than the earlier attempts made repeatedly from 1800 onwards. *Compulsory* arbitration was enacted only in wartime in the Munitions of War Act, 1915, (until 1919), and the Order of 1940 which forbade strikes and lock-outs in 'trade disputes' and set up an arbitration Tribunal. 'Trade dispute' had a definition very similar to that used in 1906; and, as the dockworkers' prosecution of 1951 showed, one curious result of that was that the Order made illegal a strike inside, but not outside, the golden formula. In 1951 the strike was against the union leadership. The jury gave a verdict so confused that the court could not accept it; and the prosecution made the best of a bad job by dropping the prosecution. It was never finally decided whether this was a trade dispute, though most people thought it was not. In the same year the Order was replaced by a modified system of compulsory arbitration (rather like that which the 1970 Bill proposed to restore to enable unions who face employers refusing negotiation to take them to unilateral arbitration on the claim); but by 1958 this had become so unpopular among employers that the Government swept it aside, as we saw in Chapter 4, p. 200.

There is left now, therefore, the availability of voluntary arbitration machinery also described in that chapter. But apart from that, the Secretary of State has certain other weapons available whereby he can encourage the parties in an industrial dispute to reach a solution without open combat. There is, for example, the standing Conciliation Service of the Ministry, which throughout the country tries to stay in close contact with unions and employers and to assist in the resolution of disputes. Furthermore, under the Industrial Courts Act, 1919, the Minister has power to inquire into any dispute and if he thinks fit to appoint a Court of Inquiry (as was done in the Seamen's Strike, 1966). He does not take this step unless conciliation has been tried and failed. The report of the Court must be laid before Parliament.

Although neither party is bound by any recommendations made by the inquiry, the reports have often commented extensively on the merits of the parties and thereby weakened or strengthened the reputation of one side or the other in the eyes of the public as a whole. The Ministry of Labour Evidence to the Royal Commission stated that a Court of Inquiry is

primarily a means of informing Parliament and the public of the facts and underlying causes of dispute ... appointed only as a last resort when no agreed settlement of a dispute seems possible and when an unbiased independent examination of the facts is considered to be in the public interest.

The power to appoint, they said, is 'used sparingly ... on matters of major importance affecting the public interest'. A court of inquiry may compel testimony; but, although there have been six occasions on which unions refused to appear, no proceedings have ever been taken. A study in 1966 found that 59 of 75 inquiries were three-man teams.[43] Of 41 such inquiries held between 1946 and 1966, 28 concerned disputes that had their origin in problems of wage payments. Many of the more famous disputes have had their Court of Inquiry, from Briggs Motors in 1964 to Port Talbot in 1969. Mr Jack Scamp, when chairman of the Motor Industry Joint Labour Council, was, on occasion, given powers of a court of inquiry. A rather less formal method, however, can be used, as in the railway docks dispute of 1964, where railwaymen complained that only T.G.W.U. men were promoted to docks foremen. The Minister set up a Committee of Investigation under the Act of 1896. This is a much less formal affair than a Court of Inquiry and its report need not even be published. The Secretary of State can also appoint a 'Committee of Inquiry' (acting either under the 1896 Act or under his 'general powers'). The famous inquiry by Lord Devlin into the labour problems of the docks was a Committee under 'general powers'. The Donovan Report thought it a 'welcome tendency' that such 'committees' had come to be given wide terms of reference and take a long-term view of the problem examined. There were 38 Committees of various types between 1946 and 1966. All these procedures illustrate the Government's opportunities of encouraging industrial peace without compulsory powers. The methods of 'public conciliation', as they have been called, have been welcomed elsewhere as preferable to 'legalistic hearing and adjudication'.[44]

From 1969 the D.E.P. would, *In Place of Strife* asserted, 'be more ready to proffer its help' and in some cases 'prompt informal investigations' to avert a strike or promote a settlement, if need be carrying out those investigations itself. The Government 'in the light of experience ... will consider whether further statutory powers are needed'. And these pieces of machinery were then joined by the C.I.R., (p. 37) whose first chairman, Mr George Woodcock, said on taking office:

We will be having to persuade people by a continuing process until agreement is reached. ... What we do will be informal and in private ... I hope in many cases [there] will not be recommendations but will be agreements accepted and supported by the people themselves.

In place of the quick and dangerous surgery of legal sanction, this approach puts its hope in the longer term and, one hopes, more durable process of inquiry, talk and gradually emergent agreement. The Commission is a body which illustrates a very different use of 'law' in industrial relations from that of which the layman usually thinks. In place of writs and wigs and injunctions is the round table provided by a law which promotes discussion.

(b) Secondly, there is social security. Parliament has tried to put the Welfare State firmly on the fence in industrial conflict – even to the extent of excluding from 'lay-off' days for redundancy, days so lost by reason of strikes in foreign lands: p. 136. Also, for instance, a person out on strike by reason of a trade dispute (defined in the usual 1906 manner) is not to be prejudiced in his use of any employment exchange facilities. On the other hand, he is refused certain social security benefits that might help to finance the strike. For instance, he is disqualified from unemployment benefit *throughout* the entire length of the stoppage *unless* he proves that he is not participating in or financing or directly interested in the trade dispute at his place of employment which caused his unemployment; and *also* does not belong to a 'grade or class' of workers who were doing so (National Insurance Act, 1965; and the Act of 1966 on earnings-related benefit).

This Act has created keen difficulty. Thus, when a skipper ordered his fellow-members of the 'Close Brethren' not to eat with the rest of his crew, and the other men struck, the Commissioner decided this was a 'trade dispute' because, although a 'personal matter', it was also concerned with the conditions of employment; and so was a stoppage about terms of employment as to union membership.[45] The Commissioners have also included a worker who was physically prevented from entering the works by pickets, saying, in any case, he must have had a trade dispute with other employees, the pickets,[46] though in 1969 this was held not to include a case where the worker was forcibly kept from work by pickets employed by another firm since he was neither participating nor interested in their dispute. What is more they put a wide meaning on 'directly interested'. The interest of the worker need not even be substantial or of great magnitude so long as it is direct. Where, in a demarcation dispute between platers and shipwrights, platers' helpers were thrown out of work by stoppage, the Commissioner decided that the latter had not proved they were not 'directly interested' in the dispute since each worked as a team with his plater and was therefore interested in the work available. The Court of Appeal, to which this case was taken twice, refused in 1964 to disturb this decision, saying that in any case the final arbiter of such matters under the Act was the Commissioner and the court could not interfere; but one judge commented that he did not disagree with the decision.[47]

There can be no doubt that this law, which penalizes the disqualified worker throughout the stoppage of work (and there are many difficult decisions on the question: when does the trade dispute stoppage 'end'?[48]), has gone far beyond 'neutrality.' The definition of 'place of employment' is unsatisfactory (both C.B.I. and T.U.C. want to change it, in different directions). Many decisions have upheld the view that a worker is 'financing' a dispute if he is a member of the trade union to which participants belong.[49] The 'direct interest' of a worker can be minimal; so the interest of a worker in the abolition of a tea break or a two-minute 'lateness allowance', where they were among subjects of disputes, was enough to bring him in. The 'interest' may even be such that the strikers' claims would *depress* his conditions, and he may be opposed to them.[50] Participation has been said to be 'always a question to be decided on all the relevant evidence', and men need not prove that they voted against a strike. But a man who refused to do the work of the strikers and one who attended work but went home thinking (wrongly) there was nothing to do, were held to have 'participated' in the strike.[51]

The Donovan Report subjected this law to a piercing analysis in perhaps its socially most valuable section on strikes. As a result of its recommendation the Labour Government planned to amend the 1965 Act and change the disqualifications, which have been much the same since the year after the General Strike. The Social Security Bill in 1970 proposed to abolish the provision concerning the same 'grade or class' of workers and to remove 'financing' from the list of disqualifications. If these amendments had been enacted they would have gone some way towards recapturing a semblance of 'neutrality'. But further amendment is needed of 'participating', 'direct interest', 'place of employment', and so on before it can be said that the State does not use such disqualifications unfairly to penalize those who lose their jobs when they are not themselves the active strikers. Moreover, a new area of dispute opened around the proposal in the same Bill to provide for a reduction in the ordinary case of one-third in any supplementary benefit allowed to men so disqualified (though not their families). No doubt tax rebates sometimes assist strikers for short periods; but the widespread notion that such men gain financially from State sources was refuted by a careful Appendix to the Donovan Report. We have a long way to go before the State is neutral with its social security payments in strikes – if, indeed, it ever can be.

THE FUTURE OF TRADE DISPUTES LAW

Everyone pays homage to the 'right to strike' but each person's social attitude, background, and values lead him to conclude just how far it should be allowed to extend. Discussion of the problem is best based on a clear expression of those assumptions in each participant, rather than upon the fortuitous appearances of legal principles. As we have seen, the apparent 'privileges' or 'immunities' of our law of industrial conflict are often no more than the British way of providing modern collective liberties for workers on their side of the bargaining table. Instead of our law establishing 'positive' rights, e.g. to strike, as has been done in other countries, such as France and Italy, the habit had grown up in Britain, before the Labour Party was ever born, of seeking from Parliament 'negative' immunities against old or new judge-made liabilities in the common law. This happened in 1871, 1875, 1906, and (as we see in the next chapter) in 1913. Thus it is of no value to present the Act of 1906 as 'conferring certain immunities' and go on to ask 'to whom should the immunities be granted? ... What should be the scope of the immunities?'[52] Those who really believe the unions are 'privileged' can be led to the most extravagant statements, such as Mr Enoch Powell who, declaring in January 1967 that Parliament was under a 'moral obligation' to end the unions' privileged position, affirmed: 'Trade Unions are the creatures of Statute'. Trade unions were created by working people. Mr George Woodcock broadly summarized the social reality, as against the legal form, when he said to the T.U.C. in 1964: 'I do not agree that the trade unions of this country have any privileges under the law of this country. It is not a privilege to be allowed to do the job you are there to do. It is your right.' With the possible exception of s.4(1), that proposition is clearly the right way in which to begin the discussions. In the main, the Donovan Report avoided the trap of talking the false legal language of 'immunities'.

Many writers (including the present author) have toyed with the idea that the traditional form of 'immunity' for those who act in trade disputes might be replaced by a code of clear, positive rights. Distinguished trade unionists wrote in 1968: 'The law ought to affirm that all employees and employers have a right to organize ...'; and workers should have legal 'rights' to elect effective shop stewards and to engage in union activities at the place of work, defined in 'A Right to Organize Act'.[53] But as the debates before the Donovan Commission developed, it became clear that, at this stage of British development, proposals for positive 'rights' were much more commonly found on the lips of those who wanted a quite new, legally regulated system of collective bargaining, in which trade unions would be constricted by many legal 'duties' as the price of the 'rights' and which would be alien to an essentially voluntary system. Such an 'interventionist' as Mr Shonfield, in his dissenting Note to the Report, supported the removal of the old language of 'immunities' (the doctrine of the 'licensed conspiracy') because he thought it appropriate to times when unions were 'weak and vulnerable' but not when they had a 'dominant role'. By that line of thought he was led to propose more extensive legal regulation.

The Report itself concluded that at present the position would not be

> improved by granting the right [to strike] in express terms. No doubt, however, if the law relating to trade disputes is codified as we recommend, the matter will receive further consideration.

The proposal for codification is most valuable. It cannot be right that strike legislation should be scattered in a jig-saw of statutes passed between 1871 and 1970. Moreover, the Report suggests that to the C.I.R. should be attached a special Industrial Law Committee to keep the legislation under constant review and work with the Law Commissions. Such a Committee is an urgent need – but it ought not to be composed (as are the Law Commissions) of lawyers alone. Given a prospect of codification, however, other objectives must be achieved.

First, the whole problem of *unlawful means* must be clarified. As the Report says: 'If the law upon the subject were clear, any ... person who adopted wrongful means would have only himself to blame'. But it is so far from being clear as to make trade unionists and employers laugh when they read the sentence. Indeed, we have seen in this chapter how the uncertainties – the residual illegality of any breach of contract after *Rookes*; the uncertain status of an act not 'actionable' in a trade dispute; the problems attaching to acts that infringe statutes or which are said to be primarily 'political'; the various new forms of 'conspiracy' or unlawful interference with business – all hang like a Sword of Damocles over the heads of those taking industrial action. They will continue to do so until a Government grasps the nettles, legislating away the new equivalence of breach of contract and violence and the other novel economic-tort liabilities, including of course the ever-expanding tort of inducing breach of commercial contract.

Secondly, action is needed to stop the growth of the 'labour injunction'. As suggested (p. 384) a reform of rules of procedure really must end the pernicious habit of granting injunctions *ex parte* in trade disputes. In many cases, when the full argument is heard for both sides, it is found that there is insufficient ground for a remedy as the evidence stands; so in such cases the union officials have had imposed on them for days an injunction for which (it turns out) there never was any legal basis. More, the labour injunction itself should be abolished in interlocutory actions. Statutory protection is, we have seen, now needed on many other aspects of the fast developing law of tort (p. 374). But, even more important, some formula is needed whereby whatever statutory liberties Parliament creates are not reduced to nought by some ingenious novel extension of the common law. The 1969 innovation of liability for mere interference with contract in the *Torquay Hotel* case (p. 334) comes to mind. It changed a critical area of the debate only a few months after Lord Donovan had blotted his signature. In 1969, Lord Reid said (in a matrimonial case) that judicial innovation should be restricted to cases of 'lawyers' law', and not extended to anything 'affecting the lives and interests of large sections of the community which raises issues of public controversy'. If that rubric is not adhered to in labour law consideration will need to be given to reducing the area over which the ordinary courts and judges have jurisdiction. Indeed some writers have seen the new restrictions on trade unions in the 1960s as part of the phenomenon that the

judiciary, in short, has no more been 'above' the conflicts of capitalist society than any other part of the State system.[54]

Even when a judge tries to innovate in order, as he sees it, to *protect* the right to strike, the sources open to him are so limited that he can easily use what looks to the lawyer the obvious method for reform, which on deeper inquiry turns out to be quite the wrong one. (The 'suspension' of employment contracts in trade disputes used by Lord Denning in *Morgan v. Fry*, 1968, is shown to be just such a case by the careful discussion in the Donovan Report, paras. 943–5; see *ante* p. 110.)

But, it is often said, 'public opinion' is in favour of clipping the wings of unions. It is difficult to test this proposition. Moreover, views are often formed not from such thorough inquiries as the Donovan Report but on the basis of the day's news of a strike or some theatrical incident which is splashed across the headlines but about which the later inquiries rarely get equivalent publicity. The 'noose trial' of 1966 was a good example. Shop stewards were said to have conducted a 'court' beneath a rope noose hanging from a beam. Fines had been levied on workers by the stewards; but the 'noose' had nothing to do with the so-called 'trial', a later inquiry revealed. The rope had hung there for over a year. One might dislike the stewards' action; but there was little to the 'trial'. Lord Lloyd wrote to *The Times* of the 'even greater evil, namely, trial by newspaper'. The union inquiry complained that 'something much less sinister than a debagging ceremony' in one of Oxford's colleges 'had been turned into a Reichstag trial' for mass consumption. Again, we have to learn to live with the simple truth that

conflict is endemic to industrial organization. It does not follow, however, that trade unions introduce conflict into the industrial scene. They simply provide a highly organized and continuous form of expression for sectional interests which would exist anyway.[55]

Moreover – and strike law has to take account of the facts of industrial life – conflict is not just strikes and lock-outs. Its methods are, Clark Kerr put it, 'as unlimited as the ingenuity of man'. Fox adds that we must re-examine the assumption that conflict is bad and harmony good. 'It may be so, but equally it may not. . . . Indeed, a vigorously overt conflict situation may be necessary for high morale.' Conflict is not necessarily 'healthy'; but we need 'painstaking inquiry into specific situations rather than . . . blanket solutions'. Legal formulae cannot paper over the cracks of social conflict; and legal 'neutrality' is hard to attain. The present writer suggested to the Royal Commission that 'one Scamp is worth a dozen injunctions'.[56] Later developments have led to only one alteration in this opinion – quadruple the figure!

Lastly we saw, in Chapter 4, that the problem of 'incomes policy' is political in the sense that it raises questions about the kind of society we want. The same is true of strike law; it partly determines the strength of the parties to collective bargaining and can affect the methods by which conflict is resolved or contained. One cannot find an easy answer by appealing to some reasonable 'public interest', for the simple reason that there is no law of reason or of nature which can tell you how much more one man should be paid than another. And the 'public interest' is no unitary third element at the bargaining table; it is a congeries of competing interests. Collective bargaining is, in truth, about distribution of income and of property (though it has influenced these much less than most people think, or than it should have, since 1918). But the merit of a flexible voluntary system is that it can allow for a shift in the relative strength of the two sides to the bargaining much more easily than one that is legally regulated. A recent attempt in Ireland to fine and then jail electricity supply workers under legislation specially passed led in 1968 to the employers having to pay their fines to end the stoppage and the legislation being revoked.

In 1969, the jailing of the veteran Australian union leader Clarence O'Shea for contempt of the Industrial Court brought the manual workers to the verge of a general strike, and a retired businessman paid £90,000 in fines to 'overcome the impasse'. The greatest merit of the Donovan Report is its rejection of such a future for Britain, and the insistence upon the rapid reform of institutions to remove the causes of strikes.[57] Such a programme needs both management and trade union initiative, and Government caution in legislating any regulatory statutes.

One impediment to such a programme will be new judge-made liabilities from courts unsympathetic to trade unions. They may once again feel (as they have felt in 1901, 1964 and 1969) that the Queensberry Rules have been altered in the middle of the bout. As we have seen, the arguments about liability that have to be carried on at the level of the common law depend on fine semantic distinctions and technical concepts. Never have men looked more puzzled than the ordinary laymen (on both sides) who heard their rights in *Rookes* v. *Barnard*, 1964, being discussed in terms of a threat to fire cannon at native traders off the Cameroons in 1793. The sociological issues of policy are decided in the interstices of such argument. That is the way of the common law. But the judges' interpretations of these technical concepts in recent years, especially in the House of Lords, make it certain that the unions could not accept them as the arbiters of a code of law that tried, as some would have it do, to bring the policy issues to the surface and decide disputes, as Viscount Radcliffe asked in *Stratford* v. *Lindley*, not by technical legal points but according to their 'substance'.* The Donovan inquiry showed that no such way of determining policy by adjudication is possible in our labour law. Indeed, it is memorable that the T.U.C. has opposed the proposed extension to all *individual* disputes of the jurisdiction of the Industrial Tribunals for fear that these tribunals would indirectly obtain a new avenue to adjudicate on collective labour problems. Even if the Government sets up new Industrial or Labour Courts, as *Fair Deal at Work* proposed, the issues of substantive law and procedure discussed in this chapter will not thereby disappear. The Donovan Report called for new facilities for training lawyers in labour law and giving them 'at least an elementary knowledge of industrial relations'. The inference is obvious, and for the most part true. But even if a new breed of lawyers is born and pervades (in time) the judicial bench there will still remain much to be said for the tradition of 'abstention' fortuitously forged by the odd legal history of British industrial conflict; and the lawyer might still do greater service here to the community by being less prominent than self-effacing.

* In effect, this would be one result of the proposals of the Conservative Government, especially by entrusting to the W.I.R.C. issues of policy on 'unfair industrial actions': Appendix, pp. 489–93; 500–522; and 524–6.

1. *Crofter Hand Woven Harris Tweed Co.* v. *Veitch* [1942] A.C. 435 at p. 463.
2. See W. E. J. McCarthy, 'Shop Stewards', *R.C. Research Paper No. 1* (1966) pp. 23–5.
3. *Report*, Cmnd 3623; paras. 70, 363, 364, 368, 380 (italics supplied).
4. H. A. Turner, *Is Britain Really Strike-Prone?* (1969, C.U.P.), p. 44. But see how W. E. J. McCarthy (1970) VIII *Brit. J. Industrial Relations* 224.
5. *The Times*, 30.12.69.
6. See H. A. Turner, G. Clack, G. Roberts, *Labour Relations in the Motor Industry* (1967).
7. J. E. T. Eldridge, 'Are Any Strikes Wildcat?', *New Society*, 17 March 1966, p. 16.
8. *Programme for Action* (1969: T.U.C.), para. 15.
9. Citrine, *Trade Union Law* (1967), pp. 14–15.
10. House of Lords: 166 *Parl. Deb.* col. 693–4, 4 December 1906.
11. *Short History of English Law* (1928), p. 337.
12. *Scala Ballroom (Wolverhampton) Ltd* v. *Ratcliffe* [1958] 3 All E.R. 220; B. Hepple, *Race, Jobs and the Law* (1970), p. 247. As to malice on the part of one or more parties to the combination, see *McKernan* v. *Fraser* (1931) 46 C.L.R. 343, 401, 407, Wedderburn, *Cases and Materials on Labour Law*, p. 449.
13. [1966] 1 All E.R. 1013 (C.A.).
14. [1969] 2 Ch. 106 (C.A.); see A. S. Grabiner (1969) 32 *Modern Law Review* 435.
15. K. W. Wedderburn (1968) 31 *Modern Law Review* 550, on the second of the two judgments in the case, 1968, S.L.T. 65.
16. [1952] Ch. 646.
17. [1965] A.C. 269 (H.L.). See (1965) 28 *Modern Law Review* 205.
18. Winn L.J., however, did not decide this point. For the discussion of the details, see Wedderburn (1968) 31 *Modern Law Review* 440; and Grabiner, op. cit. (note 14), p. 436.
19. [1898] A.C. 1.
20. Extrajudicially in 'Samples in Lawmaking' (1962), pp. 11, 12; and judicially in *Rookes* v. *Barnard* [1964] A.C. 1129 at pp. 1215–16.
21. D. F. MacDonald, *The State and the Trade Unions* (1960), p. 60.

22. *Federation News* (G.F.T.U.), 1964; Vol. 14, p. 30, p. 41. For further detailed discussion see K. W. Wedderburn (1964) 27 *Modern Law Review* 527, (1961) 24 *M.L.R.* 572; C. J. Hamson [1964] *Cambridge Law Journal* 159; L. Hoffman (1965) 81 *Law Quarterly Review* 116; C. Grunfeld, *Modern Trade Union Law* p. 435; O. H. Parsons, *The Meaning of Rookes* v. *Barnard* (1964: L.R.D.).

23. [1964] A.C. 1129 (H.L.) reversing [1963] 1 Q.B. 623 (C.A.).

24. Bohlen, *Studies in the Law of Torts*, p. 3.

25. [1968] 2 Q.B. 710 (C.A.). For a very radical extension of 'justi-fication', see *Pete's Towing Services Ltd* v. *Northern Industrial Union* [1970] N.Z.L.R. 32.

26. [1963] 1 Q.B. 623, at p. 685 (C.A.).

27. See Wedderburn (1966) 29 *Modern Law Review* 53.

28. Para. 856. See too the Commission's curious conclusion (para. 892) that it is a 'fallacy' to think it benefits employers to serve *notice* on union officials of existing commercial contracts with which a forthcoming strike will interfere. This has been done in many leading cases since 1965; and it certainly prevents the possibility of turning a blind eye! Presumably after the Alterna-tive Fuel decision, plaintiffs can warn union officials that they are *about* to negotiate such contracts.

29. See on this aspect the criticisms of V. Korah (1968) *J. Business Law* 345.

30. For the different authorities see Wedderburn (1968) 31 *Modern Law Review* p. 553; Grabiner, (1969) 32 *Modern Law Review* p. 437; Wedderburn, *Cases and Materials on Labour Law*, pp. 526–7.

31. See K. W. Wedderburn (1970) 33 *Modern Law Review* 309.

32. F. Frankfurter and N. Greene, *The Labour Injunction* (1932; 1963 ed.), p. 201.

33. Mary Southin, Q.C., 'The Courts and Labour Injunctions' (1970) *The Advocate* (Vancouver) 74, 82.

34. See *Bird Construction Ltd* v. *Patterson* (1960) 23 D.L.R. 2d. 182 (Alberta S.C. Canada). Such damages may be payable even if the judge erred in law in granting the injunction: *Griffith* v. *Blake* (1884) 27 Ch.D. 474 (C.A.).

35. *Financial Times*, 24 and 25.2.70.

36. *Brown Knight and Truscott Ltd* v. *Anderson, The Times*, 13 and 18 September 1969.

37. *Boston Deep Sea Fisheries Ltd* v. *T.G.W.U., The Times*, 13, 14,

17, 18, 20, 21 March and 9 April 1970; *Financial Times*, 10 and 19 March 1970; *Sunday Times*, 15 March 1970.

38. On the strike see Paul Foot in *The Incompatibles* (ed. R. Blackburn, 1967), pp. 169–209.

39. *National Sailors' and Firemen's Union* v. *Reed* [1926] Ch. 536, pp. 539–40.

40. Milne Bailey, *Trade Union Documents* (1929) p. 346.

41. See *Essays in Jurisprudence and the Common Law*, Chapter 11. See *D.P.P.* v. *Bhagwan* [1970] 3 All E.R. 97, H.L. (combination to act to prejudice of the State not *per se* criminal).

42. *The Times*, 18.3.70; see too 25.3.70; 23.5.70.

43. W. E. J. McCarthy and B. A. Clifford (1966) IV *Brit. J. Industrial Relations* 39.

44. K. W. Wedderburn and P. L. Davies, *Employment Grievances and Disputes Procedures in Britain* (1969), Chapter 11, 'Inquiry and Investigation', p. 240.

45. R(U) 12/62; 12/60.

46. R(U) 2/53; 3/69.

47. *Punton* v. *Ministry of Pensions* (No. 2) [1964] 1 All E.R. 448 (C.A.).

48. R(U) 1/65; 17/52; 12/60; 11/63 (the unreasonableness of management is not relevant, nor, it seems, its wrongdoing in causing a dispute: 17/61).

49. R(U) 32/53.

50. R(U) 4/62; 3/62; 25/56; 17/61.

51. R(U) 5/66; 19/55; 41/56 (see, too, 20/57 on the 'twelve days' rule; Wedderburn, *Cases and Materials on Labour Law*, p. 417).

52. Evidence of Bar Council to Royal Commission, paras. 15, 17.

53. Clive Jenkins and J. E. Mortimer, *The Kind of Laws the Unions Ought to Want* (1968), pp. 51–2.

54. R. Miliband, *The State in Capitalist Society* (1969) p. 145. For a statistical analysis of the case law, see P. O'Higgins and M. Partington (1969) 32 *Modern Law Review* 53.

55. Alan Fox, 'Industrial Sociology and Industrial Relations', *R.C. Research Paper No. 3*, p. 8.

56. *Evidence to Royal Commission*, Day 31, 1966, p. 1279.

57. See the appendix on 'The Donovan Report' in Wedderburn and Davies, op. cit., p. 279, for this thesis in relation to details of existing institutions.

CHAPTER 9

TRADE UNIONS AND MEMBERS

SINCE 1913 a 'trade union' has in law comprised any combination, temporary or permanent, under the constitution of which the *principal objects* are: *the regulation of the relations between workmen and workmen, masters and workmen, or masters and masters, or the imposing of restrictive conditions on the conduct of any trade or business*, in addition to the provision of benefits to members. (These are called the 'statutory objects'.) The definition is substantially that laid down in the Trade Union Acts 1871 and 1876, slightly amended in 1913. It applies to all unions (whether or not registered under the 1871 provisions for voluntary registration). But it is an old-fashioned description. The inclusion of employers' associations can produce oddities, as we saw in Chapter 4, p. 179. The workers' trade unions see themselves as having a much wider role. Even the Webbs' definition was, by 1920, wider: 'a continuous association of wage earners for the purpose of maintaining or improving the conditions of their working lives'.

The T.U.C.'s Evidence to the Royal Commission in 1966 listed as union objectives 'improved terms of employment (and) physical environment at work; full employment and national prosperity; security of employment and income; improved social security; fair shares in national income and wealth; industrial democracy; a voice in government; improved public and social services; public control and planning of industry'. All these are 'seen as the means to the good life'. No wonder the Donovan Commission concluded that the current definition of a 'trade union' is 'out of date'. But it also concluded that it is 'too wide' since it embraces any combination temporary or permanent whose principal constitutional objects are the statutory objects. Thus, a Joint Committee of Shop Stewards might in law be a 'trade union' so long as it had a constitution 'which it seems need not be written'. Other words in the definition cause difficulty, e.g. the '*principal* objects'.

The 1970 Bill proposed separate definitions for trade union and employers' association. The latter would include any organization of employers whose principal objects included regulation of relations between employers and workers or trade unions, or a group of such organizations. The Bill would preserve most of the advantages of the trade union Acts for such associations (e.g. freedom from restraint of trade doctrines under the 1871 Act and from tort actions under the 1906 Act) so long as they are not registered under another statute (for example, as a company or a friendly society). Such a reform would be helpful. The Donovan Report noted the chaotic situation concerning the legal status of employers' associations in 1968. The 118 associations registered as companies in 1965 could not be 'trade unions' under the current definition, since the 1871 Act made it invalid for a trade union to register as a company.[1]

The definition of *trade union* proposed by the 1970 Bill was: *an organization (whether temporary or permanent) which consists wholly or mainly of workers of one or more descriptions whose principal objects include the regulation of relations between workers of that description or those descriptions and employers or employers' associations*; or an organization, such as a federation, consisting of affiliated or constituent trade unions within that definition, which itself includes among its principal objects regulation of relations either between employers or workers or between its affiliated or constituent organizations. (This last part would apparently include the T.U.C. which, it is commonly thought, does not qualify as a trade union under the definition current since 1913.) It will be noted that the Bill proposed the useful category of 'worker' in the new definition. The separate definitions would have ended the spurious impartiality of the old one which overlooked the fact that the 'master' is normally a 'person' in law usually only because 'he' is a combination of capital personified by the law in a company.

The Donovan Report would have had trade unions compulsorily registered and incorporated. But the T.U.C. pointed out that many organizations do not have to incorporate (e.g. partnerships) and trade unions did not seek the advantages of incorporation as companies do. Although the Labour Government first toyed with compulsory registration, without incorporation, their 1970 Bill sensibly omitted both proposals. There seems to be very little to be said for compulsory registration, for even procedural problems can be solved without it (p. 451). Registration is usually proposed as part of a wider scheme for new legal controls over trade unions' rules. Moreover, the proposal is customarily linked with the compulsory enforcement of collective agreements for which compulsory incorporation of unions is a useful step.

At present, registration is *voluntary* for any seven persons who meet the old definition. There are about three large unions still unregistered; and the Report estimated that some 15 per cent of union members belonged to unregistered unions. Under the present system, before he registers a union, the Registrar must be satisfied that its principal objects are the statutory objects, and he is empowered to withdraw the registration if he is satisfied that the constitution has been altered so as to alter that state of affairs or even if the objects for which the association is actually being carried on fall outside these objects. He is also empowered to grant a certificate to an unregistered union stating that it *is* a trade union in law – a certificate which is 'conclusive for all purposes' while it is in force as to the group's status. The Registrar – in truth the Chief Registrar of Friendly Societies and his Assistant Registrars, all appointed from lawyers of many years' standing – exercises many functions similar to, though less formal than, this procedure of certification, which assist the unions in their administration. Frequently, his consultations with the unions are of primary importance. At present, the Registrar has no power to demand particular content in union rules; he merely has to see that the rules provide for the matters enumerated by the Acts. The A.E.U. Rules Revision Conference adopted new rules in 1962 which *The Times* reported to have been 'brought forward by the executive at the request of the Chief Registrar' and commented: 'It does suggest that the Registrar is examining union rules more rigidly than in the past.' Such a relationship between unions and Registrar could only be maintained if the latter had acquired and retained the fullest confidence of the former. The Chief Registrar told the Royal Commission in 1968, 'we have built up a great deal of contact with the unions and I think they will accept our suggestions'. It must be doubtful whether the same atmosphere of confidence would survive registration thrust upon unions on terms which they resented.

POLITICAL OBJECTS AND ULTRA VIRES

In the early part of this century workers' trade unions had become accustomed to support candidates for Parliament, at first as Liberals or Independents, later by supporting the new Labour Party. This was generally believed to be lawful, and a judge declared it to be so in 1907. But in the *Osborne* case, 1909,[2] the House of Lords pronounced invalid this practice of devoting union funds to political purposes. The doctrine used for the purpose was that of *ultra vires* (a doctrine of company law). The courts had since 1905 established that the *ultra vires* doctrine should apply to unions (at least if they were registered) just as it applied to companies and similar associations. If a company is set up by statute, the Act will define the powers and objects of that 'statutory company'. Under the Companies Act, a company may also be formed by registration. In the application of *ultra vires* to such companies, the doctrine means that any transaction is invalid, and can be restrained by a member, if it is outside the basic objects as laid down in the company's registered *constitution*. Thus, if the doctrine were applied in this form to trade unions, political activity would only be *ultra vires* if it exceeded the powers laid down in the union's constitution. When Osborne, a member of the railwaymen's union, challenged his union's compulsory levy to be used in support of the Labour Party, the House of Lords did not apply the doctrine in quite that form even though dealing with registered unions where the analogy (if any) must have been

413

with the registered company. All the Law Lords except one examined not the objects stated in the union constitution, but the definition set out in the Acts of 1871 and 1876. The *descriptive* terms of that definition were applied as the *restrictive* limits to the possible lawful objects of a trade union! In this decision two influences played a part, namely the desire to treat unions as corporations, and the feeling that they were still illicit, probably dangerous, associations. The aged Earl of Halsbury said: 'It is true that the [1871] Act does not make the trade union a corporation but ... it can hardly be suggested that it legalizes a combination for anything.' The question should be, said Lord Atkinson, 'whether the Legislature expressly or by fair implication has conferred upon registered trade unions power and authority to subsidize ... a scheme of parliamentary representation'. The same reasoning was later applied in Scotland to municipal representation, and even to unregistered unions. Small wonder unions are suspicious still of proposals for compulsory incorporation (especially when that very proposal had been put to – but rejected by – the 1894 Royal Commission, to bind them to collective agreements).

No more explosive decision could have been delivered in 1910 at a time when the pressure for 'direct' militant action was growing stronger inside some unions, and when an M.P. (unpaid then from any other source) might depend entirely upon funds raised from the unions. The historical novelty of the decision is often underestimated. In 1905 the House of Lords had applied the *ultra vires* doctrine against the Yorkshire Miners' Association which had paid strike pay outside the terms of its constitution. But there they had found in favour of the complaining member by using the doctrine analogous to that which would be used on a registered (not a statutory) company.[3] There can be no doubt that *Osborne* marked a new and determined departure to control the unions, though one which did not surprise trade unionists to whom judicial ingenuity was by now not unknown. The effect was, at any rate, to threaten the new Labour Party and debilitate it in the elections of 1910, for all political levies, compulsory or not, were made invalid by the judgment (and indeed, the legality of many other union activities not mentioned in the 1871–6 definition was rendered doubtful).

The result of the outcry that again followed the House of Lords judgment was the Trade Union Act, 1913. This restored to unions the *ultra vires* doctrine in the form applicable to registered (not statutory) companies, subject to certain new rules about political expenditure. Trade unions are, therefore, today able to pursue any lawful object within their constitution; but any act outside the objects of the union constitution, or what is reasonably incidental to them, is wholly null and void, and (as a consequence of the *ultra vires* doctrine) cannot be ratified as such even by unanimous vote of the members (and certainly not by that of the executive committee).

In 1952 and 1964 the House of Lords applied this reasoning, as we shall see, to the alleged, but void, 'membership' of a man apparently accepted into a union whose constitution did not permit a membership of the type attempted. If, as in the 1952 case, a man is admitted into 'temporary' membership but the union constitution makes no allowance for such a class of members, the membership is *ultra vires* and a nullity, no matter how long the man has been treated as a member. This was, said one Law Lord, 'an attempt to create a class of member outside the provisions of the rules'. This invalidity does not involve 'expulsion' of the member; it is automatic from the fact that the union has not, and never had, power to accept him into that membership. But in 1966, Scottish courts refused to apply this doctrine to dismissal of an organizer. And the Donovan Report proposed that the doctrine of *ultra vires* should not be allowed to operate if the man has been treated as a member for two years, unless he had gained admission by fraud. The law limits membership of a union today in only three serious respects. Policemen have, since 1919, been prohibited from joining a union (though if a unionist joins the police he may be given permission to remain in his old union); and the Act of 1876 (though it is not wholly clear) appears to restrict membership to those above sixteen years of age. (Some unions therefore sign up younger workers as 'associates' or 'probationers'.)

The Race Relations Act, 1968, prohibits discrimination in union admissions (and treatment or expulsion) in similar manner to the prohibition in employment generally (p. 84). But the exceptions which allow employment of a person by reason of nationality or descent for employment needing certain attributes (e.g. Chinese waiters) were not reproduced in the section dealing with trade unions and employers' associations, thereby putting in question the legality of such groups as the Indian Workers Association because the 1968 Act here applies to 'organizations of employers and workers' very generally.[4] One other charge which has been brought against unions of serious malpractice in admissions has been that levelled sometimes against the dock and printing unions, namely, nepotism in admission to a closed shop – a charge usually associated more with the boardroom than with the workbench. The 'craft' unions, however, often run into more grave criticisms in regard to refusal to admit persons trained in new ways in the trade (see p. 431).

THE POLITICAL FUND

The Act of 1913 prohibits the expenditure of funds, directly or indirectly, of any union on defined 'political' objects unless the furtherance of the political objects has been approved as an object of the union by a resolution in a ballot of members and a proper political fund has been established. The rules both for the ballot and for the separate political fund must be approved by the Registrar, who has provided a set of model rules for guidance. Political objects are defined as the expenditure of money on a Parliamentary or local government candidate's expenses; on meetings or literature in his support; on maintenance of an M.P. or councillor; in connection with registration of voters or selection of a candidate; or on the holding of 'political meetings' or distribution of 'political literature' (unless their main purpose is the furtherance of the 'statutory objects' of trade unions).

The 1913 Act went on, however, to declare that the rules must give to every member the right (of which he must be given notice) to contract out of the levy to the political fund; and that by contracting-out a member shall not be excluded from any benefits, or otherwise put under any disability or disadvantage '(except in relation to the control or management of the political fund)'. Nor may contribution to the fund be made a condition of membership. Since 1913 the only changes in this compromise structure for union political activity have been the substitution of 'contracting-in' in 1927, and the restoration of 'contracting-out' in 1946. In 1945 less than fifty per cent of relevant trade unionists paid the levy; but in 1968, the percentage of possible contributors paying it was 79·6 (about 1 per cent less than in 1965). The Donovan Report thought the 1913 scheme should be retained as it stands and strongly rejected proposals to go back to 'contracting-in'. Of course, as the figures show, the present arrangements do give the Labour Party the advantage of human apathy; but the Report pointed out that Conservative administrations could have changed the scheme between 1951 and 1964 'but this was not done'. In 1968 the average annual levy per member was just under 3s. 0d. (15p).

The individual trade union member is further protected if he ever alleges that he is 'aggrieved by a breach of any rule' made by the union under the Act. He may then complain to the Registrar who determines the dispute (even by ordering payment of benefit if he has been wrongly excluded). The Act of 1913 allows for no appeal whatever to the courts from the Registrar's 'binding and conclusive' decision (though, after the Tribunal and Inquiries Act, 1958, courts still retain a power of review if the Registrar fails to fulfil his duty properly of hearing such complaint). In 1956 a clerical worker complained that contracting-out members had voted on resolutions to nominate Aneurin Bevan as Labour Party Treasurer.[5] The Registrar decided that the union rules merely *allowed* for exclusion of a contracting-out member, but did not demand it, so there had been no breach. Similarly in 1967 the Registrar dismissed a complaint by a Mr Sharpe that his union had paid him no allowance on his appointment as chairman of Barton-on-Humber Urban District Council. The rules allowed for payments but did not compel them to be made. In *Birch*'s case, 1950,[6] however, a member was made strictly ineligible for any office that involved management of the political fund under the rules of the N.U.R. (as they then stood) if he contracted out. Birch, a branch chairman, was removed from office when it was pointed out that the branch officers controlled the fund. On a complaint to the Registrar, the latter decided that there had been no 'breach of the rules' at all. From this decision Birch could not appeal; but he next sought a declaration from the courts that the rules themselves (even though approved by the Registrar) offended against the Act. The judge agreed that they did, largely on the ground that the rules envisaged by the Act allowed discrimination only in regard to offices 'solely or mainly' concerned with management of the fund. The rules of the N.U.R. were changed after this decision so as to vest local political funds in special 'Councils'; but they retain a general restriction at national level in regard to certain union offices. Such a general discrimination against contracted-out members at national level has been said to be permitted on the ground that there is a 'necessary distinction' between union officers at local and district level and officers at the highest or national level. The latter must not be deprived of their power to guide their union's political affairs.[7] But the judge did not draw this (very reasonable) distinction in his judgment. On the contrary he treated all union offices on the same basis. It is a pity that the Donovan Report did not comment on this uncertainty in the law.

It should not be thought that the 1913 Act prohibits 'political discrimination' in unions other than that which falls strictly within the machinery described. For example, a person excluded from nomination to a conference on the alleged ground that he is 'a Conservative' or 'a Communist' is not prejudiced by reason of any contracting-out and therefore is unprotected (like the baker in 1935, alleged to be a 'disruptive element' in his union by reason of being connected with the Bakers Rank and File movement). It is also open to any union to ban persons from *office* on political or other grounds. (The Electrical, Electronic Telecommunications, and Plumbing

Trades Union has such a rule in regard to Communists and Fascists; but the T.G.W.U. rule of that kind was changed in 1968 to one giving its executive council discretion to declare persons ineligible if they belong to organizations detrimental to the union.) The Registrar has said he has no power to stop union members telling their employer that they will not work with a contracting-out member (though whether this might give rise to a right of action on the grounds of a civil conspiracy to injure may be thought an open question, as we have seen in Chapter 8). Although the political levy cannot be a *condition* of membership, it would in theory be possible for a union to refuse membership (within its rules) to someone known to be hostile to the political objects. He would not even be an aggrieved member who could complain to the Registrar, for he would never become a member at all.

MEMBERS' RIGHTS AND UNION RULES

The member has few rights accorded to him by *statute* other than those in the Act of 1913. If he is a member of a registered union, he has a special right to assign certain small sums payable at his death without making a will. The 1871 Act gives to any such member (or other person 'having an interest in the funds') a right to inspect the books and membership list; and as we shall see, an Act of 1964 entrenches a member's rights to an effective vote on an amalgamation of his union. (It may be parenthetically remarked that the annual union returns to the Registrar of funds, expenditure, and the like are open to inspection, and that the registered union must deliver to anyone on demand a copy of its rules for one shilling or less. The 1970 Bill proposed to provide stricter requirements in respect of annual financial returns, proper auditing of accounts, and the vetting of members' superannuation schemes by qualified actuaries unless the Registrar exempts them. In fact, only nine unions with more than 5,000 members did not by 1968 have professional auditors.)

The property of the union is held by the trustees on trust for the members and purposes of the union. Application outside these purposes is *ultra vires*. The registered union *must* have such trustees who control and hold the property. Thus, when in 1968 the N.U.R. – again unlucky – tried to set up a nominal company to hold its investments, thereby avoiding administrative inconveniences on a change of any one of the three trustees, the judge ruled 'reluctantly' that this scheme infringed the 1871 Act because the trustees no longer held the property (even though they controlled the company).[8] The 'corporate entity' struck again! Since 1961 it has been easier for the trustees to invest in a wider range of investments outside the traditional government and other gilt-edged securities, and considerable funds of various unions have been invested in equity shares. A Trade Union Unit Trust was even created in 1961 into which any union affiliated to the T.U.C. can put money. There has been some opposition to such a development on the ground that unions might, by increasing their stake in the employer's aggregate of capital, not remain wholly free to press the interests of the labour movement; but by 1969 fifty-seven unions had invested funds worth over £7 million. The value of the original £1,000 unit had by 1970 reached £1,565. Total funds of registered unions at the beginning of 1969 amounted to about £130 million, but it must be remembered that this represents something like £15 per member. Furthermore, few unions have large liquid assets. (The boilermakers, for example, with funds nominally at £13 12s. (£13.60) per member in 1970, had such a large amount invested in its pension fund that it estimated its liquid funds at only £6 10s. (£6.50) a head.) The expenditure on trade dispute benefit is always much lower than sickness, accident, superannuation, death and other benefits (in 1968 the registered unions' figures were 3·7 per cent and 35 per cent respectively). Members' contributions have been very low until recently. The T.S.S.A. rate of one shilling a week was stable for 33 years until it rose to 2s. 0d. in 1964, when average rates had in five years risen 'twice as fast as the increases in weekly wage rates'.[9] They needed to rise even faster. In 1956 the T.G.W.U. and G.M.W. weekly rates were still 8d. By 1970 these rates rose to 2s. 0d. (10p) and 2s. 6d. (12½p) respectively; and the A.U.E.F.W. increased its ordinary contribution to 3s. 0d.

(15p). Total income of registered unions rose from £26 million in 1957 to £44 million in 1968 (£37 million from members). Even such a strong critic of the unions as Mr Stephen Fay is of the view that 'most British trade unionists (printing workers are an exception) get trade unionism on the cheap ...'.[10] The need to improve organization and service more complicated productivity bargaining at factory level is likely to increase the need to augment union income still further.

The members' obligations to contribute to the funds and their rights over union property rest, like all their other rights, primarily on the rule book. The union rules operate as a contract, just like the articles of a company or the rules of a club. On joining the union, the member becomes a party to that contract. The 1871 Act requires that a union desirous of registration shall have rules about a number of questions (name; objects; alteration of rules; benefits; officers, committee and trustees, etc.). But the *content* under each of these headings is left to the union. An unregistered union does not, in theory, even need to have written rules. This traditional freedom to decide democratically on their own rule book is of great importance to union members. Later we shall consider new proposals to limit their choice (p. 429).

In general, therefore, a member's action to enforce the rule book will take on the appearance of an action for breach of contract. For example, in 1969, Mr Leigh, a railway guard, wished to accept nomination as candidate for president of the N.U.R. The secretary refused it, on the ground that the rules stated he must be a member of the Labour Party. Mr Leigh had been a member of the Communist Party; but six months before the nomination he had resigned and applied to join the Labour Party, though he had not yet been accepted. The judge held that the rules did not mean that candidates had to be Labour Party members at the time of nomination; Mr Leigh could get his qualification for president in time if elected.[11] The N.U.R. – third time unfortunate – was therefore banned from holding the election without including his name, since to do so would amount to a breach of the contract in the rule book. But there must be a breach of the rules before the court will act. So in cases of 1967 and 1968, two unions were held to owe certain duties under their rules to help members with legal advice. Legal aid and advice are, of course, in most unions one of the most important services to members even in this era of State legal aid. But in neither of these two cases was the union held to have broken its duty in the rules.[12] The rules are, of course, alterable in the ways allowed by the rule book so that the contract is on terms alterable from time to time, as is usual in associations.

The member can in law always restrain his union from acting unlawfully or *ultra vires*, i.e. outside the agreed objects. The case of the Yorkshire Miners in 1905 was one in which a member stopped the payment of *ultra vires* strike pay under this principle, because the union rules as drafted at the time did not permit it in the circumstances. A parallel success was registered by a Mr Lilley in 1969 when the court at his suit declared wrongful the payment by the A.U.E.F.W. of strike pay and the very calling of a strike by its Executive Council in the previous year. As for unlawful acts, in *Byrne* v. *Foulkes*, 1961,[13] the losing candidate in the election for Secretary of the E.T.U. alleged against fourteen defendants who then controlled the union a fraudulent conspiracy to rig the ballot. The court found the case proved against five defendants (members of the Communist Party) after a complex forty-two day trial – 'the biggest fraud in the history of British trade unionism', as counsel called it. In such a case the problem is not so much the law, as proof of the facts, which can be expensive and difficult. Such a fraud was an unlawful conspiracy; and damages for that tort were awarded in addition to declarations that the election was unlawful. (Costs in the action were also granted against the union, not for the tort – the Act of 1906 would not permit that – but for breach of the contract in the rule book.) It was that case that led to the rule in the E.T.U. banning Communists from holding office. Control of the union passed to a group who had exposed the fraud (many of them ex-Communists) and strained relations have produced considerable litigation about the union's affairs – the only union to be involved in such a scandal in modern British history. In declaring the method used to pass an amendment of the union's rules valid, in 1965, Mr Justice Lawton commented that there was 'no rule of the union which stated that members must love those in authority over them even though they called them brothers'. Again, if those in control of the union commit a 'fraud on the minority' (of which proof is not easy) by misappropriating the assets, any minority member may sue to stop them, and even to recover the property misappropriated for the union. Another form of wrongdoing which sometimes gave members an action against the union was 'maintenance'. Stemming from a statute of 1275, the medieval wrong, which consisted in improperly financing litigation, was abolished by an Act of 1967 as a crime or a tort. But the Act continued the principle that contracts to 'maintain' litigation were illegal. But the courts have since 1955 taken a wide view of what is a proper 'interest' in litigation, and the principle is unlikely to hamper unions in future.

Outside *ultra vires*, illegality, and fraud, however, the member's right to enforce the contract in the rules is inhibited by two principles, one of the common law, one statutory. The common law principle goes under the Dickensian title of 'The Rule in *Foss* v. *Harbottle*'. It is, once again, a company law principle, first clearly applied to trade unions in 1929 to stop members challenging decisions at the conference of the seamen's union to support a loan to the 'Miners' Non-Political Movement'. Its basis is the principle that the majority of members are to be expected to govern an association, not the court. Therefore an individual member is not to be allowed to complain of a mere 'procedural irregularity'; that is for the majority to put right. Similarly, if a wrong has been done to the association (under the control of the majority) it is for the association to sue, not the minority member (so long as illegality, fraud, or *ultra vires* are all absent). Lord Justice Russell had said in 1929 that, where the act complained of was not *ultra vires*,

the rule in *Foss* v. *Harbottle* really works by means of something in the nature of a dilemma. The only possible plaintiff to stop an *intra vires* act is the corporation itself. If an individual is in a position to be able to use the name of the corporation then the majority are in agreement with him. If he is not in a position to use that name, then the majority are in disagreement with him and he is not entitled to bring an action in his own name.

As we shall see (p. 446), that language is much more appropriate to a registered, than to an unregistered, union.

But the Rule cannot apply if the right infringed is a *personal* or 'individual' right of each member, e.g. his right to vote as the union rules prescribe. In that case he can sue for breach of contract against him personally and the *Foss* v. *Harbottle* Rule is ousted. So, in 1950, two members of the Cricklewood branch of the Vehicle Builders Union evaded the Rule and obtained a declaration pronouncing invalid proposed changes in contribution rates in their registered union. The rule book said that these rates could be changed only on a ballot of members with a two-thirds majority; but the executive had tried merely to put a simple resolution through a delegate conference. That procedure, said Lord Justice Jenkins, '... invaded the individual rights of the complainant members, who are entitled to maintain themselves in full membership ... unless and until the scale of contributions is validly altered by the prescribed majority obtained on a ballot vote. ... The gist of the case is that the personal and individual rights of membership of each of them have been invaded by a purported, but invalid, alteration of the tables of contributions. In those circumstances, it seems to me, the rule in *Foss* v. *Harbottle* has no application at all.'[14] It must be added that it is not wholly clear just which rights will be accounted 'personal' to each member or which questions 'merely procedural'. Moreover, in 1966, the High Court seemed to take inadequate account of the personal rights of a member. His union council had decided to cast its vote for Government incomes' policies at the T.U.C.; but this was a breach of the rules because of a decision at the union's own conference. The member asked for an injunction on the very morning of the T.U.C. meeting; but the judge rejected his claim in spite of the breach, saying he had no sufficient 'property right' in the matter. His personal right to have his union administered according to its rules (like the Vehicle Builders) seems to have been overlooked. The wrongdoing of union officers would normally be a wrong done to the association as such and therefore within the Rule. But in 1963 Lord Denning, Master of the Rolls, declared that 'an officer of a trade union . . . is in a fiduciary position towards the members'. In company law, directors owe their duties to the *company*, so individual shareholders cannot sue for breach of a fiduciary duty by a director, because of the Rule. But Lord Denning speaks of the duty as owed to the union *members*. That might give each member a right to sue for the officer's breach of his fiduciary duty which could be a matter of the highest importance.

The personal right to vote as the Rules provide is an individual contractual right; and allied to the right to prevent *ultra vires* or illegal acts, it constitutes the member's main power to control the administration of his union in the general interest and to prevent undemocratic practices. The Rule in *Foss* v. *Harbottle* is, in a sense, a prop to democratic control by stressing the function of majority control. As we shall see (p. 429), new legislation was suggested by the Donovan Report to break into the tradition that a union is free to choose its own method of elections (with a few statutory limitations such as an Act of 1964 on amalgamation). The question of statutory control of the rule book is bound to be a thorny point of debate in future discussions.

TRADE UNION ACT, 1871, S.4

Nothing in this Act, section 4 provides, shall enable any court to enforce directly or allow recovery of damages for breach of: (1) any agreement between trade union members as to terms on which they will transact business, employ, or be employed; (2) any agreement for payment of a subscription or penalty to a union; (3) any agreement to apply union funds for benefits to members; payments to non-members for complying with the rules; or to discharge any fine imposed by a court; or (4) any agreement between trade unions.

This section was, as we saw on p. 314, a price readily paid by the unions for the removal from their shoulders in 1871 of the burden of the 'restraint of trade' doctrine, from which they were relieved by s.3 of the Act. The main object of it is clearly to keep the agreements that are of domestic concern to trade unions out of the ordinary courts. Not only does the section not succeed in doing that entirely; but it had, as we saw in Chapter 4, some strange side-effects in the modern law (such as the application of s.4(4) to modern collective agreements made between workers' unions and certain employers' associations although that will automatically end if employers' associations cease to be 'trade unions'). What is the scope of s.4, then, in internal union affairs?

First, what is meant by 'Nothing in this Act shall enable'? We have already seen that most unions are probably still today in restraint of trade at common law. Two Law Lords thought it 'manifest' that a closed shop union would be so in 1964 (though two others left the point open). In that case s.3 of the Act is needed to allow the union and its agreements sufficient legality to come within earshot of the court. Something 'in this Act' is, therefore, brought into play, and the named agreements immediately become unenforceable under s.4. But suppose the union is 'lawful' at common law, e.g. if it has unusual rules, or if the English judges swing back into a relaxation of the 'restraint of trade' doctrine. Orthodox opinion then suggests that there is no room left for the operation of s.4, and certain judgments of the Court of Appeal support that view. But, it may be suggested, if the lawful union is sued in a *registered* name, that ability to be sued also stems wholly from the registration provisions of s.6 of the 1871 Act. If so, something 'in this Act' would again be enabling the court to pronounce; and then s.4 should apply to the named agreements.[15] Section 4 may, therefore, have a very wide reach indeed.

The oddest tangle has arisen in connection with 'direct enforcement' of the named agreements. At first the courts thought that Section 4 meant to prohibit (as it seems to do) all enforcement. Later, however, the view gained authority – and is now the law – that 'indirect enforcement' of the agreements is allowed by the section. Two lines of cases support this view. First, injunctions were granted to members seeking to prevent an *ultra vires* application of union property, as in the Yorkshire Miners' strike-pay case of 1905. An action for a declaration or injunction is not as such always 'indirect' (as in the case of the declaration refused in 1938 to a deceased member's representative directly claiming the member's superannuation benefit). But an action is not prohibited if it seeks indirect enforcement by means of a declaration or an injunction to stop *ultra vires* payments to any other person of money to which the complaining member is entitled as benefit. (Two members of the Royal Commission wanted to replace 'direct' with 'specific' – but the logic in the cases just mentioned would, one feels, still frustrate their purpose.) The second line of cases began in 1911, when Osborne successfully challenged his expulsion from the Railwaymen's Union (which had been a direct result of the previous litigation). The Court of Appeal considered that an injunction would here not infringe s.4. The plaintiff Osborne was not directly enforcing any of those specific agreements; he was defending his membership right as such by asking for a declaration and injunction against his expulsion in breach of the union rules. In 1922 the House of Lords adopted this approach. Workers had been expelled from a union for participating in 'co-partnership' schemes allegedly forbidden by the union rules. The Lords held, first, that the union executive had erred; the profit-sharing scheme in question did not, properly understood, come within the range of a 'co-partnership' aimed at by the rules. Secondly, the action for an injunction and declaration aimed at no more than maintaining the plaintiffs in membership, a construction of the rules, and an affirmation by the court that there was no power to expel. None of those objectives involved 'direct enforcements'.[16]

If s.4 does apply, the prohibition is strict. In 1963 members of the T.G.W.U. tried to sue the union and its officers, alleging that a notice for a nation-wide dock strike had been 'wrongfully cancelled' by the officers and that they were entitled to strike pay under the union rules and damages for breach of contract. The action was rapidly dismissed. The action, being in contravention of s.4(3) as an attempt to enforce directly an agreement for the application of funds to provide benefits to members, was 'wholly misconceived'. In 1912 a union was not permitted to sue for the *return* of benefit repayable under the

Rules by a member, for that would be to enforce directly an agreement within s.4(3). The 'indirect enforcement' argument, however, was employed to allow for a declaration in 1921 that certain ballots had been improperly conducted and that the union must not 'decline to receive the plaintiffs' contributions so that by virtue of the non-payment ... the plaintiffs would become liable to come out of benefit'. The court will not allow s.4, in other words, to be used as a shield by union administrators who try, in breach of the rules, to manoeuvre the member into a position where he would be vulnerable .

On the other hand, the section is only a prohibition of direct enforcement within the exact words used. Thus, in 1966, a Scottish court held easily that an action by a member claiming that the union had failed in its duty to pursue a claim for compensation after injury to the member did not fall within any of the headings of s.4. The most remarkably narrow construction of all – one which the judge thought logically 'quite untenable' but which he felt bound by previous cases to apply – is in a case of 1968.[17] There a printer left his trade to become a publican. But he remained, as the Rules allowed, an 'out-of-trade member' of his union. Six months later he wished to return to the printing trade. The union had various rules obliging it to give members details of regular and casual employment opportunities. The member here was offered only the regular jobs. He sued for damages but lost. The judge decided that this would anyway not be a breach of the, somewhat complex, rules of the union; but in passing he swept aside the defence of s.4(1) which the union had raised, on the ground that the member was trying to enforce an agreement between members concerning the terms on which any of them 'shall or shall not ... employ or be employed'. These words, he held, applied only to the conditions of an employment already in existence, not to conditions on which a man might be seeking employment in his trade. Many bizarre interpretations of s.4 have been seen in the cases, but this is perhaps the oddest.

A majority of nine Donovan Commissioners wished to repeal the whole section, seeing no reason why today 'legal contracts entered into by trade unions should be placed on a different footing from other contracts'. A minority of three favoured the section as a way of keeping internal affairs out of the courts. The 1970 Bill proposed to effect this by retaining s.4(4) as between two unions or two employers' associations, but abolishing it in regard to an agreement between a union and association. The Bill would, thus, have left the rest of the section intact, with an old problem of some interest. This is caused by the fact that s.4(1) speaks of agreements between members of the union. We shall find that, even after the House of Lords decision in *Bonsor's* case of 1956, it is still not clear whether the contract of membership of a registered union is one 'between the members' or 'between the member and the union'. The 1871 Act appears to assume the former; but if the judges say that it is the latter, s.4(1) would not apply to it. This was certainly not the intention of Parliament in 1871. In 1967, however, Mr Justice Nield spoke of a registered union having 'certain obligations to the plaintiff under the contract with her'.[18] We shall see that the insistence of some judges that a registered union is some kind of legal entity may easily lead to this kind of language. The effect upon s.4(1) of this view is, however, a death blow.

THE RULE-BOOK CONTRACT IN THE FUTURE?

By 1969 proposals had been made which would affect this structure considerably. *Fair Deal at Work* had proposed as 'minimum conditions' that the Registrar should be able to demand many types of rule – including, for example, a rule subjecting the central council of a union to re-election at 'stated intervals'; that all members should be eligible for office; an appeal for discipline to its new Industrial Court; and no clauses to 'restrict output or efficiency'. Donovan went less far but trod a similar path. The Registrar should 'advise' unions, and if necessary take them to an independent Review Tribunal to ensure that they include clear rules on such matters as the description of disciplinary offences and procedures for appeal (which must be fair); procedures for elections; and the exact status of the union's shop stewards. Moreover, the independent

Review Tribunal (a legal chairman and two wingmen from a panel of trade unionists) should also have power to hear complaints by persons against breach of the rules; unfair imposition of disciplinary penalties or expulsion; complaints under the 1913 Act or the 1964 Amalgamations Act (unhappily thereby ousting the Registrar). Such jurisdiction would, where necessary, be concurrent with that of the High Court *except* in cases of alleged unfair sanctions and expulsion.

In Place of Strife went further than Donovan in some ways. The Registrar should have power to demand that the rules 'adequately cover' certain topics (with appeal to the – old – Industrial Court against his refusal to register). The list of topics included admission, elections, discipline, expulsion, and other disputes with members (presumably including the 1913 Act), strike ballots, and the appointment and functions of shop stewards. Complaints would lie to the Registrar (who would attempt conciliation) and then to a Board by any person complaining of 'unfair or arbitrary action' by a trade union causing 'substantial injustice' in respect of either admission, discipline or expulsion and the like.

After its dispute with the T.U.C., however, the Labour Government saw matters differently and (apart from the provisions about audits and pension funds: p. 419) included none of these proposals in the 1970 Bill. There were several reasons for this. The most important was probably the understanding of the T.U.C. that these sections of *In Place of Strife* also related to 'penal clauses' on unions covered by the Government's pledge not to legislate. On its side, the T.U.C. pressed ahead with studies from which have emerged a series of detailed proposals to affiliated unions for model principles along which rule books should be clarified and reformed in connection with rules about strikes; the place of shop stewards; expulsions and membership; arrears and lapses of membership; and appeals against decisions on such matters. For example, strike procedures should be clearly stated, together with any ballots required before or during the strike; the size of the majority; and procedures for complaints; the method of election of shop stewards; their relation to union bodies; the duties and authority of stewards; the conduct of shop-floor meetings, and the running of joint shop stewards' committees. The process of reforming union rule books along such lines is proceeding; but in some cases greater speed is required.

We touch on these matters later; but it is worth pausing on the substance of some of the proposals *not* included, in the end, in the 1970 Bill. For example, the proposal to control 'arbitrary admissions' by means of appeal to a review tribunal outside the union would be a departure of the first magnitude. As we shall see, the freedom to control *admission* to the union is the mechanism whereby in a tight labour-market situation the union can exercise its share of control over 'job-entry' especially if there is a closed-shop (see p. 457 and the *Faramus* case). The Donovan Report was concerned (understandably in view of the criticism levelled at some union branches' refusal to accept 'dilutees' not trained through the normal channels) that in these days of shortage, no qualified worker should be arbitrarily denied 'the right to use the skills which he had acquired'. That was clearly the main reason for the proposed right of appeal against arbitrary refusal to admit. But if so, the law needs another amendment. A skilled man should have the right to appeal against an employer's refusal to *employ* him on suitable work. That is the other end of control of job-entry. (As usual, we come back to the right to own or control the job.) But no one has, it seems, even considered restricting by legislation the management right to refuse employment. That is to be left to, if anything, collective bargaining.

It is worthy of note here that the *courts* have made two recent forays into the field of admission to associations. In *Nagle* v. *Fielden*, 1966,[19] the Court of Appeal held that there was an arguable case for the proposition that a lady trainer, refused a licence by the Jockey Club Stewards because she was a woman, had a right at common law to have a licence because she had a right to enter a group necessary to protect her 'right to work' at the trade and should not be 'unjustly excluded from it'. But the case was settled later and a licence granted. The *Nagle* case cannot give a common law right to join a trade union whatever its rules say, unless it has torn up centuries of legal principles. This would be judicial law-making at its worst. Dr Rideout commented that 'although much of the language in the judgments is more reminiscent of the industrial scene than the turf, the actual decision cannot directly affect the unions'. Such a conclusion was, however, thrown into doubt by the astonishing dicta of the Master of the Rolls, Lord Denning, in *Edwards* v. *S.O.G.A.T.*,[20] a case where, as we shall see (p. 448), the union had wrongly excluded the member from membership in circumstances which reflected very badly upon the union. Indeed, the facts invited judicial creativity. Lord Denning not unexpectedly accepted the invitation. But he not only held that the union had acted in breach of the contract in the rule book; he went on to say that discretionary powers to expel were invalid, that rules limiting the rights of 'temporary' union members were unlawful, and even that a refusal to readmit to the union without a hearing even if allowed by the rules was wrongful if exercised 'in an arbitrary or capricious manner, or with unfair discrimination'. The theoretical basis for all this was flimsy. In effect Lord Denning was claiming, as he had since 1952, the power to revise the contract in the union rule book, the power to revise the very *content* of union rules. He would permit union power to be

exercised arbitrarily or capriciously or with unfair discrimination neither in the making of Rules nor in the enforcement of them. ... A trade union exists to protect the right of each one of its members to earn his living and to take advantage of all that goes with it. It is the very purpose of its being. If the Union should assume to make a rule which destroys that right or puts it in jeopardy – or is a gratuitous and oppressive interference with it – then the Union exceeds its powers. The Rule is *ultra vires* and invalid.

This remarkable passage would mean that few disciplinary rules, measures or expulsions could stand unless a judge sanctioned them, whatever the majority of union members democratically decided. For, effected in defence of the right of some members' right to earn their living as they wish, such actions necessarily put in jeopardy the expelled member's pursuit of his work in some way or other. Refusal to readmit, thought

Lord Denning, might 'sometimes be justified as when the trade is oversupplied with labour'. Such formulae do not begin to analyse the problem. Members of the Donovan Commission whose proposals for control of union rules were so carefully couched (and even members of the Conservative Government preparing their industrial legislation) must have despaired at the simplistic panache with which some judges suddenly seemed likely to treat these delicate social issues. What criteria, one wonders, would Lord Denning apply to decide whether (say) The Temple is 'oversupplied' with barristers? Which other bodies or arrangements are subject to this power of the courts to strike clauses out of contracts as an 'unwarranted' or 'arbitrary' interference with someone's right to work or live as he pleases? Such questions need the careful inquiry of research and the democratic decision of Parliament, not the adversary argument of counsel on which is built judicial legislation. Only two months earlier Professor Kahn-Freund, arguing for new statutory intervention which in the present writer's view might go rather further than is needed, warned:

All this should be done with caution and with a realization that the distrust of the unions against the courts and the lawyers is well grounded in the hostility which the courts have often shown to the union movement and sometimes still show.[21]

Secondly the demand for a law on strike ballots (not a demand made by Donovan) was clearly linked with the Government proposals to give the Secretary of State a power, on the advice of the C.I.R., selectively to demand the holding of a strike ballot before a strike (also firmly rejected by Donovan). One might well ask, if ballots are needed to *start* strikes, why not to *end* them? Or to 'ratify', in the American fashion, the agreements made by the union leaders? As it has been said, there is often 'inconsistency' among those who make such proposals for strike ballots; they assume that in 'unofficial strikes the union officials "know better"; yet in . . . official strikes, the rank and file members may possibly "know better" '.[22] A recent inspection of major unions' rules shows that nearly 20 per cent have *no* rules for procedures on calling strikes, and about 60 per cent did not require any ballot of members before strikes could be called. A few unions with nearly three million members, however, require a ballot of some sort before any *national* strike of members can be called; and the well-known rules of the A.E.U. give a discretion to the Executive Council on that matter, and provide for a ballot in the case of district strikes after the approval of the Executive Council. Clearly these differences reflect different conditions in various unions. As the Donovan Report put it: 'The decision on such a matter should continue to rest with the Unions'.

Thirdly, some union rule books seem to contain no clear provision about resignation from the union. The common law seems to be that a member of such a voluntary association can, in the absence of rules to the contrary, terminate his membership on one day's notice. The extent to which any rules severely restricting the right to resign might be open to legal challenge is not clear; but it does not seem objectionable for the contract in the rule book to require that a particular procedure be followed for resignation or that a reasonable period of notice be given. Such rules could be of major importance in disputes about 'poaching' of members by one union from another, discussed later (p. 464). Rules about resignation could be usefully studied by the T.U.C. They must, of course, be distinguished from rules on expulsion or lapsing, to which we turn in Chapter 10.

By 1970 the T.U.C. was strongly urging its affiliated unions to close up any loopholes which might give justification for legislation on these matters. The Donovan Report had concluded there was 'little evidence that applications for membership are dealt with unfairly or that membership is capriciously refused'. And less than 1 per cent of a sample of union members said they knew of *any* cases of unfair treatment of members by their union. On these questions the T.U.C. recommended that rule books should clearly set out provisions concerning admissions, stating clearly who is qualified; the procedures; reasons for rejection; fair procedures for informing rejected applicants and allowing them an appeal to a 'higher authority' of persons who have no 'personal interest' in the matter. Similarly on discipline there should be a clear statement of the offences for which any sanction can be applied and of procedures for hearings which comply with the principles of natural justice (see p. 451). The T.U.C. spell out such principles as including a proper notice of the charge; opportunity of being heard at a convenient time; fair hearing and an honest decision after the member's case has been fully put at the hearing. Moreover there should be a right of appeal to a 'higher authority' of the kind proposed for admissions. All these rules should be set out as an appendix to each rule book.[23] A T.U.C. survey in 1969 showed that all affiliated unions have qualifications for admission. The admission requirements are sometimes in general terms; and unions with over 7 million members had no provisions for appeals by admission applicants, but reasons for rejection were given by virtually all unions. Only three unions (12,000 members) had no expulsion or disciplinary rules, and six had no power to expel on disciplinary grounds. The 115 which had disciplinary powers had a 'blanket or general rule' putting a member open to discipline if he acted in a manner detrimental to the union. But 64 unions with 6 million members provided for an appeal to a higher body (45 through annual conference of members, and 19 to a special appeals committee).

The proposal was canvassed that the T.U.C. might set up a central appeals body for members' appeals on such questions; but this idea was dropped. This was taken by some observers to be an example of the way in which the bigger unions, (T.G.W.U., G.M.W. or A.U.E.F.W.), were not prepared to subject their autonomous procedures to an all-union tribunal. Members of the Donovan Commission were distressed that the proposal for a State-created independent Review Tribunal had been abandoned by the Government; and were prepared to face the fact that this might require financial penalties imposed on unions in such a new 'court', by whatever name it went.[24] How strong the case is for laws to ensure new types of speedy appeal against discipline or expulsion decisions (or, a different matter, to enforce certain procedures on these questions) is a matter of continuing debate. The proposals of *Fair Deal at Work* seem much too rigid for a trade union movement as diverse as the

British and might subject it to a running battle in the new Industrial Courts which would impair its efficiency as a representative of working people. No one doubts that difficult problems do arise especially where 'closed discipline' arrangements exist (p. 464). The Labour Government's change of heart on this point shows how hard it is to strike a balance. For we see in these issues the competing claims of the small minority who, here as in any walk of life, unquestionably sometimes meet with injustice, and the overall need for each union to secure its collective strength and freedom of action. To this is related the problem of the closed shop; of discipline; of union structure; and of amalgamation. All these are the subject of the next chapter.

1. See M. A. Hickling, 'Trade Unions in Disguise' (1964) 27 *Modern Law Review* 625.
2. *Amalgamated Society of Railway Servants* v. *Osborne* [1910] A.C. 87.
3. *Yorkshire Miners' Association* v. *Howden* [1905] A.C. 256.
4. See B. Hepple, *Race, Jobs and the Law* (2nd ed. 1970), pp. 105–108.
5. *In the Matter of W. F. Hobbs and C.A.W.U.*, 30 July 1956; Wedderburn, *Cases and Materials on Labour Law*, p. 563.
6. *Birch* v. *National Union of Railwaymen* [1950] Ch. 602.
7. C. Grunfeld, *Modern Trade Union Law*, p. 306.
8. *Re National Union of Railwaymen's Rules* [1968] 1 All E.R. 5.
9. J. Hughes, *Change in the Trade Unions*, 1964 (Fabian Research Series 244) 1, p. 36.
10. S. Fay, *Measure for Measure: Reforming the Trade Unions* (1970), p. 64.
11. *Leigh* v. *N.U.R.* [1969] 3 All E.R. 1249. Once again a change of rules was later proposed.
12. See, e.g., *Cross* v. *B.I.S.A.K.T.A.* [1968] 1 All E.R. 250 (and see p. 255 where Diplock L.J. leaves open whether union or member becomes the 'client' of the solicitor).
13. See C. H. Rolph, *All Those in Favour: The E.T.U. Trial* (1962).
14. *Edwards* v. *Halliwell* [1950] 2 All E.R. 1064 at p. 1067; see Wedderburn; 1957 [*Cambridge Law Journal* 194] 'Rule in *Foss* v. *Harbottle*'; *Cases and Materials on Labour Law*, p. 591; and on the company law position see Gower, *Modern Company Law* (3rd ed. 1969), Chapter 25.
15. See Wedderburn (1957) 20 *Modern Law Review* 105, pp. 120–21.
16. *Amal. Soc. of Carpenters* v. *Braithwaite* [1922] 2 A.C. 440.
17. *Andrews* v. *N.U.P.B.W.* (1968) 4 K.I.R. 121; Megaw, J. agreed with the opinion in Citrine, *Trade Union Law* (3rd ed. M. A. Hickling), p. 122, but felt bound by precedent. The Scottish courts are strangely inconsistent in their approach to S.4: contrast *M'Gahie* v. *U.S.D.A.W.*, 1966, S.L.T. 74, with *Briggs* v. *N.U.M.*, 1969, S.L.T. 30.
18. *Buckley* v. *N.U.G.M.W.* [1967] 3 All E.R. 767, 773, following Lords Morton and Porter in *Bonsor's* case, see *post* pp. 445. See Grunfeld, *Modern Trade Union Law*, p. 63 n. 20; Citrine, op. cit., pp. 122–3; Fridman, *Modern Law of Employment*,

p. 949. As will be seen, the effect of this view in destroying s.4(1) is another reason for not adopting the views of Lords Morton and Porter in the *Bonsor* case.

19. [1966] 2 Q.B. 633; R. Rideout (1966) 29 *Modern Law Review* 424 at p. 427.

20. *Edwards* v. *S.O.G.A.T.*, [1970] 3 W.L.R. 713. Lord Denning tried to establish a similar principle in 1963 but his view had been rejected by a majority of the Court of Appeal and by the House of Lords. His new view is therefore of doubtful validity: see *post* p. 458.

21. (1970) 33 *Modern Law Review*, 241, 267. This article elaborates and brings up to date the Donovan Report's argument for a carefully constructed review body to which aggrieved applicants or members might turn for redress against trade unions.

22. N. Robertson and J. L. Thomas, *Trade Unions and Industrial Relations* (1968) p. 167 (note).

23. *T.U.C. Report*, 1969, p. 141; *Report*, 1970, p. 176.

24. E. Wigham, *The Times*, 30.12.69; and now O. Kahn-Freund, 'Trade Unions, the Law and Society' (1970) 33 *Modern Law Review* 241. [Such proposals must, however, be distinguished from the more stringent legal regulations proposed by the new Government in October 1970: Appendix p. 485; on these matters p. 506.]

CHAPTER 10

THE WORKER AND THE TRADE UNION MOVEMENT

THE problems considered in this chapter form part of the picture sketched in the last. The administration of a trade union, like any other association, is bound to lead to conflicts of interest between the group and some individual members, in which each side has its arguments and merits. The common lawyer tends to respond, perhaps, more quickly to the argument advanced by the individual member, for his training and experience have attuned his ears to the cry of individual oppression. That same cry, however, may echo for many trade unionists the note of a 'blackleg' or a 'scab', someone who has let them down in crisis of battle and with whom they wish to have no more to do. Few common lawyers have the same instinctive understanding of this second response. Yet it is essential for the development of British labour law that the problems be approached with that understanding, not least where the union sees itself as defending its security against an erring member. Protection of the individual member disciplined under union rules must take account of union security for which the disciplinary rules are there. Judges sometimes criticize in the manner of one who in 1966 chastised the Building Trades Union for its 'hard-hearted' refusal of membership to a man who had lost an arm in an accident, stopping him, 'irrespective of any feeling', from entering the bricklaying trade which he had learned at his rehabilitation centre. The next week the Union, which had never been involved in the court case, stated that the man had *never* applied to join; an official at the rehabilitation centre had told him he would not get into the Union; and he had not completed the training course. The General Secretary said they had never rejected a man who had completed such a course; and he thought it 'perhaps unfortunate' that the judge saw fit to criticize the Union on the information available to him. The Donovan Report avoided the average lawyer's quick assumption that the minority is (here) always right. It went most carefully into the overall problem. Confronted, for example, by the dilemma of two Christians whose beliefs did not allow them to join a union because they could not be 'unequally yoked with unbelievers', the Donovan Report concluded that 'trade unions in the main respect genuine conscientious objections' of that kind. Where a reasonable compromise is rejected, however (such as payments to a charity in lieu of dues, in a closed shop factory) then 'some redress' should be given such persons if they lost their jobs – as we have seen, in the Report's view, before an independent review tribunal. In the rare case of a merely malicious spiteful conspiracy, the law can step in, as we saw (p. 348). Otherwise the law has traditionally intervened only when the union rules are broken, for they, after all, represent the contract made by the members.

DISCIPLINE AND EXPULSION OF MEMBERS

The courts have for long exercised general jurisdiction over the wrongful exercise of discipline in and expulsion from associations. At first this jurisdiction was said (especially in cases concerning clubs) to rest on the injured member's 'property rights' (and this old notion echoes sometimes in the courtroom even today: see p. 424). But later it came to be seen as dependent on the contract, express or implied, between the members, in the absence of which there is no basis for it. The members' contract in the rule book cannot exclude the courts' jurisdiction on questions of law. This accords with the normal limits of the law of contract. In theory, the rule book could state that it was not a contract (e.g. 'binding in honour only'). But this is unlikely ever to happen; and, once there is a legally binding contract, parties cannot wholly exclude the jurisdiction of the courts to pronounce on matters of law (as opposed to fact) for, as Lord Scrutton put it in 1922, 'there must be no Alsatia in England where the King's writ does not run'. In *Lee* v. *Showmen's Guild of Great Britain*, 1952,[1] Lord Denning remarked that the parties could make a domestic tribunal 'the final arbiter on questions of fact, but they cannot make it the final arbiter on questions of law. They cannot prevent its decisions being examined by the courts.' But what *are* 'questions of law'? As we saw in redundancy cases this is not a simple matter. In *Lee*'s case, the Guild had fined and ultimately expelled the plaintiff for acts which, it adjudged, infringed its rules of 'fair competition'. The Court, however, held that the Guild had misunderstood the true *meaning* of those words and the proper interpretation of their meaning was a matter of *law* for the court to decide. This is sometimes taken today to mean that the court can always impose its meaning on words used in the rules. That is probably not so. If in *Lee*'s case 'unfair competition', or in the case of 1922 mentioned in the last chapter (p. 427) the type of 'co-partnership', had been carefully and indisputably defined by the rules of the union, that meaning would prevail. What cannot be ousted is the right of the court, in the last resort, to enforce the rules. That does not give the court any right to re-write the rule book as we saw in *Leigh*'s case (p. 421).

Furthermore, there seems to be no objection to the union rules demanding that a member 'exhaust internal remedies' before resorting to the courts – that is to say, using all the possible internal union appeals before he brings a legal action. As we have seen, unions vary; but the 19 unions allowing an appeal to special appeal bodies include the A.E.U. and Iron and Steel Trades Confederation. In others, appeal is, we saw, to the Conference; but various trade unions seem likely in the near future to institute new appeal machinery as recommended by the T.U.C. In 1951 Viscount Simonds said that such appeals are what the member is 'bound by his contract to pursue', where there is a rule expressly demanding exhaustion of internal remedies. That would seem to fit in with the usual English view of the rule book. So he cannot sue in court before 'exhausting internal remedies' by appeal. But more recently the courts have restricted this principle to rules expressly demanding exhaustion of domestic remedies as a precondition of legal action. In the absence of such a rule, the member can start an action. Mr Justice Ungoed-Thomas, in

1965, said further that in the 1951 case the member was not expelled *during* the domestic appeal procedure. If that were not so, it might be different because 'if the court were to refuse relief until all domestic remedy had been exhausted, the remedy might be quite inadequate and substantial injustice might be suffered'.[2] And in *Leigh*'s case, 1969, the judge refused to read a rule which really tried to oust the jurisdiction of the court on the law (and was therefore invalid) as a rule requiring a member first to exhaust domestic procedures.

The basis, then, of the English court's interference is a breach of the rules. It is not 'reasonableness' but breach of contract (however technical the breach) which puts a member's case on its feet. Where the rule in question states a clear offence or procedure, the court will seize on *any* failure to observe the rule strictly. When an old member was expelled and put under 'sentence of industrial death', as the judge called it, for being twenty weeks in arrears with his subscriptions after a dispute with his union in 1923, the judge discovered that the executive had acted two days earlier than the rule allowed and stopped the expulsion on that ground. And in 1969, Mr Braithwaite, who had been expelled by the E.T.U. leadership for partaking in unauthorized meetings to protest against collective agreements made by the union leaders, succeeded in an action to have the expulsion set aside. It appeared that 'by oversight' his right to appeal in October to an Appeals Committee had been taken away in the amalgamation of the union to form the E.E.T.U.–P.T.U. A new Appeals Committee would meet next January but that was not good enough. The Court of Appeal sharply invalidated the expulsion. In the leading case of *Bonsor* v. *Musicians' Union*, 1956,[3] the expulsion arose from the member being 52 weeks in arrears – twice as long as necessary under the rules for expulsion – but the expulsion was wrongful because it was done by the local branch secretary rather than by the branch committee as the rules required. The individual member is entitled to pursue the letter of his bond with the union and the courts bring no 'Daniel come to judgment' to deprive him of a remedy if it is infringed by one jot or tittle. Many of the union's disciplinary rules will be concerned with such offences – arrears; mis-applying funds; not maintaining union discipline in industrial conflict; wage-cutting; unofficial action against the leadership; and so on. But others will be more general, e.g. expulsion for conduct in the opinion of the union committee detrimental to the interests, welfare, or reputation of the union, or some similar formula.[4]

The T.U.C. Report, 1969, discloses that the different offences and sanctions are often 'found in different parts of the rule book'. Union rule books, so often condemned as antiquated, may need not so much rewriting as *rearranging* (though, it must be added, the Royal Commission found that many did need 'complete revision'). In 1938, the Court of Appeal accepted an expulsion within a general rule when the member had disobeyed a union decision that he should accept certain work which he had refused. His disobedience had weakened the union and 'confidence . . . between the employers and the union . . . to the detriment of collective bargaining'. The committee had decided that, in refusing to agree to its decision, the member had 'knowingly acted to the detriment of the interests of the union', and in those circumstances, the rules allowed for an expulsion. Even though there was another specific rule provid-ing for mere suspension from benefit as the punishment for a member who refused to work as this worker had done, the court could not intervene just because the committee had chosen to act under the general rule permitting expulsion. (We may note that, although promoting collective bargaining, the court was, as in the *Reynolds* decisions of 1924, siding with the big battalions of employers plus union against the wildcat worker.)[5] But a much tougher attitude was evinced by Mr Justice Goff in *Silvester* v. *N.P.B.P.W.*, 1966.[6] The member was a night driver for the *Daily Mail* where various kinds of over-time were worked. He gave up overtime for domestic reasons, which the branch did not like, censuring him for it and order-ing him to work overtime. He gave notice of appeal to the Final Appeal Court of the union; but meanwhile the branch fined him £10 for failing to carry out the order, made under a rule specifying the offence of acting 'to the detriment of the interests of the union'. (The General Secretary decided his appeal could not go on until he 'carried out the provisions of the general rules'.) The only union rule on overtime was one restricting it to eight hours; and the member was not bound to work overtime under his employment contract; and it was union policy that he should not be so bound. The branch withdrew his membership card; and the Final Appeal Court in the end varied the penalty to a fine of £20. The union's actions were held to be invalid. The rule about acting to the 'detriment' of the union just could not apply to this situation. (Moreover, the General Secretary had no power to stop the appeal.)

If there is no power at all in the rules to expel, the court will not imply one. In 1912 a judge declared that the Warwickshire Miners Association was 'without power to expel' at all as its rules stood. In *Spring*'s case, 1956, the T.U.C. had, under the Bridlington Agreement, 1939 (which regulates the relations of overlapping unions and gives the T.U.C. Disputes Committee power to decide between two affiliated unions in dispute about who should organize a group of workers), resolved a dispute between two unions organizing dockworkers by declaring that workers should be transferred from one to another. A member prevented his expulsion which was necessary to put this compulsory transfer into effect. He succeeded because there was no express power in the rule book of his union to expel him merely on the ground that the T.U.C. said he ought to be expelled. (And the court could not imply any power, particularly when the worker would have said not: 'Oh! Yes! of course' to such an implied term, but: 'Bridlington Agreement? What's that?')[7] Most affiliated unions have today, however, overcome this problem by adopting a rule which gives the Executive Council power to terminate the membership of any member if that is necessary to comply with a decision of the Disputes Committee of the T.U.C. As we shall see, such power may become more important after the new T U.C. Rules on Disputes adopted at the Special Congress of 1969.

A member, then, can get the court to stop his wrongful expulsion or declare expulsion wrongful only if it would be in breach of the rules. Delay will not defeat him, so long as the issue has not become 'academic', as the court put it in 1968 when a member had only three weeks of a two-year suspension to run, but nevertheless won his remedy from the court. But in 1915 the Court of Appeal decided that a member could not be awarded damages as well for the breach of contract. The registered union was not, said the Court, a corporation and (despite the procedural devices in *Taff Vale*) could not be in law a 'party' to a contract. The union contract was between all the members. The funds belonged to all the members together. Had the other members broken that contract so that damages should be paid from the funds? No – only the committee who tried to expel him. But were not the other members liable for the committee who acted as their agents? No – because the committee, as agent for them, could make the members liable only for acts done within its authority; and it had acted 'without authority and in defiance of the rules' (Lord Justice Bankes). No damages, therefore, could be recovered from the funds. That decision stood until 1956, when the House of Lords reversed it in *Bonsor* v. *Musicians' Union*, unanimously in the result, but on two wholly opposed lines of reasoning.[3]

Bonsor recovered damages for wrongful expulsion from the union on the following arguments: two Law Lords (Morton and Porter) adopted the line of Lord Brampton in the *Taff Vale* case and said that the registered Musicians' Union was an 'entity recognized by the law'. Though it might not have 'the full powers of an incorporated society', it was 'a thing created by statute, call it what you will, an entity, a body, a near-corporation, which by statute has in certain respects an existence apart from its members'. (This, see p. 316, still rests upon an implication in the 1871 Act.) The registered union was held (for the first time) to be capable in law of being a contracting party. The expulsion of Bonsor from the 'closed shop', which had forced him to take other jobs such as removing rust from a pier, was a breach of contract by 'it', and damages could be awarded.

Lord MacDermott, however (with whom Lord Somervell agreed) refused to depart from the traditional view that a union is not sufficiently 'corporate' to be a contracting 'person' even if it is registered. The former supported his conclusions with a devastating analysis of the Acts from 1871 onwards. The contract of membership could not be with 'it' as 'it' did not exist in law. The registered name was used as a mere procedural device as in the *Taff Vale* case. Was the Court of Appeal correct, then, in 1915? No, said Lord MacDermott – because the other members were liable for the wrong done by the agents (here the branch secretary). The Union had not 'disavowed' the act of the branch secretary; it had ratified that act and done all it could to 'identify itself with the expulsion of Mr Bonsor'. Damages must therefore be paid. This reasoning is important, because it means that the union funds would not be liable in damages if the union did disavow or refused to ratify the expulsion. The importance of this for unions is considerable. Is the burden on the union to disavow the expulsion or merely not to ratify the expulsion? The duty is probably the lighter one – not to ratify. If the branch secretary had met Bonsor in the street and said: 'You're expelled', the union could not have been liable so long as it did nothing active to ratify. Lord MacDermott did not (as Lord Morton did) hold that a union guaranteed that its local officers would never expel wrongfully.

In one respect, Lord MacDermott's reasoning is unsatisfactory – largely on the ground that the only 'ratification' had been by an Executive Committee also acting in breach of the rules! There seems, after all, no basis in ordinary principles of law to say that all the members tacitly 'delegate such power' – i.e. power to approve and ratify improper expulsions – 'to their governing bodies elected to act ... on behalf of the union membership as a whole'.[8] But what mattered more was the attitude of the fifth Law Lord (Keith). Where his vote went, there the majority, and the precedent, would lie. If he agreed with Lord MacDermott about the registered union, the contract of membership would still be among the members, not with 'it'; but the decision to give damages would apply to unregistered as well as to registered unions. Unhappily Lord Keith's view is not wholly clear. He says: '... a registered trade union is a legal entity but not ... a legal entity distinguishable at any moment of time from the members ...', and it may be 'called a legal entity while at the same time remaining an unincorporated association of individuals'! Legal commentators have disagreed about the meaning of this Delphic speech.

But the Donovan Report agreed that Lord Keith joined Lord MacDermott. He stated categorically that Bonsor's 'contract of membership was a contract between himself and the other members' (not 'the union').[9] He also stressed that the union had done nothing to disavow the expulsion and that there might be cases 'where a trade union disclaims the action of an official ... and in which, accordingly, the conduct complained of cannot be said to be the act of that trade union'. In such a case, the plaintiff's claim could only be against the *individual* members who did wrong, not the union funds. This distinction would have been doubly important if the 1970 Bill had been enacted; for that proposed to clarify doubts by providing that the individual personal funds of members, officials or trustees should not be liable in any case where they were sued on behalf of a union or employers' association. It is noteworthy that behind this clause of the Bill one can see, not Lord Morton's, but Lord MacDermott's analysis of union status.

Thus, after the *Bonsor* case, damages for wrongful expulsion could clearly be recovered from a registered union if the union ratified the act. Such a right survives the member's death; and in 1968 a widow recovered over £1,392 from the painters' union for her husband's expulsion. The liability of the unregistered union would, on Lord MacDermott's argument, be substantially the same; but the difficulties of bringing an action against it would be enhanced by all the many technical problems that attend the 'representative action' procedure.[10]

A member wrongly expelled is, like any other person injured by a breach of contract, under a duty to mitigate his losses. For example, he should take reasonable steps to secure readmission to the union, and, if he has lost a job, he ought to take any other suitable job which is available. The case of the out-of-trade printer (p. 428) was one where the judge said he would have used that principle to reduce damages to a 'small' sum, had a breach been proved. Usually, the damages payable will be substantial only where the union organizes a 'closed shop', or some other 100 per cent membership practice which effectively closes the trade to the expelled member. The union will also run less risk of large damages if it can find a way merely to suspend the member until his case is decided, so that he does not have to leave work. In 1956 a worker who had refused to join his branch in a strike, called in opposition to a national agreement made by the union, was avowedly expelled by the branch for refusing to pay a £10 fine imposed upon him for bringing the union into discredit. The workers refused to work with him at the workplace. Eventually he offered to pay the £10, but the enraged local branch demanded a further £50 as the price of readmission to the union. He sued the union for wrongful expulsion, and the action was settled on the fourth day of the trial. The union paid him some £600, most of it for wages which he lost by reason of the wrongful 'expulsion', but £100 of it was by way of 'general damages' of an unspecified character.

In *Edwards* v. *S.O.G.A.T.*, 1970, the damages were higher.[11] The plaintiff, a Guyanese skilled worker in a firm with 100 per cent union membership, had once been a full member but after a dispute (unexplained in the report) became a 'temporary' member of the union. He authorized the necessary 'check-off' from his wages but the union failed to arrange this by reason of a muddle. He therefore fell into arrears and, under the rule providing for forfeiture of membership for non-payment, ceased (it was thought) to be a member. In consequence, the employer gave him notice and he lost his job. He refused to take labourer's jobs; obtained a skilled job in a non-union firm; but lost it through an argument, but without misconduct on his part. The union, which acted as an employment exchange for members and had refused to readmit him (though it did readmit four other workers), now belatedly admitted its mistake. Yet it still offered him only inferior jobs. The Court of Appeal awarded him £3,500. The exclusion from membership caused by the union's own mistake was clearly wrongful. His loss of earnings up to trial were not, the court held, to be reduced by reason of his failure to take other jobs; he had acted reasonably throughout to mitigate his damage. But the court reduced the trial judge's award of nearly £8,000 because of a second element: 'a quantification of the difference to his future earning capacity likely thereafter to result from the Union's wrongful act' (Lord Justice Sachs). Although the union now agreed to full membership, the appeal judges, by three rather different methods of calculation, added a further sum for future losses in that respect. They would not calculate loss of capacity as if he had suffered personal injury; the future loss rested, Lord Justice Megaw said, on 'hypothesis and speculation'. If future legislation does give such a worker a right to sue his employer for unjust dismissal before an industrial tribunal (p. 146), provision will have to be made for the relationship of such damages to compensation for unlawful expulsion from a union. The measure of compensation was the core of the *Edwards* case, and one appeal judge kept carefully to that issue. But public interest centred on the dicta of the other judges, as we have seen (p. 432), to which we return (p. 458).

The breach of the rules will often be (as in *Bonsor*'s case itself) a technical accident (like the branch secretary failing to call the branch committee before he acts). A survey in 1961 investigated the 40,000 workers who were voluntary branch secretaries spending on average about eleven hours a week of their own time keeping British unions running, and paid no more than £1 a week; and the 90,000 local union representatives (shop stewards and the like), four fifths of them regularly re-elected by small groups of workers at the place of work. The Donovan Report found that, with only 3,000 full-time officers, the British compared unfavourably with most other trade union movements. 'British trade unions are under-manned and under-financed', declared *In Place of Strife*. While this is clearly true there are merits in the use of part-time officials who are inevitably close to the feelings of the shop floor; and it was with this in mind that in 1956 *The Times* Labour Correspondent wrote on the new liability created by the *Bonsor* judgment:

From the trade union point of view, the danger is that they have many spare-time officials who may inadvertently break their rules and thus involve the union in damages.

The concern increased after *Rookes* v. *Barnard*, 1964. As we have seen (p. 364), the House of Lords there classified, for the first time in English law, breach of contract as wholly unlawful in character. A threat of expulsion which would be improper, therefore, might (subject to the Act of 1965, p. 371) found an action for intimidation. Further, a plaintiff might prefer to couch his action not as one for breach of contract but as one for a 'conspiracy to cause injury by illegal means, viz., the expulsion in breach of contract'. Also, since 1969, could the member ever sue for 'interference' with his contract of membership (or of employment) by union officials because of the new tort outlined by Lord Denning in the *Torquay Hotel* case? Success in such a tort action might well lead to the award of a larger sum of damages than a simple contract action could produce. In such an action, too, the liability in damages of the individual branch officers might be easier to prove.

The ways of judge-made law are hard to predict – as *Rookes* v. *Barnard* showed – but it would not be impossible for strange new fruit to be produced out of litigation which, as it were, crossed the stock of the *Rookes* and the *Bonsor* varieties of legal liability, especially if a tint of *Torquay Hotel* coloured the produce. There is an urgent need for statutory reform to pay special attention to the protection of the voluntary official who acts mistakenly but honestly. The member whose wrongful expulsion is insisted on by his union should undoubtedly have a right to claim for reasonable compensation; but the juridical basis of that liability should be made more stable and certain than the jungle of the *Bonsor* judgments.

We may here note, however, how thin are the arguments in the Donovan Report for compulsory registration and incorporation as the only proper way to solve this problem. Given that the speech of Lord MacDermott does represent the present law, there are few problems now in respect of the *registered* union. The Report, however, insists that even if all *unincorporated* bodies were given a right to sue and be sued (a step which would need only a simple amendment of the Rules of Procedure, and one which the judges have recently taken even without the amendment),[12] still 'some measure of compulsory registration' would enter in, since 'claimants would need to consult some register' of unions. The history of partnerships shows that this is just not so. Partnerships are unincorporated but have been able to sue and be sued in the 'firm name' under Rules of Procedure scarcely altered since 1891. No one has ever felt the need of any general register! There is nothing whatever in the *Bonsor* problem to support such an idea. In order to solve the *Bonsor* muddle all that is needed is a simple change in the technical Rules of Procedure.

NATURAL JUSTICE AND THE CLOSED SHOP

Expulsion and other disciplinary union rules, being drawn up by fallible men, sometimes inevitably fail to spell out everything clearly. Where the procedure for hearing a charge is not clearly specified, the judges have always implied that the 'principles of Natural Justice' must be observed. What those principles amount to is not wholly clear. There has for example been judicial disagreement in 1969 about how far they necessarily involve a right to legal representation at a hearing.[13] In 1929, Mr Justice Maugham said: 'the phrase is of course used only in a popular sense and must not be taken to mean that there is any justice natural among men'. It can only be understood in the context of the particular occasion. Union officials deciding a case can only be asked to act in good faith and not to make up their minds before the hearing, to show 'a will to reach an honest conclusion ... however strongly they had shared in previous adverse criticism of the [member's] conduct' (Viscount Simon, 1951). The law does not require even of the commercial arbitrator, said Lord Justice Bowen in 1893, 'the icy impartiality of Rhadamanthus'. So in *Maclean* v. *Workers' Union*, 1929,[14] an Executive Committee which, after a hearing, had come honestly to its decision had not (the judge held) violated Natural Justice even though its members all along had strong views about the expelled member's breach of a rule limiting circulars in union elections.

But honesty is not enough. The courts will also demand that the member be given an opportunity to be heard, with notice of the charges against him and a reasonable chance of answering them. This aspect of Natural Justice has been applied strictly to union affairs. In 1961, an expelled member of a Trinidad oilfield union appealed to the Privy Council. He had had notice of the hearing, and denied the charges; but the meeting had been adjourned to a later date, when he could not attend because of a prior engagement at a Mock Trial with a 'Girls' Group' ('a poor excuse', Lord Denning thought). At the second meeting, the charges were framed slightly differently, to allow for his expulsion. This was enough to vitiate the proceedings.[15] He should have been given adequate notice of the new charges. In England, in 1962, a member who was disciplined by the Tailors Union for writing a pamphlet, published by the Communist Party, which allegedly contravened union rules, obtained an injunction on the ground that the committee had given no notice either of the charges or of the hearing to him, in violation of the principles of Natural Justice. Moreover, the decision in *Leary* v. *The National Union of Vehicle Builders*, 1970,[16] shows that a fair domestic appeal will not, in the eyes of the law, cure an unfair hearing which violated the principles.

The member is, in fact, legally often in a superior position to the full-time union official for the latter is, in the ordinary case, an employee of the union subject to the principles of law discussed in Chapter 3. But in *Taylor* v. *National Union of Seamen*, 1967,[17] Mr Taylor was both an official of the union and a member. He was dismissed from his post as official for disobedience when he defied the General Secretary's orders on what he felt was a matter of trade union principles. Such a dismissal made him ineligible for certain posts for which union members were normally eligible. But he had a right of appeal to the Executive Council which he exercised. He appeared and answered the charges, which the rules said must be set out in full before the appeal. Then he withdrew. The General Secretary (chairman of the meeting) then addressed the Council, making further allegations, such as that he had 'communist associations' to which no opportunity to reply was ever given. Mr Justice Ungoed-Thomas had no doubt that the appeal proceedings were invalid. The General Secretary had not only acted from the chair as prosecutor (a 'role which he most amply filled'); he had even introduced new prejudicial allegations which had to remain unanswered. The problem was the remedy. As an employee, Taylor could not be granted a declaration about his contract of service (which in any case was terminable 'at pleasure' in this case). But as a *member* he could obtain a declaration protecting his full rights, including eligibility for all posts. Similarly, Mr Hiles, a carpenter, who was alleged to have broken the woodworkers' union rules by sending out a circular opposing the Government's 'wages freeze' and was expelled, obtained in 1967 an injunction to stop the union from acting on the decision. The judge thought that the rule book had not been complied with and Mr Hiles had not been given the opportunity to be heard at an appeal committee as natural justice demanded.[18]

But the procedure is ultimately controlled by the union rules. What if the rules exclude some part of 'Natural Justice'? A view has recently grown up that there is a principle of law that the rule book cannot do so and that 'Natural Justice' principles can be imposed by the court whenever it wishes. Lord Justice Denning (as he then was) said, indeed, in 1952 that such a stipulation to oust Natural Justice would be invalid. Such a view is open to question. It is undoubtedly the case that union rules mainly do adhere in practice to basic standards of Natural Justice and, despite cases like those just described, the Donovan Report agreed unions operate within them in a vast majority of cases. But infrequency of injustice is no reason for denying a remedy, though it is a good reason for fitting the remedy to the needs of overall union security. Surely, the member can always rely on Natural Justice. But there are strong reasons for believing that the rule book can control its own procedures entirely. First, the application of Natural Justice principles always depends on 'the circumstances of the case, the nature of the inquiry, the rules under which the tribunal is acting ... and so forth,' said Lord Justice Tucker in 1949.[19] The court found that the Jockey Club's rules did not demand any hearing at all by the stewards. So they could not possibly be challenged for holding a 'defective' hearing about withdrawal of a licence. If it is open to the rule book to give a committee a completely unrestricted discretion, the principles of Natural Justice cannot possibly be mandatory rules of law; for they can only apply where a hearing is required. That was the view taken in *Maclean* v. *Workers' Union*, 1929. But in *Hiles*'s case, 1967, the judge appeared to throw doubt upon the statements in *Maclean* v. *Workers' Union*. After these cases, and the *Edwards* case, 1970 (p. 432 and p. 458), it seems clear that many judges are insistent that the regulatory new view must be adopted.

Secondly, however, the new view contains a logical difficulty. The courts' jurisdiction is now based on the 'contract' in the rule book. How then can the court go on to refuse to enforce one stipulation of the parties' contract merely because it ousts 'Natural Justice'? In 1954, sensing this difficulty, Lord Justice Denning went on to claim that union rules were 'more like bye-laws than a contract ... if it should be found that any of those rules are contrary to natural justice or, what comes to the same thing, contrary to what is fair and reasonable, the court would hold them to be invalid'. This statement has vast implications, for it would mean that the courts were claiming powers to rewrite the rule book. Neither *In Place of Strife* nor even *Fair Deal at Work* suggested giving anyone that power. What is put in issue by the statement is the continued treatment of union rules as a contract made in an autonomous voluntary body – whether, in fact, the courts can themselves single out trade unions (because of their effect on workers' livelihood) for extra regulation.

In *Faramus* v. *Film Artistes Association*, 1964,[20] it was held that the courts would not go that far. In the Court of

Appeal Lord Justice Diplock declared that there is 'no principle of public policy which entitles a court to treat as void a term of a contract because it is unreasonable', and the House of Lords displayed the same attitude. It is for members, not the court, to decide what is 'reasonable'. The same case shows that whatever the right view of the rules may be, the Natural Justice argument strictly applies only to disciplinary *hearings* and the like. The Donovan Report confirmed this view by making its special 'two-year amnesty' proposal for such cases (see p. 415). The plaintiff belonged – or thought he belonged – to a union organizing all London film artistes, among whom unemployment rates would be high unless admission were severely restricted to about a quarter of the applications. The union rules aimed to exclude, amongst others, dishonest persons; but in pursuit of this aim they went so far as to declare that no person convicted of *any* criminal offence (except minor motoring offences) was *eligible* to enter or retain membership of the union. After he had been a member for some years, the union discovered that Faramus had been convicted of certain offences when seventeen years old, many years before, in Jersey.

The law report does not disclose why the union suddenly challenged Faramus's membership in this way, except that his youthful convictions had been discovered. When he signed the application forms for the union he had stated that he had never been convicted of a criminal offence specified by this rule. (This misrepresentation would give the union a right to rescind his membership on ordinary principles; but the right to rescind is subject to certain limits, and the case was not fought on that point.) The union was no doubt keen to uphold the rule book to the letter. Its membership was about 1,700; but it received some 5,000 applications a year. Lord Justice Upjohn said: 'if the membership were allowed to increase much beyond the present figures their members would hardly earn a living wage'. Lord Pearce in the House of Lords commented:

For, if all who wished were admitted, there would not be an adequate living for any. This rule is partly directed to that purpose and it is no more unfair to keep out one man because he has been convicted albeit trivially, and so to put another in his place, than to keep persons out simply because there is no room for them.

The rule, if looked at in the context of this particular union's collective needs, becomes at least intelligible, even if wider than most people would think necessary. No doubt the Committee thought it would be unfair to the man kept out to let Faramus stay in improperly. The pundits who used this (wholly unusual) rule in this rule book to pontificate on the evils of union rule books generally would have made a better case if they had advanced draft rules that were 'fairer' for excluding thousands of intending film-extras annually from their desired profession which cannot provide enough jobs for all. One suspects that some critics would introduce a 'free market' by law to allow all 5,000 into the profession, thereby driving wages down. But that is precisely what the union would not accept. And if the law were to introduce some new tribunal to adjudicate on the validity of 'arbitrary' refusals to admit (whatever the rules say) would that tribunal not be bound to become the arbiter, in a *Faramus*-type case, of the wages of film-extras?

In the 1964 case itself, Faramus's supposed membership was found *never* to have existed in law. The House of Lords had little option but to hold that his admission was *ultra vires* the union; and, therefore, he had, in law, *never been* a member at all. No question of expulsion arose. No ratification of his void membership was possible, even though he had served on the union's committee. It is arguable that a carefully drafted rule could have this same effect with existing members, making them 'ineligible' and their membership *automatically* at an end, on given events (e.g. on arrears in subscription of 26 weeks as in *Bonsor*'s case). Some lawyers think the courts might try to impose a requirement of 'Natural Justice' if the existing member is thus automatically deprived of membership rights. But it is not easy to see how they could do so if the rule book clearly provided for *automatic* ineligibility and no hearing. If it became *ultra vires* to retain him in membership, the union could not in law keep him; and no 'expulsion' or the like would be required. If disciplinary 'hearings' are subjected to outside control which the unions find oppressive, they may well turn to automatic termination rules. That very few such rules are unfairly used is a proof, as Donovan puts it, that 'it is unlikely that abuse of power by trade unions is widespread' – a modest way of putting the results of the research team's work.

These are no more than legal consequences of the *ultra vires* doctrine and of the rule book being treated like any other 'contract', a status it acquires with no greater degree of fiction than many other modern agreements. Some critics have made proposals for new judicial intervention in order to secure a 'right to work' for a worker.[21] Lord Justice Denning founded his judgment in 1952 on the notion that unions 'can deprive a man of his livelihood. ... A man's right to work is just as important to him as, if not more important than, his rights of property.' It is astonishing that English legal commentators usually discuss this 'right to work' as though it meant merely the right to do what the worker chooses to do whilst electing not to belong to a trade union. Some of those who gave evidence to the Royal Commission have even suggested that the right not to belong to a trade union should be protected by means of a new action in tort. And Mr Shonfield, questioning the Ministry of Labour witnesses about workers trained by ways other than traditional apprenticeships but refused admittance to a union, spoke of them 'really being refused the right to work'. He put it better in the previous question where he spoke of the 'right to an opportunity to try for a certain job'.[22] To most workers the 'right to work' is primarily concerned with the maintenance of full employment; the availability of suitable work for which the worker is trained; and job-security by way of protection from arbitrary dismissal. Even analytically it is wrong for lawyers to talk of any 'right' to work as our law now stands. As Dr Rideout has said: 'The "right to work" is plainly not a "right" nor is its distinction from the right to a particular job anywhere made clear, and it is not clear how far freedom to choose one's employment can be cut back before the "right" is infringed'.[23] Moreover, experience in the U.S.A. of 'right to work' laws shows that they are habitually a means for decreasing trade union power when it comes to decision-making at the place of work.

This description of the 'right to work' formula was justified anew by the remarks of Lord Denning in *Edwards* v. *S.O.G.A.T.*, 1970, [23a] a case in which the union seemed to have few merits. As we saw (p. 432), Lord Denning once again tried to reject the fiction of the rule book contract; and he was thus able to assert judicial power not merely over the exercise of union procedures but over the very content of union rules. Thus, he could say that no trade union

can give itself by its rules an unfettered discretion to expel a man or to withdraw his membership. The reason lies in the man's right to work.

With this conceptual bludgeon he struck down the S.O.G.A.T. rule that provided for automatic forfeiture of membership in cases of six weeks' arrears. The rule was 'invalid' in itself! That such rules in some form are essential to the trade union movement and its organizational efficiency (whether or not new limits should be placed on their extent) could not be a factor to be considered within the narrow judicial logic. Moreover, Lord Denning refused to allow special rules applying to 'temporary' members to curtail a worker's rights. On his view, it seems that the judges can overrule the democratic decision of a union to have any rule (as here) that temporary members shall have no right of appeal, as other members do, to the Executive Committee. Lord Denning declared all such rules that impose an 'unwarranted encroachment on the right to work' to be *ultra vires*. Clearly, on his view, all union rules about expulsion or even admission which attract judicial displeasure are unlawful. But his doctrine of a 'right to work' does not, apparently, extend to employers' control of job opportunities. One is constrained to ask why.

Lord Justice Megaw in *Edwards* wisely refused to deal with these matters in a case that was essentially concerned with computation of damages. Lord Justice Sachs also did not deal with the wider aspects of Lord Denning's statements, such as control of the power to admit to the union. But the latter *did* agree with Lord Denning on two points. Unions could deprive a worker of membership neither 'for completely arbitrary

reasons nor in a way which does not accord with natural justice'
– whatever the rules said. There must be 'some proper ground'
for termination. Thus, the disabilities of the 'temporary' member in this case were *ultra vires* the union. What, though, of the
1871 Act and of the *Faramus* case?

The latter decision (virtually ignored by Lord Denning) Lord
Justice Sachs distinguished as a case not about expulsion but
about 'eligibility' for admission. But, as we have seen, this distinction is not a logical line at which to stop once judges claim
to control the *substance* (rather than the procedural fair play)
of exclusion rules. He further held that a rule 'in these days of
closed shops' which allows a union to exclude a member 'for
any capricious reason' (including the 'colour of his skin' – a
bad example, since his lordship surely overlooked the Race Relations Act, 1968, p. 416) *is in restraint of trade*. But section 3
of the 1871 Act has for a century established that the purposes
of a trade union shall not be unlawful so as to render its
agreements (including its rules) void by reason of the *restraint
of trade* doctrine. True, Lord Justice Sachs agreed; but section
3 did not apply because:

It cannot be said that a rule that enabled such capricious and despotic action is proper to the 'purposes' of this or indeed of any
trade union.

Lord Denning, in similar vein, said a union existed to protect
the right of each member to earn his living; that was its 'very
purpose'; so rules which destroyed that right or interfered with
it 'oppressively' were invalid.

This extraordinary revival of the judicial desire to control
union rule books by way of the doctrine of restraint of trade –
for the rules which might *enable* despotic decisions must run
into thousands – seemed likely in 1970 to provoke firm trade
union opposition.

The merits of the *Edwards* case were on the face of it wholly
with the plaintiff. All the Court of Appeal had to decide was
the amount of damages. To use the opportunity to establish
new judicial control over union rules by way of the ambiguous
phrase 'right to work' and an assertion of power for judges to

say what are the 'proper' purposes of a union in terms which will scarcely seem sophisticated to students of industrial relations, is little less than a disaster for the law and its relationship with working people. It will cloud the issues in the debate about new legislation; and it will confirm the worst fears of the policies harboured by the judiciary towards trade unions. The *Edwards* case may, however, be authority for no more than its approach to quantification of damages and the proposition that union rules cannot exclude natural justice from procedures employed in excluding a member. The other dicta of Lord Denning and Lord Justice Sachs are, it is respectfully submitted, bad law in that they fly in the face of principles established in the 1871 Act and by a long period of case law culminating in the *Faramus* decision. For a century, rules for automatic forfeiture and discretionary expulsion (e.g. if the executive committee thinks it proper) have been treated as valid by both unions and courts. It is suggested that they still are valid. Were the new judgments to be upheld the judges would have succeeded in overturning the fundamental settlement of 1871 on which trade unions have grown up. Extension of judge-made law over union rules as a devious method of limiting the 'closed shop' is an unwise and improper use of judicial powers. Constitutionally and politically, whether the law is to change or remain unchanged, Parliament not the judges should be the arbiter.

Trade unionists are likely to go on seeking 100 per cent membership or other 'union security' arrangements in Britain in order to assert the right *not* to have to work with non-unionists (who nevertheless take the benefits of collective bargaining). Few non-unionists reject the wage won by union negotiators. 'Given religious and political freedom,' Professor Grunfeld puts it, 'freedom not to join a union ... amounts to freedom ... to take a free ride on the backs of one's fellow workers.' [24] Problems of great difficulty do arise in the 'closed shop', e.g. if a worker registers some truly conscientious objection to joining the union. We have seen that the Donovan Report found that trade unions 'in the main respect conscientious objectors'. Often an arrangement is made for such workers to pay to a charity, as in 1965 when the Bakers' Union agreed that conscientious objectors at a Midlands firm could pay the amount of the weekly subscription, 2s. 3d., to a charity named by the union, the district secretary, Mr Mullarkey, saying this would 'cater for those who genuinely feel that they cannot join a union and also deter those people who want something for nothing'. Where objectors are dismissed, the proposed 1970 Bill realistically proposed to give them a right to claim against the employer for unjust dismissal since it was 'to the advantage of his business' to dismiss the worker (*In Place of Strife*: see p. 144), although, as the Donovan Report said, the tribunal will clearly have to 'take into account' the worker's 'reason for refusing to join a union and whether he has in some way provoked the action of his fellow workers'. The pressure on the employer from such workers is often intense; for no one likes someone else taking a free ride on his back. In 1962, one judge in the Court of Appeal said of Rookes that he, 'whilst outside the union and avoiding its obligations, would enjoy such benefits as the union could achieve from the employers for its members. This might well not be acceptable to his colleagues.' These are, at least, not simple 'David and Goliath' problems to be solved merely by slinging pebbles at trade unions.

In his classic review of 'closed shop' practices in Britain, Dr McCarthy welcomes the possible extension of 100 per cent unionism.[25] The 'closed shop' affected in 1964 about three and three quarter million workers, about one in six of the total workforce, but about two in five of trade union members. Far more manual workers are involved than non-manual. The Donovan Report thought its total extent was about the same in 1968. About a fifth of workers in closed shops are in

some sort of pre-entry shop and are subject to various forms of entry control. About a half are in formally recognized closed shops or are employed in industries where the great majority of employers will cooperate in its implementation. [McCarthy]

He describes the functional justifications of this practice that may make it necessary for the development of sufficient collective strength at work, for 'job regulation' or the determination of conditions of employment. McCarthy rejects 'any essential difference between allowing unions to use collective sanctions in an attempt to regulate wages and conditions, and permitting the enforcement of entry control via the closed shop'. (The English courts reached that position in their conspiracy developments in the *Reynolds* (1924) and *Crofter* (1942) cases.) He also says: '... there is no convincing evidence that at present there are any industries or trades where the power of the unions, derived partly from the closed shop, is a *crucial* factor in limiting efficiency.' As for a court to control 'restrictive practices' and the like among unions, he demonstrates that the 'simple assumptions' of the Restrictive Practices Act, 1956, about competition in industry cannot be applied to the complex questions of 'determining the public interest' in the field of industrial relations and Chapter VI of the Donovan Report (with a dissent from Mr Shonfield) proves him right.

The extent of the 'pre-entry shop', extending sometimes to the running of union employment exchanges as in the cases which we met concerning printing unions, makes doubly important the discussion about new legal controls over union admissions and expulsions. Despite the undoubted need of trade unionists to protect and preserve the legality of the various forms of 100 per cent membership, there is a need also to improve the protection afforded to members in some unions. This is not just a question of better 'appeal procedures' or having 'independent appeal bodies' (like the iron and steel workers' union), though these no doubt can assist. Each union rule book needs careful consideration by the membership to see that it is suited to the union, and each section of it. The vast variety of rules discovered by the T.U.C. in 1970 about arrears and 'lapsing' disclosed a pattern more attributable to history than to logic. But once more, the T.U.C. initiative is likely to be more flexible and successful than any law.

Attention to such problems, however, is more urgently required when the trade union has made a 'closed discipline' type of agreement with employers, i.e. one where on losing union membership a man normally loses his job and *vice versa*, or where the union collaborates with the employer in enforcing disciplinary penalties against workers, e.g. by withdrawal of fringe benefits or seniority rights or even imposing fines. (The former arose in the *Edwards* case, p. 448, and the latter is illustrated by the electrical contracting industry agreements made in 1967 by the E.T.U. under which a Joint Industry Board appointed on a long-term basis by union and employers can impose a spectrum of sanctions from 'forfeiture of all or any welfare benefits' to a fine of up to £100 on a worker for any one offence or £1,000 on an employer.) In such cases, the worker must look elsewhere for his defence if his union jointly with the employer turns upon him. It is a consciousness that workers' confidence in the union may in the long term be reduced by such agreements that has led some unions to be chary of agreeing to 'penal clauses', as in the *Ford* case (Chapter 4). Thus the A.E.U. have long opposed such clauses; and in 1969, the T.G.W.U. conference unanimously passed a motion refusing to negotiate such clauses. Mr Jack Jones, its General Secretary-elect, said they would avoid them 'like the plague' because 'they weaken trade union organization at the place of work where we want organization to be strong'; and added that officials would insist that workers themselves be consulted when new agreements were negotiated – a policy which encourages hopes for the Donovan Report's policy of factory agreements in which men on the works' floor have confidence. On the other hand, employers have come to see a closed-shop arrangement as desirable where it includes clauses of this kind whereby they can have the help of the union in preventing or penalizing strikes.

Worse still, an employer who enjoys a comfortable 'closed-shop and check-off' arrangement with a union which has fallen out of touch with the spirit of a large number of its local members can be lulled into a sense of false security shattered later by an explosion of industrial conflict. Such a situation arose prior to the strike at Pilkingtons in 1970, when some 8,000 employees stopped work against the wishes of their union (G.M.W.). Eventually, the unofficial leaders and the union

collaborated in talks at the T.U.C. and in arranging a ballot
which secured a return to work. But feelings were bitter; the
union broke off the T.U.C. talks; and the unofficial leaders
threatened to lead thousands of workers out of the union. True
to their word, they delivered 4,000 workers' forms to the employer demanding cessation of their personal 'check-off' deductions. The truck legislation (p. 223) seemed to give them
the right to do so; but there was doubt whether the employer's
agreement with the union allowed it. The 'closed discipline'
situation puts a premium on the sensitivity of the union's own
officials to respond to their members' wishes. A Pilkington
manager was reported as saying: 'We would never have had
this trouble if the union had been more militant'. Other unions
said they could not take the men into membership until they
ceased to be members of the G.M.W., because that would be
'poaching' contrary to the principles of the Bridlington Agreement; and the Chemical Workers' Union secretary, apparently
relying on G. M. W. rules about lapsing, said they would remain
members of G.M.W. for 'many months'. Some 4,000 workers,
however, resigned and set up their own breakaway union, with
which management refused to negotiate. The relationship between 'poaching' and resignations appeared to need further
consideration by the T.U.C. in its proposals for reform of rule
books. Moreover, where the closed shop is buttressed by a
'check off' and a 'closed discipline' system is in operation, it
would not perhaps be unreasonable for the law to give each
worker the right to resign from his union as easily as he can
withdraw from the 'check-off' arrangement (whatever the terms
of the union rule book or of the union's closed-shop agreement
with the employer).

Cases of severe unfairness do arise, and we have seen in the
Huntley case (p. 331) and *Edwards* case (p. 448) that the
common law does not wholly lack weapons for redress. The
Donovan Report showed, however, that while the closed shop
does not always avoid injustice to individuals or harm to the
community, these are the exceptions not the rule. As for the
argument (widely accepted in Europe) that workers should have
a right *not* to belong to a union if the law gives them (as is

proposed in Britain in 1970) a right to join a union, the Report tersely destroys that false congruence, saying:

The two are not truly comparable. The former condition is designed to frustrate the development of collective bargaining which it is public policy to promote, whereas no such objection applies to the latter.

All in all, the Report demonstrates that legal 'prohibition of the closed shop must be rejected'. Any other conclusion would have set the rights of working people back forty years. There is, of course, a sense in which even one's judgement of 'functional justifications' of practices such as the closed shop will depend, in the last resort, on just how strong one thinks a trade union ought to be. But fruitful progress in trade union law will stem surely from discussion based upon the premise that, in Dr McCarthy's words: '... every worker ought to join his appropriate trade union'.

T.U.C., UNION AND MEMBER

Lastly, what is the 'appropriate' union if there are two unions in the relevant field of industry? Inter-union disputes have often caused great difficulty and, as Mr George Woodcock said in 1963 to the T.U.C., we cannot hope for a 'uniform structure, especially an industrial structure' in British unionism in the near future: 'We have to face as a fact that diversity is with us and will be with us.'

This diversity can create serious problems either because each of many occupational groups in a factory is organized by a different union, or because more than one union is claiming certain work as its right or competing for members or demanding sole right to recognition for certain workers. The need to reorganize trade unions on an 'industrial' basis, one for each industry, is sometimes described as if it were just a matter of moving workers from one organization to another by writers who would resist to the death forcible transfer from their club. In any case 'industrial unions' would entail the destruction of huge unions which have their roots either in craft (e.g. the

A.E.U.) or as general workers' unions (the T.G.W.U.). The tendencies, in fact, of all major unions have been towards becoming 'large "open" unions' which take a 'broad definition of their sector of operation' and this is 'likely to extend overlapping' among unions.[26] The old type of 'demarcation' dispute about 'who-does-what' is declining. It is not multi-unionism which is the worst problem. It is conflict and competition *between* overlapping unions.

The disputes which have caused more difficulty recently have been about competition for members and for recognition, sometimes involving rivalry between a union preferred by employers and another trying to extend its membership (an element in the background to the *Torquay Hotel* case: p. 334). The competition in 1969 between three unions to be recognized by the British Steel Corporation for white-collar workers illustrates the problem. On rare occasions the question is settled in court, as in the case of the Dock Workers Order,[27] but that is quite exceptional. In the steel dispute, involving a fight between the Clerical Workers' union, A.S.T.M.S., and I.S.T.C., (with a fourth corner occupied by the new Steel Industry Management Association), victory was won at T.U.C. level by I.S.T.C. in effect because it could bring into battle the biggest battalions, namely the bulk of the *blue*-collar steel workers, to back its claim. The situation was a good illustration of the difficulties which would beset those who want to introduce legally defined 'units' of the American type into the present British situation, units in which workers would elect only one union as their bargaining 'agent'. According to the 'units' chosen (national; local; regional; all-white-collar; or grades) one could have produced one, two, three or four unions as bargaining 'agents' for all or some of these British Steel Corporation employees. In drawing the boundaries one would be attempting to solve the dispute; but, in truth, one would lay a further time-bomb of trouble if the bargaining spread – as it would – across the election unit boundaries. The problem was bad enough without that; and it may in one sense have ended in a result which does not allow some B.S.C. white-collar workers to be represented by the union of their current choice. Since the close of (or lull in) that battle, the C.I.R. has come upon the scene and on occasion its interventions may assist the T.U.C. As Mr Wigham wrote:

In the present state of union structure the only answer ... is to say that supervisors, and other white-collar workers, should belong to the unions that most of them want to belong to. ... The worst thing that could happen would be to alienate the unions by surrendering to the clamour to give the C.I.R. 'teeth'.[28]

It is inevitable that union rivalries where they exist will show up increasingly in the sphere of white-collar workers for this is the fastest growing pool of potential recruits.

What then are the machineries at the disposal of the T.U.C.? First, there is its Disputes Committee which every year makes 'awards' between contesting unions under the Bridlington Agreement. Such contests are sometimes between a big and a small, but on occasion even between two big unions; and 'poaching' of members is by no means dead. Mr Hughes reported that cases reported to and heard by the Disputes Committee were increasing; and recent evidence indicates that this is the case. In 1956 only 4 cases were heard; in 1969 there were 23. In the years 1962 to 1965 there were 46 awards; in 1966 to 1969, 66. While this suggests an increasing problem, it also probably indicates an increasing willingness of unions to use the Disputes Committee. For whereas a study of awards made up to 1957 showed that the Committee stuck to rigid attitudes, especially on transfers of members, in later years it has adopted a more flexible approach.[29] But, of course, its 'awards' have no legal force; the only sanction is disaffiliation or suspension of an errant union. Indeed the law may obstruct the implementation of an award; we saw (p. 444) an example in *Spring*'s case, 1956. (Also in *Spring*'s case the court agreed that the Bridlington Agreement was not intended by the unions making it to be a legal contract.) In a similar case of 1955, a judge prevented expulsions forced by the T.U.C. on an 'unwilling' union (with the sanction of disaffiliation 'hanging over their heads') because that union's rules also contain no power to expel in order to obey the T.U.C. Committee. But we saw (p. 444) that many affiliated unions have today taken power to expel when an award makes it necessary to do so. In such cases, the worker's freedom to remain in the union of his choice is limited in the interests of the movement as a whole and its need to organize effectively.

Secondly, as a result of the continuing review of trade unionism set on foot at the 1962 T.U.C. there has been encouragement of amalgamation, or federation, of unions into more compact units. The General Council initiated discussions on amalgamation among various groups of unions and by 1966 Mr Hughes remarked: 'Ten years ago it would have been a brave man who would have forecast even such amalgamations and widespread discussions on structure and closer unity as have occurred'.[30]

In later years the rate of amalgamations (which may take the form of a straight merger or of a 'transfer of engagements' by one union to another) has remained steady. Between 1963 and 1969 there were 38 such amalgamations, some of them operations involving more than two organizations (such as formation of an amalgamated union in 1963 out of three unions, the Associated Blacksmiths, the Boilermakers and the Shipwrights). Some transfers involved small numbers, such as that of the Cardiff, Penarth and Barry Coal Trimmers' 50 members to the T.G.W.U. in 1968. Others were of larger unions, such as the E.T.U. amalgamation with the Plumbers in 1968 to form the E.E.T.U.–P.T.U. of some 350,000 members. The movement towards mergers continued at a galloping pace in 1970. A.S.T.M.S. took under its wing the 5,000 members of the Medical Practitioners' Union; the Prudential Insurance staff associations (5,000); and, subject to a final ballot, the Union of Insurance Staffs (16,000). The woodworkers by taking in the painters and the building technicians put their membership up to 315,000. Five footwear and leather workers' unions planned to amalgamate in a new union (N.U.F.L.A.T.; 87,000). It has become a common practice to find a larger union merging with a small one but preserving for the latter a degree of trade autonomy, and sometimes a separate group structure of its own, under the umbrella of the merged organization. Thus the Foundry Workers kept a separate identity when merging with the A.E.U. in 1967; and the A.U.E.F.W. then used similar techniques on taking in the construction engineers and D.A.T.A. in 1970, putting membership of the A.U.E.W. (as the combined union was to become) up to 1·3 million, and securing in D.A.T.A. a new platform from which to launch a drive for technical white-collar members, often in competition with such unions as A.S.T.M.S. or the T.G.W.U. The latter could absorb other unions conveniently into its different trade groups, such as the Scottish Motormen's and Amalgamated File unions in 1970, moving to over 1·5 million members. Meanwhile I.S.T.C. courted the blast-furnacemen; the seamen dallied with the T.G.W.U.; and the Vehicle Builders' union considered terms offered by both T.G.W.U. and A.U.E.W.

Until recently there have been complaints that the mergers have not taken place sufficiently quickly. Certainly some which were desired by many for a more rational structure have been thwarted, such as the amalgamation of the National Telephonists' Guild with the U.P.W. which was voted down at the last minute by the Guild's members. (The Post Office thereupon said it would not continue recognition, a situation full of the problems outlined for those who would not circumscribe sufficiently new *legal* duties of recognition: p. 165.) But the pace of mergers cannot be forced; and as Mr Hughes has said, it is faster than was once expected. The Donovan Report wanted to see an acceleration; and the T.U.C. had arranged discussion of the means for achieving this, beginning with its six national 'post-Donovan' conferences. Furthermore, the T.U.C. commented in 1968 that there should be 'more active discussion on rationalization in eliminating duplication'. In a sense, a lead has been given here both from the top and the bottom. At factory level there are 'combine committees' of shop stewards (which under the old definition are sometimes 'trade unions' in law and, as the Royal Commission suggests, should surely continue to receive the protection of the 1871 Act legalizing any 'restraint of trade'). These committees bring together stewards of many unions and sometimes many factories, for joint work. At the top, in 1964 the T.G.W.U. and G.M.W. began to negotiate a clarification of frontiers between them. By 1967, the two general unions had set up joint committees with the A.E.U. to 'deal with problems arising from conflict of interests'; and the three pledged their unions to stop mutual poaching. These committees have not always worked and there have been many unsolved allegations of 'poaching' between the three giants; but the committees have helped, and other leading unions (such as the N.U.R. and clerical workers) have in 1970 entered into similar joint committees which have even better prospects than those existing between the big three. Rumours began to abound that these three might fulfil Professor Turner's heterodox prophecy propounded some years earlier and amalgamate – dominating the T.U.C. with three and a half million members.

But this now seems very unlikely. Instead, the G.M.W. and E.P.T.U. have entered into preliminary discussions for the merger of their two organizations into a union of 1·2 million. The logic of this merger is said to be the organization of workers in certain industries (such as parts of construction and some utilities) along industrial lines, from manual workers to supervisors. But an additional explanation has been suggested, namely that the leaders of these unions felt closer to one another in policies, as against the 'left-wing' leaders of the T.G.W.U. and A.E.U. Spokesmen for the unions have denied that this is a serious motive, the G.M.W. national officer denying any plan to create 'giants of the Right against the giants of the Left'. Mr Wigham, it is true, once predicted a 'split' along those lines;[31] but the E.P.T.U.–G.M.W. merger has moved slowly since the first discussions in 1969; and it would be unfortunate if to the industrial problems of union structure were added any institutional dimensions of an ideological character.

Moreover, there are dangers of a similar character in a scramble into higgledy-piggledy amalgamations. The General Secretary of the Public Employees' union, Mr Fisher, warning against any attempt to divide the movement into two power blocs, added that, while steps must be taken to deal with competing unions,

If we are to get lasting benefits from reorganization, any mergers and amalgamations of unions must be the result of a logical identity of interests.[32]

But whose logic are we to apply? The advocates of 'general' unionism would see logic in amalgamating a whole range of workers in one union because workers have common interests; while the defenders of 'industrial' unionism would see logic lead in quite a different direction. What can be said is that 1970 has seen very little agreement among the leaders of the trade union movement as to where the right lines of development lie. One has felt that it would cause little surprise if, one morning, the Military and Orchestral Musical Instrument Makers (114 members) brought the Teston Independent Society of Cricket Ball Makers (36) into the T.U.C., merging the while with the Leeds Warpdressers, Twisters and Kindred Trades (144), the Spring Trapmakers (90) and Felt Hat Trimmers and Wool Formers (875, all ladies)! The resultant conglomerate could no doubt then negotiate good terms with a larger union. Clearly such small unions are unlikely to survive for long. The future seems to lie with a few giant 'general' unions, whatever they claim to be, with (unless they come into one or another giant) growing white-collar unions, like A.S.T.M.S., alongside them.

This prospect gives added importance to the development of joint working *arrangements*. These have proceeded at various levels and have been encouraged by the T.U.C. Some, of long standing, illustrate the flexible advantages of this approach; for example certain workers have long had, in effect, a joint membership of the Miners' Union and the T.G.W.U. In 1969 a joint committee for non-teaching university staffs was formed with representatives of N.U.P.E., N.A.L.G.O., A.S.T.M.S. and the T.U.C. itself. (The university teachers' association, A.U.T., is not affiliated to the T.U.C.; but at long last in 1970 it arranged for a – somewhat curious – form of collective bargaining for its members who teach the virtues of such a system.) Three television unions created a useful committee for joint bargaining in 1969; and in 1970 the T.U.C. cut through difficulties of long standing by inducing the E.P.T.U. and the sheet metal workers' union to sign a joint working agreement for settling the demarcation disputes which had frequently arisen between them. Of a rather different character, but fulfilling similar functions, is the formation of a federation of unions – the best known being the Confederation of Shipbuilding and Engineering Unions. Joint bargaining with employers and internal resolution of difficulties is thereby facilitated.

Even more important, perhaps, are the new initiatives which in 1970 became apparent in the T.U.C. itself. Not only did that body set up a new Collective Bargaining Committee. Plans were introduced for the formation of industrial committees. On renationalization of the industry, a Steel Committee had already been created; and a Construction Committee along the same lines was initiated. A series of industrial committees could transform the position of the T.U.C. in a world of giant 'general' unions. They might provide the bridge between the broad compass of these affiliated organizations and the bargaining at factory-floor level.

All these arrangements have occurred outside the area of the law. In its 1969 proposals and the 1970 Bill, the Labour Government suggested a statutory scheme for financial assistance of amalgamations, a 'Trade Union Development Scheme'. But from the outset trade union response was tepid, one leader saying, 'Nobody seems to know of any mergers being held up for lack of money'. But until 1964 the law had obstructed amalgamations. Any member can object to an amalgamation which is *ultra vires* or unlawful. Statutes of 1917 and 1940 demanded that union amalgamation or mergers should obtain special majorities (sometimes two thirds) in special ballots (that were sometimes required to be of 50 per cent of members voting). The Trade Union (Amalgamations) Act, 1964, reduces these legal hurdles to a more reasonable height.

The Act of 1964 permits amalgamation, or merger by transfer of engagements, after a satisfactory ballot, in which the proposal is approved by a simple majority of the votes recorded. This applies whatever the present union rules now say, although a new rule can be adopted by a union expressly excluding the new Act and imposing a higher majority if it wishes. A ballot is satisfactory only if certain minimum conditions are satisfied (e.g. each member must be entitled to vote without interference or constraint; have a fair opportunity of voting; and notice of the proposal). The Registrar must approve the notices sent out, and register the amalgamation. Arrangements are made for disposal of property and changes of name. Further, any member may complain to the Registrar if he alleges within six weeks that the voting arrangements do not satisfy the Act. The Registrar may, if he thinks fit, at the request of the union or the complainant, transfer a complaint to the High Court for its opinion on a question of law; but otherwise the validity of the resolution approving amalgamation 'shall not be questioned in any legal proceedings whatsoever' on grounds which could have been put before him. The courts are, therefore, broadly excluded from jurisdiction over the voting arrangements required by the Act except where one of the parties requests the Registrar to take the view of the judges on a matter of law. It is of no small interest that the Act passed quietly and quickly through Parliament. The trade union movement and the Government no doubt both wished to be rid of the inconvenient and archaic regulation of amalgamation by the earlier statutes; but the insertion of a jurisdiction for the Registrar was, perhaps, an additional reason for quieting any fears felt by the trade unions about an Act that does after all slightly extend statutory control over the rule book.

Some provisions have caused difficulty in the 1964 Act, such as the section stating that 'every member of the union must be entitled to vote ... without interference or constraint and must, so far as is reasonably possible, be given a fair opportunity of voting', and 'all reasonable steps must have been taken by the union to secure that, not less than seven days before voting ... begins, every member of the union is supplied' with the necessary notice in writing. This part of the Act overrides the rules if necessary. *Every* member is entitled to vote and reasonable steps must be taken to communicate with *every* member, not just members specified in the rules. Thus, it has been said that members entitled to vote include every class 'such as new members, apprentices, learners, unskilled workers or juveniles, whose right to vote on all or any matters may be limited by the rules'.[33] This approach is clearly correct. In 1969, Mr Justice Pennycuick decided that the amalgamation of the

National Graphical Association with the Lithographic Printers' Society was valid, despite the fact that the rules did not allow apprentice members to vote, when they had voted on the amalgamation. In 1967, a Mr Stevens objected to the amalgamation of his union of electrotypers, also with the N.G.A., because on 5 July 1967 the union sent out packets of notices to branches. Mr Stevens distributed them to his branch on 11 July. One member of a branch voted on 11 July; but most members voted in August. The Registrar agreed that the words of the Act ('not less than seven days before voting begins') had been broken. But the union had taken all reasonable steps; the merger had been approved by a three to one majority and only 21 members supported the complaint: so he refused to upset the amalgamation. Such decisions based on common sense would make it a pity to remove the jurisdiction of the Registrar on these matters.

Lastly there is the wider aspect of union structure. This, too, is of great concern to the individual member. As we saw in Chapter I (p. 35), the proposals of *In Place of Strife* for a new law on recognition order in multi-union situations (backed by financial penalties) were dropped in favour of the T.U.C. proposals to use voluntary methods. The proposals to revise the T.U.C. rules had been prepared anyway and were the natural outcome of the 'post-Donovan' conferences, though the process of drafting was without doubt speeded up in the battle initiated by the Government. To the special conference of 5 June 1969, the General Council proposed amendments to two rules (which were ratified in September at the annual conference). The first obliges affiliated unions to inform the Council about disputes, *including* unofficial stoppages; allows the Council to take the initiative, even in advance, and intervene; and gives it power to act under Rule 13 against a union that refuses its advice (whereby that union can be suspended or even ultimately excluded from T.U.C. membership). An even bigger amendment was made to the rule on disputes between affiliated organizations. All official stoppages resulting from *inter-union* disputes must be reported to the Council at the stage they are contemplated. No union can launch such a strike until the

Council has investigated the dispute and, if need be, referred it to the Disputes Committee. All unions must notify the Council of stoppages involving large bodies of workers 'directly or indirectly' which 'may have serious consequences' and tell the Council what it has done to secure a resumption of work. If an *inter-union* dispute leads to an unofficial strike, the unions concerned must take 'immediate and energetic steps' to obtain a resumption of work. Once again the remedy is not legal, but domestic sanctions under Rule 13, or a report to the 'next Annual Congress to deal with as may be decided upon'.

The amendments were passed by overwhelming majorities, though some delegates raised the thorny but related problem of membership of the General Council. As the motions before the 1969 T.U.C. conference showed, the representative character of this Council of 34 members will have to be insured in future if smaller unions' confidence in the use of these powers is to be retained. Furthermore, along with democracy must go a proper full-time staff (for at present the staff behind the General Council is much too small for the tasks assigned to it). As Mr Victor Feather, the new General Secretary, said in characteristic vein: 'All these things will need looking at very carefully'. But also, to avoid what it saw to be harmful and hurried 'interim' legislation, the T.U.C. on 18 June agreed to add an undertaking, which (a) repeats a large part of the amended rules; (b) states that if the Council considers it *unreasonable* to order an unconditional return to work, it will advise the unions concerned about a settlement; and (under threat of using Rule 13) states:

(c) where, however, they find there should be no stoppage of work before procedure is exhausted, they will place an obligation on the organization or organizations concerned to take energetic steps to obtain an immediate resumption of work, including action within their rules if necessary, so that negotiations can proceed.

Thus, affiliated unions can be obliged to take disciplinary action under their rules if necessary to end a stoppage; but this, as Mr Feather said, only makes 'more explicit' what was already inherent in the new rule. If a union can be made by the T.U.C. to take disciplinary action against a member under its rules for striking (perhaps against that union's better judgement) attention again focuses on the freedom of the union members to choose their own union, and within a union to choose their own rules concerning discipline and the like. The freedom to control the rule book becomes of even greater importance in the light of the new role played by the T.U.C. This is the context in which must be judged both the Conservative Government's legislation on union rules and new pronouncements in the seventies by judges. On the other hand, it is not easy to see the T.U.C. using effective powers against one of the giant affiliated organizations; and this problem (if it is one) is likely not to decrease as the affiliated units grow. But the T.U.C., from Port Talbot to Pilkingtons, showed in the first year of its new power that it trusted in the steady methods of inquiry and discussion rather than the heady wine of orders and sanctions. The traditional voluntarism of the British system of industrial relations rests, in truth, more than ever before in the hands of the central bodies, the C.B.I. and the T.U.C. The maintenance and reform of that system, with a trade union movement which enjoys both security and vigour, is in the interests of the individual worker. It was understandable for the Donovan Report itself to conclude, concerning the plans for its programme to improve British trade unions:

Carrying them through will ... demand considerable effort, imagination and initiative from trade union leaders and executive members, and a willingness to move away from accepted modes of thought and patterns of behaviour. To generate the initiative and sustain the effort we rely heavily upon the leadership of the T.U.C.

1. [1952] 2 Q.B. 329.
2. *Lawlor* v. *U.P.O.W.* [1965] Ch. 712.
3. [1956] A.C. 104.
4. See for examples, Wedderburn, *Cases and Materials on Labour Law*, pp. 657–65; R. Rideout, 'Content of Trade Union Disciplinary Rules', (1965) III *Brit. J. Industrial Relations* 153.
5. *Evans* v. *N.U.P.B.W.* [1938] 4 All E.R. 51.
6. (1966) 1 K.I.R. 679.
7. *Spring* v. *Nat. Amalgamated Stevedores and Dockers Society* [1956] 1 W.L.R. 585.
8. C. Grunfeld, *Modern Trade Union Law*, p. 168–9. Nor is the difference between Lord MacDermott and Lord Porter merely 'terminological': Citrine's *Trade Union Law* (3rd ed.), p. 175, n. 38.
9. *Report*, paras. 771–4; see K. W. Wedderburn (1957) 20 *Modern Law Review* 105. *Contra*: Lord Lloyd (1956) 19 *Modern Law Review* 121.
10. See a recent discussion in *John* v. *Rees* [1969] 2 All E.R. 274. Also, Citrine's *Trade Union Law* (3rd ed.), p. 179; Grunfeld, *Modern Trade Union Law*, p. 41; Lord Lloyd (1949) 12 *Modern Law Review* 409.
11. [1970] 3 W.L.R. 713 (C.A.).
12. See K. W. Wedderburn, 'Corporate Personality and Social Policy: The Quasi-Corporation', (1965) 28 *Modern Law Review* 62, especially pp. 65–7 where the place of the trade union cases is examined.
13. See *Pett* v. *Greyhound Racing Association Ltd* (No. 2) [1969] 2 All E.R. 221.
14. [1929] 1 Ch. 602.
15. *Annamunthodo* v. *Oilfield Workers* [1961] A.C. 945.
16. [1970] 2 All E.R. 713.
17. [1967] 1 All E.R. 767; see for critical analysis Judith Reid (1968) 31 *Modern Law Review* 214.
18. *Hiles* v. *A.S.W.* [1968] Ch. 440. See too *Breen* v. *A.E.U.* [1970] 2 All E.R. 179, which supports the traditional approach (shop steward removed from post under discretionary rules not entitled to procedures of natural justice, though committee had to act in good faith).
19. *Russell* v. *Duke of Norfolk* [1949] 1 All E.R. 109. For a

different view, see Grunfeld, *Modern Trade Union Law* (1960), p. 188; but Citrine, *Trade Union Law* (3rd ed., Hickling, 1967), p. 284, agrees that the rules can in principle exclude principles of natural justice.

20. [1963] 2 Q.B. 527 (C.A.); [1964] A.C. 925 (H.L.).

21. See, e.g., Lord Lloyd, 'The Right to Work', (1957) 10 *Current Legal Problems*, 36.

22. *Evidence to Royal Commission*, Days 2 and 3 (1965), p. 117.

23. 'Admission to Non-Statutory Associations Controlling Employment' (1967) 30 *Modern Law Review* 389.

23a. [1970] 3 W.L.R. 713 (C.A.).

24. C. Grunfeld, *Trade Unions and the Individual in English Law* (1960), p. 50.

25. W. E. J. McCarthy, *The Closed Shop in Britain* (1964); the quotations are from pp. 79; 240; 244; 259; and 281.

26. John Hughes, 'Trade Union Structure and Government', *R.C. Research Paper* No. 5, Part (i), pp. 23–25. See also Part (ii) of this paper for an important discussion of members' participation in union affairs.

27. See *Ex parte National Amalgamated Stevedores and Dockers Union*, *The Times*, 13.5.64 (dispute about which unions could nominate to local Board); and see *R. v. National Dock Labour Board* [1964] 2 Lloyd's Rep. 420 (mandamus refused).

28. *The Times*, 20.12.68.

29. Dr Shirley W. Lerner, *Breakaway Unions and the Small Trade Union* (1961); and the same author in *Industrial Relations* (1968, ed. B. C. Roberts), pp. 86–7.

30. 'British Trade Unionism in the Sixties', in *Socialist Register*, 1966 (eds. R. Miliband and J. Saville), p. 109.

31. *The Times*, 11.10.68: 'There are the beginnings of a division of the movement into two big super blocks. . . . There would develop in the movement a two-party system which could not be restricted to the top'. See on this John Hughes, *R.C. Research Paper No. 5*, Part (ii), 'Trade Union Structure and Government', p. 65 et seq.

32. *Financial Times*, 8.12.69.

33. Citrine, *Trade Union Law* (3rd ed., M. A. Hickling), p. 461.

CONCLUSION

It would be contrary to the spirit of this book to conclude it with any list of simple reforms for British labour law. Rather, it is hoped that its chapters have done something to display the interrelationship of the various parts of that law. This is not an area of law which anyone can discuss without making apparent his attitudes. It is a place where law, politics, and social assumptions meet in a man; and whoever believes that he is so 'objective' or 'impartial' as to be above policies and prejudices is either arrogantly naïve or dishonest with himself and others. Policies on labour law, as on other things, are bound to differ. What is impermissible is the pursuit of a policy in one part of labour law without account being taken of its effects in another. Whatever its faults, the Donovan Report put forward proposals which are, by that test, a success – comprehensive, consistent and realistic.

The relationship between member and union involves the structure and strength of that union, sometimes even of the whole movement (Chapters 9 and 10). The strength of the union is a key factor in collective bargaining and its legal right to take strike action and apply other forms of industrial pressure (Chapters 7 and 8) is an essential element in that method of conducting industrial relations. The legal status of the collective agreement is eventually the concern of every individual worker, unionist and non-unionist (Chapter 4), and interacts with the law concerning the individual contract of employment (Chapters 2 and 3). The legal regulation of, or support for, the method of collective bargaining (Chapter 4) touches inevitably on the adoption or rejection elsewhere of the method of legal enactment (Chapter 5). Even when the weight of legal regulation is heavy, as in safety matters and injury at work (Chapters 5 and 6), pressure for collective action breaks through. The problems of workers' representatives, on safety or on bargaining matters, industrial democracy (Chapter 1), and questions of dismissal and redundancy (Chapter 3) relate to the question whether new departures will come via collective bargaining or by legislation or by a mixture of the two (Chapter 5). Safety and medical care at work are not unrelated to industrial conflict; and the place of damages and social insurance in compensating the injured worker (Chapter 6) cannot be discussed in isolation from the rest of industrial relations. Judicial developments in the law of tort such as 'intimidation' and interference with contract impinge primarily on the right to strike (Chapter 8) but spread out their effects as far as the problem of expulsion from a union (Chapter 10), especially because so much of their novelty depends upon the expanded illegality of a breach of contract. The pattern is, in truth, that of a seamless web. At any point we are always close to lines of thought pointing back to headings we once left behind or forward to questions we have not yet reached. The law of industrial peace and of work (Chapters 1 to 6), the law of industrial conflict (Chapters 7 and 8), and 'trade union' law proper (Chapters 9 and 10) are all one.

This should not surprise us. For the law cannot escape wholly from the relationships of the workplace, and from that conflict of interests which we can scarcely hope to eradicate from our society however much we contain it within acceptable institutions. The key to the haphazard modern pattern of the law must be the legal history of the British trade union movement. Without an understanding of that history and without some sympathy with that movement, the pattern can scarcely be seen, let alone accepted. But it is a system of law that has worked. To those lawyers who in their impatience complain that the Donovan Report failed to be 'positive' in proposing a new 'rule of law' in industrial affairs, the trade unionist may be forgiven for remarking how the labours of previous commissions and the statutes they produced (which were intended to protect trade unionists) were rendered vastly uncertain and even sterile by unsympathetic legal judgments from 1872 to 1970.

In more than one chapter of labour law, we noticed that the courts in the sixties exhibited less sympathy for the defendant trade unionist engaged on a strike, and the worker plaintiff injured at work. This tendency contrasts with the enlightened attitudes of judgments given twenty years before. In 1964 the reinterpretation of strike law went so far that trade unionists justifiably felt that the 'Queensberry Rules' were being changed in the middle of the game and that old attitudes of judicial antipathy had been unearthed anew. A new Act was needed in 1965. Yet even while the Donovan Royal Commission deliberated and reported, novel developments in judge-made law were occurring, most of them to the disadvantage of workers. Nor can the influence of the courts over the interpretation of new statutes, like the Redundancy Payments Act, 1965, be said to avoid displays of a philosophy dominated by the prerogatives of management. It is still an open question whether even the new Industrial Tribunals have won the confidence of working people.

These phenomena have implications of particular importance for us lawyers, in offices, in universities, and in chambers, concerning our relationship with the ordinary citizens and workers in whose service we teach or practise the law, and concerning our own training and attitudes that often leave us unequipped to deal with the problems of labour law. They may, too, have the most profound lessons to teach concerning the sociology of law generally, and the role played by judges in all our lives. Although abstract ideas do play their part, law is not formulated in the abstract by courts and tribunals. While it is true that Parliament 'makes' law but the courts 'apply' law, its 'application' from time to time is expressed, as we have seen, in a form that is heavily influenced by the group, class, and sectional interests of real people. Lawyers, including judges, do not escape the influence of those interests on their thinking and unconscious assumptions. We have long needed, in Britain, intensified study of the law in terms of the impact of such interests – a study for which the developments in labour law provide rich material. Nor is 'the State' a piece of impartial machinery, for its power is affected by the same conflicting interests. The new interventions of 'the State' require us, in that study of labour law, to question the nature of the interventions and the purpose or assumptions of the 'law and order' which that power is often called in allegedly to sustain.

Two themes may be recalled here of special importance to labour law today. First, we have seen that the relationship between regulation by statute (with all the pressures on Parliament which that entails) and regulation by autonomous collective bargaining has never been, and is not, static. The most important questions in the next decade are whether we are to see more statutory regulation where previously collective bargaining has ruled, and, if so, where and of what character? Can bodies such as the C.I.R., T.U.C. and C.B.I. speed that reform of the institutions of collective bargaining for 'workers and their representatives to exercise their influence in the factory', in the words of the Royal Commission, in a more 'orderly' way, 'without destroying the British tradition of keeping industrial relations out of the courts'? The second theme is connected intimately with the first: the boundary round the functions that are 'exclusively management functions' is, also, not a fixed one; or, at any rate, the conditions on which management is to exercise those functions are not fixed for all time. The choice by trade unions between collective bargaining and statutory regulation will, to some extent, be made according to the extent that they formulate new demands for a share in 'management' decisions. We have seen many examples: the control of hire-and-fire, and the new notions of workers' 'property' in jobs; the demand for compulsory workers' representatives on safety at work; and so on. That *floor of rights* which is the statutory complement of a voluntary system focuses attention upon such issues. A variety of legal problems is bound to flow from any reopening of the question: Who is to control what at the place of work? The number of problems will increase if material affluence is accompanied not merely by an intensified struggle over the distribution of wealth, but also by renewed insistence on the question that is regularly put, and should be put, in any democracy: Why do *they* control *that*?

The Donovan Report concluded that the right way ahead was not to redraft the law on the basis of 'positive' rights for trade unions. It would, no doubt, be fitting in modern society to recognize positively the role and place of workers' collective organization, to welcome it and to strengthen it by law, rather than to leave it cloaked merely in the apparent 'immunities' and ostensible 'privileges' which were, as we have seen, the legal form in which the trade union movement had to gain its liberty of action, and in which that liberty always rests on the uncertain goodwill of the judiciary. But such an innovation, the present writer has been convinced, would be used to threaten today the more valuable tradition of non-intervention by the law. The urgent and immediate task of reform is to be approached by grafting new features on to that traditional structure, using law where necessary to create the machinery (and the C.I.R. shows it is not always needed), rather than by making a dash for short-cut solutions by imposition of legal sanctions. That tradition cannot be lightly discarded. For it expounds, after all, the simple truth that industrial disputes can never be settled in the last resort with writs and injunctions. Collective bargaining must be reformed, and through it a rapid advance be made towards industrial democracy. Then may come the time for the law to be redrawn on the basis of 'positive' rights. Success in these ventures might do something to improve the unhappy relations – all too often the conflicts – between the worker and the law.

APPENDIX

THE following proposals of the Government to introduce strong legal regulation into the British industrial relations system were published as this edition was in the press. The Government stated that they definitely represented the structure of a new Bill which it intended to enact. In order to assist the reader who wishes to contrast particular points in these proposals with the existing law and with earlier suggestions for its reform, a few notes have been added referring to passages in the main text of this book. The proposals as a whole should, however, be weighed against the general structure of our labour law developed since the Trade Union Act, 1871, as described in the preceding chapters.

9 October 1970 K.W.W.

INDUSTRIAL RELATIONS BILL
CONSULTATIVE DOCUMENT

I. INTRODUCTION

1. The Government has made clear its intention to introduce a comprehensive Industrial Relations Bill during the present session of Parliament.

2. This document sets out the principles on which the Government proposes that the Bill should be based, and the main provisions which it proposes to include. It is intended to serve as a basis for consultations with the Trades Union Congress and the Confederation of British Industry; the Government wishes to start these consultations without delay. The Government will also welcome comments from other interested organizations and individuals. Details of where to send these comments, and of how to obtain further copies of the document, will be found at the end.

3. The improvement of industrial relations is of great importance both from an economic and from a social point of view.

Poor industrial relations adversely affect output, raise industrial costs, damage the balance of payments, and inhibit industrial investment. They also restrict people's opportunities of finding satisfaction in their work, and create avoidable conflicts and hostilities in the workplace and in society as a whole. They dissipate the energies of management and unions alike, which are needed for more constructive purposes.

4. Poor industrial relations are not to be equated simply with strikes. They include many other kinds of failure in human relations in employment. The remedies are primarily the responsibility of management, in whose hands rests the initiative for any improvements that the circumstances may permit.

5. Strikes are, however, often an important symptom of poor industrial relations. And they can make poor industrial relations still worse, particularly when agreed procedures for resolving disputes are ignored, or when one group's pursuit of its sectional interests leads to conflict with other employees. Unions and employees have a responsibility, as well as management, to see that their actions are directed towards securing and maintaining good industrial relations.

6. Whatever changes are made, the present widespread shortcomings of industrial relations in Britain cannot be expected to disappear overnight. But they will not disappear at all unless managements, and the representatives of employees, intensify their efforts to identify and resolve the problems that arise between managements and employees. The improvement and strengthening of machinery for negotiation and consultation, for example, is crucial. Where such efforts have been forthcoming, substantial improvements in industrial relations have been secured.

7. For its part, the Government will continue to encourage progress towards better industrial relations by the example it sets as an employer and by the help and encouragement it can give through its specialist services which provide advice and conciliate in disputes.

8. But more is required. Government has a responsibility to make clear the standards to which, on behalf of the country as a whole, it expects the conduct of industrial relations to con-

form, to establish safeguards for the individual and the community, and to provide the means for resolving disputes over the machinery of industrial relations and the behaviour of the parties to it. The proposed Industrial Relations Act will be the Government's main instrument in achieving these objectives.[1]

9. The Government therefore sees the proposals set out for comment in this document as complementary, and essential, to a continuing and necessarily long-term exercise in the reform and improvement of human relations in the factory, shop, and office. They are not and cannot be an immediate or self-sufficient solution to our problems of deteriorating industrial relations. Nor are the proposals framed with any wish to encourage litigation about industrial relations questions as anything but a last resort. But the Government believes that legislation has an essential and positive role to play in the improvement of industrial relations; that the clear statement of fundamental rights and obligations in this field, in what will be the first comprehensive Industrial Relations Act that this country has ever had, will itself help to persuade managements and unions towards fairer and more constructive methods of conducting their relations and resolving their differences.

10. Thus the improvement of industrial relations in Britain can only be secured by collective effort on the part of Government, managements, unions and workers within a new framework of law which:

(i) sets national standards for good industrial relations;

(ii) safeguards those who conform to them;

(iii) protects individual rights in employment; and

(iv) provides new methods of resolving disputes over the conduct of industrial relations.

11. It is against this background that the proposals which follow should be seen.

1. This Bill will thus represent the first attempt ever to regulate British industrial relations by law as a 'main instrument' of general reform. See O. H. Parsons, *Tory Threat to the Unions* (Labour Research Dept. 1970).

II. GENERAL PRINCIPLES

12. It may be useful to set out at once the principles that the Government regards as fundamental. They are:

(i) That every individual should have a right to join a trade union and participate in trade union activities, and an equal right not to do so.

(ii) That workers, where they so wish, should have the right to negotiate collectively, through their trade union or unions, with their employer.

(iii) That the worker should be free to withdraw his labour, subject only to the requirements of his individual contract of employment.

(iv) That employers and their associations, and trade unions and their members, should have clearly defined rights and obligations towards each other, and obligations towards the general public, in the conduct of industrial relations; and that there should be clear, fair and readily available ways of securing those rights and enforcing those obligations.

III. INDUSTRIAL RELATIONS PRACTICE

13. It is proposed that the Secretary of State should be required, within a year from the passage of the legislation, to prepare and lay before Parliament a Code of Industrial Relations Practice. The objectives and the purposes of the Code would be to:

a. encourage the development of free and responsible collective bargaining, in which each party recognizes and respects the legitimate rights and objects of the other;

b. encourage the establishment, within undertakings, of effective means of communication, including the provision of information, between management and workers at all levels so as to involve them more fully in the operations of their firms;

c. encourage and promote the development and observance

of orderly and peaceful procedures for resolving differences between employers and unions, without damaging the public interest, and taking full advantage of the facilities for conciliation and advice provided by the Secretary of State and others;

d. promote the freedom and security of individual workers; and

e. develop trade unions and employers' associations as representative, responsible and effective bodies for conducting relations between employers and workers.

14. All those concerned with industrial relations would be expected to conform to the Code. It would not be directly enforceable, but in any proceedings before the proposed National Industrial Relations Court or the Industrial Tribunals (see Part IV) compliance or non-compliance with it could be adduced in support or rebuttal of the case put forward by either party. If the Court or Tribunal found that any person had complied or failed to comply with the Code, in relation to the matter at issue, it would take that into account in determining any liability or compensation.

IV. STATUTORY AGENCIES

15. The substance of the Government's proposals will be found in later parts of this document. But in order to make clear the framework within which these proposals would operate, it begins by outlining the agencies that will be concerned.

IVa. *The National Industrial Relations Court and the Industrial Tribunals: Structure*

16. The Government proposes to establish a new system of adjudication for industrial relations matters consisting of courts specially suited, by their composition and experience, to deal with such matters. This would have as its higher level a new National Industrial Relations Court (NIRC) of equivalent status to the High Court, and as its lower level the present Industrial Tribunals (ITs) which would be given new functions

and considerably expanded to deal with the additional work.[2]

17. It is intended that access to the NIRC and the ITs should be easy and their proceedings relatively informal; that they should include people with specialist and practical experience of industrial relations on both sides of industry, with a lawyer as chairman; and that they should be able to apply their practical experience to the matters that come before them.

18. The NIRC would thus consist of a President and other members of the higher judiciary in England and Scotland, and 'lay' members with relevant industrial relations experience.

19. The NIRC would be able to sit in more than one division and in various parts of the country. Although it would probably be based in London, it would normally sit at appropriate regional and local centres if that would meet the convenience of the parties.

20. There would be a right of appeal from the NIRC on a point of law to the Court of Appeal (in Scotland to the Court of Session).

IVb. *NIRC and ITs: Jurisdiction*

21. It is the Government's intention that, generally speaking,[3] legal cases about industrial relations matters should be heard by the new NIRC, and on some matters the ITs. The NIRC and ITs would therefore have jurisdiction in respect of any proceedings about:

    a. the inducement of, or any threat to induce, a breach of contract in contemplation or furtherance of an industrial dispute;[4]

2. See pp. 127 and 150. The function of lay 'wingmen' is likely to be even more slender in the NIRC where the chairman is a High Court judge. As to appeals see paras. 20 and 24; and above p. 148.

3. The problem of overlapping jurisdictions is left obscure in the proposals. See for other examples, paras. 67 and 99.

4. Actions in respect of other industrial torts might, on *this* wording, still go to the High Court. See Chapter 8 on conspiracy; unlawful interference with contract and business; intimidation (the Trade Disputes Act, 1965, is to be repealed: para. 70). On other tort liabilities, see pp. 375-7. As to breach of employment contracts, see paras. 61-70.

b. any of the unfair industrial actions mentioned in these proposals (see next paragraph);

c. any breach of a legally enforceable collective agreement;

d. any infringement of a contract between trade unions or between a trade union and its members;

e. any infringement of rights to be secured by the legislation or any action in relation to which a remedy was expressly created by the legislation;

f. the matters for which the ITs are responsible at present.

22. The Government proposes that a number of actions by employers, employers' associations, trade unions and others involved in industrial relations, which it considers to be seriously contrary to the standards which should be observed in the conduct of industrial relations, should be 'unfair industrial actions'. Each is mentioned at the appropriate place in this document.[5] Anyone claiming he had been injured, or was threatened with injury, as a result of an unfair industrial action directed against him would be able to bring a complaint in the NIRC or ITs, which would be able to grant any of the remedies proposed in paragraph 30. Where it would be an unfair industrial action to organize a strike or lock-out for a particular purpose, it would also be an unfair action:

- to threaten a strike or lock-out for that purpose;
- to organize or threaten any other concerted industrial action for that purpose;
- to put pressure for that purpose, by industrial action or the threat of it, on an employer not himself a party to the dispute.

23. The general principle governing the allocation of functions between the ITs and the NIRC would be that issues which involved an individual would be dealt with by the ITs whilst collective issues (e.g. about enforcement of bargaining rights, or about legally enforceable collective agreements) would be decided by the NIRC. However, there would be provision for individual cases which were expected to be long or

5. Paragraphs outlining the main points concerning UIA's and related liabilities are: 14, 21, 22, 47, 48, 49, 55, 67, 69, 70, 71, 74, 75, 81, 90 (vii), 99, 109, 110, 115, 117, 122, 125, 131, 143, 151, 153 and 169.

complex, or which had important wider implications, to be transferred from the ITs to the NIRC.

24. The NIRC would take over the present responsibilities of the High Court and the Court of Session in Scotland for appeals from the ITs on points of law – except those under the Industrial Training Act and (for the present) the Selective Employment Payments Act.

IVc. *NIRC and ITs: Procedure and Remedies*

25. It is proposed that the procedure of the NIRC and ITs should be as informal and free from technicalities as possible, although they would of course give reasons for their decisions. Power would be taken to lay down rules of procedure for the NIRC by statutory instrument.

26. As in the ITs at present (and also in the present Industrial Court), parties to cases would be allowed to be represented by lawyers or by other persons (e.g. trade union officers) or to represent themselves as they wished.

27. There would be a discretionary power to award costs, but only when the NIRC or IT considered that the party concerned had acted frivolously or vexatiously, or, in appeals and comparable cases, had no reasonable grounds for bringing the case.[6]

28. The NIRC and ITs would have power to require the attendance of witnesses and the disclosure of documents, and to hear evidence on oath.

29. The NIRC and ITs would be required to afford opportunities for conciliation between the parties before a case was heard. Information given or obtained in the course of conciliation, and the positions taken by the parties during conciliation, would not be admissible as evidence in the proceedings.

30. The NIRC and the ITs would be able:
  – to award compensation
  – to determine the rights of a party
  – to make orders to refrain from unfair industrial action
  – to make speedy but temporary orders.

6. An extension of the present power of tribunals which extends only to frivolous or vexatious claims.

The NIRC would have power to enforce any of these orders.'

31. In the Government's view, the NIRC should never grant an interim remedy (i.e. what is at present described as an *ex parte* injunction) that would restrain industrial action without giving those who would be affected an opportunity to put their case. Such a remedy would not be granted before the NIRC had given any registered trade union or employers' association that appeared to it to be directly concerned an opportunity to put its case.[8]

32. The NIRC would have power to enforce its own decisions. Orders of the ITs would be enforced through the NIRC, rather than through the County Courts as at present. But the collection of debts arising out of cases in the NIRC and the ITs would continue to be a matter for the County Courts.

33. It is proposed that the ITs should be given a limited power to review their decision if fresh facts come to light.

IVd. *The Commission on Industrial Relations*[9]

34. The Commission on Industrial Relations (CIR) would as at present be primarily concerned to assist employers and unions in the voluntary reform of industrial relations, institutions and procedures. This would continue to be its main function. But it is proposed to give it the additional responsibilities indicated in Part VII of these proposals, and to put it on a statutory basis (at present it is a Royal Commission).

35. The Secretary of State would continue to be responsible for appointing the Chairman and members, and he (alone or with other Ministers) would initiate references (apart from those initiated by the NIRC under the proposals in Part VII).

36. The CIR would be enabled to hold such inquiries as it considers necessary or desirable for the performance of its functions; to examine witnesses on oath; to hear evidence in

---

7. By imprisonment for contempt of NIRC. These orders would be a new form of labour injunction: pp. 379–384.

8. See p. 379.

9. See p. 38; the 'additional responsibilities' would radically alter the position of the CIR.

private if this is requested; to require people to attend, or to produce documents or furnish information relevant to the inquiry; and to conduct ballots.

37. The CIR would be enabled to do what it could to help to remedy the defects which it finds in existing arrangements.

38. The CIR would make a report to the Secretary of State and any other Ministers who had initiated a reference.

39. The CIR would be required to make an annual report to the Secretary of State on its activities. This would include a general review of the development of collective bargaining during the year and would draw attention to any problems that the Commission regarded as being of special importance.

IVe. *The Registrar of Trade Unions and Employers' Association*

40. Under existing law the rules and conduct of trade unions and employers' associations are, in some limited respects, subject to independent scrutiny and supervision by the Registrar of Friendly Societies. But the Government considers the existing provisions inadequate. They do not ensure that the membership can exercise reasonable democratic control, or give the individual member (or applicant for membership) sufficient safeguards against unjust treatment.

41. It therefore proposes to create a new office of Registrar of Trade Unions and Employers' Associations. The Registrar would take over the present responsibilities of the Registrar of Friendly Societies in relation to trade unions and employers' associations and would have the additional functions outlined in Part VI.

42. The Registrar's main responsibilities would be to ensure that trade union rules conformed to standards laid down in the legislation, and that unions observed their rules and were properly administered, in order to safeguard the public interest and protect the rights of union members and applicants for membership. In order to carry these out effectively, he would have authority to conduct preliminary enquiries and to call for documents. He would be able to initiate enquiries, either at the request of individual members or applicants for membership,

or on the basis of any information he received from elsewhere. If he felt, following enquiries, that an allegation of malpractice was justified, he would have discretion to resolve the matter himself by conciliation and advice to the parties. In the last resort, however, the member (or the Registrar after an investigation which he had initiated himself) would be able to take a case to the NIRC for adjudication. (See also Part VId.)

IVf. *Arbitration Board. Courts of Inquiry* [10]

43. To avoid confusion, the existing Industrial court would be renamed the Arbitration Board. Its present functions would remain substantially unchanged, but Section 8 of the Terms and Conditions of Employment Act 1959 would be amended so that only registered trade unions could initiate a reference under that section. The Board would in addition be responsible for arbitration in cases referred to it by a registered union authorized to do so by the NIRC under Part VII d and e of these proposals.

44. It is proposed that the Secretary of State should retain his existing powers in industrial disputes, including in particular his powers to arrange for conciliation under the Conciliation Act 1896 and to refer matters to arbitration and commission inquiries under the Industrial Courts Act 1919.

V. WORKERS' RIGHTS

Va. *In relation to trade union membership, non-membership and activity*

45. In the Government's view each worker should have an unqualified right to choose whether or not to join a trade union.

46. The Government therefore proposes to make provision in the Industrial Relations Bill to secure the right of an individual to belong to an independent registered trade union and to take part in that trade union's activities. Equally the Bill would

10. See pp. 197 and 395.

secure the right of an individual to choose not to belong to a trade union.[11]

47. Under these provisions an individual would be able to seek redress for any action of his employer which was designed to deter him from joining a registered trade union, continuing in membership of such a union, or taking part in that union's lawful activities, or which penalized or discriminated against him for these reasons. This protection would similarly apply where an individual was penalized or discriminated against for refusing to join or continue membership of a trade union. Compensation could be awarded, if appropriate, against anyone who had put pressure on the employer, as well as the employer himself.

48. It is also proposed to make it an unfair industrial action to organize, or threaten to organize, a strike to put pressure on an employer to discriminate against an individual because of his membership or non-membership of a registered trade union.

49. There would be corresponding provisions to protect people seeking employment.

50. Claims about infringement of the right to belong or not to belong to a registered trade union would be dealt with by the ITs.

Vb. *In relation to unfair dismissal*[12]

51. At present an employee may seek damages if he is dismissed in breach of contract, and the Redundancy Payments Act 1965 provides protection for the employee dismissed on account of redundancy. But an employee has no redress against his employer for unfair dismissal.

52. Britain is one of the few countries where dismissals are a frequent cause of strike action. It seems reasonable to link this with the fact that in this country, unlike most others, the law provides no redress for the employee who suffers unfair or arbitrary dismissal, if the employer has met the terms of the

11. See pp. 80 and 460–65. The second proposal, together with para. 48, would abolish the right not to work with non-unionists. Compare para. 70.
12. See pp. 143–9.

contract, e.g. with regard to giving notice. Thus if an employee is dismissed without reasonable cause, and though this may severely prejudice his future livelihood, the law gives him no right of appeal against his dismissal. Both on grounds of principle and as a means of removing a significant cause of industrial disputes, the Government proposes to include provisions in the Industrial Relations Bill to give statutory safeguards against unfair dismissal.

53. It is proposed that employees should have a right to appeal to an IT if they consider that they have been unfairly dismissed. Initially, because of limitations on the rate at which the ITs can be expanded for their additional functions, this right would have to be limited to employees with two or more years' service in their employment; but the intention would be to extend the right to other employees later. Remedies would be available in respect of dismissals for reasons of membership or non-membership of a registered trade union or for participation in trade union activities without the need for any such two-year qualifying period.

54. A dismissal would be fair if the employer had acted reasonably and had dismissed the employee because, for example, of redundancy or the employee's conduct or capability.[13] Where an IT found a dismissal unfair it would be able to recommend reinstatement or, alternatively, to award compensation. Neither the employer nor the employee could be compelled to accept an IT's recommendation of reinstatement, but any reasonable refusal could be reflected in the award of compensation. Compensation would be awarded on the basis of assessment of past and probable future loss, broadly as at common law (taking account of the ordinary duty of a claimant to mitigate his loss so far as possible). Any award would, however, be subject to a limit (as suggested by the Donovan Commission) of two years' wages or salary, disregarding any wages or salary in excess of £40 per week.

55. It would be an unfair industrial action to induce, or threaten to induce, a strike to secure the unfair dismissal of an

13. The effect seems to be to put the burden of proof generally on the employee: contrast pp. 144–5.

employee.[14] The IT would, where it considers it appropriate, be able to award compensation for unfair dismissal against any others who had put pressure on the employer to dismiss, as well as against the employer himself.

56. Some employees already have the benefit of voluntary procedures which provide them with safeguards against unfair dismissal. The Government is anxious to encourage such responsible self-government within industry and therefore proposes to provide for the exemption from the statutory machinery of voluntary procedures which provide adequate protection against unfair dismissal for the employees covered by them.

Vc. *Under the Contracts of Employment Act 1963*

57. The Contracts of Employment Act prescribes minimum periods of notice of termination for employers and employees. In the case of the employee these periods of notice vary from one to four weeks, depending on his length of service.

58. The Government considers that the periods of notice provided by the Act should now be increased for long service employees, by providing for a minimum of 6 weeks' notice after 10 years' service and 8 weeks' notice after 15 years' service. The period of service qualifying both employer and employee to an entitlement of a minimum of one week's notice would be reduced from 26 to 13 weeks.[15]

59. The provisions of the Act under which employers are required to give their employees a written statement of their main terms of employment would be amended to ensure that employees are given adequate information about any terms and conditions affecting their proposed basic right to choose whether or not to belong to a trade union, and about the steps which they should take to bring any grievance to the notice of the employer.[16]

Vd. *Conciliation*

60. Wherever possible it is intended to promote the voluntary

14. Contrast p. 144. Much will turn on the definition of 'strike'.
15. See p. 117.   16. See p. 72.

settlement by conciliation of complaints about unfair dismissal or other infringement of individual rights. The Secretary of State would be responsible for providing a conciliation service in relation to such complaints. The Bill would provide for this service to be informed when a complaint was lodged with the ITs and for conciliation officers to seek to obtain a voluntary settlement between the parties before the matter came for hearing before the IT. It is hoped that this would encourage the early settlement of such disputes, without the need for a case to be heard before an IT.

Ve. *Alleged breaches of contracts of employment*

61. The Government considers that employees might often find the ITs, with their practical, and comparatively informal, approach to questions of employment and industrial relations, a more convenient and accessible forum for cases about alleged breach of a contract of employment than the Courts. It therefore proposes to carry out the recommendation of the Donovan Commission that provisions should be made for the ITs to hear such cases.

62. This could not be introduced straight away, however, since the capacity of the ITs would first have to be expanded sufficiently to deal with the additional cases (and with the other new functions which it is proposed to give to them). The Government therefore proposes that power should be taken to extend the ITs' jurisdiction in this way by statutory instrument.[17]

63. This power would not, however, extend to cases in which damages are claimed for personal injuries or death; nor would it permit any remedy other than compensation; nor would it give the ITs an exclusive jurisdiction in this field.

Vf. *Overlap with Race Relations Act 1968*

64. Some of the proposals in this document overlap with the Race Relations Act 1968, e.g. in relation to claims that dismissal by an employer, or discriminatory action by a trade union (whether registered or not), was due to colour, race, or

17. See p. 149.

ethnic or national origins. Where the remedies to be provided by the Industrial Relations Bill are more generous to the aggrieved individual than those provided by the Race Relations Act, it is intended that the Government's proposals should take the place of the Act. It is proposed, however, that in such cases the Race Relations Act machinery should still be available for securing an assurance of no further acts of discrimination and for dealing with breaches of such assurances.

Vg. *Rights in relation to the present law*

65. The legislation would make it clear that no court or tribunal will have power to compel an individual worker to remain at work against his will, or to compel him, whether directly or indirectly, to refrain from working in accordance with his contract of service. Thus a worker who was on strike could not be compelled by the courts to return to work; nor could they compel a worker to take strike action.

66. It is proposed to keep in force the existing provisions protecting trade unions and their members from proceedings for being in unlawful restraint of trade (section 2 of the Trade Union Act 1871)[18] and protecting individuals who join together in an industrial dispute from actions for criminal or civil conspiracy (section 3 of the Conspiracy and Protection of Property Act 1875 and section 1 of the Trade Disputes Act 1906). It is also proposed to implement the recommendation of the Donovan Commission that, since it is not a tort for individual employees to go on strike in breach of their contracts of employment, any danger that an agreement between them to do so might be actionable as a tort should be removed.[19]

67. Those involved in industrial disputes would retain all their

18. The protection against unlawful *civil* status for 'restraint of trade' given by s.3 of the 1871 Act, p. 314 and p. 459, is omitted. This intention seems to be confirmed by para. 108. Unregistered groups thus have no right to organize.

19. This removes the possible liability for conspiracy based on *Rookes* v. *Barnard*: p. 377. But, since the Act of 1965 (p. 371) is to be repealed, *a threat* to strike in breach of employment contracts is, despite para. 69, a possible ground of liability both, it seems, in the NIRC and the High Court; see pp. 366–70; and paras. 71, 75, 109.

existing immunities from legal action in the existing courts, since it is the Government's intention to give the NIRC and ITs, generally speaking, an exclusive jurisdiction in civil cases arising from industrial disputes (paragraph 21).[20] Registered trade unions and other industrial relations organizations (see Part VI) would however, as the Donovan Commission proposed, lose their present immunity in the ordinary courts (under section 4 of the Trade Disputes Act 1906) from actions in tort not connected with an industrial dispute.[21]

68. In addition, it is proposed to have a provision in relation to the NIRC and ITs, comparable to the second part of section 3 of the Trade Disputes Act 1906, that an act done by a person in contemplation or furtherance of an industrial dispute is not actionable on the ground only that it is an interference with the trade, business or employment of some other person, or with some other person's right to dispose of his capital or his labour.[22]

69. Registered trade unions, and their officials and members acting with their authority, would enjoy in the NIRC and the ITs a protection comparable to that which they have at present (under sections 3 and 4 of the Trade Disputes Act 1906) from actions in tort connected with an industrial dispute – although they would not enjoy any immunity in relation to unfair industrial actions and in the other ways proposed in this document (e.g. Part VId). It is however intended to provide that a threat of industrial action would be regarded as unfair only if the proposed industrial action itself be unfair. There would also be an upper limit on awards of compensation against registered trade unions (paragraph 86).

70. Other industrial relations organizations and individuals, however, would not enjoy any special immunity in the NIRC and ITs. In particular it would be an unfair industrial action

20. If a plaintiff brings suit in the High Court, whose job is it to see if it 'arises from an industrial dispute'? And is this phrase coterminous with the existing concept of acts *in contemplation or furtherance of a trade dispute* (p. 327)? The proposals say nothing about the definition of 'trade dispute', see p. 336 and p. 374.

21. See pp. 319–21.

22. See p. 368 for the way in which this part has lost meaningful effect.

for any such organization or individuals to induce workers to go on strike in breach of their individual contracts of employment, or to threaten to do so (paragraph 110). This would have the effect of removing (in the NIRC and ITs) the protection which such organizations or individuals at present enjoy under the first part of section 3 of the Trade Disputes Act 1906, and under the Trade Disputes Act 1965 (which would be repealed). There would also be no upper limit on awards of compensation against unregistered industrial relations organizations.

71. The following kinds of 'secondary' industrial action would be unfair industrial actions. First, to threaten or induce industrial action in support of any such action which is itself unfair (for any of the reasons given elsewhere in this document). Secondly, even when the original industrial action was not unfair, the Government intends that it should be unfair for anyone to threaten or induce industrial action to persuade any other person not to enter into or perform a commercial contract, unless that person is himself participating in, or directly interested in, or supporting any party to the industrial dispute which gave rise to the original industrial action. This would mean, for example, that an attempt to threaten or induce industrial action to persuade one company not to supply goods to another where the latter but not the former was involved in a dispute would be actionable before the NIRC.[23]

72. The Government has reviewed the role of the criminal law in industrial disputes. It considers that it has no place except in relation to situations involving violence or threats of it, or risk of serious injury.

73. The necessary safeguard against industrial action leading to serious harm is provided by section 5 of the Conspiracy and

23. On interference with commercial contracts, existing and future, compare p. 351 and pp. 375–87. This proposal would produce an English version of sections 8(b)(4)(B) and 8(e) Labor Management Relations Act 1947 (amended 1959) in the USA, which make many forms of 'secondary boycott' illegal. 'To curtail secondary boycotts is to deprive unions of an element of their strength, to make them enter the economic struggle with one hand tied'; C. Summers and H. Wellington, *Labor Law* (1968), p. 280. The American litigation illustrates the difficulty of defining primary employers 'directly interested'. See too p. 336.

Protection of Property Act 1875 which makes it a criminal offence for any person wilfully and maliciously to break a contract of service or of hire, if he knows or has reasonable cause to believe that the consequence of his doing so will be to endanger human life or to cause serious bodily injury or to expose valuable property to destruction or serious injury. The Government proposes to retain this section which is of general application. Section 4 of the same Act, as amended, which includes rather comparable provisions in respect of the gas, electricity and water industries, would however be repealed. The Government considers that the provisions of section 5, taken together with the other proposals in this document, make it unnecessary and unjustifiable to retain selective criminal provisions relating to the employees of these three industries.[24]

74. The Government proposes that the protection which the law gives to peaceful picketing (section 2 of the Trade Disputes Act 1906) should not apply to the picketing of a person's home.[25]

75. The Bill would protect people who wish to exercise their rights under it from any attempt to put pressure on them not to do so. It would therefore make it an unfair industrial action to take, induce or threaten any action to prevent or hinder any person from exercising or asserting any right or performing any duty under it. It would also make void any agreement not authorized under it, which excluded or limited the operation of any right under it.[26]

VI. TRADE UNIONS AND EMPLOYERS' ASSOCIATIONS

VIa. *Registration and status*

76. At present the additional rights which trade unions and employers' associations gain by registration, and the additional duties which they accept, are relatively limited. Legal status as a trade union, and many associated advantages, are available

24. See p. 388.   25. See p. 324.

26. Although not couched in terms of conspiracy, this paragraph could form a springboard for extensions of illegality of the kind described on pp. 376–7. It is the exact opposite of the 'model' on p. 385.

equally to registered and unregistered bodies. In the Government's view, the substantial new rights which it proposes for trade unions should only apply to those which, by registering, accept statutory minimum standards in relation to their rules and the rights of their members.

77. It therefore proposes to introduce a new system of registration which will limit legal status as a trade union or employers' association to registered organizations. The rights and privileges accorded to trade unions and employers' associations in the Bill would accordingly only be granted to those which are registered. Registration would also enable the organization to hold property in its own name.

78. Registration as a trade union would be available only to workers' organizations, and registration as an employers' association only to employers' organizations; the test would be whether the membership was composed wholly or mainly of workers, or of employers, in each case.

79. Federations or other joint organizations of trade unions, or of employers' associations, would be eligible for registration in a separate section of the register and would be granted legal status as a trade union or employers' association, as the case may be. Such federations would have to be composed wholly of registered organizations.

80. Further conditions of eligibility would be:

(i) that one of the principal objects of the organization is the regulation of relations between employers and workers. (Organizations with other objects besides the regulation of relations, for example some professional associations, would therefore be eligible to register providing they satisfy the other conditions.)[27]

(ii) that the constitution of the organization gives it adequate control over the determination of its objects and procedures, and over the purposes for which funds may be used, to be able to meet the requirements of registration. (Branches of registered trade unions or employers' associations would therefore not be eligible for separate registration; unions consisting of several auto-

27. Compare p. 411.

504

nomous parts would be eligible only for registration as federations.)[28]

(iii) if the organization is a trade union or federation of unions, that it is not under the domination or control of an employer or employers.

81. It is proposed that it should be an unfair industrial action for an employer or a number of employers or an employers' association to seek to dominate a registered trade union, or to take any action to interfere with the administration of a registered trade union which is calculated or intended to bring it under the domination or control of an employer or a number of employers or an employers' association.[29]

82. Trade unions, employers' associations and federations which are registered as trade unions under the Trade Union Act 1871 would, if they satisfy the new conditions of eligibility, be transferred to the appropriate section of the new register. Other organizations seeking registration would have to make an application, supported by a copy of their constitution and rules and other necessary information.

83. Registered organizations would be required to make an annual report to their members.

84. Registered trade unions and employers' associations, and their officials, would continue to enjoy immunity from actions in tort in respect of acts done in contemplation or furtherance of an industrial dispute. But they would no longer have their present immunity in respect of other tortious acts; nor would they have any immunity before the NIRC and ITs in relation to unfair industrial actions and in the other ways proposed in this document (e.g. Part VI d).

85. A registered organization would be able to avoid liability in any proceedings before the new agencies if it was able to show that it had used its best endeavours to fulfil its obligations and to prevent any continuation or repetition of the acts complained of.[30]

28. The demand for 'adequate control' appears to limit the extent to which a registered union could give 'authority' to officials or members to act, which is critical to para. 69. As to federations, see para. 93.

29. See p. 80.   30. See p. 180; but see para. 115.

86. There would be upper limits on the compensation that could be awarded against a registered trade union in any proceedings before the NIRC or the ITs. Subject to this, all the funds of a union that were available to finance industrial action would be treated as available for the payment of compensation awards.

VIb. *Rules*

87. It is proposed that registered organizations should be required to have rules which do not conflict with basic principles affecting members' rights, and which deal adequately with subjects specified in the Bill. The Registrar would have discretion to allow a reasonable period for each organization to meet these requirements; he would also have power to waive a specific requirement in a particular case.

88. Failure to meet the requirements in the time allowed would lead to cancellation of registration. Provision would also be made for cancellation of registration if, in the Registrar's opinion, the organization ceased to be eligible for registration under the criteria set out in paragraphs 78–80.

89. All decisions of the Registrar concerning registration, cancellation of registration, or rules requirements would be subject to appeal to the NIRC.

90. It is proposed that the Bill should set out the following basic principles to ensure that members of a registered trade union (and of any other organization with similar purposes) enjoy equal rights to participate in the affairs of the organization and to receive fair treatment in their relations with it (even if its rules provide to the contrary):

 (i) the organization must not arbitrarily or unreasonably exclude from membership anyone who is reasonably qualified to undertake a kind of work ordinarily done by members of the union;[31]

 (ii) if a member has met his obligations (e.g. as to subscriptions), the organization must not restrict his right to resign;

 (iii) every member must have an equal right to hold office,

31. Compare the jurisdiction claimed by judges in *Edwards* v. *SOGAT*, p. 458.

to nominate candidates, to vote in elections or ballots, to attend meetings and to participate in the business of meetings – subject to reasonable rules determined by the organization;

(iv) subject to reasonable rules, all members must have an equal right to vote in any situation where a vote is taken; they must also have a fair and reasonable opportunity to vote without interference or constraint; and where the voting is by ballot, its secrecy must be properly secured;

(v) no member of an organization may be disciplined, suspended, expelled or have his membership terminated (other than for non-payment of subscription) unless he has been given written notice of the charge brought against him, a reasonable time to prepare his defence, a full and fair hearing and a written statement of the findings;

(vi) no organization may limit the right of any member to institute proceedings in any court or tribunal or his right to appear as a witness in any proceedings;

(vii) no member who refuses to participate in any industrial action which is deemed unfair by the Bill may be expelled, disciplined or discriminated against by the organization, notwithstanding anything in its rules.

91. Registered organizations would be required to have rules which deal adequately with specified matters, although the organization would remain free to draw up its own rules on these matters. Different requirements would be laid on trade unions and employers' associations on the one hand, and federations on the other.

92. The rules of registered trade unions and employers' associations would be required to make adequate provision for a more comprehensive list of subjects than is contained in the Trade Union Act 1871. This would be based on the recommendations of the Donovan Commission that rules should deal adequately with admission, discipline, disputes between unions and their members, the procedure for elections, the determination of objects, the method of government and the conduct of business.

93. The rules of federations would be required to deal with broadly similar matters, but excluding those relating to the interests of individual members, notably those relating to admission and discipline.

94. Further details of the proposed provisions mentioned in paragraphs 92 and 93 are given in Appendix I.[32]

VIc. *Audit of accounts and investigation of superannuation schemes*

95. Registered trade unions are at present required by the Trade Union Act 1871 to have their accounts audited and to submit an annual statement of accounts to the Registrar of Friendly Societies. The Donovan Commission agreed with the Registrar's recommendation that all but the smallest trade unions should be required to appoint professional auditors and to have members' superannuation schemes periodically investigated by an actuary.

96. The Government therefore proposes that registered trade unions and employers' associations should be required to maintain proper accounting records, appoint professionally qualified auditors to audit the accounts; and submit these accounts in an annual return to the Registrar of Trade Unions and Employers' Associations together with a copy of the auditor's report. Smaller unions would be exempted from the requirement to employ auditors who are professionally qualified but they would still be required to have their accounts audited and submit them to the Registrar.

97. Registered trade unions and employers' associations possessing superannuation schemes for their members would have to have them examined by a qualified actuary at stated intervals to ensure that the schemes are viable. They would be required to set up separate superannuation funds if they do not have them at present. Copies of the actuary's report would

32. The Appendix, not here reproduced, would demand rules on many subjects but leave their content to the choice of union members. By contrast para. 90(i)(ii)(iii) and (vii) would limit severely the power of a union to determine the content of its own rules. Compare p. 412. The overriding nature of the 'basic principles' is brought out by para. 100.

have to be sent to the Registrar and supplied to members of the union on request.

VId. *Complaints*

98. In the Government's view, individuals who consider that they have grounds for complaint against a trade union about certain matters (particularly those that may affect their employment, or that concern the democratic running of the union) should in the last resort have a right to have their complaint heard by an independent body not connected with the union.

99. It therefore proposes that members of registered trade unions and employers' associations should be given access to the Registrar, and to the ITs and in some cases the NIRC, to complain about such matters. Access would also be available for former members and persons seeking membership. Complaint could be made in this way about any acts which are in breach of the basic principles set out in the Bill, or which are in breach of the rules of the organization. Members of other organizations with purposes akin to those of a trade union would have similar rights, although they would not be able to complain to the Registrar about alleged breaches of the rules.

100. ITs (and the NIRC) would have power to refer a complaint from a member of a registered organization to the Registrar of Trade Unions and Employers' Associations. The Registrar could also take action on such complaints made direct to him by the member. He would have power to investigate alleged breaches of the basic principles or of the rules at his own initiative if he had reason to believe that there had been serious or persistent breach of the basic principles or of its rules by a registered organization.

101. If the Registrar were unable to settle the matter the IT (or the NIRC) would hear the matter. The case would be brought by the complainant or, if the Registrar had initiated the investigation, by the Registrar himself. If the IT or NIRC found the complaint justified, it would have power to order a remedy, including the award of compensation where appropriate. Compensation for loss of employment resulting from wrongful termination of, or exclusion from, membership would

be calculated on the same basis as for unfair dismissal. In the last resort, if there were serious and persistent breaches of these requirements, the union could be deregistered.

102. The ITs and the NIRC would be able to refuse to consider a complaint which was not made within a reasonable time, and to defer the hearing of a complaint until the complainant had made use of his organization's internal appeals procedure.

VIe. *Employers' associations*

103. It is proposed that the Bill should provide for employers' associations to be treated as a separate category, instead of continuing to be covered by the definition of 'trade union' as under the present law. This was one of the recommendations of the Donovan Commission.

104. The requirements of the Bill about registered employers' associations would correspond generally to those about registered trade unions, except where this was clearly inappropriate.

105. The requirements about an annual report to members, an annual return to the Registrar, the submission of information to the Registrar, and audit and superannuation would apply to employers' associations as to trade unions.

106. Registered employers' associations, like registered trade unions, would be required to have rules on specified subjects and to cover particular matters on these subjects. The Registrar would have power to waive requirements about rules in a particular case if they were clearly inappropriate.

VIf. *Other combinations of workers*

107. As explained above, it is proposed to confine the title and status of 'trade union' to those organizations that register as such. However, as was recognized by the Donovan Commission (and by the House of Lords in the Harris Tweed case, 1942) there are likely to be occasions when a group of workers combine together to advance or defend their own lawful interests in a way which, in essence, involves the regulation of relations between themselves and their employers. This might happen, for example, in the course of organizing a new trade union. As explained in paragraph 66 above, the Government

proposes that the members of such a combination should continue to enjoy their present protection from proceedings for criminal or civil conspiracy.

108. There is, however, no reason why such a combination, which has not yet accepted the responsibilities implied in registration, should enjoy the other benefits or privileges proposed in this document for registered trade unions. An organization of this kind would, therefore, have to register as a trade union before it acquired the right to commence proceedings or make any claim before any of the new agencies proposed in this document. Only after registration, for example, could such an organization put a claim for recognition to the NIRC (Part VIId) or operate an agency shop (Part VIIf). And only then would its members have the protection proposed for the right to join and take part in the activities of a trade union.

109. But it would not be right for such a combination to be any less accountable than a registered trade union. It is proposed to provide, therefore, that such an organization should be subject to the same liabilities as a registered trade union (for example in respect of unfair industrial actions).[33] It is proposed to enable proceedings to be commenced and enforced against the funds of such an organization without the necessity for bringing a representative action against some of its members. And if, before registration, the organization operated a political fund, it would (like registered trade unions) be subject to the appropriate provisions of the Trade Union Act 1913.

110. It is proposed to provide that it should be an unfair industrial action for organizations and individuals, other than registered trade unions and employers' associations (and their officials and authorized agents), to induce (or threaten to induce) workers, in the course of an industrial dispute, to break their contracts of employment. This change is necessary because the existing immunity in these circumstances has increasingly been abused in sudden unofficial strikes, and because a clear distinction must be drawn between the privileges of a registered organization (which would, under these proposals, have

33. The UIA is, once more, only an 'example' of a ground of liability, which confirms that existing tort liabilities would remain.

accepted certain basic obligations) and the position of any comparable organization that had not yet accepted such obligations.[34]

111. Once such an organization had registered it would, of course, secure the limitation of liability and the other advantages proposed for registered trade unions in paragraphs 84–86 above.

VII. COLLECTIVE BARGAINING

VIIa. *Legal status of collective agreements*[35]

112. At the present time collective agreements between employers and unions have a doubtful status in law. In principle there is no reason why a collective agreement, like any other valid contract, cannot be made legally binding; but in practice the attitude of the parties to collective agreements, the lack of any clear indication that they are to be legally bound, and the form and language of agreements have encouraged the view (which has been accepted by the courts in some cases) that most collective agreements are not intended to have the force of legally binding contracts.

113. In the Government's view this is an unsatisfactory state of affairs. First, it is essential that the legal status of collective agreements should be clear and unambiguous. Secondly, it is highly desirable that agreements should be expressed in language which makes quite clear what it is the parties have agreed to. Thirdly, the parties should regard – or come to regard – the signing of agreements as a responsible act which binds them in law to honour their commitments.

114. The Government therefore proposes that the Bill should create a presumption that any written collective agreement entered into after a given date should be a legally binding and enforceable contract unless there is an express written provision to the contrary in the agreement itself. In this way the presumption would be rebutted, as with a commercial agreement,

34. This proposal, together with para. 69, introduces far more severe control than any of the recommendations in the Donovan Report: see p. 385.

35. On the existing law, see p. 171; and on the policy issues, pp. 180–85.

only by clear evidence that the parties did not intend to enter into legal relations. The provision in section 4(4) of the Trade Union Act 1871 which prevents the courts from enforcing directly an agreement between a trade union and an employers' association would be repealed.

115. There would be an obligation on the parties to a legally binding collective agreement to use their best endeavours to avoid or end any industrial action which was in breach of the agreement or which, if undertaken by a party to it, would have been a breach of it.[36]

116. Any action about the alleged breach of a legally binding collective agreement would be heard by the NIRC or the ITs.

117. It would be an unfair industrial action to induce a party to a legally enforceable collective agreement to break it.[37]

VIIb. *Selective introduction of enforceable procedures*

118. Despite these provisions, there may still be no legally enforceable procedure agreements, or indeed no satisfactory procedure agreements at all in some sectors of industry for some time to come. In some cases this may be an important contributory factor to poor industrial relations. This possibility has led the Government to examine other proposals for securing the introduction of clear and legally enforceable procedural provisions.

119. The Government therefore proposes that an employer or a recognized registered trade union (or the Secretary of State) should be able to apply to the NIRC for a reference to the CIR to review existing procedures, or the absence of procedures, with a view to producing new or improved procedural provisions which could if necessary be made legally binding. If the NIRC were satisfied, on the evidence brought before it and in accordance with specified criteria, that the development or maintenance of orderly industrial relations in the undertaking concerned had been seriously impeded by recourse to industrial action in breach of the procedure agreement, or in

36. See p. 180. The last words are quite extraordinary.
37. Is NIRC likely to demand a technical 'breach' or would 'interference' be enough? Compare pp. 357, 375, 377.

the absence of any effective agreement, it would refer the matter for investigation by the CIR.

120. The CIR would then have the task of examining any existing procedural provisions and:

    a. indicating which (if any) of these provisions could form part of a clear, effective and suitable procedure agreement;

    b. insofar as it considered any existing procedure agreement was deficient, or found that there was no procedure agreement, promoting discussion between the parties with a view to their agreeing to suitable provisions to make good the deficiency;

    c. if suitable provisions could not be agreed by the parties, recommending provisions which should be incorporated in the agreement.

121. The CIR would report to the NIRC, indicating what it considered to be suitable and effective procedure provisions – and whether or not these were incorporated in an existing agreement or had been agreed in discussions between the parties.

122. Any of the parties concerned would have the right to apply to have the CIR's recommendations made legally binding by order of the NIRC. When such an application was made, the NIRC would have to notify all the other parties (and the Secretary of State) and would conduct a hearing if any of the parties so requested.

123. At such a hearing, any party could ask for the application to be turned down on the ground that it was not necessary, in order to establish orderly industrial relations and secure the observance of procedure agreements, to make the provisions legally enforceable.

124. Any party could also argue that the provisions were insufficiently clear to be made legally enforceable. If the NIRC agreed, it could seek the agreement of the parties to clearer provisions and, if they did not agree, could refer the matter back to the CIR for further consideration.

125. Unless the NIRC rejected the application or referred it back to the CIR, it would make an order declaring the

provisions legally enforceable against the specified parties.[38]

126. There would be appropriate provisions for the modification of provisions made legally enforceable by such an order, and for application to have the order revoked when no longer needed.

VIIc. *Notification of procedure agreements and arrangements*

127. The Government proposes to continue the existing scheme for the voluntary notification of procedure agreements and arrangements to the DEP. The intention is to use the information obtained by notification to identify areas where procedures can be improved. It is proposed to take reserve powers to make this notification a statutory obligation. It is however hoped that, as in the past, the vast majority of employers will continue to co-operate on a voluntary basis without any use of these powers.

128. The proposed reserve powers would enable the Secretary of State to make regulations specifying the classes of employers to whom they applied and requiring them to notify the DEP of procedure agreements and arrangements at plant and company level to inform the DEP of any national or industry-wide procedure agreements or arrangements which they observe. The regulations would have to allow at least six months for this information to be supplied. Employers who had already supplied the information on a voluntary basis could be exempted.

VIId. *Recognition and bargaining rights*

129. It is of first importance to satisfactory collective bargaining and healthy industrial relations to establish a stable and effective bargaining structure. This implies, on the one hand, a readiness on the part of employers to negotiate seriously and responsibly with unions which (singly or together) represent and enjoy the support of a substantial body of em-

38. Once it was legally enforceable, actions interfering with the imposed procedure would attract the dangers of para. 75. The power whereby the Minister can, via NIRC, impose procedure in law renders of less value the power permitted to employers and unions to specify that a procedure shall not be legally binding.

ployees; and, on the other hand, workable and dependable arrangements and machinery through which employers and employee representatives can communicate, negotiate and resolve their disputes.

130. In the Government's view, disputes about bargaining rights and bargaining structure can be most satisfactorily resolved by the parties themselves (where necessary with help of conciliation) who will generally recognize their joint interest in achieving a good working relationship with one another. There are, however, situations where – because of the unwillingness of the employer to concede recognition to one or more unions, because disputes between unions over the right to represent particular groups of employees are not resolved, or because of the fragmentation of bargaining – the strain on industrial relations becomes excessive and the parties are entirely unable to compose their differences or to contemplate a fundamental change in the bargaining structure. It is in these situations that the Government believes that the possibility of recourse to independent investigation may prevent destructive conflict and a breakdown in industrial relations. It is to prevent such an outcome that the proposals in this section are directed.

131. The Government proposes to provide that any registered trade union, any employer or registered employers' association, a substantial proportion of the employees concerned, or the Secretary of State, could make a claim to the NIRC to have any dispute over a trade union's claim for recognition, or over bargaining structure, examined by the CIR. It would be an unfair industrial action to call a strike (or lock-out) over any question of recognition or bargaining rights while it was before the NIRC or the CIR and for a period after the CIR reported. The NIRC would refer the matter to the CIR if it were satisfied that no further progress could be made by discussions between the parties and/or conciliation, and that such a reference would help the development or maintenance of stable and effective bargaining arrangements.

132. The CIR would then investigate the problem and recommend:

i. an appropriate bargaining unit or units;

ii. a bargaining agent for each unit;

iii. any conditions which should be satisfied before recognition was granted to the bargaining agent.

133. The 'bargaining unit' would mean the employees, or a group of the employees, of a single employer or group of associated employers, whose terms and conditions of employment should, in the view of the CIR, be determined in the same negotiations.

134. The 'bargaining agent' would be the registered union, or the joint negotiating panel of registered unions, which should have sole negotiating rights for all employees within a bargaining unit. The CIR would not be able to recommend more than one bargaining agent for a bargaining unit.

135. The terms 'bargaining unit' and 'bargaining agent' have, for convenience, been borrowed from United States law and practice. The Government proposes that these concepts should be applied only in the specific situations described in this document, where this is necessary to promote the development of stable and effective collective bargaining; it does not envisage that they should be generally applied as in the United States.[39]

136. A joint negotiating panel would be a body in which a number of registered unions had vested appropriate authority to enter into collective agreements on their behalf and whose entry into such an agreement would commit each of the constituent unions as if it were a direct party to the agreement. The CIR would be able to recommend, and to assist with, the creation of a joint negotiating panel. It would specify, in its recommendations, which unions should belong to the panel – though obviously, in doing so, it would take account of any successful existing arrangements, and the readiness of unions to work together.

137. In considering whether a union or joint negotiating

39. The problem of how to delimit the boundaries of an appropriate bargaining 'unit' has given rise to a bewildering maze of decisions in the USA by both National Labor Relation Board and the courts: Summers and Wellington, op. cit., pp. 511–548. Merely to 'borrow' the machinery and use it only in selected cases will not by any means avoid this problem: pp. 167, 182, 464–6. The borrowed items would best be returned.

panel should be a bargaining agent, the CIR would take account of the extent to which the union or joint panel:

    i. has the support (not necessarily membership) of a substantial proportion of the employees affected; and

    ii. has the resources and organization that would enable it effectively to represent the employees.

138. The CIR would be able to recommend that no bargaining agent should be recognized if the union or unions concerned, or any feasible joint negotiating panel, did not (or would not) have substantial support from employees or had not (or would not have) the resources and organization to enable it to represent employees effectively.

139. The CIR could, where appropriate, specify conditions which must be fulfilled by the union or joint panel before statutory bargaining rights could be granted. Such conditions might, for example, relate to making sufficient trained officials and shop stewards available to participate in negotiations; or to an agreement not to pursue a claim for negotiating rights elsewhere in the undertaking.

140. The purpose of the CIR's examination would be to try to produce a durable solution to the dispute which gave rise to the reference. In general, if the CIR found that settled recognition arrangements were working well, it would be unlikely to disturb them.

141. The CIR would prepare a document embodying its recommendations and would send it to the NIRC, with copies to the Secretary of State, the employer, and the unions concerned in the reference.

142. The employer or the recommended bargaining agent could then apply to have the CIR's recommendations made enforceable; and the NIRC would enforce the recommendations if the employees concerned voted, by a majority in a secret ballot, to endorse the CIR's recommendations.

143. After the NIRC had made an order making the CIR's recommendations enforceable, the employer would be required to negotiate seriously with the bargaining agent. It would be an unfair industrial action for him to fail to do so, or to negotiate with anyone else in respect of the bargaining unit or any part

of it; and for anyone else to threaten industrial action, or to induce the employees to take industrial action, to disrupt in any way the statutory bargaining structure. If the NIRC found that an employer had failed to negotiate seriously, it could give the union a right unilaterally to refer a claim for improved terms and conditions of employment for the employees concerned to the Arbitration Board, whose award would be binding.[40]

144. There would be appropriate provisions for recognition orders to be modified or revoked when necessary. In particular, if, after a suitable minimum period, a large proportion of the employees were dissatisfied with the bargaining agent, they would be able to reopen the matter and secure a further ballot on whether its position as bargaining agent should be ended or transferred to another union.

VIIe. Disclosure of information by employers [41]

145. The Government considers that it is an essential part of the successful conduct of collective bargaining that the employer should not unnecessarily withhold information about his undertaking that the trade union representatives need in the course of negotiations.

146. It therefore proposes that the Code of Industrial Relations Practice (which the Secretary of State would have to prepare, as explained in Part III) should give guidance on the principles and practice to be applied by employers in relation to the disclosure of information about their undertakings to trade union representatives with whom they negotiate. This part of the Code would provide guidance about the disclosure of information without which trade union representatives would be impeded in their conduct of negotiations.

147. If an employer failed in the course of negotiations to

40. See p. 167, mentioning the complex litigation in the USA since 1935 on the 'duty to bargain in good faith'. The meaning of the duty to bargain 'seriously' is critical. 'What is at stake, of course, is the extent of governmental control over the subjects of collective bargaining and ultimately over the terms of the collective agreement': Summers and Wellington, op. cit., p. 636.

41. See pp. 46 and 169–70.

disclose information in accordance with the Code to representatives of a registered trade union that he recognized, the union could complain to the NIRC. If its complaint were upheld, the Court could grant the union the right unilaterally to refer a claim for improved terms and conditions of employment for the employees concerned for arbitration by the Arbitration Board, whose award would be binding.

148. In the Government's view, the employees of the larger employers should be entitled to some basic information about the undertaking, just as shareholders are in the case of public companies. The provision of this information to employees would recognize the interest which they have in the progress of the undertaking for which they work, and would acknowledge its obligations towards them.

149. It is therefore proposed that the Secretary of State should have power to require employers of a certain size or type, by regulations which would be subject to the approval of Parliament, to disclose specified information to their employees at stated intervals.

150. Appropriate provisions would be made for the protection, both in this case and in that of disclosure to trade unions, of confidential personal information and information the disclosure of which would be seriously prejudicial to the interests of the employer's undertaking.

VIIf. The 'closed shop' and the 'agency shop'

151. The Government is opposed to the 'pre-entry closed shop' which can exclude an individual from entering certain employments if he is not a member of any or of a particular trade union. It considers that an employer should be free to employ anyone who has the necessary skills. It proposes that the Industrial Relations Bill should contain provisions making any pre-entry closed shop agreement or arrangement void, and that any strike action (or threat of strike action) to enforce the continuation of, or to induce an employer to enter into, such an agreement should be an unfair industrial action.[42]

152. On the other hand the Government believes there is

42. Compare pp. 346; 454–65.

much to commend 'agency shop' agreements, whereby a registered trade union represents all the employees in a particular undertaking or establishment or part of it, and is supported financially by all of them. It considers, however, that employees should have the opportunity to choose whether or not such an agreement should govern their own place of employment or continue to do so, and that the individual should have a right, while paying for the services the union provides, to choose not to be a member of the union.

153. It is proposed to provide, therefore, that the introduction or continuation of an agency shop agreement reached between a union and an employer should be subject to the 20 per cent of the employees covered by the agreement to request a secret ballot to determine whether a majority of those employees favour the agency shop. The Government also proposes that it should be open to an employer resisting a union's claim to an agency shop or to a registered trade union pressing such a claim, to request a secret ballot to determine the wishes of employees. (Industrial action over an agency shop dispute whilst the CIR was organizing and conducting a ballot would be unfair.) If the ballot showed that a majority of those eligible to vote were in favour of the introduction of an agency shop, the employer would be obliged to enter into an agreement with the appropriate registered trade union to introduce it. If he failed to do so the trade union would be able to seek an order from the NIRC requiring him to do so. If, on the other hand, there was no majority in favour of an agency shop the employer and union would be prevented from introducing an agency shop agreement for two years; and it would be an unfair industrial action during that period for an employer to introduce an agency shop or for the union to call a strike to force the employer to do so. Only a registered trade union would be entitled to continue or secure an agency shop agreement.

154. Applications for agency shop ballots would be dealt with by the NIRC and, where an application was approved by the NIRC, the CIR would be responsible for supervising or arranging the ballot.

155. Where an employer entered into an agency shop agreement with a registered trade union he could require the employees concerned, after an interval of time, to join that trade union or to pay a regular contribution in lieu of the union's membership subscription. Anyone who did not follow either course would be liable to dismissal. The appropriate contribution would be in respect of the services provided by the trade union, and would be comparable to the subscription which the ordinary member of the union would be required to pay, less any optional elements. The payment of this contribution would not, however, entitle the employee as of right to all the benefits of membership of the trade union and it would not constitute a contract of membership. Where an individual had an objection on conscientious grounds both to belonging to a trade union and to paying any contribution to its funds there would be provision to allow him to contribute the appropriate amount to an appropriate charity.

156. Disputes about the level of the appropriate contribution to be paid by a non-member, about whether an employee has a genuine conscientious objection to contributing to a trade union's funds, and about what is an 'appropriate charity', would be for determination by an IT.

VIIg. *Wages Councils*[43]

157. The Government believes that greater progress can now be made in promoting the growth of voluntary arrangements for collective bargaining in Wages Council industries, and accelerating the abolition of councils which have outlived their usefulness, by amending the Wages Councils Act, 1959, and the Terms and Conditions of Employment Act, 1959, broadly on the lines recommended by the Donovan Commission.

158. As recommended by the Donovan Commission it is proposed to amend the Wages Councils Act to provide that trade unions should be able to apply unilaterally for the abolition of a council, provided that the union or unions are repre-

43. See p. 207.

sentative of a substantial proportion of the workers in the trade or industry concerned. (The Secretary of State would retain his present power to take the initiative in proposing the abolition of a council despite the absence of any application.)

159. It is proposed that the Act should be amended to provide that the only condition to be satisfied before a wages council can be abolished should be that the council is no longer necessary to maintain reasonable standards of remuneration among the workers within its scope.

160. Under present legislation, questions concerning the establishment, abolition or variation of the field of operation of a wages council are resolved by reference to ad hoc commissions of inquiry consisting of independent members and representatives of employers and workers. The establishment of the CIR makes it unnecessary to set up ad hoc bodies to decide these questions. It is proposed therefore that the Act should be amended to provide that the CIR should have power to perform all the functions at present undertaken by ad hoc commissions of inquiry.

161. The present legislation specifies in detail the criteria, concerning the extent and adequacy of existing negotiating machinery, to be applied by ad hoc commissions of inquiry. With the change in the grounds for abolition and the substitution of the CIR for ad hoc commissions of inquiry, these provisions would no longer be relevant and it is proposed to remove them from the Act.

162. It is proposed that the employers' side and the wages council concerned as a whole (i.e. including the independent members) should be consulted before action is taken to abolish a council. In cases of doubt or dispute the issue would be referred to the CIR.

163. Section 8 of the Terms and Conditions of Employment Act, 1959, which provides for the adjudication of the present Industrial Court – the future Arbitration Board – on a claim that an employer is not observing 'recognized' terms and conditions of employment, denies access to the Court if the claim concerns workers whose remuneration, or minimum remuneration, is fixed by or under any other enactment. It is proposed

to remove this exclusion so far as workers covered by wages councils are concerned.[44]

164. However, only registered trade unions would in future have the right (in wages council industries as elsewhere) to put claims under section 8 to the Arbitration Board.

VIII. NATIONAL EMERGENCIES AND STRIKE BALLOTS

165. Disputes sometimes arise where – whatever the merits and demerits of the case – the Government's prime duty and responsibility is to protect the public interest. At present, this can be done only by proclaiming a State of Emergency and, in the last resort, calling upon the armed services to secure essential supplies and services. The value of this safeguard is limited by the fact that the Emergency Powers Act 1920 cannot be invoked solely on the ground that the national economy is endangered.[45]

166. The Government regards this situation as unsatisfactory and proposes that the Secretary of State should have additional powers to intervene in disputes which may seriously threaten the national health, safety, or economy and/or the livelihood of a substantial portion of the community. He would, however, have to act through the NIRC; he would have no power to intervene directly. The present provisions of the Emergency Powers Act would remain.

VIIIa. *National emergencies*

167. The Government proposes that where industrial action has begun, or is likely to take place, which would deprive the community of the essentials of life or seriously endanger the national health, security, or economy, the Secretary of State should be able to apply to the NIRC for a restraining order against any union, employer, or employers' association, or any other person.

44. See p. 200 and p. 211. See, too, on s.8, the proposal in para. 43.
45. See p. 394. The proposed new pattern here again is the Taft–Hartley law of 1947 in the USA.

168. Before applying for such an order the Secretary of State should take account of the extent to which agreed or customary procedures for settling disputes have been adequately [*sic*] and of any representations made by the parties concerned.

169. Unless the NIRC, after considering the application in relation to relevant criteria, were not satisfied that there were grounds for the application, it would make an order restraining named organizations and/or persons from taking steps to call, induce, or finance the industrial action. Any strike calls already issued would be required to be withdrawn.

170. The order would be effective for a period of up to 60 days – during which the NIRC would be able to make appropriate orders (expiring at the same time as the original order) against other organizations or persons who were found to be instigating action relating to the same dispute. While the orders were in force all appropriate action would be taken to effect a settlement. The order could be renewed if the initial order were for a shorter period than 60 days, but could not be extended beyond, or renewed at or after, the end of the 60 days.

171. The order would not compel individuals to return to, or to remain at, work. There would be no sanctions against any individual solely on the ground that he participated in industrial action. This conforms to the general principles set out in Part II.

VIIIb. *Strike ballots*

172. There are sometimes cases where industrial action would deprive the community, or a substantial part of it, of the essentials of life, or seriously endanger the national health, security, or economy, or the safety or livelihood of a substantial portion of the community, but where there is doubt whether such industrial action has the support of the majority of workers involved. In such circumstances the Government proposes that the Secretary of State, after taking account of any representations made by the parties concerned, should be able to apply to the NIRC for an order for a secret ballot to be held.

173. The NIRC, after considering the application in relation to relevant criteria, would make such an order for a ballot unless it were not satisfied that there were grounds for it. The order would prohibit calling or inducing industrial action over the matter at issue till the ballot was held. Once again, however, the order would not compel individuals to return to or remain at work.

174. The issue to be decided by the ballot would be whether or not a majority of the workers concerned were in favour of industrial action on the matters and in the circumstances specified in the NIRC's order. The order would also make clear who was to be balloted.[46]

175. The ballot result would be notified to NIRC and the Secretary of State, and would be published.

176. The result of the ballot would not be binding and the NIRC's order would lapse once the ballot had been held.

IX. SCOPE AND INTERPRETATION

177. In general it is proposed to exclude from the scope of the proposals in this document:

(i) workers ordinarily employed outside Britain, except when they are in Britain (but merchant seamen ordinarily resident in Britain and employed on ships registered in Britain will be covered);

(ii) the armed forces and the police.

It is also proposed to exclude from certain of the proposals (e.g. those on unfair dismissals):

(i) part-time workers employed less than 21 hours a week;

(ii) employees in small establishments (whose definition might vary for different parts of the provisions);

(iii) workers employed by their husband or wife or a close relative;

46. The NIRC appears to have complete control as to what question should be put to the workers. Under the Taft–Hartley law, after 60 days of a national emergency injunction the National Labor Relations Board conducts a ballot on the employer's 'last offer'. The 'criteria' mentioned here and the power to frame the question will similarly affect the conduct of employers in collective negotiations.

(iv) share fishermen wholly remunerated by a share of the catch.

178. In general it is proposed that the provisions should apply to persons employed under a contract personally to do work (i.e. certain sorts of self-employed people) in the same way as to those employed under a contract of employment, except where (e.g. in relation to unfair dismissal) this is clearly inappropriate.[47]

179. The Government is consulting with the Government of Northern Ireland about how far (if at all) the proposed legislation should apply to Northern Ireland.

Department of Employment and   5 October 1970
Productivity

47. See p. 61 on self-employment.

SELECTED BIBLIOGRAPHY

This bibliography contains some but not all of the works cited in the notes to each chapter. Its aim is to provide those interested in pursuing topics further with a reading list for their studies.

1. GENERAL

Aiken, O., and Reid, J., *Labour Law*, Vol. I., *Employment, Welfare and Safety at Work* (forthcoming).

Carby Hall, J. R., *Principles of Industrial Law* (1969).

Citrine, N. A., *Trade Union Law* (1960, 3rd ed. 1967: M. A. Hickling) (textbook on trade unions and strikes).

Cooper, Mansfield, and Wood, J. C., *Outlines of Industrial Law* (1966, 5th ed.).

Cronin, J. B., and Grime, R. P., *Labour Law* (1970).

Drake, C. D., *Labour Law* (1969) (brief textbook).

Fridman, G. H. L., *The Modern Law of Employment* (1963, 2nd supp., 1966) (legal reference textbook).

Grunfeld, C., *Modern Trade Union Law* (1966) (textbook on trade unions and strikes).

Kahn-Freund, O., 'Labour Law', lecture in Ginsberg, M. (ed.), *Law and Opinion in England in the 20th Century* (1959) (development of labour law in Britain).

Kahn-Freund, O., *Labour Law, Old Traditions and New Developments* (1968) (review of current trends in Britain).

Miller, I. R., *Industrial Law in Scotland* (1970).

Sim, R. S., and Powell Smith, W., *Casebook on Industrial Law* (1969).

Wedderburn, K. W., *Cases and Materials on Labour Law* (1967).

2. DONOVAN REPORT, ASSOCIATED MATERIALS, AND PROPOSALS

(a) Royal Commission on Trade Unions and Employers' Associations (1965–8); Chairman: Lord Donovan. (June 1968, Cmnd 3623, H.M.S.O.).

(b) Research Papers published by the Royal Commission:
 (1) *The Role of Shop Stewards*, W. E. J. McCarthy;

(2) Part 1: *Disputes Procedures*, A. I. Marsh;
Part 2: *Disputes Procedures*, A. I. Marsh and W. E. J. McCarthy;

(3) *Industrial Sociology and Industrial Relations*, A. Fox;

(4) i. *Productivity Bargaining*; ii. *Restrictive Labour Practices*; by the Commission's Secretariat;

(5) *Trade Union Structure and Government*, J. Hughes:
Part 1: *Structure and Development*;
Part 2: *Membership Participation and Trade Union Government*;

(6) *Trade Union Growth and Recognition*, G. S. Bain;

(7) *Employers' Associations:*
Part 1: V. G. Munns;
Part 2: W. E. J. McCarthy;

(8) *Three Studies in Collective Bargaining:*
1. *Grievance Arbitration in the U.S.*, J. Stieber;
2. *Compulsory Arbitration in Britain*, W. E. J. McCarthy;
3. *Check-off Agreements in Britain*, A. I. Marsh and J. W. Staples;

(9) *Overtime Working in Britain*, E. G. Whybrew;

(10) *Shop Stewards and Workshop Relations*, W. E. J. McCarthy and S. R. Parker;

(11) *Two Studies in Industrial Relations:*
1. *The Position of Women in Industry*, Nancy Seear;
2. *Changing Wage Payment Systems*, R. S. McKersie;

(12) Social Survey Report, *Workplace Industrial Relations* (S.S. 402; 1968, H.M.S.O.).

(c) Evidence to Royal Commission: Selected Items:

(Entries in square brackets indicate separate publication; the full minutes of written and oral evidence and a volume of *Selected Written Evidence* are all published by H.M.S.O.)

Ministry of Labour [H.M.S.O. 1965], Minutes, Days 2, 3; *Selected Written Evidence*, Part 1.

National Coal Board, Day 4.

London Transport, Day 5.

Confederation of British Industries [1965], Days 6, 9, 22, 69; *Selected Written Evidence*, Part 5.

Chief Registrar of Friendly Societies [H.M.S.O. 1965], Day 8.

Dr R. W. Rideout, Day 15.

Department of Economic Affairs, Day 18.

Engineering Employers' Federation [1965], Day 20; *Selected Written Evidence*, Part 6.

Motor Industry Employers [1965], Day 23.

Amalgamated Engineering Union [*Trade Unions and the Contemporary Scene*, 1965], Day 24.

Massey-Ferguson (U.K.) Ltd, Day 25.

National Association of Local Government Officers, Day 26; *Selected Written Evidence*, Part 3.

Transport and General Workers' Union [1966], Day 30.

Professor K. W. Wedderburn, Day 31.

Society of Independent Manufacturers, Day 32.

Professor B. C. Roberts, Day 33.

Swedish Employers' Confederation, Day 34.

Inns of Court Conservative Society, Day 35.

Professor H. H. Wellington, Day 41.

Bar Council, Day 43.

Sir Roy Wilson, Q.C., Day 45.

Shipbuilding Employers' Federation, Day 48.

Law Society, Day 52; *Selected Written Evidence*, Part 8.

A.S.S.E.T. [1966, *100 Years On*], Day 53.

Haldane Society, Day 56.

Trades Union Congress [*Trade Unionism*, 2nd ed. with supp., 1967], Days 61, 65; *Selected Written Evidence*, Part 4.

Allan Flanders, Day 62; *Selected Written Evidence*, Part 9.

Professor G. H. Camerlynck, Day 66.

Kodak Ltd, Day 67.

Professor H. A. Turner, *Selected Written Evidence*, Part 14.

(d) Other Works (see, too, 6(d) and 9 *infra*):

British Journal of Industrial Relations: Special Issue on Donovan Report (November 1968) Vol. VI, (especially, General Commentary 275; C. Grunfeld, 'The Legal Aspects', 316; H. A. Turner, 'The Research Papers', 346).

Commission on Industrial Relations, *Report No. 1* (*Associated Octel*; Cmnd 4246); *Report No. 4* (*Birmid Qualcast*; Cmnd 4264); *Report No. 5* (*BSR Ltd*; Cmnd 4274); *Report No. 9* (First General Report; Cmnd 4417).

Confederation of British Industries, *Disputes Procedures* (1970; report on reform of procedures).

Conservative Political Centre, *Fair Deal at Work* (1968).

Fay, S., *Measure for Measure: Reforming the Trade Unions* (1970).

Jenkins, C., and Mortimer, J. E., *The Kind of Laws the Unions Ought to Want* (London, 1968).

Kahn-Freund, O., 'The Shifting Frontiers of the Law and Custom in Labour Relations' (1969) 22 *Current Legal Problems* 1.

Kahn-Freund, O., 'Industrial Relations and the Law – Retrospect and Prospect' (1969) VII *Brit. J. Industrial Relations* 301.

Labour Government White Paper, *In Place of Strife*, Cmnd 3888 (1969, H.M.S.O.).

McCarthy, W. E. J., 'Nature of Britain's Strike Problem' (1970) VIII *British J. Industrial Relations* 224.

Parsons, O. H., *The Donovan Report* (London, 1968).

Paynter, W., *British Trade Unions and the Problem of Change* (1970; by member of C.I.R.).

Roberts, B. C., 'Fair Deal at Work – A Review' (1968) VI *Brit. J. of Industrial Relations* 360.

Schmidt, Folke, 'Royal Commission on Trade Unions and Employers' Associations' (1969) 32 *Modern Law Review* 65.

Trades Union Congress, *Action on Donovan* (1968).

Trades Union Congress, *Programme for Action* (1969).

Turner, H. A., *Is Britain Really Strike-Prone?* (1969, C.U.P.).

Wedderburn, K. W., 'Report of the Royal Commission on Trade Unions and Employers' Associations' (1968) 31 *Modern Law Review* 674.

Wood, J. C., 'Law and Industrial Relations' (1969) *J. Bus. Law* 93.

Woodcock, G., 'Role of Commission on Industrial Relations' (1969) 78 *Employment and Productivity Gazette* 116.

3. CONTRACT OF EMPLOYMENT, ETC. (See too 6(c), p. 537)

Batt, F. R., *Law of Master and Servant* (ed. G. J. Webber, 5th ed. 1967, effectively 1965).

Bayliss, F. J., *British Wages Councils* (1962).

Brown, D., 'The Test of Service' (1969) *J. Bus. Law* 177.

Casey, J. P., 'Unemployment Benefit and Damages: Need for a New Approach' (1969) *Juridical Review* 206.

Clark, G. de N., 'Remedies for Unjust Dismissal: Proposals for Legislation' (P.E.P. 1970 Broadsheet No. 518).

Clark, G. de N., 'Industrial Law and the Labour Only Sub-Contract' (1967) 30 *Modern Law Review* 6.

Clark, G. de N., 'Unfair Dismissal and Reinstatement' (1969) 32 *Modern Law Review* 532.

Counter, K. N. S., 'Preservation of Pension Rights' (1968) *J. Bus. Law* 229.

Drake, C. D., 'Wage Slave or Entrepreneur?' (1968) 31 *Modern Law Review* 408.

Drake, C. D., 'Wrongful Dismissal and "Sitting in the Sun"' (1969) *J. Bus. Law* 113.

Freedland, M., 'Straightening out the Kinks in the Law of Contract' (1969) 32 *Modern Law Review* 314.

Freedland, M., 'Dismissal in Redundancy Payments Act 1965' (1970) 33 *Modern Law Review* 93.

Freedland, M., 'The Equal Pay Bill, 1970', *Industrial Law Society Bulletin, No.* 7 (1970), p. 3.

Ganz, G., 'Public Law Principles Applicable to Dismissal from Employment' (1967) 30 *Modern Law Review* 288.

Gardiner, Gerald, (1959) 22 *Modern Law Review* 652, '*Lister* v. *Romford Ice and Cold Storage Company Ltd*: Report of the Inter-Departmental Committee' (Note).

Goodhart, A. L., 'Damages and Pensions' (1967) 83 *Law Quarterly Review* 492.

Grime, R. P., 'Two Cultures in the Court of Appeal' (1969) 32 *Modern Law Review* 575 (summary dismissal).

Heydon, J. D., 'Frontiers of Restraint of Trade Doctrine' (1969) 85 *Law Quarterly Review* 229.

Kahn-Freund, O., 'Note on Status and Contract in British Labour Law' (1967) 30 *Modern Law Review* 635.

Logan, D., 'A Civil Servant and His Pay' (1945) 61 *Law Quarterly Review* 240.

Melville, L., '*Coco* v. *Clark*' (1968) 118 *New Law Journal* 924 (confidential information).

Ministry of Labour, *Sick Pay Schemes* (H.M.S.O. 1964).

National Joint Advisory Council (Min. of Labour), 'Dismissal Procedures' (H.M.S.O. 1967).

National Joint Advisory Council (Min. of Labour), 'Preservation of Pension Rights' (H.M.S.O. 1966).

North, P. M., 'Disclosures of Confidential Information' (1965) *J. Bus. Law* 307, (1966) 31, (1968) 32.

O'Higgins, P., 'The Contracts of Employment Act 1963' [1964] *Cambridge Law Journal* 220.

O'Higgins, P., 'When is an Employee not an Employee' [1967] *Cambridge Law Journal* 27.

Redgrave, *Factories Acts* (eds. Fife and Machin, 21st ed. 1966) Part IV on 'Truck Acts'.

Reid, Judith, 'Report on Dismissal Procedures' (N.J.A.C.) (1968) 31 *Modern Law Review* 64.

Rideout, R. W., 'The Contract of Employment' (1966) *Current Legal Problems* 111.

Samuel, P., and Lewis, R., 'Building's Bedouin Arabs' *Personnel,* Vol. I, p. 20 (1968).

4. STATUTES AND EMPLOYMENT (including 'Floor of Rights' Statutes, Redundancy, etc.)

D.E.P. 'Employment and the Race Relations Act 1968' (1970) 79 *Employment and Productivity Gazette* 100.

Drake, C. D., 'Labour Mobility' (1969) 5 *Ind. Law Soc. Bull.* 2.

Freedland, M., 'Redundancy Payments Act of 1965 and the Policy of Labour Mobility' (1969) 5 *Ind. Law Soc. Bull.* 23.

Fridman, G. H. L., 'Employment Law and Redundancy Payments' (1967) *New Law J.* 117, 375, 403, 425, 602, 701, 850, 935, 1005, 1036, 1187.

Gilbert, B. B., *The Evolution of National Insurance in Great Britain* (1966).

Government Interdepartmental Working Party Report, *National Minimum Wage* (1969, 'Green Paper', H.M.S.O.).

Hall, J. S., 'Selective Employment Tax' (1967) *J. Bus. Law* 7.

Hepple, B.A., *Race, Jobs and the Law in Britain* (2nd ed. 1970).

Hepple, B. A., 'Race Relations Act of 1968' (1969) 32 *Modern Law Review* 181.

Jenkins, E. (ed.), *Digest of Commissioners' Decisions* (National Insurance, Industrial Injuries, and Family Allowances Acts), Vols. I & II, 1964 and Supplements; 1969 Supp. 13.

Kahn-Freund, O., 'Tangle of the Truck Acts' (1949) 4 *Industrial Law Review* 2.

Mann, F. A., 'Redundancy Payments Act of 1965 and Conflict of Laws' (1966) 82 *Law Quarterly Review* 316.

Redgrave, *Factories Acts* (eds. Fife and Machin, 21st ed. 1966; Part IV 'Truck Acts').

Reid, Judith, 'Cases on Selective Employment Tax' (1969) *Brit. Tax Review* 343.

Rideout, R. W., *Reforming the Redundancy Payments Acts* (Instit. Personnel Management, 1969).

Samuels, A., 'Government Participation in Private Industry' (Industrial Expansion Act of 1968) (1968) *J. Bus. Law* 296.

Samuels, H., and Stewart-Pearson, N., *Redundancy Payments* (2nd ed 1970).

Trades Union Congress, *Low Pay* (1970: useful discussion document on problems of minimum pay statute).

Wedderburn, K. W., 'Redundancy Payments Act of 1965' (1966) 29 *Modern Law Review* 55.

5. ACCIDENTS AND INDUSTRIAL INJURY

Allsop, P. (ed.), *Encyclopedia of Factories* (looseleaf) (1963 et seq.)

Atiyah, P. S., 'Collateral Benefits Again' (1969) 32 *Modern Law Review* 397 (damages).

Atiyah, P. S., *Accidents, Compensation and the Law* (1970).

Bell, J., *How to Get Industrial Injuries Benefits* (1966).

Calabresi, G., *The Costs of Accidents* (Yale, 1970).

Clark, G. de N., 'Labour-Only and Safety' (1968) 31 *Modern Law Review* 74.

Curson, C., 'Compensation for Accidents at Work', *D.E.P. Gazette* July 1969, p. 624 (H.M.F.I.'s paper attacking civil action for damages).

Dias, R. W. M., 'Consent of Parties and Voluntas Legis (*Shatwell* v. *I.C.I.*)' [1966] *Cambridge Law J.* 75.

Dias, R. W. M., 'Kind and Extent of Damage in Negligence' [1970] *Cambridge Law J.* 28.

Fife, I., and Machin, E. A., *Offices, Shops, and Railway Premises Act of 1963* (1963).

Fleming, J., 'The Collateral Source Rule and Loss Allocation' (1966) 54 *California Law Review* 1478.

Fridman, G. H. L., 'Security in Mines' (1969) 32 *Modern Law Review* 174.

Hendy, J., 'Limiting the Uncertainty of Foreseeability' (1969) 32 *Modern Law Review* 438.

Hepple, B. A., 'Employers' Liability: Defective Equipment' [1970] *Cambridge Law J.* 25.

Howells, R. W. L., 'Industrial Accidents: Education and Enforcement' (1970) 33 *Modern Law Review* 89.

Howells, R. W. L., 'Accidents and the Law', *New Society*, 23 Sept. 1965.

Howells, R. W. L., 'New Wave of Interpretations of the Factories Acts' (1962) 25 *Modern Law Review* 98.

Howells, R. W. L., '*Priestley* v. *Fowler* and the Factory Acts' (1963) 26 *Modern Law Review* 367.

Hunter, D., *Health in Industry* (1959) (Industrial Diseases).

Industrial Law Society *Bulletin No. 6* (1969): 'Personal Injuries – Social Insurance or Tort Liability' (A. Sapper; P. S. Atiyah; B. Thompson; B. Mathieson).

Ison, T. G., 'Tort Liability and Social Insurance' (1969) 19 *Univ. Toronto Law J.* 614.

Ison, T. G., *The Forensic Lottery* (1967).

Jenkins, E. (ed.), *Digest of Commissioners' Decisions* (National Insurance, Industrial Injuries, and Family Allowances Acts), Vols. I and II and Supplements.

Jolowicz, J. A., 'Damages; Collateral Benefits' [1969] *Cambridge Law J.* 183.

Labour Lawyers Society, *Occupational Accidents and the Law* (Fabian Society, 1970. Research Series 280).

Munkman, J., *Employers' Liability at Common Law* (1966).

Redgrave, *Factories Acts* (eds. I. Fife and E. A. Machin, 21st edn., 1966) (legal reference book).

Reid, Judith, 'Industrial Injuries and the Tea Break' (1966) 29 *Modern Law Review* 389.

Reid, Judith, 'The Duty to Fence' (1967) 30 *Modern Law Review* 455.

Samuels, H., *Factory Law* (1969, 8th ed.).

Street, H., *Justice in the Welfare State* (1968).

Thomson, B. and R., *Accidents at Work* (1968, 3rd ed.).

Williams, J. L., *Accidents and Ill Health at Work* (1960).

Young, A. F., *Industrial Injuries Insurance* (1964).

6. LEGAL ASPECTS OF COLLECTIVE BARGAINING

(a) Collective Agreements and Related Statutes, etc.:

Asmal, K., 'Collective Agreements and Contractual Obligations' 14 *Leargus: Public Affairs Review* 15: ibid. 8.

Clark, G. de N., 'The *Ford* Case' (1970) 33 *Modern Law Review* 117.

Foster, K., 'The Ford Case and After' (1969) 113 *Solicitors' Journal* 295.

Hepple, B. A., 'Intention to Create Legal Relations' [1970] *Cambridge Law J.* 122 (on the *Ford* case).

Kahn-Freund, O., 'Legislation Through Adjudication: Legal Aspects of Fair Wages Clauses' (1948) 11 *Modern Law Review* 269 and 429.

Selwyn, N., 'Collective Agreements and the Law' (1969) 32 *Modern Law Review* 377 (criticism of *Ford* case).

Wedderburn, K. W., 'The Legal Force of Plant Bargains' (1969) 32 *Modern Law Review* 99.

Wedderburn, K. W., 'British Unions Beware', *New Society*, 4 Dec. 1969 (on problems of legal right to recognition and bargaining).

Weisbard, S., 'Legal Consequences of Collective Agreements' (1970) 120 *New Law J.* 98.

(b) Prices and Incomes Policies:

(1) Selected Reports of National Board for Prices and Incomes: 1966–9 Annual General Reports; and especially:

No. 89, *Office Staff Employment Agencies, Charges and Salaries*, Cmnd 3828 (1968);

No. 101, *Pay of Workers in Agriculture*, Cmnd 3911 (1969);

No. 68, *Agreements Between Engineering Firms and D.A.T.A.*, Cmnd 3632 (1968);

No. 63, *Municipal Busmen*, Cmnd 3605 (1968);

No. 65, *Payments by Results Systems*, Cmnd 3627 (1968);

No. 27, *Workers in Retail Drapery, etc., Trades*, Cmnd 3224 (1967);

No. 123, *Productivity Agreements*, Cmnd 4136 (1969, second report on productivity bargains);

No. 132, *Salary Structures*, Cmnd 4178 (1969).

(2) British Journal of Industrial Relations (1964), 'Symposium on Incomes Policy', II, No. 3, 309–78.

Cliff, T., and Barker, C., *Incomes Policy, Legislation and Shop Stewards* (1966).

Drake, C. D., 'Prices and Incomes Act of 1967' (1968) *J. Bus. Law* 120.

Fleeman, R. K., and Thompson, A. G., *Productivity Bargaining: A Practical Guide* (1970).

Labour Government White Papers, *Productivity, Prices, and Incomes Policy 1968 and 1969*, April 1968, H.M.S.O., Cmnd 3590 and December 1969, Cmnd 4237.

Lewis, N., 'Prices and Incomes Act' (1967) 30 *Modern Law Review* 67.

McCarthy, W. E. J. (ed.), *Ditchley Paper* 15, 'Role of Government in Industrial Relations' (1968).

Topham, A., 'Productivity Bargaining', *Trade Union Register 1969*.

(c) Grievance Procedures, Arbitration, and Labour Tribunals:

Aaron, B. (ed.), *Disputes Settlement Procedures in Five West European Countries* (1969) (comparative lectures by X. Blanc Jouvan, G. Giugni, T. Ramm, F. Schmidt, K. W. Wedderburn).

Amulree, Lord, *Industrial Arbitration in Great Britain* (1929: historical).

Anderman, S. D., *Voluntary Dismissal Procedures and the New Legislation* (P.E.P., forthcoming 1970).

Givry, J. de, 'Labour Courts: an International Review' (1968) VI *British Journal of Industrial Relations* 364.

Hughes, H. D., 'Settlement of Disputes in the Public Service' (1968) *Public Administration* 45 (comparative – Great Britain, Australia, and Canada).

National Joint Advisory Council (Ministry of Labour), *Dismissals Procedures*, H.M.S.O. (1967).

Plumridge, M., 'Disciplinary Practice' (1966) XLVIII *Personnel Management* 138.

Rideout, R. W., 'The Industrial Tribunals' (1968) 21 *Current Legal Problems* 178–94.

Sharp, I. G., *Industrial Conciliation and Arbitration in Great Britain* (1950).

Wedderburn, K. W., and Davies, P. L., *Employment Grievances and Disputes Procedures in Britain* (Univ. of California Press, 1969).

Weisbard, S., 'Industrial Tribunals' (1969) 119 *New Law J.* 916.

(d) Industrial Democracy (Workers, Corporations, and the State, etc.) (see too *infra* p. 544 (Section 11 (1) General):

Banks, J. A., *Industrial Participation* (1963).

Blumberg, P., *Industrial Democracy* (1968).

Clegg, H. A., *A New Approach to Industrial Democracy* (1960).

Coates, K., and Topham, A., *Industrial Democracy in Great Britain* (1968) (readings). [New ed. 1970: *Worker's Control*]

Coates, K., and Topham, A., 'The Ambiguities of Workers' Participation' (1967) 22 *International Socialist Journal* 622.

Flanders, A., Pomerans, R., and Woodward, J., *Experiment in*

Industrial Democracy (1968, London; report on the 'John Lewis Partnership').

Galbraith, J. K., *The New Industrial State* (1967).

Gower, L. C. B., *Modern Company Law* (3rd ed., 1969) Chapter 3, pp. 57–64. (Company law and workers).

Industrial Relations: Symposium, Vol. 9 (1970), pp. 117–214: 'Workers' Participation in Management; International Comparison'.

Institute for Workers' Control, New Series, various pamphlets on workers' control; including H. Scanlon, 'The Way Forward' (1968).

Kendall, W., 'Workers' Participation' (1970) 2 *Bulletin of Institute for Workers' Control* 7.

Kindleberger, C. P., (ed.), *The International Corporation* (1970, U.S.A.).

Labour Party, *Industrial Democracy* (Working Party Report, 1967).

Miliband, R., *The State in Capitalist Society* (1969).

Pribicevic, B., *Shop Stewards' Movement and Workers' Control 1910–1922* (1959).

Selsnick, P., *Law Society and Industrial Justice* (1969, New York).

Shonfield, A., *Modern Capitalism* (1965; new ed. 1969).

Sturmthal, A., *Workers' Councils* (1964).

Turner, L., *Politics and the Multi-national Company* (1969, Fabian Society, Research Series 279).

Walker, K. F., *Industrial Democracy: Fantasy, Fiction or Fact?* (1970; *Times* lecture).

7. STRIKES AND INDUSTRIAL CONFLICT

Christie, I. M., 'Inducing Breach of Contract in Trade Disputes (England and Canada)' (1967) 13 *McGill Law J.* 101.

Dean, M., 'Recklessness and Inducing Breach of Contract' (1967) 30 *Modern Law Review* 208.

Goodhart, A. L., 'The Legality of the General Strike', Chapter XI in *Essays in Jurisprudence and the Common Law*; and (1927) 36 *Yale Law J.* 464.

Guest, A. G., and Hoffmann, L. H., 'When is Boycott Unlawful?' (1968) 84 *Law Quarterly Review* 310.

Grabiner, A. S., 'There is a Tort of Interference with Contractual Relations' (1969) 32 *Modern Law Review* 435.

Hamson, C. J., 'A Further Note on *Rookes* v. *Barnard*' [1964] *Cambridge Law J.* 159.

Hamson, C. J., 'Inducing Breach of Contract – Interference with Business' [1968] *Cambridge Law J.* 190.

Heydon, J. D., 'Justification in Intentional Economic Loss' (1970) 20 *Univ. Toronto Law J.* 139.

Hickling, M. A., '*Tynan* v. *Chief Constable of Liverpool*' (1965) 28 Act' (1966) 29 *Modern Law Review* 32.

Hickling, M. A., '*Tynan* v. *Chief Constable of Liverpool*' (1965) 28 *Modern Law Review* 707 (picketing).

Hoffmann, L. H., '*Rookes* v. *Barnard*' (1965) 81 *Law Quarterly Review* 116.

Hughes, A. D., 'Liability for Loss Caused by Industrial Action' (1970) 86 *Law Quarterly Review* 181.

Industrial Law Soc. Supp. to Bulletin No. 5, 1969, 'Law and Industrial Conflict – Symposium' (Prof. R. Blanpain; S. D. Anderman; W. Paynter; Prof. K. W. Wedderburn).

Kahn-Freund, O., '*Rookes* v. *Barnard* – and After', Vol. 14, *Federation News*, April 1964 (article in *Journal of General Federation of Trade Unions*).

Lewis, N., 'Strikes and Contracts of Employment' (1968) *J. Bus. Law* 24.

O'Higgins, P., and Partington, M., 'Industrial Conflict and Judicial Attitudes' (1969) 32 *Modern Law Review* 53.

O'Higgins, P., 'Legal Effect of Strike Notice [1968] *Cambridge Law J.* 223.

Parsons, O. H., *The Meaning of* Rookes *v.* Barnard: *Trade Unions Hamstrung* (Labour Research, 1964).

Picciotto, S., and Davies, P. L., 'Sit-ins and the Law', *New Society*, 16 April 1970 (on injunction procedure).

Simon, Sir John, *The General Strike* (1926: three speeches).

Smith, D. W., '*Rookes* v. *Barnard*: An Upheaval in the Common Law Relating to Industrial Disputes' (1966) 40 *Australian Law J.* 81, 112.

Thompson, A. W. J., 'Injunction in Trade Disputes in Britain Before 1910' (1966) *Industrial and Labour Relations Review* 213.

Wedderburn, K. W., 'Inducing Breach of Contract and Unlawful Interference' (1968) 31 *Modern Law Review* 440.

Wedderburn, K. W., 'Intimidation and the Right to Strike' (1964) 27 *Modern Law Review* 257 (on the House of Lords decision in *Rookes* v. *Barnard*).

Wedderburn, K. W., 'Labour Injunction in Scotland' (1968) 31 *Modern Law Review* 550.

Wedderburn, K. W., 'The Right to Threaten Strikes' (1961) 24 *Modern Law Review* 572 (on *Rookes* v. *Barnard* in High Court).

Wedderburn, K. W., 'Trade Disputes Act of 1965' (1966) 29 *Modern Law Review* 53.

Wedderburn, K. W., 'Torts out of Contracts: Transatlantic Warnings' (1970) 33 *Modern Law Review* 309 (on interference with contract).

Wedderburn, K. W., '*Stratford* v. *Lindley*' (1965) 28 *Modern Law Review* 205.

Weir, J. A., '*Rookes, Stratford* – Economic Torts' [1964] *Cambridge Law J.* 225.

8. TRADE UNION LAW (MEMBERSHIP AND ADMINISTRATION)

Goodhart, A. L., 'The Right to Work' (1966) 82 *Law Quarterly Review* 319.

Grunfeld, C., 'Political Independence in British Trade Unions' (1963) I *Brit. J. Industrial Relations* 23.

Grunfeld, C., *Trade Unions and the Individual in English Law* (1963: Institute of Personnel Management).

Hall, J. S., 'Right to Work' (1967) 117 *New Law J.* 961.

Hickling, M. A., 'Legal Personality of Trade Unions in the British Isles' (1964) 4 *Western Law Review* 7.

Hickling, M. A., 'Right to Membership of a Trade Union' (1967) *Univ. Brit. Columbia Law Review* 243.

Hickling, M. A., 'Trade Unions in Disguise' (1964) 27 *Modern Law Review* 625.

Kahn-Freund, O., 'The Illegality of a Trade Union' (1943) 7 *Modern Law Review* 192.

Kahn-Freund, O., 'Trade Unions, the Law and Society' (1970) 33 *Modern Law Review* 241.

Lloyd, D., 'The Right to Work' (1957) 10 *Current Legal Problems* 36.

Lloyd, D., 'Damages for Wrongful Expulsion from a Trade Union' (1956) 19 *Modern Law Review* 121.

Reid, Judith, 'Dismissal of the Paid Union Official' (1968) 31 *Modern Law Review* 214.

Rideout, R. W., 'Admission to Non-Statutory Associations Controlling Employment' (1967) 30 *Modern Law Review* 389.

Rideout, R. W., 'Content of Trade Union Disciplinary Rules' (1965) III *Brit. J. Industrial Relations* 153.

Rideout, R. W., 'Responsible Self Government in British Trade Unions' (1967) V *Brit. J. Industrial Relations* 74.

Rolph, C. H., *All Those in Favour – the E.T.U. Trial* (1962).

Wedderburn, K. W., 'The Bonsor Affair – A Postscript' (1957) 20 *Modern Law Review* 105.

Weir, J. A., 'Discrimination in Private Law' [1966] *Cambridge Law J.* 165 (admission to associations).

9. INDUSTRIAL RELATIONS – MODERN BACKGROUND

Allen, V. L., *Trade Unions and the Government* (1960).

Bain, G. S., *The Growth of White-Collar Unionism* (1970).

Barratt Brown, M., 'The Trade Union Question' (1967) 38 *Political Quarterly* 156.

Blackburn, R., and Cockburn, A., *The Incompatibles* (1967).

Blumler, J. G., and Ewbank, A. J., 'Trade Unionists, Mass Media and Unofficial Strikes' (1970) VIII *Brit. J. Industrial Relations* 32.

Burns, T. (ed.), *Industrial Man* (1969).

Clack, G., *Industrial Relations in a British Car Factory* (1968).

Clegg, H. A., *The System of Industrial Relations in Great Britain* (1970: the major modern textbook).

Clegg, H. A., and Adams, R., *The Employers' Challenge* (1957) (a study of the engineering strike).

Clegg, H. A., Killick, A. J., and Adams, R., *Trade Union Officers* (1961).

Coates, K., Topham, T., and Barratt Brown, M., *Trade Union Register 1970*.

Committee of Inquiry under Prof. Phelps Brown, *Labour in Building and Civil Engineering*, Cmnd 3714, 1968.

Dunlop, J. T., and Chamberlain, N. W. (eds.), *Frontiers of Collective Bargaining* (1967).

Dunlop, J. T., *Industrial Relations Systems* (1958).

Eldridge, J. E. T., *Industrial Disputes* (1968).

Flanders, A., 'Collective Bargaining – a Theoretical Analysis' (1968) VI *Brit. J. Industrial Relations* 1.

Flanders, A., *Collective Bargaining: Prescription for Change* (1967).

Flanders, A., *Industrial Relations: What is Wrong with the System?* (1965).

Flanders, A., *Trade Unions* (1968 ed.) (the best short introduction).

Flanders, A., *Collective Bargaining* (1969: very useful selected readings especially on Britain and U.S.A.).

Flanders, A., 'Changing Character of Collective Bargaining', (1969), 78 *Employment and Productivity Gazette*, 1100.

Fox, A., 'Managerial Ideology and Labour Relations' (1966) IV *Brit. J. Industrial Relations* 366.

Fox, A., and Flanders, A., 'Reform of Collective Bargaining: From Donovan to Durkheim' (1969) VII *Brit. J. Industrial Relations* 151.

Goldthorpe, J. H., Lockwood, D., Bechhofer, F., and Platt, J., *The Affluent Worker: Industrial Attitudes and Behaviour* (1968).

Hughes, J., *The T.U.C.—A Plan for the 1970s* (1969, Fabian Tract 397).

Jenkins, C., and Mortimer, J. E., *British Trade Unions Today* (1965).

Jenkins, P., *The Battle of Downing Street* (1970).

Knowles, K. G. J. C., *Strikes* (1952).

Lerner, S. W., *Breakaway Unions and the Small Trade Unions* (1961).

Lewis, R., 'Report of Phelps Brown Committee' (1969) 32 *Modern Law Review* 75.

Marquand, Judith, 'Which are the Lower Paid Workers?' (1967) V *Brit. J. Industrial Relations* 359.

Marsh, A., *Industrial Relations in Engineering* (1965).

Martin, R., and Fryer, R. H., 'Management and Redundancy: Planned Change' (1970) VIII *Brit. J. Industrial Relations* 69.

McCarthy, W. E. J., (ed.), *Industrial Relations in Britain* (1969, London: introductory).

McCarthy, W. E. J., *The Closed Shop in Britain* (1964).

Mortimer, J. E., *Industrial Relations – The Role of the Trade Unions* (1968).

Roberts, B. C., (ed.), *Industrial Relations* (1968, revised).

Roberts, B. C., *Trade Union Government and Administration in Great Britain* (1956).

Robinson, O., 'Representation of the White Collar Worker' (Bank Staffs) (1969) VII *Brit. J. Industrial Relations* 19.

Ross, A. M., and Hartman, P. J., *Changing Patterns of Industrial Conflict* (1960).

Sayles, L., *Behaviour of Industrial Work Groups* (1958).

Stieber, J., 'Unauthorised Strikes in American and British Industrial Relations' (1968) VI *Brit. J. Industrial Relations* 232.

Topham, T., 'Package Deals in British Collective Bargaining' (1964) 5 *International Socialist Journal* 520.

Thomas, R. (ed.), *An Exercise in Redeployment* (Report of Trade Union Study Group: 1969).

T.U.C. Annual Reports, especially for 1964, 1967, 1968 and 1969.

Turner, H. A., 'British Trade Union Structure: A New Approach?' (1964) II *Brit. J. Industrial Relations* 165.

Turner, H. A., *Is Britain Really Strike Prone?* (1969).

Turner, H. A., Clack, G., and Roberts, G., *Labour Relations in the Motor Industry* (1967).

Wedderburn, Dorothy, 'Redundancy', in Pym, D. (ed.), *Industrial Society* (1968).

Wedderburn, Dorothy, 'Workplace Inequality', *New Society*, 9 April 1970.

Wedderburn, Dorothy, *Redundancy and the Railwaymen* (1965).

Westergaard, J. H., 'Rediscovery of the Cash Nexus', *Socialist Register 1970*, p. 111.

Woodward, Joan, *Industrial Organization* (1965).

Young, A. F., *Social Services in British Industry* (1968).

10. HISTORICAL BACKGROUND

Arnot, R. Page, *The Miners* (Vols. I–III).

Askwith, Lord, *Industrial Problems and Disputes* (1920).

Aspinall, A. L., *The Early English Trade Unions* (1949).

Bealey, F., and Pelling, H., *Labour and Politics: 1900–1906* (1958).

Clegg, A. H., Fox, A., and Thompson, A. F., *A History of British Trade Unions 1889–1910* (1964).

Cole, G. D. H., 'Some Notes on British Trade Unionism in the Third Quarter of the Nineteenth Century', in Carus-Wilson (ed.) *Essays in Economic History* (1962).

Cole, G. D. H., *Short History of the British Working Class Movement* (1947).

Cole, G. D. H., and Filson, A. W., *British Working Class Movements: Select Documents 1789–1875* (1951) (a useful source book).

Hammond, J. L. and B., *Lord Shaftesbury* (Factories Acts) (1923).

Hedges, R. V., and Winterbottom, A., *Legal History of Trade Unionism* (1930) (the best legal history to that date).

Hilton, W., *The Truck System* (1960).

Hobsbawm, E. J., *Labouring Men* (1964) (valuable collection of essays).

Hutchins, B. L., and Harrison, A., *A History of Factory Legislation* (1903; 3rd ed. 1926, reprinted 1966) (the leading history of the factory enactments).

Jenks, *Short History of English Law* (1934), pp. 320–40.

Milne-Bailey, W., *Trade Union Documents* (1929).

Orton, W. A., *Labour in Transition* (1921) (the First World War).

Pelling, H., *A History of British Trade Unionism* (1963).

Pelling, H., *Origins of the Labour Party* (1954).

Phelps Brown, E. H., *The Growth of British Industrial Relations* (1959) (a study of 1906–14).

Pritt, D. N., and Freeman, R., *The Law Versus the Trade Unions* (1958).

Roberts, B. C., *The Trades Union Congress 1868–1921* (1958).

Saville, J., 'Trade Unions and Free Labour' in Briggs, A., and Saville, J., (eds.), *Essays in Labour History* (1960) (the background to *Taff Vale*).

Symons, J., *The General Strike* (1957).

Thompson, E. P., *The Making of the English Working Class* (1963) (early nineteenth century).

Turner, H. A., *Trade Union Growth Structure and Policy* (1962) (study of the cotton unions).

Webb, S. and B., *History of Trade Unionism* (1920).

Webb, S. and B., *Industrial Democracy* (1914) (still a very useful source).

11. COMPARATIVE AND FOREIGN

(1) General or of Special Interest:

Aaron, B. (ed.), *Dispute Settlement Procedures in Five Western European Countries* (U.C.L.A., 1969: X. Blanc-Jouvan, G. Giugni, F. Schmidt, T. Ramm, K. W. Wedderburn).

Aaron, B., 'Labour Courts: Western European Models and the U.S.' (1969) 16 *Univ. California Los Angeles Law Review* 847.

Casey, E. Riley, and O'Neill, B. J., 'Comparisons of Law and Labor Relations in U.S.A. and U.K.' (1969) 44 *Tulane Law Review* 67 (introductory).

Christie, I. M., *Liability of Strikers in Tort* (England and Canada) (1967).

Galenson, W., and Lipset, S. M., *Labor and Trade Unionism* (1960) (interdisciplinary reader).

Garbarino, J. W., 'Managing Conflict in Industrial Relations' (U.S.A. and Britain) (1969) VII *Brit. J. Industrial Relations* 317.

International Institute for Labour Studies, Bulletin 6 (1969), *Workers' Participation in Management* (Country Studies Series): France 54; Germany 93; U.S.A. 149; ibid. Bulletin 5 (1968) Poland 188.

Johnston, G. A., 'The Influence of International Labour Standards on Legislation and Practice in the U.K.' (1968) 97 *Int. Lab. R.* 465–88.

Kahn-Freund, O., *Labour Relations and the Law* (1964) (papers on nine systems of collective agreement, and strike law, given in 1962).

Kamin, A. (ed.), *Western European Labor and the American Corporation* (1970).

Levy, H. M., 'Role of Law in U.S. and England in Protecting Workers from Discharge or Discrimination' (1969) 18 *International and Comparative Law Quarterly* 558.

Lowry, J. P., *Greener Grass?* (London, 1970: report on U.S. Labour Law for British engineering employers).

O'Higgins, P., 'Labour Law'. Chapters in *Annual Survey of Commonwealth Law* (1965; 1966; 1967), and (with B. A. Hepple) ibid. (1968; 1969).

(2) Commonwealth and Irish:

Adell, B., 'Collective Agreement and the Right of Employee to Sue Employer' (1967) 45 *Canadian Bar Review* 354.

Arthurs, H. W., 'Collective Bargaining in the Public Service of Canada – Bold Experiment or Act of Folly?' (1969) 67 *Michigan Law Review* 971.

Arthurs, H. W., 'Developing Industrial Citizenship' (1967) 45 *Canadian Bar Review* 786.

Arthurs, H. W., 'Right to Strike in Common Law Provinces of Canada', *4th Internat. Symposium on Comparative Law*, 187 (1969).

Arthurs, H. W., and Crispo, J. M. G., *Law and Labour Relations*, Toronto Conference, 1966, Centre for Industrial Relations, Univ. of Toronto.

Bretten, G. R., 'The Right to Strike in New Zealand' (1968) 17 *International and Comparative Law Quarterly* 749.

Brissenden, P. F., *Settlement of Labour Disputes of Rights in Australia* (1966), Monograph 13, Univ. of California, Los Angeles Institute of Industrial Relations.

Carrothers, A. W. R., *Collective Bargaining in Canada* (Toronto, 1965) (textbook).

Carrothers, A. W. R. (ed.), *Report of a Study on the Labour Injunction in Ontario*, 2 vols. (Toronto, 1966).

Casey, J. P., 'The Injunction in Labour Disputes in Eire' (1969) 18 *International and Comparative Law Quarterly* 347.

Crispo, J. M. G., and Arthurs, H. W., 'Industrial Unrest in Canada: Diagnosis of Recent Experiences' (1968) 23 *Relations Industrielles* 237.

Dey, J. F., and McKenzie, D. B. (eds.), *Outline of Industrial Law* (Australia, 1964).

Finkelman, J., 'Law of Picketing in Canada' (1937) 2 *Univ. Toronto Law J.* 67 and 344 (British and Canadian: a classic article).

Foenander, O. de R., *Trade Unionism in Australia* (1962).

New Zealand ('Woodhouse') Royal Commission: *Compensation for Personal Injury* (Wellington, 1967).

New Zealand: Ministry of Labour: *Commentary on Royal Commission of Inquiry into Compensation for Personal Injury* (Wellington, 1969).

Sams, K. I., 'Appeals Board of Irish Congress of Trade Unions' (1968) VI *Brit. J. Industrial Relations* 204.

Southin, Mary, Q.C., 'The Courts and Labour Injunctions' (1970) 28 *The Advocate* (Vancouver Bar Association) 74.

Sykes, E. I., *Strike Law in Australia* (1962).

Sykes, E. I., *The Employer, the Employee and the Law* (2nd ed., Sydney, 1964).

Szakats, A., *Trade Unions and the Law* (New Zealand, 1968).

Woods, H. D., et al., *Task Force Report: Problems in Industrial Relations* (Canada, 1968).

(3) European:

Aaron, B. (ed.), Blanc-Jouvan, X., Ramm, T., Giugni, G., and Schmidt, F., *Labor Courts and Grievance Settlement in Western Europe* (Univ. of California Press, 1971).

Adlercreutz, A., 'Rise and Development of Collective Agreements' (1958) 2 *Scandinavian Studies in Law* 9 (on Sweden, Denmark, France, Britain).

Blaise, J., *La Régulation du Travail et de l'Emploi* (Dalloz, 1966) (France).

Blanpain, R., *Les Conventions Collectives de Travail* (1964) (Belgium).

Boldt, H., et al., *Le Contrat de Travail* (1965) (Common Market countries).

Camerlynck, G. H., *Le Contrat de Travail* (Dalloz, 1967) (France).

Camerlynck, G. H., and Lyon-Caen, G., *Droit de Travail* (1967) (best short French textbook).

Cartwright, H. A., 'Law of Obligations in England and Germany' (1964) 13 *International and Comparative Law Quarterly* 1316 (accident insurance: 1320–24).

Despax, M., *Les Conventions Collectives* (Dalloz, 1967) (France).

Edlund, S., 'Settlement Through Negotiation of Disputes on the Application of Collective Agreements' (1968) 12 *Scandinavian Studies in Law* (ed. F. Schmidt) 9.

Farnsworth, G., 'Employees with Rights', 65 *Law Society Gazette* 541 (Germany).

Feldesman, W., 'Yugoslav Labor Relations Law and Practice' (1969) 21 *Syracuse Law Review* 9.

François, L., *La Distinction Entre Employés et Ouvriers* (La Haye, 1963) (Germany, Belgium, France, Italy).

Giugni, G., 'Recent Developments in Collective Bargaining in Italy' (1965) 91 *International Labour Review* 273.

Hellner, J., 'Damages for Personal Injury and Victim's Private Insurance' (1970) 18 *American J. Comparative Law* 126 (Sweden; see on Norway: Selmer, K. S., ibid. 145).

Kolaja, J., *Workers' Councils: Yugoslav Experience* (1965).

Lyon-Caen, G., 'La Convention Collective de Travail en Droit International Privé (1964) *Journal du Droit International* 1.

Lyon-Caen, G., *Les Salaires* (Dalloz, 1967) (France).

McPherson, W. H., and Meyers, F., *French Labour Courts: Judgment by Peers* (1966).

Meyers, F., 'Role of Collective Bargaining in France' (with special reference to unemployment insurance) (1965) III *British Journal of Industrial Relations* 363.

Panayotopoulos, M., *Le Contrôle Judiciaire du Licenciement* (Paris, 1969) (Common Market countries and Greece).

Peterson, R. B., 'Swedish Experience with Industrial Democracy' (1968) VI *Brit. J. Industrial Relations* 185.

Ramm, T., 'La Situation Actuelle du Droit du Travail en Allemagne' (1967) *Droit Sociale* 624.

Schmidt, Folke, *The Law of Labour Relations in Sweden* (1962) (includes texts of basic collective agreements).

Sinay, H., *La Grève* (Dalloz, 1966) (France).

Singleton, F., 'Workers' Self-Management in Yugoslavia', *Trade Union Register 1970*, 231.

Spiro, H. J., *The Politics of German Co-determination* (1957).

Szubert, W., 'Contract of Employment in Polish Labour Law' (1962) 25 *Modern Law Review* 36.

Troclet, L. E., and Vogel Polsky, E., *Le Travail Intérimaire* (Brussels, 1968).

Vagts, D., 'Reforming the Modern Corporation – Perspectives from the German' (1966) 80 *Harvard Law Rev.* 23.

Verdier, J. M., *Syndicats* (Dalloz, 1967) (France).

(4) United States:

Aaron, B., 'Judicial Intervention in Labor Arbitration' (1967) 20 *Stanford Law Rev.* 41.

Aaron, B., 'Labor Relations Law', in *Challenges to Collective Bargaining* (ed. L. Ulman) (1967).

Aaron, B., 'Union's Duty of Fair Representation' (1968) *Journal of Air Law and Commerce* 167.

Abodeely, J. E., 'The National Labor Relations Board and Unit Clarification' (1969) 117 *Univ. Pennsylvania Law Review* 1075.

Asher, L., 'Secondary Boycotts – Allied, Neutral and Single Employers' (1964) 52 *Georgia Law J.* 406.

Blackman, J., *Presidential Seizure in Labor Disputes* (1967).

Bok, D., and Dunlop, J. T., *Labor and the American Community* (1970).

Burton, J. F., and Krider, C., 'Role of Strikes by Public Employees' (1970) 79 *Yale Law J.* 418; (reply by Wellington and Winter, ibid. 441).

Christensen, T. G., 'Labor Arbitration and Judicial Oversight' (1967) 19, *Stanford Law Review* 671.

Cox, A., and Bok, D., *Labor Law* (1970) (major casebook).

Edwards, H. T., and Bergman, E. W., 'Legal and Practical Remedies to Enforce No-Strike Commitment' (1970) 21 *Labor Law J.* 3.

Fleming, J., *The Labor Arbitration Process* (1965).

Gould, W. B., 'Public Employment: Mediation, Fact Finding and Arbitration' (1969) 55 *American Bar Assoc. J.* 835.

Gould, W. B., 'Status of Unauthorized and Wildcat Strikes under the N.L.R.A.' (1967) 52 *Cornell Law Quarterly* 672.

Gould, W. B., 'Black Power in the Unions: Impact upon Collective Bargaining' (1969) 79 *Yale Law J.* 46.

Gould, W. B., 'Labor Arbitration of Grievances involving Racial Discrimination' (1969) 118 *Univ. Pennsylvania Law Review* 40.

Gregory, C. O., *Labor and the Law* (1961) (U.S. historical and readable introduction).

Kuhn, J. W., *Bargaining in Grievance Settlement* (1961).

Meyers, F., *Ownership of Jobs* (California, 1964) (survey of U.S.A., Britain, France, Mexico).

Meyers, F., *Right to Work in Practice* (1959) (U.S.A.).

Moore, J. E., 'N.L.R.B. and Supervisors' (1970) 21 *Labor Law J.* 195 (on exclusion of foremen from bargaining rights).

Note (Anon.), 'Fair Representation and Union Discipline' (1970) 79 *Yale Law J.* 730.

Passman, E. H., 'Notice Requirements Under Taft–Hartley' (1970) 21 *Labor Law J.* 39 (compulsory 60-day notice to end collective agreements).

Platt, E., 'Duty to Bargain as Applied to Management Decisions' (1968) 19 *Labor Law J.* 113.

Stedman, J. C., 'The Employed Inventor' (1970) 45 *New York Univ. Law Review* 1.

Summers, C. W., 'American Legislation for Union Democracy' (1962) 25 *Modern Law Review* 273.

Summers, C. W., 'Collective Agreements and the Law of Contracts' (1969) 78 *Yale Law J.* 525.

Summers, C. W., 'Exclusive Representation by Majority Unions: A Unique Principle of American Labor Law' in *Hedendaags Arbeidsrecht* (Papers for Prof. M. Levenbach: 1966, Amsterdam) p. 304 (very useful introduction).

Summers, C. W., and Wellington, H. H., *Labor Law* (1968) (major casebook).

Wellington, H. H., 'Function of Contract and the Collective Bargaining Agreement' (1964) 112 *Univ. of Pennsylvania Law Rev.* 467.

Wellington, H. H., *Labor and the Legal Process* (1968) (very readable critique of U.S. labour law).

Wellington, H. H., and Winter, R., 'Limits of Collective Bargaining in Public Employment' (1969) 78 *Yale Law J.* 1107; and (1970) ibid. 805.

TABLE OF STATUTES

TABLE OF CASES

INDEX

MORE ABOUT PENGUINS
AND PELICANS

Penguinews, which appears every month, contains details of all the new books issued by Penguins as they are published. From time to time it is supplemented by *Penguins in Print*, which is a complete list of all books published by Penguins which are in print. (There are well over three thousand of these.)

A specimen copy of *Penguinews* will be sent to you free on request, and you can become a subscriber for the price of the postage. For a year's issues (including the complete lists) please send 20p if you live in the United Kingdom, or 40p if you live elsewhere. Just write to Dept EP, Penguin Books Ltd, Harmondsworth, Middlesex, enclosing a cheque or postal order, and your name will be added to the mailing list.

Some other books published by Penguins are described on the following pages.

Note: *Penguinews* and *Penguins in Print* are not available in the U.S.A. or Canada

A HISTORY OF BRITISH TRADE UNIONISM

Henry Pelling

'A genuine and worthwhile addition to the growing literature on trade unionism' – George Woodcock in the *Sunday Times*

Today trade unionism plays a more important part in the nation's economy than ever before, and its problems of internal reform and its relations with the government and the public are constantly under discussion. But its present structure can only be understood in relation to its long history.

Henry Pelling, a Fellow of St John's College, Cambridge, and author of *The Origins of the Labour Party*, leads the reader through a vivid story of struggle and development covering more than four centuries: from the medieval guilds and early craftsmen's and labourers' associations to the dramatic growth of trade unionism in Britain in the nineteenth and twentieth centuries.

He shows how powerful personalities such as Robert Applegarth, Henry Broadhurst, Tom Mann, Ernest Bevin, and Walter Citrine have helped to shape the pattern of present-day unionism; and also how the problems of today's leaders stem from the need to adapt attitudes and structure moulded in the conflicts of earlier generations.

'Readable and intelligent' – *The Times Education Supplement a Pelican Original*

FREEDOM, THE INDIVIDUAL AND THE LAW

Harry Street

Civil Liberties are very much in the news. At the heart of every incident that concerns the rights and obligations of the individual lies a conflict, sometimes muted, sometimes violent, between competing interests: freedom of speech v. security of the state, freedom of movement v. public order, the right to privacy v. the demands of a vigilant press. Every day brings fresh reports of 'punch-up' politics, banning of controversial posters, abuse of telephone tapping, contempt of Parliament ... the headlines never stop.

Yet Professor Street's *Freedom, the Individual and the Law* is the first comprehensive survey of the way English law deals with the many sides of Civil Liberty. After an introductory description of the powers of the police, Professor Street addresses himself in detail to the main areas of freedom of expression, freedom of association, and freedom of movement. Protection against private power, the right to work, and other subjects of contemporary importance make up the citizen's first guide to the theory and practice of Civil Liberty.